Personal Finance
An Integrated Planning Approach

SEVENTH EDITION

Personal Finance
An Integrated Planning Approach

BERNARD J. WINGER

RALPH R. FRASCA

UNIVERSITY OF DAYTON

Prentice Hall
UPPER SADDLE RIVER, NEW JERSEY 07458

TO THOSE WE LOVE:

Sue, Mike, and Bob
Crystal, Matthew, Anthony, Michael, and Christina

Library of Congress Cataloging-in-Publication Data

Winger, Bernard J.
    Personal finance: an integrated planning approach/Bernard J. Winger, Ralph R.
Frasca.—7th ed.
      p. cm.
    Includes bibliographical references and index.
    ISBN 0-13-185619-7 (alk. paper)
    1. Finance, Personal.   I. Frasca, Ralph R.   II. Title.
HG179.W545 2005
332.024—dc22

2004061117

Executive Editor: David Alexander
Acquisitions Editor: Jon Axelrod
Editorial Director: Jeff Shelstad
Assistant Editor: Francesca Calogero
Senior Media Project Manager: Nancy Welcher
Marketing Manager: Sharon Koch
Marketing Assistant: Tina Panagioutou
Managing Editor (Production): Cynthia Regan
Production Editor: Melissa Owens
Permissions Supervisor: Charles Morris
Manufacturing Buyer: Michelle Klein
Design Manager: Maria Lange

Designer: Michael Fruhbeis
Cover Design: Kiwi Design
Cover Photo: Kelvin Murray / Stone / Getty Images, Inc
Director, Image Resource Center: Melinda Reo
Manger, Rights and Permissions: Zina Arabia
Manager, Visual Research: Beth Brenzel
Manager, Cover Visual Research & Permissions:
  Karen Sanatar
Manager, Print Production: Christy Mahon
Composition/Full-Service Project Management:
  Laserwords/Progressive Publishing Alternatives
Printer/Binder: Courier Westford

Credits and acknowledgments borrowed from other sources and reproduced, with permission, in this textbook
appear on appropriate page within text.

Pearson Education LTD.
Pearson Education Singapore, Pte. Ltd
Pearson Education, Canada, Ltd
Pearson Education—Japan

Pearson Education Australia PTY, Limited
Pearson Education North Asia Ltd
Pearson Educación de Mexico, S.A. de C.V.
Pearson Education Malaysia, Pte. Ltd

10 9 8 7 6 5 4 3 2 1
ISBN 0-13-185619-7

Brief Contents

PART 1 THE BASIC FRAMEWORK:
Organizing and Managing Your Financial Resources   *1*

  1   Financial Planning: Why It's Important to You   2
  2   The Time Value of Money: All Dollars Are Not Created Equal   21
  3   Financial Statements and Budgets: Where Are You Now and
       Where Are You Going?   46
  4   Taxes: The Government's Share of Your Rewards   79

PART 2 LIQUIDITY MANAGEMENT:
Managing Current Assets and Current Liabilities   *111*

  5   Cash Management: Funds for Immediate Needs   112
  6   Short-Term Credit Management: Consumer Credit   135

PART 3 BUYING NOW AND PAYING LATER:
Managing Your Long-Term Liabilities   *169*

  7   Consumer Durables: The Personal Auto   170
  8   Housing: The Cost of Shelter   193

PART 4 INVESTING FOR THE FUTURE:
Growing Your Financial Resources   *225*

  9   Financial Markets and Institutions:
       Learning the Investment Environment   226
  10   Investment Basics: Understanding Risk and Return   250
  11   Stocks and Bonds: Your Most Common Investments   270
  12   Mutual Funds and Other Pooling Arrangements:
       Simplifying and (Maybe) Improving Your Investment Performance   300

PART 5 PROTECTING YOUR WEALTH:
Insurance and Retirement Planning   *325*

  13   Property and Liability Insurance: Protecting Your Lifestyle Assets   326
  14   Health Care and Disability Insurance:
       Protecting Your Earning Capacity   355
  15   Life Insurance and Estate Planning: Protecting Your Dependents   380
  16   Retirement Planning: Planning for Your Long-Term Needs   415

appendix   Time-Value-of-Money Concepts   446

Contents

Preface   xv

PART 1   THE BASIC FRAMEWORK:
Organizing and Managing Your Financial Resources   1

1   **Financial Planning: Why It's Important to You   2**
Why Study Personal Finance?   3
   Your Goals in Life 3   •   Important Economic Trends 5
Achieving Financial Goals through Planning   7
   Life-Cycle Planning 8   •   Major Financial Planning Areas 8   •
   A Planning Approach 10
Making Financial Decisions   11
   Some Helpful Economic Insights 11
The Building Blocks of Success   12
Appendix 1.1   A Closer Look at Career Planning   19

2   **The Time Value of Money: All Dollars Are Not Created Equal   21**
Compounding (Finding Future Values)   22
   Future Value of a Single Payment 22   •   Future Value of an Annuity 25
Discounting (Finding Present Values)   26
   Present Value of a Single Payment 26   •   Present Value of an Annuity 28   •   More
   Applications of Future and Present Values 28   •   Approximation Methods
   with Annuities 29
Goal Planning for the Steeles   31
   Making Goals Concrete 31   •   Adjusting for Inflation 32   •   Determining a Savings
   Schedule 32   •   A Final Note on Goal Planning 36
Appendix 2.1   Interpolation Techniques   44

3   **Financial Statements and Budgets: Where Are You Now and Where Are You
Going?   46**
The Balance Sheet   47
   Assets 48   •   Liabilities 49   •   Net Worth 50
The Income Statement   52
   Income 52   •   Expenses 52   •   Contribution to Savings 53
Evaluating Past Financial Performance   53
   Matching or Beating the Inflation Rate 54   •   Maintaining Adequate Liquidity 57   •
   Avoiding Excessive Amounts of Debt 58   •   Review of the Steeles' Financial Situation 60
Achieving Goals through Budgeting   60
   Goal Setting 61   •   Preparing the Annual Budget 62   •   Monitoring and Controlling
   Activities 65

4 **Taxes: The Government's Share of Your Rewards 79**

Determining Your Federal Income Tax 80

Gross Income Items 80 • Adjustments to Income 81 • Adjusted Gross Income 84 • Taxable Income 84 • Determining Your Tax Liability Before Tax Credits 86 • Tax Credits 88 • Do You Get a Refund or Owe More Taxes? 88 • Determining the Steeles' 2004 Income Tax 88

Other Aspects of the Federal Income Tax 92

Capital Gains and Losses 92 • Alternative Minimum Tax 93 • The Role of the Internal Revenue Service 94 • Getting Outside Help 96 • Special Considerations for Students 97

Planning to Reduce Your Income Taxes 99

Invest Where You Receive Tax-Advantaged Income 99 • Take Capital Losses Quickly 100 • Split Your Income 100 • Stagger Income and Expenses 101 • Defer Income to Later Years 101

Other Important Taxes 102

Social Security Taxes 102 • State and Local Taxes 103 • Death and Transfer Taxes 104

PART 2   LIQUIDITY MANAGEMENT:
Managing Current Assets and Current Liabilities   111

5 **Cash Management: Funds for Immediate Needs   112**

Meeting Cash Needs 113

Why Hold Cash? 113 • Fundamental Deposits 114 • Other Deposits 116

Using Your Checking Account 117

Selecting a Bank 117 • Checking Account Procedures 118 • End-of-Month Activities 122 • Checks That Guarantee Payment 124 • Electronic Banking 126

Understanding How Your Account Earns Interest 127

How Interest Is Calculated 127 • Determining Interest on Your Account 128

Cash Management Strategy 128

Interest Rate Volatility 130

6 **Short-Term Credit Management: Consumer Credit   135**

Arranging and Using Credit 136

Reasons for Using Credit 136 • Disadvantages of Using Credit 137 • How to Get Credit 138

Sales Credit 141

Kinds of Accounts 143 • Credit Cards 146 • Protection against Credit Card Fraud 149 • Correcting Credit Card Mistakes 150 • Credit Cards Contrasted with Debit Cards 152

Cash Credit 153

The Contract 153 • How Interest Charges Are Determined 154

Obtaining Credit and Resolving Credit Problems 157

Sources of Credit 157 • A Credit Management Strategy 161 • Resolving Personal Debt Problems 162

PART 3   BUYING NOW AND PAYING LATER:
Managing Your Long-Term Liabilities   169

7 **Consumer Durables: The Personal Auto   170**

Major Household Purchases and the Electronic Market 171

Electronic Purchases 172 • Online Auctions and Electronic Payments 173 • Warranties 174

Selecting an Automobile   176

    Pricing Information 176   •   Rebates and Dealer-Supplied Financing 177

The Costs of Owning and Operating an Automobile   179

    The Cost of Ownership 179   •   The Cost of Operation 181   •   The Total Cost of Ownership and Operation 181   •   The Mass-Transit Alternative 182

The Leasing Alternative   182

    The Closed-End Lease 183   •   The Open-End Lease 183   •   Evaluating a Car Lease 184   •   A Lease/Buy Comparison 186

What If You Bought a Lemon?   188

    Secret Warranties 188   •   Alternative Dispute Resolution 188   •   Lemon Laws 189

8   Housing: The Cost of Shelter   193

Rent or Buy?   194

    Determining What You Can Afford 196   •   Types of Housing 198   •   A Cost Comparison 200

The Real Estate Transaction   204

    The Appraisal 204   •   The Real Estate Agent 206   •   The Home Inspection 207   •   The Purchase Contract 207   •   The Title Search 208   •   The Closing 208   •   Warranties 210

Financing the Purchase   211

    Fixed Rate Mortgages 211   •   Adjustable Rate Mortgages 213   •   Specialized Mortgage Formats and Creative Financing 216   •   Reading the Fine Print 216   •   Insured Mortgages 217   •   Refinancing 218   •   What If You Can't Meet Your Mortgage Payments? 219

PART 4   INVESTING FOR THE FUTURE:
Growing Your Financial Resources   225

9   Financial Markets and Institutions: Learning the Investment Environment 226

Goals and Investment Alternatives   227

    What Are Your Needs? 227   •   Basic Investment Alternatives 229

Securities Markets   232

    Organized Exchanges 232   •   Over-the-Counter Markets 234

Regulation of the Securities Industry   234

    Federal Legislation 234   •   State Law and Self-Regulation 236

Using the Services of a Stockbroker   237

    Selecting a Stockbroker 237   •   Kinds of Accounts 239   •   Kinds of Positions 240   •   Kinds of Orders 241   •   Do Things on Paper First 243

Finding Investment Information   243

    Company Sources 244   •   Investment Advisory Services 245   •   Newspapers and Magazines 245   •   Internet Data Sources 246

10   Investment Basics: Understanding Risk and Return   250

Risk and Return   251

    What Is Risk? 251   •   Sources of Risk 252   •   How Much Return Do You Need? 253

The Rewards of Diversification   255

    Why Diversification Works 256   •   Diversification Guidelines 257

Applying a Risk-Return Model   258

    Eliminating Random Risk 258   •   Managing Market Risk 258   •   Making Stock Selections 261

Building and Changing a Portfolio   262
  Acquiring Securities 263   •   Selling Securities 264   •   Economic Changes and the
  Portfolio 265

11 **Stocks and Bonds: Your Most Common Investments   270**
  An Overview of Common Stocks   271
    Characteristics of Common Stock 271
  Fundamental Analysis of Common Stocks   276
    Application of the CAPM 276   •   Price-to-Earnings Analysis 278   •   The PEG
    Ratio 280   •   Fundamental Value and Book Value 280
  Corporate-Issued Bonds   282
    Your Rights as a Bondholder 282   •   Payment Characteristics of Bonds 282   •
    Retirement Methods 283   •   Investing in Corporate Bonds 284
  Government-Issued Bonds   284
    U.S. Treasury Securities 284   •   U.S. Agency Bonds 286   •   Municipal Bonds 287
  Return and Risk Characteristics of Bonds   287
    Expected Return from Bonds 287   •   Risks of Bond Investment 290
  Preferred Stock   291
    Characteristics of Preferred Stock 291   •   Expected Return from Preferred Stock 293

12 **Mutual Funds and Other Pooling Arrangements: Simplifying and (Maybe)
  Improving Your Investment Performance   300**
  Mutual Funds   301
    Characteristics of Mutual Funds 301   •   Important Mutual Fund Services 305   •
    Selecting a Mutual Fund 306
  Other Pooling Arrangements   309
    Unit Investment Trusts (UITs) 309   •   Exchange-Traded Funds 311   •   Real Estate
    Investment Trusts (REITs) 312   •   Limited Partnerships 313   •   Investment Clubs 315
  Constructing and Maintaining Your Personal Portfolio   315
    Portfolio Construction 315   •   Maintaining Your Portfolio 318   •   Asset Allocation
    Mutual Funds 318   •   Mutual Funds Management in the 401(k) Retirement Plan 319

PART 5   PROTECTING YOUR WEALTH:
         Insurance and Retirement Planning   325

13 **Property and Liability Insurance: Protecting Your Lifestyle Assets   326**
  Fundamental Insurance Concepts   327
    Risk 327   •   Risk Management 329
  Homeowners' Insurance   330
    The Terminology of Homeowners' Policies 330   •   Property Coverage 333   •   Liability
    Coverage 335   •   Policy Format 336   •   Specialized Insurance 339   •   Selecting
    Homeowners' Insurance 340   •   Making Sure You Collect on a Loss 341
  Automobile Insurance   342
    Who Needs Auto Insurance Coverage? 343   •   Coverage Under Your Auto Policy 343   •
    The Cost of Auto Insurance 347   •   Before, At, and After the Accident 349

14 **Health Care and Disability Insurance: Protecting Your Earning Capacity   355**
  Health Care Insurance   356
    Types of Coverage 357   •   Important Provisions 360   •   Insurance Providers 362   •
    Employment Related Health Care Insurance 363   •   Publicly Provided Health Services 366
    •   Individually Selected Health Care Insurance 367
  Disability Income Protection   369
    Sources of Disability Income 369   •   Insurance Clauses Affecting Disability Benefits 372
    Determining Disability Income Insurance Requirements 374

15 Life Insurance and Estate Planning: Protecting Your Dependents   380

Estimating Your Life Insurance Needs   381

  The Transition Fund 382 • The Family Maintenance Fund 383 • Specialized Funds 387 • The Insurance Protection Gap 388

The Special Language of Life Insurance Policies   389

  The Basic Policy 389 • Special Provisions 390

Kinds of Insurance Protection   391

  Term Insurance 391 • Cash Value Insurance 395

Selecting the Right Policy   399

  Selecting the Type of Policy 399 • Term or Cash Value Insurance? 399 • Comparison Shopping 401

Estate Planning   404

  The Last Will and Testament 405 • Transferring Your Estate Outside the Will 409

16 Retirement Planning: Planning for Your Long-Term Needs   415

Saving and Investing for Retirement   417

  Company Pension Plans 417 • Other Company Retirement Plans 427 • Individual Retirement Plans 428

Establishing a Personal Retirement Plan   434

  Social Security Benefits 434 • Estimating and Saving for Your Retirement Needs 438

Appendix: Time-Value-of-Money Concepts   446

Index   455

Boxed Features

CHAPTER 1

Box 1.1 Saving Money, Earn Less, Save More, Be Happy
Box 1.2 Financial Planning for Young Adults, Five Simple Steps to Start Your Financial Lift
Box 1.3 Finance News, What's a Professional Financial Planner—And Do You Need One?

CHAPTER 2

Box 2.1 Saving Money, Time Value of Money—Big Bore or Big Help?
Box 2.2 Financial Planning for Young Adults, Focus on the Asset, Not on the Daily Savings
Box 2.3 Finance News, Retirement: A Distant Goal or a Distant Dream?

CHAPTER 3

Box 3.1 Financial Planning for Young Adults, Pay Yourself First
Box 3.2 Finance News, What's Happening to Savings?
Box 3.3 Simplifying Financial Planning, Budgeting with Envelopes and Play Money

CHAPTER 4

Box 4.1 Simplifying Financial Planning, How Do Your Deductions Compare?
Box 4.2 Saving Money, Do Your Own Tax Return
Box 4.3 Finance News, IRS Clarifies Innocent and Injured Spouse Relief

CHAPTER 5

Box 5.1 Finance News, Indexed U.S. Savings Bonds
Box 5.2 Saving Money, Check Cashing—Your Bank Wants a Piece of the Action
Box 5.3 Simplifying Financial Planning, Banking by Computer: Has Electronic Banking Finally Arrived?
Box 5.4 Financial Planning for Young Adults, Stored Value Cards: Don't Pay for a Picture

CHAPTER 6

Box 6.1 Simplifying Financial Planning, A Credit Card Register
Box 6.2 Finance News, Scores Revealed
Box 6.3 Financial Planning for Young Adults, Student Loan Consolidation
Box 6.4 Saving Money, Use Your Credit Card Wisely

CHAPTER 7

Box 7.1 Finance News, The No-Call List
Box 7.2 Saving Money, Use Your Home Equity to Finance Your Car
Box 7.3 Financial Planning for Young Adults, First Job, Time to Buy a New Car?

CHAPTER 8

Box 8.1 Finance News, Beware Predatory Lending
Box 8.2 Financial Planning for Young Adults, Where Do You Get the Down Payment?
Box 8.3 Saving Money, Biweekly Mortgages

CHAPTER 9

Box 9.1 Finance News, Human Frailties: Why Smart People Make Dumb Investments
Box 9.2 Saving Money, Who Is Your Best Protector Against Dishonest Brokers? You!
Box 9.3 Financial Planning for Young Adults, Investing over the Internet
Box 9.4 Simplifying Financial Planning, Your Broker—Your Banker

CHAPTER 10

Box 10.1 Financial Planning for Young Adults, Do Small Investors Have a Chance?
Box 10.2 Simplifying Financial Planning, Are You Losing Sleep over Underdiversification?
Box 10.3 Finance News, Dogs of the Dow: Using a High-Yield Method to Select Stocks
Box 10.4 Saving Money, Have Your Cake and Eat It, Too? Get a MITT

CHAPTER 11

Box 11.1 Finance News, Financial Analysts: Do They Help or Hinder?
Box 11.2 Financial Planning for Young Adults, How About $766 Million for a $100 Investment?
Box 11.3 Simplifying Financial Planning, Buy Treasuries Directly
Box 11.4 Saving Money, No Reason to Settle for 90 Percent

CHAPTER 12

Box 12.1 Financial Planning for Young Adults, Want to Invest in a Mutual Fund? Just Do It!
Box 12.2 Saving Money, Focus on Loads and Annual Expenses

Box 12.3 Finance News, What's a Hedge Fund?
Box 12.4 Saving Money, Can You Profit from Market Overreactions?

CHAPTER 13

Box 13.1 Finance News, Insurers Use Credit Report to Determine Risk Exposure
Box 13.2 Financial Planning for Young Adults, A Property Insurance Protection Checklist for College Students
Box 13.3 Saving Money, Holding Down Insurance Costs for Young Drivers

CHAPTER 14

Box 14.1 Finance News, Health Savings Accounts
Box 14.2 Financial Planning for Young Adults, Insurance Options for Young Adults
Box 14.3 Saving Money, A Flexible Spending Account for Medical Expenditures
Box 14.4 Simplifying Financial Planning, Having a Living Will

CHAPTER 15

Box 15.1 Financial Planning for Young Adults, Do Children and Young Adults Need Life Insurance?
Box 15.2 Finance News, Living Benefits Insurance and Life Settlements
Box 15.3 Simplifying Financial Planning, Borrowing Your Cash Value
Box 15.4 Saving Money, Staying Healthy

CHAPTER 16

Box 16.1 Finance News, Employers Expand the Number of Cash Balance Plans
Box 16.2 Saving Money, Consolidating Pension Accounts through Rollovers

Preface

As the economy moves along in its usual cyclical fashion, financial planning continues to be important. Equally important is how personal finance instructors prepare their students to meet the challenges of a constantly changing economy. In our view, the most critical tasks are twofold: First, to have students appreciate the importance of planning and have a basic understanding of planning techniques; and second, to develop students' abilities to think critically and to make effective decisions. A course in Personal Finance obviously includes other features and topics, many descriptive in nature. These make the course more in touch with current events and also make it lively. The instructor is the artist who blends all topics together to create the course that is appropriate for his or her audience, and we believe the 7th edition of our text will give instructors the complete set of materials to craft their courses most effectively.

SIGNIFICANT CHANGES IN THE SEVENTH EDITION

We have added a number of new topics to this edition. Additionally, we have revised and altered other topics. The changes are detailed below.

New Topics

1. A set of forms has been created to guide and assist students in creating their own financial plans. These forms will be helpful to instructors in assigning semester-long projects. These forms are available electronically from the Winger/Frasca Web site (**www.prenhall.com/winger**). You must have a valid access code to access these forms.
2. A goal planning excercise for a young adult has been added and appears in Chapters 1, 2, and 3.
3. A new theme for boxed items—Financial Planning for Young Adults—has been included.
4. Stored value cards issued now by both employers and retail merchants are explained in Chapter 5.
5. Student loan consolidation and student loans are examined in Chapter 6.
6. The current topic of predatory lending is introduced in Chapter 8.
7. Hedge funds, which are growing rapidly in popularity, are covered in Chapter 12.
8. Insurers increasingly rely on an insurance risk score when setting premiums. This is now discussed in Chapter 13.

9. Prescription drug cards are listed under publicly funded programs in Chapter 14. Also included in this chapter are new boxed items on recently introduced Health Savings Accounts and Health Insurance Options for Young Adults.

Significantly Revised Topics

1. Tax changes through 2004 are included in Chapter 4 and injured spouse relief is highlighted in a boxed feature.

2. The costs of owning and operating an automobile are updated in Chapter 7.

3. The buy versus rent comparison in the housing chapter has been revised so that rental cost and ownership costs are more easily identified.

4. All tables on Social Security benefits now include the percent of income replaced by Social Security benefits.

5. Stock and bond returns in Chapter 10 are updated through 2003; other economic and financial data in Chapter 1 are updated through July 2004.

Alterations and Deletions

1. Techniques of interpolation have been moved from the body of Chapter 2 to Appendix 2.1.

2. The Appendix on the Rule of 78 has been deleted from Chapter 6.

3. The multiple of salary approach to estimating life insurance needs has been deleted from Chapter 15.

DISTINGUISHING FEATURES OF THE TEXT

A Flexible Outline Realizing that not all students have the same needs, we have designed the text to be used in different settings, the most common being a sixteen-week semester where the instructor seeks reasonably full topical coverage in both breadth and depth. However, Personal Finance has a unique situation in that it is frequently offered as a survey course, or as a course in a Life Skills program. Here, full coverage may be difficult to achieve, or perhaps not warranted. In these situations the following adjustments will lead to a streamlined coverage and still provide strong training in personal finance skills.

- Chapter Two dealing with time value of money concepts can be omitted without losing continuity.
- Chapter Eleven on stock and bond investment can be shortened considerably by deleting all or parts of the sections: Fundamental Analysis of Common Stocks, Return and Risk Characteristics of Bonds, and Preferred Stock. An overview of stocks and bonds is presented in both Chapters 9 and 10.

Most of the chapters and many chapter sub-parts (such as Estate Planning in Chapter 15) are self-contained units, making their coverage an instructor's option.

Decision-Making Approach We continue using a four-part approach to decision making that involves setting goals, listing alternatives, measuring performance, and evaluating achievement. Important in this process are the concepts of opportunity costs and marginal analysis. These topics are introduced and explained in Chapter 1 and are used extensively throughout the text.

An Emphasis on Risk and Return At the core of financial decision making is the balancing of risk and return. This concept applies in particular to investments, but it is also useful in other decisions that involve uncertainty; thus, there is an expanded discussion of risk management in the insurance section. In the investment section, we treat risk in such a way that students can use the concept when making investment decisions. Readers, thus, gain a practical tool as well as an understanding of the basic principles.

Integration with the Internet The Internet is thoroughly integrated throughout the sixth edition. Noted previously are the Internet exercises. In addition, we continue to feature Topic Links, which you will find identified in the margins throughout each chapter. Whenever you see the Topic Links icon, go to the Winger/Frasca Web site (**www.prenhall. com/winger**) for a direct hyperlink to a topic source.

Focus on the Time Value of Money The growing importance of achieving long-term goals through investing has increased the need for students to grasp the time value of money. Our explanation and use of these techniques are simple and well within the grasp of most students.

An Illustrative Family As part of the decision-making approach, we continue to highlight a typical American family, the Steeles. Their financial situation is far from perfect, and, like most of us, they make mistakes. The Steeles' financial situation has been updated and revised. They still manage to live a reasonably comfortable and financially secure life, but they are encountering growing financial pressures as they consider their future needs to educate their children and to provide an income for themselves in retirement. The Steele family appears in every chapter, where they encounter problems common to most families. As they deal with them and make decisions, so does the reader.

A Goal Planning Exercise for a Single Mother The Marie Wilson Goal Planning Exercise gives students an opportunity to participate in the important job of framing goals, planning to achieve them, and budgeting properly to afford them. The exercise spans Chapters 1, 2, and 3 with Excel worksheets available at the Winger Web site. Marie Wilson is a single adult with a four-year old son, trying to get ahead financially on a limited income.

Boxed Features Each chapter contains featured items that have been selected specifically for this edition to add interest and to provide background. All boxes have been selected to fit into four themes: Financial Planning for Young Adults, Saving Money, Simplifying Financial Planning, and Personal Finance News. These themes focus student attention and often include practical and useful information.

The Use of Color, Graphics, and Other Visual Aids The sophisticated graphic treatment in this text is meant to heighten interest in the topic at hand and to illustrate the concept in a concrete and effective way. The illustrations are both analytical and inviting.

An Informal Writing Style To help the reader comprehend the many complex aspects of personal finance, we employ an informal writing style that brings the student into the discussion without simplifying the concepts involved. We have been careful to explain new or unfamiliar terms, to use examples where appropriate, and to speak engagingly to the student.

A Complete Complement of End-of-Chapter Learning Aids Each chapter concludes with the following aids:

- **Key Terms** A list of important concepts in each chapter, accompanied by the page number where each key term is introduced and defined. To help the reader locate them, the key terms appear in boldface type within the chapter.

- **A Follow-Up on the Steeles** Thought-provoking questions designed to stimulate students to think about solutions to specific financial planning problems.

- **Problems and Review Questions** A list of questions meant to provide the basis for a review of textual material and to stimulate thought and discussion on the chapter's content. New to this edition: The list of questions and problems has been expanded. Also, all items have been updated to reflect changes in the financial environment.

- **Cases in Personal Finance** Two cases that, when completed, provide additional insight into the topics covered. These study aids are more challenging than the problems and review questions, requiring a firm grasp of the fundamentals and more computation. New to this edition: All cases have also been revised to reflect changes in the financial environment.

- **Working Out on the Web** Exercises designed to show students how the Internet can be used as a financial planning tool. The exercises are linked to informational sources on the Internet.

Supplementary Materials This text is accompanied by a complete list of supplementary teaching aids for both the instructor and the student. As with the sixth edition text, the Internet is a major component of this ancillary package.

FOR THE INSTRUCTOR

- **Instructor's Manual** The Instructor's Manual, written by the authors, is designed to assist instructors in their preparation of teaching activities. Each chapter of the Instructor's Manual includes key concepts for that chapter, a brief explanation of major topics, a detailed outline for the chapter, further insights on how the Internet may be used to enhance the current topic and, of course, the answers to the end-of-chapter questions and sample solutions for the cases.

- **Test Item File** The Test Bank, written by the authors, contains over 1400 questions that vary in rigor and type.

- **Test Gen EQ** The print Test Banks are designed for use with the TestGen-EQ test generating software. This computerized package allows instructors to custom design, save, and generate classroom tests. The test program permits instructors to edit, add, or delete questions from the test banks; edit existing graphics and create new graphics; analyze test results; and organize a database of tests and student results. This new software allows for greater flexibility and ease of use. It provides many options for organizing and displaying tests, along with a search and sort feature.

- **PowerPoint Lecture Notes** This lecture presentation, prepared by Gayle Russell of Eastern Connecticut State University, includes about 30–40 slides per chapter. Each chapter presentation includes an introduction to the chapter, chapter objectives, and a detailed outline of the chapter.

- **IRCD** This CD-ROM contains the Computerized Test Bank files, Test Item File (in Microsoft Word), Instructor's Manual (in Microsoft Word), and PowerPoint Lecture files.

- **Companion Website** (**www.prenhall.com/winger**). Companion Websites provide an interactive learning environment for students and provides a link to the electronic Instructor Resources. Every Companion Website integrates Syllabus Manager, an online tool that provides instructors with an easy, step-by-step process to create and revise syllabi, with direct links into Companion Website and other online content. Students access Syllabus Manager directly from within the Companion Website, providing quick access to course assignments.

FOR THE STUDENT

CONGRATULATIONS!! If you bought a new copy of this textbook, you should have also received an Access Code Card. The code on this card allows you to access the Personal Planning Worksheets called "Your Financial Review," which are available on the Winger/Frasca Companion Website (**www.prenhall.com/winger**).

If you have purchased a **used** copy of this textbook, you will need to purchase a new Access Code Card to get access to this resource. You can do this buy purchasing a separate access code card from your bookstore (ISBN: 0-13-187255-9) or you can order the access code card online by logging on to **www.prenhall.com/finance** and entering the access code card ISBN (0-13-187255-9) in the search bar located at the top of the page.

- **Companion Website** (**www.prenhall.com/winger**). The Companion Website includes: *online study guide*, which offers different types of self-assessment exercises with immediate feedback, *web destination links*, which are hyperlinks to the "Workout on the Web" exercises from the textbook as well as links to the "Topic Links" that are highlighted in the margins of the text. This Companion Website also includes "Your Financial Review" worksheets, created by the authors.
- **"Your Financial Review" Financial Planning Worksheets** This set of twenty forms covers a wide array of topics, ranging from setting goals to evaluating individual stocks. The forms can assist students in preparing their own financial plans, or instructors can use them in conjunction with specific assignments.

We usually learn by doing, and this text gives students plenty of opportunities to both do and learn. The decision-making approach enlivens the classroom, simplifies the teaching process, and encourages independent analysis on the part of the student. *Personal Finance: An Integrated Planning Approach* presents personal finance in a way that is easy to understand, easy to teach, and interesting to learn. We hope that you enjoy this text.

Acknowledgments

This edition is a collaborative effort of many people—teachers, students, and financial planners—who have contributed numerous suggestions, criticisms, and helpful insights. To begin with, we are grateful to Anna Boulware (St. Charles Community College), Margaret L. Burk (Muskingum College), Craig Bythewood (Florida Southern College), Stephen G. Chambers (Johnson County Community College), Caroline S. Fulmer (University of Alabama), Sam S.P. LaMartina (MidAmerica Nazarene University), Frances Lawrence (Louisiana State University), Kenneth L. Mark (Kansas City, Kansas Community College), Manouchehr Mokhatari (University of Maryland), Cynthia Overgard (University of Connecticut), Ted Pilger (Southern Illinois University), Edward Stendardi (St. John Fisher College), Dick Verrone (University of North Carolina at

Wilmington), Bashar Zakaria (Sacramento City College and California State University, Sacramento), Jim Bryan (Manhattanville College), Anthony Avallone (National University), Robert Emmer (University of California at Berkeley), Chris Austin (Normandale Community College), Deborah Kailer (Allegheny Community College), Abbas Mamoozadeh (Slippery Rock University), Dan M. Khanna (Golden Gate University), and Kyle Mattson (Weber State University), who provided important contributions to this edition. We also wish to thank those who have been so helpful on previous editions: Rick Deus (Sacramento City College), David D. O'Dell (McPherson College), Steven E. Huntley (Florida Community College), Daniel T. Winkler (University of North Carolina–Greensboro), Clarence C. Rose (Radford University), Cliff Olson (Southern College), Robert C. Waldron (Southern Illinois University–Carbondale), William S. Tozer (Washington State University), Richard Trieff (Des Moines Area Community College), Paul Allen (Sam Houston State University), Anne Bailey (Miami University), Emerson R. Bailey III (Casper College), James W. Baird (Community College of the Finger Lakes), A. Frederic Banda (The University of Akron), Robert J. Bond (Los Angeles Valley College), Benny D. Bowers (University of North Carolina at Charlotte), Patrick J. Cusatis (Pennsylvania State University), Mary Ellen Edmondson (University of Kentucky), Loren Geistfeld (Ohio State University), George L. Granger (East Tennessee State University), Vickie L. Hampton (University of Texas at Austin), Donald Johnson (College for Financial Planning), Walter H. Johnson (Cuyahoga Community College), Jerry L. Jorgenson (University of Utah), Robert F. Kegel, Jr. (Cypress College), Robert W. Kilpatrick (University of Connecticut), Anthony J. Lerro (Winthrop College), Joseph T. Marchese (Monroe Community College), William C. Marrs (Morton College), Jerry Mason (Texas Tech University), Randolph J. Mullis (University of Wisconsin), Emily Norman (Delta State University), Dennis D. Pappas (Columbus State Community College), Myron S. Pharo (Penn State University), J. Franklin Potts (Baylor University), Jean R. Robinson (Cornell University), Joe Samprone (Purdue University), Michael Solt (University of Santa Clara), Mary J. Stephenson (University of Maryland), Skip Swerdlow (University of Nevada–Las Vegas), and Rosemary Walker (Michigan State University).

Finally, the Prentice Hall finance team—David Alexander, executive editor, Francesca Calogero, assistant editor, and Nancy Welcher, media project manager—should be recognized for their excellent work and, more important, for their enthusiasm for the project. Special thanks is also due to Melissa Owens, our production editor, who deserves credit for the outstanding quality of the text.

Bernard J. Winger
Ralph R. Frasca

PART 1

The Basic Framework

ORGANIZING AND MANAGING YOUR FINANCIAL RESOURCES

Chapter 1
Financial Planning: *Why It's Important to You*

Chapter 2
The Time Value of Money: *All Dollars Are Not Created Equal*

Chapter 3
Financial Statements and Budgets: *Where Are You Now and Where Are You Going?*

Chapter 4
Taxes: *The Government's Share of Your Rewards*

We usually think of financial success as making the most of what we have. We can achieve it through planning: setting goals, establishing priorities, and making effective decisions. Our goals are likely to be both financial and nonfinancial. Indeed, nonfinancial goals—those pertaining to love, family, and religion—are probably more important. But our success in achieving financial goals often enables us to enrich the nonfinancial aspects of our lives.

Part 1 deals with effective planning techniques, the key to financial success. We begin, in Chapter 1, by outlining the planning process and presenting several basic concepts that can help you effectively evaluate financial choices. Among other issues, we consider the uneven match between income and needs during the life cycle, which requires us to respond by shifting resources through time to accommodate present and future needs.

This time shifting of resources creates an important need to understand the time value of money, which is covered in detail in Chapter 2. Here we explain the processes of compounding and discounting, and how knowledge of each helps us in making financial decisions.

Long-run financial success is usually accomplished by achieving short-run goals. Budgets and financial statements, the subjects of Chapter 3, help you do just that. Financial statements show you where you are now so that you can plan effectively for the future; they help determine your existing worth and show how you managed your income in the past. Budgeting, on the other hand, helps you manage your future income, thereby increasing your net worth.

Part 1 concludes with a discussion of taxes emphasizing the federal personal income tax. Chapter 4 familiarizes you with tax law as well as tax minimizing strategies.

1

Financial Planning

WHY IT'S IMPORTANT TO YOU

OBJECTIVES

1. To understand why setting goals is an important first step in financial planning

2. To appreciate that trends in the financial environment—inflation, taxes, and economic cycles—affect financial success and enhance the need for planning

3. To see why life-cycle financial planning is important and to understand the nature of a planning approach

4. To understand what is meant by marginal analysis and opportunity costs and to know how these concepts are used in financial decision making

5. To appreciate that financial success builds on a strong foundation and follows a building-block approach through time

6. To meet the Steeles, a family we will follow through the text

TOPIC **LINKS**

Follow the **Topic Links** in each chapter for your interactive Personal Finance exercise on the Web. Go to: **www.prenhall.com/winger**

Steele FAMILY

The Steeles—Arnold (37), Sharon (35), Nancy (9), and John (7)—are a typical American middle-class family. By most measures, the Steeles have achieved a certain level of success. Arnold is a chemist with a major paint manufacturer and is currently next in line for vice president of plant operations. Sharon is a CPA and works part time at a local accounting firm. As the demands on her time by Nancy and John have diminished, she has steadily expanded her work hours. Eventually, she hopes to return to full-time employment.

The Steeles have thought about the future mostly in terms of aspirations and dreams. Nancy has shown an aptitude on the piano and the family would like to continue her music lessons, which could be expensive. Arnold and Sharon hope that both kids go to college and they expect to help them financially when each starts. The family vacations often, usually camping in the Smoky Mountain National Park. If their resources were adequate, they would like to buy a vacation condominium near Pigeon Forge, Tennessee, and they also have thought about a family vacation in Hawaii. As empty-nesters, Arnold and Sharon have dreamed of traveling extensively in Europe and, of course, they hope to enjoy a long retirement with a living standard comparable to the one they now experience. Finally, if everything works out well, they would like to leave a substantial estate for Nancy and John.

Arnold grew up in the town in which they now live, but Sharon is from Pittsburgh. Both Arnold's and Sharon's parents are living and in reasonably good health, given their ages. Each family is self-sufficient but not by any means wealthy. Arnold has a brother, Dave (33), who is divorced from his wife. His income is not substantial and he currently is taking classes at a local university with the hope of eventually earning a bachelor's degree in business management. The divorce has been reasonably amicable and he and his wife have joint custody rights of their two children. Arnold and Sharon try to help Dave raise the kids, who often are visitors at the Steeles' home. Arnold also has a much younger sister, Jody (22), who will finish college in the spring with a degree in education. She plans to teach kindergarten in the local school district.

As we start our journey into personal financial planning, we would like to introduce you to the Steele family. You will meet them often in the succeeding chapters as they help us illustrate the application of financial planning techniques. After you finish a chapter, we encourage you to read some follow-up questions on the vignette in the chapter-end materials. As you will learn throughout the text, the Steeles are not experiencing any unusual financial stress. However, they have done virtually no financial planning for the future—an omission that many families make and one that could prove costly in the long run.

Like the Steeles, many of us would prefer avoiding financial problems or turning them over to someone else. Managing financial resources is time consuming, usually difficult, and sometimes not successful. We have often asked the federal, state, and local governments for help; Social Security retirement and federally funded health care are examples. But there is growing evidence that governments are no better—and perhaps are worse—at solving these problems than we are. If you are a young adult ready to start pursuing the American Dream, you will face some challenges far more formidable than those that faced your parents. The dream is becoming ever more elusive.

Many people of your parents' generation never worried much about health care and retirement. If they had a job, their employers provided health insurance, and Social Security will be waiting for them at retirement. Many of you are unlikely to have these assurances. If there is one dominant social theme in recent years it is *self-reliance*. Self-reliance, though, is not a trait inherited at birth; rather, it is an acquired skill. This leads us to personal finance. Becoming self-reliant financially begins with knowledge, and your decision to take a personal finance course was a wise one; it may be one of the most important decisions in your life.

WHY STUDY PERSONAL FINANCE?

You probably decided to take a personal finance course because financial success is important to you and you realize that in most cases it doesn't come easily. But what is financial success, and how is it measured? To some, it means making a lot of money—the sooner, the better. If that is your goal, then we are afraid this text won't help you very much; nor, we might add, will any other. You might as well save your time and go to Las Vegas or Atlantic City and hope for the best. **Financial success,** often elusive to define, is usually thought of as *obtaining the maximum benefits from limited financial resources*. This means you can be a financial success (or failure) regardless of your income level. A widow with many children and an income below the poverty line may be quite successful in allocating her very limited resources to achieve the goals her family feels are important, whereas a millionaire might misallocate most of his resources and achieve nothing.

Financial success: Obtaining maximum benefits from limited financial resources.

Your Goals in Life

If personal finance deals with achievement of goals, then you might ask: What goals does it try to achieve? Does it suggest, for example, that we all should save as much as we can? Do we measure success in terms of our weekly contributions to the bank account? Not necessarily. Obviously, what we plan to do during our lifetimes differs considerably. You may want to have a big family and enjoy entertainment activities with the kids while they are young and growing; you might also want to provide for their education. We, on the other hand, might be skinflints who love money for money's sake and have virtually no other

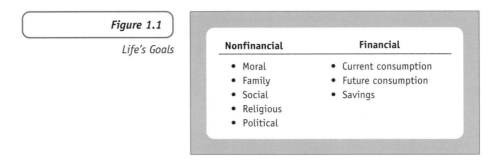

Figure 1.1

Life's Goals

Nonfinancial	Financial
• Moral	• Current consumption
• Family	• Future consumption
• Social	• Savings
• Religious	
• Political	

interests in life. (We're really not.) As Figure 1.1 indicates, we can categorize goals as either nonfinancial or financial.

Nonfinancial Goals

We should realize that many of our aspirations in life are nonfinancial. We hold moral, family, social, religious, or political ideals that have little or no connection to finance. You can't put a price tag on these goals, and you don't try. On the other hand, the extent to which we succeed in achieving our financial goals might determine how much time and energy are available to pursue the nonfinancial aspirations. Sociologists tell us, for example, that one of the primary reasons for divorce is financial stress in the family. Achieving financial goals doesn't assure a happy life, but the evidence suggests that it helps far more than it hinders.

Financial Goals

Financial goals form the basis for financial planning. Indeed, without financial goals, planning is impossible. Setting goals and incorporating them in annual budgeting are important topics discussed in depth in Chapters 2 and 3. However, it is useful to introduce the topics here.

Saving money $

BOX 1.1

Earn Less, Save More, Be Happy

Does more money always bring more happiness and do we ever have enough money? The answer to these question seems to be "no." Actually, regardless of our income level, most of us think we need 20 percent more wealth than what we currently have, according to Harvard University sociologists who asked people how much it would take to make them "perfectly happy."

Another researcher, Richard Easterlin from the University of Southern California, notes that this perception leads us to chase a moving target. The result? We never hit it, even though we spend valuable time and effort trying, and we wind up being perpetually unhappy even though our incomes are constantly rising. Apparently spending time with family and friends carries too high a price when that time can be spent earning more income. Easterlin's research, though, indicates that it is precisely good health and quality time with loved ones that make us happy.

Ironically, financial planning, which many people view as the primary tool of the wealth chaser, can play a critical role in shaping family happiness. When used properly, and when family members share common values, it forces us to put a price tag on our activities. Is it Yellowstone next year or a pool in the backyard? Or, should all of us work a little less and spend a few evenings in the park? The very act of asking these questions and then incorporating our answers into a family budget might slow the chase for more income. At the very least, it should help us determine what truly makes us happy.

Finally, perhaps the simplest way to save money is to realize we may not need as much of it as we think. Again, by having a firm grip on our financial situation, by making realistic plans for the future, and by providing adequately for emergencies, we will have a clearer idea of when we have enough money and that it is unnecessary to pursue the 20 percent "more."

Very broadly, one might list the most important financial goal as **financial independence,** that is, to have enough income or resources to be self-reliant. However, a goal defined this broadly really doesn't help us plan for the future. What does self-reliant mean? You might understand it as having a job with little threat of a layoff, while someone else sees it as never going into debt. Actually, there are two more concrete goals to shape financial plans: a consumption goal—current and future—and a savings goal.

Financial independence: Having sufficient income or resources to be self-reliant.

Current Consumption. Current consumption refers to goods and services that we use in a current period of time, such as this year. These goods and services measure our scale of living. A low consumption budget means we use fewer of them and (probably) have a lower level of satisfaction than someone with a high consumption budget. If Mary's consumption budget is twice that of John's, chances are very good she has more consumption satisfaction than he. But she might not have twice as much. Economists often point out the **principle of diminishing marginal satisfaction,** which means that current consumption satisfaction increases as current income increases but usually at a decreasing rate. This principle explains why we begin to look more favorably at future consumption after we have achieved reasonable levels of current consumption.

Current consumption: Goods and services used in a current time period.

Principle of diminishing marginal satisfaction: A decreasing *rate* of satisfaction in relation to increasing income.

Future Consumption. Future consumption refers to goods and services to be used in future periods. By itself, future consumption is less desirable than current consumption. Would you rather enjoy a good meal today or 20 years from today? In fact, if your annual income were to remain constant throughout your life, you might very well choose to spend a higher proportion on consumption while you are young, rather than waiting until you are old. But our incomes are seldom the same from year to year. Usually, they are quite low when we start our careers, increase substantially as we move into our most productive years, and then decline as we enter retirement. If we were forced to consume all our income each year, a very uneven consumption pattern would result. Fortunately, there is no such requirement. We try to smooth current consumption over time in order to get the highest overall consumption satisfaction throughout our lifetimes. This means we borrow heavily when we are young and repay our debts in later years.

Future consumption: Goods and services to be used in future periods.

Savings. Savings is simply the portion of our income *not* spent on current consumption. We have just mentioned one important reason for saving—to enjoy future consumption, perhaps in retirement—but there are others. One of the more important of these is to leave an estate to our heirs. Another might be to increase our investment assets, thereby gaining greater financial independence.

Savings: The portion of current income *not* consumed.

Important Economic Trends

Achieving financial goals would be much simpler if we lived in a predictable economic environment. But we don't. There are, however, certain trends that are likely to continue in the future. Let's see what they are.

TOPIC **LINKS**
Find current economic data at Economic Statistics Briefing Room.

Continuing Inflation

As Figure 1.2 shows, recent inflation rates are substantially lower than those in the past; indeed, they have declined so much that some economists are concerned that we may be entering periods of deflation (falling prices). Since the last time we experienced deflation was in the Depression of the 1930s, it is not a familiar situation, which would make financial planning even more difficult if it were to occur. However, the consensus of economists is that modest inflation, with rates between 1 and 3 percent, is the more likely long-run scenario. Although these numbers suggest a tame inflationary environment, over long periods

TOPIC **LINKS**
Visit the St. Louis Fed's site.

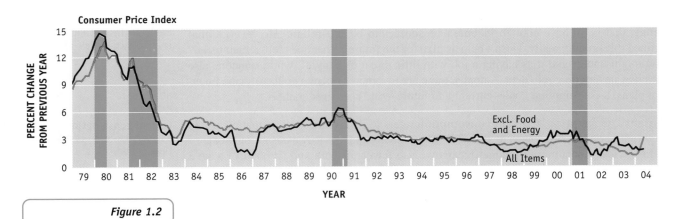

Consumer Price Index

Figure 1.2

Annual Inflation Rates

Source: Federal Reserve Bank of St. Louis, National Economic Trends, *July 2004, p. 8.*

of time they can seriously erode the value of your savings. Your investments must earn more than the inflation rate if you hope to grow your wealth in real terms. Unfortunately, many people have been content to leave too much of their money in low-yielding savings accounts that often only match, or fall short of, inflation rates. We hope you won't make that mistake.

Persistent Business Cycles

Figure 1.3 provides a measurement of our economy's performance since 1979. As you see, there were four recessions, each of which had a serious impact on many American families, in terms of layoffs, reduced incomes, and spending cutbacks. There is no reason to suspect the pattern of recessions will stop, so you should develop financial plans that allow for economic instability. Build enough wealth to survive a financial shock and hold it in investments that aren't devastated in value by the cycle.

If you will soon be a college graduate, you are likely to find the job offers fewer in number and perhaps for less money than offers made to graduates during boom years. Unfortunately, college recruiting is one of the quickest and easiest ways for companies to cut expenses.

Figure 1.3

Changes in Real Gross Domestic Product (GDP)

Source: Federal Reserve Bank of St. Louis, National Economic Trends, *July 2004, p. 4.*

Continued Instability in Financial Markets

The crash of the stock markets in 2000 should be a lesson that investment risk is still very much alive and a force to be considered in making plans for the future. The robust and consistent gains in stock prices prior to the crash created a type of investment euphoria where

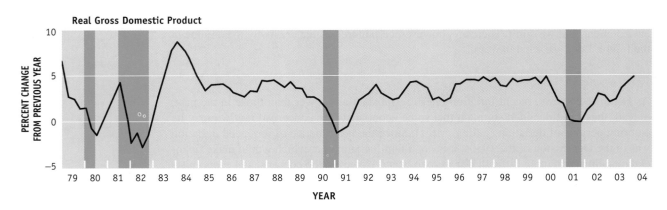

Real Gross Domestic Product

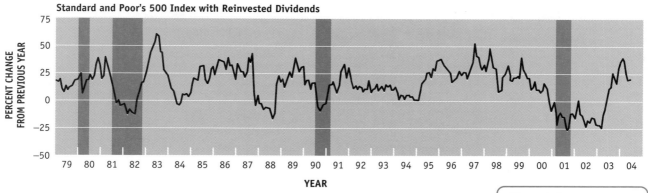

Standard and Poor's 500 Index with Reinvested Dividends

Figure 1.4

Stock Returns: Standard and Poor's 500 Index with Reinvested Dividends

Source: Federal Reserve Bank of St. Louis, National Economic Trends, *July 2004, p. 7.*

20 to 30 percent gains each year were to be considered the norm. If you really wanted to get rich, you were urged to put your money in Internet stocks, which virtually doubled in price every three months. When it was all over, many of the Internet start-ups were bankrupt and even the blue-chip technology stocks, such as Intel, had lost 50 percent or more of their value. The popular Nasdaq index, loaded with big technology companies, declined to 1620 from its record high of almost 5000 one year earlier; and, as Figure 1.4 shows, returns on an index of 500 large companies have been very volatile over time. Note the significant negative returns in 2000, 2001, and 2002.

A High and Selectively Rewarding Tax System

Despite whichever party wins the presidency or holds a majority in Congress, we can usually count on two outcomes where taxes are concerned—rates will be high and the tax law will grow more complex. Indeed, it is already referred to as "the full employment act for accountants." From a financial planning perspective it is appropriate to focus attention on attributes of the tax law that favor some courses of action over others. For example, the law encourages people to save and invest for their eventual retirement by allowing certain income tax deductions for contributions made to qualified retirement plans, such as IRAs (explained and discussed in later chapters). Put simply, not to take advantage of such plans—and many people do not—is poor financial practice. Buying or selling your home or investment securities also has potential tax savings or pitfalls, which you should research before making decisions. Finally, it is important to follow the financial news to be aware of changes that could impact your financial plans.

ACHIEVING FINANCIAL GOALS THROUGH PLANNING

Planning is the key to personal financial success. Without it, your situation resembles that of an empty, rudderless ship floating on a lake. You can't tell where the ship has been or where it's going. Few people live this aimlessly, but many have only very hazy and poorly defined ideas about what they hope to accomplish financially. Waking up one morning in your mid-forties and realizing you'd better do something about retirement is a poor approach. You may not have enough time to accumulate an adequate retirement nest egg, and you also lose all the income tax advantages that were available during the previous years, plus the earnings that earlier investments could have provided. A dollar saved and properly invested in your twenties could easily be the equivalent of $10 saved and invested during your forties. This view of planning as a lifelong process is called **life-cycle planning.**

TOPIC **LINKS**

Examine an overview of financial planning.

Life-cycle planning: A view of financial planning as a lifelong process.

Figure 1.5

Life-Cycle Financial Planning

Life-Cycle Phases	Financial Planning Areas
Young adult (18–25)	Consumption and savings
	Debt
Family formation (26–35)	Insurance
Family development (36–49)	Investment
	Retirement
Family maturity (50–60)	Estate
Retirement (60–?)	Income taxes

Life-Cycle Planning

People go through different phases during their lives, as Figure 1.5 shows. Goals change in importance as we enter different phases, but the key to life-cycle planning is that *all* our lifelong goals are recognized and attended to at *each* phase in the cycle. The sooner a goal is stated and solidified, the better. Retirement (as in the preceding example), the children's educations, or a trip to Tahiti is more easily and effectively accomplished when lead times are longer.

Major Financial Planning Areas

Certain areas require constant attention in all life-cycle phases. These areas are consumption and savings planning, debt planning, insurance planning, investment planning, retirement planning, and estate planning. Threaded throughout all of these areas is income tax planning. The government's share of your success is a fact of life that is probably already familiar to you. It certainly will become more familiar as this course progresses. The sections that follow discuss each type of planning.

Consumption and Savings Planning

Consumption and savings planning is an integral part of your strategy to achieve lifelong goals. As mentioned previously, you must decide each year how much of your income to allocate to current consumption and how much to save for the future. The topic of saving to acquire future goals is covered in Chapter 2. Also, two important activities related to consumption and savings planning are preparing periodic personal financial statements—an income statement and a balance sheet—and an annual budget. The latter is the instrument you use most often to make sure you are moving toward your goals. Financial statements and budgeting are covered in Chapter 3.

Debt Planning

Very few people avoid debt throughout their lives—nor should they. Debt is the vehicle that allows us to even our lifelong consumption. In addition, it is a shopping convenience, and it can help us hedge against inflation by permitting us to buy assets that match or beat the inflation rate. But debt must be managed carefully. We must avoid excessive debt and make sure we tap the lowest-cost sources of credit. Why borrow at 18 percent if you have access to funds costing 8 percent or less? Unfortunately, many Americans do. Debt management is discussed in Chapters 6 and 7.

Insurance Planning

Life's uncertainties create continuous insurance needs. As a young adult with few obligations and no dependents, your primary asset is your ability to work and earn income. Therefore, you must protect yourself against the loss of that ability; that is, you need disability insurance. As you go through later phases of the life cycle, other insurance needs increase in importance. The needs of your dependents in the event of your death create a demand for life insurance, and as you accumulate assets—a house, automobiles, household furnishings, and others—you need more property and personal liability insurance. And, most important, you need medical insurance to protect against health or accident problems. The "average" illness can lead to hospital and doctor bills large enough to wipe out your entire savings, and then some. Insurance planning is explained in Chapters 13, 14, and 15.

Investment Planning

While saving part of our income each year, we must decide how to invest it. Choices here seem almost limitless, ranging from simply letting our bank account grow to speculating in raw land or commodity futures contracts. Successful investment often spells the difference between achieving our lifelong goals (and maybe even exceeding them) and failing to do so. An important first investment goal is to provide sufficient liquidity; this topic is discussed in Chapter 5. You can then turn your attention to riskier investments that offer potentially higher returns, as discussed in Chapters 9, 10, 11, and 12.

Retirement Planning

Retirement planning consists primarily of estimating future consumption and other needs and then determining how you will meet those needs when you are no longer working. Most of us rely on Social Security and employer-sponsored retirement plans for retirement income, but we also realize that supplemental sources may be necessary to maintain a suitable lifestyle in retirement. We must invest during our working years to accumulate a retirement nest egg. The federal government has recognized these supplemental retirement efforts and has enacted favorable tax legislation to help achieve them. Retirement planning is the subject of Chapter 16.

Estate Planning

If you live forever, you can avoid the problem of estate planning: how to minimize taxes while giving away your wealth. Since the odds in favor of earthly immortality are not encouraging, your next best strategy is to make sure you have your financial house in order when you make the grand exit. Essential to this plan are a proper will and a sound tax strategy, which might mean distributing part of your wealth in the form of gifts while you are still alive. Estate planning is, appropriately enough, our final subject, and it appears in Chapter 15.

Income Tax Planning

Almost no aspect of our financial lives is untouched by federal income taxes. The federal government will become a partner in all the income you earn. There are ways to minimize the tax bite, but it is up to you to find out what they are and how and when to use them. Two people with identical incomes and family situations could wind up with $100,000 difference in their assets after 30 years or so because of effective versus ineffective tax planning. With this much at stake, it's worth your effort to become familiar with the income tax law, and Chapter 4 will give you a good start.

Career Planning

Choosing a career is clearly an important decision, not only financially but also in terms of mental and emotional health. To many people, their careers define them as persons and represent sources of both enjoyment and frustration. Moreover, career planning is not a one-time effort during senior year in college but, rather, it goes on throughout the whole life cycle, as people change careers or temporarily leave and then return to the labor market. Although career planning is a topic generally outside the area of personal finance, because of its importance, some advice is provided in Appendix 1.1 to this chapter.

A Planning Approach

As shown in Figure 1.6, planning involves four steps. First, you must state your broad goals in specific and concrete terms. For example, if buying a home is an important goal, you must decide eventually when you will buy it, how much to pay for it, the size of your down payment, and how to finance it. The second step is to create an action plan, which sets out in detail how you will achieve your goal. To achieve the goal of buying a home, you must save a portion of your income each year and invest the funds temporarily. After you have set a specific date to buy a home, you can decide which temporary investments are best suited to help achieve the goal. If the purchase date is relatively far in the future (say, five years or longer), you might choose investments that are somewhat riskier (with potentially higher yields) than you would choose if you intended to buy next year. The third step in the planning process involves evaluating your performance toward the goal. This step would be unnecessary if we lived in an unchanging world—but we do not. The type of home you want might increase in price, or financing costs might go up, or other changes could frustrate your effort to buy the home. The fourth and final planning stage forces us to decide if the goal is still worth achieving or if we should abandon it and search for another broad goal. If you decide the home is still worth the effort, for example, you must then revise your action plan by increasing the annual savings or perhaps by choosing other temporary investments offering higher returns. (The latter approach could be very risky, though.)

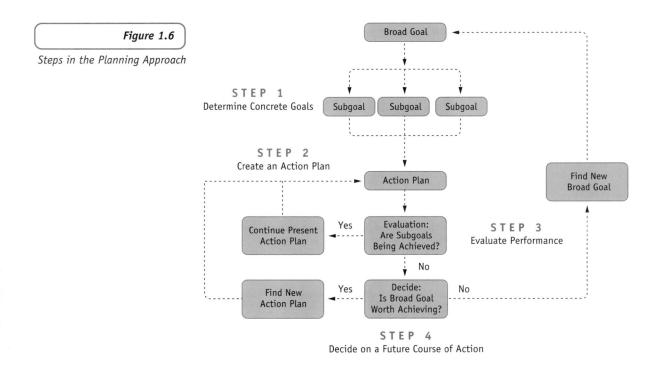

Figure 1.6

Steps in the Planning Approach

STEP 1
Determine Concrete Goals

STEP 2
Create an Action Plan

STEP 3
Evaluate Performance

STEP 4
Decide on a Future Course of Action

Using the four steps shown in Figure 1.6 does not guarantee success, but you will certainly achieve goals far more easily if you use this method rather than a haphazard approach. Effective planning puts you at the rudder of the ship on the lake, and it gives you the navigational aids you need to bring the ship to its destination.

MAKING FINANCIAL DECISIONS

Making a decision is a complex process. To decide is to choose among alternatives. You probably have encountered many situations in which making a choice was difficult; indeed, your biggest problem may have been simply identifying what choices were available. Then you had to find some basis for evaluating the expected outcomes of each alternative. With all that done, you must pick one alternative as the best. Consider how difficult choosing a major in college can be; unfortunately, we face equally difficult financial decisions most of our lives. We can make better decisions if we follow guidance provided by basic economic theory, and we'll probably attain a more secure future if we follow a conservative approach when we build for it.

Some Helpful Economic Insights

Economists have pioneered in the field of decision making. Two concepts—marginal analysis and opportunity costs—are useful to anyone who must make important decisions. Each is explained in the following sections.

Marginal Analysis

Marginal analysis means looking at *changes* in important variables that are related to changes in decision inputs you can control. For example, suppose you are ready to graduate and you are investing in a wardrobe you will need for your first job. You know that two good business suits are a must, but a third might be a luxury. To decide whether to buy the third suit requires that you compare the benefits it provides against its cost. If you think the added benefits are worth it, buy the third suit; if not, then don't buy it. But definitely do not consider benefits that the first and second suits provide, because they are totally irrelevant to the decision.

Marginal analysis should always be employed whenever a decision involves comparing different approaches to a problem. For example, suppose you are considering buying two different automobile insurance policies that differ with respect to coverage and cost. The two plans have the same basic coverage, but one includes protection against certain perils whereas the other does not. The former also has a higher yearly premium. In deciding between the two, you don't have to look at the total coverages and total premiums of each; all you have to do is to compare the extra (marginal) coverage with the extra (marginal) premium. Then decide if the more comprehensive policy is worth the extra cost.

Marginal analysis: Evaluating *changes* in important variables in relation to controllable decision inputs.

Opportunity Costs

Opportunity costs are benefits that you give up when you choose one alternative over another. If you decide to work during the Christmas holidays, you might give up a skiing trip to Colorado. The opportunity cost of the job is the fun you lose by not choosing the skiing trip, and the opportunity cost of the skiing trip is the income you won't earn by turning down the job. Sometimes opportunity costs are obvious; at other times they are identified only by thoughtful consideration. For example, what is your opportunity cost of taking a course in personal finance, assuming you need the hours for graduation? It is not the

Opportunity costs: Benefits given up when one alternative is chosen over another.

tuition cost of the course; rather, it is the information and learning offered by another course that you can't take because you are taking this one.

These examples might seem trivial, but opportunity costs arise in big decisions as well as small. Examples: What are the opportunity costs of choosing one career over another? What are the opportunity costs of your undergraduate education? What are the opportunity costs of renting versus buying a home? Consider carefully your responses to these questions. Some of the costs are clearly economic and probably easy to measure; others involve personal preferences and can be measured only by expressing personal value judgments. To get on the right track when using this technique, ask the following question: What do I give up if I choose one alternative over another? The answer will give you the opportunity cost for the alternative under consideration.

THE BUILDING BLOCKS OF SUCCESS

An important part of financial planning is setting priorities. All through life you will encounter both opportunities and risks, and you need to put them in perspective. Suppose you are a young person with family obligations and very little savings. A friend, who has recently become a securities salesperson, calls and tells you how you can double your money in a speculative investment. There is a strong temptation to take the offer, even though you know if it fails you will have to give up or delay other important goals. But if it succeeds, you can do so much more! Most financial advisers will tell you to forget risky

Finance News

BOX 1.3

What's a Professional Financial Planner—And Do You Need One?

The growing complexities of financial planning over the past 20 years have created a demand for a new professional—the **financial planner.** This person has a broad understanding of tax laws, insurance, investments, and finance in general. He or she is not necessarily an expert in any one area but is sufficiently knowledgeable in all to recognize problems and to suggest specialized professional help if it is needed. The planner's main function is to create a financial plan to help clients achieve their goals. This profession is not yet as organized and regulated as other professions, such as medicine, law, or accounting, and anyone can adopt the title of professional planner. But there is a growing trend toward regulation and, as the following table shows, there are a number of self-regulatory organizations that are active in establishing standards and a professional code of ethics.

Do you need a professional planner? Of course, the answer to that question depends on the complexity of your financial situation and how much of your own time you are willing to devote to the job. Assuming you have an average financial situation and you carefully complete this text (and the course, if you are using the text as part of a course), you should be able to develop your own financial plans. However, the professional planner may be able to add insights to a problem or use a computer to develop and evaluate your financial plans. These services could be worth their costs, which usually start at about $300 for a simple evaluation and could go to several thousand dollars for someone with complex financial problems.

Some companies provide financial planning services to their employees as a fringe benefit. If you use this service, make sure the contact person is truly a financial planner and not a commissioned salesperson who may promote his or her products, whether they are appropriate for you or not.

Organization	Certification/Membership
International Board of Standards and Practices	Certified Financial Planner (CFP)
American College of Bryn Mawr, PA	Chartered Financial Consultant (ChFC)
International Association of Financial Planning	Member of the Registry
International Association of Registered Planners	Registered Financial Planner (RFP)
National Association of Personal Financial Advisors	Association of Fee-Only Planners
American Institute of Certified Public Accountants—Personal Financial Planning Division	Certified Public Accountant—Accredited Personal Financial Planning Specialist (CPA–APFS)

propositions such as this until you have satisfied those goals you have already decided are the most important.

Setting priorities and sticking to the long-run plan suggests a **building-block approach to financial planning,** as illustrated in Figure 1.7. You begin with the lowest blocks, which means you first build a strong foundation of support. You proceed to the first investment level *after* the lowest blocks are secure. Likewise, go to riskier investments only after you have a suitable level of safe ones, deferring the very riskiest until last. Remember that if you fail at a higher level, the goals supported by success at the lower levels will not be achieved. You might have decided, for example, to invest in government bonds that will guarantee enough future return to put your kids through the state university. If you abandon this plan and put the money instead in speculative growth stocks, you might eventually have enough to put them through Harvard—or you might have to tell them there is very little available to support their educations anywhere. You must make the choice, but at least understand the risks involved and the potential consequences of your choice.

Building-block approach to financial planning: Sequential investing, starting with a low-risk foundation and then moving to riskier investments.

Financial planner: A professional who helps clients create, maintain, and execute a financial plan, designed to achieve their financial goals.

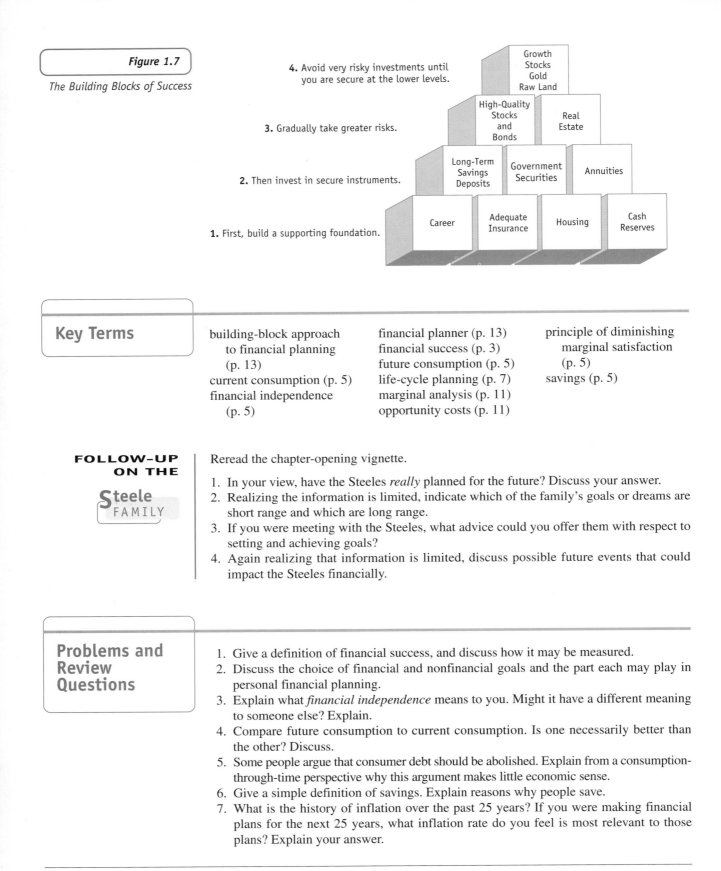

Figure 1.7

The Building Blocks of Success

4. Avoid very risky investments until you are secure at the lower levels.

3. Gradually take greater risks.

2. Then invest in secure instruments.

1. First, build a supporting foundation.

Growth Stocks Gold Raw Land

High-Quality Stocks and Bonds

Real Estate

Long-Term Savings Deposits

Government Securities

Annuities

Career

Adequate Insurance

Housing

Cash Reserves

Key Terms

building-block approach
to financial planning
(p. 13)
current consumption (p. 5)
financial independence
(p. 5)

financial planner (p. 13)
financial success (p. 3)
future consumption (p. 5)
life-cycle planning (p. 7)
marginal analysis (p. 11)
opportunity costs (p. 11)

principle of diminishing
marginal satisfaction
(p. 5)
savings (p. 5)

FOLLOW-UP ON THE

Steele FAMILY

Reread the chapter-opening vignette.

1. In your view, have the Steeles *really* planned for the future? Discuss your answer.
2. Realizing the information is limited, indicate which of the family's goals or dreams are short range and which are long range.
3. If you were meeting with the Steeles, what advice could you offer them with respect to setting and achieving goals?
4. Again realizing that information is limited, discuss possible future events that could impact the Steeles financially.

Problems and Review Questions

1. Give a definition of financial success, and discuss how it may be measured.
2. Discuss the choice of financial and nonfinancial goals and the part each may play in personal financial planning.
3. Explain what *financial independence* means to you. Might it have a different meaning to someone else? Explain.
4. Compare future consumption to current consumption. Is one necessarily better than the other? Discuss.
5. Some people argue that consumer debt should be abolished. Explain from a consumption-through-time perspective why this argument makes little economic sense.
6. Give a simple definition of savings. Explain reasons why people save.
7. What is the history of inflation over the past 25 years? If you were making financial plans for the next 25 years, what inflation rate do you feel is most relevant to those plans? Explain your answer.

8. What has been the history of the overall economy over the past 25 years? Explain if you think recessions no longer plague our economic growth.
9. Some people believe that the stock market is a safe place to put your money. Do you agree, particularly if the money might be needed on short notice?
10. Suppose that you are planning for your retirement in 30 years. What rate of return on stock investments is reasonable to use in making such plans?
11. Is our current income tax law neutral in terms of financial planning; that is, can you make such plans without considering tax impacts? Discuss.
12. What are the phases of the life cycle, and how are they related to financial planning?
13. Explain the steps involved in financial planning, and list the eight major planning areas.
14. Explain marginal analysis and opportunity cost, and then indicate why they are important concepts in financial decision making.
15. How would you measure the cost of spending a night at home watching television?
16. Martin has been asked by Jan to deliver a package on his way home for Christmas break. The trip would take him a total of 200 miles out of his way. Jan has offered to pay $40 for the service.
    (a) What marginal costs of operating his car do you think Martin should consider in deciding to accept or reject Jan's offer?
    (b) Identify an opportunity cost to Martin himself that might sway his decision.
17. What is a building-block approach to financial planning?
18. Bryan has saved $2,000. His friend Chris has told him he should put it in a savings account because Bryan has very little cash reserves. Bryan wants to speculate in the stock market by trading biotech stocks. What's your view on this matter? Discuss.

Case 1.1
The Haggertys' Financial Planning

Jan and Mickey Haggerty graduated from college several years ago. Each majored in biology, and they were fortunate to receive good job offers at graduation; their combined income last year was over $100,000. The Haggertys enjoy a high level of current consumption, but they also have saved about $6,000, which is invested in a bank savings account. They would like to buy a house eventually, but they are not certain when. Jan thinks they should have a definite plan for buying the house. This plan would indicate the date of purchase, the down payment, the expected purchase price, and other important details. Jan is so enthusiastic over the purchase that she thinks they should take their money out of savings and invest in growth stocks. She has heard that they ought to get 20 percent on these stocks, which certainly beats the 2 percent they are getting at the bank.

Mickey thinks Jan worries too much about buying a house. He questions the necessity of a financial plan, believing instead that they should just continue saving in the future as they have in the past. Besides, he heard at work that a recession could be coming, and, if it does, he thinks it might be a good idea to delay buying stocks until their prices come way down. He heard you make money in the stock market by buying low and selling high. Jan would like to buy the house within five years; Mickey thinks setting a date is not wise. If the stocks work out well, they can get it sooner; if not, they have to wait. Besides, a friend of Mickey's told him he should worry more about all the income taxes he and Jan are paying, since they already are in a 28 percent tax bracket.

Questions
1. Without knowing more about the Haggertys, would you say they might benefit from financial planning? Cite specific examples.
2. What do you think of Jan's idea of investing in growth stocks? What additional information about the Haggertys would you like to have before you give a final answer to this question?

3. What is your opinion of Mickey's idea to delay buying common stocks until their prices fall? Do you think his source of information at work is a reliable forecaster? And do you think it's a good idea in general to base the success of your financial plans on accurately forecasting future economic events? Explain.

Case 1.2
Lou Pirella and Vicki Wright: Two College Students

Lou Pirella and Vicki Wright are taking a course in computer science together. They have been good friends for some time, and each will graduate at the end of the current term. Lou is going directly into the workforce, and Vicki plans to earn an M.B.A. degree at a university near her hometown. She is trying to convince Lou to join her, but he feels four years of college is enough—at least for a while.

Lou and Vicki have been talking quite a bit about their plans after graduation. Vicki is relying on her M.B.A. to earn a good income in the future, although she also plans to invest, but only in very secure investments. Lou will take a more aggressive approach to investing, and he told Vicki he will probably earn considerably more than she each year. Lou has opened an account at a stock brokerage firm and plans to begin investing as soon as he can.

Neither Lou nor Vicki currently has life insurance or very much money in checking and savings accounts. Moreover, neither has given much thought to future housing needs. Both have fairly sizable student loan amounts outstanding and Lou has a credit card balance of $4,300 on which he makes monthly payments. He knows he pays interest on unpaid balances, but he isn't sure of the interest rate.

Questions
1. How should Vicki look at the opportunity costs of her M.B.A. degree? Explain.
2. Suppose that when Vicki registers at the university, she learns that she can pay a flat tuition of $3,000 a semester and take up to 15 credit hours (but no more). Or she can elect simply to pay $250 per credit hour and take as many hours as she wants each semester. Assuming it takes 60 hours to graduate, and also assuming she could handle 20 hours a semester without threatening her grades, what is the marginal cost of the second option—that is, paying $250 per credit hour? What might be the opportunity costs of the first option? Explain.
3. What advice can you give Lou with respect to financial planning? Touch on specific topics in your answer.

Marie Wilson Goal-Planning Exercise Setting Goals

Marie Wilson is a very good friend of yours. Married at 19, she is currently 28 years old, divorced for the past two years, and has a 4-year-old son, Jake. She has a reasonably good relationship with Jake's father, who contributes to his son's support. Marie is employed full time as a paralegal in a large law office. Her salary this year is $32,000. While Marie enjoys her job, she would like to achieve a more rewarding position in the future, perhaps one day becoming an attorney.

Marie has recently earned a two-year paralegal degree from a local community college. She has tentative plans to start a four-year program with a major in either economics or political science. If she pursues this goal, Marie would take evening classes at the local university. She hopes that she could earn a degree in four years, if she can find the time and financial resources to support her efforts.

Marie lives close to town and commutes to work by bus. However, she owns a 1994 Grand Marquis that is used on weekends and shopping trips. The car does not get very good gas mileage and seems to be in frequent need of repairs. The local university is located outside the city and not conveniently accessed by public transportation. Marie believes that she will need a new car within the next three years.

Marie likes her neighborhood, particularly its school system; however, she is cramped in her current apartment. Larger apartments are available, but Marie would prefer not moving until she could afford buying a condominium. There are a number available in the area, unfortunately, at prices that she cannot afford at the present time.

Marie tries to be active in the community and is a choir member at a local church. The church runs a two-week summer touring program to various cities, but Marie has been unable to go because of the cost. She very much would like to join the group next year. She also enjoys doing things with Jake, particularly outdoor activities. Jake shows strong athletic skills, and Marie would like to enroll him in a golf clinic when he is eight or nine. Of course, a clinic is expensive and she would probably need to buy a set of clubs.

Marie has given no thought to eventual retirement, hoping that Social Security funds will be adequate when retirement arrives. She feels that retirement is so far in the future that it is unwise to worry about it now. Marie has a strong relationship with her parents and a sister, but they are in no position to help her financially. Marie has considerable debt (credit card and school loans) and virtually no savings. On occasion, she is depressed by what she believes will be a bleak financial future, and she has often discussed this topic with you. You would like to help Marie, and you are excited by the opportunity to apply much of what you will learn in your Personal Finance course.

You will gain additional data about Marie as you go through the next two chapters. We will give you hints and perhaps suggestions at various points, but it will be your job to help Marie start a solid financial plan by framing financial goals, determining the required savings to achieve them, and incorporating a savings amount into her annual budget. The first task you should undertake is to prepare a list of financial goals, using Form 1.1.

Form 1.1

Identifying Financial Goals
Current Date: Month_____Day_____Year_____

	Date to Achieve	Number of Years in the Future
A. Short-range goals (to be achieved within two years)		
_____		
_____		
_____	_____	_____
B. Intermediate-range goals (to be achieved in two to ten years)		
_____		
_____		
_____	_____	_____
C. Long-range goals (to be achieved in periods over ten years)		
_____		
_____		
_____	_____	_____
Discussion of goals		
_____		
_____		
_____	_____	_____

Exercises to Strengthen Your Use of the Internet
(Internet links for the following exercises can be found at **www.prenhall.com/winger**.)

Exercise 1.1 Getting Financial Planning Information
The American Association of Retired Persons (AARP) is concerned about family finances for all families, not only for those who are retired. Visit its Web site and learn more about financial planning.
Q. Click on "Financial Planning" and then choose "Be Cautious When Doing Business On Line." Discuss several precautions indicated by AARP.

Exercise 1.2 Visit the White House for Financial News
The White House gathers a wide array of financial and economic news used by the president and his advisers in making important political decisions.
Q. Click on "Income" and find the most current value for household income. Then click on the graphic and determine if household income is rising or falling.

Exercise 1.3 Following the Economy
Keep up with current economic events by using the Bureau of Labor Statistics data and choosing the series of interest to you. Click on the graphic for a graph of the series, which gives the information more effectively than the tables. For the following question choose the "Unemployment Rate" series.
Q. What has been the highest unemployment rate since 1992. Suppose the unemployment rate is 10 percent at the time you graduate. What implication might such a rate have with respect to your job-search efforts?

Exercise 1.4 Finding a Financial Planner
You may want the assistance of a professional financial planner. Visit the Forum for Investor Advice and see its comments on finding a financial planner who is right for you.
Q. Review the questions you should ask the planner in your initial interview.

Appendix 1.1
A Closer Look at Career Planning

Career planning is a complicated process in which you must consider your preferences, aptitudes, and current resources. Your school placement counselor and your state bureau of employment are good starting points for formalizing career plans. If you decide to use a private counselor, be sure to check out references and review his or her credentials. The International Association of Counseling Services and the National Board of Certified Counselors are the top accrediting services for career counselors.

Sources of Information

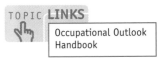

TOPIC **LINKS**

Occupational Outlook
Handbook

The best source for a summary description of over 250 occupations is the *Occupational Outlook Handbook,* by the U.S. Department of Labor. This handy guide is available on the Internet and in print. For each occupation, you can discover the educational requirements, working conditions, and average earnings. The job outlook for each occupation is highlighted, along with sources of additional information.

The introduction to the *Occupational Outlook Handbook* contains a review of tomorrow's jobs. It shows occupations that are expected to grow the fastest over the next few years and those that will decline as a percentage of the workforce. Market wages are set by supply and demand, and it is likely that occupations experiencing the greatest increase in demand will also reflect the largest increases in wages.

Other useful publications by the U.S. Bureau of Labor Statistics include the *Career Guide to Industries* and the *Occupational Outlook Quarterly*. The *Career Guide to Industries* reviews occupations from an industry perspective, indicating the kinds of occupations that can be found within a given industry. For in-depth articles on specific occupations or job-search strategies, you should examine previous issues of the *Occupational Outlook Quarterly*.

Potential Salaries

The U.S. Census Bureau publishes an update to *What's It Worth: Field of Training and Economic Status* every few years. Here you can find earnings by both undergraduate and advanced degrees. For the most recent information on salary offers for new graduates, go to Jobweb on the Internet for a quarterly salary survey. Additional salary information on recent graduates can be found at the National Association of Colleges and Employers. More comprehensive, but less recent, data are contained in the National Compensation Survey conducted by the U.S. Bureau of Labor Statistics.

TOPIC **LINKS**

National Association of Colleges and Employers

Your potential salary is only one of many factors you should consider when choosing a career. The same caution applies when deciding among competing salary offers. Consideration should be given to relative working conditions, opportunities for advancement, job-related learning experiences, and most importantly, nonwage fringe benefits.

Fringe Benefits

In its survey of the employer cost of employee compensation the U.S. Department of Labor indicates that over 25 percent of total employee compensation consists of fringe benefits. Typically, the most valuable components of the fringe benefit package are the health and pension benefits. In most cases, these and related benefits are either tax deferred or tax exempt. Tax-deferred benefits are those for which taxes come due only at some future date, the most common being employer contributions to pension plans. The tax on such contributions typically does not become due until you retire and are likely to be in a lower tax bracket.

TOPIC **LINKS**

Employee Benefits Survey at the BLS

Tax-exempt benefits are those that avoid taxes completely. One of the most important of these benefits is employer contributions to health and life insurance plans. Since a tax is never imposed, the dollar value of tax-exempt fringe benefits will understate the value it would cost employees if they were to purchase similar benefits with after-tax wages. For example, suppose you are in the 28 percent marginal tax bracket. This means that if you earn another dollar, you will have to pay the government 28 cents. You get to keep only 72 cents as after-tax income. Now suppose the prospective employer offers to provide $1,000 of medical insurance payments. In the 28 percent marginal tax bracket, you would have to earn $1,388.89 before taxes to provide these same benefits out of after-tax income. The before-tax cost may be calculated using the following formula.

$$\text{Before-tax cost} = \frac{\text{tax-free fringe benefit}}{(1 - \text{marginal tax rate})}$$

$$\$1,388.89 = \frac{\$1,000}{(1 - 0.28)}$$

Regional Cost-of-Living Comparisons

If you are comparing salaries in two different regions of the country, you should consider differences in relative costs of living. It can cost more than twice as much to live in New York City and maintain the same living standard as living in a midsized midwestern city

TOPIC LINKS

Cost of Living at Datamaster

such as Dayton, Ohio. The difference will depend on whether you rent or buy a home, how you commute to work, your tax bracket, and your particular lifestyle. There are a number of salary comparison calculators on the Internet. Because each uses a slightly different method for weighting the relevant factors, the results, as illustrated in the following table, can diverge widely. Datamaster provides a much higher relative income for New York City because it assumes you will live in Manhattan, the most expensive area in the five New York City boroughs.

	Dayton, OH	Los Angeles	New York City	Miami
Datamaster	$50,000	$81,501	$113,515	$53,340
Homefair	$50,000	$73,151	$ 71,461	$61,356
Yahoo	$50,000	$71,506	$ 79,032	$47,850

2

The Time Value of Money

ALL DOLLARS ARE NOT CREATED EQUAL

OBJECTIVES

1. To gain a general understanding that monies received or paid out at different points in time have different values and that these values can change dramatically depending on interest rate levels and the points in time when they are received or paid

2. To understand the process of compounding and to be able to compute a future value of a single payment or of an annuity

3. To understand the process of discounting and to be able to compute the present value of a single payment or of an annuity

4. To be able to find approximate values for unknown interest rates or unknown holding periods when the values for other financial variables are known

5. To recognize the importance of planning in the effort to achieve future goals

6. To be able to compute a required annual savings amount to meet future goals

7. To be able to construct a savings plan designed to show how savings will grow over time and be used to meet future goals

TOPIC **LINKS**

Follow the **Topic Links** in each chapter for your interactive Personal Finance exercise on the Web. Go to: **www.prenhall.com/winger**

Steele FAMILY

Sharon Steele participated in a lunch discussion about the pending retirement of one of the CPA firm's partners. The talk was lively and there was spirited give-and-take on the topic of the amount of money needed to provide a comfortable retirement for a typical couple. Amazingly, the estimates varied from $100,000 to well over $1,000,000. Of course, although people were making different assumptions, Sharon had no doubt that coming up with a reasonable amount was not a back-of-the-envelope calculation. More importantly, as Sharon listened, it dawned on her that she and Arnold had a poor grasp of how much they might count on from Social Security and from Arnold's retirement plan. Would the two be enough?

She later discussed her concern with Arnold and, as they pursued the issue further, it became clear that not only were they unsure about retirement funds, but also they had virtually no idea of how much would be needed to finance other desired activities. A particularly troublesome part of the planning involved estimating values through time. Sure, they could determine how much one year at State U might cost for Nancy and John if they started school today; but what will be the cost when they actually enroll in eight and ten years, respectively? Then, after these amounts are somehow calculated, how much must they invest each year to achieve them? Arnold and Sharon aren't going to kid themselves; they must allow a considerable amount of time to become familiar with time-value-of-money techniques.

Perhaps one of the most difficult parts of financial planning is estimating future funds requirements. The Steeles aren't alone in their inability to measure a retirement need or the amount needed for future college costs. Many families experience similar problems. The trouble lies in two areas: First, since expenses occur in the future, sometimes the very distant future, the impact of rising prices over time makes it difficult to determine how much the expenses actually will be. Second, knowing how much to invest periodically to meet the expenses is equally difficult since actual earning rates on the investments may not be known.

This chapter presents a basic treatment of approachs designed to measure the value of money over time, which are usually referred to as time-value-of-money techniques. There are two fundamental activities—compounding and discounting. Each is explained and the chapter concludes by applying these techniques to the Steeles' goal-planning situation.

COMPOUNDING (FINDING FUTURE VALUES)

Compounding: The process of accumulating value over time from a single payment.

Annuity: A series of equal payments.

Compounding refers to the process of accumulating value over time. Two cases are considered: first, the accumulation of value from a single payment (*payment* is a more general term than *investment*); second, the accumulation of value from a series of equal payments, called an **annuity.**

Future Value of a Single Payment

Future value: A sum of money received or paid in the future.

A sum of money received or paid in the future is called a **future value.** For example, you might be considering an investment that costs $1,000 today and returns the same amount to you at the end of three years. Is it a good investment? Of course not! Why be content just to get your money back when other investments pay interest? If someone wishes to use our money, we insist on a return—one at least as good as those available on equal-risk, alternative investments. Suppose the borrower offered to give your $1,000 back at the end of three years along with $200 in interest. Is that acceptable, if you think you could earn 10 percent annual interest somewhere else? To answer the question we must calculate the future value (*FV*) of $1,000 invested elsewhere. This calculation follows.

TOPIC **LINKS**

Use a future value calculator.

$$FV \text{ at end of year } 1 = \$1,000 + 0.10(\$1,000) = \$1,100$$

$$FV \text{ at end of year } 2 = \$1,100 + 0.10(\$1,100) = \$1,210$$

$$FV \text{ at end of year } 3 = \$1,210 + 0.10(\$1,210) = \$1,331$$

An alternative quick calculation is:

$$FV = (\$1,000)(1.0 + i)(1.0 + i)(1.0 + i)$$

where i = your required investment rate each period. Then

$$FV = (\$1,000)(1.1)(1.1)(1.1) = (\$1,000)(1.331) = \$1,331$$

Compound interest: A future value that includes interest on interest.

Simple interest: An assumption that interest earned in a period is withdrawn in that period.

In the preceding example, your $1,000 grows to $1,331 if you can invest it (and all the subsequent interest earned) at 10 percent. Comparing $1,331 with the $1,200 offered by the other investment tells us the other investment should be rejected.

The $331 of interest as calculated is called **compound interest.** It includes "interest on interest," which means that interest earned in earlier periods is assumed to be reinvested to earn interest in future periods. **Simple interest** assumes that interest earned in each period is withdrawn and not reinvested. The following formula is used to calculate simple interest:

Simple interest = (principal) × (rate) × (time)

Using the preceding data, simple interest would be $300 as calculated here:

$300 = ($1,000) × (0.10) × (3)

You can use either method to calculate interest, depending on which one is more appropriate to what you actually will do with earned interest. However, in most financial planning illustrations the compound method is used.

The Importance of Additional Yield

The future values of different investments are crucial to many financial decisions. For example, suppose you are considering investments A and B. A offers an 8 percent yield and has virtually no risk on either a short- or long-term basis. B offers a 10 percent yield and is about as risky as A on a long-term basis but somewhat riskier in the short term. (You might pay a penalty for early withdrawal, for example.) Since you plan to hold each investment for a long period of time, B's added risk is not of major concern to you. On the other hand, you aren't sure that a mere two percentage points is enough marginal yield to pick B over A. By looking only at the difference of two percentage points, you may fail to see the substantial difference in future values between the two. Figure 2.1 shows this difference in dramatic detail. (The amounts were calculated using the compound interest techniques explained earlier.) At the end of three years, you will have only $71 ($1,331 minus $1,260) more with investment B, but at the end of 40 years you will have an extra $23,533—more than twice as much!

The Importance of Additional Time

Figure 2.1 also dramatizes the importance of investing early to achieve certain goals, such as retirement. Suppose you are 25 and plan to retire at age 65. You are considering investing

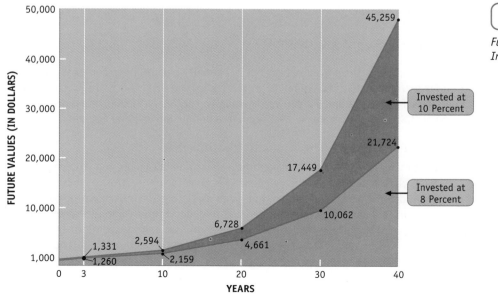

Figure 2.1

Future Value of $1,000 Invested at 8 and at 10 Percent

	Table 2.1		Interest Rate		
		Number of periods (*n*)	6%	8%	10%
Portion of a Future Value-of-$1 Table		1	1.0600	1.0800	1.1000
		3	1.1910	1.2597	1.3310
(See Appendix, Table A.1 for an expanded table.)		10	1.7908	2.1589	2.5937
		20	3.2071	4.6610	6.7275
		30	5.7435	10.0620	17.4490
		40	10.2850	21.7240	45.2590

now for retirement but wonder how much difference it would make if you waited 10 years to start. Assuming the 10 percent investment rate, the answer is $27,810 ($45,259 minus $17,449). You accumulate considerably more in the last 10 years than do you in the first 30!

Time-Value-of-Money Tables

Future value calculations are easy to make with a hand calculator, following the procedures just explained. As an alternative, many people use a *future-value-of-$1 table*. A portion of such a table is shown as Table 2.1. (More detailed tables appear in the Appendix at the end of the text.) A future-value table shows the future value of $1 invested for a specified number of periods and at a specified investment rate each period. To use the table, simply multiply the future value of $1 by the number of dollars you invest. If you invest $100, multiply $100 times 1.3310; if $200, multiply $200 times 1.3310, and so forth. You can see from Table 2.1 how the values in Figure 2.1 were determined.

The Rule of 72

The rule of 72: A simple technique to determine how long it takes to double an investment's value.

A popular technique for examining the relationship between a future value and its associated interest rate is the **rule of 72.** It's quite simple to use. For example, suppose you would like to double the amount of funds you have placed in an investment. The length of time needed to accomplish this goal depends on the rate of interest you earn. If you suppose you can earn 6 percent, how long will it take to reach your goal? The answer is found by dividing the interest rate into the number 72; so, 72/6 = 12, or 12 years. A general formula is

Doubling time (*DT*) = 72/interest rate

An answer is always an approximation, but it is usually close enough for most problems. If you refer to Table A.1 in the Appendix at the end of the text, you will see that the future value factor for 6 years and 12 percent is actually 1.9738. A $1,000 investment grows to only $1,973.80, rather than the $2,000 needed to double the original amount.

Time-Value of Money Calculations on the Internet

TOPIC LINKS

Bloomberg
MMIS
OBANet
Martindale's
SmartCalcs
Money Advisor

A number of very good Web sites make time-value calculations for you. You enter the necessary data, click a button, and the calculation is done instantly. Most of these calculators are structured for a particular application, such as saving for retirement or paying off a mortgage loan. As such, they have limited use in general time-value-of-money situations that are presented here. However, once you have a basic understanding of the concepts, you probably will be interested only in specific applications as they arise. The dedicated-function calculators then will be most useful to you. We listed some of the better Web sites in the margin on this page, and we will refer to these sites again in future chapters as needed.

Future Value of an Annuity

Recall that an annuity is a series of equal payments. Many financial products, such as investments and insurance policies, involve making annual payments. So, suppose an investment requires a payment of $1,000 a year for the next three years, with payments made at the *end* of each year. How much will this investment accumulate at the end of the three years, assuming an annual investment rate of 10 percent?

Let's break the investment down to three separate single payments—one occurring a year from now (with two years to accumulate), one occurring two years from now (one accumulation year), and one occurring three years from now (no accumulation time). The accumulations are as follows:

$$\text{First payment: } \$1,000 \times 1.1 \times 1.1 = \$1,210$$
$$\text{Second payment: } \$1,000 \times 1.1 = \quad 1,100$$
$$\text{Third payment: } \$1,000 \times 1.0 = \quad \underline{1,000}$$
$$\text{Total } \$3,310$$

The answer is $3,310. It could have been found much more quickly by referring to a future-value-of-$1-annuity table, an example of which appears in Table 2.2. As you see, the future value of a $1 annuity invested at 10 percent for three years is 3.310. Multiply this figure by the annuity amount—$1,000—and you have your answer. You have found the future value of an ordinary annuity *(FVOA)*.

If payments take place at the end of the period, the annuity is called an **ordinary annuity;** if they take place at the beginning of a period, it is called an **annuity due.** An annuity due simply involves one more compounding period than an ordinary annuity, thereby increasing the total accumulation. Let's return to the preceding example and calculate the accumulation:

$$\text{First payment: } \$1,000 \times 1.1 \times 1.1 \times 1.1 = \$1,331$$
$$\text{Second payment: } \$1,000 \times 1.1 \times 1.1 = \quad 1,210$$
$$\text{Third payment: } \$1,000 \times 1.1 = \quad \underline{1,100}$$
$$\text{Total } \$3,641$$

The sum—$3,641—is called the future value of an annuity due *(FVAD)*. Of course, there is a much easier way to find this value. Simply find the accumulation with an ordinary

Sidebar notes:

TOPIC **LINKS** Use a future-value-of-an-annuity calculator.

Ordinary annuity: An annuity with end-of-period payments.

Annuity due: An annuity with beginning-of-period payments.

Number of periods (*n*)	Interest Rate		
	6%	8%	10%
1	1.0000	1.0000	1.0000
3	3.1836	3.2464	3.3100
10	13.1800	14.4860	15.9370
20	36.7850	45.7620	57.2750
30	79.0580	113.2800	164.4900
40	154.7600	259.0500	442.5900

Table 2.2

Portion of a Future-Value-of-$1-Annuity Table

(See Appendix, Table A.2 for an expanded table.)

annuity and multiply it by 1.0 plus the interest rate (i, expressed as a decimal); that is,

$$FVAD = (1.0 + i) \times FVOA = (1.0 + 0.10) \times FVOA$$
$$FVAD = (1.10) \times \$3,310 = \$3,641$$

Since converting a *FVOA* to a *FVAD* is so easy, we present only a *FVOA* table in the Appendix at the end of the text.

DISCOUNTING (FINDING PRESENT VALUES)

Discounting: The process of reducing future values to present values.

In compounding we are finding future values, given present values; in contrast, **discounting** is the process of reducing future values to present values. Again, two cases are considered: first, finding the present value of a single sum that will be received or paid in the future; and second, finding the present value of an annuity to be received or paid in the future.

Present Value of a Single Payment

Discounting is simply the reverse process of compounding. So, revising the preceding example, suppose an investment that requires an immediate $1,000 payment will pay us $1,331 three years from now. Is it a good investment? The answer depends on the interest rate (now called a discount rate) we think should apply to the investment. Let's find the present value (*PV*) of the $1,331 future value (*FV*), discounting at 10 percent (*i*).

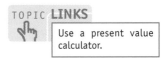

TOPIC **LINKS**

Use a present value calculator.

Using a Present Value Table

The easiest approach is to use a present-value-of-$1 table, an example of which appears in Table 2.3. As you see, the present value of $1 received three years in the future and

	Interest Rate		
Number of periods (n)	**6%**	**8%**	**10%**
1	0.9434	0.9259	0.9091
3	0.8396	0.7938	0.7513
10	0.5584	0.4632	0.3855
20	0.3118	0.2145	0.1486
30	0.1741	0.0994	0.0573
40	0.0972	0.0460	0.0221

Table 2.3

Portion of a Present-Value-of-$1 Table

(See Appendix, Table A.3 for an expanded table.)

discounted at 10 percent is $0.7513 (about 75 cents). Multiplying 0.7513 times the future value of $1,331 gives us the present value of the investment—$1,000.

The answer should reinforce the foregoing statement that discounting is simply the reverse process of compounding. We showed earlier that $1,000 *compounds* to $1,331 when invested at a 10 percent annual rate for three years. Clearly, then, $1,331 *discounts* to $1,000 when it is received three years from now and 10 percent is the annual discount rate.

Is the investment a good one, then? Actually, it's right at the margin between good and bad—a situation we often describe as a "fairly priced" asset. For example, if you use an 8 percent discount rate, you get a present value of $1,056.55 (0.7938 × $1,331). Now, we could say the investment is a good one because the present value exceeds the $1,000 required to buy it. In contrast, if you discount at 12 percent, the investment turns bad because the present value is now only $947.41 (0.7118 × $1,331).

Present Value Graph

Figure 2.1 illustrates how $1,000 *grew* in value over time. Figure 2.2 shows how $1,000 *depreciates* in value over time. Two discount rates—10 percent and 4 percent—are used in the illustration. As you see, the depreciation rate is much faster with the 10 percent rate. For example, the $1,000 received 10 years from now is worth only $386 today if the 10 percent rate is used; with the 4 percent rate, the present value is $676. No one should be indifferent as to when he or she receives money in the future. The rule is always the sooner,

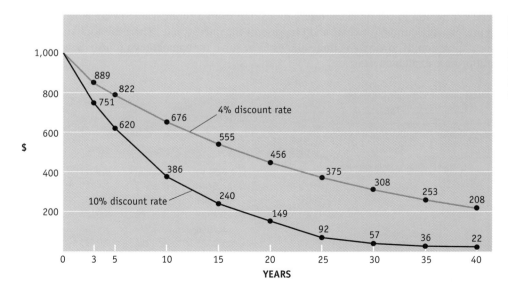

Figure 2.2

Present Value of $1,000 Received in the Future and Discounted at 10 Percent and at 4 Percent

the better. Moreover, no one should take lightly the interest rate used in the discounting process, since higher rates always lead to more rapid erosion of value. See Box 2.1 for a real-world example involving a discounting situation.

Present Value of an Annuity

Finally, we can find the present values of ordinary annuities and annuities due. Again, the easiest method is to use the present-value-of-$1 annuity table (see Table 2.4). As an example, suppose you are evaluating an investment that pays you $5,000 a year (end of year) for the next three years. What is the present value of the investment (ordinary annuity), assuming an annual discount rate of 6 percent? From Table 2.4, we find the discount factor for three years and 6 percent; it is 2.6730. So, the present value of an ordinary annuity $(PVOA)$ = 2.6730 × $5,000 = $13,365.

Table 2.4 shows discount factors for ordinary annuities. If the investment required beginning-of-year payments, its present value $(PVAD)$ would be $14,166.90. As before:

$$PVAD = (1.0 + i) \times PVOA = (1.0 + 0.06) \times PVOA$$

$$PVAD = (1.06) \times \$13,365 = \$14,166.90$$

Is this a good investment? The answer depends on its cost. Suppose the cost is $13,700 and payments are received at the end of three years. Then it is a bad investment because the present value of what you receive is only $13,365; in effect, you lose $335 ($13,365 − $13,700) if you buy it. But if payments begin immediately (annuity due), it's a good investment and you make $466.90 ($14,166.90 − $13,700.00). Receiving the payments one year earlier makes the difference.

More Applications of Future and Present Values

We can express the relationship between a present value (PV) and a future value (FV) as follows:

$$FV = [FV \text{ of } \$1 \text{ factor: } n, i] \times PV$$

The expression in the brackets refers to a value from a future-value-of-$1 table, where n represents the number of years and i represents the interest rate. There are four variables in the expression. Knowing any three allows us to solve for an unknown fourth. Several illustrations are explained next.

Table 2.4

Portion of a Present-Value-of-$1 Annuity Table

(See Appendix, Table A.4 for an expanded table.)

| Number of periods (n) | Interest Rate | | |
	6%	8%	10%
1	0.9434	0.9259	0.9091
3	2.6730	2.5571	2.4869
10	7.3601	6.7101	6.1446
20	11.4699	9.8181	8.5136
30	13.7648	11.2578	9.4268
40	15.0463	11.9246	9.7791

Finding an Unknown Interest Rate

Suppose we have the following problem. What interest rate must be earned to achieve a $6,000 goal in five years, assuming $4,000 is invested today? Rather than solving for a future value, we now must solve for an interest rate. Let's plug values into the preceding formula, knowing that $FV = \$6,000$, $PV = \$4,000$, and $n = 5$.

$$\$6,000 = [FV \text{ factor}] \times \$4,000$$

$$[FV \text{ factor}] = \$6,000/\$4,000 = 1.5$$

Now, refer to Table A.1 in the Appendix at the end of the text. Go to the five-year row and go across the row until you find the closest value to 1.5. You should see that this value is 1,4683, which is found in the 8 percent column. So, the answer is approximately 8 percent.

Since 1.4683 is a bit smaller than 1.5000, the actual rate is a bit more than 8 percent. (We can get a more accurate answer by using interpolation techniques, which are covered in Appendix 2.1.)

Finding an Unknown Number of Years

Let's try another problem. You hope to earn 20 percent on a somewhat risky investment. You will put $3,000 into the investment and will "cash out" when the investment value reaches $10,000. How long will that take? Again, we go back to the basic formula and insert values.

$$\$10,000 = [FV \text{ factor}] \times \$3,000$$

$$[FV \text{ factor}] = \$10,000/\$3,000 = 3.3333$$

Returning to Table A.1, go to the 20 percent column and go down until you find the number closest to 3.3333. It is seven years, which has an FV factor value of 3.5832. Since 3.5832 is a bit larger than 3.3333, the actual number of years is a bit less than seven. (An interpolated answer is shown in Appendix 2.1.)

Approximation Methods with Annuities

The preceding examples relate to a single payment. However, we can also use approximation methods when annuities are involved. Again, two basic equations apply:

$$FV = [FV \text{ of } \$1 \text{ annuity: } n, \ i] \times \text{annuity payment}$$

$$PV = [PV \text{ of } \$1 \text{ annuity: } n, \ i] \times \text{annuity payment}$$

An Example Using a Future Value

We will illustrate with an example. You are committed to saving and investing $2,500 annually over the next 10 years. If you hope to accumulate $50,000 at the end of the period, what interest rate must you earn? Since the problem deals with compounding, refer to Table A.2 in the Appendix at the end of the text.

$$\$50,000 = [FV \text{ factor}] \times \$2,500$$

$$[FV \text{ factor}] = \$50,000/\$2,500 = 20.000$$

Go to the 10-year row and move across until you reach the number closest to 20.000; it is 20.303, which is associated with 15 percent. Since 20.303 is a bit more than 20.000, the actual rate is a bit less than 15 percent.

An Example Using a Present Value

You are thinking of buying a lottery ticket that will provide you with either a lump-sum payment of $2,000,000 right after you win or an annual payment of $160,000 for the next 20 years. You must make a choice at the time you purchase the ticket. What is the implied rate of interest embedded in the lottery payoffs? Since the $2,000,000 is a present value, use Table A.4.

$$\$2,000,000 = [PV \text{ factor}] \times \$160,000$$

$$[PV \text{ factor}] = \$2,000,000/\$160,000 = 12.500$$

Go to the 20-year row and go across until you reach the number closest to 12.5000; it is 12.4622, which is associated with a 5 percent interest rate. (An interpolated answer is shown in Appendix 2.1.)

Knowing that the embedded rate is about 5 percent should help you decide how to take the money after you win. If you think that you could invest over the 20 years at rates higher than 5 percent indicates that you want the lump-sum payment. If you can't earn more than 5 percent elsewhere, take the extended payout.

Financial PLANNING for Young Adults

BOX 2.2

Focus on the Asset, Not on the Daily Savings

Most of us establish daily consumption routines that on the surface seem trivially inexpensive. Two dollars for coffee, five or more for lunch, and maybe a snack or two at the vending machine. Add smoking to the mix and you can spend easily $10 to $20 every day. What's it worth to you to save some of this outlay, maybe by giving up smoking or by brown-bagging it for lunch? Aside from considerable health benefits gained, assuming you invest the savings, you can create an asset that is much larger than you might think. If you haven't been successful in the past breaking these "inexpensive" habits, you might have more luck if you focus on the asset you're giving up, rather than the small daily savings.

As an example, suppose you can save $15 a week. The table opposite shows potential future values using weekly compounding and assuming different investment rates and periods of time that the asset is held. As you can see, the results are impressive. So, don't look at the $15 a week you can save; rather, plan on how you'll spend $307,533 when you are in your early sixties.

(If you think $15 is too low—or too high—you can adjust the table amounts by multiplying them times your number over 15. For example, if you think $20 is a better estimate, multiply by 20/15, or 1.333.)

Changing a lifestyle is not easy. Moreover, the physical act of depositing money in an investment account involves some time and effort. The candy bar gives us immediate satisfaction; the investment only gives us numbers to look at. We must decide their relative importance, but at least this little exercise shows the long-run impact of what we are giving up as we munch on our Tootsie Rolls.

Years Held	Investment Rates		
	3%	6%	9%
10	$ 9,093	$ 10,680	$ 12,633
20	21,367	30,131	43,682
40	60,293	130,103	307,533

GOAL PLANNING FOR THE STEELES

Time-value-of-money techniques are useful tools for determining the required amount of funds to achieve future goals, some taking place 20 to 30 years in the future. The application of these tools in the Steeles' case is illustrated in the following sections.

In the plan, the Steeles' last goal is 28 years away, when Arnold begins retirement. You might question the realism of trying to determine goals and preferences so far in the future. Who knows if either Arnold or Sharon will live for 28 more years? So why go to all the bother? But what is the alternative? You can't ignore the future, unless you are not particularly concerned about what happens to you or people you care about when the future arrives. The odds are very high that Arnold and Sharon will live well past the estimated retirement date. The odds are also good that both Nancy and John will go to college. So, the Steeles can either plan for these very important events, or they can "wing it" and hope the money is there when the time comes.

Making Goals Concrete

The first phase in the planning process involves identifying particular goals, setting the future years when the goals are to be achieved, and establishing an initial dollar amount for each goal. You should understand that a goal is something far more concrete than a dream. While there is nothing wrong with the latter—indeed, most goals probably begin as dreams or wishes—a goal implies a commitment toward its achievement. Moreover, you should only set goals for activities that are very important. If these can be achieved through a savings plan, then you can add other less important goals over time.

What and When?

Table 2.5 illustrates the first phase in columns 1 and 2. The Steeles have specified four major goals.

1. Providing four years of college education to Nancy and John, starting 8 years from the present and ending in 13 years.
2. Adding a greenhouse to the home 18 years in the future.
3. Taking a European vacation 20 years in the future.
4. Accumulating a retirement nest egg 28 years in the future.

Although these are the most important goals, the list could be expanded if the Steeles determine that these goals can be achieved without undue stress on their yearly budget, which is a topic we explore in the next chapter.

How Much If Undertaken Today?

The amount of funds needed to achieve a goal is established initially by determining the cost of the activity if it were undertaken today. These amounts appear in column 3 of Table 2.5. So, if Nancy started college in the current year, the associated costs would be $12,000 for the year. It takes $48,000 for Nancy's four years, and a similar amount for John's education. If each can finish in four years, the annual outlays cover a six-year period, beginning in eight years. There are two years when both kids are at the university together. Also, as you can see, the greenhouse would cost $40,000 to install today and the European vacation would cost $10,000. Finally, Arnold and Sharon would like to have $100,000 to use in a variety of ways if they were to retire this year. They might spend all of it before their deaths, or they might save it as a legacy for Nancy and John.

(1) Goals	(2) Years Until Goal Is Achieved	(3) Amount Required	(4) Inflation Rate	(5) Future-Value-of-$1 Factor	(6) Inflation-Adjusted Amount (3) × (5)	(7) Future-Value-of-$1 Annuity Factor (8% rate)	(8) Required Annual Savings (6)/(7)
1. Nancy starts college:							
year 1	8	$ 12,000	6%	1.5938	$ 19,126	10.636	$ 1,798
year 2	9	12,000	6%	1.6895	20,274	12.487	1,624
2. John joins Nancy at college:							
year 3	10	24,000	6%	1.7908	42,979	14.486	2,967
year 4	11	24,000	6%	1.8983	45,559	16.645	2,737
3. John finishes college:							
year 5	12	12,000	6%	2.0122	24,146	18.977	1,272
year 6	13	12,000	6%	2.1329	25,595	21.495	1,191
4. Add greenhouse to home	18	40,000	3%	1.7024	68,096	37.450	1,818
5. Take European vacation	20	10,000	3%	1.8061	18,061	45.762	395
6. Accumulate retirement							
nest egg	28	100,000	3%	2.2879	228,790	95.338	2,400
Totals		$246,000			$492,626		$16,202

Table 2.5

Determining Required Savings Amounts

Adjusting for Inflation

Unfortunately, since these goals take place at very distant future points in time, inflation will most likely increase their costs above the amounts specified in column 3. So the costs must be adjusted to reflect inflation. The assumed inflation rates are shown in column 4. Arnold and Sharon expect that the overall rate of inflation over the planning period will be 3 percent. However, college costs have been increasing in recent years at about twice the overall inflation rate, and there is no indication that this rate will diminish. Therefore, college costs are presumed to increase at a 6 percent rate.

Determining an inflated amount is accomplished by using the *compounding process*, discussed earlier in this chapter. An inflation rate (or, more generally, a growth rate) works the same as an interest rate. If inflation is 6 percent, an item costing $100 today will cost $106 a year from today. You should see that this is the same as saying that $100 invested today at 6 percent interest will be worth $106 a year from today. Recognizing this similarity, we can then calculate the inflated amounts by using the future-value-of-$1 tables.

For example, Nancy's first year in college is eight years in the future and the $12,000 cost will grow 6 percent a year. From Table A.1 in the Appendix at the end of the text, we find the future-value-of-$1 factor for eight years, 6 percent is 1.5938. Therefore, the inflation-adjusted amount is $19,126 (1.5938 × $12,000). Similar calculations are made for the remaining items in Table 2.5. You might note the severe impact of inflation over time, which just about doubles the cost of future goals for the Steeles ($492,626 versus $246,000). The lesson is simple: Ignore inflation at your own peril!

Determining a Savings Schedule

By far the most difficult part of the planning process is determining how much must be saved each year to achieve the goals. Usually, planners go through a series of attempts (trial and error) until a workable saving schedule is reached. Column 8 of Table 2.5 shows a step in a first trial, one the Steeles are *not* likely to accept.

Required Annual Savings

A required annual savings amount is determined by using the compounding process again, only this time we use the future-value-of-a-$1 annuity. Assuming that the Steeles will earn 8 percent on their savings, we can illustrate one of the calculations. For example, the Steeles have 18 years to save for the greenhouse; so we find from Table A.2 in the Appendix the future-value-of-a-$1-annuity factor for 18 years and 8 percent. It is 37.450. Divide this figure into the inflation-adjusted cost of $68,096 and arrive at the required annual savings of $1,818.

Summing the amounts for all the activities gives a total required annual savings of $16,202. However, this is *not* an amount that must be saved each year over the next 28 years. Indeed, as each goal is achieved, the need to save for it is eliminated. The process is illustrated in Table 2.6.

A First Trial

As you see in column 2 of the table, an annual savings amount of $16,202 lasts for only eight years, after which Nancy's first year in college is over. Thus, the $1,798 of annual savings to meet the first year's cost of $19,126 is no longer needed. In year 9, then, the required deposit to the savings account falls to $14,404 ($16,202 − $1,798). As all the

Year	Deposit	Interest Earned (8% Rate)	Withdrawals	Ending Balance
1	$ 16,202	$ —	$ 0	$ 16,202
2	16,202	1,296	0	33,700
3	16,202	2,696	0	52,598
4	16,202	4,208	0	73,008
5	16,202	5,841	0	95,051
6	16,202	7,604	0	118,857
7	16,202	9,509	0	144,567
8	16,202	11,565	19,126	153,209
9	14,404	12,257	20,274	159,595
10	12,780	12,768	42,979	142,164
11	9,813	11,373	45,559	117,791
12	7,076	9,423	24,146	110,144
13	5,804	8,812	25,595	99,165
14	4,613	7,933	0	111,711
15	4,613	8,937	0	125,261
16	4,613	10,021	0	139,895
17	4,613	11,192	0	155,699
18	4,613	12,456	68,096	104,672
19	2,795	8,374	0	115,841
20	2,795	9,267	18,061	109,843
21	2,400	8,787	0	121,030
22	2,400	9,682	0	133,112
23	2,400	10,649	0	146,161
24	2,400	11,693	0	160,254
25	2,400	12,820	0	175,475
26	2,400	14,038	0	191,912
27	2,400	15,353	0	209,665
28	2,400	16,773	228,790	49

Table 2.6

The Steeles' Savings Plan: First Trial

goals are eventually reached, the savings account is depleted at the end of 28 years. (The $49 remaining in the account is trivial and due to rounding.)

Note that we are assuming end-of-year deposits (ordinary annuities—not annuities due). Thus, the interest of $1,296 earned in year 2 is based on year 1's deposit of $16,202. Also note that the ending balance of $33,700 consists of the $16,202 deposit made in years 1 and 2 and the interest earned in year 2 ($16,202 + $16,202 + $1,296 = $33,700).

The Steeles are not likely to follow this savings plan since it requires the most savings in the early years, when their incomes are probably lower than what they will be in more distant years. Generally, our incomes rise as we advance in our careers or become more skilled at trades. Even though the plan is rejected, its creation is still worth the exercise because it serves as a test for accuracy in the construction of Table 2.5. If our ending balance were not close to zero, we would know a mistake was made.

A Second Trial

Sharon decided to create a spreadsheet in an effort to find a workable savings plan. In a second trial, she and Arnold decided to set the initial annual savings amount at $8,000 and then increase it by $1,000 every four years. They felt that these amounts would likely be around 10 percent of their pretax incomes. This is not an unduly high savings goal but, as we shall learn in the next chapter, it is one that far exceeds their present savings effort.

Table 2.7 shows the results of the second trial, and the picture is not good. As you see, a negative balance of $8,081 appears by year 12. Of course, a negative figure could not

Table 2.7

The Steeles' Savings Plan: Second Trial

Year	Deposit	Interest Earned (8% Rate)	Withdrawals	Ending Balance
1	$ 8,000	$ —	$ 0	$ 8,000
2	8,000	640	0	16,640
3	8,000	1,331	0	25,971
4	8,000	2,078	0	36,049
5	9,000	2,884	0	47,933
6	9,000	3,835	0	60,767
7	9,000	4,861	0	74,629
8	9,000	5,970	19,126	70,473
9	10,000	5,638	20,274	65,837
10	10,000	5,267	42,979	38,125
11	10,000	3,050	45,559	5,616
12	10,000	449	24,146	−8,081
13	11,000	(646)	25,595	−23,322
14	11,000	(1,866)	0	−14,188
15	11,000	(1,135)	0	−4,323
16	11,000	(346)	0	6,331
17	12,000	506	0	18,838
18	12,000	1,507	68,096	−35,751
19	12,000	(2,860)	0	−26,612
20	12,000	(2,129)	18,061	−34,801
21	13,000	(2,784)	0	−24,586
22	13,000	(1,967)	0	−13,552
23	13,000	(1,084)	0	−1,637
24	13,000	(131)	0	11,232
25	14,000	899	0	26,131
26	14,000	2,090	0	42,222
27	14,000	3,378	0	59,599
28	14,000	4,768	228,790	−150,423

exist in the real world. It actually implies that the Steeles would have to borrow an amount to make up any deficiency. The savings account is then replaced by a loan account, and interest earned becomes interest owed. This situation is not acceptable to the Steeles.

A Third Trial

Arnold and Sharon did not believe they could increase their savings above the 10 percent of income target. This decision implies that they must cut back on one or several of their goals. Fortunately, the Steeles have accumulated some investments (we'll learn more about these in the next chapter) that are worth approximately $25,000. The Steeles were thinking of using these funds for a Hawaiian vacation and/or a down payment on a vacation condo in the Smoky Mountains. However, it now appears that one or both of these dreams must be abandoned. Thus, Sharon made the assumption that $18,000 of the $25,000 is transferred to the savings account related to their goal-planning activity.

Table 2.8 shows a third trial at a savings plan, which will serve as the final version. Sharon assumes the $18,000 deposit is made immediately and so earns interest for a full year. At the beginning of year 1, then, there is $18,000 in the account, which earns interest of $1,440 during year 1. The Steeles are satisfied with this third trial since there are no negative years and only a small surplus of $4,865 at the end year 28. Given this final version of their savings plan, they will budget in the upcoming year to save and invest $8,000.

Year	Deposit	Interest Earned (8% Rate)	Withdrawals	Ending Balance
1	$ 26,000*	$ 1,440	$ 0	$ 27,440
2	8,000	2,195	0	37,635
3	8,000	3,011	0	48,646
4	8,000	3,892	0	60,538
5	9,000	4,843	0	74,381
6	9,000	5,950	0	89,331
7	9,000	7,146	0	105,478
8	9,000	8,438	19,126	103,790
9	10,000	8,303	20,274	101,819
10	10,000	8,146	42,979	76,986
11	10,000	6,159	45,559	47,585
12	10,000	3,807	24,146	37,246
13	11,000	2,980	25,595	25,631
14	11,000	2,050	0	38,681
15	11,000	3,095	0	52,776
16	11,000	4,222	0	67,998
17	12,000	5,400	0	85,438
18	12,000	6,835	68,096	36,177
19	12,000	2,894	0	51,071
20	12,000	4,086	18,061	49,096
21	13,000	3,928	0	66,023
22	13,000	5,282	0	84,305
23	13,000	6,744	0	104,050
24	13,000	8,324	0	125,374
25	14,000	10,030	0	149,404
26	14,000	11,952	0	175,356
27	14,000	14,028	0	203,384
28	14,000	16,271	228,790	4,865

* Consists of beginning-of-year deposit of $18,000 and end-of-year deposit of $8,000.

Table 2.8

The Steeles' Savings Plan: Final Version

A Final Note on Goal Planning

It is important to recognize that the usefulness of goal planning depends to a large extent on the validity of the assumptions embedded in the plans. In the Steeles' case, the two major assumptions are the inflation rates (3 percent and 6 percent) and the earning rate (8 percent). How realistic is it that any of these rates will not change over the plan's life? It is in fact totally unrealistic. Inflation may increase or abate, and earning rates are very likely to change over the period. Does this make planning a fruitless endeavor? No, it means simply that planning is not some activity undertaken once and then left unchanged. Rather, it is an ongoing process as we discussed in Chapter 1.

The Need to Monitor Progress

Sharon and Arnold must constantly monitor progress toward achieving their goals, and they must respond immediately to changes in the financial environment. Rising inflation rates or falling investment rates will increase the need to save more each year; if the situations reverse, the need to save each year lessens. Sharon's spreadsheet is an extremely useful tool in terms of simplifying the planning activity. It only takes a few seconds to enter different numbers and observe the changes in required annual savings.

Finance News

BOX 2.3

Retirement: A Distant Goal or a Distant Dream?

Some 80 million Americans, those born between 1946 and 1962, are in deep trouble. A generation not accustomed to the word *no* where spending is concerned are getting ever closer to retirement with very little in savings. And it's starting to dawn on them that $2,000 a month from Social Security is petty cash to a family used to spending $5,000 a month to keep happy.

Put simply, too many families are not saving enough for retirement. A recent study by the Employee Benefit Research Institute shows the average balance in a 401(k) plan for workers investing since 1999 or earlier was $76,809 in 2003. This figure was up sharply over the previous year, largely on the strength of big gains in the stock market. Unfortunately, the study also shows that only 54 percent of workers between ages 25 and 34 work for employers who offer such plans. More unfortunately, other studies indicate that perhaps less than 50 percent of such workers participate in the plans when offered the opportunity. While $76,809 is hardly a large number, the data imply that it applies to roughly only one in four workers. What do the other three in four have? Apparently, not much. The Federal Reserve Consumer Finance Survey showed that the median amount invested in retirement assets by all U.S. families was a mere $29,000 in 2001 (the most recent survey year).

Unfortunately, many families pursue retirement planning as though they live in Oz. Some plan to *never* retire; now, that's a realistic approach, particularly if you have a job that is physically or emotionally demanding and not much fun. Others are counting on Mom and Dad to leave them a bundle. True, trillions of dollars of savings are held by the over-55 generation, but most of that belongs to a handful of very wealthy families. The average baby-boomer family will probably get around $25,000—just enough to buy a new car. And, no kidding, some families actually believe that a winning ticket in the state lottery will bail them out in the end.

Avoiding such a situation requires a thoughtful savings-investment plan. As the following table shows, the sooner you start, the easier the task. A $250,000 nest egg is not an excessive amount for two spouses who are likely to live 15 to 20 years beyond age 65. The 4 percent column is the most realistic when inflation is taken into consideration, but no tax-savings retirement plans (such as IRAs or 401(k)s) are used; if such plans are available, you could achieve the 6 or 8 percent columns. You would have to be very lucky to earn an inflation-adjusted 10 percent rate of return.

Required Monthly Savings to Accumulate $250,000 by Age 65

Age you begin to invest	Interest rate earned on investments			
	4%	6%	8%	10%
25	$ 211	$ 125	$ 71	$ 39
35	359	248	167	110
45	680	539	422	327
55	1,692	1,518	1,358	1,210

How Should the Steeles Invest?

We shall defer a complete discussion of this question to various chapters later in the text. At this point we can make some general observations. First, the rate earned on savings must be an after-tax rate; that is, the Steeles must net 8 percent. If it were a pretax rate, then the amount remaining after taxes would be inadequate to fund the goals. Earning an after-tax rate of 8 percent is not all that easy unless you use certain tax shelters, such as IRAs, tax-deferred annuities, or State Higher Education plans.

Second, the Steeles might want to set up specific savings/investment accounts for each goal. This would be a requirement for the tax-sheltered plans mentioned earlier, but it might be a good idea even if there were no legal requirement. For example, the Steeles can probably afford to take greater investment risks with funds specified for the very long-run goals. The long investment horizon—a period in which the funds are not needed and can remain invested—allows the Steeles to, say, put all the funds in growth stocks in which they might achieve a return greater than 8 percent. On the other hand, the investment vehicles selected to fund Nancy's and John's education will probably be more conservative and will probably earn less than 8 percent. Finally, if different earning rates are planned, Sharon will need to revise her spreadsheet, which now assumes only one rate.

Key Terms

annuity (p. 22)   compounding (p. 22)   ordinary annuity (p. 25)
annuity due (p. 25)   discounting (p. 26)   rule of 72 (p. 24)
compound interest (p. 22)   future value (p. 22)   simple interest (p. 22)

FOLLOW-UP ON THE Steele FAMILY

Much of this chapter has dealt with the Steeles' goal-planning activities. You may need to refer back to some of the material to answer the following questions.

1. Table 2.5 assumes inflation rates of 6 percent and 3 percent. Granting that these are perhaps the best estimates, nevertheless, rework columns 6 and 8 assuming college costs increase 8 percent annually and that all other costs increase at a 5 percent annual rate. How much must the total required annual savings be, assuming the investment rate remains at 8 percent?
2. Continuing with Table 2.5, don't change the inflation rates. Now let's consider the possibility that the Steeles can do better than 8 percent on some of their investments. Specifically, assume they continue to earn 8 percent on investments held for the kids' education but they can earn 10 percent on investments for the greenhouse and the European vacation, and they can earn 12 percent on their retirement investments. Now determine the required annual savings.
3. The Steeles abandon the first savings plan (shown in Table 2.6) because it places too great a strain on their incomes over the next 8 to 13 years. However, by going to the savings plan shown in Table 2.8, aren't they introducing greater risk into the process, in the sense that one never knows what can happen in the future, and saving greater amounts earlier in their lives provides a cushion in later years if something goes wrong? Discuss this point, addressing both sides of the issue.

1. What is compounding?
2. What is compound interest? How does it differ from simple interest?
3. Suppose you invest $5,000 for five years at an interest rate of 8 percent. How much simple interest will you earn over the five years? How much compound interest would you earn? What is the explanation for the difference between these two amounts?
4. What is a future value?
5. Suppose you can earn 10 percent on an investment rather than 8 percent. After 20 years, the future value will be 25 percent greater. True or false? Explain.
6. Future values always grow larger the longer an investment is held. But do they grow proportionately larger? For example, if you hold an investment for 40 years, do you earn twice as much as if you held it for 20 years? Discuss.
7. You want to double your money in six years. Approximately what rate of interest must you earn?
8. If inflation in the future runs at a 3 percent annual rate, how long will it take for prices to double?
9. What is an annuity? What is meant by the future value of an annuity?
10. How does an ordinary annuity differ from an annuity due? Which one provides the larger value in a compounding situation?
11. Explain the difference between compounding and discounting.
12. Find the following future values, using Table 2.1 or 2.2:
    (a) $500 invested today at a 6 percent rate and held for 20 years,
    (b) $800 invested at the end of each of the next 10 years to earn 10 percent,
    (c) $300 invested at the beginning of each of the next 40 years to earn 8 percent.
13. Find the following present values, using Table 2.3 or 2.4:
    (a) $6,000 received 30 years from now, discounted at 10 percent,
    (b) $4,000 to be received at the end of each of the next 10 years, discounted at 6 percent,
    (c) $2,000 to be received at the end of each of the next three years, discounted at 8 percent.
14. Suppose an investment has been offered to you that requires an initial outlay of $10,000. Ten years from now the investment will pay you $20,000. If you think an investment of this type should offer a return of 8 percent, should you make the investment? Explain, showing your analysis.
15. You can buy an annuity contract that will pay you $1,000 a year (end of year) for the next 10 years. The contract costs $6,000 today. If you think you should earn 6 percent on such investments, should you buy the contract? Explain, showing your analysis.
16. You have $15,000 to invest today. You hope to buy a new car that costs $25,000 in four years. What approximate rate of interest must you earn to achieve your goal?
17. You can invest $40,000 today toward your eventual retirement that will earn 14 percent interest over the period. You want to have $500,000 at the retirement date. How many years away from retirement are you?
18. You can invest $3,000 annually at the end of each of the next 12 years. You hope to have $60,000 in the investment account by then. What rate of interest must you earn to meet this goal?
19. Your grandmother died recently. She named you as a beneficiary on an insurance contract that will pay you $60,000 immediately. However, the contract gives you the alternative of taking $20,000 a year (end of year) for the next five years. You think that you will earn 6 percent on your investments over this period of time. Given this information, what is the better choice—immediate cash or the extended payout? Explain.
20. Distinguish between a goal and a dream.

21. The first phase of goal planning involves three steps. List them.
22. How is inflation handled in the goal-planning process? Explain.
23. Explain, as best you can, what is meant by a required annual savings amount.
24. What is a savings schedule?
25. Explain why it is necessary to monitor a savings plan over time.

Case 2.1
Judy Shipley Plans for the Future

Judy Shipley graduated recently from Columbia University with an M.B.A. degree. Judy had five years of experience with a stockbrokerage firm before she entered Columbia, and this experience plus a very salable degree have landed Judy a fantastic position as an assistant portfolio manager with a mutual fund company. Her starting salary will be $110,000. Judy is unmarried and not contemplating marriage in the immediate future. She currently has no debts and no significant assets. Judy will move to Philadelphia shortly, with all moving expenses paid by her new employer.

Judy has assembled a list of goals that she would like to achieve over the next 10 years. The list does not include a retirement goal because her employer has a 401(k) plan in which she will participate. Judy hopes that her high income will support an ambitious goal plan because she wants to avoid any short-term debt. Judy anticipates an inflation rate of 4 percent on all the activities except the down payment on the town house. She has learned that housing prices in the neighborhood she favors have been increasing at an 8 percent rate. She will use that figure. Because Judy intends to make rather conservative investments, an investment rate of 6 percent seems reasonable to use.

Intended Activity	Future Date	Amount
1. Trip to Asia	2 years	$ 20,000
2. Purchase a new Lexus for cash	4 years	60,000
3. Make a down payment on a town house	6 years	80,000
4. Furnish the town house	8 years	100,000

Questions
1. Using Table 2.5 as a guide, prepare a similar schedule and calculate a required annual savings amount for each activity. How much must Judy save and invest each year (assume end-of-year payments) to achieve all of her goals?
2. Using your analysis from question 1, prepare a savings schedule similar to the one in Table 2.6.
3. Do you think that Judy will be able to meet her savings requirements, assuming taxes and 401(k) contributions will take about 40 percent of her income? Discuss your response.

Case 2.2
The Rohrbachs Plan for Retirement

Herman and Grace Rohrbach are in their mid-thirties. They are reasonably well off financially insofar as Grace's mother has established a trust fund to educate their two children, Barbara and Frances. The Rohrbachs lead rather simple lives and have no desires for lavish spending. However, they do face one major financial challenge: how to have sufficient resources in their retirement years. Herman owns his own camera shop and Grace has no employment income, although she often works in Herman's store.

The Rohrbachs have accumulated around $50,000 in savings, which is invested in a bond mutual fund, currently earning 5 percent after taxes. They have no other savings programs, either personal or through the business. If Herman retired today, his only income would be Social Security, which he estimates to be $18,000 annually. He would sell the business immediately prior to retirement. He has no idea what it will be worth then, but he believes he could get $100,000 for it today. To live a comfortable retirement, the Rohrbachs think they need an annual income comparable to their current one, which is $60,000 after income taxes. The Rohrbachs clearly need help to determine if they need to increase their annual savings to meet their retirement goal. Finally, the Rohrbachs will live off Social Security and interest from accumulated savings available at retirement. They will not touch any principal in their savings accounts, preferring instead to leave that money to their children. Retirement is planned in 30 years.

Questions
1. Social Security is indexed to inflation. If the inflation rate is 3 percent over the next 30 years, how much Social Security income will the Rohrbachs receive? How much will their income (currently $60,000) need to be at that time, assuming it grows at the 3 percent rate? How much, then, will be the shortfall—the difference between the two?
2. How much will be in the bond fund at retirement, assuming that it continues to earn 5 percent?
3. Herman has a very good location for his camera shop and can renew the lease indefinitely into the future. Suppose that its value increases by 10 percent annually over the next 30 years. How much will it then be worth?
4. Combine your answers to questions 2 and 3. The total represents an amount available to the Rohrbachs at the beginning of retirement. Now assume they sell the camera shop and put the proceeds into the bond fund, and the fund continues to earn 5 percent during their retirement years. Are these annual earnings sufficiently high to meet the income shortfall determined in question 1? Your answer should be "no." Determine how much they must invest each year to accumulate a sufficient amount, which can also be deposited into a bond fund. Assume they earn 12 percent on these annual (end-of-year) investments.

Marie Wilson Goal-Planning Exercise **Preparing a Savings Schedule**

Marie appreciates the help you have given her in formulating financial goals. By putting the goals within specific time frames, she has a sharper focus on the savings effort she must make to achieve her goals. Her current problem is one of estimating an amount to save each year. At first, this task seemed relatively easy, but its complexity began to grow when certain financial factors were considered. These factors are the expected inflation rate on the costs of goals and the rate of return she might earn on periodic savings.

Some of the goals you and Marie have discussed must be achieved out of current income or with borrowed funds; these include pursuing a college degree, buying a new car, and paying off college loans. Marie will focus on these goals later when she attempts to prepare a budget. Also, although Marie thought retirement planning was out of the question, you have convinced her that she should consider it, even though her retirement date is probably 40 years away.

Marie has four goals that she will consider in her current savings plan: (1) sending Jake to a golf clinic five years from now at a cost of $4,000; (2) making a $14,000 down payment on a condo 10 years from now; (3) saving $32,000 for Jake's four years of college costs ($8,000 a year) beginning 14 years from now; and (4) accumulating $50,000 in a fund to be used when retirement begins in 40 years.

Assist Marie in preparing saving schedules for the planned goals. First, complete a simple schedule (Form 2.1) that ignores inflation and interest earnings. (This schedule will show a required annual savings amount of $2,500 ($100,000/40). Also, negative account balances will appear in years 16 and 17. This means Marie must borrow to meet her goals. For simplicity, assume that she will do this, but ignore any interest on the loans.

Goals in Action	Year	Amount Required	Planned Savings	Account Balance
	1	$	$2,500	$2,500
	2		2,500	5,000
	3			
	4			
Golf Clinic	5	4,000		
	6			
	7			
	8			
	9			
	10			
	11			
	12			
	13			
	14			
	15			
	16			
	17			
	18			
	19			
	20			
	21			
	22			
	23			
	24			
	25			
	26			
	27			
	28			
	29			
	30			
	31			
	32			
	33			
	34			
	35			
	36			
	37			
	38			
	39			
	40			
Totals				

Form 2.1

A Simple Savings Schedule

Second, complete a schedule (Form 2.2) that shows a required annual savings amount when inflation and interest are considered. Assume an overall inflation rate of 3 percent and an investment-earning rate of 6 percent. The total required annual savings should be $5,386.

Since Marie expects that her income will increase over time, she will not start her savings amount at $5,386 per year. Instead, she will begin her savings plan at $2,000 for each of the first five years and then increase the annual amount by $500 in each of the following five-year intervals. Use Form 2.3 to determine if this is a workable plan.

Form 2.2

Determining an Annual Savings Amount

(1) Goals	(2) Years Until Goal is Achieved	(3) Amount Required	(4) Inflation Rate	(5) Future Value of $1 Factor	(6) Inflation Adjusted Amount	(7) Future Value of $1 Annuity Factor	(8) Required Annual Savings
1. Golf clinic							
2. Condo down payment							
3a. College Year 1							
3b. College Year 2							
3c. College Year 3							
3d. College Year 4							
4. Funds in retirement account							
Totals							

Year	Deposit	Interest Earned	Withdrawals	Ending Balance	Form 2.3
1					*Determining a Savings Plan*
2					
3					
4					
5					
6					
7					
8					
9					
10					
11					
12					
13					
14					
15					
16					
17					
18					
19					
20					
21					
22					
23					
24					
25					
26					
27					
28					
29					
30					
31					
32					
33					
34					
35					
36					
37					
38					
39					
40					

Exercises to Strengthen Your Use of the Internet

(Internet links for the following exercises can be found at **www.prenhall.com/winger**.)

Working Out on the Web

Exercise 2.1 Using a Financial Calculator

There are many great calculators on the Net, and most are designed to deal with a particular type of financial calculation. Visit OBA Net's Calculator Package and review its offerings. *Q. Click on "Simple Savings Calculator" to determine how long it will take to achieve a savings goal. Assume a target savings of $10,000, $30 weekly savings, and an interest rate of 6 percent. Your answer should be 281.92 weeks (5.42 years).*

Exercise 2.2 Saving for College

You may be advising someone about saving for college. These calculations can be somewhat extended and difficult, but FinAid offers considerable help with a really great Internet site.

Q. Click on "Savings Plan Designer" and notice the financial variables involved. Let's make some assumptions: Current savings are $2,000, interest rate is 8 percent, 10 years to enrollment, 100 percent of projected college costs, one year costs are $20,000, increasing at 6 percent. Find that monthly savings must be $826.68 to finance the future college costs.

Exercise 2.3 Finding the Future Value of a Single Payment and Annuity

Several of the calculators can be used for time value problems in general. For example, go to Centura Financial Calculators. Go to "Savings Calculators" and then "How much, at what rate, when?" to answer the first question and "How much faster will my money grow?" to answer the second.

Q. You hope to receive $5,000 in graduation gifts, which you will invest for your retirement in 30 years. If you can earn 12 percent each year, how much will you have in the retirement fund at the end of 30 years?

Q. You want to buy a $20,000 car in three years. If you can invest $6,300 a year and earn 8 percent each year, will you have enough funds at the end of three years?

Exercise 2.4 Finding the Present Value of a Single Payment

Money received in the future has less value than money available today. RF Investment has a calculator that finds the discounted value of a future payment.

Q. Assume today's date is 01/01/02 and you will receive a gift of $1,000 on 01/01/08. If the discount rate is 10 percent, what is the present value?

Appendix 2.1
Interpolation Techniques

While handheld calculators and computers are used frequently to make time-value-of-money calculations, when we begin studying time value of money, it is helpful to use tables. Unfortunately, tables often provide answers that are not as accurate as we might like them. Interpolation techniques add considerable accuracy to our calculations. Some examples from Chapter 2 are illustrated.

Finding an Unknown Interest Rate

FV at 5 years, 8% = 1.4693

FV at 5 years, 9% = 1.5386

Difference = 0.0696 (call this the *total difference*)

Then find:

FV at 5 years, 8% = 1.4693

FV at 5 years, ?% = 1.5000

Difference = 0.0307 (call this the *partial difference*)

Now solve:

Rate = lower rate + (partial difference/total difference) × rate increment

Rate = 8% + (0.0307/0.0693) × 1%

$$= 8\% + (0.443) \times 1\% = 8\% + 0.443\%$$
$$= 8.443\%$$

A financial calculator shows the actual rate is 8.447 percent; so, the approximation is very close.

Finding an Unknown Number of Years

20%, 7 years	= 3.5832
20%, 6 years	= 2.9860
Total difference	= 0.5972

20%, 6 years	= 2.9860
20%, ? years	= 3.3333
Partial difference	= 0.3473

$$\text{Number of years} = 6 + (0.3473/0.5972) \times 1.0 \text{ year}$$
$$= 6 + 0.5815$$
$$= 6.5815 \text{ years}$$

A financial calculator gives an answer of 6.6036 years. Again, the approximation method provides a fairly close answer.

An Example Using Present Value

20 years, 4%	= 13.5903
20 years, 5%	= 12.4622
Total difference	= 1.1281

20 years, 4%	= 13.5903
20 years, ?%	= 12.5000
Partial difference	= 1.0903

$$\text{Rate} = 4\% + (1.0903/1.1281) \times 1\%$$
$$= 4\% + 0.9665\%$$
$$= 4.9665\%$$

3

Financial Statements and Budgets

WHERE ARE YOU NOW AND WHERE ARE YOU GOING?

OBJECTIVES

1. To understand the importance of the balance sheet as a tool for measuring personal wealth

2. To prepare a balance sheet by identifying and valuing assets and liabilities

3. To prepare an income statement and to recognize its role in measuring financial performance

4. To evaluate financial performance by using appropriate financial ratios

5. To prepare an annual budget by constructing a master budget worksheet and a monthly income and expense plan

6. To monitor monthly activities by creating a system for recording actual income and expenses and then comparing them with budgeted amounts

7. To evaluate and control expenses during the year through a monthly review process

TOPIC LINKS

Follow the **Topic Links** in each chapter for your interactive Personal Finance exercise on the Web. Go to: **www.prenhall.com/winger**

The Steeles' failures at budgeting and their lack of personal financial information are not characteristics unique to them. Indeed, many, if not most, families probably share the Steeles' experiences. Successful financial planning begins with a clear assessment of where you are and where you hope to be in the future.

You learned in Chapter 1 that financial planning is a four-stage process: First, financial goals are set; second, action plans are devised for achieving those goals; third, a system is developed to measure the degree to which success is achieved; and fourth, on the basis of an evaluation of achievement, goals and action plans are reexamined to determine whether they should be dropped, modified, or left unchanged. In this chapter, our attention is directed toward the third task—measuring achievement. We are helped in this effort by accountants, who have devised three particularly useful statements that measure success. These are the balance sheet, the income statement, and the cash budget. Each is structured to answer a specific question about financial performance. The balance sheet determines your financial position *at a particular point in time,* usually at the end of the year. The income statement shows your income, expenses, and contribution to savings *over a past period of time,* usually the preceding year. The cash budget details estimates of your income, expenses, and contribution to savings *in the upcoming period,* usually the next year. Each of the three statements plays an important role in helping us achieve our financial goals.

THE BALANCE SHEET

What are you worth? It's a good practice to ask yourself this question periodically. A loan officer at a bank most certainly will ask it if you apply for a loan. She will also ask you to prepare a **personal balance sheet** to aid her in determining whether you should get the loan. The balance sheet is designed to determine someone's wealth. It has three components: **assets,** items that are owned and are measured by their fair market values; **liabilities,** bills and other obligations owed creditors that must be paid in the future; and **net worth,** the difference between assets and liabilities. (*Net worth* is actually the accounting term for wealth.) A simple balance sheet for Mike Mason, a second-year college student, appears in Figure 3.1. Mike has only a few assets, the most important being his stereo unit and tape and record albums, and he has only two liabilities—$20 he owes Ed Bates and the balance due on his Visa card. Since the total value of Mike's assets is $1,311, and his liabilities are only $96, he has a net worth of $1,215 ($1,311 − $96) on December 31, 2005.

The word *balance* in balance sheet suggests a particular relationship among its three components. As Figure 3.1 shows, the balance is between assets on the one hand and the sum of liabilities and net worth on the other. Arithmetically, it is shown by the equation

Assets = liabilities + net worth

The equality always holds, because net worth can be either positive or negative. It is positive when the market values of assets are greater than the total value of all liabilities; it is negative when the reverse is true.

Personal balance sheet: A statement designed to measure someone's wealth.

Assets: Items of value owned by the balance sheet preparer.

Liabilities: Bills and other obligations of the balance sheet preparer.

Net worth: Wealth of the balance sheet preparer (assets minus liabilities).

Assets		Liabilities and Net Worth	
Cash on hand	$ 18.00	Loan from Ed Bates	$ 20.00
Balance in the checking account	75.00	End-of-month balance on Visa card	76.00
Clothing inventory	237.00		
Textbooks, school supplies, and similar items	81.00	Total liabilities	$ 96.00
Stereo unit and tape and record albums	900.00	Net worth	$1,215.00
Total assets	$1,311.00	Total liabilities and net worth	$1,311.00

Figure 3.1

A Balance Sheet for Mike Mason Prepared as of December 31, 2005

Listing liabilities ahead of net worth on the right-hand side of the balance sheet is done for a purpose, too: It reflects the legal claims creditors have on assets. Specifically, it means that in most cases (except bankruptcy), their claims to your assets rank before your own claims. This relationship can be seen with an example. Suppose you purchase a new car for $10,000, putting down $2,000 and financing $8,000 with a local bank. If we ignored all other balance sheet items, immediately after the purchase your balance sheet would appear as follows:

$$\$10,000 (\text{assets}) = \$8,000 (\text{liabilities}) + \$2,000 (\text{net worth})$$

After the first year of ownership, you may have paid off $2,000 of the loan, but if the car depreciated by $3,000, the new balance sheet would be:

$$\$7,000 (\text{assets}) = \$6,000 (\text{liabilities}) + \$1,000 (\text{net worth})$$

If the car had to be sold at this point to raise cash, the bank's $6,000 loan balance would be satisfied first. After that is taken care of, then you can take what is left—in the preceding example, $1,000. You should also be able to see how negative net worth arises. If the car depreciated by $5,000 in the first year while the loan payoff remained at $2,000, net worth would now be a negative $1,000. Before we look more closely at assets, liabilities, and net worth, it should be remembered that financial planning aims to maximize net worth; it does not attempt to maximize assets. As you can see, regardless of how much your assets are worth, if your liabilities are greater, you have negative net worth. Technically and legally, you're insolvent.

Assets

Assets are things you own that have market value. They might have physical substance, such as jewelry or a house; or they may be pieces of paper, such as stocks and bonds, that give you rights to receive income or other benefits. Determining the total value of your assets takes two steps. First, you must identify and count all the items you own, and second, you need to determine each item's market value. This second step is often harder, even though some assets' values are easily determined: For example, a quick glance at the morning newspaper will tell you what a share of IBM stock is worth. But other assets, such as a diamond engagement ring purchased many years ago, have market values that can be only roughly approximated unless an expert is consulted.

Assets and liabilities are often grouped on the balance sheet to make evaluation easier. In this respect, there are three asset categories: assets to satisfy liquidity needs, assets that are a part of our lifestyles, and investment assets that can increase net worth or provide income for current use or for retirement. We now take a closer look at these three categories.

Liquid Assets

Liquid asset: Cash or any other asset easily convertible to cash with no loss in market value.

A **liquid asset** is cash or any other asset that can be converted to cash with a minimum amount of inconvenience and with no loss in market value. Examples of liquid assets are currency, checking accounts, savings accounts, money market deposits, and certificates of deposit. Managing liquid assets is a very important part of personal financial management, and the topic is discussed thoroughly in Chapter 5.

Figure 3.2 shows a comprehensive balance sheet for Arnold and Sharon Steele. Arnold and Sharon have $16,240 in liquid assets, with most of it being held in their passbook savings account and certificates of deposit.

Lifestyle (Use) Assets

Things that help us achieve the quality of life we want are our **lifestyle assets** (also called use assets). Most families hold the greatest percentage of their total assets in them. This is particularly true if a house is purchased, since it is such a large investment. But many other similar assets are also "big ticket" items, such as household furniture and furnishings, appliances, automobiles, and possibly hobbies like coin and stamp collections. Naturally, ownership of these assets varies considerably from one family to another, depending on family members' interests and activities.

Referring to Figure 3.2, you can see that of the Steeles' total lifestyle assets of $261,500, $205,000 is in their home. They determined this value by observing the selling prices of homes similar to theirs and then deducting 7 percent to allow for a realtor's commission.

Lifestyle assets: Things that help us achieve our desired quality of life.

Investment Assets

Investment assets are purchased for the purpose of providing additional income or increasing your net worth over time. There are many different kinds of investment assets, as Figure 3.2 shows, and the Steeles have accumulated a reasonable amount of them. However, the Steeles realize that they must increase their investment assets substantially if they are to achieve their retirement goal and the goals they have for educating John and Nancy.

Adding the total of investment assets to the total of lifestyle assets and liquid assets determines total assets. As you can see in Figure 3.2, for the Steeles this was $325,540.

Investment assets: Assets that provide income or increase our net worth.

Liabilities

At any point in time, most people have debt obligations. These obligations arise for a variety of reasons. You might use a bank credit card because of its convenience. If you don't want to use all your liquid assets to pay for one item, you might arrange an installment loan. Because you simply don't have enough resources, you obtain a mortgage loan to buy a house. Liabilities such as these are usually arranged on the balance sheet as current or noncurrent.

Current Liabilities

A **current liability** is any debt that must be paid within one year. There are two sources of current liabilities. First are unpaid bills. These come from your use of credit cards, or from direct purchases, as in the case of gas, electric, and telephone bills. The Steeles had $2,180 ($460 + $1,720) of these items. The second source consists of portions of installment loans that are due within one year. The Steeles are paying off two car loans over four years. The current liability portion is $4,424. We distinguish between current and noncurrent liabilities in order to better evaluate the Steeles' liquidity position, a topic we'll explain in more detail later in this chapter.

Current liability: A debt that must be paid within one year.

Noncurrent Liabilities

Noncurrent liabilities are all debt obligations beyond one year, and they are also of two types. The first type represents the noncurrent portion of loans with specific repayment schedules. Examples are installment loans on automobiles, furniture, and major appliances, or credit card balances being paid off on an installment basis. To illustrate, one of the Steeles' car loans extends into 2008 with portions payable in 2007 and 2008, which explains their $4,966 noncurrent liability. Another important example is a mortgage loan

Noncurrent liabilities: Debt obligations beyond one year.

Figure 3.2

Balance Sheet for the Steele
Family

BALANCE SHEET at _December 31, 2005_

For _Arnold & Sharon Steele_

ASSETS

Liquid Assets:

Coins and currency on hand	$ 240
Checking account balances	2,400
Other deposits at financial institutions:	
Savings account	5,600
42-month certificate of deposit	5,000
	—
Money market mutual funds	—
U.S. Series EE or HH bonds	3,000
Other liquid assets:	
none	—
none	—
Total liquid assets	$ 16,240

Lifestyle Assets:

Residence	205,000
Vacation home	—
Furniture, household furnishings, and appliances	20,000
Automobiles and recreational vehicles:	
2004 Voyager van	16,000
2002 Honda sedan	11,000
2000 Coleman camper	2,100
Jewelry	4,000
Clothing	1,400
Sporting equipment	600
Hobbies and collections _(stamp collection)_	400
Other lifestyle assets:	
2003 Toro riding mower	1,000
Total lifestyle assets	$ 261,500

Investment Assets

Preferred stocks	$ —
Common stocks	16,000
Corporate bonds	—
Government bonds	—
Mutual funds _200 shares of Fidelity Fund_	6,800

on a house or other property. The second kind of noncurrent liability consists of loans that do not have repayment schedules. A loan on your life insurance policy, such as the $2,000 loan the Steeles have on Arnold's policy, is an example. While these loans do not require repayment, you do pay interest on them periodically. Adding noncurrent and current liabilities gives total liabilities; for the Steeles, this figure is $168,149 ($8,354 + $159,795).

Net Worth

TOPIC **LINKS**

Determine your net worth.

As indicated previously, net worth is the difference between total assets and total liabilities. Even though this form of measurement has its problems, it is still the single best

Figure 3.2

Business interests			—
Cash value of life insurance			4,000
Cash value of annuities			—
Cash value of employer's retirement fund			21,000
Individual retirement accounts (IRAs):			
Arnold — none			—
Sharon — none			—
Total investment assets	(c)	$	47,800
TOTAL ASSETS = (a) + (b) + (c) =	(d)	$	325,540
LIABILITIES			
Current Liabilities:			
Unpaid bills *Gas and Electric, Telephone*		$	460
Credit card balances due			1,720
Estimated taxes due			1,750
Installment loan balances due in one year:			
Autos			4,424
Others:			
none			—
Other current liabilities:			
none			—
Total current liabilities	(e)	$	8,354
Noncurrent liabilities:			
Installment loan balances due after one year:			
Autos			4,966
Others:			
none			—
Mortgage loans			152,829
Loans on life insurance policies			2,000
Debit balances on margin accounts with stockbrokers			—
Other noncurrent liabilities:			
none			—
Total noncurrent liabilities	(f)	$	159,795
TOTAL LIABILITIES = (e) + (f) =	(g)	$	168,149
NET WORTH = (d) – (g) =	(h)		157,391
TOTAL LIABILITIES AND NET WORTH = (g) + (h) =	(i)	$	325,540

estimate of one's wealth. The Steeles' net worth at December 31, 2005, was $157,391. This figure was calculated in Figure 3.2 by subtracting total liabilities (item *g*) from total assets (item *d*). Net worth plays a crucial role in estimating financial strength, so we need to understand how it can change from one period to the next. Net worth can be changed in the following two ways.

First, net worth increases whenever cash income exceeds cash expenses during a period. This situation is called a **positive contribution to savings;** conversely, if expenses exceed income, a negative contribution—call it **dissavings**—occurs, and it reduces net worth. Second, changes in net worth also occur when the market values of assets you own at the beginning of a period increase or decrease during the period. For example, if you

Positive contribution to savings: Increase in net worth.

Dissavings: Reduction in net worth.

own a home that increases in value, your net worth increases by an equal amount. (This assumes, of course, that you do not increase your mortgage or other loans.)

THE INCOME STATEMENT

Income statement: Detailed breakdown of cash income and expenses over a past period.

The **income statement** (sometimes called the statement of cash flows) presents a detailed breakdown of cash income and expenses over a past period. In doing this, it also provides a figure for the period's contribution to savings and, thus, it becomes an important companion statement to the balance sheet. The income statement provides the opportunity to review how well you have done financially in the past period and to help you budget your income and expense items for the upcoming period. The Steeles' income statement for 2005 is shown in Figure 3.3 and discussed in the following sections.

Income

Income: Cash inflows, consisting primarily of salaries and wages.

Income usually consists of cash inflows. As Figure 3.3 shows, there are many potential sources of income. For many people, Arnold and Sharon included, by far the largest percentage of their total income consists of wages and salaries. Arnie has a full-time position with InChemCo, but Sharon works only during the tax season—roughly January through April—with a CPA firm. The data arrangement in Figure 3.3 shows gross wages rather than after-tax, or take-home, wages. You probably will do your financial planning with the take-home figure, but it is also instructive to detail the actual amount of taxes you pay. This puts the total expense in perspective and underscores the need for effective tax planning. It is surprising how few people actually know how much in total taxes they pay—much less their effective tax rates—because they focus exclusively on take-home pay. You should look carefully at both.

TOPIC **LINKS**

Determine your cash flow.

The Steeles' total wages in 2005 were $75,600. Deducting from this the total payroll taxes of $14,570 leaves their combined take-home salary of $61,030. Arnold's and Sharon's salaries have increased rather nicely in the last several years, making it easier for them to achieve their financial goals.

The Steeles' $937 of interest income came from their passbook savings account, certificates of deposit, and U.S. Series EE bonds. They did not actually withdraw the interest earned on any of these deposits (you have limited access to the latter two) but instead allowed it to accumulate. The $1,090 of dividend income was earned on their common stocks and Fidelity Fund shares, and they did receive those dividends in cash. Adding the interest and dividends to their wages and salaries gives their total income of $77,627.

Expenses

Expenses: Cash outflows that sustain our scale of living.

Expenses are cash outflows that sustain our scale of living. They do not include all cash outlays, however. You would not, for example, consider the purchase of investment assets as expenses. Payments made on installment and mortgage loans are viewed as expenses even though formal accounting rules would probably require us to distinguish between payments of interest and payments of principal in measuring income. (We are required to do this for tax purposes, because interest is an itemized deductible expense whereas principal payments are not. But our focus here is not on taxes.)

The breakdown of expenses in Figure 3.3 is typical of most income statements you are likely to encounter in loan applications and elsewhere. The list of expenses is fairly comprehensive, although you might prefer to arrange them differently. We'll distinguish between inflexible and flexible expenses when budgeting is discussed later, but it is useful to introduce and explain these terms here.

Inflexible Expenses

Inflexible expenses (also called fixed expenses) are often defined as those over which you have very little control in the short run. Some expenses are perfectly inflexible, meaning they never change in amount. Such expenses arise typically from contractual arrangements requiring payments of so much per period. As you review the expense categories in Figure 3.3, you most likely will pinpoint the following as examples: the mortgage payments of $18,285, the automobile loan payments of $5,688, and maybe the life insurance premiums of $480. These expenses are often called **sunk costs** because the fixed amount must be paid regardless of what happens in the future; the only way out of them is to drop, pay off, or renegotiate the underlying contracts. Other inflexible expenses are not fixed in amount from period to period, but they are nevertheless difficult to control. The Steeles' taxes of $18,070 are a good example of this type; we know they must be paid each year, but the actual amounts might differ each year, or even in each month of the year.

Flexible Expenses

Flexible expenses (also called variable expenses) are those over which you have some control, at least in the short run. A good example is home maintenance. Of course, some of these expenses are more flexible than others. Home maintenance expenses, along with doctors' and dentists' bills, are very irregular and are the most troublesome to deal with in budgeting. Others, however, are far more predictable, such as purchases of food and household supplies. Some flexible expenses might be paid in such a way that they become inflexible expenses. For example, gas and electric usage can be billed in equal monthly payments regardless of seasonal variations. Also, some flexible expenses go up or down along with your income. For example, if you use your car on the job, and you work more hours during a period, your car expenses will increase as your income rises.

Figure 3.4 shows a breakdown of the Steeles' $75,033 of total expenses in 2005. As you can see, the larger percentage is in the inflexible category, indicating that quite a bit of their expenses were set and uncontrollable during the year.

Contribution to Savings

As explained earlier in this chapter, the excess of income over expenses is a positive contribution to savings (or savings, for short). It increases net worth and is a source of increases in assets or reductions in liabilities. In 2005, the Steeles made a positive contribution to savings of $2,594. This amount is 3.3 percent of their gross income, which puts them a bit under the national savings rate that is currently about 4 percent. However, the amount of their income exceeds the national average; so, they should be able to save considerably more—a goal they have set for the future.

EVALUATING PAST FINANCIAL PERFORMANCE

Ultimately, your financial performance can be judged successful or unsuccessful only within the framework of your personal goals. If your plans call for buying a house or a new car, or saving $5,000, then you are successful if you achieve those goals. Apart from this personal evaluation, however, there also are objective yardsticks, called **financial ratios,** to measure present financial strength and its growth over time. Actually, to an outsider, such as a bank from which you are seeking a loan, your personal goals are not important. The bank must evaluate your request with an impersonal, objective attitude, asking whether you are a good credit risk. Periodically, you should use similar objective criteria to assess your situation. Three areas that are particularly important to evaluate are your financial performance as compared with the annual inflation rate, the liquidity of your assets, and your level of debt.

Inflexible expenses: Expenses that are hard to control in the short run.

Sunk costs: Costs that cannot be avoided regardless of what happens in the future.

Flexible expenses: Expenses that are generally controllable in the short run.

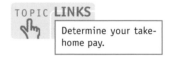
TOPIC **LINKS**
Determine your take-home pay.

Financial ratios: Yardsticks to measure financial strength and progress.

Figure 3.3

Income Statement for the Steele Family

INCOME STATEMENT for the Period ___Year Ended 12/31/05___

For ___the Arnold and Sharon Steele Family___

INCOME

Wages and Salaries:

				Percent
Arnold — InChemCo		$	60,200	
Sharon — Todd and Talbot CPAs			15,400	
Total wages and salaries	(a)		75,600	97.4%

Other Income:

Interest		$	937	
Dividends			1,090	
Capital gains or (losses)			none	
Others			none	
Total other income	(b)	$	2,027	2.6%
TOTAL INCOME = (a) + (b) =	(c)	$	77,627	100.0%

EXPENSES

Housing:

Rent		$	none	
Mortgage payments			18,285	
Maintenance fees on condo or cooperative			none	
Maintenance and home furnishings			3,500	
Total housing expenses	(d)	$	21,785	28.0%

Transportation:

Automobile loan payments		$	5,688	
Gas, oil, other maintenance and repairs			2,100	
License, parking, and other auto			210	
Other transportation			none	
Total transportation expenses	(e)	$	7,998	10.3%

Food and Other Consumption Items:

Food and household supplies		$	6,300	
Meals eaten out			1,210	
Personal care—barbers and beauticians			720	
Others			none	
Total food and other consumption items	(f)	$	8,230	10.6%

Utilities:

Telephone		$	540	
Gas and electric		$	2,280	
Water and sanitation			510	
Garbage pickup			none	
Cable TV			420	
Others			none	
Total utilities	(g)	$	3,750	4.8%

TOPIC **LINKS**

Find the current inflation rate.

Matching or Beating the Inflation Rate

It is always sound financial management to compare the annual inflation rate with annual changes in both your income and net worth. In periods of high inflation, such as the early 1980s, it is doubly important, because failure to match inflation will lead to an eroding scale of living and a diminished real net worth.

Figure 3.3

				Percent
Taxes:				
Payroll		$	14,570	
Real estate and personal property			3,500	
Others			none	
Total taxes	(h)	$	18,070	23.3%
Insurance:				
Health and medical withheld from wages		$	none	
Life			480	
Property and liability		$	570	
Automobile			1,470	
Disability			none	
Others			none	
Total insurance	(i)	$	2,520	3.3%
Leisure and Entertainment:				
Theater and sporting events		$	870	
Health club memberships			none	
Newspapers, magazines, etc.			430	
Vacations			2,380	
Hobbies			280	
Sporting equipment			160	
Others *Family Christmas gifts*			890	
Total leisure and entertainment	(j)	$	5,010	6.5%
Clothing:				
New clothing			1,830	
Laundry and dry cleaning			290	
Others			none	
Total clothing	(k)	$	2,120	2.7%
Others:				
Gifts and charitable contributions		$	2,080	
Dues and subscriptions			200	
Tuition, books, other education expenses			390	
Babysitters			540	
Family members' personal allowances			1,300	
Unreimbursed medical–dental			1,040	
			—	
			—	
			—	
Total others	(l)	$	5,550	7.2%
TOTAL EXPENSES = (d) + (e) + (f) + (g) + (h) + (i) + (j) + (k) + (l) =	(m)		75,033	96.7%
CONTRIBUTION TO SAVINGS = (c) – (m) =	(n)	$	2,594	3.3%

Income and the Inflation Rate

Let us suppose that your **nominal income** (the amount you actually receive) increases by 5 percent during a year when prices in general are increasing by 10 percent. In real terms—that is, in terms of what your nominal income buys—your **real income** (the amount your nominal income is worth) has declined by 5 percent. You are worse off this year because you have not kept up with the inflation rate. You may not feel much worse off, at least not

Nominal income: Actual income received.

Real income: Nominal income adjusted for inflation.

Figure 3.4

A Breakdown of the Steeles'
2005 Expenses

Inflexible Expenses		Flexible Expenses	
Mortgage payments	$18,285	Family members' allowances	$ 1,300
Automobile loan payments	5,688	Leisure and entertainment	5,010
Car licenses	210	Home maintenance and furnishings	3,500
All utilities	3,750	Gas, oil, and car repairs	2,100
All taxes	18,070	All food and other consumption items	8,230
All insurance	2,520	Clothing, laundry, and dry cleaning	2,120
Dues to professional societies	200	Gifts and charitable contributions	2,080
Tuition and books	390	Babysitters	540
		Medical-dental expenses	1,040
Totals	$49,113		$25,920
Total Expenses			

$75,033

Percentages
Inflexible = $49,113/$75,033 = 0.66, or 66%
Flexible   = $25,920/$75,033 = 0.34, or 34%

immediately, because some items in your budget are fixed, as we explained earlier. So, you will continue to make the same payments on your auto or furniture loans, or on your home loan, as you did in the past, and you may continue to meet your savings goals. But eventually many of the items being financed will need to be replaced, and we then confront the reality of a deteriorated financial condition.

Financial PLANNING for Young Adults

BOX 3.1

Pay Yourself First

Most financial planners agree that if saving money is truly important to you, then put savings in a proper focus—first, and not last—in the budget. In short, pay yourself first out of each paycheck. Seriously, when you get paid, take whatever percentage amount you have targeted and put it in a savings vehicle; then spend the rest.

This strategy works even better if you never get your hands on the money. So consider using a "forced-savings" approach. For example, many employers let you channel funds into U.S. savings bonds, mutual funds, or optional retirement plans. Or your bank may have automatic transfer plans that reposition cash from your checking account to a savings account. If you own mutual fund shares, choose the option to reinvest all dividends and capital gain distributions. Also, some companies have dividend-reinvestment plans; if you own shares in them, take the option. If you are very poor at voluntary savings, consider buying whole life, rather than term insurance. This type of policy has a built-in savings feature.

Millions of Americans willingly choose to have more taxes withheld from their paycheck than the IRS requires and then count on the tax refund for extra spending or saving funds. Of course, this is the least effective way to do it, since you give up interest on money that could go into interest-earning assets. If you are currently allowing overwithholding, check with your employer to see if an alternative savings arrangement is available.

Finally, some people argue that buying a home is the ultimate forced savings, since living in rented housing produces nothing more than canceled checks. Frankly, this argument stretches the point a bit. Buying versus renting is a complex problem, where the forced-savings feature might be considered, but should not dominate, in making a decision.

An important first test, then, is to compare your increase in nominal income with the inflation rate for the year. The simplest approach is first to calculate a percentage change in nominal income, as shown here:

$$\% \text{ change in nominal income} = \left(\frac{\text{this year's nominal income}}{\text{last year's nominal income}} \right) - 1.0$$

After you have this figure, compare it with the inflation rate (which is frequently reported in the newspaper and on television) to judge your relative performance. Using the Steeles as an example, and assuming that the 2005 inflation rate was 4 percent, we have

$$\% \text{ change in nominal income} = \frac{\$77,627}{\$71,788} - 1.0 = 1.0813 - 1.0 = 0.0813, \text{ or } 8.13\%$$

Thus, we know that the 8.13 percent increase in the Steeles' nominal income was about twice the inflation rate.

Net Worth and the Inflation Rate

Inflation's impact is not limited to your income. If the market values of your assets do not increase at inflation's rate, your real net worth will decline. The same arithmetic procedures shown earlier can be used to calculate the change in real—as opposed to nominal—net worth. To prevent a decline in net worth, you must own assets that appreciate in value equal to the inflation rate. In the past, personal residences and common stocks have performed well in this respect.

Maintaining Adequate Liquidity

Adequate liquidity means having sufficient liquid assets to pay your bills on time. You may have a very high net worth, but if most of it is represented by assets with poor liquidity, such as your house, you still could be illiquid. To avoid becoming illiquid we often hold a portion of our total assets in cash or other liquid assets, such as savings accounts. Two ratios are frequently used to measure liquidity: the ratio of liquid assets to take-home pay and the ratio of liquid assets to current liabilities.

Liquid Assets to Take-Home Pay

Financial advisers often use the rule of thumb that you should hold liquid assets equal to three to six months of take-home pay to serve as a buffer. If you have good loss-of-income protection through your employer or union, then the low figure might be adequate. If protection is poor, you should strive for the higher amount.

Using data for the Steeles, we can calculate their **liquid assets to take-home pay ratio.** Recalling (from page 48) that their 2005 take-home pay was $61,030 and their liquid assets at December 31, 2005, were $16,240 (see Figure 3.2), we have:

Liquid assets to take-home pay ratio: A liquidity measurement.

$$\frac{\text{Liquid assets to}}{\text{take-home pay ratio}} = \frac{\text{liquid assets}}{\text{take-home pay}} = \frac{\$16,240}{\$61,030} = 0.266$$

The number can then be expressed as months of the year; for example, 0.266 means about 27 percent of 12 months, or about 3.2 months. (Notice that an answer of 0.5 indicates half the year, or six months.) Thus, the Steeles fall at the lower rule-of-thumb figure of three months, suggesting they should build their liquid reserves. Since Arnold does have rather good loss-of-income protection at InChemCo, the lower figure is the more appropriate one for them to use. (We should note that take-home pay is an appropriate value to use if there are no other major sources of income, as in the Steeles' case. If there are other major sources, they should be included in the denominator, after allowing for related income taxes.)

Liquid Assets to Current Liabilities

The ratio of liquid assets to take-home pay does not consider the level of existing liabilities. Another family may show an identical ratio to the Steeles but be in far worse shape because their existing current liabilities are much greater. To augment the first ratio, then, it is helpful to calculate another ratio, called the **liquidity ratio,** which measures liquid assets against current liabilities. For the Steeles, it is:

$$\text{Liquidity ratio} = \frac{\text{liquid assets}}{\text{current liabilities}} = \frac{\$16,240}{\$8,354} = 1.94$$

This number tells us the Steeles have $1.94 of liquid assets for every $1.00 of existing current liabilities. There is no hard-and-fast rule indicating what this ratio should be, but any number greater than 1.0 shows fairly good strength, assuming the ratio of liquid assets to take-home pay is also adequate. Of course, the larger the number, the better the liquidity. With a ratio of 1.94, the Steeles are in reasonably good shape.

Avoiding Excessive Amounts of Debt

Adequate liquidity protects you from temporary cash emergencies, and liquidity ratios are designed to warn you of liquidity problems. However, they do not tell us whether total debt is being used properly or is excessive. *Excessive* doesn't mean too much debt in absolute dollars but rather in relation to your underlying assets and income that support the debt. Two important ratios are often used to evaluate total debt: the ratio of total liabilities to total assets and the ratio of take-home pay to debt repayment obligations.

Total Liabilities to Total Assets

Technically, you are judged insolvent when your total liabilities exceed your total assets. Being insolvent doesn't automatically mean you are illiquid; you might still have sufficient cash to pay your bills for a while. What it does mean is that, unless the situation changes, you will ultimately not have enough assets to pay all your bills. Many people in this position eventually file bankruptcy as a means of settling with creditors or establishing an orderly plan for paying their bills over an extended period of time.

Bankruptcy (discussed more fully in Chapter 6) is not to be taken lightly or viewed as a convenience to avoid paying obligations. You should look for early signals of impending troubles. The **debt ratio,** which measures total liabilities against total assets, is one such signal. Using the Steeles' data from Figure 3.2 as an example, it is calculated as follows:

$$\text{Debt ratio} = \frac{\text{total liabilities}}{\text{total assets}} = \frac{\$168,149}{\$325,540} = 0.517$$

This number tells us that the Steeles have about $0.52 in total debts for each $1.00 of total assets. Looking at it in another way, the value of their assets could shrink up to 48 percent $(1.00 - 0.52)$ before the Steeles would encounter insolvency problems. The

Finance News

BOX 3.2

What's Happening to Savings?

Clearly, Americans are saving less and less of their incomes, to such an extent in recent years that savings have actually turned negative during some months. The last time we saw negative savings was back in the 1930s during the Great Depression. In contrast, the 1995 to 2000 period showed some of the strongest economic gains on record. Yet savings fell dramatically. (See the accompanying graphic, which shows personal saving as a percentage of disposable personal income.)

All sorts of explanations of the phenomenon have come forth. A current popular idea is the so-called "wealth effect"—Americans have built considerable wealth in their homes and stock portfolios through rising market values, making savings less needed as a mechanism to build wealth. Indeed, many families continually refinance their homes, drawing out the built-up equity to finance even more spending.

No doubt, we have become a nation of spenders. Mom and Dad want $60,000 Saabs and Porsches, and the kids want $200 gym shoes. Many families earn the incomes to afford such luxuries if they don't worry about retirement. But, of course, that's when the fiddler gets paid. Saving 0 percent of our incomes, coupled with collapsing stock prices in our retirement accounts, is not exactly how one goes about building a retirement nest egg.

Of course, when retirement comes, we can simply refinance the house again, or sell it for a king's ransom. The house should last almost forever, shouldn't it? And housing prices never go down, do they? Frankly, if our retirement funds must come from a highly mortgaged house, we are in very bad shape.

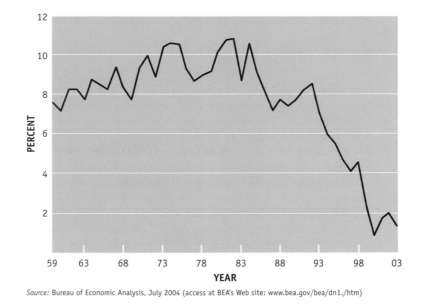

Source: Bureau of Economic Analysis, July 2004 (access at BEA's Web site: www.bea.gov/bea/dn1./htm)

smaller the ratio, the better from a safety point of view, but again, there is no iron-clad rule telling us what the ratio should be in every instance. The less volatile the market prices of your assets, the higher the ratio could be, all other things considered. In general, we like to see ratios below 0.5 to be on the relatively safe side. The Steeles are right at the margin.

Debt Service Coverage

Your capacity to carry debt is reflected not only in the market value of assets you own but also by the relationship of your take-home pay to your total debt-servicing charges. By debt service, we mean monthly (or yearly) payments of both principal and interest on those loans requiring periodic repayment. The debt service coverage ratio measures take-home pay against total debt service charges. The Steeles have two auto loans and their home mortgage. In addition, they borrowed $2,000 on Arnold's life insurance policy. Although this loan does not require periodic repayments, they pay interest of $160 each year. The total annual payments are $24,133 ($18,285 + $5,688 + $160), and the following **debt service coverage ratio** can be calculated:

$$\text{Debt service coverage ratio} = \frac{\text{take-home pay}}{\text{debt service charges}} = \frac{\$61,030}{\$24,133} = 2.53$$

This number indicates that the Steeles earned $2.53 in take-home pay for each $1.00 of required debt repayment and interest. Higher ratios, of course, indicate greater debt-carrying capacity than low ones. A ratio of 1.0 means that all of your after-tax income is needed to repay existing debts, and a ratio less than 1.0 indicates that your income will not even cover your existing repayments. (Again, if other major sources of income exist, they should be included, on an after-tax basis, in the numerator.)

A single number is never enough to distinguish strength from weakness, but it is usually felt that a ratio of 3.0 or better signals adequate strength and reasonable flexibility in future budgeting. In such a situation, a large portion of your income will not be committed to repaying existing debt. The Steeles' ratio of 2.53 indicates some weakness in this area.

Review of the Steeles' Financial Situation

Now that you have learned about financial statements and have seen them applied to the Steeles' financial situation for 2005, what impression do you have? Are they a wealthy family? Are they "sailing right along" with few financial concerns? Actually, their situation is not quite so successful as it might first appear.

True, they have a net worth of over $157,000. But there are a number of areas of concern. First, their residence of $205,000 is almost two-thirds of their total assets. Housing prices do often increase over time at the inflation rate or greater, but real estate markets can become very soft in the short run. A decline of 10 or 20 percent over several years, while not likely, would decrease their net worth substantially.

Second, Arnold and Sharon have $27,000 invested in late-model automobiles, which depreciate in value rather rapidly. If they continue to turn over their cars after three or four years, they will perpetually carry a rather high amount of expensive installment debt. As our ratio analysis revealed, they are probably already at their debt limit, and it would be helpful to reduce debt somewhat.

Third, and most important, the Steeles are enjoying a high-consumption budget that produces very little savings in relation to their income. At their current pace, they will not accumulate sufficient funds to educate Nancy and John or to achieve other important future goals. Put simply, the Steeles must rethink their priorities, become smarter consumer-investors, or do both. We will follow them in this process as the remaining chapters unfold. But their most pressing immediate need is to learn the budgeting process.

ACHIEVING GOALS THROUGH BUDGETING

What is a **budget?** Put very simply, a budget is any plan—simple or complex—that expresses your financial goals and how you will allocate your limited resources to achieve them. A budget can be so simple that you keep it on the back of an envelope to monitor your monthly progress with checkmarks. Or it can be as complex as the one the federal government prepares each year, detailing how over $2 trillion will be spent. But size is no guarantee of success. Your envelope approach might work, and there are many critics who feel the federal budget never has. We'll discuss principles of effective budgeting in this chapter, but before doing so, we will set forth some simple rules for budgeting success. Our discussion will revolve around these rules:

TOPIC **LINKS**

Compare your spending to that of others like you.

- *Set realistic budget goals.* The plural is important here. The budget is a device for achieving all your important goals; it is not a straitjacket to produce only savings.
- *Stick to simple procedures.* A $25 journal or an expensive computer is nice if you use it properly, but a waste of money if you don't. Trying to categorize every conceivable expense misses the whole point of budgeting and creates an unnecessary work burden that makes budgeting unpleasant.
- *Use the budget to control and direct expenses.* The main strength of a budget does not lie with its record-keeping function, although that is a necessary part. A budget allocation, say, for dining out, is a commitment you and your family make to an underlying activity. If you exceed the budget amount, ask yourself why. If the answer is because you want to, then you need to reexamine your goals to see if more funds should be allocated to this activity and less to others. If the answer reflects a temporary "overindulgence," then cut back next month to bring the activity back within budget. The simple acts of knowing you have exceeded budget and then deciding what to do about it are the essence of successful budgeting.

Goal Setting

When you set goals, you are effectively managing your finances rather than merely letting them take place as you go about your routine activities. Actually, **goal setting** is a rather complex process, and it has been studied by professionals from many disciplines, including social psychology, economics, and behavioral management. Goals can be viewed in a type of hierarchy, with very general and abstract goals at the top and more specific and tangible ones at the bottom. Figure 3.5 illustrates such a hierarchy of financial goals. At the top is the general goal of attaining financial independence for each member of the family. But what does this mean? You might understand it to mean sufficient wealth to be self-reliant; another person might understand it as having a job free of possible firing or other layoffs. To be meaningful, the general goals must be expressed in specific terms. For example, in Figure 3.5 financial independence is structured into three distinct goals: to enjoy a current living scale that reflects a moderate to high level of consumption, to provide a college education for the children, and to achieve a scale of living in retirement that

Goal setting: A complex process that involves a hierarchy of wants—abstract at the top and tangible at the bottom.

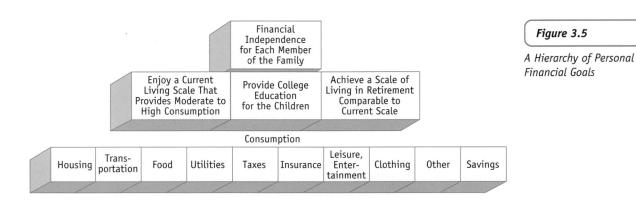

Figure 3.5

A Hierarchy of Personal Financial Goals

is on a par with the current living scale. As we move to the lowest level on the triangle, goals become even more specific and can be broken down to yearly savings and current consumption targets. Things to be acquired in the future—the children's education and retirement funds—must be saved for out of current income. Savings must be budgeted if these goals are to be achieved. As we saw in Chapter 2, the Steeles are planning to save $8,000 in the upcoming year.

Preparing the Annual Budget

TOPIC **LINKS**

See a sample budget.

Master budget worksheet: Budget allocations detailing planned income, expenses, and contribution to savings.

Monthly income and expense plan: A monthly breakdown of amounts listed on the master budget worksheet.

Armed with a clear understanding of the importance of expressing goals, you are in position to prepare the annual budget. It is this budget and your willingness to stick with it that will determine your success in goal achievement. There are two parts to budget preparation: the **master budget worksheet,** which details planned income, expenses, and contribution to savings in total for the budget year; and the **monthly income and expense plan,** which shows how each month's income, expenses, and contribution to savings will take place.

The Master Budget Worksheet

Budgeting begins each year by trying to forecast what your total income and expenses will be in the budget year. Some income and expense items are easy to forecast because they are known in advance (recall our previous discussion of fixed expenses): your mortgage payments on the house, for example. Others can vary widely and will be much more difficult to estimate: Dentist or doctor bills are good examples here, as is home maintenance. Despite the difficulties, estimates must be made and the budget finished.

Figure 3.6 on pages 64–65 illustrates a master budget worksheet the Steele family prepared for 2006. You probably recognize immediately that the budget has the same format as the income statement shown in Figure 3.3. The budget for a year should lead directly to the same kind of actual income and expense items after the year is over. In fact, budgeted and actual figures should be compared very closely at the end of a budget year, both for evaluating results for the year just ended and for preparing a budget for the upcoming year.

It goes almost without saying that budget figures should be determined as realistically as possible. Each line item should be reviewed and some reason found for making the estimate; that is, your figure should be defensible. A common mistake is to set a consumption item unrealistically low. If you think there is a good chance you will spend $40 a week on dining out and if that is what you want to do, then don't budget this activity at $20 a week. Doing so will only lead to frustration and eventual discarding of the budget.

The Monthly Income and Expense Plan

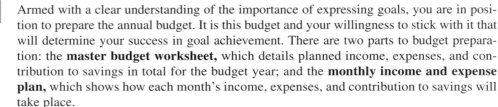

TOPIC **LINKS**

Complete a spending personality assessment.

After the master budget worksheet has been prepared, the next budgeting step is to determine how income and expense items will occur during the year. Usually, this is done on a monthly basis. Some expenses occur sporadically and in rather large amounts. It is important to plan for these expenses so that sufficient funds are available when these expenses must be paid. The monthly income and expense plan details income, expenses, and contribution to savings on a month-to-month basis. Arnold and Sharon Steele programmed their personal computer to show their monthly income and expense plan; it is shown in Figure 3.7.

Estimating the Monthly Activity

TOPIC **LINKS**

See how other people spend their money.

Some of the expense items were estimated in total by determining a budget monthly figure and then multiplying by 12. The monthly allocation, then, is this same monthly figure. For example, the Steeles' telephone bill was budgeted at $45 a month, so that figure is entered for each month. Notice in Figure 3.7 those expenses that do not occur uniformly. For example, all the insurance bills come in January and February; real estate taxes are paid in February and August, and dental–medical bills are expected in February and September. Notice further that Sharon's salary comes only in January through June and again in December and that dividends are received quarterly. In planning the monthly activity, you should try to determine as well as you can when the expected income or expense will occur.

Getting Through the Lean Months. Because of the irregularity of some income and expense items, it is possible that your expenses will exceed your income in a given month. Of course, you must have the funds available to meet the deficit, and you may have to borrow to do so. In looking at Figure 3.7 you see that the Steeles will have five deficit months. The other seven months show positive contributions to savings. By knowing they are likely to need extra funds in these five months, the Steeles can be alert to the need for effective cash management. For example, if we assume that their checking account balance is at a bare minimum as they begin 2006, then they should be careful how they deposit the expected surplus of $1,157 in January. It would not be wise to put all

Simplifying FINANCIAL Planning

Budgeting with Envelopes and Play Money

At first glance, the bulletin board in Mark and Carla Spielman's kitchen looks pretty much like anyone else's—but there's a difference. Along with the reminders, recipes, and other assorted notes usually adorning bulletin boards, theirs has nine letter-size envelopes, one for each of the most important ways the Spielmans spend money; there's also a red envelope for savings, red meaning: "Stop before entering." In each of the 10 envelopes Mark and Carla put a predetermined amount of play money at the beginning of each month, which represents their monthly allotment for the activity marked on the envelope; for example, the Entertainment envelope starts each month with $200 in it.

These envelopes are the Spielmans' complete budgeting system. Every evening they go together to the bulletin board and withdraw money from the appropriate envelopes to represent the money they spent that day, whether by check or cash. At the end of the month all the envelopes should be empty, except those that include things such as vacations, where funds are being temporarily saved for later use. If all goes exactly to plan, every envelope should be empty, except savings, on December 31. But what happens if the money runs out before a month is over? Unless they come up with a good reason for transferring

BOX 3.3

from one envelope to another (but never from the red one unless it's an absolute emergency), that activity is shot for the month. So if $200 is taken out of the Entertainment envelope by midmonth, the Spielmans watch a lot of television or find other things to do for the rest of the month.

The envelope system of budgeting probably dates back to the time envelopes were invented. Of course, the system itself doesn't guarantee success, but supposedly the discipline you gain by touching and feeling the money as you slip it out of the envelope makes you more budget conscious than do other approaches, such as writing things down on a budget worksheet, or, in today's environment, punching data into your home computer. But what about play money? Will you have the same emotional reservations about spending it as you have about spending real money? Some financial planners think so, and if you haven't done well at budgeting in the past, it's worth a try. It has several big advantages over the real thing: It's not that important if you lose some, and hardly anyone wants to steal it. And, just as important, you can leave your actual cash in the bank to earn interest. Don't take this last advantage lightly. If you have an expense budget of $5,000 a month and pay expenses uniformly over a month, your average balance for the month—and for the year as a whole—is $2,500. If you had a bank account earning 4 percent, you would give up $100 a year by stuffing cash in those envelopes. So, use play money and sleep at night—and have a good night on the town with the interest you earn.

Figure 3.6

Master Budget Worksheet for the Steeles

MASTER BUDGET WORKSHEET for the period   *Upcoming Year 2006*

For   *the Arnold and Sharon Steele Family*

INCOME

   Wages and Salaries:

      Arnold—*expect 5% raise this year* .... $ 63,216

      Sharon—*expect 10% raise and more hours* 18,000

     Total wages and salaries .... (a) 81,216

   Other Income:

     Interest   *should be about 7% on average balance* .... $ 984

     Dividends   *expect 10% increase* 1,200

     Capital gains or (losses) .... *none*

     Others .... *none*

      Total other income .... (b) $ 2,184

TOTAL INCOME = (a) + (b) = ... (c) $ 83,400

EXPENSES

   Housing:

     Rent .... $ *none*

     Mortgage payments   *fixed* 18,285

     Maintenance fees on condo or cooperative .... *none*

     Maintenance and home furnishings   *cut back a bit* 2,400

      Total housing expenses .... (d) $ 20,685

   Transportation:

     Automobile loan payments   *fixed* .... $ 5,688

     Gas, oil, and other maintenance and repairs   *say $200 a month* 2,400

     Licenses, parking, and other auto   *should be about $20 a month* 240

     Other transportation .... *none*

      Total transportation expenses .... (e) $ 8,328

   Food and Other Consumption Items:

     Food and household supplies   *about $550 a month* .... $ 6,600

     Meals eaten out   *lets budget $80 a month* 960

     Personal care—barbers and beauticians   *about $60 a month* 720

     Others .... *none*

      Total food and other consumption items .... (f) $ 8,280

   Utilities:

     Telephone   *this should be $45 a month* .... $ 540

     Gas and electric   *last year was $190 a month; go higher* 2,400

     Water and sanitation   *last year was $128 a quarter; go higher* 720

     Garbage pickup .... *none*

     Cable TV   *$35 a month last yaer; will go higher* 480

     Others .... *none*

     Total utilities .... (g) $ 4,140

of it into some type of account—say, a certificate of deposit—that is not readily available for withdrawals, because they will need $1,673 in the next month. Unquestionably, the year's activity will not unfold exactly as the Steeles see it in Figure 3.7; there are sure to be some surprises along the way to change things, but the Steeles are now in a far better position to cope with these changes than they would be without their monthly income and expense plan.

Figure 3.6

Taxes:		
Payroll *estimates based on 2006 estimated income*	$	15,600
Real estate and personal property *last year's; didn't go up*		3,500
Others		none
Total taxes	(h) $	19,100
Insurance:		
Health and medical withheld from wages *InChemCo pays*	$	none
Life *fixed; don't anticipate more insurance*		480
Property and liability *budget 5% over last year*		600
Automobile *budget 5% over last year*		1,560
Disability *InChemCo pays*		none
Others		none
Total insurance	(i) $	2,640
Leisure and Entertainment:		
Theater and sporting events *budget $70 a month*	$	840
Health club memberships *not interested*		none
Newspapers, magazines, etc. *budget $40 a month*		480
Vacations *count on four weeks camping*		1,800
Hobbies *buy one small antique*		240
Sporting equipment *soccer shoes, tennis equipment*		240
Others *Christmas gifts*	$	800
Total leisure and entertainment	(j) $	4,400
Clothing:		
New clothing *let's budget $150 a month*		1,800
Laundry and dry cleaning *estimate $20 a month*		240
Others		none
Total clothing	(k) $	2,040
Others:		
Gifts and charitable contributions *budget $180 a month*	$	2,160
Dues and subscriptions *last year's amount*		200
Tuition, books, other education expenses *expect big increase*		480
Babysitters *estimate at $50 a month*		600
Family members' personal allowances *we agree on this*		1,200
Unreimbursed medical–dental		—
InChemCo pays all		—
figure the worst on braces		1,200
		—
Total others	(l) $	5,840
TOTAL EXPENSES = (d) + (e) + (f) + (g) + (h)		
+ (i) + (j) + (k) + (l) =	(m) $	75,453
CONTRIBUTION TO SAVING = (c) – (m) =	(n) $	7,947

Monitoring and Controlling Activities

With the master budget worksheet and the monthly income and expense plan finished, the first phase of budgeting is completed. You now have a road map to guide your financial activities through the year. The second phase of budgeting begins as the year unfolds and events take place. This phase involves three separate tasks: First, you need a system to record your actual income and expenses. Second, you must periodically update your

Income	Jan	Feb	Mar	Apr	May	June	July	Aug	Sept	Oct	Nov	Dec	Total
Arnold's salary	5,268	5,268	5,268	5,268	5,268	5,268	5,268	5,268	5,268	5,268	5,268	5,268	63,216
Sharon's salary	2,000	3,000	4,000	4,000	2,000	1,000	—	—	—	—	—	2,000	18,000
Interest	82	82	82	82	82	82	82	82	82	82	82	82	984
Dividends	—	—	300	—	—	300	—	—	300	—	—	300	1,200
Total income	7,350	8,350	9,650	9,350	7,350	6,650	5,350	5,350	5,650	5,350	5,350	7,650	83,400
Expenses													
House mortgage	1,524	1,524	1,524	1,524	1,524	1,524	1,524	1,524	1,524	1,524	1,524	1,524	18,285
Maintenance and furnishings	200	200	200	200	200	200	200	200	200	200	200	200	2,400
Auto loan	474	474	474	474	474	474	474	474	474	474	474	474	5,688
Gas, oil, maintenance	200	200	200	200	200	200	200	200	200	200	200	200	2,400
Licenses, parking	20	20	20	20	20	20	20	20	20	20	20	20	240
Food, household items	550	550	550	550	550	550	550	550	550	550	550	550	6,600
Meals eaten out	80	80	80	80	80	80	80	80	80	80	80	80	960
Personal care	60	60	60	60	60	60	60	60	60	60	60	60	720
Telephone	45	45	45	45	45	45	45	45	45	45	45	45	540
Gas and electric	200	200	200	200	200	200	200	200	200	200	200	200	2,400
Water, garbage	180			180			180			180			720
Cable TV	120			120			120			120			480
All payroll taxes	1,400	1,500	1,700	1,600	1,400	1,200	1,100	1,100	1,100	1,100	1,100	1,300	15,600
Real estate taxes		1,800						1,700					3,500
Life insurance	480												480
Property insurance		600											600
Auto insurance		1,560											1,560
Theater, sports	70	70	70	70	70	70	70	70	70	70	70	70	840
Newspapers, magazines	40	40	40	40	40	40	40	40	40	40	40	40	480
Vacations				300		400	600					500	1,800
Hobbies, Christmas gifts				120				120				800	1,040
Sporting equipment				120				120					240
New clothing	150	150	150	150	150	150	150	150	150	150	150	150	1,800
Laundry, dry cleaning	20	20	20	20	20	20	20	20	20	20	20	20	240
Gifts, contributions	180	180	180	180	180	180	180	180	180	180	180	180	2,160
Dues and subscriptions	50				50		25	25	25	25			200
Tuition, books, etc.								480					480
Babysitters	50	50	50	50	50	50	50	50	50	50	50	50	600
Personal allowances	100	100	100	100	100	100	100	100	100	100	100	100	1,200
Dental–medical		600							600				1,200
Total Expenses	6,193	10,023	5,663	6,403	5,413	5,563	5,988	7,508	5,688	5,388	5,063	6,563	75,453
Contribution to Savings	1,157	–1,673	3,987	2,947	1,937	1,087	–638	–2,158	–38	–38	287	1,087	7,947

Figure 3.7

Monthly Income and Expense Plan for the Steele Family for 2006

income and expense accounts to see if actual amounts received and spent are in line with amounts planned. (This is usually done on a monthly basis.) Third, you need to evaluate and control activities as the year progresses.

Recording Income and Expenses

Record keeping is perhaps the most unpleasant aspect of budgeting, but it is necessary. Our concern should be primarily with how to do it most efficiently, since most people resent doing extensive bookkeeping each evening or weekend. The following list of suggestions might help you simplify the work.

Don't Use Cash. Pay as many bills as you can with checks or by charges to your credit cards (assuming neither method induces you to spend more). These will give you a written record of expenses that can be recorded at the end of the month. Paying bills with cash means, in effect, that you must create your own record, either by saving invoices or by writing things on odd pieces of paper. Both of these activities are time consuming, and the records are easily lost. Whenever you do pay with cash, standardize the recording by creating your own little voucher, which can be a small piece of paper like the one shown in Figure 3.8. You can make many of these if you have access to a copying machine. Stick a few in your pocket each day and get in the habit of using them.

Code Income and Expense Accounts. Assign an account number to each line item (particularly those used frequently), and, as you pay a bill, code the check stub with the appropriate number. This practice will facilitate summing expenses by category each month. Also, code your income items as you make bank deposits in order to identify the income source. If you receive a check from someone and cash it instead of depositing it, you also will have to record the amount received and identify the source. It is almost always better to deposit all checks and cash to your checking (or other) account so that they can be identified; if you need cash, write a check to get it.

See If Your Bank Can Help. Ask if your bank provides computerized services in summarizing your checks and deposit slips. Some banks do (and the trend is growing), and if you simply number-code your checks and deposits for each income and expense classification, the bank's monthly statement can provide you with the following information: (*a*) income and expense by each code number, (*b*) number of entries in each code number, (*c*) a percentage breakdown of income and expenses by code number for the month, and (*d*) an update of income and expense items by code number for the year. There probably will be a modest charge (say, $6 to $12 a month) for this service.

Date	6/8/XX
Amount Paid	$12.50
To Whom	Burger King
For What	Eating Out

Figure 3.8

A Simple Voucher to Record Cash Expenses

	January				
Income	Budgeted	Actual	Variance	Cumulative Variance	Budgeted
Arnold's salary	$5,268	$5,268	$ 0	$ 0	$ 5,268
Sharon's salary	2,000	2,375	375	375	3,000
Interest	82	84	2	2	82
Dividends	0	0	0	0	0
Total Income	$7,350	$7,727	$ 377	$ 377	$ 8,350
Expenses					
House mortgage	$1,524	$1,524	$ 0	$ 0	$ 1,524
Maintenance and furnishings	200	188	12	12	200
Auto loan	474	474	0	0	474
Gas, oil, maintenance	200	210	−10	−10	200
Licenses, parking	20	23	−3	−3	20
Food, household items	550	548	2	2	550
Meals eaten out	80	88	−8	−8	80
Personal care	60	73	−13	−13	60
Telephone	45	41	4	4	45
Gas and electric	200	195	5	5	200
Water, garbage	180	188	−8	−8	0
Cable TV	120	120	0	0	0
All payroll taxes	1,400	1,531	−131	−131	1,500
Real estate taxes	0	0	0	0	1,800
Life insurance	480	480	0	0	0
Property insurance	0	0	0	0	600
Auto insurance	0	0	0	0	1,560
Theater, sports	70	62	8	8	70
Newspapers, magazines	40	37	3	3	40
Vacations	0	0	0	0	0
Hobbies, Christmas gifts	0	0	0	0	0
Sporting equipment	0	40	−40	−40	0
New clothing	150	161	−11	−11	150
Laundry, dry cleaning	20	27	−7	−7	20
Gifts, contributions	180	180	0	0	180
Dues and subscriptions	50	50	0	0	0
Tuition, books, etc.	0	0	0	0	0
Babysitters	50	67	−17	−17	50
Personal allowances	100	100	0	0	100
Dental–medical	0	0	0	0	600
Total Expenses	$6,193	$6,407	$−214	$−214	$10,023
Contribution to Savings	$1,157	$1,320	$ 163	$ 163	$−1,673

Figure 3.9

Monthly Budget Update for the Steeles for the First Quarter, 2006

Use a Personal Computer. If, like the Steeles, you have a personal computer, determine if a home budgeting software package will be helpful. These vary in capability, but all provide data manipulation similar to the bank's service mentioned earlier. In addition, your personal computer has capabilities to store all the data and make them readily available for other purposes, such as comparing one month's expenses in a given category with similar monthly expenses of the previous year. And much more can be done; for example, the budget can be connected directly to your year-end balance sheet and income statement, so that making entries on the computer keyboard is virtually all you ever have to do for the entire financial recording process. All data manipulation and storage—and even printed copies—are provided automatically by the computer.

Updating Income and Expense Accounts

After all income and expense items have been accounted for, the next step is to update your monthly income and expense plan by recording actual amounts and then comparing them with the budget. This is usually done monthly, and it is done best with an income and

February				March		
Actual	Variance	Cumulative Variance	Budgeted	Actual	Variance	Cumulative Variance
$ 5,268	$ 0	$ 0	$ 5,268	$ 5,268	$ 0	$ 0
3,475	475	850	4,000	4,425	425	1,275
80	−2	0	82	77	−5	−5
0	0	0	300	300	0	0
$ 8,823	$ 473	$ 850	$ 9,650	$10,070	$ 420	$ 1,270
$ 1,524	$ 0	$ 0	$ 1,524	$ 1,524	$ 0	$ 0
160	40	52	200	230	−30	22
474	0	0	474	474	0	0
225	−25	−35	200	232	−32	−67
27	−7	−10	20	24	−4	−14
596	−46	−44	550	593	−43	−87
102	−22	−30	80	91	−11	−41
66	−6	−19	60	63	−3	−22
43	2	6	45	43	2	8
208	−8	−3	200	176	24	21
0	0	−8	0	0	0	−8
0	0	0	0	0	0	0
1,647	−147	−278	1,700	1,910	−210	−488
1,800	0	0	0	0	0	0
0	0	0	0	0	0	0
620	−20	−20	0	0	0	−20
1,630	−70	−70	0	0	0	−70
80	−10	−2	−70	−76	−6	−8
37	3	6	40	56	−16	−10
0	0	0	0	0	0	0
0	0	0	0	0	0	0
0	0	−40	0	0	0	−40
133	17	6	150	174	−24	−18
28	−8	−15	20	26	−6	−21
178	2	2	180	173	7	9
0	0	0	0	0	0	0
0	0	0	0	0	0	0
64	−14	−31	50	79	−29	−60
100	0	0	100	100	0	0
470	130	130	0	0	0	130
$10,212	$−189	$−403	$ 5,663	$ 6,044	$−381	$−784
$−1,389	$ 284	$ 447	$ 3,987	$ 4,026	$ 39	$ 486

expense plan update, such as the one shown in Figure 3.9. If the actual amount for a line item differs from the budgeted figure, it is called a **variance.** Variances can then be either favorable—meaning they assisted in the saving effort—or unfavorable—meaning they detracted from it. An **income variance** is favorable whenever actual exceeds budgeted; it is unfavorable when the reverse is true. An **expense variance** is favorable whenever actual is less than budgeted, and it is unfavorable in the reverse case. Unfavorable variances are indicated in Figure 3.9 by a minus sign in front of the amount. The **cumulative variance** figure results from adding the current month's variance to variances of previous months; thus, the cumulative variance for maintenance—the second expense item—in February is a favorable $52, which is the sum of the favorable $40 variance in February and the favorable variance of $12 in January. In March, maintenance showed an unfavorable variance of $30, and subtracting this from February's cumulative variance gives a new cumulative variance of $22 at the end of March.

Figure 3.9 shows the Steeles' activity for the first three months of 2006. Although you see all three months at once, you should assume that each month's activities were

Variance: Actual income or expense item that differs from the budgeted amount.

Income variance: Income item variance—favorable when actual exceeds budgeted; unfavorable in the reverse situation.

Expense variance: Expense item variance—favorable when actual is less than budgeted; unfavorable in the reverse situation.

Cumulative variance: Monthly accumulation of variances.

recorded separately. The flow of data gives you a fairly good picture of how the Steeles' financial events took place during the quarter. Sharon began working more hours than she anticipated, which led to most of the favorable income variance in January, and this continued in February and March. By the end of the quarter, Sharon had earned $1,275 more than budgeted. The estimates for Arnold's salary and dividends were accurate, and the interest variance is trivial.

Evaluating and Controlling Activities

Being able to stay within budget means you are continuously adjusting your expenses during the year. Evaluating and controlling activities really make the budget work; an elaborate recording system does little good if we choose to ignore the information it provides. For example, the Steeles went $11 over their budget for new clothing in January. This tells them they have only $139 ($150 − $11) to spend in February. You must subtract the cumulative variance (add, if it's favorable) from the current monthly budget figure to determine how much of current funds is available for a given line item. In February, the Steeles went $17 under budget for new clothing, which offset the unfavorable $11 variance, leaving a $6 favorable variance for March. However, March's figure was $24 over budget, meaning the Steeles ended the first quarter with a cumulative unfavorable variance of $18 in this account. Unless their goal is changed here, they should try to reduce this variance to zero by the end of June.

Even though you are monitoring activities and calculating cumulative variances at the end of each month, a year-end review can be helpful. It serves mainly to assist in making budget estimates for the next year. It also provides an opportunity to prepare the current year's income statement, because the figure for each line item on this statement is simply the budget amount for the year plus its cumulative variance at December 31.

Key Terms			
	assets (p. 47)	income (p. 52)	monthly income and
	budget (p. 60)	income statement (p. 52)	expense plan (p. 62)
	cumulative variance (p. 69)	income variance (p. 69)	net worth (p. 47)
	current liability (p. 49)	inflexible expenses (p. 53)	nominal income (p. 55)
	debt ratio (p. 58)	investment assets (p. 49)	noncurrent liabilities
	debt service coverage ratio	liabilities (p. 47)	(p. 49)
	(p. 60)	lifestyle asset (p. 49)	personal balance sheet
	dissavings (p. 51)	liquid asset (p. 48)	(p. 47)
	expense variance (p. 69)	liquid assets to take-home	positive contribution to
	expenses (p. 52)	pay ratio (p. 57)	savings (p. 51)
	financial ratios (p. 53)	liquidity ratio (p. 58)	real income (p. 55)
	flexible expenses (p. 53)	master budget worksheet	sunk costs (p. 53)
	goal setting (p. 61)	(p. 62)	variance (p. 69)

FOLLOW-UP ON THE

Steele
FAMILY

This entire chapter has focused on the Steeles. If you have read it carefully, you should have a good understanding of their present financial situation and what they hope to accomplish in the upcoming year. Let's consider a few other points.

1. The Steeles saved $2,594 in 2005 and plan to triple this amount in 2006. Judging from your own experiences at saving money, do you feel the Steeles will accomplish their goal?

2. Reviewing their expense allocations in the master budget worksheet, in what area(s) do you think the Steeles are likely to go "over budget" during the year?
3. The review of the Steeles' situation on page 60 of the text seems rather harsh. Do you agree with it? Explain.
4. Your family background may be quite different from the Steeles. Without interjecting personal value judgments, how would you compare your family situation with the Steeles'?

Problems and Review Questions

1. Explain the following elements of a balance sheet and give an example of each:
   (a) liquid assets
   (b) investment assets
   (c) lifestyle assets
   (d) current liabilities
   (e) noncurrent liabilities
2. Explain how asset values are determined on the balance sheet and whether these valuations are made easily.
3. What is net worth? Does it have anything to do with wealth? Explain two factors that can change net worth from one period to the next.
4. Explain the difference between a current and a noncurrent liability. Give an example of each. Explain whether liability amounts are difficult or easy to determine.
5. Lisa Rich spent every cent she had and then borrowed $1,000 to purchase an elaborate wardrobe worth $2,000. Ignoring all of Lisa's other assets and liabilities, construct her balance sheet after the purchase. Suppose that, a year later, Lisa's wardrobe—now completely out of style—is worth only $100. If Lisa has paid off $500 of her loan, what does her balance sheet look like now? Comment on her present financial position.
6. What is an income statement, and what are its component parts? In your answer, distinguish between flexible and inflexible expenses.
7. Would you classify the following expense items as flexible or inflexible? Which one(s) would you consider sunk costs?
   (a) property taxes
   (b) house mortgage payments
   (c) clothing
   (d) car licenses
   (e) insurance
   (f) family members' personal allowances
8. Explain how planned savings differs from savings as something left over.
9. The following items, arranged alphabetically, belong to either the income statement or the balance sheet. Put them in their correct place and then construct each statement. (You must also calculate net worth and contribution to savings.)

Automobile (2003 Ford)	$ 6,000
Automobile loan payments	1,200
Cash value of life insurance	2,000
Coins and currency	300
Credit card balances due	500
Federal income taxes withheld from wages	4,000
Food and household supplies	6,000
Gas and electric expenses	2,200
Gifts	400

Hobbies and collections	650
Installment loan balances due in one year	1,200
Interest	700
Jewelry	850
Mortgage loan on residence	60,000
Mortgage payments	6,200
Property and liability insurance	300
Real estate taxes	1,200
Residence	80,000
Telephone	240
Theater and sporting events	700
Tuition	1,100
U.S. Series EE bonds	1,600
Unpaid bills	700
Wages and salaries	26,000

10. You are given the following data for Kim Zerussen:

	2004	2005
Income during the year	$30,000	$32,000
End of year: Assets	50,000	60,000
Liabilities	40,000	49,000

Assuming that inflation was 10 percent during 2005, evaluate Kim's financial performance for that year.

11. Explain a financial ratio and then identify the following ratios, indicating what they are supposed to test. How would you evaluate each, given its specific numbers? After you complete that assignment, discuss whether you think the person to whom these ratios apply is a good credit risk.
    (a) liquid assets to take-home pay $= 0.08$
    (b) liquidity ratio $\qquad = 0.75$
    (c) debt ratio $\qquad = 1.20$
    (d) debt service coverage ratio $\quad = 1.10$

12. Explain three simple rules that often lead to success in budgeting. Do you agree that the more complex a budget is, the more successful it will be? Explain.

13. Discuss the process of setting goals. List several general goals that you think will be important to you after graduation and then indicate which specific goals you will use in your annual budgets.

14. Describe the master budget worksheet, indicating some expenses you believe might be easy to forecast and some that are more difficult.

15. Explain how you would forecast the following expense items for an upcoming budget year:
    (a) mortgage payments
    (b) food and household items
    (c) income and other payroll taxes
    (d) family members' personal allowance

16. How does a monthly income and expense plan help in managing your cash and checking account?

17. Explain how a budget helps achieve effective cash management.

18. Briefly describe four procedures that might simplify bookkeeping activities connected with recording monthly income and expense amounts.
19. Explain the relationship among the budget, the income statement, and cumulative variances. Also discuss possible situations that might warrant making changes in a budget during the year.
20. Following are budget and actual figures for selected income and expense accounts for the month of June and cumulative variances for each account through May. (Parentheses indicate an unfavorable variance.)

	Cumulative Variance Through May	June Budgeted	June Actual
Salaries	$(1,600)	$3,000	$3,400
Expenses:			
Rent	(100)	300	320
Transportation	85	200	215
Food	125	550	575
All others	(160)	850	780
Payroll taxes	400	900	1,000

Answer the following, assuming that the foregoing list of accounts is all that needs to be considered.
(a) Calculate June's variances and the cumulative variances through June.
(b) If the budgeter planned at the beginning of the year to save an equal amount each month and has not revised that plan, how much has he or she actually saved through June? (Show your work.)

Case 3.1
Can Arnold and Sharon Afford a Vacation Condominium?

At the end of 2004, Arnold and Sharon Steele were considering buying a condominium in Gatlinburg, Tennessee. Gatlinburg is a resort town next to the Great Smoky Mountain National Park area, where the Steeles have often camped. The condo they particularly liked was priced at $67,000, and the seller offered to finance 90 percent of the purchase price with a first mortgage loan requiring monthly payments of $597 during the first year. To make the $6,700 down payment and $2,200 of closing costs, the Steeles planned to sell both their Coleman camper (which would have been worth $2,500 at that time) and their U.S. Series EE bonds (then worth $2,800). The balance of $3,600 would be borrowed from Sharon's parents, who would not expect regular repayments of the loan but would charge interest of $288 each year. Arnold and Sharon decided against the purchase for a number of reasons, one of which involved finances. They felt that the condo would have placed an excessive strain on their budget, given their alternative goal of adding to their investments and liquid assets.

Questions
1. Using the data given in this case and elsewhere in this chapter, calculate what the Steeles' contribution to savings would have been in 2005 if they bought the condo on January 1, 2005. (Assume that expenses, including income taxes, not related to the purchase remain the same.)

2. Prepare a new balance sheet at December 31, 2005, for the Steeles, again assuming that they made the purchase on January 1, 2005, and that total interest payments on the mortgage loan were $6,935 and payments of principal were $229 for the year.
3. Using the four ratios given in this chapter to evaluate liquidity and total debt, make new calculations for the Steeles, assuming the condo purchase, and compare them with those calculated in the chapter. Discuss the comparisons.
4. Do you agree with the Steeles that the purchase would have been a financial strain for them? Explain your answer.

Case 3.2
The Terrels' Budget for 2006

Donna and Sherman Terrel are preparing a budget for 2006. Donna is a systems analyst with an airplane manufacturer, and Sherman is working on a master's degree in educational psychology. The Terrels do not have any children or other dependents. Donna estimates her salary will be about $36,000 in 2006; Sherman expects to work only during the summer months, doing painting and remodeling work for a building contractor. He anticipates an income from those activities of $2,400 a month in June, July, and August. Sherman does have a scholarship that pays his tuition and also provides $2,400 a year, payable in equal amounts in October and February. The Terrels don't expect to have any other income in 2006.

Donna and Sherman have listed their expected total expenses in 2006 as follows:

Housing (rent)	$5,760
Transportation	4,800
Food (includes dining out)	7,920
Utilities	2,880
Payroll taxes:	
Donna	10,800
Sherman	1,200
Insurance:	
Life—payable in May	600
Auto—payable in January	1,320
Leisure and entertainment:	
Vacation in May	1,152
All others	1,728
Clothing	1,296
Others	$3,840
Total Expenses	$43,296

The Terrels will begin 2006 with about $1,200 in liquid assets, and they prefer not to draw this balance below $600 at any time during the year.

Questions
1. Prepare a monthly income and expense plan for the Terrels in 2006.
2. On the basis of the plan you have just prepared, discuss the Terrels' expected financial situation in 2006. Explain if you foresee any difficulties.
3. During the quarter break in April, Sherman's employer landed a major remodeling project and asked for Sherman's help. Sherman agreed, and he expects to earn $1,800 from the job before taxes but probably won't receive a check until early June. Discuss how this unexpected event might affect the Terrels' activities and their budget for the balance of 2006. It is not necessary to prepare a revised monthly income and expense plan, but do refer to specific accounts and amounts (make appropriate assumptions) in your discussion.

Marie Wilson Goal-Planning Exercise Preparing a Budget

You have helped Marie establish financial goals and prepare a plan for achieving them. A tentative plan requires that Marie save $2,000 annually over the next five years. Since Marie has saved very little until now, she is concerned that this amount may be excessive. She has asked your help in preparing a budget for the upcoming year.

Form 3.1

Budget

	Amounts	Percent
Income		
Salaries and wages: earner 1	$_____	_____
Salaries and wages: earner 2	_____	_____
Total salaries and wages	$_____	_____
Other income		
Interest	_____	_____
Dividends	_____	_____
Capital gains	_____	_____
Alimony/ support payments	_____	_____
Others	_____	_____
_____	_____	_____
Total other income	$_____	_____
Total income	$_____	100%
Expenses		
Housing		
Rent or mortgage payments	$_____	_____
Maintenance	_____	_____
Home furnishings	_____	_____
Other housing -	_____	_____
Total housing	$_____	_____
Transportation		
Auto loan payments	$_____	_____
Gas, oil, maintenance	_____	_____
Licenses, parking fees	_____	_____
Other transportation	_____	_____
Total transportation	$_____	_____
Food and other consumption items		
Food and household supplies	$_____	_____
Meals eaten out	_____	_____
Personal care—barbers, beauticians	_____	_____
Total food and consumption	$_____	_____
Utilities		
Telephone	$_____	_____
Internet connection	_____	_____
Gas and electric	_____	_____
Cable	_____	_____
Water	_____	_____
Other utilities	_____	_____
Total utilities	$_____	_____

	Amounts	Percent
Taxes		
Payroll	$_____	_____
Real estate	_____	_____
Other taxes	_____	_____
Total taxes	$_____	_____
Insurance		
Health and medical	$_____	_____
Life	_____	_____
Auto and property	_____	_____
Disability	_____	_____
Other insurance	_____	_____
Total insurance	$_____	_____
Leisure and entertainment		
Theater, sporting events	$_____	_____
Memberships	_____	_____
Newspapers, magazines	_____	_____
Hobbies	_____	_____
Other leisure and entertainment	_____	_____
Total leisure and entertainment	$_____	_____
Clothing		
New clothing	$_____	_____
Dry cleaning	_____	_____
Other clothing	_____	_____
Total clothing	$_____	_____
Other expenses		
Baby sitting and child care	$_____	_____
Educational outlays	_____	_____
Charitable gifts	_____	_____
Personal allowances	_____	_____
Unreimbursed medical and dental		
student loans		
_____	_____	_____
_____	_____	_____
_____	_____	_____
Total other expenses	$_____	_____
Total Expenses	$_____	_____
Contribution to Savings	$_____	_____

Marie expects to earn $32,000 next year in salary and $6,000 in support payments from Jake's father. Other income is minimal and can be disregarded. Her monthly rent is $400 and she estimates a gas and electric bill of $150 a month. Payroll taxes have been about 10 percent of her gross salary and her employer withholds $200 a month for health insurance. Last year, she paid baby-sitters $4,800, and she paid $1,200 on her student loans. Her telephone bill is $20 a month and she pays another $18 a month for Internet service. While she hasn't kept good records, Marie estimates she spends about $400 a month on auto expenses (not counting auto and property insurance of $1,500 a year) and about $6,000 yearly on food, both at home and dining out.

Marie realizes that the previous list is not inclusive, and she expects that you can help her identify possible outlays related to other areas. Explain to Marie why you believe these areas are important. However, do not consider any expenses related to Marie's intent to begin law school. Marie feels this goal is very important but first she must determine if it can be accommodated within her budget. Use Form 31 to help her prepare an annual budget. Try to be as realistic as possible in setting expense items. After finishing the budget, prepare a report on Marie's financial situation. Discuss whether she will have adequate financial resources to pursue the goals identified in Chapter 1.

Internet Exercises to Strengthen Your Use of the Internet

(Internet links for the following exercises can be found at **www.prenhall.com/winger.**)

Working Out on the Web

Exercise 3.1 What Is Your Spending Personality?

Your spending personality assessment may be revealed by answering a questionnaire from *HealthyCash*.

Q. What are your buying habits? Explain if you may have shopping problems that can hinder your saving effort.

Exercise 3.2 Is Your Income Matching the Inflation Rate?

Find the most recent inflation rate by consulting Economic Statistics Briefing Room. Scroll down and choose "Prices."

Q. How much must your income increase each year to match the most recent inflation rate, as measured by the "Consumer Price Index"? Also, click on "Chart" to see recent trends in the CPI.

Exercise 3.3 Setting Up a Budget

Along with the text's treatment, some additional help in setting up a budget is provided by Household Budget Management. Choose "What Is a Household Budget." Then scroll down and choose "A Sample Budget."

Q. Compare its sample budget to the one in this chapter.

Exercise 3.4 How Do Other People Spend Their Money?

The BLS Consumer Expenditure Survey (choose "Consumer Expenditures in 1999") shows expenditures for the average American family. The Steeles spent 28 percent of their income on housing.

Q. What percentage does the average family spend on housing? Suppose your rent is 40 percent of your income. What problems can this create in your effort to balance your budget?

Exercise 3.5 Do You Have a Typical Budget?

Money Online has a budget maker that allows you to enter your personal data and then analyze your spending. Click on "Making a Budget" then "Evaluating Them."

Q. Enter appropriate data for the Steeles and then compare their spending to that of other people shown in the example.

4

Taxes

THE GOVERNMENT'S SHARE OF YOUR REWARDS

Steele FAMILY

This is the weekend Arnold and Sharon have reserved for filing their taxes. As usual they have waited until the week of April 15. Tax-filing season typically puts the Steeles in an unpleasant mood. However, the task is less time consuming now that they are using computer software to fill in their federal and state tax forms. Given the appropriate information, the software program automatically computes a number of entries such as their tax credits and tax liability. In addition, it also simultaneously completes both federal and state forms, reducing the need to manually repeat the process on their state income tax form.

Last year they purchased a computer program to aid them in filing their taxes. This year they bought the annual update. The updated program for the current year eases some of the time burden by accessing the personal data from last year's tax forms and automatically entering them on this year's forms. It keeps track of the previously entered data to ensure the entry of repeat information in the current year. For example, if they claimed a home interest deduction in the previous year, the program automatically prompts them for information in the current year.

The Steeles feel well prepared to tackle this year's taxes. In addition to using computer support, they have also been keeping track of their tax-deductible expenses. Receipts for expenses that might be deductible, such as medical and child care expenses, have been filed in special folders. They have also been noting tax-deductible items on check stub memos and credit card statements.

OBJECTIVES

1. To understand the basic approach used by the Internal Revenue Service to determine your yearly federal income tax liability

2. To be able to calculate your yearly federal income tax liability following directions and guidelines provided by the Internal Revenue Service

3. To recognize the role the Internal Revenue Service plays in enforcing the income tax law and to know when to seek professional help in income tax matters

4. To understand and use important strategies that help you save federal income taxes or defer them to later years

5. To identify other important taxes that you currently pay or will pay in future years

TOPIC **LINKS**

Follow the **Topic Links** in each chapter for your interactive Personal Finance exercise on the Web. Go to: **www.prenhall.com/winger**

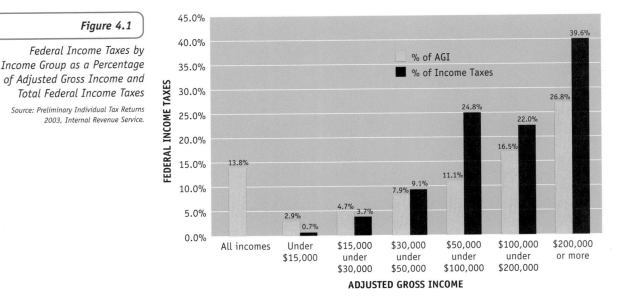
Taxes are an important part of our everyday lives. We pay sales and excise taxes on many items that we purchase to consume. Our houses, automobiles, and other assets—tangible and intangible—are subject to property taxes. The income we earn is taxed, and when we die, our estates are taxed. Figure 4.1 indicates the size of the "tax bite" in relation to income; note that the table considers only so-called direct federal taxes levied on households. When all taxes are considered, the percentages are considerably higher. Indeed, the Tax Foundation estimates that the average family must work about 101 days each year to support government services. The largest single tax is the federal income tax, and Figure 4.1 gives a clear indication of the federal government's role in American society. Not only does its size make it important, but it is structured such that most people can reduce their tax liability through effective tax planning.

TOPIC **LINKS**

Tax Foundation

DETERMINING YOUR FEDERAL INCOME TAX

Almost all individuals with moderate levels of income are required to file a federal income tax return. In the year 2004, single individuals with more than $7,800 in taxable income and married couples living together with more than $15,600 in taxable income were required to file federal tax returns. There is a different income threshold for those age 65 or older and dependents. In addition, those owing special taxes, such as Social Security and Medicare, must also file a return. Even when it is not required, you may want to file a return to receive a refund for an overpayment of withholding taxes or a tax credit.

The federal income tax follows the steps illustrated in Figure 4.2. The entire process is explained in greater detail in the following sections, and later we'll illustrate the topic by showing Arnold and Sharon Steele's income tax return.

TOPIC **LINKS**

See IRS Pub. 17 "Your
Federal Income Tax."

Gross Income Items

Gross income items: Sources
of income that are subject to
the federal income tax.

Nontaxable exclusions: Items
that are *not* includable as
gross income.

Global income: Income from
all sources.

To begin with, many items that you might look on as part of your **global income** (income from all sources) are not considered taxable income by the Internal Revenue Service (IRS). A partial list of included items is shown in Figure 4.3. Specifically excluded from global income are those items listed in Figure 4.4.

Some of the excluded items are important in tax strategy. Notice that municipal bond interest is an excluded item. All other factors being the same, it is to your advantage

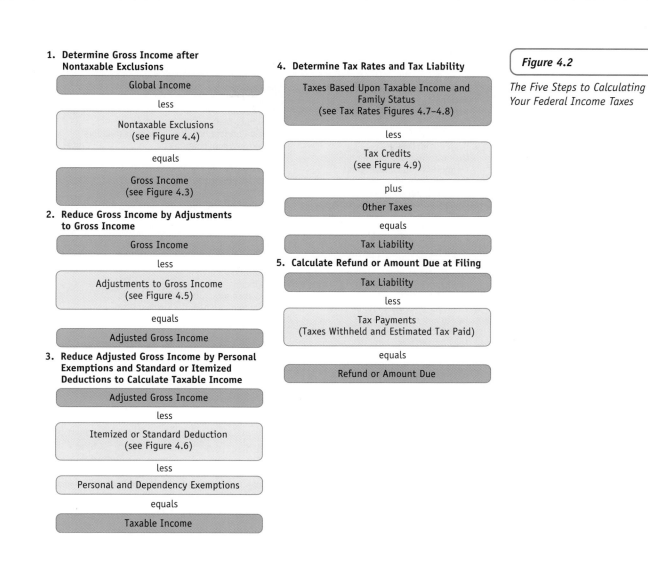

1. Determine Gross Income after Nontaxable Exclusions

Global Income

less

Nontaxable Exclusions
(see Figure 4.4)

equals

Gross Income
(see Figure 4.3)

2. Reduce Gross Income by Adjustments to Gross Income

Gross Income

less

Adjustments to Gross Income
(see Figure 4.5)

equals

Adjusted Gross Income

3. Reduce Adjusted Gross Income by Personal Exemptions and Standard or Itemized Deductions to Calculate Taxable Income

Adjusted Gross Income

less

Itemized or Standard Deduction
(see Figure 4.6)

less

Personal and Dependency Exemptions

equals

Taxable Income

4. Determine Tax Rates and Tax Liability

Taxes Based Upon Taxable Income and Family Status
(see Tax Rates Figures 4.7–4.8)

less

Tax Credits
(see Figure 4.9)

plus

Other Taxes

equals

Tax Liability

5. Calculate Refund or Amount Due at Filing

Tax Liability

less

Tax Payments
(Taxes Withheld and Estimated Tax Paid)

equals

Refund or Amount Due

Figure 4.2

The Five Steps to Calculating Your Federal Income Taxes

to own municipal bonds as opposed to those whose interest payments are fully taxable. Also, such items as group term life insurance and health insurance are often offered as fringe benefits by employers (or as part of a salary-reduction plan). If you had to purchase these items with after-tax income, they may cost you considerably more. For example, if you are in a 28 percent tax bracket, you must earn $1,389 to net $1,000. (You get this figure by dividing the $1,000 by 1.00 minus the tax bracket; that is, $1,389 = 1,000/[1.00 - 0.28]$.) Clearly, if your employer gives you a choice between the $1,000 or a nontaxed fringe benefit, choose the latter if you intend to buy the benefit anyway.

Adjustments to Income

Adjusted gross income is equal to gross income less certain adjustments permitted by the tax law. These are significant adjustments because they reduce your income before you itemize deductions. A partial list of adjustments is shown in Figure 4.5. The education-related adjustments are discussed in a later section of this chapter. A discussion of some of the other important adjustments follows.

Adjusted gross income: Gross income plus or minus certain adjustments.

Figure 4.3

A Partial List of Gross Income Items

Alimony
Awards, prizes, and lottery winnings
Back pay
Bargain purchase from employer
Bonuses
Breach of contract damages
Business income
Cash gift from employer
Clergy fees and contributions
Commissions
Compensation for services
Damages other than personal injury
Death benefits
Debts forgiven
Director's fees
Dividends
Embezzled funds
Employee awards
Employee benefits (excepting certain fringe benefits)
Employer-paid disability benefits
Estate and trust income
Farm income
Fees for services
Gains from illegal activities
Gains from sale of property
Gambling winnings

Group term life insurance, premium paid by employer (coverage over $50,000)
Hobby income
Interest income
Jury duty fees
Living quarters, meals (unless furnished for employer's convenience)
Mileage allowance
Military pay (unless combat pay)
Partnership income
Pensions
Professional fees
Punitive damages
Reimbursement for moving expenses
Rent
Retirement pay
Rewards
Royalties
Salaries
Severance pay
Social Security benefits (partial inclusion)
Strike and lockout benefits
Supplemental unemployment benefits
Tips and gratuities
Travel allowance
Unemployment compensation
Wages

Health and Medial Savings Account Deduction

If you satisfy certain IRS requirements, you may be able to set up a special account. Funds in this account are an adjustment to your gross income and can be used to pay for qualified medical expenses. These are explained in IRS Publication 969, "Health Savings Accounts" and IRS Publication 502, "Medical and Dental Expenses." These accounts are also discussed in Chapter 14, "Health Care and Disability Insurance."

Figure 4.4

A Partial List of Exclusions from Gross Income

Accelerated death benefits and long-term care benefits
Accident insurance proceeds
Annuities (to a limited extent)
Casualty insurance proceeds
Child support payments
Cost-of-living allowance (for military)
Damage for personal injury or sickness
Disability benefits you paid for
Disability pensions (to a limited extent)
Fellowship grants (to a limited extent)
Gifts
Health insurance proceeds not deducted as a medical expense
Inheritances
Life insurance paid on death
Long-term capital gain on personal residence

Meals and lodging (furnished for employer's convenience)
Military allowances
Municipal bond interest
Qualified employer contributions (to a limited extent) for
— adoption expenses
— educational expenses
— long-term care service
— moving expenses
— pension benefits
— health, life, and disability benefits
— health and medical savings accounts
Relocation payments
Scholarship grants (to a limited extent)
Survivor benefits for public safety officers
Veterans' benefits
Welfare payments
Workers' compensation

Figure 4.5

A Partial List of Adjustments to Income

Alimony paid
Contributions to health savings account
Contributions to individual retirement plans
Moving expenses
Penalty for early withdrawal of savings
Qualified educational expenses
Self-employed health insurance deduction
Self-employment tax (half)
Student loan interest

Moving Expenses

You can deduct certain moving expenses if your new job is at least 50 miles from your previous home and these expenses are incurred within one year of the date on which you began your new job. These deductions are available to both individuals changing jobs and those entering the job market for the first time. Generally, you can deduct the cost of traveling to your new home and the cost of moving your furnishings.

IRAs and Keogh Plans

IRAs and **Keogh plans** will be explained in greater detail in Chapter 16, but a few words about each are appropriate here. A Keogh plan can be established by anyone with self-employed income (i.e., income from a business). This plan is used by many small business operators and professionals, such as artists and writers. Allowable contributions to a Keogh are considerably greater than IRA contributions, so if you earn self-employed income, you should become familiar with the Keogh provisions.

IRAs and Keogh plans: Retirement plans that reduce gross income.

The tax-deductible IRA (Individual Retirement Account) can be used by anyone (employed or self-employed) whose income does not exceed certain limitations. Its intent is to encourage individual retirement planning, and it accomplishes this aim by allowing deductions to qualified IRA investments. Most investments people make—such as deposits in banks and savings and loans, common and preferred stocks, bonds, certain partnership interests, and more—are qualified investments. Generally, the contribution limits out of earned income are as follows; however, taxpayers over age 50 can contribute additional amounts.

TOPIC **LINKS**

See IRS Pub. 590 "Individual Retirement Arrangements."

Tax Year	Maximum Contribution
2005–2007	$4,000
2008	$5,000

It goes almost without saying that the IRA is one of the easiest and most generous tax concessions provided by Congress. Many tax advisers call it the best tax shelter for the middle-income family. Not only is the IRA a generous deduction but it's also virtually the only one you can take even after the tax year is over, since you have until April 15 of the following year to make your investment. Unfortunately, if your income exceeds certain limits and you have an employer-sponsored retirement plan, the deductibility of an IRA is gradually eliminated. The current limits can be found in IRS Publication 590, "Individual Retirement Arrangements."

There are also two special IRAs: one is called the Roth IRA and the other is an "education IRA." These are both more fully explained later in the text. Briefly, neither of these provides an immediate tax deduction. However, the funds accumulate tax free, and if they are properly distributed, the withdrawals are nontaxable.

Alimony Paid

In general, **alimony payments** must be included as income by the person receiving them and are deductible by the ex-spouse making them. Such payments must be the result of a

Alimony payments: Added to gross income of the receiver but a reduction of the payer's gross income.

court decree of divorce or separation and also must satisfy all of the following requirements. Divorce or separation often involves deep emotional feelings, and the last thing on the spouses' minds is how to structure the divorce to minimize future tax liabilities. This is unfortunate, because a cooperative approach can benefit each partner. You need good tax advice in this area, and it's usually worth retaining an attorney or CPA to help with the settlement.

Adjusted Gross Income

Gross income less adjustments is adjusted gross income. This is an important figure because some itemized deductions are phased out if your adjusted gross income exceeds annually determined limits.

Taxable Income

Taxable income consists of adjusted gross income less **personal and dependency exemptions** and deductions for personal expenses. This latter item consists of either taking a standardized amount or itemizing allowable deductions.

Personal and Dependency Exemptions

Taxable income: Adjusted gross income less personal and dependency exemptions and allowable personal expense deductions.

The law allows most taxpayers a personal exemption. The amount was $3,100 in 2004. It is *indexed* to the price level; therefore, the exemption is adjusted upward each year to reflect the current cost of living. Each spouse on a joint return is entitled to the exemption, and it also applies to any of the taxpayer's dependents. Therefore, a married couple with two dependents could claim $12,400 in exemptions for tax year 2004.

Personal and dependency exemptions: Deductions from adjusted gross income based on the number of people in a household, their ages, and eyesight quality.

It is important to note that someone claimed as a dependent on another's return, such as parents claiming a dependent child, cannot also take the personal exemption. A working college student, for example, might provide most of his or her own support, thereby earning the exemption amount but preventing the parents from taking it. If the parents are in a high tax bracket, this is poor tax strategy.

Personal and dependency exemption deductions are gradually eliminated when taxable income exceeds certain limits. In 2004, the threshold level of income was $214,050 for married couples filing a joint return and $142,700 for single filers.

The Standard Deduction

Standard deduction: Deduction from adjusted gross income based on the taxpayer's filing status.

In addition to personal and dependency exemptions, the law also allows a **standard deduction** for personal expenses. The deductible amount depends upon taxpayer filing status as indicated later. Standard deduction amounts also are inflation indexed. Age and impaired sight allow taxpayers *additional* standard deduction amounts beyond those just described. If you are claimed as a dependent on your parents' tax return, you still receive a small standard deduction of about $800 in 2004.

TOPIC **LINKS**

See IRS Pub. 501 "Exemptions, Standard Deduction, and Filing Information."

If you are:	Standard Deduction Amount 2004
1. Married filing jointly, or a qualifying widow or widower	$9,700
2. Head of a household	7,150
3. Single	4,850
4. Married filing separately	4,850

Simplifying **FINANCIAL Planning**

BOX 4.1

How Do Your Deductions Compare?

Below are average amounts written off by taxpayers who claimed these deductions on 2003 returns filed in 2004. Note: This does not mean that taxpayers with $50,000 to $99,999 in income averaged $5,672 in medical deductions. Most such persons did not qualify for medical write-offs. The figure instead is the average deduction among those who *could* deduct medical expenses.

			Size of Adjusted Gross Income				
			$15,000	$30,000	$50,000	$100,000	
Item	**All Returns**	**Under $15,000[1]**	**Under $30,000**	**Under $50,000**	**Under $100,000**	**Under $200,000**	**$200,000 or More**
Student loan interest deduction:	$671	$468	$622	$699	$746	$546	
Tuition and fees deduction:	$1,792	$1,864	$1,542	$1,462	$1,816	$2,210	
Medical savings account deduction:	$2,009	$1,205	$1,075	$1,451	$2,269	$2,571	$2,768
Medical and dental expenses deduction:	$6,083	$7,400	$5,890	$4,994	$5,672	$10,969	$28,305
Interest paid deduction:	$9,150	$7,043	$6,453	$6,850	$8,364	$11,825	$21,998
Charitable contributions deduction:	$3,372	$1,423	$1,890	$2,006	$2,530	$3,875	$17,354

Source: Preliminary Individual Income Tax Returns, 2003, Internal Revenue Service.

Itemized Deductions

Itemized deductions: Deductions from adjusted gross income based on actual amounts spent by a taxpayer.

If your **itemized deductions** are greater than your standard deduction, you may take these as an offset to adjusted gross income instead of the standard deduction. In general, the IRS does not allow personal expenses as deductions except in those cases where the tax law clearly indicates to the contrary. Most allowable itemized deductions reflect activities regarded as socially desirable (giving to charity, for example) or alleviating undue financial hardship (medical expenses). Some are allowed probably because strong vested interests were influential in having them included in the tax law. Figure 4.6 indicates the more common deductions. While it is important to keep good records to support all items on your tax return, it is particularly so in the case of itemized deductions. A lack of supporting evidence—canceled checks, invoices, or carefully written logs—will often lead to a disallowance of the claimed deduction.

There are limits on the amounts you can deduct for medical expenses, charitable contributions, casualty losses, and miscellaneous expenses. You can take only amounts greater than 7.5 percent of your adjusted gross income for medical expenses, which include hospital and doctor bills and drugs and medicines. Special rules apply if charitable contributions exceed 20 percent of adjusted gross income. Also, for a charitable contribution to qualify, it must be made to an IRS-recognized charity; gifts made to individuals do not count as deductions. You may claim a deduction for a contribution of $250 or more only if you have a receipt from a qualified charitable organization.

As is the case with personal and dependency exemptions, taxpayers lose a portion of itemized deductions when their incomes exceed certain limits. The elimination of these tax preferences at high incomes is scheduled to be gradually phased out after 2005.

Figure 4.6

Frequently Claimed Itemized Deductions

Medical expenses (including payments to medical insurance) in excess of 7.5% of adjusted gross income
State and local income taxes
Property taxes
Personal property taxes
Interest on home mortgage (possible limitations)
Charitable contributions (subject to limitations)
Casualty and theft losses (subject to limitations)
Miscellaneous expenses in excess of 2% of adjusted gross income:
    Union dues
    Professional dues and subscriptions
    Certain educational expenses
    Tax return preparation fee
    Investment counsel fees
    Unreimbursed business expenses

Determining Your Tax Liability Before Tax Credits

Many taxpayers can proceed directly to the tables excerpted in Figure 4.7 (if their taxable income is less than or equal to $100,000) or the tax schedule in Figure 4.8 (if their income is above $100,000) to calculate their income tax before tax credits. For example, a married couple with taxable income of $50,911 would have had a corresponding tax of $6,924 in 2004. If you have qualifying dividends or capital gains, you must use a special worksheet for computing your tax instead of the tax tables.

Figure 4.7

A Portion of the 2004 Tax Table

2004 Tax Table—Continued

If line 42 (taxable income) is—		And you are—			
At least	But less than	Single	Married filing jointly *	Married filing separately	Head of a house-hold
			Your tax is—		
50,000					
50,000	50,050	9,244	6,789	9,244	8,106
50,050	50,100	9,256	6,796	9,256	8,119
50,100	50,150	9,269	6,804	9,269	8,131
50,150	50,200	9,281	6,811	9,281	8,144
50,200	50,250	9,294	6,819	9,294	8,156
50,250	50,300	9,306	6,826	9,306	8,169
50,300	50,350	9,319	6,834	9,319	8,181
50,350	50,400	9,331	6,841	9,331	8,194
50,400	50,450	9,344	6,849	9,344	8,206
50,450	50,500	9,356	6,856	9,356	8,219
50,500	50,550	9,369	6,864	9,369	8,231
50,550	50,600	9,381	6,871	9,381	8,244
50,600	50,650	9,394	6,879	9,394	8,256
50,650	50,700	9,406	6,886	9,406	8,269
50,700	50,750	9,419	6,894	9,419	8,281
50,750	50,800	9,431	6,901	9,431	8,294
50,800	50,850	9,444	6,909	9,444	8,306
50,850	50,900	9,456	6,916	9,456	8,319
50,900	50,950	9,469	6,924	9,469	8,331
50,950	51,000	9,481	6,931	9,481	8,344

Figure 4.8

If Your Taxable Income Is Over	But Not Over	Your Tax Is This	Plus This %	Of the Excess Over
Single				
$0	$7,150	0	10%	0
$7,150	$29,050	$715	15%	$7,150
$29,050	$70,350	$4,000	25%	$29,050
$70,350	$146,750	$14,325	28%	$70,350
$146,750	$319,100	$35,717	33%	$146,750
$319,100	—	$92,592	35%	$319,100
Married filing jointly or widow(er)				
$0	$14,300	0	10%	0
$14,300	$58,100	$1,430	15%	$14,300
$58,100	$117,250	$8,000	25%	$58,100
$117,250	$178,650	$22,787.50	28%	$117,250
$178,650	$319,100	$39,979.50	33%	$178,650
$319,100	—	$86,328	35%	$319,100
Married filing separately				
$0	$7,150	0	10%	0
$7,150	$29,050	$715	15%	$7,150
$29,050	$58,625	$4,000	25%	$29,050
$58,625	$89,325	$11,393.75	28%	$58,625
$89,325	$159,550	$19,989.75	33%	$89,325
$159,550	—	$43,164	35%	$159,550
Head of household				
$0	$10,200	0	10%	0
$10,200	$38,900	$1,020	15%	$10,200
$38,900	$100,500	$5,325	25%	$38,900
$100,500	$162,700	$20,725	28%	$100,500
$162,700	$319,100	$38,141	33%	$162,700
$319,100	—	89,753	35%	$319,100

2004 Tax Rate Schedules

Federal marginal tax rates can be found in column 4 of Figure 4.8. The federal marginal tax rate on taxable income ranges from zero percent when your taxable income is zero to 35 percent at the top bracket. Within the income bracket defined in the first three columns, the marginal tax rate is the percent of each addition dollar of income that you owe in federal taxes. As indicated in Figure 4.8, if you are single tax filer with taxable income of $30,000 you are in the 25 percent marginal tax bracket. You only get to keep 75 cents of each additional. Your overall marginal tax rate, which includes payroll taxes (FICA) and state income taxes, will be higher. Moreover, the phase out of deductions at high incomes will also increase the effective marginal tax rate.

Tax Credits

A **tax credit** is a direct reduction against your tax liability. It provides a dollar-for-dollar offset to your tax liability. Tax credits can be either nonrefundable or refundable. The size of a "nonrefundable" tax credit is limited by the taxes you owe. If a "refundable" tax credit exceeds the taxes you owe, the excess is returned in a check from the government. Many

Tax credit: A dollar-for-dollar offset against the tax liability.

Figure 4.9

Partial List of Tax Credits

Adoption credit
Child and dependent care
  expenses credit
Child tax credit
Earned income credit
Education credit
Elderly or disabled credit
Foreign tax credit

low-income families with one adult over age 24 qualify for the Earned Income Tax Credit (EITC). Because it is a refundable tax credit, low income earners who owe little or no tax on their income can receive a refund check. Most of the other popular tax credits, such as the child care credit and the educational expense credits are nonrefundable. A partial list of tax credits is in Figure 4.9.

Your tax liability for the year is determined by subtracting the total of your credits from the taxes you calculated using the tax table or one of the schedules. This tax liability is an important figure—one you should be very much aware of as you make financial decisions. An even more important figure to know is the marginal tax rate on your last income dollar.

Do You Get a Refund or Owe More Taxes?

The amount you receive or pay depends on how much tax has been withheld from your wages or, if you earned income not subject to withholding, how much you have paid in estimated taxes. (By the way, if you expect to earn such income, you are required to file an estimated tax. Failure to do so can lead to both penalties and interest.) If withholding was greater than your tax liability, you are entitled to a refund; if the reverse is true, you must pay additional tax. Every employer is required to provide employees an annual report of their wages and all the taxes (and possibly other items) withheld from their wages. This report is called a **W-2 form,** and you should review yours each year to make sure it is correct. You need to attach copies to your federal and state income tax returns.

W-2 form: A form prepared by an employer showing an employee's earnings and withholdings.

W-4 form: A form signed by an employee to claim exemption allowances for payroll withholding purposes.

The IRS will charge you penalties if you withhold sustantially less than you should during the tax year. On the other hand, the IRS does not pay interest on excess withholding. Despite this fact, many taxpayers claim fewer exemptions than they need to on withholding forms filed with their employers (called a **W-4 form**). They do this because it is a form of forced savings or because they enjoy getting a big refund. Actually, this is very poor financial management. You can do better if you invest the money in a way that offers you a return.

Determining the Steeles' 2004 Income Tax

In 2005, Arnold and Sharon Steele had the following items to consider in preparing their 2004 income tax return. Arnold earned $55,380 at InChemCo and had $3,600 of federal income tax withheld from his salary. Sharon earned $13,800 at Todd and Talbot and had $233 of such taxes withheld. They received $861 in interest on savings accounts and $812 in dividends on stocks they owned. During the year they sold some stocks Sharon received from her parents as a gift. There was a long-term $2,935 taxable gain on the sale. The

Steeles itemized their deductions and arrived at an allowable total of $16,477. They also paid $1,600 in child-care expenses. With the preceding information, the Steeles are ready to prepare their return. They used Form 1040 (the so-called long form), which is shown in Figure 4.10.

TOPIC **LINKS**

Get IRS Forms and Publications.

Filing Status and Exemptions

The Steeles are filing a joint return, and they are claiming four exemptions. They could have filed under option 3—married filing separate returns—but they found their tax liability would have been greater. This isn't always the case, so you should check your liability each way to determine the appropriate option.

Total Income

The Steeles' total income was $69,180.

Adjustments to Income

None.

Tax Computation

The Steeles' adjusted gross income is reduced first by their net itemized deductions of $16,477. Then this subtotal of $53,311 is further reduced by the $12,400 of exemptions (four exemptions claimed times $3,100 per exemption) to arrive at their taxable income of $44,911. Their Line 43 tax liability before tax credits is $5,648. Because they had qualifying dividends and capital gains, they had to determine the Line 43 tax using a special tax worksheet.

Credits and Refund

The Steeles had two credits in 2004. The first was for a dependent care tax credit and the second was for a child tax credit. The credit for child and dependent care expenses is related to your total qualifying expenses and level of adjusted gross income. The maximum is $3,000 if you have one qualifying dependent, and $6,000 if you have two or more. The Steeles' credit was 20 percent of the $1,600 of qualifying expenses, or $320.

The Steeles were also eligible for a $1,000 child tax credit for each child. The child tax credit is phased out for upper-income couples and individuals. Given the Steeles' income for 2004, they were entitled to the entire child tax credit for each child.

At this point, Arnold and Sharon reflect on their tax situation. Their tax liability is $3,328 out of their pretax total income of $73,788. Therefore, they paid 4.5 percent ($3,328/$73,788) of their total income in 2004 in federal income taxes. This is their **average tax rate,** but a far more useful figure is their **marginal tax rate.** This rate is more or less buried in the tax table. Arnold and Sharon found it by using the tax rate schedules in Figure 4.8 to calculate their tax. This schedule clearly highlights their marginal rate, which is 15 percent. The marginal rate, as you should see, is the rate being applied to the bracket in which taxable income falls. If the Steeles' taxable income rose enough to put them into the next higher bracket, their marginal rate would jump to 25 percent. The marginal rates are the ones to consider in making financial decisions concerning future sources of income or deductions, because additional income will be taxed, or additional deductions will save taxes, at the marginal rate. For example, suppose Sharon has considered working additional hours at Todd and Talbot, and she could earn $1,000 more by doing so. Should she work the additional hours? If she does, the Steeles' taxable income will increase by $1,000. Assuming that everything else remains the same, they will pay $150 more in federal taxes, and their after-tax income will increase by only $850. They must decide if the additional $850 is worth the extra time and effort on Sharon's part. Of course, this does not

Average tax rate: Total tax liability divided by total income.

Marginal tax rate: Additional tax liability divided by additional income.

Form 1040   Department of the Treasury—Internal Revenue Service

U.S. Individual Income Tax Return 2004   (99)   IRS Use Only—Do not write or staple in this space.

For the year Jan. 1–Dec. 31, 2004, or other tax year beginning _____, 2004, ending _____, 20 ___   OMB No. 1545-0074

Label

(See instructions on page 16.)

Use the IRS label. Otherwise, please print or type.

Your first name and initial **Arnold S.**	Last name **Steele**
If a joint return, spouse's first name and initial **Sharon P.**	Last name **Steele**

Your social security number **000 00 0000**

Spouse's social security number **000 00 0000**

Home address (number and street). If you have a P.O. box, see page 16.   **496 Mulberry Lane**   Apt. no. ___

City, town or post office, state, and ZIP code. If you have a foreign address, see page 16.   **Middlebury, Missouri 64131**

Important! You **must** enter your SSN(s) above.

Presidential Election Campaign
(See page 16.)

Note. Checking "Yes" will not change your tax or reduce your refund.
Do you, or your spouse if filing a joint return, want $3 to go to this fund?   You ☑Yes ☐No   Spouse ☐Yes ☑No

Filing Status

Check only one box.

1. ☐ Single
2. ☑ Married filing jointly (even if only one had income)
3. ☐ Married filing separately. Enter spouse's SSN above and full name here. _____
4. ☐ Head of household (with qualifying person). (See page 17.) If the qualifying person is a child but not your dependent, enter this child's name here. _____
5. ☐ Qualifying widow(er) with dependent child (see page 17)

Exemptions

6a ☑ **Yourself.** If someone can claim you as a dependent, **do not** check box 6a
b ☑ **Spouse**
c **Dependents:**

If more than four dependents, see page 18.

(1) First name Last name	(2) Dependent's social security number	(3) Dependent's relationship to you	(4)☑ if qualifying child for child tax credit (see page 18)
Nancy T. Steele	000 00 0000	Daughter	☑
John L. Steele	000 00 0000	Son	☑
			☐
			☐

d Total number of exemptions claimed

Boxes checked on 6a and 6b   **2**
No. of children on 6c who:
lived with you   **2**
did not live with you due to divorce or separation (see page 18)
Dependents on 6c not entered above
Add numbers on lines above   **4**

Income

Attach Form(s) W-2 here. Also attach Forms W-2G and 1099-R if tax was withheld.

If you did not get a W-2, see page 19.

Enclose, but do not attach, any payment. Also, please use Form 1040-V.

7	Wages, salaries, tips, etc. Attach Form(s) W-2	**7** 69,180 00
8a	**Taxable** interest. Attach Schedule B if required	**8a** 861 00
b	Tax-exempt interest. **Do not** include on line 8a **8b**	
9a	Ordinary dividends. Attach Schedule B if required	**9a** 812 00
b	Qualified dividends (see page 20) **9b** 812 00	
10	Taxable refunds, credits, or offsets of state and local income taxes (see page 20)	**10**
11	Alimony received	**11**
12	Business income or (loss). Attach Schedule C or C-EZ	**12**
13	Capital gain or (loss). Attach Schedule D if required. If not required, check here ☐	**13** 2,935 00
14	Other gains or (losses). Attach Form 4797	**14**
15a	IRA distributions **15a** b Taxable amount (see page 22)	**15b**
16a	Pensions and annuities **16a** b Taxable amount (see page 22)	**16b**
17	Rental real estate, royalties, partnerships, S corporations, trusts, etc. Attach Schedule E	**17**
18	Farm income or (loss). Attach Schedule F	**18**
19	Unemployment compensation	**19**
20a	Social security benefits **20a** b Taxable amount (see page 24)	**20b**
21	Other income. List type and amount (see page 24) _____	**21**
22	Add the amounts in the far right column for lines 7 through 21. This is your **total income**	**22** 73,788 00

Adjusted Gross Income

23	Educator expenses (see page 26) **23**	
24	Certain business expenses of reservists, performing artists, and fee-basis government officials. Attach Form 2106 or 2106-EZ **24**	
25	IRA deduction (see page 26) **25**	
26	Student loan interest deduction (see page 28) **26**	
27	Tuition and fees deduction (see page 29) **27**	
28	Health savings account deduction. Attach Form 8889 **28**	
29	Moving expenses. Attach Form 3903 **29**	
30	One-half of self-employment tax. Attach Schedule SE **30**	
31	Self-employed health insurance deduction (see page 30) **31**	
32	Self-employed SEP, SIMPLE, and qualified plans **32**	
33	Penalty on early withdrawal of savings **33**	
34a	Alimony paid b Recipient's SSN _____ **34a**	
35	Add lines 23 through 34a	**35**
36	Subtract line 35 from line 22. This is your **adjusted gross income**	**36** 73,788 00

For Disclosure, Privacy Act, and Paperwork Reduction Act Notice, see page 75.   Cat. No. 11320B   Form **1040** (2004)

Continued

Figure 4.10

1040 U.S. Individual Income Tax Return

Tax and Credits

37	Amount from line 36 (adjusted gross income)	37	73,788 00

38a Check if: ☐ **You** were born before January 2, 1940,   ☐ Blind.   **Total boxes**
☐ **Spouse** was born before January 2, 1940,   ☐ Blind.   checked   38a ☐

Standard Deduction foró

b If your spouse itemizes on a separate return or you were a dual-status alien, see page 31 and check here   38b ☐

People who checked any box on line 38a or 38b **or** who can be claimed as a dependent, see page 31.

39	**Itemized deductions** (from Schedule A) **or** your **standard deduction** (see left margin) .	39	16,477 00
40	Subtract line 39 from line 37	40	57,311 00
41	If line 37 is $107,025 or less, multiply $3,100 by the total number of exemptions claimed on line 6d. If line 37 is over $107,025, see the worksheet on page 33	41	12,400 00
42	**Taxable income.** Subtract line 41 from line 40. If line 41 is more than line 40, enter -0- .	42	44,911 00
43	**Tax** (see page 33). Check if any tax is from: **a** ☐ Form(s) 8814 **b** ☐ Form 4972 . .	43	5,648 00
44	**Alternative minimum tax** (see page 35). Attach Form 6251	44	
45	Add lines 43 and 44	45	5,648 00

All others:

Single or Married filing separately, $4,850

Married filing jointly or Qualifying widow(er), $9,700

Head of household, $7,150

46	Foreign tax credit. Attach Form 1116 if required . . .	46	
47	Credit for child and dependent care expenses. Attach Form 2441	47	320 00
48	Credit for the elderly or the disabled. Attach Schedule R .	48	
49	Education credits. Attach Form 8863	49	
50	Retirement savings contributions credit. Attach Form 8880 .	50	
51	Child tax credit (see page 37)	51	2,000 00
52	Adoption credit. Attach Form 8839	52	
53	Credits from: **a** ☐ Form 8396 **b** ☐ Form 8859 . .	53	
54	Other credits. Check applicable box(es): **a** ☐ Form 3800 **b** ☐ Form 8801 **c** ☐ Specify name:	54	

55	Add lines 46 through 54. These are your **total credits**	55	2,320 00
56	Subtract line 55 from line 45. If line 55 is more than line 45, enter -0-	56	3,328 00

Other Taxes

57	Self-employment tax. Attach Schedule SE	57	
58	Social security and Medicare tax on tip income not reported to employer. Attach Form 4137	58	
59	Additional tax on IRAs, other qualified retirement plans, etc. Attach Form 5329 if required .	59	
60	Advance earned income credit payments from Form(s) W-2	60	
61	Household employment taxes. Attach Schedule H	61	
62	Add lines 56 through 61. This is your **total tax**	62	3,328 00

Payments

If you have a qualifying child, attach Schedule EIC.

63	Federal income tax withheld from Forms W-2 and 1099 .	63	4,983 00
64	2004 estimated tax payments and amount applied from 2003 return	64	
65a	**Earned income credit (EIC)**	65a	
b	Nontaxable combat pay election 65b		
66	Excess social security and tier 1 RRTA tax withheld (see page 54)	66	
67	Additional child tax credit. Attach Form 8812 . . .	67	
68	Amount paid with request for extension to file (see page 54)	68	
69	Other payments from: **a** ☐ Form 2439 **b** ☐ Form 4136 **c** ☐ Form 8885 .	69	
70	Add lines 63, 64, 65a, and 66 through 69. These are your **total payments**	70	4,983 00

Refund

Direct deposit? See page 54 and fill in 72b, 72c, and 72d.

71	If line 70 is more than line 62, subtract line 62 from line 70. This is the amount you **overpaid**	71	1,655 00
72a	Amount of line 71 you want **refunded to you**	72a	1,655 00

b Routing number ☐☐☐☐☐☐☐☐☐   **c** Type: ☐ Checking ☐ Savings

d Account number ☐☐☐☐☐☐☐☐☐☐☐☐☐☐☐☐☐

73 Amount of line 71 you want **applied to your 2005 estimated tax**   73

Amount You Owe

74	**Amount you owe.** Subtract line 70 from line 62. For details on how to pay, see page 55	74	
75	Estimated tax penalty (see page 55) 75		

Third Party Designee

Do you want to allow another person to discuss this return with the IRS (see page 56)? ☐ **Yes.** Complete the following. ☐ **No**

Designee's name   Phone no. ( )   Personal identification number (PIN) ☐☐☐☐☐

Sign Here

Joint return? See page 17.

Keep a copy for your records.

Under penalties of perjury, I declare that I have examined this return and accompanying schedules and statements, and to the best of my knowledge and belief, they are true, correct, and complete. Declaration of preparer (other than taxpayer) is based on all information of which preparer has any knowledge.

Your signature *Arnold Steele*	Date 4/15/05	Your occupation **Engineer**	Daytime phone number (000) 000-0000
Spouse's signature. If a joint return, **both** must sign. *Sharon Steele*	Date 4/15/05	Spouse's occupation **Accountant**	

Paid Preparerís Use Only

Preparer's signature	Date	Check if self-employed ☐	Preparer's SSN or PTIN
Firm's name (or yours if self-employed), address, and ZIP code		EIN	
		Phone no. ( )	

Form **1040** (2004)

Figure 4.10

take into account payroll taxes or state and local income taxes that would further increase the effective marginal tax rate.

Finally, since the Steeles had $4,983 of taxes withheld from their wages, they overpaid their 2004 tax liability by $1,655. They could have applied this overpayment to a 2005 estimated tax but chose a refund instead.

OTHER ASPECTS OF THE FEDERAL INCOME TAX

In addition to understanding how the federal income tax formula is used to determine your tax liability, it is important to be familiar with other aspects of the tax. In the following sections we will explain capital gains and losses and the role of the Internal Revenue Service (IRS). Finally, we discuss the issue of seeking outside help in preparing your return.

Capital Gains and Losses

As your income and wealth increase, you can expect to have a growing number of transactions involving the sale or exchange of capital assets. Almost always, an exchange results in either a gain or a loss that may have to be reported in filing your annual return.

What Is a Capital Gain or Loss?

Capital gain or loss: Gain or loss resulting from the sale of a capital asset.

A **capital gain or loss** results whenever you sell a capital asset for more or less than what you paid for it (or your "adjusted basis" in the asset when special tax rules apply). The next logical question is: What are **capital assets?** For the most part, everything you own and use for personal purposes, pleasure, or investment is a capital asset. Examples are stocks, bonds, and other securities; your house, car, and household goods; or your hobbies, such as stamp and coin collections, and fishing gear.

Capital assets: Assets held for personal pleasure or investment.

Tax Treatment of Capital Gains and Losses

On certain assets the tax on capital gains is reduced below the tax on ordinary income. Whether the gain or loss qualifies for a lower tax rate depends on the holding period. Changes in the value of assets held for one year or less are termed *short-term* capital gains or losses. These are evaluated at ordinary income tax rates. The appreciation or depreciation in the market value of assets held for a longer period qualifies as a *long-term* capital gain or loss. For most financial assets, such as stocks and bonds, the maximum tax rate on long-term capital gains is either 5 percent if you are in the 15 percent marginal tax bracket or 15 percent if you are in a higher tax bracket. This does not apply to collectibles (items such as stamps, coins, and rare wines) or depreciated real estate, which have higher maximum rates.

Any gain on the sale of property held for personal use—your car, for example—must be reported and is taxed in full. Losses on the sale of such assets, however, cannot be deducted against other income. Of course, you seldom sell personal property at a gain, but it is possible.

Investment assets are treated similarly to personal-use assets but with one distinction: You can deduct up to $3,000 of any losses. If losses in a year exceed $3,000, the unused portion can be carried forward to future years and taken as deductions. However, the maximum allowable deduction in any year is $3,000. This includes carry-forward amounts and current-year losses. There are special tax loss regulations for deductions by individuals who actively manage a business. These are explained in the IRS Publication 925, "Passive Activity and At-Risk Rules."

TOPIC **LINKS**

See IRS Pub. 925 "Passive Activity and At-Risk Rules."

Selling Your Home

Your home is a personal property, so it is also subject to capital gain taxation. However, special provisions have been written into the law to soften the tax's impact. Under most circumstances you can exclude a $250,000 ($500,000 for married couples) gain on the sale of your main home. To qualify you must have owned the home for at least the past two years and have used it as your main home for two years. In addition, you must not have excluded the gain from the sale of another home within the past two years. If you lived in the home for less than two years, you may qualify for a partial exclusion. You cannot deduct a loss from the sale of your main home.

TOPIC **LINKS**

See IRS Pub. 523 "Selling Your Home."

It is obvious that a home is a tax-advantaged investment. This feature, coupled with the fact that home prices have generally increased over the years, has made home ownership a very solid investment. This aspect is explained more fully in Chapter 8.

Alternative Minimum Tax

The stated purpose of the **alternative minimum tax (AMT)** is to ensure that the rich pay at least something. In effect, the AMT computation eliminates many deductions and credits and creates a tax liability for those who would otherwise pay less in taxes. Those above the income limit must pay at least the AMT. Because the income limits have been stated in dollar terms that are not adjusted for inflation ($58,000 for a married couple and $40,250 for a single filer in 2004), an increasing number of individuals who are not rich now have to undertake an additional calculation of their federal taxes. The procedures for calculating the AMT are difficult and time consuming. This one calculation may make tax preparation software worth the cost.

Alternative Minimum Tax (AMT): Alternative tax calculation to ensure upper income families pay a minimum tax.

The Role of the Internal Revenue Service

The **Internal Revenue Service (IRS),** a division of the Treasury Department, is the federal agency assigned the task of administering the federal income tax. Two of its most important functions are providing taxpayer assistance and auditing tax returns. In addition to understanding these functions, you should be aware of the filing deadline and extensions and the statute of limitations as it applies to the federal income tax.

Taxpayer Assistance

The IRS attempts to make filing your return as easy as possible. (Don't blame the IRS if the return itself is difficult to complete; blame Congress, because the tax law is its responsibility.) If you have filed a return in the past, you are automatically sent a tax form for the current year. If you have never filed a return or if you need to file one different from the previous year, you can find forms at practically every public library and many banks or savings and loans. Forms and instructions are also available from the IRS home page on the Internet (www.irs.gov). In addition to Form 1040 (illustrated with the Steeles' example), there are two simpler forms—1040A and 1040EZ—that many taxpayers can use.

It is often helpful to read IRS publications to handle a tax item properly. The instruction booklet that accompanies your tax return contains a list of IRS publications and forms and shows where to write in your state to get them. We strongly recommend Publication 17, "Your Federal Income Tax," as a handy and reliable general reference on many tax matters. If you file Form 1040EZ or Form 1040A, the IRS will figure the tax for you, if you wish. You must provide all the relevant information, however. The IRS will also figure your tax on Form 1040 if you meet certain tests.

TOPIC **LINKS**

See IRS Pub. 17, "Your Federal Income Tax."

TOPIC **LINKS**

See IRS Pub. 967, "The IRS Will Figure Your Tax."

IRS Audits

The strength of our tax system rests on the integrity of millions of taxpayers to file an honest and reasonably correct return. An important function—the IRS audit—is to ensure that such filing takes place. The IRS has three basic audit approaches: the field audit—where an IRS agent visits your premises to examine your return; the office audit—where you visit an IRS center; and the self-audit—where the IRS essentially questions some aspect of your return and asks you to examine the item again to determine its appropriateness.

An audit may involve questioning just one item on your return, or the whole return might be audited, which means you must have documentary support for each line item. Returns selected for audit are determined by a formula (known only to the IRS) and random procedures. Generally, as indicated in Figure 4.11 your chance of audit increases significantly with income and self-employment. The high rate at the lower incomes was a result of special audits of the Earned Income Tax Credit.

It is illegal to file a fraudulent return or not to file a return at all, and stiff penalties can be assessed in each case. A mistake or an alternative interpretation of the law may not lead to a penalty, but you will pay interest on any deficiency. The interest rate changes periodically, depending on market rates of interest. For assessments of additional taxes, the interest period begins on the due date of the return—not from the time the deficiency is found.

Filing Deadline and Extensions

Your tax return must be filed before April 16. If you can't meet that deadline, you can get an **automatic extension** for four months. However, before April 16 you must file Form 4868 asking for the extension. Remember, though, an automatic filing extension does not extend the time you have to pay your tax. You must estimate your tax for the year and pay

Figure 4.11

IRS Examination Coverage: Fiscal Year 2003

Source: 2003 IRS Annual Data Book.

Individual Income Tax Returns	Percent Audited
Form 1040A with income under $25,000	0.51
All other returns by income	
Under $25,000	1.09
$25,000 under $50,000	0.30
$50,000 under $100,000	0.41
$100,000 or more	0.98
Self-Employed Schedule C Returns	
Under $25,000	3.00
$25,000 under $100,000	1.33
$100,000 or more	1.47

any tax due along with Form 4868. There is a penalty for late payment unless you have reasonable cause for not paying your tax when due. You can request extensions beyond the automatic four-month extension, but you must meet certain tests before the IRS will grant them.

Electronic Filing

As an alternative to mailing in your tax return, you can have it electronically filed. If you would otherwise file Form 1040EZ, you can do this yourself by using a touch tone telephone and the IRS's Telefile system. The IRS mails informational packages to those who may be eligible. To use the system, you dial an IRS toll-free number and punch in responses to a computer-automated series of questions. The program immediately tells you if you owe taxes, how much you owe, or how much you overpaid. The personal ID contained in the informational package serves as your signature. You can have your refund directly deposited in your bank account or you can pay the taxes you owe by either debit or credit card.

If you need anything more complicated than a 1040EZ, you will have to use the IRS e-file program. In at least 37 states you can simultaneously electronically file both your federal and state returns. You can do this through your personal computer or through a professional preparer. To do it yourself, you need a computer, an Internet connection, and tax preparation software that offers the IRS e-file option. The two major software packages, Intuit's Turbo Tax and Kiplinger's TaxCut, allow you to file one free electronic return. There are also a number of sites on the Internet that let you prepare your tax forms and calculate many of the entries online.

For a fee, taxes due can be paid with a credit card. If you are owed a refund, you typically receive your return within two to three weeks, instead of the usual five to six weeks for a mailed return. If you can't wait that long, a number of preparers will make you a **refund anticipation loan** of $300 to $3,000. In this case, you receive a direct deposit following the acknowledgment by the IRS that you have filed a valid return. Naturally, you should determine if the fees associated with electronic filing and a refund anticipation loan are worth the benefit. Unless you need the refund desperately, determine the equivalent annual interest on the latter item. For most individuals, this will be an unreasonably high rate. Consequently, it has not proven popular among middle- and upper-income tax filers.

The Statute of Limitations

The **statute of limitations,** as it generally applies to the federal income tax law, gives the IRS three years from the time a return is filed to impose additional tax liabilities. This fact suggests that tax records should be kept at least this long. But a special six-year limitation

TOPIC **LINKS**
Explore the IRS e-file options.

TOPIC **LINKS**
Get a list of companies and software accommodating electronic returns.

TOPIC **LINKS**
Go to online tax preparation sites.

TOPIC **LINKS**
Download federal fill-in forms.

Refund anticipation loan: A loan provided by a tax preparation service based on a taxpayer's refund.

Statute of limitations: A period of three years given the IRS to impose additional taxes on a filed return.

applies if you omit a gross income item that is greater than 25 percent of reported total gross income. Moreover, the statute of limitations does not apply if a return is never filed or if a fraudulent return is filed.

Also, be forewarned that if you overpaid taxes in a given year, you must file a claim for a refund within three years from the date the return was filed or two years from the date the tax was paid, whichever is later. Failure to file within these periods usually leads to loss of the refund.

Getting Outside Help

Preparing returns has become a very big business, and you are probably familiar with H & R Block, the largest tax preparation service in the United States. Should you use an outside firm? The answer to that question depends on several factors. If you have a rather complex tax question that cannot be answered by referring to Publication 17 or a tax reference manual at the public library, and if the item is large enough to matter, then an expert's opinion is needed. Second, you may not care to spend the time doing your return. There are two broad types of preparers: the tax service companies such as H & R Block and professionals such as CPAs and attorneys.

Tax Service Companies

Many tax service companies open their offices in January and close them in May. Others remain open all year in some of their locations. Fees for their services vary, but a Form 1040 with several supporting schedules will usually cost between $50 and $100. The short forms cost less, but there are additional charges for state and local income tax returns. While most of these companies do a good job in filing your return, you should know that most of their work consists of simply entering the data you give them in appropriate places on the return. While they claim their staff is instructed to ask the right questions to save you taxes, you shouldn't count on it.

After you finish this chapter, if you get Publication 17 and also keep reasonably alert to newspaper and magazine articles on how to reduce your taxes, you will have a good chance of doing a better job on your return than many of these preparers will. Actually, you're more likely to save taxes by planning throughout the year rather than finding clever loopholes at year's end.

CPAs and Attorneys

CPAs and attorneys with specialized training in federal income taxation are the tax experts. If you are fortunate to have a high income, or if you are involved in activities with many income tax implications (running a business, for example), you probably need a professional. As just mentioned, you may want his or her services to guide you throughout the year. You most likely want assistance not only in preparing the return but also in setting up trusts or gifts or advising you about the income tax implications of various investments, including self-employed retirement plans (if they are applicable). Fees for these services are very high: Count on $100 to $200 an hour or an annual retainer of $1,000 as a minimum.

Financial Planners

Many financial planners do not specialize in income tax advice, although they may have contact with people who do. Also, a number of business firms are now engaging financial planners to advise their employees on financial planning. Their services are offered as a fringe benefit to employees. You might ask if this service is available at your company and, of course, take advantage of it if it is. The financial planner may not do tax returns, but he or she should be able to help with tax planning.

Tax Publications and Software

If you decide to prepare your own tax return, consider buying books that offer tax advice. The oldest, and still one of the best, is J. K. Lasser's *Your Income Tax*. However, there are several other excellent guides at modest prices.

Using computer software to prepare your return can save you considerable time. A good program will lead you through the return by providing information on likely deductions and signaling probable omissions. Intuit's TurboTax and Kiplinger's TaxCut are the two major competitors in this market. Both are excellent programs and each allows you to electronically file one return for free. When selecting software, be sure to check out the following features:

- The ability to complete both federal and state tax returns. (Most software packages charge an extra price for a state module.)
- The capability of importing data from your existing word processing or spreadsheet programs into the tax software. Some tax packages accept data directly from the popular budget management programs.
- Telephone support providing information on both software and tax questions.
- The cost of an annual upgrade.

The tax law has become increasingly complicated over the last decade. It is no surprise that more people than ever before are using tax preparation software to ease that burden. It represents a nice solution for middle-income individuals who have to fill out more than the 1040EZ but who do not have a special tax situation that requires expert advice.

Special Considerations for Students

TOPIC **LINKS**

See these IRS publications on educational expenses.

Congress has enacted several tax incentives to encourage expenditures on education. Further information can be found in specialized IRS publications for students. These are explained in IRS Pub. 508, "Tax Benefits for Higher Education."

If you are under age 24 and a full-time student, you may be claimed as a dependent on your parents' return. This is typically advantageous, because they are likely to be in a higher marginal tax bracket. Being listed as a dependent on your parents' tax form does not necessarily relieve you of the responsibility of also filing a return. In general, you must file a federal income tax return if you had earned income of more than $4,750 (2004) or if you had unearned income of more than $750. However, you should file if you are due a refund on taxes withheld from your paycheck.

Scholarships, Grants, and Fellowships

Scholarships, grants, and fellowships may or may not be included in taxable income. If you are in a degree program and those awards cover purely educational expenses such as tuition, fees, books, supplies, and equipment, then they are most likely tax exempt. However, awards for noneducational living expenses such as room and board are taxable. One exception is an ROTC subsistence allowance paid to students participating in advanced training.

Employment-Related Advantages

A qualified tuition reduction for either graduate or undergraduate studies is tax free. This is a reduction in tuition provided to an employee, or the wife and child of an employee, by the educational institution.

Work related educational expenses that meet certain restrictive requirements are deductible. The education must be required by your employer or serve to maintain or improve your skills in your present work. It doesn't qualify if it is needed to meet minimum educational requirements for your present job or if its purpose is to prepare you for a new trade or business. This deduction reduces your taxable income only if you itemize and your total job-related deductions exceed 2 percent of your adjusted gross income.

Some employers pay for part-time schooling under a qualified educational assistance plan. Either a portion or all of these payments up to $5,250 may be tax exempt. Your employer can tell you if the plan is qualified. If you do receive tax-exempt payments, you cannot receive both a reimbursement and a tax deduction for the identical expense.

Tax Credits

The Hope Scholarship Credit and the Lifetime Learning Credit are available for qualified educational expenses. For each eligible student you may only claim one of the tax credits. The Hope is available for the first two years of postsecondary education. For additional years of schooling, you may be entitled to a Lifetime Learning Credit. Both credits are eliminated for higher-income households.

To qualify for the Hope Scholarship Credit you must be enrolled at least half time in one of the first two years of higher education. In addition, you must be enrolled in a program leading to a degree, certificate, or other recognized educational credential. In the years in which you are not entitled to Hope Credit, you may still receive a Lifetime Learning Credit. If you are claiming a Hope Scholarship Credit for a particular student, none of that student's expenses for that year may be applied toward the Lifetime Learning Credit.

Tuition and Fees Deduction

If you do not use either of the tax credits listed previously, you may be eligible to deduct some of your or your dependent's educational expenses. Subject to income limits, $4,000 of annual expenses are deductible in 2004 as an adjustment to gross income. This deduction can be claimed regardless of whether you itemize.

Coverdell Education Savings Account

Subject to income restrictions on contributors, you can contribute up to $2,000 each year in a Coverdell Education Savings Account meant to fund the qualified educational expenses of a designated beneficiary. These funds can be used for qualified primary, secondary or college expenses. Deposits in a Coverdell account are not tax deductible but they grow tax free until distributed. Withdrawals are taxable if they are used for non-qualified expenses.

Qualified Tuition Programs

Several state-run programs let you either prepay college expenses or contribute to an account to pay for a future education. The contributions to a qualified state tuition program are not tax deductible, but there is no tax on distributions for qualified educational expenses. Unlike an Education Savings Account, there are no income restrictions on contributors and there is no limit on contributions so long as they do not exceed the amount of potential educational expenses.

Early Distributions from IRAs

A tax penalty is generally levied on distributions from an IRA before age 59 1/2. However, funds withdrawn to pay for qualified educational expenses are exempt from the penalty. Withdrawals from a traditional IRA will be taxed at ordinary income rates in the year they are disbursed.

Student Loan Interest

Generally, personal interest you pay on a loan, other than mortgage interest, is not tax deductible. There is an exception for interest you pay on a qualified student loan used for qualified educational expenses by yourself or a dependent. The student loan interest deduction is taken as an adjustment to income. Therefore, you get the tax benefit even if you do not itemize your deductions. The amount you can deduct is limited and is phased out at higher incomes.

Education Savings Bonds You can exclude from your gross income interest on qualified U.S. savings bonds, if you have qualified higher educational expenses during the redemption year. The savings bond must be a Series EE U.S. savings bond issued after 1989. The bond must be issued in your name and you must be at least 24 years old before the bond's issue date. This exemption is subject to limits on your income.

PLANNING TO REDUCE YOUR INCOME TAXES

Effective tax planning is an ongoing process. Among other things, it requires selecting investments carefully, holding them for a sufficient length of time, and then selling them at the most opportune time for tax purposes. It also means that you must use provisions of the income tax law that are specifically designed to lower your tax liability. Tax planning attempts to either avoid taxes altogether or defer them to a later time. It works within the tax law, not outside of it as is the case with tax evasion. Following are some of the more common and useful tax-planning techniques.

Invest Where You Receive Tax-Advantaged Income

The tax law favors some forms of income over others. You can reduce your taxes by investing first in those favored investments, which are discussed here.

Buy Municipal Bonds

All interest on **municipal bonds** is tax exempt. These bonds are explained in more detail in Chapter 11, but you should see at this point that the after-tax yield on a municipal bond is the same as its pretax yield.

Municipal bonds: Bonds paying interest that are exempt from federal income tax.

Buy a Home

We have already explained the income tax treatment of your personal residence. In effect, you can enjoy a $250,000 tax-free, long-term capital gain each time you replace your principal residence. It's hard to beat that anywhere. Also, most mortgage interest is deductible as an itemized expense.

Actively Invest in Real Estate

Despite the disadvantage of limited deductibility of business losses, actively managing your own business, such as real estate, offers certain tax advantages for most taxpayers. The appeal of real estate rests in the fact that a large portion of many losses is represented by a noncash charge called depreciation. This means that even though the property shows a loss for tax purposes, you might still have a decent cash return.

Plan for Retirement

Many types of tax-advantaged retirement accounts, discussed in this and later chapters, defer taxes on contributions and earnings until they are withdrawn after age 59 1/2. If your marginal tax rate is lower in your retirement years than it is now, the difference will result in a net savings.

Take Capital Losses Quickly

If you have a capital loss, it is usually to your advantage to take it before a tax year ends. Even if you believe the security's price might rebound and eliminate the loss, you should consider selling the security you own and replacing it with a similar security. For example, suppose you buy Exxon common stock, and after your purchase, its price falls to half of what it was. You believe the international oil companies will do well in the future, but the year is about to end. Consider selling Exxon and buying Mobil, another international oil. You will then be able to deduct all the loss in Exxon (up to $3,000), and the tax savings will enable you to buy that many additional shares of Mobil. Why not just sell Exxon and buy it right back? You can't; that's called a *wash sale*. You must wait at least 30 days, which also may not be a bad idea if you think Exxon is a far better stock than Mobil over the long run. This strategy works well for stocks, but it works even better with bonds since their characteristics are more similar from one bond to another.

The general rule of thumb is that you take your losses quickly and let your gains run. Remember, deductible short-term losses provide tax savings at ordinary income tax rates, whereas long-term gains are taxed at lower statutory limits.

Split Your Income

Dividing income among family members so that it is taxed at a collectively lower marginal rate is a favorite tax-avoidance technique. If you are in a 28 percent tax bracket and your child is in a 15 percent tax bracket, then the family will save 13 cents on each dollar of income earned by the child rather than the parent. This approach is used often when people wish to establish educational funds for their children. It can also be used to create retirement income for aging parents, who may also have high medical expenses. The two most frequently used techniques are making outright gifts and setting up trusts.

Gifts

Custodial account: An account set up by parents in their children's names.

A husband and wife can give someone as much as $22,000 a year without incurring any gift tax; and since it is a gift, it is not income to the recipient. Regardless of the amount given, any future earnings on the invested funds become income of the recipient. Suppose you are interested in providing funds for your child's future support. It's a simple matter to set up a **custodial account** (at a bank or other financial institution) and make a gift each year, the amount depending on how much you wish to accumulate. For minors under 14 years of age, the first $800 of income from gifted assets (or any assets) is tax free by virtue of a modified standard deduction. The tax consequences for unearned income above that amount are complicated (see IRS Publication 929, "Tax Rules for Children and Dependents").

Keep in mind that once you make gifts to your children, they become the children's property. In effect, you lose control of the money and cannot legally get it back. Finally, anyone who sells securities that have appreciated in value to finance their children's college costs is simply throwing money down the drain. At the very least, they should give the securities to the children, who can then sell them.

Trusts

A trust is a legal arrangement that allows assets to be managed by a trustee for the benefit of individuals called beneficiaries. Trusts are more expensive to establish than a gifting program, but they can be structured in many ways, making it wise to seek legal advice in establishing one. Trusts are often used to provide income for someone who is aged or infirm and in need of medical or other care. Funds provided the beneficiary are derived from income earned on trust assets, which is taxed at a lower rate than the one applying to the trust creator.

Stagger Income and Expenses

If you can control the timing of expenses and income, you may be able to reduce taxes. For example, you may have a very large doctor or hospital bill that can be paid in either 2005 or 2006. But you might find that even by paying the bill in 2005, you don't have enough other itemized expenses to exceed the standard deduction. If you pay the bill in 2005 anyway, you may lose benefit of the deduction in 2006. By delaying payment you hold the expense until 2006, when you may be able to itemize.

Even if you itemize in both years, it could be advantageous to stagger as many itemized expenses as you can into one of the two years. Again, this difference results from the income tax's progressive rate structure: A large total in one year could put you in a lower tax bracket that year, whereas taking an approximately even amount each year might leave you in the same bracket each year. As the months of November and December get closer, you should review your tax situation and see if expenses can be staggered profitably. Of course, staggering income—if that's possible—should also be considered.

Defer Income to Later Years

Deferring income to be taxed in later years is different from avoiding taxes altogether. However, deferring can be as attractive as avoidance for several reasons. First, deferred income is free to accumulate, and it will grow to a substantially larger sum than income that is taxed each year. Second, your marginal tax rate on deferred income (usually during retirement) might be lower than your current marginal rate. Some commonly used income-deferring investments are IRAs and Keogh and 401(k) plans; tax-deferred annuities; and U.S. Treasury Series EE bonds. In addition to these formal plans, any investment that defers your return to the future offers tax advantages. For example, a growth stock typically pays little or no current dividends that would be taxable. Rather, you can enjoy your total return as a capital gain when you sell the stock in the future. True, you might pay the same amount of tax as you would with, say, a savings account, but with the growth stock, taxes are deferred until the stock is sold. The "saved" taxes can be invested and earn a return during the entire investment period.

IRAs, Keoghs, and 401(k) Plans

We will discuss each of these in far greater depth in Chapter 16. Certainly one of the major advantages of these plans is the deduction against current income of amounts invested.

With regular IRAs, you should be aware you can always take your money out before retirement. Withdrawals, however, must be included in determining taxable income in the withdrawal year. (Remember: You excluded the IRA contribution in the year you made it.) If you do so before age 59 1/2, you must pay a 10 percent penalty unless the withdrawal was for some exempted reason.

Tax-Deferred Annuities

A **tax-deferred annuity** is an investment that is usually written by an insurance company. It also defers income to later years, but in contrast to IRAs, Keoghs, and 401(k)s, you cannot take a deduction on your current return for amounts invested, which makes them less attractive.

Tax-deferred annuity: An investment, usually sold by insurance companies, that allows tax deferral on current interest earned.

IRS Clarifies Innocent and Injured Spouse Relief

You trusted your spouse and your spouse betrayed your trust. Now after the divorce you find that in addition to cheating on you, your spouse also cheated the government. Your name was on the return and now the IRS wants to be paid. It could hold you responsible for the entire amount due even though it is owed on your spouse's income.

If you are a truly innocent spouse, the IRS just might have a soft spot in its heart for you. To find out if you qualify for special tax relief, visit the IRS's Innocent Spouse Web site **(www.irs.gov/individuals/innocent)**. Basically, to be entitled to innocent spouse relief, the errors that caused the understatement of taxes must have been your spouse's and you must not have had knowledge of the understatement at the time the joint return was signed. The tax liability may have resulted from erroneous items such as unreported income or an incorrect deduction, credit or basis for a capital gain.

If you succeed in convincing the IRS that it would be unfair to hold you responsible for the tax liability, then your spouse or former spouse will be liable for all taxes, interest, and penalties on the improperly reported or omitted items. The IRS indicates

it will consider the following factors when determining whether it would be unfair to hold you responsible:

- Whether you received a significant benefit either directly or indirectly, from the understatement
- Whether your spouse (or former spouse) deserted you
- Whether you and your spouse have been divorced or separated
- Whether you received a benefit on the return from the understatement

Remember, as with all tax matters, the burden is on you to prove your innocence and not on the IRS to prove your guilt.

Closely related to innocent spouse relief is an injured spouse claim. Suppose you file a joint return with your spouse, but your spouse has an outstanding claim for past taxes, child support, spousal support, or student loans. The government may intercept a refund on your taxes to pay for those debts. If the refund in used to pay claims against your spouse from before you got married or to pay claims that are the sole responsibility of your spouse, you might be an injured spouse. To apply for status as an injured spouse you must file Form 8379, "Injured Spouse Claim and Allocation." If the IRS decides you are an injured spouse, the refund on your portion of the household income will not be used to pay debts that are the sole responsibility of your spouse. For low-income couples, this can result in the injured spouse receiving a portion of the Earned Income Credit.

U.S. Treasury Series EE Bonds

Series EE bonds give you the option of either reporting income as it accrues on the bond each year or reporting it when you cash the bond. The main advantage of this bond is its flexibility. You choose when to cash it and pay the tax, and choosing a year when your marginal tax rate is low can save taxes. These bonds are explained further in Chapter 11.

OTHER IMPORTANT TAXES

Although the federal income tax is the most important tax to most of us, others should also be understood. For example, people in low- or middle-income brackets might pay more in Social Security taxes than in personal income taxes; if you are very wealthy, you may pay substantial estate and inheritance taxes when you die or gift taxes if you try to give the estate away before you die. The growing fiscal needs of state and local governments have brought forth an array of income, sales, and property taxes at these levels.

Social Security Taxes

Most of us are familiar with the Social Security system. We are counting on it as an important part of our retirement income or for survivor benefits to our families if something happens to us. But, as you probably also know, it has come under financial stress because benefits seem to be outpacing revenues. As a result, Social Security taxes have escalated rapidly and will continue to do so in the future.

The taxes withheld from your wages for Social Security are called **FICA taxes;** FICA denotes taxes collected under the Federal Insurance Contributions Act. FICA taxes consist of three components; health insurance (HI), old age and survivor's insurance (OASI), and disability insurance (DI). HI is paid for by a 1.45 percent tax on all wages. There is an annually adjustable limit on the taxable base for OASI and DI taxes. In 2004, wages up to $87,900 were taxed at 6.2 percent pay for these components. Accordingly, at below the adjustable limit, FICA taxes add up to 7.65 percent of your wages.

FICA taxes: Taxes collected for Social Security purposes.

It is important to realize that you might overpay FICA taxes. This could happen if you change employers during the year or if you work for two or more employers. You can claim excess payments as a credit against your federal income tax liability at the time you prepare your return. By all means, check the W-2 forms your employer gives you in January to make sure you have not overpaid. However, both spouses must pay the full amount of the tax, so you cannot have an overpayment simply because the sum of the two exceeds the maximum.

Also, you should be aware that your employer must pay FICA tax equal to the amount withheld from your wage. This is an expensive payroll cost for employers. Self-employed individuals must also pay both the employer's and employee's portions of the tax.

State and Local Taxes

The maze of state and local taxes in most states not only takes a fairly large amount from your bank account but also creates considerable confusion as to what is being taxed and for how much. Very few people thoroughly understand all these taxes; in fact, some of the taxes are buried in the prices of items that we buy. There is little that can be done about the situation except to make the best of it. Table 4.1 gives an indication of how tax burdens vary among different cities. Of course, governments that collect high taxes may also provide high levels of services. In this sense, then, high taxes aren't necessarily bad.

City	Total Taxes Paid as Percent of Gross Income			
	$25,000	$50,000	$75,000	$100,000
Atlanta	7.9	9.9	11.0	11.2
Baltimore	7.5	11.2	11.9	11.9
Chicago	9.9	9.9	10.4	10.0
Detroit	9.9	10.5	11.0	10.9
Milwaukee	7.9	10.3	11.3	11.3
New York	7.1	12.0	14.0	14.2
Philadelphia	11.3	13.2	13.0	12.6
Portland	10.3	11.8	12.4	12.6
Seattle	7.3	6.5	6.5	6.1
Washington, DC	6.6	9.2	10.1	10.5
Median	7.0	8.1	9.1	9.4

Table 4.1

Estimated State and Local Taxes Paid by a Family of Four in Selected Cities: 2003

Source: Tax Rates amd Tax Burdens in the District of Columbia: A National Comparision, 2003.

TOPIC LINKS

Find state income tax rates.

Income Taxes

All the states except Alaska, Florida, Nevada, South Dakota, Texas, Washington, and Wyoming levy income taxes. These are usually withheld from your wages, but you must file an annual return, similar to the federal return, to calculate your tax liability and to determine any over- or underpayment. The tax bases and rates vary among the states, and they can be quite high. A New York City resident whose income is in the highest bracket will pay over 20 percent in combined state and city income tax.

Many local governments—mostly cities and villages—impose income taxes. While these are often called payroll taxes, they are imposed on all forms of income. These also require filing an annual return if you have taxable income not subject to withholding. It is not uncommon for someone (such as a sales representative) to file more than a dozen returns if he or she earned income in 12 different communities. To make matters more confusing, there is always the question of whether you pay tax to the city where the income was earned or the city in which you live, assuming they are different. In general, the tax follows the place of employment unless the city of residence imposes a higher tax rate; then you usually pay the difference between the two rates to the city of residence. Of course, you must file a tax return with that city.

Property Taxes

Property taxes are still the mainstay of local governments, particularly school districts. All states have taxes on real property (houses and buildings), and most also tax personal property (equipment, furniture, fixtures, and the like) of businesses; some also tax household personal property. Many impose taxes on intangible property, such as stocks and bonds. The property tax rate that you pay depends very much upon the community where the property is located. You'll pay an effective tax rate of about $38.60 per $1,000 in Bridgeport, Connecticut, and $3.80 per $1,000 in Honolulu, Hawaii.

Sales Taxes

Forty-five states and the District of Columbia have sales taxes. Some tax all consumption items—services as well as commodities—and others omit services. Some tax necessities, such as food; others do not. The sales tax rates vary among states, and even within states when local governments enact their own taxes to "piggyback" the state tax.

DEATH AND TRANSFER TAXES

If you think you can avoid paying taxes by dying, you are wrong. Those who have been lucky enough to accumulate a sizable estate at death may have to share their financial success with the government. Some call this double taxation, since it was already taxed once when it was earned. With proper estate planning, however, even wealthy individuals can significantly reduce their tax liabilities at death. Through the use of life transfers and special trusts they can ensure that their wealth is transferred intact to desired beneficiaries. The strategies for accomplishing this objective for high-income individuals are too complicated for us to discuss in this introductory text. You need the help of estate planning professionals if you find yourself in this category. Nevertheless, a basic understanding of estate and transfer taxes can benefit most individuals. With it, even moderate-income individuals may avoid tax liabilities and know when to seek professional financial help.

Federal Gift and Estate Tax

Federal estate tax: A tax levied on a decedent's estate.

The **federal estate tax** is a tax that is levied on the value of a decedent's estate at the time of death. The **federal gift tax** is an excise tax charged on the transfer of property by a living

Tax Year	Top Rate	Estate Exemption Amount
2005	47%	$1.5 million
2006	46%	$2 million
2007	45%	$2 million
2008	45%	$2 million
2009	45%	$3.5 million
2010	repealed	
2011	55%	$1 million

Table 4.2

Planned Changes in the Estate Tax

Source: Joint Committee on Taxation.

donor. A gift tax is necessary to supplement an estate tax; otherwise, you would be able to transfer wealth during your lifetime and, therefore, avoid the estate tax. The federal gift allows a "modest" nontaxable gift each year of $11,000 per donee ($22,000 for husband and wife donors). For most families the "modest" gift provision allows a substantial transfer of their wealth each year.

Federal gift tax: Excise tax levied on the transfer of property; supplements the federal estate tax.

The interaction of the federal estate and gift tax is fairly complicated. However, the tax is only applied to large gifts and estates because of a rather large tax credit on taxable transfers and specific exclusions. The most notable is the marital exclusion that permits an unlimited nontaxable transfer to a living or surviving spouse. Taxable gift transfer above the annual exclusion and taxable death transfers above allowable exclusions are subject to a unified tax and a unified credit. This means that the tax and the credit are applied to the combined value of the taxable gift and death transfers. Under the Tax Relief Act of 2001, the unified credit gradually increases over the next few years until the unified tax is entirely eliminated in 2010. However, the present law does retain a separate gift tax in 2010 in order to reduce the incentive for transferring income-generating property from high-rate taxpayers to low-rate taxpayers. Given the planned expansion in the unified credit, taxable transfers below the amounts listed in Table 4.2 will be exempt from gift and estate taxes. If Congress does nothing, which is unlikely, the estate tax will be reinstated in 2011.

State Death Taxes

A tax on the property transferred or received upon the death of the owner is known as a death tax. There are two types of death taxes: an estate tax and an inheritance tax. An estate tax is imposed on the property of the deceased before it is transferred; an **inheritance tax** is levied on the property when the beneficiary receives it. At the federal level, only an estate tax exists. However, state governments impose either estate or inheritance taxes, and sometimes both.

Inheritance tax: State tax levied on the heirs to an estate.

Each state has its own inheritance or estate tax. The exact tax rate and the exemption accorded each beneficiary differ from state to state. About one-third of states have inheritance taxes. These are levied somewhat differently than estate taxes in that heirs are classified according to their relationship to the decedent. Inheritance tax statutes generally segregate beneficiaries into classes similar to the following:

- Class 1: Spouse
- Class 2: Parents, children, grandparents, lineal descendants
- Class 3: Brothers and sisters, aunts and uncles
- Class 4: Children of brothers and sisters, children of aunts and uncles
- Class 5: All others

The tax rates on classes of beneficiaries are structured so that the larger the estate and the more distant the relationship to the deceased, the higher is the tax rate. Inheritance taxes play an important role in estate planning by providing an incentive to leave property to closer relatives. Furthermore, because exemptions are low—in one state $5,000 for a spouse—and because rates can be high on large estates, approaching 30 percent, inheritance taxes also provide an incentive for lifetime gifts.

Transfers of Appreciated Property

Most of us are not wealthy enough to worry about the gift or estate tax. However, the method in which our property is distributed can still be important because it can affect the federal income taxes paid by beneficiaries. In some situations it may be preferable to let the property transfer at death rather than as a gift. This is because the property of the deceased receives a stepped-up cost basis for tax purposes at death. This means that the cost basis for valuing the taxable capital gain is set at the market value of the property at the time of death rather than what it cost when it was initially purchased by the deceased.

If you were lucky enough to buy stock in Microsoft when it was first issued, you probably own some shares that are worth a lot more than you previously paid for them. If you sold them today, you would have to pay a tax on that capital gain. If instead those shares transferred to your children at your death, your children would receive a new cost basis in the stock valued at the time of your death. Consequently, the entire appreciation in the value of the stock that occurred while you were alive would escape taxation. Regrettably, new rules will go into effect when the federal estate tax is eliminated in 2010. With some modification, beneficiaries will have to pick up the cost basis of the deceased.

If you gift property to others while you are alive, the recipient of a gift must assume your cost basis when the property has appreciated in value. Therefore, if you gift your children that Microsoft stock, they will have to pay a capital gain tax on the entire appreciation in the value of the stock from the time you purchased it. The basic rule of thumb is that you let those goods that have appreciated in market value transfer at death rather than as gifts. In this way a new cost basis is established, and potential capital gains taxes are eliminated.

Alternatively, don't bequeath property that has depreciated in value. The beneficiary will not be able to receive the tax benefit from the capital loss. Don't give depreciated property away, either. The best strategy is to take the capital loss yourself. On gifts that have depreciated in value, the cost basis to the recipient is the lower of the cost to the donor or the fair market value at the time the gift was made. Thus, the recipient of a gift that has depreciated in value since its initial purchase would not be able to take the reduction in value before the property was transferred as a loss for tax purposes.

Key Terms

adjusted gross income (p. 81)
alimony payments (p. 83)
alternative minimum tax (AMT) (p. 93)
automatic extension (p. 94)
average tax rate (p. 89)
capital assets (p. 93)
capital gain or loss (p. 92)
custodial account (p. 100)
federal estate tax (p. 104)
federal gift tax (p. 105)

FICA taxes (p. 103)
global income (p. 80)
gross income items (p. 80)
inheritance tax (p. 105)
Internal Revenue Service (IRS) (p. 94)
IRAs and Keogh plans (p. 83)
itemized deductions (p. 85)
marginal tax rate (p. 89)
municipal bonds (p. 99)
nontaxable exclusions (p. 80)

personal and dependency exemptions (p. 84)
refund anticipation loan (p. 95)
standard deduction (p. 84)
statute of limitations (p. 95)
taxable income (p. 84)
tax credit (p. 87)
tax-deferred annuity (p. 101)
W-2 form (p. 88)
W-4 form (p. 88)

Reread the chapter-opening vignette.

1. The Steeles postponed filing their federal return until the last possible date. Was this a wise strategy?
2. How do you find the Steeles' marginal tax rate?
3. What tax strategies can you offer the Steeles for reducing their future tax liabilities?

**Problems
and Review
Questions**

1. Arrange the following items in their appropriate sequence according to the federal income tax formula:
   (a) adjusted gross income
   (b) adjustments to income
   (c) itemized deductions
   (d) tax credits
   (e) gross income items
   (f) nontaxable exclusions
   (g) federal income taxes withheld
   (h) exemptions
2. What is the amount allowed for a personal exemption? Is the exemption amount indexed? Explain what this means.
3. Suppose you and your spouse work and have wages of $16,000 and $5,000, respectively. Calculate the maximum deduction for IRAs. Calculate it if your income was $21,000 and your spouse's was zero.
4. Chrissy, Jack, and Janet are friends. Jack and Janet have grown fond of each other and are thinking of marrying. Chrissy has told them, however, that if they do, their income taxes will increase. Jack and Janet don't see how that's possible. Assume each made $37,000 and took the standard deduction in 2004. Using the tax schedules in Figure 4.8 to approximate their taxes, determine whether Chrissy is right.
5. John and his wife Clara had $26,000 of adjusted gross income in 2004. They filed a joint return and took the standard deduction. Is it likely they had to pay any taxes? If so, how much?
6. Steve has a 28 percent marginal tax rate. What is it worth to him to have:
   (a) an additional itemized deduction of $100?
   (b) an additional $100 invested in a tax-deductible IRA?
   (c) an additional tax credit of $100?
7. Explain the tax treatment for capital gains and capital losses.
8. Miguel purchased a home in 1985 for $30,000. He sold it in 1990 for $70,000 and immediately purchased another one for $80,000, which he sold in 2004 for $135,000. How much taxable capital gain, if any, does Miguel have?
9. Identify, explain, or elaborate upon the following items:
   (a) functions of the IRS
   (b) automatic extension of time for filing
   (c) statutes of limitations
   (d) assistance in tax-return preparation
   (e) income splitting
   (f) staggering expenses
   (g) avoiding taxes
   (h) deferring taxes

10. How are FICA taxes calculated? Is it possible to overpay them? If your answer is yes, what should you do?
11. What are estate, gift, and inheritance taxes?
12. Identify frequently levied state and local taxes.

Case 4.1
Preparing Becky Sell's First Tax Return

Becky Sell graduated from a midwestern college in 2004 and began work as a marketing manager trainee for a large consumer products company. Becky had never prepared her own tax return before, but she was determined to do it for the first time. Becky got all pertinent information together in February 2005, and it appears as follows:

A. Data on two W-2 forms (Becky worked part-time prior to graduation) showed wages of $44,000 and federal income tax withheld of $4,600. In addition, they showed she paid $1,600 in state and city income taxes and $3,366 in FICA taxes.
B. Becky paid most of her bills with checks and kept all canceled receipts for purchases. Examination of these and her check stubs shows the following major classifications of expenses: rent = $5,000; charitable contributions = $500; interest on installment loans = $1,900; food and clothing = $8,000; dues to professional marketing society = $200; hospital and doctor's bills = $1,000; state sales tax = $600; contributions to a political candidate in her hometown = $110; contributions to a panhandler she often sees outside the office of the political candidate = $50.
C. Becky received $12,000 in gifts at graduation, and with it she purchased shares of GM stock in April. Three months later she sold these shares for $8,500.

Becky wants to file a return that will minimize her 2004 tax liability. She has cash from the GM stock sale that could be used for an IRA investment, but she isn't sure of the maximum allowed.

Questions
1. If Becky itemized personal expenses, how much can she deduct? How much is her standard deduction?
2. Using the schedules in Figure 4.8, and taking the standard deduction, determine Becky's 2004 tax liability. (Assume she will make a $2,000 tax deductible IRA investment.) How much will Becky owe or have refunded?
3. Determine Becky's marginal tax rate and explain to her what this rate means.
4. Becky worked for two employers; did she overpay her FICA taxes? Explain.

Case 4.2
The Brittens' Investment Alternatives

Bernie and Pam Britten are a young married couple beginning careers and establishing a household. They will each make about $50,000 next year and will have accumulated about $40,000 to invest. They now rent an apartment but are considering purchasing a condominium for $100,000. If they do, a down payment of $10,000 will be required.

They have discussed their situation with Lew McCarthy, an investment adviser and personal friend, and he has recommended the following investments:

1. The condominium—expected annual increase in market value = 5 percent.
2. Municipal bonds—expected annual yield = 5 percent.
3. High-yield corporate stocks—expected dividend yield = 8 percent.
4. Savings account in a commercial bank—expected annual yield = 3 percent.
5. High-growth common stocks—expected annual increase in market value = 10 percent; expected dividend yield = 0.

Questions

1. Calculate the after-tax yields on the foregoing investments, assuming the Brittens have a 28 percent marginal tax rate.
2. How would you recommend the Brittens invest their $40,000? Explain your answer.

Exercises to Strengthen Your Use of the Internet

(Internet links for the following exercises can be found at **www.prenhall.com/winger.**)

Working Out on the Web

Exercise 4.1 Keeping Up with Changes in the Tax Code

Each year Congress makes at least minor changes in the tax code. Those people who are aware of the changes can often modify their personal financial plans so that the changes work in their favor. Money Central, an MSN Microsoft Web site, highlights recent changes in the law that affect individuals.

Q. How might recent changes in the tax law influence your current or future financial decisions?

Exercise 4.2 What's an Enrolled Agent (EA)?

If the IRS audits you, an enrolled agent can appear at the IRS in your place. How do you locate an enrolled agent? The answers to this and other questions concerning enrolled agents appear at the Web site for the National Association of Enrolled Agents.

Q. How does one become an EA, and what are the entry requirements for this profession?

Exercise 4.3 Getting the Tax Information You Need

The IRS Web site contains electronic copies of its publications in print. Many are in HTML format that can be directly viewed. Go to IRS Publications. Open Publications 17 "Your Federal Income Tax." Most taxpayers will not have to look beyond this publication for information on filing their tax returns. At the beginning of this booklet is a section that highlights the important changes for the most recent tax year.

Q. What are the most important changes for the latest tax year?

Exercise 4.4 Locating Information on State Taxes

The IRS provides tax forms, informational publications, and tax tips. Determine what type of information is available from your state government. In your hunt, you can use a general search program link at Google, or you can use one of the special pages with state government links. For example, try Federal Tax Administrators or the Tax Sites State Government Tax List.

Q. Can you electronically access information on your state taxes? If so, at what site can you access this information?

Exercise 4.5 Determining the Top State Marginal Tax Rate

Most states tax income in a manner consistent with the federal government's taxation of income. If your state has an income tax, what is its top marginal tax rate and at what level of taxable income does this rate become effective? Which state has the top marginal tax rate in the nation? This information is available from the Federation of Tax Administrators, an association of major state tax collection agencies.

Q. If your state has an income tax, what is the top marginal rate in your state, and at what level of taxable income does this rate become effective?

PART 2

Liquidity Management

MANAGING CURRENT ASSETS AND CURRENT LIABILITIES

Chapter 5
Cash Management: Funds for Immediate Needs

Chapter 6
Short-Term Credit Management: Buying Now and Paying Later

The management of any unit—business, government, or family—having financial transactions recognizes the need to maintain adequate liquidity. Cash is received from employment or other sources, held for a while, then used to pay bills or invested in savings accounts or other financial assets. Managing these cash flows should be undertaken in a way that embraces both a cash management strategy and a short-term credit management strategy. Together, these strategies aim to reduce the overall costs of liquidity, which can be explicit costs, such as interest expenses on amounts borrowed, or opportunity costs, such as interest-earning opportunities forgone because cash is deployed in other ways.

Chapter 5 focuses on cash management. It discusses some basic features of cash-type assets, such as savings accounts, certificates of deposit, and U.S. savings bonds. For readers with poor familiarity with checking accounts, the chapter provides specific steps in managing a checking account properly. The topic of how interest is determined on savings accounts is also discussed, and the chapter concludes with a discussion of cash management strategy.

Chapter 6 examines short-term credit, which can be viewed broadly as simply another source of cash to pay bills or make investments. But it can be an expensive source and not one to be taken lightly or overused. The chapter focuses on various sources of credit and how to manage credit effectively. It also highlights courses of action if credit is denied, or if borrowers' rights are abused by lenders or by credit card fraud. Finally, advice is offered for resolving personal debt problems.

5

Cash Management

FUNDS FOR IMMEDIATE NEEDS

OBJECTIVES

1. To identify the important deposits for holding cash balances and the advantages and disadvantages of each

2. To determine how much liquidity is usually necessary, given your income and preferences for safety

3. To decide on the appropriate type of checking account and to learn how to make transactions with your account and reconcile it each month

4. To understand how compounding makes your deposits grow over time and why deposits with long maturities are riskier than those with short maturities

5. To devise a strategy for managing your total liquid asset portfolio

TOPIC LINKS

Follow the **Topic Links** in each chapter for your interactive Personal Finance exercise on the Web. Go to: **www.prenhall.com/winger**

Steele FAMILY

Arnold and Sharon Steele are increasing their familiarity with financial planning. They have prepared and analyzed financial statements recently, which have uncovered some financial strengths and weaknesses. Their liquidity position seems satisfactory but not strong. They have $16,240 in liquid assets that were accumulated more or less at random. They have a savings account that was opened right after their marriage, and it has been untouched since then. They recently put funds into certificates of deposit because of an advertisement they read in the newspaper, and they invested in savings bonds because of certain tax advantages they hoped to achieve with them. Finally, they had $2,400 in their checking account at year-end. This amount varies from month to month and, on average, is considerably more than they need to have on hand. However, they occasionally buy an antique and must have sufficient funds to make the purchase.

The Steeles are trying to resolve two issues with respect to their liquid assets: First, is the current amount adequate, or should they hold more or fewer such assets? Sharon is concerned about the safety of their investments, particularly those earmarked for John and Nancy's education. Most liquid assets are very safe, an appealing feature to Sharon, who feels that a good portion of their future savings should be allocated to them. Arnold leans more toward minimizing their liquid asset holdings in favor of greater allocations to long-term investments, such as stocks, bonds, and mutual funds.

The second issue the Steeles need to resolve is the selection of specific liquid assets. Should they continue to hold the current mix, or should they look for alternatives? How much additional yield can they reasonably expect to achieve by rearranging the liquid asset mix? And does the greater yield bring greater risks?

Like the Steeles, many people do not seem overly concerned about managing liquidity. Perhaps they view liquid assets as a temporary reservoir that grows higher occasionally because they can't spend their incomes fast enough. Since these assets have a short "shelf life," why worry about achieving high relative returns? The money won't be there long enough to matter anyway.

This is a poor approach to liquidity management. What is needed is a **cash management strategy,** which is a plan determining how much cash to hold, in what form, and in which financial institutions. This chapter discusses the important aspects of cash management.

Cash management strategy: A plan determining how much cash to hold, in what form, and in which financial institutions.

MEETING CASH NEEDS

Few of us hold the same amount of cash. Your income might be far greater than mine, or you might be more conservative in your financial outlook. Despite such differences, people share some common characteristics that determine their cash needs. And to satisfy them, most of us keep some pocket money and hold the rest of our cash in either checking or savings accounts.

Why Hold Cash?

There are three reasons why people hold cash: to undertake transactions, to have a cash reserve in case of an emergency, and to have a temporary store of value. Each of these will now be examined.

Undertake Transactions

Each day you make small transactions. You may have bought lunch at the cafeteria; perhaps you stopped at a vending machine to buy a candy bar or some other item. It took cash—specifically, **pocket money** (coins and currency)—to do these things. How much pocket money do most people have on hand? Normally, they keep enough to get through a week or two; so, if you spend an average of $10 a day, you might cash a check each week for $70. Or if you have access to an automated teller machine (ATM), you can use your bank card to make withdrawals, and this method is usually more convenient than cashing a check. Actually, it is convenience, along with safety, that dictates how much pocket money to have on hand: The more convenient it is to get it, the less you need to hold. Since pocket money is easily lost or stolen, it is usually worthwhile to put up with some inconvenience to keep your balance low.

Pocket money: Coins and currency a person holds.

These inconveniences lead most people to open a **checking account** to pay larger monthly bills, such as the rent or utilities. You wouldn't want the risk of losing currency in the mail or the inconvenience of visiting the creditor just to pay the bill in cash. Moreover, a canceled check serves as evidence of having paid the bill. The advantages of checking accounts so heavily outweigh any of their disadvantages that a much larger portion of our total liquid assets is held in them than in coins and currency.

Checking account: Funds held with a financial institution and available upon demand.

Emergency Reserves

In addition to needing cash for everyday transactions, most people want to hold a portion of their assets in liquid form in case of emergencies. An illness, the loss of a job, or any other unfortunate event can severely strain a family's budget, and without some liquid assets, the family could be forced to sell other assets, such as the house or automobile, to

Emergency reserves: Liquid deposits held to meet unexpected cash needs.

meet daily living expenses. While most people agree that some cash should be held for **emergency reserves,** *how much* should be held isn't clear. Individual circumstances must dictate the amount. If you have disability income insurance or other protection that would maintain your income at close to its previous level while you are unemployed, you need a smaller emergency reserve than does someone whose income stops altogether. Important, too, is the amount of medical insurance carried: The more you have, the less cash you need. Many financial planners recommend a reserve equivalent to three to six months' after-tax income; so if you take home $2,000 a month, a reserve of $6,000 to $12,000 is suggested. Remember, though, this is only a rule of thumb.

Since emergency reserves are not intended to be used for making transactions, they should be held in deposits that offer the highest potential return consistent with reasonable liquidity. Holding them in a checking account that pays no interest, for example, would be a mistake.

Store of Value

You may be saving to make a major purchase in the future: a house, a new automobile, a personal computer, or a vacation. Until you have enough money, you need to save each pay period and then hold your savings in a form that will earn a return. You should be aware, though, that if you are holding funds for a fairly long period of time, the return on your deposits may not match the inflation rate on the item you are saving to buy. In this case, the deposit has not served well as a store of value. It is important to balance earnings against liquidity in the savings effort; to achieve your target, you may have to give up some liquidity to capture a higher return.

In addition to saving for a major purchase, some people hold cash balances as temporary "parking places" for their money. They really plan to reinvest their funds in less liquid investments in the future but are waiting for the investment environment to improve. Whatever the motive for holding cash, it must be held in specific kinds of deposits, to which we now turn our attention.

Fundamental Deposits

TOPIC **LINKS**

Find current rates on savings assets.

Many people meet their cash needs by holding deposits in checking and NOW accounts and passbook savings accounts. These are the basic deposits, but other types are often used as well. Table 5.1 shows frequently used deposits and grades them in terms of availability, safety, liquidity, and yield. In this section and the next we will explain these deposits, but first, remember that what makes a deposit liquid is your ability to withdraw it easily, with no delays or other complications, and your ability to withdraw it with *no loss in principal*. This last feature rules out many kinds of investments for serving liquidity needs. Common stocks, for example, can be sold quickly and relatively inexpensively—but there is never a guarantee they can be sold without loss, so they fail the liquidity test. Some of the deposits examined later are much more liquid than others. Certificates of deposit are the least liquid because of their interest penalties for early withdrawal.

Closely related to the issue of losing principal is the question of safety. Many depositors view safety as their most crucial concern because a large portion of their total investments may be in liquid accounts. Certainly a major advantage of holding deposits in most banks, savings and loans, and credit unions is the availability of federal insurance.

Indeed, the failures of major financial institutions in the past clearly indicate that you could make a tragic mistake by using a nonfederally insured institution. Be sure, then, to look for the following abbreviations when opening an account.

Deposit	Availability	Safety	Liquidity	Yield (average rate)[a]
Regular checking account	A+ (no minimum)	A+	A+	F (0.0%)
Savings account	A+ (no minimum)	A+	B+	D (1.23%)
NOW account	A (small minimum)	A+	A+	D (0.25%)
Money market deposit account	C (fairly large minimum)	A+	B+	B− (1.49%)
Money market mutual fund	B+ (minimum varies)	A to C (depending on securities held)	A+ to B (depending on checkwriting privileges)	B− (1.12%)
Certificates of deposit (CDs)	A (minimum varies)	A+	C (early withdrawal penalties)	A (2.93%)[b]
Series EE bonds	A (small minimum)	A+	B	B+ (4.38%)

[a]Approximate amounts at August 1, 2004. Rates vary considerably within and among regions, making comparative shopping very important. Helpful information can be found at www.bankrate.com/brm/default.asp.

[b]On 60-month CDs; longer maturities offered higher rates, shorter maturities less.

Table 5.1

A Scorecard for Liquid Deposits and Accounts

- *FDIC* (Federal Deposit Insurance Corporation)—insures commercial banks
- *SAIF* (Savings Association Insurance Fund)—insures savings and loans and mutual savings banks
- *NCUA* (National Credit Union Administration)—insures credit unions

It is important to know also that insurance is provided up to $100,000 for the *depositor,* not for the deposit. So, if you are fortunate enough to have more than $100,000, you should open a second account with a different institution, or you could make additional deposits with the same institution in another person's name.

Checking and NOW Accounts

Checking and NOW accounts are used primarily to satisfy transaction needs. While there is a slight technical difference between a regular checking and a **NOW (negotiated order of withdrawal) account,** for all practical purposes they are identical. Their major difference to you is that a NOW account pays interest on balances in the account, whereas a regular checking account does not. Most banks advertise their NOW accounts with names such as *Checking Plus* or *Checking Plus More,* to indicate that interest is earned on the account. The interest may be paid in several ways. Amounts below a minimum earn interest at a relatively low rate, and amounts above the limit earn higher rates. The higher rates are usually pegged to current money market rates, which means the interest you receive depends on the level of interest rates in general; as these go up, so does the amount earned. Of course, the reverse is also true.

If you can meet the minimum balance requirement of a NOW account, it is usually the best choice. However, get complete information on all accounts the bank offers before making a choice. Then compare their benefits and costs.

Savings Accounts

Many Americans have had a **savings account** at one time or another. They were often called passbook accounts because a record of your activity in the account was recorded in

NOW (negotiated order of withdrawal) account: Interest-earning checking account, usually with a minimum balance requirement.

Savings account: Account with virtually no restrictions but with no checkwriting privileges.

a passbook. These books are now mostly replaced by the type of statements used for checking accounts. However, the rate of interest earned on passbook accounts is still called the **passbook rate.** Because these accounts require no minimum balances, they are used frequently when only small deposits can be made. The passbook rate is generally the lowest rate of interest available, and it may be to your advantage to invest funds in alternative liquid accounts if you have enough cash to qualify for one of them. But shopping around may be to your advantage, even with savings accounts. For example, your credit union might offer a higher rate than your bank or savings and loan.

Passbook rate: Interest rate on a savings account; usually the lowest savings rate offered by a financial institution.

Other Deposits

In addition to checking and savings accounts, investors have access to a variety of other deposits. These are explained briefly in the following sections.

Money Market Deposit Accounts

Money market deposit accounts (MMDAs) offer current money market rates and easy access through checkwriting privileges, usually limited to three checks (or six transfers in total) a month. Federal depository insurance also enhances their appeal, as does access through automated teller machines. Unfortunately for small depositors, they have minimum deposit balances.

Money market deposit account (MMDA): Savings account with an interest rate that is tied to money market rates of interest.

Money Market Mutual Funds

Money market mutual funds pool the resources of many investors to purchase short-term securities issued by the U.S. Treasury, large commercial banks, and financially strong corporations (more information about mutual funds is provided in Chapter 12). Most people cannot afford to purchase such securities directly because they are sold only in very large denominations, such as $10,000 for a U.S. Treasury bill and $100,000 for a commercial bank certificate of deposit. Since most of these investments are very safe, so too are the money market mutual funds that invest in them. Nevertheless, your deposit is not insured as it is in a money market account or other federally insured deposit. All money market mutual funds have a minimum balance requirement, which is usually $1,000, although some are as low as $500.

Money market mutual fund: Pooling arrangement that invests in money market securities having very large denominations.

Certificates of Deposit

Certificates of deposit (CDs) are somewhat different from money market deposit accounts or money market mutual funds. When you buy CDs, you are in effect freezing your money for the maturity of the deposit, which can vary from seven days to eight years, or even longer. For instance, a 60-month deposit of $1,000 might be purchased to yield 6 percent. At the end of 60 months you will get $1,338.23, which is the principal plus interest (assuming annual compounding). But suppose you need the money before the 60 months end. You will then pay an interest penalty, the amount depending on when withdrawal takes place. A very early withdrawal can mean you get less back than your initial deposit. Naturally, this penalty discourages investors from using these deposits indiscriminately to obtain higher rates. The interest rate at the time of purchase is locked in for the entire term of the deposit. If interest rates fall during that period, you benefit by having your money invested at the higher rate. But if interest rates rise, the certificates will have been a poor choice.

Certificate of deposit (CD): Savings account with a set maturity and restricted access to funds until maturity.

U.S. Series EE Bonds

U.S. Series EE bonds are very attractive short-term investments, particularly for small investors. They now offer returns pegged to interest paid on U.S. Treasury securities. If you

U.S. Series EE bonds: Treasury-issued bonds with indexed interest rates, low denominations, and other attractive features.

hold these bonds for five years or longer, their yield is set at 90 percent of *five-year* Treasury securities. If you hold them for less than five years, you forfeit interest for the three most recent months. Yields are determined twice a year, at May 1 and November 1.

The interest you earn on Series EE bonds is free of state and local income taxes and can be deferred for federal income tax purposes until you redeem the bonds. Moreover, federal income taxes may be avoided altogether if interest on the bond is used to pay for a child's college or vocational education. Currently, single individuals earning $58,500 or less and married couples jointly earning $87,750 or less earn a full exclusion of all Series EE bond interest. For incomes from $58,500 to $73,500 (single return) and $87,750 to $117,750 (joint return), partial exclusion is available; and for incomes over $73,500 and $117,750, no exclusion is allowed. Clearly, this possible avoidance of taxes on Series EE bonds makes them very attractive.

Interest is earned on the Series EE bond by redeeming it for an amount greater than what was paid to purchase it. Another important consideration in purchasing Series EE bonds is their widespread availability. They can be bought or redeemed at most federally insured commercial or mutual savings banks or savings and loans.

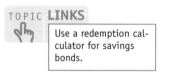

TOPIC **LINKS**

Find information on U.S. savings bonds.

TOPIC **LINKS**

Use a redemption calculator for savings bonds.

U.S. Series HH Bonds

The Treasury no longer issues Series HH bonds. We mention them here since previously issued bonds are still outstanding. If you own any of them, you should consult your local bank for advice on whether to hold or sell them. Their current interest rate of 1.5 percent makes them unattractive.

USING YOUR CHECKING ACCOUNT

The convenience of paying bills by checks, rather than with cash, was noted earlier in this chapter. Maintaining a checking account properly, however, involves some work. Care must be taken in making deposits and writing checks, and it is important to keep an adequate balance in the account, both to avoid overdrafts and to stay above any minimum that applies to the account. In addition, each month the bank will provide a statement of activity in the account, which you should reconcile with your activity records to ensure that neither you nor the bank has made a mistake. The first order of business, though, is to select a bank. We use the term **bank** to refer to any financial institution that offers checking account services. These could be commercial banks, savings and loans, mutual savings banks, or credit unions.

Bank: Any financial institution offering checking account services.

Selecting a Bank

A variety of factors usually determines your choice of a bank. Perhaps the most important of these is convenience, but consider also the range of services provided by the bank. Finally, you must evaluate what the bank charges to service the account and what it offers in interest on average balances. Shop around to find a checking account that fills your needs best.

TOPIC **LINKS**

Find banking information for various states and for various financial institutions.

Geographic Convenience

Depositors often cite geographic convenience as an important factor in choosing one bank over another. Although many transactions can be made indirectly through such means as preauthorized savings or bill payments, people nevertheless still conduct most of their banking business by direct contact with the bank. They visit it frequently to cash checks,

Indexed U.S. Savings Bonds

For a variety of very good reasons, many investors choose U.S. savings bonds as a primary vehicle to provide liquidity or to save for a child's education. Recently, the government has provided still another reason—inflation protection. The Treasury now issues inflation-indexed savings bonds, whose redemption values adjust semiannually to reflect the rate of inflation in the previous six months. Here's how they work.

Suppose you buy a bond with a $1,000 face value and a 2 percent semiannual interest rate. Suppose in the following six-month period inflation is 1.5 percent. Then your bond's face value "indexes" up to $1,015. Also, the bond's interest rate applies to the new value; so, you would earn interest of $20.30 in the second six-month period as opposed to $20.00 in the first six months. While $0.30 hardly seems earth shaking, remember that this process continues until you cash in the

bond. If inflation heats up, the accumulation derived from indexing could be substantial.

The new savings bonds also offer the same attractive features of the old savings bonds, such as being free of state and local taxes on interest, federal income tax deferral and possible avoidance if the bonds are used to finance a child's higher education, and widespread availability at banks and other financial institutions. Also, as with the old bonds, interest is not paid to you but rather accumulates in the bond's redemption value.

So, should investors rush out and buy as many of the new bonds as they are allowed in any calendar year ($30,000)? Maybe not. Unfortunately, the indexed bonds offer lower interest rates than the present variety. Suppose you can earn 3 percent annually on them versus 5 percent on the existing bonds. Now you must forecast future inflation rates. If you think they are likely to average more than 2 percent (the difference in yields), take the indexed bond; in the reverse case, the nonindexed bonds are a better choice. As usual, making a personal financial decision is not easy.

make deposits, pay off loans, and so forth. It's not surprising, then, that geographic convenience still matters the most. But closely related to the geographic convenience of the main office and branches is the existence of automated teller machines at convenient locations. Many people now rely on them as a source of cash and as a means of making other transactions. Finally, convenience and courtesy at the bank will probably influence your choice to open or keep an account there. Drive-in window facilities are obviously important to many of us, judging by the long lines of automobiles we often see at banks.

TOPIC **LINKS**

Visit First Star Bank's Web site.

Bank Services

Full-service banks and many other institutions now offer a wide array of services to their depositors, as Figure 5.1 shows. You might notice the items of convenience, such as the arrangements available for paying bills and transferring funds.

Service Charges and Earned Interest

Competition among banks has led to significant differences in service fees and interest paid on deposits. So comparative shopping is essential. There is little reason to pay any fee, no matter how small, for a service, when you can get the same service free elsewhere. However, if a bank's charges are low for some services, they might be high for others. Decide which services are important and then do your shopping.

Checking Account Procedures

Using a checking account is a relatively simple process if you are careful. Once an account is opened, you will make periodic deposits to increase your balance, and you will draw it down by writing checks. A record of these transactions is kept in a check register, which

Savings/Investing

- Passbook accounts
- Money market deposit accounts
- Certificates of deposit—maturities of one week to 10 years
- Savings reserve, to protect against accidental overdrafts
- IRAs
- Mutual funds
- Annuity products
- Brokerage services

Loans

- Personal loans—autos, trucks, recreational vehicles, home improvements
- Business loans—lines of credit, term loans
- Mortgage loans—business and residential (conventional, FHA, VA)

Major Credit Cards

- American Express Gold Card/Executive Credit
- MasterCard/Visa

Other Services

- Internet banking
- Bill-paying services
- Automated teller machines
- Safe deposit boxes
- Trust services
- Business services—payroll, accounting, leasing, direct deposit
- Preauthorized savings—automatic transfers from checking to savings
- Direct deposit of retirement checks (Social Security, Civil Service, or Railroad Retirement)
- Direct deposit of payroll checks
- Wire transfers
- Bank by mail
- Money orders, cashier's checks, traveler's checks
- Utility payments

may be a journal but is more often simply stubs to the checks written. Regardless of what forms are used to keep records, it is a good idea to take a little extra time to record all pertinent data. Very often a check is written in haste at a crowded checkout line, for example, and the stub is left for our memory to fill in later. Unfortunately, memories fade with time, particularly with respect to the exact amount of the check, and after several such instances, we have no idea how much is in the account. Along with filling out the stub completely as the check is written, it is also a good idea to earmark certain expenditures if they have particular importance. For example, many people use a checkmark or other symbol to identify tax-deductible expenses. This identification helps when next year's tax return needs to be filed.

Opening the Account

Opening a checking or savings account requires nothing more than filling out a simple signature card. If a joint account is opened, both (or all) signatures are required. It is important to use your legal name on any account. A married couple should consider a joint account rather than separate accounts for several reasons. First, the monthly service charges on two accounts are generally higher than for only one account. Second, and more important, if one of the spouses were to die, the funds in a joint account would pass immediately to the remaining spouse. This right of survivorship is associated with most bank accounts. However, in some states a joint account that does not specifically state **right of survivorship** will presume that **tenants in common** applies, in which case the survivor

Right of survivorship: An owner of an account has access to all funds upon the death of a co-owner.

Tenants in common: An owner of an account has a legal claim only to his or her share of an account upon the death of a co-owner.

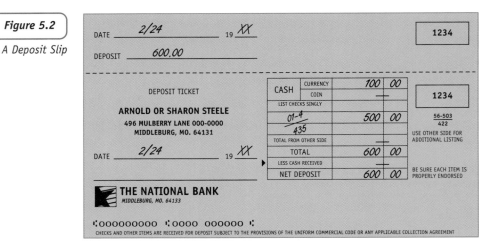

Figure 5.2

A Deposit Slip

DATE _____ 2/24 _____ 19 XX   1234

DEPOSIT _____ 600.00 _____

DEPOSIT TICKET

ARNOLD OR SHARON STEELE
496 MULBERRY LANE 000-0000
MIDDLEBURG, MO. 64131

DATE _____ 2/24 _____ 19 XX

THE NATIONAL BANK
MIDDLEBURG, MO. 64133

CASH	CURRENCY	100	00
	COIN		
LIST CHECKS SINGLY			
01-4		500	00
435			
TOTAL FROM OTHER SIDE			
TOTAL		600	00
LESS CASH RECEIVED			
NET DEPOSIT		600	00

1234

56-503
422

USE OTHER SIDE FOR
ADDITIONAL LISTING

BE SURE EACH ITEM IS
PROPERLY ENDORSED

⑆000000000 ⑆0000 000000 ⑈

CHECKS AND OTHER ITEMS ARE RECEIVED FOR DEPOSIT SUBJECT TO THE PROVISIONS OF THE UNIFORM COMMERCIAL CODE OR ANY APPLICABLE COLLECTION AGREEMENT

receives only his or her share of the account. Be sure to inquire about right of survivorship when you open an account.

Making Additional Deposits and Endorsing Checks

Making deposits to a checking account is a regular activity. These deposits consist of currency, coins, and checks written to you. Deposits are made with a deposit slip, such as the one illustrated in Figure 5.2. Notice that the deposit is for $600, consisting of $100 in currency and a check for $500. The arrangement of numbers 01-4/435 is the bank transit number on the check deposited. This number is of no particular importance to you, but it is used in the Federal Reserve's check-clearing process, and it should be listed carefully to help this process. Also, use a separate line for each check deposited even if all the checks are from the same bank.

Checks can be endorsed (signed on the back) in three different ways, as shown in Figure 5.3. You use a **blank endorsement** when withdrawing cash from the account, but remember that once you sign a check it becomes a negotiable instrument and can be used as such by anyone. If you happen to lose the check, all the finder needs to do is sign it under your signature and cash it. As a safeguard, don't sign the check until you are at the bank and ready to make the withdrawal. A **restrictive endorsement** limits the use of the check to a single purpose. "For deposit only" is written on a check when it is deposited by mail. If the check is lost in the mail and subsequently found, it cannot be cashed. A **special endorsement** is used when you use the check to pay someone else. All that you need do is indicate the payee and sign, as shown in Figure 5.3. It is usually not a good idea

Blank endorsement: Unrestricted endorsement of a check; anyone possessing the check can cash it.

Restrictive endorsement: Limits the use of a check to a single purpose, usually to make a deposit.

Special endorsement: Using a check to pay a third party.

Figure 5.3

Ways to Endorse a Check

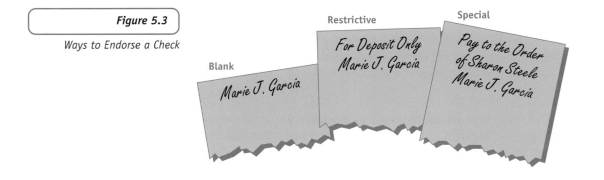

Restrictive

Special

Blank

Marie J. Garcia

For Deposit Only
Marie J. Garcia

Pay to the Order
of Sharon Steele
Marie J. Garcia

Check Cashing—Your Bank Wants a Piece of the Action

What does Wells Fargo (a major U.S. bank) and Cash America International (a pawnshop operator) have in common? They have formed an alliance to bring check-cashing services through vending machines in grocery and convenience stores. This union is further evidence that major banks plan to tap into a very lucrative market, one they had disdained in the past as perhaps too "seamy" for blue-blooded bankers.

Well, the lure of huge profits is enough to make any banker rethink his or her bloodlines. But what's good for bankers and pawnshops is definitely very bad for the rest of us. Consider that the going charge to cash a check (most often a payroll check) is 2 to 3 percent of the check amount plus transaction fees. Let's take the 2 percent figure, ignore the transaction

fee, and assume that you cash a $500 check each week. That's $10 a week, or $520 a year. Of course, what you really have here is a perpetual short-term loan of $490 (the interest is paid in advance), and the annual rate of interest is about 106 percent a year! Even the Shylock in *Get Shorty* would go for this deal.

As banks probe more deeply into the market, they have learned that many customers are not poor; indeed, Fisca (a check-cashers trade group) reports that 60 percent of them have accounts at banks or credit unions. Why then use such an exorbitant source of cash? Convenience. Apparently, we like to get our cash when it's convenient for us, not for bankers. We sometimes want it at night or on weekends.

Once in a while we all slip and find ourselves short on cash. Look at the outrageous fee, then, as the price of forgetfulness. It won't break our budget or put us in the poorhouse. But, if we use check cashers on a routine basis, we're certainly heading for trouble and might as well forget the budget.

to pay bills in this manner, however, since you will not have a record of the payment unless you take the time to make one. Remember, the check will be returned to the person who issued it, not to you.

Writing Checks

Writing a check is a simple procedure illustrated in Figure 5.4. As mentioned earlier, the stub should be filled in at the same time the check is written, and, naturally, they should be in agreement. Your account number is printed on the bottom of the check, as well as on the deposit slip. This number identifies the account and is needed whenever inquiries about the account are made. As a safeguard, the amount of the check is indicated both numerically and in written form. Be particularly careful about the written amount, because it is the legally binding figure. Also, your signature should appear exactly as you signed the signature card to open the account.

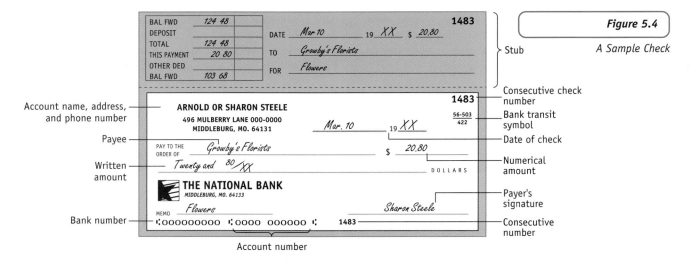

Figure 5.4

A Sample Check

"Bouncing a Check"

Overdraft (bounced check):
A check lacking sufficient funds to cover it.

If you happen to write a check without sufficient funds to cover it, you will have an **overdraft,** commonly referred to as a **bounced check.** It's an expensive oversight, since most banks charge about $30.00 for each such check. Moreover, it can lead to a poor credit rating. Either of these factors should motivate you to balance your account accurately on a timely basis. After writing one or two overdrafts, some people go to the opposite extreme and keep an excessive balance to avoid the problem in the future. But this practice is costly if the account does not pay interest. Another precautionary step is to arrange a savings reserve that ties the checking account to a savings account and automatically transfers funds from the latter to the former whenever an overdraft takes place. Although this arrangement is better than "overloading" the checking account, it too has a drawback if interest earned on the savings account is only at the passbook rate. You might get a better rate than this in another account. A third alternative is to arrange for a loan that will cover the overdraft. This is the worst alternative, since interest is typically charged at your credit card rate, which is usually 18 percent or more.

Availability of Funds

TOPIC **LINKS**

See Sovereign Bank's funds availability policy.

Current federal law requires all banks to comply with the following standards in making funds available after deposits have been made to the account: Cash, wire transfers, government checks, cashier's checks, and certified checks must be available on the next business day. Checks written on a local bank or other local financial institution must be available two business days after the deposit day, and checks written on a nonlocal financial institution must be available five business days after the deposit day. However, in some situations, a bank may hold the funds for longer periods. It is a good idea to check your bank's policy if you intend to write checks against a current deposit.

Stopping Payment on a Check

Stop-payment order: Directive to a bank not to pay a check.

Sometimes it is necessary to stop payment on a check already issued. Perhaps you paid someone for merchandise and after inspection found it defective or incomplete. You simply go to the bank and fill out a form, called a **stop-payment order,** directing the bank not to pay the check. You are charged for this service, so it shouldn't be used casually. It's a better idea not to issue a check until you are satisfied with the service or merchandise in question.

You may not have to issue a stop-payment order for a lost or stolen check. Contrary to what you may have heard, such checks are the bank's responsibility and not yours; that is, the bank is supposed to verify your signature before honoring a check. However, you may incur liability if you were negligent in handling your checks. So, to avoid problems inform the bank and close the old account while opening a new one (which may involve a charge). Also, don't issue a stop payment for a check you forgot to sign. Let it process, and the bank may honor the check anyway. If it doesn't, write another check to the payee.

End-of-Month Activities

At the end of each month, the bank will send you a monthly statement showing all transactions the bank has recorded in your account. It is important to reconcile this statement each month, both to update and audit your records for accuracy and to make sure the bank hasn't made a mistake.

Bank Reconciliation

Bank reconciliation: End-of-month analysis comparing the cash balance per bank statement with the cash balance per checkbook.

A **bank reconciliation** means that the end-of-month balance as shown on the bank statement is the same as the end-of-month balance shown in the check record. Figures 5.5, 5.6,

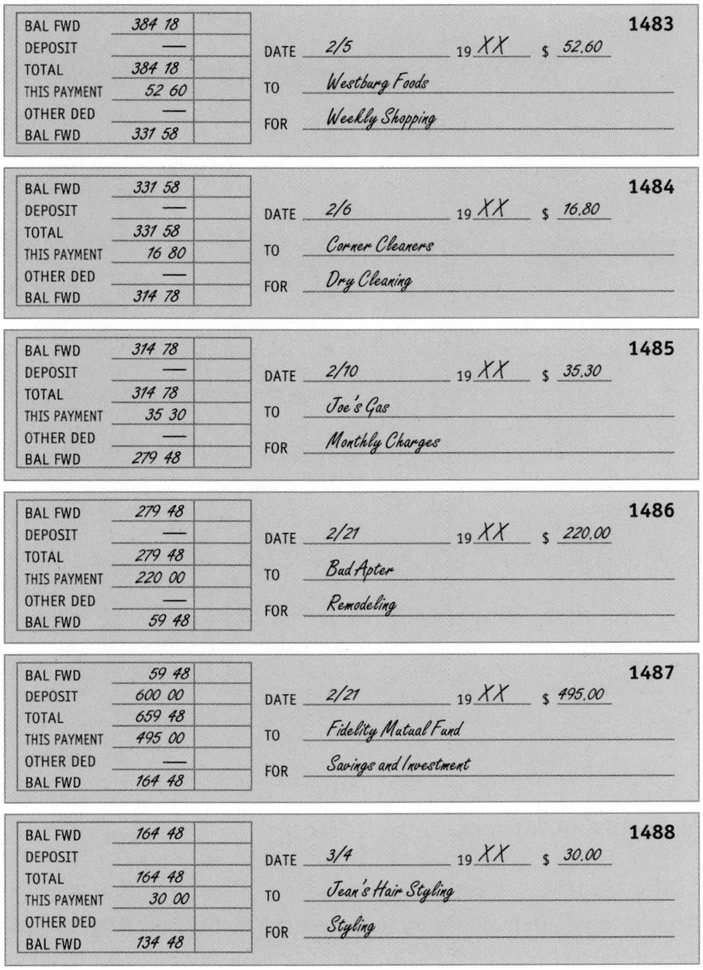

BAL FWD	384 18	**1483**
DEPOSIT	—	DATE 2/5 19XX $ 52.60
TOTAL	384 18	
THIS PAYMENT	52 60	TO Westburg Foods
OTHER DED	—	
BAL FWD	331 58	FOR Weekly Shopping

BAL FWD	331 58	**1484**
DEPOSIT	—	DATE 2/6 19XX $ 16.80
TOTAL	331 58	
THIS PAYMENT	16 80	TO Corner Cleaners
OTHER DED	—	
BAL FWD	314 78	FOR Dry Cleaning

BAL FWD	314 78	**1485**
DEPOSIT	—	DATE 2/10 19XX $ 35.30
TOTAL	314 78	
THIS PAYMENT	35 30	TO Joe's Gas
OTHER DED	—	
BAL FWD	279 48	FOR Monthly Charges

BAL FWD	279 48	**1486**
DEPOSIT	—	DATE 2/21 19XX $ 220.00
TOTAL	279 48	
THIS PAYMENT	220 00	TO Bud Apter
OTHER DED	—	
BAL FWD	59 48	FOR Remodeling

BAL FWD	59 48	**1487**
DEPOSIT	600 00	DATE 2/21 19XX $ 495.00
TOTAL	659 48	
THIS PAYMENT	495 00	TO Fidelity Mutual Fund
OTHER DED	—	
BAL FWD	164 48	FOR Savings and Investment

BAL FWD	164 48	**1488**
DEPOSIT		DATE 3/4 19XX $ 30.00
TOTAL	164 48	
THIS PAYMENT	30 00	TO Jean's Hair Styling
OTHER DED		
BAL FWD	134 48	FOR Styling

Figure 5.5

Sample Check Stubs

and 5.7 illustrate the steps in the reconciliation process. Figure 5.5 shows the stubs from a series of checks, numbers 1483 through 1488, written from the account. Notice that the running balance is maintained and that the end-of-month balance is $134.48. Figure 5.6 shows the bank statement sent to the depositor at the end of the month. A glance at it reveals several bits of information. First, the bank has deducted a service charge of $2.00, which wasn't known and, therefore, was not recorded up to now. So the first task is to reduce the book balance from $134.48 to $132.48. Second, you can see that of the six checks written during the month, only four have cleared; checks 1486 and 1488 are still outstanding. That is why the bank's balance is so much greater than the book balance. Figure 5.7, shown on page 125, is a reconciliation form that appears on the back of this particular bank statement. By following steps 1 through 4, you should be able to reconcile the statement. Notice that after the outstanding checks are deducted from the bank's balance, the book balance (after the service charge has been deducted) of $132.48 is confirmed. This reconciliation is a fairly simple one, since there are only six checks to review, no deposits in transit, and no other activity to make things more difficult. However, before you start a reconciliation, it is a good idea to compare each cleared check with the data recorded on the stub, because errors seem to occur no matter how carefully we try to keep our books. Cross-checking before you start

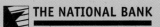

THE NATIONAL BANK

YOUR BANKING NO. 211 4003

ARNOLD OR SHARON STEELE
496 MULBERRY LANE
MIDDLEBURG, MO 64131

STATEMENT PERIOD	PAGE
FROM 2/04/XX TO 3/07/XX	1

CHECKING

TYPE	PREVIOUS BALANCE	DEPOSITS & CREDITS		CHECKS & DEBITS		NOW INTEREST	SERVICE CHARGE	CURRENT BALANCE
		NUMBER	AMOUNT	NUMBER	AMOUNT			
FREE&EASY 02	384.18		600.08	1	601.70		2.00	382.48

DAY	AMOUNT	CHECK NO. OR DESCRIPTION	DAY	AMOUNT	CHECK NO. OR DESCRIPTION	DAY	AMOUNT	CHECK NO. OR DESCRIPTION
07	2 00	SERVICE CHARGE						
05	52 60	1483						
08	16 80	1484						
18	35 30	1485						
24	600 00	DEPOSIT						
25	495 00	1487						

Figure 5.6

Sample Bank Statement

to reconcile can prevent a headache later on if the two balances fail to agree after a first reconciliation attempt.

Filing and Storage

Truncation: The bank retains a payer's checks.

After reconciliation, the bank statement can be filed for later reference. Most banks will return the canceled checks along with your statement, although the trend today is toward **truncation,** which simply means that the payer's bank retains the checks and forwards only a bank statement. This statement, however, does indicate the name of the payee on each check, along with the check number and dollar amount. Many depositors prefer truncation because it reduces the bulky records they must keep. Be careful to save whatever documents the bank returns to you. These items—not your check stubs or other documents that you generate—are necessary to support a claim that payment has been made. For example, the Internal Revenue Service requires these source documents to support your personal income tax deductions.

Moreover, new legislation, called Check 21, went into effect on October 28, 2004. Under this law, banks have a choice of returning actual checks or so-called "substitute checks," which may be electronic images of one or both sides of the check. We'll see how banks respond to the new law.

Checks That Guarantee Payment

On occasion you may need a check that guarantees payment. Maybe you are buying something from a person who doesn't know you and is also not familiar with your bank. Conversely, there are instances when you want to be sure a check you are receiving will not bounce. There are three popular approaches to guaranteeing a check: have a personal check certified, buy a cashier's check, and buy traveler's checks.

To balance your checking account:

Step 1 Subtract from your checkbook balance all charges or other transfers that are shown in the checking section on the front of the statement such as Service Charges, Automatic Transfers, Reorder of Checks, or Others. Your Checking Plus Loan Payment is shown in the bottom right section on the front of your banking statement. Subtract only the payment amount from your checkbook balance. Add your NOW Account Interest to your checkbook balance.

Step 2 Compare checks shown on this statement to your checkbook records and list checks outstanding by dollar amount.

Checks Outstanding		
Date or No.	1486	$ 220.00
	1488	30.00
Total		$ 250.00

Step 3 Enter Current Balance shown on this statement. $ _____ 382.48

Add Deposits made after Statement Period. $ _____ —

Total $ _____ 382.48

Subtract total of checks outstanding. $ _____ 250.00

Step 4 This Balance should agree with your checkbook. $ _____ 132.48

Figure 5.7

A Bank Reconciliation

Certified Check

A person can take a personal check to his or her bank and ask to have it certified, making it a **certified check.** This means that the bank will verify that sufficient funds are in the account to cover the check. After this verification, the bank deducts the amount of the check from the account, making the funds immediately available to the payee. A certification is then stamped on the check.

Certified check: Bank verification that a payer has sufficient funds to cover a specific check.

Cashier's Check

People without checking accounts often use a **cashier's check** to pay bills. Such a check is also used when the amount involved is very large. It is written by a bank against itself and is accordingly much more acceptable than a personal check. There is a small service charge for a cashier's check unless you are a special customer to the bank, in which case the charge might be waived.

Cashier's check: A check issued by a bank against itself.

Traveler's Checks

A **traveler's check** is generally used when you are traveling away from home. These checks can be purchased at any bank or other financial institution in denominations that usually range from $10 to $100. At the time you buy these checks, you sign each one in the presence of a bank officer; later, when you cash one of them, you sign again in the presence of the person cashing it. The payees can thus compare signatures to guard against forgery. You also get a small journal to record the check serial numbers and other pertinent information. It's a good idea to keep this journal somewhere other than where you keep the

Traveler's check: Check purchased from a bank, usually when a payer is traveling away from home.

checks, since theft or loss of the checks must be reported to the bank to stop payment. If the journal and checks are lost or stolen together, you may not know what specific checks are actually missing. Traveler's checks are accepted practically everywhere throughout the world. They are a wise purchase (some banks will provide them free) whenever you travel.

Electronic Banking

TOPIC **LINKS**

Review Atlanta Bank's Internet features.

Automated teller machines (ATMs): Machines that perform certain banking functions.

Electronic funds transfer systems (EFTS): Electronic payment of bills and other transfers of cash.

TOPIC **LINKS**

Review Check Free Corporation's Internet bill-paying features.

Growing computer and electronics technologies have created important changes in the way banking transactions can be made. As mentioned before, it is now possible to do much of your banking business with your telephone hooked up to your personal computer. Most of us are already familiar with **automated teller machines (ATMs).** With these, you use a plastic ID card and a personal access code to conduct a number of bank activities such as withdrawing cash (in limited amounts only), transferring funds from one account to another, or paying routine monthly bills. You should exercise care in using an ATM, because it is a fertile area for consumer fraud and theft. For example, don't leave your access card in the machine or in other unprotected places, and don't use obvious code numbers such as your street address or phone number.

Electronic funds transfer systems (EFTS) extend beyond ATM services. The same access card can also be used to pay bills at stores that have point-of-sale terminals. In this way, funds are transferred automatically from your account to the vendor's. There are still other forms of electronic transfers: You may have an arrangement whereby your payroll check is wired directly to your bank; or, if you are a retiree, you may receive your Social Security check through an electronic transfer. Although electronic banking lacks a personal touch, it does add convenience.

Simplifying FINANCIAL Planning

Banking by Computer: Has Electronic Banking Finally Arrived?

About a dozen years ago, we heard that banking by phone was the wave of the future. It never happened. Now we hear that in the near future most U.S. families will bank by computer, and there is growing evidence that indeed they will. The pieces are all coming together: First, more than 70 percent of all U.S. homes own personal computers; second, the number of homes hooking up to the Internet is growing rapidly; and, third, easy-to-use software such as Intuit's Quicken is being integrated into online banking services.

The big advantage of computerized banking is the ease of paying bills. With a PC, you pay bills by writing checks on the

BOX 5.3

screen and clicking a payment box. Data for payees that you pay frequently, such as the telephone company, are held in memory, which means you don't even have to write the on-screen check—just click another box. Your electronic check can be sent in one of two ways. You may have a service that actually writes a check and mails it to the payee. Or the payee may have an electronic hookup to your bank, in which case the funds are simply transferred from your account to the payee's.

Naturally, computer banking involves charges. In some cases you pay a fee to the online provider in addition to its regular monthly fee. Also, there is usually a per-check charge for all checks above a minimum number. A ballpark estimate of cost is $9 to $15 a month for 30 checks. This method offers scant dollar savings over the old way, but it should save you time. Moreover, you may have instant access to your account to determine its balance, outstanding checks, or other information. Last, but not least, you avoid licking those gruesome postage stamps.

UNDERSTANDING HOW YOUR ACCOUNT EARNS INTEREST

What does a financial institution mean when it offers to pay you, say, 12 percent interest on your account? On the surface, this looks like a simple enough calculation: If you put $1,000 in the account, you get back $1,120 a year later, which is the initial $1,000 plus $120 (0.12 × $1,000) of earned interest. Simple as it seems, complications can arise if your account is structured differently from the one just mentioned, and many are.

TOPIC **LINKS**

Make compound interest calculations.

One source of confusion in the simple interest calculation is that it assumes that interest is paid only once—at the very end of the year. But you probably have seen accounts that advertise interest paid weekly, daily, or even continuously. Do you earn more with these accounts? If so, how much more? To answer these questions we need an understanding of basic interest calculations. Finally, suppose you make periodic deposits and withdrawals to and from an account. Will interest be earned on the deposit balance at the beginning of the month, at the end of the month, on the average for the month, or just what? Clearly, these questions, too, must be asked before you open an account.

How Interest Is Calculated

The actual interest dollars (I) earned on a deposit depend on three factors: the amount you invest (P); a stated interest rate (i), expressed in decimal form; and the length of time (t) the deposit is held, expressed as a fraction or multiple of a year. This relationship is shown as follows:

$$\$I = (\$P)(i)(t)$$

Thus, in the earlier example we have

$$\$120 = (\$1,000)(0.12)(1)$$

If the deposit were held for only six months, then the interest earned would be

$$\$60 = (\$1,000)(0.12)\left(\frac{6}{12}\right)$$

The future value (FV) of any deposit is simply the sum of principal invested and interest earned; that is,

$$\$FV = \$P + \$I$$

The FV for the deposit held 12 months is $1,120 ($1,000 + $120), and it is $1,060 ($1,000 + $60) for the six-month deposit. Which of these two deposits would you rather have? If you thought that at the end of six months you could take the $1,060 and reinvest it at a 12 percent annual rate for another six months, you would clearly prefer the two six-month deposits to the one 12-month. Why? To find out, calculate the FV of the six-month deposit at the end of the second six months. You must first calculate I, which is

$$\$63.60 = (\$1,060)(0.12)\left(\frac{6}{12}\right)$$

Then FV is $1,123.60 ($1,060 + $63.60). What you have determined is the future value of a deposit with a 12 percent stated interest rate (also called the *nominal rate*)

Table 5.2

Future Values of $1,000 Invested at 8 Percent Stated Rate with Interest Calculated Under Various Compounding Periods

Frequency of Compounding	Number of Years Deposit Is Held				
	1	**2**	**4**	**8**	**16**
Annually	$1,080.00	$1,166.40	$1,360.49	$1,850.93	$3,425.94
Semiannually	1,081.60	1,169.86	1,368.57	1,872.98	3,508.06
Quarterly	1,082.43	1,171.66	1,372.79	1,884.54	3,551.49
Weekly	1,083.22	1,173.37	1,376.79	1,895.55	3,593.11
Daily	1,083.28	1,173.49	1,377.08	1,896.35	3,596.13
Continuously	1,083.30	1,173.51	1,377.13	1,896.48	3,596.62

compounded semiannually. In comparison with the annual compounding, it provided $3.60 more over the one-year holding period. From this illustration, you probably also recognize that the more often compounding takes place, the greater is the future value of any given deposit for any given stated interest rate. Table 5.2 shows future values for a $1,000 deposit and an 8 percent stated rate for various compounding periods, assuming the deposit is held for 1, 2, 4, 8, or 16 years. As you see, more frequent compounding leads to greater future values. The table also shows a fairly common phenomenon in compounding. Small differences compounded over a long period of time eventually become a big difference. For example, daily compounding added only $3.28 more than annual compounding for one year, but over 16 years the difference grows to $170.19 ($3,596.13 − $3,425.94). *Continuous compounding* may not be familiar to you. It assumes that interest is calculated even more frequently than every second of every day. It sounds impressive but, as Table 5.2 shows, it adds little above daily or weekly compounding.

Table 5.3

Quarterly Interest Earned Under Four Determination Methods with a 6 Percent Stated Interest Rate

Activity in the Account

Day	Deposit (Withdrawal)	Balance
1	$1,000	$1,000
30	1,000	2,000
60	(900)	1,100
90	Closing	1,100

Interest Calculations

1. Day of deposit to day of withdrawal:
   a. $1,000 × 30/360 × 0.06 = $ 5.00
   b. $2,000 × 30/360 × 0.06 = $10.00
   c. $1,100 × 30/360 × 0.06 = $ 5.50
   Total $20.50

2. Minimum balance:
   $1,000 × 90/360 × 0.06 = $15.00

3. FIFO:
   a. $ 100 × 90/360 × 0.06 = $ 1.50
   b. $1,000 × 60/360 × 0.06 = $10.00
   Total $11.50

4. LIFO:
   a. $1,000 × 90/360 × 0.06 = $15.00
   b. $ 100 × 60/360 × 0.06 = $ 1.00
   Total $16.00

Determining Interest on Your Account

All savings accounts are not alike in the way interest is determined on them. Differences arise with respect to the length of time balances in the account are judged to qualify for earning interest. In some cases, if a deposit is not held for an entire quarter, it earns no interest at all, even if it was withdrawn on the very last day of the quarter. Four different methods are in general use: (*a*) day of deposit to day of withdrawal (or daily interest), (*b*) minimum balance, (*c*) FIFO, and (*d*) LIFO. Table 5.3 illustrates those four methods. It is assumed that a deposit of $1,000 is made on the first day of the quarter; another $1,000 is made on the 30th day; and a $900 withdrawal takes place on the 60th day. The account has a stated interest rate of 6 percent.

Most banks use the daily interest method. However, some do not, making it important for you to ask how your bank determines interest.

CASH MANAGEMENT STRATEGY

At the beginning of this chapter we said that the object of cash management is to minimize cash balances while maintaining an adequate level of liquidity. By now you can see that the problem is made more complex by the many forms of liquid deposits. No one would argue against keeping currency and coin holdings to a minimum, but differences of opinion arise over how other cash should be held. If you want to manage your cash actively rather than putting it all into one account, then you should follow these steps:

1. Resolve to your own satisfaction which direction you think interest rates will move in the planning period.
2. Obtain current information about various deposit accounts, particularly current interest rates and possible account restrictions.
3. Allocate your liquid funds among the accounts to satisfy your preferences for yield, safety, and liquidity.

Financial PLANNING for Young Adults

BOX 5.4

Stored Value Cards: Don't Pay for a Picture

A recent but rapidly growing phenomenon is the use of stored value cards. Technically, these are debit cards that consumers use in a variety of ways, such as making purchases at retail outlets or withdrawing cash at ATMs; some value cards may also be recharged. Well over 1,000 companies now offer such cards to their employees, and the number is growing rapidly. The cards are convenient, particularly to transient workers or young adults who may not have checking or savings accounts, and who may find it difficult or expensive to cash a payroll check.

Another form of stored value cards is the gift card, which various companies issue as a substitute for the old form of gift certificate. These cards can be insidiously expensive. For example, there may be a transaction fee or a shipping fee. Equally bad, after a year or two, unused balances on the cards (called "breakage") are frequently confiscated by the issuer through steep monthly service charges. *Money* magazine noted (December, 2003; p. 37) that breakage in 2004 could be as high as $4 billion. The article also cited the Hilary Duff card as an example of outrageous expenses—$4.50 transaction fee and $2.50 shipping fee on a $25 gift card.

As with cash itself, you need to be careful with any stored value card. Anyone who finds a lost card may use it. Also, these cards could induce extra spending because of their convenience. Finally, think twice: Is Hilary Duff's (or another celebrity's) picture worth $7?

Keep in mind: The more yield you want, the less safety and liquidity you must take. These three aspects are brought together in the action plan for the Steele family, but we should emphasize the instability of interest rates.

Interest Rate Volatility

TOPIC **LINKS**

See Treasury bill rates over the past six years.

The advent of money market funds introduced many of us to the volatile behavior of interest rates. Up to that time, most saving deposits were in passbook accounts with their virtually constant rates. However, when yields on money market funds rose into the double-digit range in 1979 and then almost to 18 percent by mid-1981, deposits by the billions flowed out of passbook accounts and into the funds. But these exceptionally high rates didn't last; by the end of 1982 they were down to around 8 percent, and by the end of 1993 they were down to about 3 percent. While the trend in interest rates since 1981 has been downward, there have been periods of sharp increases. For example, rates skyrocketed during 1994, and many funds were offering close to 6 percent by year end—almost twice their yields of a year earlier. Interest rates spiked up again to almost 7 percent in late 1999.

Such volatility in rates makes cash management very difficult. For example, when rates are low, there is a temptation to shift your money into higher-yielding accounts, such as two-year certificates of deposit, to "pick up" the higher yield. But doing that could be a mistake if rates then increase.

Key Terms

automated teller machines (ATMs) (p. 126)
bank (p. 117)
bank reconciliation (p. 122)
blank endorsement (p. 120)
cashier's check (p. 125)
cash management strategy (p. 113)
certificate of deposit (CD) (p. 116)
certified check (p. 125)
checking account (p. 113)
electronic funds transfer systems (EFTS) (p. 126)

emergency reserves (p. 114)
money market deposit account (MMDA) (p. 116)
money market mutual fund (p. 116)
NOW (negotiated order of withdrawal) account (p. 115)
overdraft (bounced check) (p. 122)
passbook rate (p. 116)
pocket money (p. 113)

restrictive endorsement (p. 120)
right of survivorship (p. 119)
savings account (p. 115)
special endorsement (p. 120)
stop-payment order (p. 122)
tenants in common (p. 119)
traveler's check (p. 125)
truncation (p. 124)
U.S. Series EE bonds (p. 116)

Reread the chapter-opening vignette.

A breakdown of the Steeles' $16,240 of liquid assets at December 31, 2005 is as follows:

Account	Amount
Coins and currency	$ 240
Regular checking	2,400
Savings account	5,600
60-month CDs	5,000
U.S. Series EE bonds	3,000
Total	$16,240

The Steeles like to shop at flea markets and antique malls where purchases must often be made in cash. So, they typically keep about $1,800 or more in their checking account than would otherwise be necessary. Also, as you may recall from their budget in Chapter 3, there are two months—February and August—that show sizable negative cash flows of $1,673 and $2,158, respectively.

1. Does the total liquid asset amount of $16,240 seem adequate for the Steeles, considering their income?
2. Is the Steeles' reason for keeping an excessive checking account balance sensible? Can you offer a better approach, assuming they will continue their shopping habits?
3. Assume that the deposit rates shown in Table 5.1 exist at December 31, 2005. How would you advise the Steeles to allocate the $16,240 among the various types of deposits? Show the specific amounts you suggest for each type of deposit. If you think the appropriate amount is zero, so indicate.
4. Hopefully, your plan created in your answer to question 3 shows superior returns to the Steeles' existing arrangement. Show the enhanced yield, but also discuss whether or not your plan offers more or less safety and more or less liquidity.

1. Explain the reasons for holding cash. How much pocket money (coins and currency) should most people hold? What advantages does a checking account have over pocket money?
2. List and briefly explain three fundamental deposits and five other popular types of deposits, ranking them according to availability, safety, and liquidity.
3. What is a *federally insured* deposit? Is deposit insurance important to you? Explain.
4. Explain all the advantages of U.S. Series EE bonds. Identify several advantages that are most important to you.
5. A local bank offers a "free" checking account if you maintain a minimum balance of $1,000. Is the account really free? Explain.
6. What institutions are "banks"? What makes an institution a bank, according to the text?
7. Discuss factors that should be considered in choosing a bank.
8. Identify or explain the following items:
   (a) Certificate of deposit
   (b) bank

**Problems and
Review
Questions**

(c) right of survivorship

(d) bounced check

(e) stop-payment order

(f) truncation

(g) certified check, cashier's check, traveler's check

(h) ATM

(i) EFTS

9. Explain three ways to endorse a check; explain which is the riskiest and why.

10. Explain what is meant by interest rate volatility and then discuss the risk of investing in CDs in periods of interest rate volatility.

11. Juan Mendez has just opened a savings account that pays interest at a 4 percent annual stated rate, compounded semiannually. If he puts $1,000 in the account, how much will he get back a year later? After he opened the account, Juan learned that another account was also available that quoted a rate of 4.25 percent, compounded annually; now he isn't sure whether he got the best deal. Did he?

12. Which method of determining interest is the most favorable to consumers?

Case 5.1
Mark's First Checking Account

During his junior year in college, Mark Sutherland opened a checking account at the First National Bank of Westerly, Nebraska. His account does not have a minimum balance requirement, but he does pay a monthly service charge of $3.00. Mark has just received his first monthly bank statement and notices that the end-of-month balance on the statement is quite different from the end-of-month balance he shows in his check record. He has asked your help in explaining this difference and has provided you with the following bank statement and check record.

ACCOUNT:	Mark J. Sutherland		PERIOD:	January 3, 2005
ACCOUNT #:	43967			through
				January 31, 2005

Bank Statement of Activity This Month

Beginning Balance		Deposits and Other Credits to Your Account	Checks and Other Charges to Your Account	Ending Balance
	00.00	300.00	163.80	136.20
03	Deposit	300.00		
05	100	16.50		
07	101	20.00		
12	103	42.96		
14	104	16.87		
17	105	5.00		
17	106	11.43		
19	107	25.00		
24	108	14.04		
28	109	9.00		
31	Service Charge	3.00		

Mark's Check Record

Date	No.	Payee	For	Amount	Balance
1/3		Deposit		300.00	300.00
1/3	100	Harmon Foods	food	16.50	283.50
1/4	101	Cash		20.00	263.50
1/5	102	VOID			
1/7	103	Mel's Sporting Goods	gym shoes	42.96	220.54
1/10	104	Valley Cleaners	dry cleaning	18.67	201.87
1/13	105	Sharon Mackey	birthday present	5.00	196.87
1/14	106	University Bookstore	supplies	11.43	190.44
1/14	107	Cash		25.00	175.44
1/19	108	Harmon Foods	food	14.04	161.40
1/24	109	Mom	repay loan	9.00	152.40
1/25	110	Poindexter's Cafe	Sharon's birthday party	20.00	132.40
1/26		Deposit		50.00	182.40
1/28	111	Exxon	monthly statement	12.96	169.44

Questions

1. Reconcile Mark's account for him, and explain the difference between his balance of $169.44 and the bank's balance of $136.20.
2. How careful was Mark in keeping a record of his checking activities? Discuss.

Marcia and Phil Helm have been married for several years. They have no children, and each has a professional career. Marcia is a trainee for a management position at a large department store, and Phil is an engineer at an electronics firm. Their careers have promising futures, but neither has exceptionally good income protection in the event of a layoff. The Helms have saved around $8,000, and $7,400 of it is in a 3.5 percent savings account at the credit union where Phil works. They have about $600 in a regular checking account (with Mid-City Bank) that doesn't have a service charge or monthly minimum requirement but also doesn't pay any interest. The Helms' combined take-home pay is about $5,000 a month, and Phil thinks they should take the $7,400 out of their savings and invest in the stock market to earn a better return. He points out that, excluding their life insurance policies, they have no other investments. Marcia thinks this plan might be too risky, but she does agree that the 3.5 percent yield is not very good. Recently, at a party, a friend suggested they take out certificates of deposit (CDs) with long maturities, since they were paying around 6 percent. The Helms liked her advice and stopped at Phil's credit union to get more information on the CDs. After talking with the office manager for a while, though, they became even more confused. He didn't favor CDs, although the union had them available. He pointed out that interest rates on the new money market accounts were around 4 percent and didn't require "freezing" your money for a year or more. He also indicated that the union could offer a super NOW account that would allow the Helms to close their current unproductive checking account with Mid-City. This account would give them unlimited checkwriting privileges with no service charges and would pay 3 percent interest; however, it would require a minimum balance of $2,500. If their balance went below the minimum in a month, interest would be only 2 percent.

The Helms left the credit union without taking any action. They have asked you for advice on managing their liquid deposits.

Case 5.2

Choosing Liquid Accounts for Marcia and Philip Helm

Questions

1. Do you feel the Helms' $8,000 liquid balance is adequate? Explain.
2. Explain the relative risks and potential advantages of CDs. Explain under what condition(s) you would recommend them for the Helms.
3. Do you agree with Phil that some of their funds should be invested in the stock market? Explain.
4. Prepare and defend a cash management plan that you think is most appropriate for the Helms.

Working Out on the Web

Exercises to Strengthen Your Use of the Internet

(Internet links for the following exercises can be found at **www.prenhall.com/winger.**)

Exercise 5.1 How Can You Join a Credit Union?

If your employer does not have a credit union, you still may have an opportunity to join one. Consult CUNA & Affiliates and answer the following question.

Q. What are the seven ways to find a credit union?

Exercise 5.2 Where Can You Earn the Highest Returns on Your Cash Deposits?

USA Today helps you find financial institutions offering the highest yields on bank deposits, money market funds, and Treasury securities. Choose "CD and Loan Rates," then "CD, Savings."

Q. Suppose you are helping your parents invest $80,000 over the next six months. Where can you get the highest return with a six-month CD in your state? Find the phone number of the offering institution, and then call to determine if the account has federal insurance.

Exercise 5.3 What Is the Trend in Short-Term Interest Rates?

Interest rates are often volatile over time. **Economagic.com** provides an array of interest rate data. You can use this site to examine the trend in financial data.

Q. What is the current trend in the one-year treasury bill rate (auction average)?

Exercise 5.4 Can I Pay Bills over the Internet—and How Much Does It Cost?

You can use the Internet to pay bills. Many banks, such as Bank One, provide this service.

Q. Click on "Site Map," and then scroll down to "On Line Banking." Then, scroll down to find the monthly fee for the Online Bill Payment feature. At this price, would you find this service useful?

Exercise 5.5 Finding Nominal and Effective Yields

What is the effective yield on an account that compounds more frequently than once a year? Consult Money Advisor, go to "Loans and Savings Calculators," and click on "Nominal and Effective Rates."

Q. Enter: 3425.94 for future value, 1000 for present value, 16 for years, and 1 for compounding frequency. What are the nominal and effective rates? Now enter 3596.13 for future value, 1000 for present value, 16 for years, and 365 for compounding frequency. What are the nominal and effective rates? Compare your answers.

6

Short-Term Credit Management

CONSUMER CREDIT

OBJECTIVES

1. To evaluate reasons for and against using credit and decide whether credit is appropriate for you

2. To be able to take the necessary steps to establish credit and develop a credit history

3. To identify what is meant by sales credit and how it is used

4. To understand how to use credit cards properly and to know your legal rights as a borrower against credit mistakes

5. To identify the important characteristics of installment loans

6. To compare the various sources of credit and to learn what to do if you experience credit problems

Steele FAMILY

"Just when you think everything is going fine, something comes along to upset your day," Sharon thought, as her car was towed away. A call from the mechanic brought more bad news. The transmission was shot and it would cost $3,000 to repair. The transmission was out of warranty; therefore, the Steeles would have to decide how to finance the payment. They thought the car was running fine and had not planned for this expense. Being short of cash and with other major bills, such as property taxes coming due in the next few months, the Steeles are worried about how they are going to pay for the repairs. There is no way they could get by with just one car.

Their credit card carries a substantial credit limit. They could charge the repairs to the credit card and pay it off over the next few months. However, the APR on the card is 16 percent, which seems high to the Steeles. The Steeles are also considering the sale of a few shares of stock, but this would trigger some capital gains taxes. Another option they have is to take out a temporary home equity loan. For a $50 application fee, Arnold's credit union will provide him with a $10,000 line of credit on his home equity. Amounts borrowed on this line of credit will carry an 8 percent APR.

TOPIC **LINKS**

Follow the **Topic Links** in each chapter for your interactive Personal Finance exercise on the Web. Go to: **www.prenhall.com/winger**

When you are faced with unexpected expenses, like the Steeles' situation, credit can be a useful tool for managing your expenses and your household budget. There are, however, unfortunate examples of those who have let credit work against them rather than for them. With some care, credit can become a useful instrument in financial planning. Borrowing to purchase assets, such as a home, which are likely to increase in value, can be a wise investment strategy. On the other hand, borrowing to increase present consumption, or to purchase assets that will decrease in value, places a burden on our future ability to consume. Too much, and it can result in a vicious cycle, with an ever-increasing burden of obligations as we attempt to repay old debts with new loans.

All of us use credit in one form or another. When the paper boy or girl delivers your newspaper each day and stops by only at the end of the month to collect, he or she extends credit to you for the month's bill. The same is true for the local gas and electric company or any other business that does not demand immediate payment for its product or service. Much of this credit—called **service credit**—we take for granted, probably because it is readily available and usually provided without cost. The forms of credit we are more aware of—sales credit and cash credit—are more difficult to obtain and often carry interest and other expenses; these forms of credit are the topics of this chapter.

Service credit: Credit extended by the merchant from whom you have purchased the good or service.

TOPIC **LINKS**

Review a Credit Guide from the Federal Reserve Bank.

ARRANGING AND USING CREDIT

Before applying for credit, you should consider carefully why you want it and what possible disadvantages are connected with its use. It is important to avoid too much debt, as this often leads to serious financial problems, including the possibility of bankruptcy.

Reasons for Using Credit

People sometimes think that the only reason for using credit is a lack of sufficient cash to pay for a purchase. Although this factor can be important, it may not be the only one. Furthermore, your lack of sufficient cash does not necessarily mean that the item's cost exceeds all the cash you have. You may have more than enough to pay for it, but in so doing you would reduce your cash reserves below what you consider a safe level. Furthermore, you would give up the financial return on those reserves. So you may choose not to use cash to maintain adequate liquidity and earnings. You might choose credit over cash for other reasons, too, and these are discussed next.

As a Shopping Convenience

Using credit instead of cash can make shopping much more convenient. You avoid the risks of loss or theft associated with carrying cash, and your end-of-month statement provides a clear and complete record of expenses to help with budgeting and income tax preparation. A credit card also simplifies shopping by phone or returning merchandise. A national credit card, such as Visa or MasterCard, allows you to enjoy many of these advantages throughout the entire United States, even throughout the world.

To Increase Total Consumption Benefits

Borrowing allows people to consume in a given year at a level greater than their incomes would otherwise permit. This consumption in turn can lead to a higher scale of living and greater satisfaction from total consumption over time. This point is illustrated in Figure 6.1, in which we show a four-year period to keep things simple. Assume that you would like to have an even amount of consumption over the four years, as indicated by the line *AB*, and also assume your total consumption for the four years equals your total income; that is, assume zero savings over the four years. If your income is low at the beginning and then rises, as shown by the line *CD*, and if your consumption is tied to your income, it would also be low at the start and higher at the end. However, borrowing allows you to even out

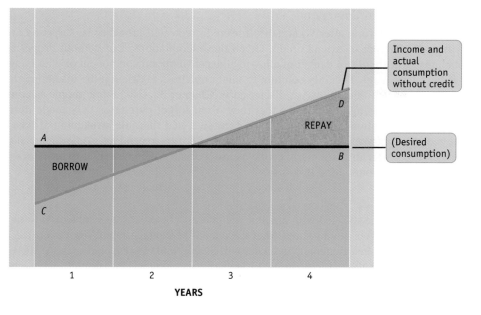

Figure 6.1

Consumption and Credit over Time

consumption and achieve your goal. You borrow in years 1 and 2 and repay the loans in years 3 and 4. The illustration does not consider interest, which would reduce total consumption, since part of your income would be needed to pay it, but the added satisfaction you gain from an even level of consumption might far outweigh the satisfaction you lose by paying interest.

As an Inflation Hedge

When the rate of inflation increases, many people tend to use credit in an effort to soften its impact. We hear such expressions as "paying back your debt with cheap dollars" and "buy now and avoid higher future prices." All too often, these words have been true and symbolic of a high-consumption approach toward life. Credit makes this approach possible. Buying now to avoid higher future prices, however, is often not as simple as it appears, since a high inflation rate is almost always accompanied by a high rate of interest on money borrowed.

As a Source of Emergency Funds

Having easy and quick access to credit gives you funds that could be used in case of emergency if your available liquid assets were not adequate. Some people regard this feature as the single most important advantage of credit, since it allows them to hold a larger portion of their total investments in nonliquid assets, where yields have historically been higher. It would be a mistake, though, to rely upon credit too much or for too long a period of time. Borrowed funds must be repaid, meaning that eventually you must sell nonliquid assets and suffer potential losses if their prices are low when you sell them.

Disadvantages of Using Credit

After considering the reasons for using credit, you should also become aware of some of its disadvantages. The final decision to use credit—and how much to use—rests on a comparison of its advantages and disadvantages. The most important disadvantages are discussed in this section.

A Temptation to Overspend

As mentioned before, after you qualify for credit, you will probably be surprised at how willing lenders are to extend credit. Given these temptations, and without proper credit planning, you are in real danger of allowing the consumption component of your budget to get far out of hand. The only solution to this problem is to develop the discipline to stay within a planned budget, as we discussed in Chapter 3. Also, some people become so accustomed to using credit cards that they often forget purchases they made during a month. Consumption naturally becomes excessive, and the rude awakening arrives with the monthly statement. To guard against this form of overspending, some financial planners urge you to maintain a credit card expense journal, which is similar to the check stubs in a checking account. (See Box 6.1)

Credit Costs

The biggest cost associated with credit is the interest you pay, if your loan carries interest. At a minimum, you should know what the annual percentage rate (APR) is on the loan, how interest will be calculated, and what will be the total interest paid over the life of the loan. We'll cover those topics in detail later in this chapter. Occasionally there may be expenses directly connected with credit, such as an annual maintenance fee on your account.

    Indirect costs can be important, too. If your loan involves a credit card, you must be concerned about its safety: If your credit card is lost or stolen, it can be used by someone else, with you paying the bill. The **Truth in Lending Act (TILA)** limits your loss to $50 per account, but this amount could be substantial if you lost five or six cards. You will also have the aggravation of notifying creditors and taking other steps to be protected under the law. Another indirect cost is the time it takes to review creditors' monthly statements for accuracy and then to write and mail your checks. Many people are not concerned with these indirect costs, but they may be important to you.

Less Flexibility with Future Budgets

The more we spend in one period, deferring payment until a later one, the less flexible is our future budget. In effect, we increase the fixed-expense component of the future budget. By itself, this practice isn't necessarily bad; but it sometimes happens that items purchased with credit fail to satisfy us as we thought they might at the time we purchased them. Holiday gifts usually come to mind as examples here. In these cases, we are left with the bills to pay, along with the temptation to buy new items to satisfy current consumption demands. An overreliance on credit can strain your future budget.

How to Get Credit

Having decided you want credit, the next step is to apply for it. You can apply in person or by mail, but in either case, you probably will be asked to complete an application form that asks for personal and financial information. It is important to know what a lender looks for in a credit applicant and what steps you can take to begin a credit record. If you are a woman, you may face special problems in this effort.

What the Lender Looks For

Put simply, the only concern of the lender is your ability to repay the loan along with any related expenses. To assess this ability, lenders often look at the three Cs of credit—your *character, capital,* and *capacity.* Character has to do with how you have handled yourself in previous financial dealings. Do you have checking and savings accounts and use them regularly? Have you used credit properly by repaying your debts on a timely basis? These

Truth in Lending Act (TILA): Sets rules regulating credit market. It also sets limits on your credit-related financial responsibilities.

TOPIC **LINKS**

A summary of consumer credit laws.

BOX 6.1

A Credit Card Register

If you update the register each time you write a check, your check register should indicate just how much you have in your checking account. Unless you or the bank makes a mistake, you are not likely to be surprised by your monthly checking account statement. The same people, however, who keep excellent check registers are often surprised by the outstanding balance on their charge account, because they fail to keep similar information on their credit card use.

The first sign of credit card misuse is an expectedly large credit card balance. If you use "plastic money" often, you are likely to forget just how much you have charged. You might keep the receipts in your wallet with the good intention of periodically totaling your charges, but somehow that gets put off until the credit card statement arrives. But then it is too late: You have already overspent your budget.

You may have heard of food diets in which you are required to keep a running list of everything you eat. If each little snack is added to the list, you may eventually come to the realization that all those little snacks add up to one big eating spree. The same should hold true for a credit diet. If you maintain a running tally of your credit charges, you must inevitably confront your own excesses and reduce your overspending. You can do this by creating a credit register that you update just as you would a check register.

Credit card companies do not supply a credit card register. However, you can create your own out of an unused check register by using the accompanying illustration as a guide. Each time you charge a purchase, receive a credit for returned merchandise, or make a monthly payment, enter the transaction in the register and update the outstanding balance. If you get in the habit of making entries with each use of the account, you will eliminate the unexpected by knowing just how much you owe at any time.

Date	Description	Credit for Returns and Payments	Amount of Charge	Balance $74.20
1/2/02	Marshalls—sweater		$56.19	130.39
1/6/02	Sunoco—gas and milk		18.75	149.24
1/8/02	Kmart—return of defective garden hose	$11.08		138.16
1/9/02	Lotus Blossom—dinner with the Williams		48.96	187.12

are some of the questions lenders frequently ask to judge creditworthiness. Capital refers to your financial strength, usually measured by net worth, a topic discussed in Chapter 3. Capacity means your ability to repay debt out of your future income. Here the lender looks not only at the amount of such income but also at future commitments that might restrict it.

Lenders may apply rules of thumb before granting a loan. For example, only consumers with monthly mortgage loan payments less than 25 percent of income and total loan payments less than 30 percent of income may be deemed creditworthy. Others may use a more specific evaluation technique to weigh important factors in the credit-granting decision and arrive at a numeric guide as to whether credit should be made available to you (see Box 6.2 on credit scoring). The scoring system will be based on the lender's bad-loan experience. Factors that are likely to weigh in your favor include home ownership, residential and job stability, education, and income.

Regardless of the system lenders use to evaluate your credit application, the **Equal Credit Opportunity Act (ECOA)** insists that fairness be applied. You cannot be discriminated against because of race, color, age, sex, marital status, or related other factors. This does not mean that someone is automatically given a loan because of one or several of these characteristics; what it does mean is that lenders may not *deny* him or her a loan because of any one of them. ECOA also ensures that lenders do not use such factors in credit-scoring formulas.

TOPIC **LINKS**

Know your credit rights.

Equal Credit Opportunity Act (ECOA): Ensures that you cannot be denied credit because of your race, color, age, sex, or marital status.

Beginning a Credit Record

Being aware of the factors lenders look at to assess your creditworthiness helps you improve your score and your chances of receiving credit. Here are some practical things you can do.

- Open both checking and savings accounts (if you don't already have them) and, of course, use them properly. This means no "bounced checks" and a history of regular deposits to the savings account.
- Open a retail charge account with a local store or major oil company. These accounts are often easier to obtain than other loans. Then use the card and make sure you are prompt in remitting the monthly balance due. Not all creditors report to credit bureaus. Make sure that yours do. In this way you will begin to build a credit history.
- Qualify for a small installment loan. Repaying such a loan promptly each month helps establish a good credit record.
- If you have recently moved, write for a summary of any credit record kept by a credit bureau in your former town. It will be helpful in establishing credit in your new town.
- Have a telephone installed; this item often appears as a factor in credit-rating formulas.
- Don't overly apply for credit. Too many credit applications can hurt your credit worthiness.

Special Concerns for Married Women

You may face special problems in getting credit if you are a woman, so you should take additional steps:

- Always use your own name when applying for credit. If you are Nancy Brown, who marries Edward Hall, you should use *Nancy Hall* or *Nancy Brown Hall* as your legal name, if you choose to use your husband's last name. You are not required to do so, however, and you can continue to use your maiden name. But definitely do not use a social title such as *Mrs. Edward Hall*. Not only could other women have this name, but also any credit information under it goes to your husband's credit file and does not benefit you individually.
- Make sure all credit information is reported under your name as well as your husband's. With a **joint credit account** both spouses are responsible for the debt. Obviously, if you are separated or divorced, you should immediately cancel all joint accounts. On an **individual credit account** only you are responsible for the debt, and the account will appear only on your credit report.
- If you are recently married, inform creditors accordingly and indicate that you wish to maintain your own credit record. For individuals who live in a community-property state, a creditor may consider your spouse's credit history. Nevertheless, you should make certain that the local bureau has a separate file in your name.

The Role of the Credit Bureau

Once you begin using credit, you will establish a credit history. It contains a record of credit previously granted you and how responsible you were in handling that credit. Many lenders do not maintain their own credit-investigating facilities but instead use such services provided by major credit bureaus. In all likelihood, one or more of these bureaus will keep your credit history.

The United States has approximately 2,000 credit bureaus that function as clearinghouses for information about borrowers' credit histories. These bureaus are connected by computer, so if you wish to make a credit card purchase in California, the seller can check your credit history even if you have never used your card outside of New York. The three major national credit bureaus are Equifax (www.equifax.com), Experian (www.experian.com), and Transunion (www.transunion.com).

TOPIC **LINKS**
Credit and divorce

Joint credit account: Both spouses are responsible for the debt.

Individual credit account: Only you are responsible for the debt.

The largest of these firms, Experian, maintains over 90 million credit files. It is sometimes believed that the credit bureau decides whether you receive credit, but this is not true. A credit bureau only stores information about how you have handled credit in the past and any legal actions that might impair your financial strength in the future. Lenders may buy a credit report from the credit bureau. They use this report in their decision to extend you credit, although it is not the only factor they consider, and a good credit record doesn't automatically guarantee that credit will be given.

The credit report includes the credit accounts that you have with banks, retailers, credit card issuers, and other lenders. Information on each account states your credit limit, the loan amount, the account balance, and your payment history. Public record information such as bankruptcies, tax liens, and monetary judgments are also included. Bankruptcy information may remain on your credit report for up to 10 years, and other negative information may remain up to seven years. The report also indicates if anyone besides you is responsible for paying the account. Finally, it lists all credit inquiries over the last year, and all employment related inquiries over the past two years.

If You Are Denied Credit

According to the Federal Reserve Bank of Chicago, the following are the most common reasons for being denied credit.

- Too little time in current job or at current residence
- Too much outstanding debt
- Unreasonable purpose for requesting credit
- Cosigner cannot take on additional debt liability
- Errors on applicant's credit record
- Strictness of creditor's standards

Under the **Fair Credit Reporting Act**, you are entitled to one free report each year from each of the three major credit bureaus. They must each maintain a toll-free number for requesting your free report. In addition, they are required to notify you in writing the first time they add negative information to your file.

If you are denied credit, insurance, or employment because of your credit report, the creditor must give you the name, address, and telephone number of the credit-reporting agency that supplied the report. Review your credit report and insist that any incorrect information be removed from the file. If the facts are correct, but you feel they do not fairly present your side of the story, you may submit your own statement to be included in the file. You can also insist that all those who have requested your file within the last six months be notified of any unsubstantiated or incorrect entry.

You can review your credit report even if you are just curious about it. The bureaus in your area can be found in the Yellow Pages under such headings as "Credit" or "Credit Reporting Agencies." They can also be found on the Internet.

A **secured credit card** can be helpful if you are trying to reestablish a good credit record. The card is secured by funds that you have on deposit at the bank, assuring the bank repayment for your purchases. Consequently, banks that might not consider issuing you a typical credit card will have no problem granting you a secured credit card.

SALES CREDIT

Sales credit arises from the sale of merchandise or services. Traditionally, most of this credit was offered by merchants, such as department stores, major oil companies, automobile dealerships, and furniture and appliance dealers, in an effort to expand their sales.

TOPIC **LINKS**
Credit reporting agencies and a sample credit report

Fair Credit Reporting Act (FCRA): Sets down your rights to a fair and accurate credit report and establishes procedures for correcting an inaccurate report.

TOPIC **LINKS**
Obtain a credit report.

Secured credit card: A credit card secured by funds held at the bank issuing the card. Useful for those who are establishing credit or who are trying to overcome a poor credit history.

Sales credit: Any credit arising from the sale of merchandise or services.

Finance News

BOX 6.2

Scores Revealed

For several years, you have been able to get a copy of your credit report. Until recently, however, credit reporting agencies were prohibited from making credit scores available to consumers. Your credit score is a single number that summarizes and grades your creditworthiness. The most commonly accepted summary grade is your FICO score. It is named after Fair, Isaac & Co., the originator of the scoring methodology.

For a small fee you now can obtain both your credit report and your FICO score from a credit reporting agency. Your credit score is a three-digit number from 300 to 900, which may determine whether you get that car loan or home mortgage. It may even influence whether you get that next job. If you are not denied credit, it may influence how much you will pay in loan origination fees and on interest rates. Potential borrowers with scores above 700 may get preferential treatment, whereas those with scores of less than 600 are likely to be placed in the high-risk category.

The credit agencies will not tell you how they determine the score.

However, it is generally understood that your credit score will be based upon the following factors. Fair, Isaac reports that it weights each of these factors by the indicated percentage.

- A history of on-time payments (35%) and the length of your credit history (15%)
  The longer your credit history and the longer your track record of on-time payments, the higher your score
- Your amount owed (30%)
  The smaller your use of credit relative to your credit limit, the higher your score.
- New credit (10%)
  The fewer the number of inquiries, the higher your score.
- Types of credit in use (10%)
  The larger the variety of debt (auto loans, mortgages, credit cards) you have successfully managed, the higher your score.

You can obtain your credit score at any time for a small fee. You must have free access to your credit score when you apply for a home mortgage and if you are denied credit. Having a good credit score is really no secret. You can estimate your own score at www.myfico.com. Paying your bills promptly and avoiding excessive debt is the basic recipe for good credit

Ranges of credit worthiness

Range	Credit Worthiness
720–850	Very Good to Excellent • Best interest rates on loans. • Your mailbox will be overflowing with credit offers. • Average score is about 720.
650–720	Good • Likely to get credit, but not the best interest rate.
630–650	Fair • May get credit but your creditor will take a second look at your ability to handle the risk.
580–630	Poor • Missed payments or lack of credit record. • May get credit but only at higher rate.
350–580	Bad • Likely to be denied credit by all but a high cost lender. • Your mailbox will be overflowing with offers from credit repair services.

TOPIC **LINKS**

Score Power

While they are still important in supplying such credit, the major bank credit cards—Visa and MasterCard—are the primary sources. Sales credit is often symbolized by a credit card that is used to make service or merchandise transactions, although many of these cards can now be used for financial transactions as well, such as making a cash loan.

Kinds of Accounts

You can obtain sales credit in three different forms: (1) as a regular (or 30-day) account; (2) as a revolving account; and (3) as a retail installment account. The first two are called open-end credit accounts; they are discussed next. The third is referred to as a closed-end account, and it is discussed in a later section. When you establish an **open-end account,** you sign an agreement that covers all credit purchases and cash advances made in the account. This one agreement is binding as long as the account is open. In contrast, a **closed-end account** requires a separate retail installment contract for each purchase; consequently, these are usually for large amounts and longer periods of time.

Regular Charge Account

People who use a **regular charge account** are typically those who view credit as a shopping convenience. Your purchase transactions for a month are accumulated and sent to you at the end of the month. You agree with the terms of this account by paying the total amount billed within 10 to 30 days after the billing date, and generally you avoid interest by so doing. Interest can be charged for late payment, however.

Revolving Account

A **revolving credit account** allows you to make purchases up to a credit limit that is usually determined by your credit record and net worth. If you then pay the full amount due at the end of the month, you are using the account as a regular charge account. You must at least make a partial payment. The minimum amount depends on how much credit you have used and the interest charged on the account. As the balance is reduced by payments, you may again make purchases up to the limit, so the account may never actually be paid off. Interest is charged each month on the unpaid balance.

Your monthly payments are presumed to cover interest first. If the payment exceeds the interest charge, the excess reduces the principal that you owe. The creditor must inform you each month as to the interest rate applicable that month, the applicable rate expressed as an annual percentage rate (APR), and the method used to determine the balance on which the monthly rate is applied. A revolving credit agreement will also include information about:

- the time available to pay your balance due without being charged interest
- the minimum amount you must pay each month, and what happens if you don't pay it
- permission you give the creditor to investigate your credit history

You will receive a monthly statement for each credit account you have. An example of such a statement is shown in Figure 6.2, where the period covered is the month of July. This statement is patterned after one used by a major bank card but it is typical of most monthly statements. Notice that the borrower made three purchases during the month and one payment; there were no credits for returned merchandise. The lender charged interest of $4.32 for the month, based on the monthly rate of 1.65 percent (which is an annual percentage rate of 19.80 percent). The sum of this interest and purchases was $92.61 ($4.32 + $88.29). Subtracting the $20.00 payment made during the month gives the net change during the month of $72.61; this amount is then added to the $215.00 beginning-of-the-month balance to arrive at the end-of-the-month balance of $287.61. This amount or the minimum monthly payment of $20.00 must be paid by August 15. Also notice that the borrower has a credit limit (the most that can be borrowed) of $2,000, and there is $1,712.39 ($2,000 − $287.61) of credit available at the beginning of August. You may have outstanding charges up to this amount. Charges in excess of the credit limit may result in a penalty.

Open-end account: A credit agreement that establishes an ongoing line of credit covering future purchases. One agreement may cover a multitude of purchases.

Closed-end account: A credit agreement covering a single purchase with a set repayment schedule.

Regular charge account: A credit account with a merchant in which complete payment at the end of the billing cycle usually avoids all interest charges.

Revolving credit account: An open-end account with an established line of credit and rules for minimum monthly payments and interest charges on the unpaid balance.

Reference Number	Date	Description of Transaction		Amounts (Credits indicated by−)
89453987	7/05	Walmart 7549	Centerville, OH	$ 38.15
42874908	7/10	Payment		20.00−
69426933	7/12	Days Inns 033M	McDonough, GA	32.50
75538521	7/20	Mendelsons Retail	Dayton, OH	17.64

FINANCE CHARGE	Computed on an Average Daily Balance of	MONTHLY PERIODIC RATE	ANNUAL PERCENTAGE RATE	Payment Due Date	Statement Closing Date
$ 4.32	$ 261.83	1.65%	19.80%	8/15/XX	7/31/XX

Previous Balance	Payments	Credit Transactions	Debit Transactions	FINANCE CHARGE	New Balance
$ 215.00	$ 20.00	$ -0-	$ 88.29	$ 4.32	$ 287.61

Credit Limit: $2,000
Available Credit: $1,712.39
Minimum Monthly Payment: $20.00

Figure 6.2

A Monthly Statement for a Revolving Credit Account

We mentioned earlier that it might be the borrower's intent to use a revolving account as a somewhat permanent form of credit. Before doing that, a person should consider other sources of credit that might be less expensive. In the preceding example, the APR was a rather high 19.80 percent. Generally, revolving credit is expensive credit if it is used on a permanent basis.

Determining Interest on a Revolving Account

Interest on a revolving charge account is determined by applying the monthly rate to the balance in the account. It seems simple enough, except that there are various ways of determining what this balance is. The three most commonly used methods are the previous balance method, the adjusted balance method, and the average daily balance method. The method used by the card issuer should be prominently displayed on the contract. Using data from Figure 6.2, each of these methods is illustrated in Table 6.1.

The **previous balance method** is the simplest of the three. The rate is applied to the balance at the end of the previous month. As you see in Table 6.1, this means you multiply the rate, 1.65 percent, by the previous balance, $215.00, to arrive at the month's interest of $3.55. This method works to your advantage if you have considerable charges in the current month.

The **adjusted balance method** is more favorable than the previous balance method. The adjusted balance is equal to the previous balance less any payments or returns you made during the current billing cycle. Thus, in Table 6.1, the adjusted balance is simply $215 less the credit payment of $20. Applying 1.65 percent to $195 determines a finance charge of $3.22. This is the most advantageous method for cardholders.

There are two variations to the **average daily balance method;** one includes purchases for the current billing cycle, the other does not. The *average daily balance method including current purchases* gives the most correct balance for applying interest. In this procedure, you weight a balance for the number of days it is outstanding. In the example, the beginning balance of $215.00 was applicable only for the four days, 7/1 through 7/4. Thereafter, other balances were appropriate for varying numbers of days. By weighting each balance for the number of outstanding days, you arrive at the total weighted balance

Previous balance method: The interest rate is applied to the outstanding balance at the end of the previous billing period.

Adjusted balance method: The interest rate is applied to the previous balance less any payments or returns made during the current billing cycle.

Average daily balance method: The interest rate is applied to the average outstanding balance over the billing cycle.

Table 6.1

I. Previous Balance Method

Interest is charged on the previous balance

$$1.65\% \times \$215.00 = \boxed{\$3.55}$$

II. Adjusted Balance Method

Interest is charged on the previous balance less any current credits

$$1.65\% \times (\$215.00 - \$20.00) = \boxed{\$3.22}$$

III(a). Average Daily Balance Method (including current purchases)

Interest is charged on the updated balance considering the day a charge or credit takes place

Period	(a) No. of Days	(b) Balance	(c) (a) × (b)
7/1–7/4	4	$215.00 + $ -0- = 215.00	$ 860.00
7/5–7/9	5	215.00 + 38.15 = 253.15	1,265.75
7/10–7/11	2	253.15 − 20.00 = 233.15	466.30
7/12–7/19	8	233.15 + 32.50 = 265.65	2,125.20
7/20–7/31	12	265.65 + 17.64 = 283.29	3,399.48
	31		$8,116.73

$$\text{Average daily balance} = \frac{\$8,116.73}{31} = \$261.83$$

$$1.65\% \times \$261.83 = \boxed{\$4.32}$$

III(b). Average Daily Balance Method (excluding current purchases)

Interest is charged on the updated balance considering the day a current payment is made but ignoring current purchases or returns

Period	(a) No. of Days	(b) Balance	(c) (a) × (b)
7/1–7/9	10	$215	$2,150.00
7/10–7/31	21	$215.00 − $20.00 = 195	4,095.00
			$6,245.00

$$\text{Average daily balance} = \$6,245.00/31 = \$201.45$$

$$1.65\% \times \$201.45 = \boxed{\$3.32}$$

of $8,116.73, which is then divided by 31 to arrive at the $261.83 average daily balance. This figure multiplied by 1.65 percent gives the interest amount of $4.32.

The other variation is the *average daily balance method excluding current purchases.* Again an average daily balance is computed. However, in this variation of the average daily balance method, the finance charge is less because new purchases are not included in the daily balance. As indicated in Table 6.1, the finance charge is only $3.32 when new purchases are excluded.

Lenders traditionally provide a **grace period** of 25 days during which interest on the loan balance is forgiven. This usually applies only when you have fully paid off the previous month's balance. The grace period normally lasts between the statement closing date and the payment due date. Recently, some lenders have eliminated the grace period; others have offered their customers a choice between credit accounts with or without a grace period. Finance charges on the account with the grace period are based on a higher annual percentage rate, making it less desirable for someone who does not regularly pay off the entire amount due.

Grace period: Period in which interest charges are forgiven on the condition that the outstanding balance is fully repaid.

Two-cycle average daily balance method: Collects interest over two billing periods when an unpaid balance is begun.

Some major card issuers are now applying a **two-cycle average daily balance method.** This eliminates any grace period applied in a previous month when you fail to completely pay off the balance in the present month. Thus, the creditor can in effect go back two months to collect interest on unpaid balances. If you pay your balance in full each month or you carry a balance from month to month, your interest payments are the same as under the one-cycle average balance method. Those hit the hardest with increased interest charges are consumers who pay off their balances in alternating months.

For each revolving account you have, you should determine how the monthly balance is calculated and verify the monthly statement to make sure it is correct. Of course, you aren't likely to go through all the calculations for the average daily balance method, and it may not be necessary that you do. A quick glance between this month and last month should indicate if the number is approximately correct. A last piece of fairly obvious advice is to use those accounts that determine the monthly balance to your best advantage.

Credit Cards

"Plastic money" is indeed an appropriate name for what we use to purchase many goods and services. About one-half of all families hold at least one retail store card. Most retail store cards are charge cards issued in conjunction with a regular charge account. An even larger percentage of all households have at least one bank credit card. The major names of issuers include Visa, MasterCard, and Discover.

Credit Card Issuers

Bank credit cards: Credit cards, such as MasterCard and Visa, that are issued by banks.

The **bank credit cards**—MasterCard and Visa—are by far the largest suppliers of consumer installment credit. When you use one of these cards, you are actually borrowing from a bank, perhaps a local one, or you may have a card issued by one of the major banks, such as Bank One. We illustrated and discussed a typical credit card account earlier, which showed how the card is used to make purchases. But bank cards can also be used to make financial transactions. For example, you may be able to get cash advances from money machines with your card, and in some places you can use it to buy securities, such as stocks or bonds. A checklist, like that in Figure 6.3, can be used to compare the costs and benefits of various cards.

TOPIC **LINKS**

Locate credit card companies.

Specialty Cards

Affinity card: Returns a small percentage of sales to the sponsoring organization.

A bank card that carries the name of a sponsoring organization is known in the industry as an **affinity card.** The card's sponsor receives a small percentage of card sales. Part of this may be returned to cardholders in the form of frequent flyer miles, discounts on purchases, or a cash rebate. Some sponsors, such as environmental groups and alumni organizations, use the revenues from affinity cards to support socially desirable causes. Visa estimates that 22 percent of their cardholders have these cards.

Travel and entertainment (T&E) cards: Credit cards issued by finance companies catering to businesspeople and travelers.

Traditionally, **travel and entertainment (T&E) cards,** such as American Express and Diners Club have catered to travelers—usually businesspeople—who frequently buy goods and services away from their hometowns. The cards are used to pay for hotel and motel accommodations, to buy airline tickets, and to pay restaurant bills. However, the T&E cards are expanding their services. The usual annual fee of $50 or more for a T&E card is much higher than that of a bank credit card, and it is questionable whether it is worth it, since bank credit cards are so universally acceptable.

Figure 6.3

Cost Comparison Checklist

Charge	Description
Annual membership fee[a]	Typically about $25 for bank credit cards and higher for travel and entertainment cards.
Annual percentage fee[a]	One-twelfth of the annual rate is applied to the outstanding balance to determine the monthly finance charge. If an introductory rate is offered, the regular rate should also be disclosed. The APR on cash advances is likely to be higher than the APR on credit purchases. Some issuers also practice *tier pricing*, whereby the APR is higher on balances above a certain amount.
Variable rate information[a]	If the interest rate is variable, the disclosure will indicate the index or formula and the spread or margin that determine the APR. If there is a cap or a floor on the APR, this should also be indicated.
Grace period[a]	The free period within which the credit extended must be repaid to avoid finance charges will be indicated. If the card issuer does not provide a grace period, that fact must be disclosed.
Balance computation method[a]	Method used to compute the balance upon which finance charges will be based.
Minimum finance fee[a]	Minimum fee applied whenever there is a finance charge.
Transaction fee[a]	Fee applied to each purchase.
Cash advance fee[b]	Fee imposed for an extension of credit in the form of cash.
Late payment fee[b]	Fee imposed for late payment of minimum monthly payment.
Over-the-limit fee	Fee imposed for exceeding the credit limit.
Replacement fee[c]	Fee for replacing a lost credit card.
Return check charge	Fee for a check returned because of insufficient funds.
Copy charge[c]	Fee for receiving a photostatic copy of receipt on sales or cash advance.
Fees for optional services[c]	May include such things as credit life insurance, disability insurance, unemployment insurance, and credit card registration. See the benefits section for a description of some of these benefits.

Continued

We mentioned earlier that many retail establishments issue their own credit cards, known as private-label cards. These stores generally prefer that you use their card rather than a bank card (many will not accept bank cards), since consumer credit is often a profitable part of their business.

Selecting a Credit Card

Many people who are good credit risks find their mailboxes overflowing with solicitations from credit card companies. Their major problem is not in getting credit but rather in

Figure 6.3

Continued

Benefit Comparison Checklist	
Benefit	**Description**
Credit limit	If your credit balance exceeds this amount, you will be charged an over-the-limit fee.
Credit life insurance	Pays off the outstanding balance up to some set limit at the time of death.
Total disability insurance	May pay off your account balance or make minimum monthly payments if you become totally disabled.
Unemployment insurance	If you are involuntarily terminated from your employment, this may cover your minimum monthly payment during the period of unemployment.
Rebates and discounts	Some cards offer a small percentage rebate on all credit purchases. Others offer discounts on special purchases such as airline tickets.
Purchase price protection	If you charge something and then see the same product advertised elsewhere at a lower price within a specified time period, your account will be credited with the difference. This may be difficult to document and inconvenient to collect. In addition, there may be a limit on refunds.
Accident insurance	Small amounts of coverage for accidental injuries.
Rental car collision insurance	This may already be provided under your personal auto insurance.
Merchandise warranty protection	The period of warranty may be extended by the card issuer.
Credit card registry	Service that arranges for cancellation and replacement of credit cards in the event of loss.
Merchandise loss protection	Replaces the cost of lost or stolen items that were charged up to a specified limit. Insurance lasts for only a specified period after purchase and may be secondary to protection under other insurance policies.

[a]Information must be disclosed in a prominent table.
[b]Information must be disclosed somewhere on the application form.
[c]Information need be provided only upon request.

selecting the best credit from among the numerous offers. In order to make comparison shopping easier and also to eliminate potentially misleading sales practices, Congress empowered the Federal Reserve Board to set down rules governing the information that credit card companies must furnish potential consumers. The rules enacted under this law have provided for detailed and uniform disclosure of rates and other cost information in applications and solicitations to open credit and charge card accounts.

The Federal Reserve Board periodically collects and publishes information on credit card plans offered by major financial institutions. The Bankrate Monitor also provides a survey of recent rates. The cost of credit can vary significantly among issuers and over time in response to changing conditions in credit markets. In addition to interest charges, the cost of using a credit card will include maintenance fees and other specialized charges. Many of these costs are described in the credit card comparison checklist Figure 6.3. Information on most of the items listed is typically disclosed prominently on the application form.

TOPIC **LINKS**

Review the FRB credit card survey and the Bankrate Monitor.

Do not ignore the fees listed in Figure 6.3. An increasing share of the revenues from credit cards comes from these items. Cardweb.com reports that, as a percent of revenue, these fees rose from only 17.3 percent in 1994 to 33.4 percent in 2003. This increase has placed an increasing burden on those who do not use credit wisely

The benefit section of the checklist in Figure 6.3 indicates the many types of services that card issuers have provided in an effort to attract customers. The value of many of these items is rather small. You would be wise to select from among offers of credit cards on the basis of an assessment of the relative costs itemized in the cost section of the checklist.

The best credit card for you will depend on your credit practices. If you intend to pay off the entire balance each month, a card with a grace period and a low annual membership fee would be favored. Given the high cost of finance charges on credit cards and the relatively lower cost of credit from other sources, this is probably the best strategy for most people. However, if you do intend to incur finance charges on your credit card, then you may be better off by paying a higher annual membership fee in exchange for a lower APR. For example, if your average outstanding balance is $1,000, then a 1 percent reduction in the APR would save you $10 a year. Therefore, if the annual membership fee on this card is no more than $10 above the fee on a card with a higher APR, it could be your best choice.

Credit Cards for College Students

Given the financial characteristics of the typical college student, you would probably think that he or she would find it difficult to get credit. Many college students have no employment and a limited credit history. To overcome these seeming obstacles, some issuers use a special credit scoring formula for college students that minimizes these factors. In fact, the U.S. General Accounting Office reports that college students represent a prime market for credit card issuers. Both mail solicitations and on-campus presentations are commonplace. College students are viewed as good and responsible customers who will continue to have a lifelong need for credit. The issuers anticipate retaining these students after graduation when these accounts will become more valuable. Some universities have entered into financial arrangements with card issuers to provide an affinity card that bears the logo of the university in return for a payment.

Students who run up excessive debt or make late payments can impair their credit card rating in the future. However, the majority of these students seem to pay off their balance in full. Only about 5 percent of college students have an outstanding balance of $3,000 or more. Unfortunately, those students with large outstanding balances will have their financial problems compounded by interest charges. At a minimum monthly payment of $60, a $3,000 balance could take 100 months to pay off and generate about $3,000 in additional interest payments at a 19 percent APR (see Figure 6.4).

TOPIC **LINKS**

Download a payback spreadsheet.

Protection Against Credit Card Fraud

We mentioned previously that the Truth in Lending Act limits your losses from unauthorized uses of your credit cards to $50 per card; but, if your purse or wallet is stolen and if it contains several cards, your loss can be more than trivial. So it pays to be careful with them, and the following are suggestions that can help in this effort.

- Immediately sign a new credit card when it arrives. Record card numbers, their expiration dates, and the phone number and address for each card company and keep this information in a safe place.

Monthly Payment	Number of Months	Total Interest
$ 60	100	$ 2,991
75	64	1,790
100	42	1,102
125	31	804

Minimum payments are typically 2 percent of the outstanding balance or $10, whichever is higher.

- Don't leave blank lines above the total on a credit card slip. Draw a line through any blank line above the total. Make sure the sales check you sign is completed correctly, including the addition of separate line items; then save your receipts, compare them with your monthly bill, and report any discrepancy immediately.
- Watch clerks carefully while they are using your card to make sure they do not run impressions on other sales checks. Of course, ask the clerk to return your card immediately after it has been used.
- Destroy old bills and receipts. Also destroy all credit cards you do not use. Be extra careful in giving your number over the phone unless you initiate the phone call and want to charge the purchase. Any calls purporting to be "conducting a credit card survey" should be completely avoided.
- Don't provide your credit card number, bank account information, or Social Security number over the phone or on the Internet, unless you know you are dealing with an honorable business.
- Don't pay for credit preapproval on a loan. It is against the law for anyone to ask you to pay before your loan or credit is approved.
- Don't lend your credit card to anyone. Your credit history is too important.
- If your cards are stolen or lost, contact each issuer immediately. This means keeping a list of addresses and phone numbers in a convenient and safe place; but remember that accidents such as these often happen on vacation, and your list will not do much good if it is at home. Although getting ready for a vacation is hectic enough, try to remember the list and don't store it in your wallet or purse, because that is what is usually lost or stolen.

Correcting Credit Card Mistakes

Despite the care taken by you or the credit issuer, mistakes do occur. It is important for your sake that they are corrected immediately, not only to save money if it's an overcharge but also to protect your good credit rating. Both the Truth in Lending Act and the Fair Credit Billing Act give you considerable legal protection against mistakes on open-end accounts. Since it is very important that you understand what your protections are, some of them—billing errors, defective goods, prompt payment, and credit blocking—are discussed next. This material is adapted from the *Consumer Handbook to Credit Protection Laws*, published by the Board of Directors of the Federal Reserve System.

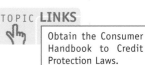

TOPIC **LINKS**

Obtain the Consumer Handbook to Credit Protection Laws.

Correcting Billing Errors

If your credit card statement contains a billing error, notify the creditor *in writing* as soon as you discover it. You may want to call the card company to correct the problem, but phoning is not sufficient to cover your legal safeguards. Compose a letter similar to that in Figure 6.5 and send it by certified mail with return receipt requested.

Pay all parts of the bill that are not in dispute. The creditor should acknowledge your letter within a month or two, but in no case more than 90 days. If the creditor made a mistake, you do not have to pay finance charges on the disputed amount. If the creditor disagrees with you, the creditor must explain the basis for the disagreement.

A creditor may not threaten your credit rating while you're resolving a billing dispute. Once you have written about a possible error, a creditor is prohibited from giving out information to other creditors or credit bureaus that would damage your credit reputation. And, until your complaint is answered, the creditor also may not take any action to collect the disputed amount.

After the creditor has explained the bill, you may be reported as delinquent on the amount in dispute, and the creditor may take action to collect if you do not pay in the time allowed. Even so, you can still disagree in writing. Then the creditor must report that you have challenged your bill and give you the name and address of each person who has received information about your account. When the matter is settled, the creditor must report the outcome to each person who has received information. Remember that you may also place your own side of the story in your credit record.

Defective Goods or Services

Under most circumstances you may withhold the remaining payment on any damaged or shoddy goods or poor-quality services purchased with a credit card. However, you must first make a real attempt to solve the problem with the merchant. Your withholding of payments results in what is called a **chargeback,** whereby the card issuer charges the disputed amount back to the merchant. At this point the merchant can dispute the chargeback. The card issuer must then decide whether to reissue the bill to you or to proceed against the merchant for repayment.

Chargeback: A disputed amount charged back to the merchant by the credit card company.

Date

Your Name
Your Address
Your City, State, Zip Code

Complaint Department
Name of Credit Reporting Agency
Address
City, State, Zip Code

Dear Sir or Madam:

I am writing to dispute the following information in my file. The items I dispute also are encircled on the attached copy of the report I received. This item (identify item(s) disputed by name of source, such as creditors or tax court, and identify type of item, such as credit account, judgment, etc.) is (inaccurate or incomplete) because (describe what is inaccurate or incomplete and why). I am requesting that the item be deleted (or request another specific change) to correct this information. Enclosed are copies of (use this sentence if applicable and describe any enclosed documentation, such as payment records, court documents) supporting my position. Please reinvestigate this (these) matter(s) and (delete or correct) the disputed item(s) as soon as possible.

Sincerely,
Your name

Enclosures: (List what you are enclosing)

Figure 6.5

Sample Dispute Letter

Source: Federal Trade Commission, "Building a Better Credit Record."

Prompt Credit Payments and Refunds for Credit Balances

To avoid finance charges on your account within a certain period of time, it is obviously important that you get your bills, and get credit for paying them promptly. If your account is one on which no finance charge is added before a certain due date, then creditors must mail their statements at least 14 days before payment is due.

Creditors must credit payments on the day they arrive, as long as you pay according to payment instructions. Stores often give you a credit on your bill instead of cash when you return a purchase. If this results in a credit balance on your account, a store must make a refund in cash if you request it.

Credit Blocking

Credit blocking: Credit limit is reduced by the amount of the expected purchase.

If you were ever in the embarrassing position of having a purchase denied because you had exceeded your credit limit, you may have been a victim of **credit blocking.** This is a perfectly legal practice. It can happen when you use your credit card to check into a hotel or to rent a car. The clerk will contact the card issuer with the estimated cost. Your line of credit is then reduced by this amount with what is termed a "block" or "authorization." When you pay your bill with the same credit card, the block is typically removed in a few days. However, using a card different from the one you used to initiate the transaction could create a credit problem. The credit limit on the first card might remain blocked for as long as 15 additional days. Consequently, if you use a different card to pay the bill, be sure to tell the clerk to unblock the first card.

Credit Cards Contrasted with Debit Cards

Debit card: Unlike a credit card, the price of a purchase is deducted immediately from your bank deposit.

A credit card should not be confused with a debit card even though they may look identical. For example, the MasterCard II—a **debit card**—is a perfect clone of the MasterCard credit card. It is unfortunate that they look alike, because they are different in terms of their impact on your cash flow and on the protection you have under federal law. You can use a debit card at an automated teller machine or point-of-sale terminal. Whenever you use the card, your bank deposit is reduced immediately. By contrast, a credit card transaction puts you in debt to the bank; you reduce the debt later by paying your monthly statement. A debit card is actually a form of checking account, which is how you should view it when considering its use.

Over the last decade, there has been tremendous growth in debit card transactions. They are convenient for the consumer because using them reduces trips to the bank or money machine and time at the checkout counter. The convenience, however, comes at the cost of giving up some of the benefits related to credit card use. Most credit cards have a grace period over which no interest is charged. Depending on when the purchase is made and when the bill comes due, this grace period can provide the consumer with up to a month's free credit. Electronic transfers, which clear over a much shorter period, leave little or no room between expenses and revenues. On the other hand, for consumers who have had trouble controlling their expenditures, replacing a credit card with a debit card can be a plus. Available funds must exist before the purchase is made.

Automatic teller machine (ATM) cards sometimes function as debit cards. Unlike credit cards, losses resulting from lost or stolen ATM and debit cards are regulated by the Electronic Fund Transfers Act. With an ATM or debit card, your losses are limited to only $50, if you report the loss within two days. If you fail to notify the debit card issuer within two business days after learning of the theft, you can lose up to $500. Furthermore, if you wait until 60 days or more after a bank statement has been mailed, your losses may be unlimited. This is greater than your potential loss on a credit card, which is limited to a

$50 maximum under the Truth in Lending Act. Given a choice between using a debit or credit card, it is hard to see why you shouldn't always choose the credit card.

CASH CREDIT

Cash credit simply means borrowing money; as we have seen, sales credit involves borrowing in connection with buying something. The distinction is a tenuous one, since in most cases cash borrowed is also used to make purchases. The major distinction between sales and cash credit is the way you repay the debt. Cash credit is repaid either with a single payment at the end of a period of time or by a series of uniform payments called installments.

Cash credit: Credit extended in the form of cash.

You might remember that earlier we said a form of sales credit is the retail installment account. This account is virtually identical to an installment cash loan, which is why it is explained now rather than before. Over the last few decades, the use of revolving charge accounts has displaced a large percentage of installment sales of consumer durables such as furniture and appliances. Installment sales are now reserved for the more expensive items on which you desire to spread out payments over time.

The Contract

The agreement between you and a person selling an item is called a **retail installment contract.** If you purchase the item by obtaining a cash loan from a bank, savings and loan, consumer finance company, or credit union, the agreement is called a **promissory note.** Although promissory notes can be unsecured—and in fact, many are—their use in consumer credit is almost always on a secured basis, with the purchased item serving as collateral. The retail installment contract is always on a secured basis. The creditor obtains a security interest in the property with the **security agreement,** which is a separate instrument.

Retail installment contract: A contract between a borrower and a lender establishing periodic repayment of the amount borrowed.

Promissory note: A contract binding a borrower to future repayment of the amount borrowed.

Security agreement: Establishes the creditor's security interest in the good for which the credit was extended.

Information That Must Be Provided

The Truth in Lending Act requires that each credit contract gives you the following information:

- The amount financed
- The total number of payments, the amount of each payment, and due dates
- Finance charges expressed both as a dollar amount and as an annual percentage rate
- The date when finance charges begin if that date is different from the transaction date
- An itemized list of all charges not included as part of the finance charge
- The charges for late payments or default
- A description of security held by the creditor
- How finance charge refunds are determined in the case of prepayments
- A description of prepayment penalties, if any

Creditors are also required to supply the following additional information when merchandise is purchased on time:

1. A description of the merchandise
2. The cash price
3. The deferred payment price
4. The down payment, including any trade-in

How Interest Charges Are Determined

TOPIC **LINKS**

Read "The ABCs of Calculating Interest."

Although the Truth in Lending Act requires lenders to state in writing the interest you must pay on a loan—both in dollars and as an annual percentage rate (APR)—it is still important that you know how these calculations are made. Three approaches are in general use: the simple interest method, the discount method, and the add-on method. These are explained next.

Simple Interest Method

Simple interest method: The interest payment is computed by applying the annual percentage rate to the outstanding loan balance.

Under the **simple interest method,** the interest payment is computed by applying a percentage rate to the outstanding loan balance during each payment period. This is the usual method for calculating a finance charge on a revolving credit account like that discussed earlier. It is also used by many banks and credit unions for computing the interest due on automobile installment loans and home mortgages.

Suppose you have a $1,000 loan with monthly payments and an annual percentage rate (APR) of 12 percent. Monthly interest charges are equal to 1 percent (12 percent/ 12 months) of the outstanding balance. You could pay off this loan in 12 equal monthly payments of $88.85. The formula for estimating the monthly payment is complicated. Thankfully, you can easily calculate the needed payment with a handheld or online financial calculator by entering $1,000 for the amount borrowed, 12 for the number of periods, and 1 percent for the periodic interest rate.

TOPIC **LINKS**

Use an online calculator.

How interest accrues and the balance is reduced over the loan's 12-month duration is illustrated in Figure 6.6. Using the simple interest method, the monthly finance charge in column 3 is equal to the outstanding balance in column 1 times the monthly interest charge of 1 percent. The excess of the monthly payment in column 2 over the finance charge in column 3 serves to reduce the outstanding balance. You should notice that as the loan is repaid, the finance charge in column 3 declines. You should also notice that, given the equal monthly installments and the declining monthly finance charge, a larger portion of each subsequent monthly installment is devoted to loan repayment. Thus, the loan is paid off more rapidly toward the end of the monthly payments.

Figure 6.6

A 12-Month Installment Loan with Annual Simple Interest of 12 Percent, or 1 Percent Monthly

Month	(1) Outstanding Balance	(2) Monthly Payment	(3) Monthly Finance Charge	(4) Monthly Loan Repayment
1	$1,000.00	$ 88.85	$10.00	$ 78.85
2	921.15	88.85	9.21	79.85
3	841.51	88.85	8.42	80.43
4	761.08	88.85	7.61	81.24
5	679.84	88.85	6.80	82.05
6	597.79	88.85	5.98	82.87
7	514.92	88.85	5.15	83.70
8	431.22	88.85	4.31	84.54
9	346.68	88.85	3.47	85.38
10	261.30	88.85	2.61	86.24
11	175.07	88.85	1.75	87.10
12	87.97	88.85	0.88	87.97
Total		$1,066.19	$66.19	$1,000.00

Discount Method

Under the **discount method,** the lender deducts the interest to be paid on the loan from the credit extended to you at the beginning of the loan. Therefore, the face amount of the loan will exceed the amount you want to finance. To finance a purchase of $1,000, you have to borrow more than $1,000. On a one-year loan, your total payments are determined by the following formula:

Discount method: The interest payment is deducted from the credit extended at the beginning of the loan.

$$\text{Total payments on discount loan} = \frac{\text{amount financed}}{1 - (\text{discount rate} \times t)}$$

$$\$1,136.36 = \frac{\$1,000}{1 - (0.12 \times 1)}$$

where t is the term of the loan in years. Thus, to finance a $1,000 purchase for one year at a discount rate of 12 percent, you must repay $1,136.36. If this were a 12-month installment loan, you would owe $94.70 ($1,136.36/12) per month. The true interest rate on this discount installment loan would be much higher than 12 percent, because you would not have the full use of $1,000 during the entire year. As indicated in the cost comparison in Figure 6.7, the annual percentage rate on this loan is 24.28 percent, about twice the discount rate.

Add-On Method

The add-on method is by far the most widely used method for determining finance charges on consumer loans. Under the **add-on method,** the lender adds the interest to the value of the purchase you are financing to determine your total payments using the following formula:

Add-on method: Interest is added to the amount financed in order to determine total payments.

$$\frac{\text{Total payments}}{\text{on add-on loan}} = \text{amount financed} \times [1 + (\text{add-on rate} \times t)]$$

$$\$1,120 = \$1,000 \times [1 + (0.12 \times 1)]$$

If the add-on rate is 12 percent per year and you intend to borrow $1,000 for one year, the interest charge of $120($1,000 $\times$ 0.12 $\times$ t), where t is the term of the loan in years, is added to the original principal of $1,000 to determine total repayments of $1,120 ($1,000 + $120). The monthly payments would equal $93.33 ($1,120/12). You should notice that an add-on rate of 12 percent is more costly than a similar loan with a simple interest rate of 12 percent. The monthly payments of $88.85 on the simple interest loan are $4.48 less per month than the $93.33 monthly payment for a comparable add-on loan.

As with the discount loan, the true interest rate on an add-on loan is far greater than the add-on rate of 12 percent. Again, you are being charged as if you had the full use of $1,000 for the entire year. However, you have the use of a full $1,000 only for the first month.

Method	Contract Rate	APR	Monthly Payment	Total Interest Paid
Simple interest	12%	12.00%	$88.85	$ 66.19
Discount interest	12%	24.28%	94.72	136.36
Add-on interest	12%	21.46%	93.33	120.00

Figure 6.7

Comparative Interest on Credit of $1,000 to Be Repaid in 12 Equal Monthly Installments

Since you repay principal with each payment, the total amount borrowed declines with each payment. In the current example, an add-on rate of 12 percent would entail the same monthly payments as a simple interest rate of 21.46 percent.

Annual Percentage Rate

Annual percentage rate (APR): The rate charged on the outstanding balance; the ratio of the finance charge to the average amount of credit extended over the life of the loan expressed as a rate.

TOPIC **LINKS**

Download a financial calculator.

Regardless of how the lender determines the interest charge, the government requires that the lender provide the borrower with the information on the true interest rate, or what is officially termed the annual percentage rate. The **annual percentage rate (APR)** is the ratio of the finance charge to the average amount of credit extended to you over the life of the contract, expressed as a percentage rate per year. Since the simple interest charge is also based on the amount of credit extended in each period, the annual simple interest rate and the APR are the same.

There is nothing simple about calculating the APR on installment loans. However, inexpensive financial calculators will provide either the APR or monthly payments given the amount and term of the loan. In addition, interactive calculators on the Internet and software that can run on your personal computer.

The APR is the rate you should use to judge the relative cost of credit. As indicated in Figure 6.7, identical contract rates can result in widely different interest payments and annual percentage rates. If you are comparing loans for identical amounts of credit and identical maturities, the loan with the lower APR will also have the lower finance charge.

Areas of Special Concern

In addition to recognizing how the finance charges are computed, it is important that you read the entire credit agreement carefully and understand each of the several clauses that may be included in the contract. The areas discussed in the following paragraphs should receive special consideration.

Rule of 78: A method for computing the interest refunded upon early repayment. This method is highly favorable to lenders.

Prepayment and the Rule of 78 Credit agreements will include a statement indicating how interest is to be calculated if you decide to repay the loan at any date that is earlier than scheduled. Agreements that utilize the add-on method for computing installment payments usually determine your interest refund by the so-called **rule of 78.** This method for computing the interest refunded upon early repayment depends on a difficult calculation that is favorable to lenders, because it penalizes early loan repayment.

Acceleration clause: A late payment entitles the lender to demand that the entire unpaid balance be paid immediately.

The Acceleration Clause If you miss just one payment on a loan, the **acceleration clause** makes the entire unpaid balance due immediately. If you can't pay this entire amount, you stand a chance of having the loan collateral repossessed. Repossession is guided by state law, but it usually means the lender is free to sell the item for its best market price. From this amount are deducted any expenses connected with the sale, and the difference is applied to the credit balance. If it is greater, the lender remits the difference to the borrower; if it is less, the borrower is still required to pay the difference. Your main concern here is the price the lender receives in selling the repossessed item. Under forced sale conditions, it could be very low, and you would bear the loss. Lenders do not usually apply the acceleration clause immediately, preferring instead to rely upon penalties for late payments, but it is not a factor to take casually.

Add-on clause: Allows the lender to repossess all goods financed under the agreement in the event of a missed payment.

The Add-On Clause Suppose you purchase some kitchen appliances from an appliance dealer and finance the deal with an installment loan for one year. Six months later you return to the same dealer and purchase a television set and tape recorder as part of an add-on to your earlier agreement. Eight months after that purchase, financial problems set in and you stop making payments on the loan. With an **add-on clause,** the dealer can repossess all the appliances he or she sold you, even though your total payments may have been more than enough to have paid for the earlier purchase. Fortunately, courts seldom enforce this clause.

The Balloon Payment The **balloon payment** is usually the last installment payment, and it is for an amount much greater than the other monthly payments. The problem with the balloon is that borrowers may not prepare sufficiently to make the payment and so may require new financing when it is due or may have the item repossessed. Balloon clauses sometimes were used in the past as a means of defrauding borrowers, and this abuse led some states to make them illegal.

Balloon payment: An amount larger than other periodic payments that is due as the last installment payment.

OBTAINING CREDIT AND RESOLVING CREDIT PROBLEMS

Once you understand how credit works, the next step is to find a lender. After you are successful in arranging credit, the final step is to use it properly to avoid credit problems. Unfortunately, even the most financially prudent people can face these problems, and you should know how to deal with them.

Sources of Credit

There are many suppliers of credit, ranging from commercial banks at the top of a list to friends and relatives at the bottom. The discussion that follows will not attempt to explain detailed features of each but will focus instead on their most important characteristics. Comparative shopping is important in the credit market. We are in an era of volatile interest rates, and although it is true that similar lenders tend to charge about the same rates for similar loans, differences can exist. And don't underestimate the importance of saving 1 or 2 percent on the loan. For example, a 48-month installment loan for $5,000 will cost about $250 more at 16 percent than at 14 percent.

Interest rates charged on consumer loans in a recent period are illustrated in Figure 6.8. Rates on credit cards are typically above other types of personal loans. Highly collateralized loans, such as car loans, tend to be significantly lower. Over this recent period, there was almost a six-point differential between credit card rates and the rates on new car loans. Before you run up that balance on your credit card, it would be wise to check out less expensive sources of credit.

Be sure you adhere to the following dos and don'ts before you take out a loan.

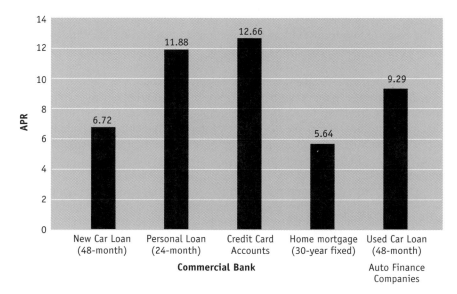

Figure 6.8

Interest Rates on Consumer Loans (February 2004)

Source: Federal Reserve Bank.

Loan Dos

- Do shop around for a loan
- Do read the loan application form
- Do get copies of all forms you sign

Loan Don'ts

- Don't be talked into falsifying information on a loan
- Don't accept larger monthly payments than you can afford
- Don't accept last minute changes in the terms of the loan
- Don't sign a blank form

Personal Lines of Credit and Banking Institutions

Commercial banks, savings and loan associations, and credit unions all compete for your consumer credit dollar with similar offers. In addition to credit cards, these institutions generally provide revolving credit at lower interest rates in the form of overdraft protection credit lines, unsecured personal credit lines, and home equity credit lines.

Overdraft protection credit line: Credit is automatically extended to cover excess withdrawals from a checking account.

The financial institution where you have a checking account may offer you an **overdraft protection credit line.** If you write a check for an amount that exceeds the funds available, the bank automatically extends you a loan to cover the excess amount up to some predetermined credit limit. In addition to providing you with a convenient source of credit, the overdraft protection credit line has the advantage of saving you the embarrassment and cost of a bounced check.

Unsecured personal credit line: An unsecured credit line upon which you can withdraw cash.

An **unsecured personal credit line** is separate from your checking account. You must apply for it by submitting a loan application. After you are approved for an unsecured personal credit line, you access the credit line by writing specially issued checks or utilizing a special credit card. Each month you receive a statement indicating the amount you owe, the amount of credit still available, your finance charges, and your minimum monthly payment.

Home Equity Loans

Home equity loan: A loan secured by the ownership in your home in the form of a second mortgage.

With a **home equity loan,** your credit is secured by your ownership in your home. Banks typically let you borrow up to 75 to 80 percent of the equity in your home. Home equity loans come in two forms: closed-end credit and open-end credit. With an *open-end home equity line of credit*, you can borrow up to a predetermined credit limit on a revolving charge account. A *closed-end home equity loan* is the same as a second mortgage on your home. You borrow a fixed amount for a set period of time.

Home equity loans have become extremely popular because interest charges on home equity loans up to $100,000 for a married couple may be taken as an itemized deduction on federal income tax returns. Interest payments on all other consumer loans are nondeductible. Moreover, home equity loans are typically available at much lower interest rates than other consumer loans, and repayment can be stretched out over a longer period.

The Federal Trade Commission enforces a three-day cancellation rule on home equity loans. You have the right to cancel the loan within three days of signing the contract on your principal home. Beware of home equity scams listed in Figure 6.9. Predatory lenders may target homeowners for subprime loans. These are high-risk loans at high interest rates to borrowers with minimal debt repayment capacity. Such loans have been used to fund shoddy or nonexistent home repairs.

Figure 6.9

Home Equity Scams

Source: FTC Consumer Alert, "Avoiding Home Equity Scams."

Equity Stripping: The lender gives you a loan based on the equity in your home, not on your ability to repay based on your income. If you can't make the payments, you could end up losing your home.

Loan Flipping: The lender encourages you to repeatedly refinance the loan and often to borrow more money. Each time you refinance, you pay additional fees and interest points. That only serves to increase your debt.

Credit Insurance Packing: The lender adds credit insurance to your loan, which you may not need.

Bait and Switch: The lender offers one set of loan terms when you apply, then pressures you to accept higher charges when you sign to complete the transaction.

Deceptive Loan Servicing: The lender doesn't provide you with accurate or complete account statements and payoff figures. That makes it almost impossible for you to determine how much you have paid or how much you owe. You may pay more than you owe.

Used wisely, paying off higher-interest-bearing debt with funds from a low-interest, tax-advantaged home equity loan could be a good decision. On the negative side, home equity loans may entice some consumers into making long-term payments on purchases that provide short-lived satisfaction and may place home equity at risk.

Consumer Finance Companies

There are two types of consumer finance companies: those that offer specialized loans, such as GMAC on General Motors automobiles, and those that offer general-purpose loans, both secured and unsecured. The specialized lenders are dominant forces within their particular areas, and they usually offer interest rates at or below bank rates. Sometimes they are substantially below bank rates when they are part of auto dealers' sales promotion programs. Of course, the question then is whether you are getting the best price on the item purchased. Try to bring financing into the discussion as a separate topic after the price has been agreed upon. The objective is to get the best price *and* the best financing.

The general-purpose consumer finance companies are more willing to loan to first-time borrowers and to make loans on unsecured terms. Their administrative costs tend to be higher because they make many small loans, and their delinquency costs are also higher because of the poorer quality of the loans they make. As a result of these factors, you can expect their interest rates to be higher on these kinds of loans.

Student Loans

Credit cards should only be used to finance your short-term credit needs. Obviously, it is the wrong source of credit for a college education, which provides delayed long-term benefits. A prolonged outstanding balance on a credit card should signal the need to rethink your budget. Student loans are a preferred source for funding your income expenditure gap.

Stafford loans are provided through the federal student loan program. There are both subsidized loans and unsubsidized loans. On subsidized loans the government pays the interest while you are in college. On unsubsidized loans you pay all the interest. Both loans are based on financial need. The interest rate on these loans is tied to that on short-term government securities. This rate is likely to be significantly less than that on other types of credit. For those in significant need, Perkins loans may be available through the school financial aid office. The interest on these loans is also subsidized while the student is in school. In addition, some or all of this loan may be forgiven for employment in public service. See Box 6.3 for loan consolidation strategies.

BOX 6.3

Financial
PLANNING
for Young Adults

Student Loan Consolidation

You generally have to start paying back student loans six months after leaving school. These loans initially have a maximum repayment term of 10 years. By arranging a loan consolidation, you can typically extend the repayment period to 30 years at a fixed rate. This can significantly lower your monthly payments. For example, on a 5% loan, this can cut your monthly payments almost in half. If you are just starting out with relocation expenses and initial household expenses, smaller monthly payments can reduce the strain on your budget. Of course, your total interest payment on the loan will be greater over the extended period. However, you should have the option of making larger monthly payments and paying off your loan earlier.

Both the government and private lenders offer loan consolidations. In addition to an extended term of repayment, lenders may offer other repayment options. These may include a graduated payment plan (payments are set to increase over time), an income-sensitive program (payments are tied to the size of current income), and an income-contingent program (payments are tied to your future income).

If you are out of school, in school but attending classes less than half-time, or in school with direct federal loans, you probably qualify for a loan consolidation. In many cases you don't even have to have more than one loan to consolidate. If you are thinking of entering graduate school, you may be able to consolidate your undergraduate loans while continuing your education.

Generally, the fixed interest rate on the consolidated loan is the weighted average of the variable rates on your separate loans. For example, when a $40,000 loan at 4% is consolidated with a $10,000 loan at 5%, the consolidated $50,000 loan will have a rate of 2% (40/50*4% + 10/50*5%). This rate is fixed for the life of the loan and cannot exceed a set maximum.

The variable rate on initial student loans is tied to short-term interest rates on government securities. Whether changing variable rate loans for a fixed rate is a good strategy will depend on what happens to future interest rates. In the summer of 2004, student loan rates hit a 39-year low. If rates rise, a lock in at a low fixed rate could save you thousands of dollars. On the other hand, a drop in interest rates could mean losing a potentially lower variable rate.

Web sites with additional information:

Direct Consolidation Loans	**loanconsolidation.ed.gov**
College Funding Services	**www.cfsloans.com**
Federal Consolidation.Org	**www.federalconsolidation.org**
SallieMae	**www.salliemae.com**

If educational needs exceed Stafford loan limits, parents of students can consider a PLUS (Parent Loan for Undergraduate Student) loan. These are less attractive than Stafford loans and the parent is responsible for repayment. The rates on these should be compared with other potential sources of funding, like a home equity loan.

Repayment of any outstanding student loans should also be a part of your credit management strategy. High cost credit should always be paid off first. Credit cards and personal loans are likely to have higher interest rates than student or home equity loans. In addition, interest on student loans and home equity loans may be tax deductible, whereas interest charges on personal credit are not.

Other Sources

Some sources are not typical lenders to consumers but are nevertheless important. You can borrow on your ordinary life insurance policy up to its loan value, usually at a rate that could be far lower than any other available rate if the policy is older than, say, 10 years. These loans are exceptionally easy to make, requiring you to do nothing more than write a letter. Although you never have to repay them, if you die, your beneficiaries will receive only the face value of the policy less the amount of the loan outstanding.

If you own stocks or bonds, you can consider using them as collateral for a loan. A bank will accept securities as collateral, or you can open a margin account with a stock-brokerage firm. In either case, you can usually borrow up to 50 percent of the market value of the securities pledged. The interest rate on such a loan will probably be one to two points above the prime rate (the rate a bank charges its most creditworthy customer). This arrangement can be risky in a volatile market. Should the market price of the stocks fall, you may get a call for additional collateral. If you fail to provide the requested funds, the broker may force the sale of your stocks at a market low.

If you are really desperate and have something of value, consider a pawnshop. Pawnbrokers are willing to make loans on practically any item they feel can be resold if you fail to reclaim it after a specified period of time, usually 60 to 90 days. You will be able to borrow only a fraction of the item's market value and can expect to pay the very highest interest rates allowed. They are bad places to borrow, but pawnshops can be good places to buy if you are willing to take some risks on product quality and service.

As a last (or maybe first) resort, friends and relatives might extend credit to you. Before taking this alternative, bear in mind that credit misunderstandings have ended many friendships. The best advice if you do borrow (or lend) is to put the arrangement in writing, complete with all pertinent details that are found on other credit contracts. A "pay-me-back-when-you-can" loan is bad for both the borrower and the lender, because neither knows how to budget for the loan. Also remember that if either borrower or lender dies, heirs will be left to resolve the loan. Although the two parties involved may know and trust each other, their heirs may not.

Another option is to have a creditworthy friend or relative cosign a loan for you. However, should you default on the loan, the individual who cosigned the loan will be financially responsible for the remaining payments and any penalties or collection charges. In most states, the lender has the same rights to collect from the cosigner as the initial borrower. This means the lender can collect from the cosigner without first attempting to collect from the borrower. If you are asked to cosign a loan, remember the reason the borrower needs a cosigner is that he or she has been deemed a poor credit risk.

A Credit Management Strategy

Credit management is similar in many respects to cash management, discussed in the previous chapter. There the objective was to maximize the return on short-term investments while achieving a reasonable degree of liquidity. Here the objective is to minimize the cost of credit while simultaneously achieving both the target amount needed and a reasonable level of shopping convenience. Since we differ in how much credit we want and in our attitude toward convenience, our strategies for managing credit will also differ, but the following guidelines apply in most cases.

1. Use as much of the grace period as you can, but be sure to avoid late payment penalties. You can thus keep your money in an interest-earning account longer than if you pay bills with cash.
2. Use revolving charge accounts, as a 30-day account. We mentioned previously that most often this is expensive credit, and it should be used only if other credit is unavailable.
3. Take a broad view toward credit; that is, do not think in terms of borrowing here to buy this or borrowing there to buy that, but think instead of a total borrowing requirement. Then search for the cheapest sources of credit to meet this requirement. For example, you might take a home equity mortgage and with it buy a car, send your kid to summer camp, and enjoy a vacation. The interest on this loan could be far less than an installment loan on the car and personal loans for the other two activities—and no riskier.
4. Be careful of variable-rate loans if you think that interest rates may rise. The initial interest rate on a variable-rate loan is lower than on a fixed-rate loan. The variable rate, however, is indexed to other market rates of interest and automatically rises as they do.

Saving money $

BOX 6.4

Use Your Credit Card Wisely

If you follow these few simple rules, using your credit card can save you money.

- Use a credit card with a low or zero annual fee and a grace period.
- Keep a running balance of your charges so that you are not surprised by the amount you owe on your monthly statement.
- Use credit instead of cash whenever you can.
- Pay off your outstanding balance each payment period.
- Compare your credit card statement with your own list of charges each month.
- Immediately report and challenge any billing errors

You must, however, follow all of these rules. If you don't pay off your balance each month, then a card with a low annual fee, but a high interest rate on the outstanding balance may not be a wise choice.

By using the zero interest credit during the grace period, you can keep additional financial assets in an interest earning account. If you can shift $1,000 out of cash into a financial asset earning only 5 percent, you can earn an extra $50 a year. With compounding, that would add up to an extra $629 after 10 years. That may not sound like a lot of money. But by making a number of sound financial choices on how you handle your credit, the financial benefits can add up.

Compare this virtuous cycle to the vicious cycle that can result from a growing outstanding balance and late payments. Running a $1,000 outstanding balance on your credit card will cost you finance charges and may lower your credit score. Moreover, at a high interest rate, that outstanding balance will rapidly grow. At a 16 percent APR, that outstanding balance will double in less than four and one-half years.

Using your credit card wisely and paying off your monthly balance can improve your credit score and result in lower interest rates on car loans and home mortgages. In addition, a good credit score can even lower your insurance premiums and increase your chances of employment.

Under all circumstances you should try to avoid getting into a vicious credit cycle. This occurs when the interest payments on the debt become a burden, forcing you to search for other sources of credit just to repay the previous debt. Keeping track of your personal debt ratios can help you avoid this trap.

Resolving Personal Debt Problems

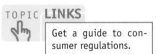

TOPIC **LINKS**

Get a guide to consumer regulations.

The easiest way to resolve a credit problem is not to let it begin in the first place. This means limiting your credit to an amount your income can support. Credit counselors often feel this limit is about 20 percent of your take-home pay for consumer credit, not including your home mortgage. The 20 percent is applied in two ways: First, your monthly credit payments should not exceed 20 percent of your monthly take-home pay; and second, your total consumer credit should not exceed 20 percent of your total take-home pay for the year. If you exceed either one of these limits, you are courting financial danger. You can keep credit within the 20 percent limit by always figuring the impact of any new credit arrangement on your budget *before* you take out a loan.

Despite all precautions, you may still run into credit problems. As indicated in Figure 6.10, medical institutions initiated over half of the collection actions for bad debts. No doubt most of these problems resulted from unexpected circumstances and inadequate health coverage. If you find yourself confronting a financial crisis, the first step is to contact the creditor. You cannot resolve a credit problem by avoiding creditors. Explain the reasons for your temporary difficulties and try to work out a modified payment plan that fits your budget. Most lenders prefer being paid in full, even if extra time is needed. In bankruptcy they may only collect a fraction of the amount due. Also, the Fair Debt Collection Practices Act protects you from lender harassment at all times. If you are unable to obtain relief from the lender, seek credit counseling. A personal bankruptcy should only be considered after all other attempts to resolve your problem have failed.

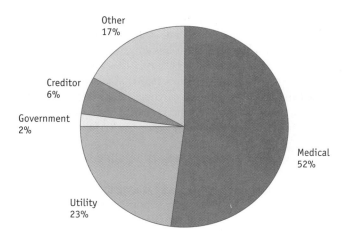

Figure 6.10

Collection Actions by Type

Source: "An Overview of Consumer Data and Credit Reporting," Robert B. Avery, Paul S. Calem and Glenn B. Canner, Federal Reserve Bulletin, February 2003.

Pie chart labels:
Other 17%
Creditor 6%
Government 2%
Medical 52%
Utility 23%

Credit Counseling

Beware of advertisements promoting debt relief. Some companies may be selling debt consolidation in a single high-interest loan or may be offering bankruptcy services. You cannot change your credit history, only your future.

The Federal Trade Commission warns you to beware of companies that:

- Want you to pay for credit repair services before any services are provided
- Do not tell you your legal rights and what you can do yourself for free
- Recommend that you not contact a credit bureau directly
- Suggest that you try to invent a new credit report by applying for an Employer Identification number (EIN) to use instead of your Social Security number
- Advise you to dispute all information in your credit report or take any action that seems illegal, such as creating a new credit identity

If you have a credit problem, contact the Better Business Bureau or the chamber of commerce in your town and inquire about credit counseling assistance. Avoid any private credit counselor who supposedly specializes in working out your credit problems. The fee for this service can be as high as 35 percent of your total debt.

Recognizing their common interest in helping troubled borrowers, many lenders support the activities of **credit counseling** services sponsored by the National Foundation of Consumer Counseling. These counseling centers provide two levels of service. First, they work with the borrower to develop a reasonable plan for repaying debts. This plan often includes a budget. Second, if this budget indicates that income will not be sufficient to meet both living expenses and the existing debt repayment load, the counselor will attempt to negotiate a more reasonable repayment plan with lenders. The borrower then gives the counselor a certain percentage of each week's income, and this in turn is given to the lenders. This service is essentially free to borrowers, regardless of their income, as are other counseling services.

Bankruptcy

About 1.5 million Americans file for bankruptcy each year. Many people continue to regard bankruptcy as a calamity to be avoided at any cost. Others view it as an easy way to avoid all the bills that result from an enjoyable buying binge. Regardless of your viewpoint, bankruptcy is a serious step, and you should seek credit counseling before taking it.

TOPIC **LINKS**
National Foundation of Consumer Counseling

Credit counseling: Helps consumers with credit problems by rescheduling loans and eliminating negative behaviors.

You can file for bankruptcy under either Chapter 7 of the bankruptcy code, called a straight bankruptcy, or under Chapter 13 of the bankruptcy code, called a wage earner plan. In most instances, neither can be used to avoid payments for alimony, child support, fines, taxes, or recent student loans.

Over 70 percent of personal bankruptcies are filed under Chapter 7 as **straight bankruptcies.** This discharges all of your debts and thus provides you a fresh start. A straight bankruptcy may require you to sell off most of your assets. However, you are not left a complete pauper, and in most cases few assets are actually sold. Under federal exemptions, which may be more or less generous than state laws permit, you may keep from creditors a portion of homeowner's equity or personal property and additional amounts of specific assets.

If you have been through a straight bankruptcy, you cannot file again for another six years, and the record of the bankruptcy remains on your credit report for 10 years. During this period it may be difficult for you to get credit or enter into normal everyday contracts such as rental agreements or purchase contracts. It may even hurt your employment prospects if potential employers access your credit records.

Under a Chapter 13 filing, the court creates a **wage earner plan.** This is a court approved and administered repayment schedule for employed persons with regular income. This allows debtors to retain most of their property and to repay all or part of their obligations over a three- to five-year period with protection from creditors. It will remain on your credit report for seven years. On the plus side, it indicates that by filing under Chapter 13 rather than Chapter 7, you made a sincere attempt to repay your debts.

Bankruptcy is a financial tool of last resort. It should only be entered into when all else fails. Since it is likely to come to the attention of both future creditors and employers, it can hinder your attempts to obtain future sales credit, a mortgage, insurance, and even employment. In addition, income taxes, child support payments, alimony, student loans, debts incurred in anticipation of bankruptcy, and court awards may all survive a bankruptcy.

Protection from Lender Harassment

The **Fair Debt Collection Practices Act** entitles borrowers to be treated fairly by debt collectors. You are entitled to a written notice from the debt collector describing your debt in detail and what to do if you feel you do not owe the debt. You then have 30 days to send a letter to the debt collector denying the debt. The debt collector cannot continue collection efforts until you receive a written verification of the debt. Among other things, the debt collector cannot use abusive language, threaten you, harass you at work, or attempt to collect the bill through trickery. Finally, you can keep a debt collector from communicating with you by providing written notification that all contacts must cease. This does not eliminate the debt. You can still be sued.

Straight bankruptcy: A Chapter 7 bankruptcy in which most assets are sold off, most debts are discharged, and a fresh start is provided.

Wage earner plan: A repayment schedule established under Chapter 13 bankruptcy that allows debtors to retain their property while repaying all or part of their obligations.

TOPIC **LINKS**

Visit the chat room at Debt Counselors of America.

Fair Debt Collection Practices Act: Limits the tactics that creditors may employ in attempting to collect overdue loans.

Key Terms

acceleration clause (p. 156)
add-on clause (p. 156)
add-on method (p. 156)
adjusted balance method (p. 144)
affinity card (p. 146)

annual percentage rate (APR) (p. 156)
average daily balance method (p. 144)
balloon payment (p. 157)
bank credit cards (p. 146)

cash credit (p. 153)
chargeback (p. 151)
closed-end account (p. 143)
credit blocking (p. 152)
credit counseling (p. 163)
debit card (p. 152)

discount method (p. 155)
Equal Credit Opportunity
   Act (ECOA) (p. 139)
Fair Credit Reporting Act
   (FCRA) (p. 141)
Fair Debt Collection
   Practices Act (p. 164)
grace period (p. 145)
home equity loan (p. 158)
individual credit account
   (p. 140)
joint credit account
   (p. 140)
open-end account (p. 143)

overdraft protection credit
   line (p. 158)
previous balance method
   (p. 144)
promissory note (p. 153)
regular charge account
   (p. 143)
retail installment contract
   (p. 153)
revolving credit account
   (p. 143)
rule of 78 (p. 156)
sales credit (p. 141)
secured credit card (p. 141)

security agreement (p. 153)
service credit (p. 136)
simple interest method
   (p. 154)
straight bankruptcy (p. 164)
travel and entertainment
   (T&E) cards (p. 146)
Truth in Lending Act
   (TILA) (p. 138)
two-cycle average daily
   balance method (p. 146)
unsecured personal credit
   line (p. 158)
wage earner plan (p. 164)

Reread the chapter-opening vignette.

1. What are the pros and cons of borrowing on a credit card to pay for auto repairs?
2. What are the pros and cons of borrowing on home equity to pay for auto repairs?
3. How would you advise the Steeles to finance the auto repairs? What alternative sources of financing might you consider? Does selling off some stock holdings seem like a good idea?

FOLLOW–UP ON THE

Steele FAMILY

Problems and Review Questions

1. Explain how credit serves as
   (a) a shopping convenience
   (b) a means to increase total consumption benefits
   (c) a hedge against inflation
   (d) a source of emergency funds
   What are several disadvantages of credit?
2. Describe the three Cs of credit and why lenders feel they are important in evaluating a loan request. Then list five steps you can take to begin a credit record; list three extra steps that might be necessary if you are a woman.
3. What function does the credit bureau perform in the lender's evaluation of your credit application?
4. How do you obtain your credit score? How do you improve your credit score?
5. How does a credit card differ from a debit card? Explain.
6. List steps you can take to protect yourself against credit card fraud.
7. Suppose you review your monthly statement of credit card activities and discover that you have been charged for an item you didn't buy. What should you do?
8. Describe the information a lender must provide you on a credit contract. Why should you be particularly concerned about the following items?
   (a) the rule of 78
   (b) the acceleration clause
   (c) the add-on clause
   (d) a balloon payment

9. Explain several steps you can take to avoid credit problems.
10. If a good friend of yours has had serious financial misfortunes lately and is unable to meet her debt payments, what advice can you give? Be sure to include the topic of bankruptcy, since she has heard that it eliminates all your credit problems. In your discussion, distinguish between straight bankruptcy and a wage earner plan.
11. Indicate the actions you should take if you are denied credit or employment because of an unfavorable credit report.
12. Which method for determining the outstanding balance on a revolving credit account is likely to determine the lowest outstanding balance? Which method is likely to determine the highest outstanding balance?
13. Under what circumstances would you decide to obtain a credit card with a lower APR but a higher annual maintenance fee?
14. Suppose you were deciding whether to prepay a loan. Discuss the important facts that must be taken into consideration in order to make the least-cost decision.
15. Explain why home equity loans have become an important source of consumer credit.

Case 6.1
Helen's Debt Repayment Choices

As a graduation present, Helen received a $5,000 cash gift from her grandparents. She has no immediate need for these funds. Therefore, she plans to either invest these funds or use them to reduce some of her outstanding debt. Her debt includes an outstanding balance on her credit card, a used car loan, and a student loan. All of these loans are at current average market rates.

Questions
1. Given Helen's three sources of debt, which is likely to carry the highest APR and which is likely to carry the lowest APR?
2. Which of these debts should Helen consider paying off first? Why?
3. She has to decide whether it is best to use these funds for debt repayment or investment. What factors should she take into consideration?
4. Are there special strategies she should consider with regard to her student loan?

Case 6.2
Evaluating Nancy Tai's Revolving Account

Nancy Tai has recently opened a revolving charge account with MasterCard. Her credit limit is $1,000, but she has not charged that much since opening the account. Nancy hasn't had the time to review her monthly statements promptly as she should, but over the upcoming weekend she plans to catch up on her work.

In reviewing October's statement she notices that her beginning balance was $600 and that she made a $200 payment on November 10. She also charged purchases of $80 on November 5, $100 on November 15, and $50 on November 30. She can't tell how much interest she paid in November because she spilled watercolor paint on that portion of the statement. She does remember, though, seeing the letters APR and the number 16 percent. Also, the back of her statement indicates that interest was charged using the average daily balance method, including current purchases, which considers the day of a charge or credit.

Questions
1. Assuming a 30-day period in November, calculate November's interest. Also calculate the interest Nancy would have paid with: (*a*) the previous balance method, (*b*) the adjusted balance method.

2. Going back in time to when Nancy was just about to open her account, and assuming she could choose among credit sources that offered the different monthly balance determinations, and assuming further that Nancy would increase her outstanding balance over time, which credit source would you recommend? Explain.

3. In talking with Nancy, you have learned that she can also get credit through her credit union. An advertisement from the union shows that Nancy could take a personal cash loan at 14 percent on a discount basis or an installment loan at 12 percent add-on. Each is a one-year loan. Would you advise Nancy to use one of these to pay off her November balance with MasterCard? (Assume the 14 and 12 percents are not APRs.) Nancy doesn't believe she will have enough funds to reduce the November balance until the end of next October.

Exercises to Strengthen Your Use of the Internet
(Internet links for the following exercises can be found at **www.prenhall.com/winger**.)

Exercise 6.1 Obtain a Credit Report
You can link to Trans Union, TRW (Experian), and Equifax for information on obtaining your credit report.
Q. Where and how can you obtain a credit report? How much will it cost you?

Exercise 6.2 Comparing Credit Card Offers
The Bank Rate Monitor provides information on numerous credit card offers. For each, the terms and conditions are listed. Select two of the offers and compare the terms and conditions.
Q. Given your expenditure habits, which is the preferred choice for you?

Exercise 6.3 Should You Prepay a Loan?
This utilizes another one of the great financial calculators from Hugh Chou. The Prepayment vs. Investment Calculator determines when it is beneficial to make early payments on a mortgage. However, the results can be extended to any installment-type loan with simple interest payments.
Q. Using your best estimate of current interest rates, is it better to prepay your loan or invest in a money market fund? How about prepaying your loan versus investing in risky stocks? What part does risk play in your decision?

Exercise 6.4 How the Interest Rate Affects Your Debt Repayments
The interest rate can significantly influence the size and term of your debt repayments. This can be illustrated with the aid of several financial calculators on the Internet. The most appropriate one for this project is the Unknown Loan Variables Calculator from Bank 2000. Assuming compounding with simple interest, this program can calculate the number of periods needed to pay off a loan given the monthly dollar payments. You can also calculate the monthly dollar payment needed to pay off a loan in a given number of installments. Calculate the monthly payment on a 24-month installment loan of $5,000 at both an 18 percent annual rate of interest and a 15 percent annual rate of interest.
Q. At the lower interest rate, how much do you save on monthly payments and total interest payments?

Calculate how long it would take to pay off a $5,000 loan balance with monthly payments of $100 at both 18 percent and 15 percent annual rates of interest.

Q. How much longer does it take to pay off the loan at the higher interest rate, and how much more do you pay in total interest payments?

Exercise 6.5 Interest Rate Comparisons
Using the Bank Rate Monitor Home Equity Loan page, find the lowest rate on a home equity loan in the closest geographic market. Compare this with the lowest rate on a credit card in the same geographic market from the Bank Rate Monitor Credit Card home page.
Q. Which is the better deal?

Exercise 6.6 Changes in Interest Rates
The Federal Reserve Bank publishes data on the types of loans listed in Figure 6.8. These are placed on the Internet at the Board of Governors Web site for the Federal Reserve Bank. Compare data on the most recent rates with those listed in Figure 6.8.
Q. Does the comparison indicate an increasing or a falling trend in interest rates? Given the historic trend in interest rates, how do you expect interest rates to change in the future?

Exercise 6.7 The Card You Pick Can Save You Money
Every six months the Federal Reserve System collects data on credit cards offered by major financial institutions. The data are published in a bulletin and on the Internet under the title "The Card You Pick Can Save You Money." The survey reveals a variety of offers over a wide range of interest rates and annual fees.
Q. What are the highest and lowest interest rates in the latest survey? What are the highest and lowest annual fees in the latest survey?

PART 3

Buying Now and Paying Later

MANAGING YOUR LONG-TERM LIABILITIES

Chapter 7
Consumer Durables: The Personal Auto

Chapter 8
Housing: The Cost of Shelter

The previous section concentrated on management of short-term assets and liabilities. Liabilities that last longer than a year are long-term liabilities. Some of the techniques discussed in the previous chapter can be applied to the management of long-term assets. For example, installment loans often last more than a year. Such loans are typically used to finance the purchase of consumer durables. A consumer durable is any good that provides benefits lasting more than one year.

Consumers often incur long-term liabilities to purchase consumer durables such as home furnishings. The logic of purchasing consumer durables with long-term credit is that you match the future stream of benefits with a future stream of financial obligations. Using long-term financing to purchase goods that offer only immediate and short-term benefits is unwise in most instances. It locks you into continuing payments that extend way beyond any enjoyment you may have derived from the product. Consumers that use long-term credit to finance temporary pleasures may find themselves on a financially disastrous treadmill. They become immersed in ever-increasing amounts of debt to sustain an overly high standard of living.

In this section we focus on two major lifestyle purchases that provide long-term benefits; the family auto and the family home. In Chapter 7 we first discuss the new expanding electronic marketplace and your rights as a consumer. We then look at strategies for selecting the family auto. We also weigh the relative benefits of leasing versus purchasing.

Chapter 8 examines the most long-lasting and expensive asset you are likely to own, the family home. Where you live should complement your desired lifestyle, but it also must be constrained by how much you can afford. This will depend on the cost of the home and the cost of financing. Accordingly, you must know how to shop for a home and shop for financing. The home mortgage market offers a wide selection of mortgage formats. Mortgages can have fixed or variable interest rates and the payments can be structured over various time frames. By the end of the chapter, you should be able to intelligently assess your buying and borrowing opportunities.

7

Consumer Durables

THE PERSONAL AUTO

OBJECTIVES

1. To recognize the importance of budgeting consumer durables

2. To understand the rules governing electronic transactions

3. To describe the characteristics of warranties

4. To obtain information on new and used car prices

5. To calculate the cost of owning and operating an automobile

6. To evaluate the lease–buy decision

7. To explain the complaint process for correcting auto defects

8. To understand your rights under lemon laws

Steele FAMILY

Given the recent problems with Sharon's auto, the Steeles now expect they may have to replace Sharon's car sooner than they had previously thought. They are wary of buying a new car and committing themselves to large monthly payments. They could purchase a slightly newer used car, but they worry that might result in taking on someone else's problem.

At work, Sharon uses one of the company cars to visit clients. Every few years, the company vehicles are replaced with the latest models. When she asked her boss how much this cost, she was told that the company leases rather than purchases its fleet of cars. She was shocked to find that the monthly payments on these leases were substantially less than the Steeles were paying on their car loans. Sharon wonders whether they should consider leasing their next car as a way of holding down monthly expenses. The morning paper contains numerous ads by car dealers listing leasing arrangements requiring little money down and low monthly payments.

After the family home, your auto is probably your next most expensive purchase. The auto is one member of a class of products called **consumer durables.** These are defined as goods that provide consumer benefits lasting at least one year. Purchasing decisions regarding consumer durables deserve more attention than you devote to purchasing everyday consumables. The negative impact of a wrong decision may be more expensive and more long lasting. Such goods make possible our high standard of living; however, they also make significant demands on both our financial resources and our available time.

About 10 percent of consumer expenditures are devoted to household furnishings, appliances, and automobiles. When you consider the ongoing costs of operations and maintenance for these same items, their proportionate impact on the household budget is much greater. In one way or another, one dollar out of every four dollars that consumers spend is somehow related to the purchase of consumer durables or the operation and maintenance of consumer durables.

Consumer durables give rise to multiple entries on the household budget. A product that is purchased with savings is listed as an expense at the time of purchase. If it is financed through borrowing, however, it will create inflexible future expenses until the loan is repaid. The continuing outflow required for maintenance and operations must also be budgeted. Moreover, additional expenses will most likely show up in separate household accounts for utilities and fuels.

Given our large discrete expenditures on consumer durables and their interrelatedness with other household expenditures, it is easy to see that consumer durables create special budgeting problems. Without adequate planning, repair or replacement is likely to be an unexpected event that creates havoc with the household budget.

Using your own funds to finance your purchases will save on finance charges. You can budget for these expenditures by creating replacement funds for goods that are on a regular replacement cycle, such as the roof on your home or the family auto. An emergency fund can be used to pay for unexpected replacements. Don't assume the use of your own money is costless. You are giving up interest income you could have earned on these funds. In addition, money in replacement funds may be limited to short-term, lower-yielding investments.

On products that have a trade-in value, you may want to calculate **net replacement cost.** This is equal to replacement cost less the market value of the trade-in. Consumer durables depreciate in market value over time because of wear or simply because the product no longer embodies the latest technology or fashion. Some consumer durables, such as cars, experience a rapid decline in market price after the initial purchase. Others, such as computer equipment, may be highly affected by changes in technology.

Most of this chapter is devoted to the most expensive consumer durable you probably will purchase—the automobile. You must decide what auto best fits your needs and how much you can afford. You have a choice of either leasing the auto or financing a purchase. To avoid unexpected surprises, you must then budget for the maintenance and operation of the vehicle. Before we take a closer look at those decisions, we want to review some concerns that apply to all major household purchases and the new electronic marketplace.

Consumer durables: Consumer goods that provide benefits that extend over a period of at least one year.

Net replacement cost: Replacement cost less trade-in value.

MAJOR HOUSEHOLD PURCHASES AND THE ELECTRONIC MARKET

An efficient selection process must include gathering and evaluating information. Information can be gained from talking to friends, visiting retail outlets, and reading such consumer-oriented magazines as *Consumer Reports* and *Consumer Research* or purchasing one of the numerous buyer's guides. Today the Internet is an important tool for researching prices and products. There are numerous shopping robots on the Web that will summarize prices at numerous online stores and provide buyer's guides on products. In addition, manufacturer's Web sites often provide additional information on technical specifications, instruction manuals, and warranty coverage.

The Internet has significantly lowered the cost of comparison shopping. Most major chains and even many local stores now list their prices on Web sites. Shopping services by all the major Internet portals, such as Yahoo! and Google, provide instant price comparisons

TOPIC **LINKS**

Product review and price comparison Web sites.

on products and retailers. It is likely that the ready availability of pricing information has made the entire retail sector more competitive.

There are many Internet sites that specialize in product reviews. Individuals that previously purchased the product or dealt with a particular merchant often post reviews. The product reviews can be helpful in judging the product's qualities. On the other hand, you must be careful not to place too much weight on the experiences of a small number of customers. It is unfortunate that the Internet has also created numerous opportunities for criminals. Figure 7.1 lists the top 10 Internet frauds.

Electronic Purchases

The first rule you should adhere to when shopping on the Internet is to know with whom you are dealing. Several sites rate online retailers on honesty, convenience, and on-time delivery. Merchant reviews are essential when dealing with a new online store that is not backed up by a brick-and-mortar site. CNET (**shopper.cnet.com**), BizRate.com (**www.bizrate.com**), and Nextag (**www.nextag.com**) all provide information on online merchants and rate customer service. Local stores are likely to work with you to correct mistakes and ensure customer satisfaction. Although it may be more convenient to shop electronically, it may be much less

Figure 7.1

Top 10 Internet Frauds

Source: National Fraud Information Center,
Trends January-December 2003

Auctions 89%
    Never delivered or misrepresented goods or services

General Merchandise 5%
    Sales of everything from T-shirts to toys that are never delivered or are not as advertised

Nigerian Money Offers 2%
    False promises of riches if consumers pay to transfer vast fortunes to their accounts

Information/Adult Services 1%
    Cost of services misrepresented or services never provided

Internet Account Services 1%
    Cost of Internet access misrepresented or services never provided

Computer Equipment/Software .2%
    Sales of computer products never delivered or misrepresented

Work-at-Home Plans .2%
    Kits sold on false promises of big profits from working at home

Lotteries .2%
    False promises to help consumers win money or claim winnings from foreign lotteries

Fake Checks .2%
    Consumers are paid with phoney checks for items they've sold or work performed, with instructions to wire some of the money back to the con artists

Advance Fee Loans .1%
    False promises of personal or business loans, even if credit is bad, for a fee paid up-front

convenient to return unsatisfactory merchandise. For both local and online merchants, be sure to check out return policies. Some may refuse to accept returned merchandise and others may charge a hefty restocking fee on returns.

The **Mail Order Merchandise Rule** was initially issued by the Federal Trade Commission to cover telephone and catalog sales. This regulation is now applied to all electronic sales, including purchases through the Internet or by fax. Unless the seller states otherwise, the "30-day rule" applies. After accepting your order, the retailer must ship the product within 30 days or obtain your consent to delay shipment. This may be extended to 50 days if the retailer is providing a new line of credit. Should the retailer not obtain your consent to a delayed shipment, the seller must promptly refund your money, including all related sales charges. This rule covers only merchandise; it does not cover services such as photo finishing. If you receive merchandise you have not ordered, you may legally consider it a gift.

Online fraud and deception account for over one-quarter of consumer complaints received by the Federal Trade Commission. The top complaint is identity theft. This is when someone uses your identity to run up fraudulent purchases. Crooks don't need the Internet to steal your identity. They can rob you of your wallet or go through your garbage. Unfortunately, criminals are increasingly using the Internet as a source of personal information. The best advice is to follow the Federal Trade Commission's rules for "paying safe" in Figure 7.2.

Mail Order Merchandise Rule: Protects customers against the untimely shipment of products.

TOPIC **LINKS**

National Fraud Information Center and FTC online fraud sites.

Online Auctions and Electronic Payments

The Internet Fraud Watch reports that about 89 percent of all Internet-related fraud complaints were about online auctions. Eighty percent of the online auction complaints involved the use of money orders and checks. Only 6 percent involved credit cards. A survey sponsored by the National Consumers League indicated that 41 percent of buyers on online auctions encounter a problem. A startling 10 percent received damaged items and another 10 percent never received the item won at auction.

Figure 7.2

Paying Safe

Source: Federal Trade Commission, "Guide to Online Payments."

When you make purchases online, make sure your transactions are secure, your personal information is protected, and your fraud sensors are sharpened. Although you can't control fraud or deception on the Internet, you can take steps to recognize it, avoid it, and report it. Here's how:

- Use a secure browser—software that encrypts or scrambles the purchase information you send over the Internet—to guard the security of your online transactions.
- Keep records of your online transactions. Read your e-mail—merchants may send you important information about your purchases.
- Be prompt about reviewing your monthly bank and credit card statements for any billing errors or unauthorized purchases. Notify your credit card issuer or bank immediately if your credit card or checkbook is lost or stolen.
- Read the policies of Web sites you visit—especially the disclosures about a Web site's security, its refund policies, and its privacy policy on collecting and using your personal information.
- Keep your personal information private. Don't disclose your personal information—your address, telephone number, Social Security number, and e-mail address—unless you know who's collecting the information, why they're collecting it, and how they'll use it.
- Give payment information only to businesses you know and trust and only in appropriate places such as order forms.
- Never give your password to anyone online, not even to your Internet service provider.
- Do not download files sent to you by strangers or click on hyperlinks from people you don't know. Opening a file could expose your system to a computer virus.

Auctions can be divided into "business-to-person" auctions and "person-to-person" auctions. In the "business-to-person" format, the auction site has control of the merchandise and ensures that it is delivered to the buyer. It is the latter category of auctions, "person-to-person" auctions, that have been the source of most consumer complaints.

Internet auction sites for person-to-person auctions claim they are not responsible for the quality of the merchandise or the representations made by sellers. However, as an aid to consumers, most sites post feedback on a seller's previous transactions. You should review the posted comments and examine the seller's track record. Be aware that shills can manipulate these posts and a dishonest seller can generate a good track record before cashing in on a major scam. Some auction sites provide fraud insurance protection for buyers. The maximum payout on fraud protection is usually limited to modest amounts after a small deductible.

To protect market participants, auction payments are increasingly being completed through a financial intermediary such as PayPal. A financial intermediary accepts credit card payments from buyers and makes cash payments to sellers. The service is paid for by about a 3 percent deduction from the amount paid sellers. PayPal protects you from credit card fraud by ensuring that your financial information is not disclosed to the seller. An intermediary that functions as an escrow service may provide additional protection for both buyers and sellers. The escrow service holds the buyer's payment until the goods arrive and the buyer approves the transfer. If problems occur, the escrow service attempts to negotiate a compromise. The service is paid for with a fee that may range from 2 to 5 percent of the purchase price.

Warranties

Whether you make an online purchase or a store purchase, it is important that you check out the product's warranty. Most consumers do not bother to read warranties. They should, because the terms of a warranty can often provide sufficient reasons for selecting one product over another. **Warranty** and **guarantee** have the same meaning. They represent the seller's assumption of responsibility for the quality, character, or suitability of the goods sold. In a world of imperfect information, the buyer cannot know everything about the product being purchased. Therefore, the consumer requires some protection in the event the product does not perform as expected. It is the warranty that provides the needed protection.

Warranty or guarantee: The seller's assumption of responsibility for the quality, character, or suitability of goods sold.

Implied and Express Warranties

All products, except those sold **"as is,"** carry implied warranties. An implied warranty is imposed upon the seller by law. In other words, the law sets down certain requirements that the seller must live up to. The **implied warranty** will consist of a warranty of merchantability and a warranty of fitness for purpose. *Merchantability* means that the buyer has the right to expect that the good is generally of the same quality as similar goods in its class and that it does what it was built to do. A buyer has the right to expect that a washing machine washes clothes. *Fitness of purpose* means that if the buyer is relying on the seller to select a good for a particular purpose, and the seller has reason to know of that purpose, the good should prove suitable. For example, if the seller knows that the buyer wants a washing machine to wash rugs, then the machine should be able to handle difficult tasks such as cleaning heavy rugs.

"As is": The seller bears absolutely no responsibility for the quality or performance of the good.

Implied warranty: A warranty created by the operation of the law when no express warranty exists.

Not all products carry an **express warranty.** An express warranty is contractual; that is, it depends on the written or oral agreement between the buyer and seller. An express warranty need not be in writing, nor is it even necessary for the seller to intend to guarantee the item for an express warranty to exist. Statements of fact and promises expressed by the sales agent or manufacturer either at the time of the sale or in previous advertisements can form the basis for an express warranty. However, you must carefully distinguish statements of fact from what is called **puffery.** This is typical sales talk meant to persuade the customer by overly praising the good. Statements such as "This is a good buy" are mere puffery and do not carry an express warranty.

The **Magnuson-Moss Warranty Act of 1975** regulates express written warranties. Before passage of this act, many written warranties contained clauses that relieved the seller of an implied warranty. Consequently, some consumers would have been better off without an express warranty. One of the purposes of this act was to make such clauses ineffective by prohibiting written warranties from limiting the implied warranty to a shorter period than that covered by the written warranty. However, the seller can still avoid an implied warranty by selling the product "as is."

Express warranty: An oral or written agreement between buyer and seller concerning the character or performance of the good.

Puffery: Persuasive sales talk overly praising the good.

Magnuson-Moss Warranty Act of 1975: Federal law regulating the conditions and limitations contained in express warranties.

Full and Limited Warranties

Another purpose of the Warranty Act was to set down requirements for full and limited warranties. It is now necessary that all written warranties be labeled either *limited* or *full*.

The **full warranty** label means that consumers are entitled to full remedies for a specified period of time. They may even request a replacement or refund if the warrantor has been given a reasonable number of attempts to fix the product and has been unsuccessful. This provision is termed **lemon protection,** and it is included only in full warranties. The *full* label also means that, during the period specified, consumers will not be charged for parts or labor, or associated transportation and travel. In addition, a full warranty cannot disclaim or limit the duration of implied warranties, be limited to the original owner, require a registration card to provide the date of purchase, or impose an unreasonable requirement as a condition of warranty coverage. Any warranty that does not meet these standards must be labeled a **limited warranty.**

Many products will carry both limited and full warranties. For example, the first year of ownership may be covered by a full warranty, with coverage reduced to a limited warranty in subsequent years. It is also possible that some components will be covered by a full warranty, while others will have limited coverage or none.

Full warranty: During a specified time period, purchases are entitled to full protection, including lemon protection and all repair-related costs.

Lemon protection: If the merchandise cannot be repaired after a reasonable number of attempts, the customer can elect to receive either a replacement or a refund.

Limited warranty: Any express warranty that does not meet all of the necessary conditions for a full warranty.

Should You Purchase a Service Contract?

Whenever you purchase a major home appliance or a car, the salesperson will usually try to sell you a **service contract** or what is also called an **extended warranty.** This is because service contracts have proved to be highly profitable for sellers and not so profitable for buyers. Unless you are particularly hard on the products you use, the expected cost of repairs is typically much less than the cost of the service contract. For example, an MIT study for the National Science Foundation revealed that the cost of a service contract for a color TV set was almost 10 times the expected cost of repairs, and for a refrigerator it was about 16 times the expected cost of repairs.

A service contract is, in effect, the same as an insurance policy. You are insuring yourself against repairs on your consumer durables. The manufacturer or retailer is betting that the equipment won't break down, and you are betting that it will. In subsequent chapters

Service contract or extended warranty: For an initial fee, the seller agrees to repair the merchandise, either without charge or a set charge, for a period beyond the initial warranty.

we will discuss the basic principles of insurance protection. One such principle is that you should concentrate on insuring yourself against major financial calamities and bear any small risks yourself. The breakdown of the washing machine may seem major at the time it happens, but it is really minor relative to other financial losses you may suffer.

SELECTING AN AUTOMOBILE

TOPIC LINKS

Check out car guides on the Internet.

The decision to buy or lease an auto will lock you into future finance, maintenance, and insurance payments. Finding the right car takes more than just finding the best buy. You must decide which car best fits your needs. You can buy an expensive car that impresses your friends but drains your bank account, or you can more modestly satisfy your needs. In this section you will find help on the purchase versus lease decision and on how to correct problems after the purchase. Selecting a car and selecting auto insurance are not separate decisions. Consequently, you might also want to read Chapter 13 on property and liability insurance before you purchase that next car.

Pricing Information

The current practices accompanying automobile sales seem to have evolved from the horse trading of the past. A car is one of the few purchases we make that still involves haggling over price. In such market encounters, the person with the best information will usually have the advantage. If you don't do some comparative shopping, you give the seller the advantage.

Monroney sticker price:
Legally required price information adhered to the windows of all new cars.

New Cars

Each new car must have the **Monroney sticker price** on a side window. This shows the base price, the manufacturer's installed options with the manufacturer's suggested retail price, the manufacturer's transportation charge, and the fuel economy. The **base price** is the cost of the car without options but includes standard equipment and factory warranty. Some new cars may also have a **dealer sticker price.** This will include such extras as dealer-installed options, additional dealer markup (ADM), dealer preparation, and undercoating. The dealer rarely gets the sticker price for the car.

The most important piece of information you can have when bargaining with the dealer is the **invoice price.** This is the price the manufacturer charges the dealer for the car. However, on some cars the invoice price may be greater than the dealer's final cost. This is because the dealer may receive rebates, allowances, discounts, and incentive awards from the manufacturer.

Invoice costs and a wealth of other data are available at no charge over the Internet. You can even get a price quote from a regional dealer. If you use invoice cost as a bargaining chip in the showroom, it is suggested that you first ask the salesperson for the minimum markup over invoice that is acceptable to the dealership. If this markup is favorable relative to other dealers you have visited, add it to their indicated invoice cost and make a firm offer. Don't waiver from your initial offer. If your money doesn't talk, be ready to walk.

The salesperson is likely to offer you an extended warranty for an additional charge. For the same reasons stated previously, it is usually not a good buy. Moreover, to a considerable degree the extended warranty may cover repairs already provided for under the regular warranty. A four-year, 48,000-mile extended warranty on a car that has a manufacturer's three-year, 36,000-mile regular warranty extends coverage by only one year and 12,000 miles. The limited additional coverage, however, has not deterred dealers from charging exorbitant prices. The New York attorney general's office found that over half the consumers in that state who purchased extended warranties were charged more than the manufacturer's suggested retail price.

Used Cars

If you are considering buying, selling, or trading in a used car, the two most commonly used sources of pricing information are the *National Automobile Dealers Association Official Used Car Guide* and the *Kelley Blue Book Used Car Guide*. These are on hand at most libraries and at banks where car loans are made. In addition, online versions are available on the Internet. They contain the average trade-in or wholesale price and the retail price for many different makes of used cars. Also included are estimated prices for optional equipment.

Your best buy is typically a two- to three-year-old used car. This is because the annual percentage depreciation in price is greatest over the first few years. Before selecting a model, you should consult the *Consumer Reports* readers' survey on frequency of repair records also published in the April issue. Obviously, try to avoid makes and models that are not on their recommended list.

A used car at a dealer should have a large sticker called the "Buyers Guide" posted in the window. This will indicate whether the car is covered by a warranty, and if it is, what the warranty includes. About one-half of used cars are sold "as is," meaning there is no warranty. When you purchase a car "as is," you are fully responsible for any needed repairs. For those cars that are sold with a warranty, the previous discussion on warranties applies. If the car is still covered by an unexpired manufacturer's warranty, then the manufacturer, not the dealer who sold you the car, is responsible for fulfilling the terms of this warranty. If you have any questions concerning warranty coverage, be sure to ask the dealer to explain the terms of the contract. Also be sure that all the dealer's promises are included in the written warranty.

Rebates and Dealer-Supplied Financing

Manufacturer's rebates and low-interest dealer financing are widely used advertising gimmicks. Once in the showroom, the consumer often finds that these items are being offered

Base price: Price of the car without optional features.

Dealer sticker price: Monroney sticker price plus dealer add-ons.

Invoice price: The price the manufacturer charges the retailer for the car.

TOPIC **LINKS**
Get the invoice price and a price quote.

TOPIC **LINKS**
Find the current market value of your car.

in place of the typical dealer discount. The true cost of the car may be unchanged or even greater.

A Federal Trade Commission investigation of promotions for dealer financing turned up numerous examples of unethical and possible illegal activities. In some cases consumers were offered the low rate on only a few cars and only if they made an unusually large down payment. In other cases the typical cash discount was unavailable, and the car was loaded with high-cost options. The latest promotional strategy is to apply the low advertised rate only on loans of unusually short duration. Watch out for last-minute changes in what you were previously promised. It is a sure sign you are being taken for a ride.

The Bank Rate Monitor can provide you with information on interest rates in your area. Using a financial calculator or Table 7.1 you can calculate your total payments at alternative interest rates. You may then judge any trade-off between a lower interest rate and a higher purchase price. Remember, if you trade in the car before the loan matures, you lose the subsequent benefits of a lower interest rate.

A word of caution: Sometimes a lender will offer a loan at an attractive interest rate and then tack on to the monthly payment a charge for credit life insurance. This insurance will pay off the remaining principal on the loan in the event of your death. In many states it is illegal to require that the borrower accept the **credit life insurance.** It is often unnecessary, high-cost insurance, the purpose of which is actually to increase the interest return to the lender. If credit life is being forced upon you, be sure to compare loans according to total monthly payments, including the credit life premium.

Credit life insurance: Pays off the remaining loan balance upon one's death.

Saving
money $

Use Your Home Equity to Finance Your Car

Rates on home equity loans are about the same as on auto loans. However, they have one big advantage, the tax advantage. Interest on home equity loans up to $100,000 is tax deductible. If you itemize your deductions (if you have a home, you probably do), this can be a substantial savings.

A homeowner can take out a loan by borrowing against the equity in the home, the difference between the market value on the home and the remaining balance on the mortgage. Of course, if you default, you can lose your home. Defaults, however, are low on home equity loans. This is why lenders can offer attractive rates.

One important concern is that you don't trade off long-term home equity debt for short-term enjoyment. With most auto loans the outstanding balance is typically less than the market value of the car. When you use a home equity loan, the repayment schedule is not necessarily tied to the life of the auto. Unless you monitor both your loan balance and the value of the car, you could find yourself in an ever-increasing financial quagmire. You may be burdened with debt on a car you no longer own.

BOX 7.2

In the past, lenders would not make a home equity loan if your total "loan-to-value" ratio was above 80 to 85 percent. This value provided the lender with a cushion should you not be able to repay your loan. Home prices could fall 15 to 20 percent in a declining market without endangering the loan collateral. Lately, lenders have been making home equity loans that take total outstanding loans up to 100 percent of the appraised value of the home. The catch is that these loans carry a higher interest rate to offset the greater risk of default.

TOPIC **LINKS**

View current interest rates.

Representative Loan Rates (September, 2004)	
Credit card rate (fixed)	12.68%
New car loan (48 month)	5.89%
Home equity loan (30K)	6.45%
1-year adjustable rate mortgage	4.37%
30-year fixed rate mortgage	5.37%

Annual Percentage Rate	Term of Loan (Months)			
	24	36	48	60
3%	$42.98	$29.08	$22.13	$17.97
4%	43.42	29.52	22.58	18.42
5%	43.87	29.97	23.03	18.87
6%	44.32	30.42	23.49	19.33
7%	44.77	30.88	23.95	19.80
8%	45.23	31.34	24.41	20.28
9%	45.68	31.90	24.89	20.76
10%	46.14	32.27	25.36	21.25
11%	46.61	32.74	25.85	21.74
12%	47.07	33.21	26.33	22.24
13%	47.54	33.69	26.83	22.75

Table 7.1

Monthly Payments on Each $1,000 Borrowed

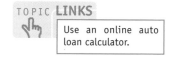
TOPIC **LINKS**

Use an online auto loan calculator.

THE COSTS OF OWNING AND OPERATING AN AUTOMOBILE

When deciding whether to purchase a car, and when planning your household finances, you will need information on the cost of ownership and operation. Runzheimer International, a management consulting firm, specializes in the collection of data on travel and living costs. Its estimates for the cost of owning and operating selected vehicles are given in Figure 7.3. For the owner who purchases a new car and trades it in after 36 months and 60,000 miles, the cost of owning and operating an automobile is a significant expense. As indicated in Figure 7.3 the owner of even a modestly priced new car would incur over $6,000 a year in expenses. For budgeting purposes, these expenses may be separated into the fixed cost of ownership and the variable cost of operation.

TOPIC **LINKS**

See what else Runzheimer International has to offer.

The Cost of Ownership

Ownership costs are fixed; that is, they do not vary with usage. No matter how much or how little you use the car, these expenses will remain relatively constant. Each of the following is considered a **cost of ownership**: auto insurance, license, registration, taxes, depreciation, and finance charges.

Cost of ownership: Fixed costs that do not vary with usage.

Insurance

The cost of insurance will depend upon the amount and type of coverage. For a detailed discussion of auto insurance, see Chapter 13.

License, Registration, Taxes

The state in which you live will impose these fees. Each state has its own formula for determining the cost of a license. This can vary depending on the vehicle's weight and type and your intended use of the motor vehicle.

With the purchase of a car you should receive a **certificate of title.** This authenticates your ownership of the car and should be kept in a safe place. Never leave it in the car, since

Certificate of title: Legal evidence of your ownership of a motor vehicle.

Figure 7.3

Projected Ownership and Operating Costs for Selected 2004 Cars, Standard City, USA

All four-door vehicles similarly equipped including automatic transmission, power steering, power disc brakes, air conditioning, tinted glass, AM/FM stereo, body side moldings, speed control, left-hand remote control mirror, rear window defogger, pulse windshield wipers, antilock brakes, driver and passenger air bags, and tilt steering.

Costs include operating expenses (fuel, oil, maintenance, & tires), fixed expenses (insurance, depreciation, financing, taxes, and licensing) and are based on a 36-month/60,000 mile retention cycle.

*20,000 mile annual usage

Source: Runzheimer International. These data are presented with permission from Runzheimer International, the Rochester, Wisconsin-based management consulting firm.

MAKE & MODEL	ANNUAL COSTS			Cost Per Mile*		
	Operating Costs (Variable)	Ownership Costs (Fixed)	Total Costs	Operating Costs (Variable)	Ownership Costs (Fixed)	Total Costs
BMW 540I	$3,760	$12,840	$16,600	$0.19	$0.64	$0.83
Lincoln Town Car Exec.	3,850	12,652	16,502	0.19	0.63	0.83
Cadillac DeVille	3,760	12,893	16,653	0.19	0.64	0.83
Buick Park Avenue Ultra S.C.	3,610	12,054	15,664	0.18	0.60	0.78
Buick LeSabre Limited	2,890	9,386	12,276	0.14	0.47	0.61
Mercury Grand Marquis GS	3,340	7,708	11,048	0.17	0.39	0.55
Dodge Intrepid SE	2,950	7,373	10,323	0.15	0.37	0.52
Buick Century Custom	2,990	7,223	10,213	0.15	0.36	0.51
Ford Taurus SE	3,010	6,951	9,961	0.15	0.35	0.50
Chevrolet Impala	2,950	6,949	9,899	0.15	0.35	0.49
Chevrolet Malibu	2,990	6,597	9,587	0.15	0.33	0.48
Chevrolet Malibu LS	2,990	6,829	9,819	0.15	0.34	0.49
Pontiac Grand Prix SE	3,140	6,945	10,085	0.16	0.35	0.50
Pontiac Grand AM SE	2,620	6,597	9,217	0.13	0.33	0.46
Toyota Camry LE	2,760	6,073	8,833	0.14	0.30	0.44
Honda Accord LX	2,700	6,023	8,723	0.14	0.30	0.44
Chevrolet Cavalier	2,560	6,045	8,605	0.13	0.30	0.43
Ford Focus SE	2,450	5,748	8,198	0.12	0.29	0.41
Honda Civic LX	2,300	5,175	7,475	0.12	0.26	0.37
Toyota Corolla CE	2,330	5,127	7,457	0.12	0.26	0.37

Certificate of registration: A document indicating that your car is properly registered with the state motor vehicle department.

the car may be stolen. Another important document is the **certificate of registration,** which indicates that the vehicle has been properly registered with your state motor vehicle department. This document should remain in your car.

Depreciation

Depreciation: The reduction in the market value of a motor vehicle due to passage of time, mechanical and physical condition, and number of miles driven.

Depreciation is the reduction in the market value of the vehicle due to passage of time, mechanical and physical condition, and number of miles driven. Although depreciation does vary with usage, it is dependent primarily upon time for autos; therefore, it can be considered a fixed cost for any given year.

Your average annual depreciation will depend on the age of your car and your holding period. If you purchased a new car each year for $20,000 and traded in the old car each year for $15,000, your average annual depreciation would be $5,000. Alternatively, if you purchased a new car every other year for $20,000 and traded in the two-year-old car for $12,000, the depreciation over the two-year period would be $8,000. After the total depreciation is divided by 2, the length of the holding period, the average annual depreciation is $4,000. The difference between average annual depreciation of $5,000 and average annual depreciation of $4,000 represents a yearly savings of $1,000. This is the dollar advantage of having a two-year holding period rather than a one-year holding period. The longer you hold the car, the smaller is your average annual cost of depreciation.

Finance Charges

Estimates of finance charges included in Figure 7.3 assume that each car is purchased with a 20 percent down payment and financed with a 36-month loan at a competitive market rate. If you purchase the car out of savings, you can eliminate these explicit finance charges; however, you give up the interest income you could have earned on those savings. This lost interest would also represent a cost of ownership. Consequently, whether or not you intend to finance the purchase with borrowed funds, you should consider the Runzheimer estimate of finance charges as a real cost of ownership. Runzheimer estimates that depreciation and finance charges make up more than 50 percent of auto costs.

Other Costs of Ownership

Any additional fixed costs that are incurred because of car ownership should also be considered. For example, if you rent a garage to house your car, the rental payments should be included in the cost of ownership. On the other hand, if you would normally live in a home with a garage, whether or not you own a car, then your additional or marginal cost of storage would be zero.

The cost of accessories may also be included. These may consist of such things as extra wheels for snow tires, radios, and trailer hitches. Items that have an effect on mechanical operation can be included under the maintenance component of operating expenses.

The Cost of Operation

Costs that are related directly to usage are called *variable costs*. The **cost of operation** includes all variable costs. Your cost of operations will be directly related to how much you use your car.

Cost of operation: Variable costs that are directly related to usage.

Gasoline and Oil

After the cost of depreciation, this is likely to be your next largest vehicle expense. Your costs should be based on your regional cost of fuel and your car's fuel economy.

Maintenance and Tires

The owner's manual or your local mechanic should be able to recommend a maintenance schedule based on the miles you typically drive. Maintenance and tires are not generally covered under an automobile warranty and therefore should be included in the household budget. For older cars on which the warranty has expired, unscheduled repairs and parts replacement should also be given consideration when estimating expenditures.

Other Operating Costs

Metered curb parking, fees charged for parking lots, and toll charges for highways, tunnels, and bridges may all represent additional operating costs. In an urban environment these costs should not be overlooked; they can represent a significant cost of commuting.

The Total Cost of Ownership and Operation

By adding together the fixed cost of ownership and the variable cost of operation, you can calculate the total cost of the family car. The cost of ownership generally represents a larger portion of total auto expenditures than the cost of operation.

On a per-mile basis, the total cost per mile of the midsize car driven 20,000 miles per year is about 50 cents. This consists of 15 cents per mile in operating costs and 35 cents per mile in ownership costs. At this level of usage, ownership cost represents about 70 percent of your auto-related transportation expenses. However, if the car is driven an additional mile, the variable cost of operations will increase by about 15 cents, while the fixed cost of ownership will remain relatively stable. This means that as the car is used more often, the relative importance of ownership cost will decline.

The Mass-Transit Alternative

In highly congested New York City, about 44 percent of the workforce uses public transportation to get to work. In less densely populated Indianapolis, only about 3 percent of the workforce uses public transportation. This difference can be explained in terms of relative availability, relative cost, and relative convenience of mass transit in each of these cities. If you have a mass transit alternative in your city, you should compare the costs of using a private auto with those of using public transit.

When judging the relative merits of public transit, you should first decide whether you could do without owning a motor vehicle. If you can rely solely on mass transit, you may weigh the cost of public transit against the total cost of ownership and operation. Alternatively, if you find you need the car anyway, then you should weigh the cost of public transit only against the cost of vehicle operation. This is because the cost of ownership is a **sunk cost:** It is something you have to pay whether or not you use the car. Therefore, if you own the car and want to know whether to drive it an additional mile or to use public transit to go the same mile, you should consider only the **marginal,** or additional, **cost** you will incur. In most circumstances, the least costly alternative will depend upon the necessity of car ownership.

Sunk cost: A cost that has already been incurred and, therefore, cannot be changed.

Marginal cost: Additional or incremental cost that will be incurred.

THE LEASING ALTERNATIVE

If you find that you do need a car, but the need exists only for an occasional trip, you might consider an occasional rental as a practical alternative to ownership. By renting you avoid the high fixed cost of ownership, an exorbitant expense for a car that is seldom used.

If you need a car for longer periods of time but wish to hold down the high initial cost of ownership, you might consider leasing. Your current expenses and your periodic payments will be less than if you purchased the same car on credit. When you lease a vehicle, you are only paying rent for the car's long-term use. Your payments are determined primarily by the difference between the initial price of the car and the resale value of the car at the termination of the lease. If you finance a purchase, on the other hand, you are building equity as you pay off the loan principal. When you complete your car loan payments, you own the car. If you sell the car before all the loan payments are completed, you should receive any amount in excess of the loan balance.

A vehicle lease is a contract between the lessor (the property owner) and the lessee (the user) that sets out the terms and limitations on the use of the vehicle and the payment.

There are two types of leasing contracts: closed end and open end. Both are covered by regulations specified in the Consumer Leasing Act of 1977 and by the Federal Reserve Board under Regulation M. Some of these regulations may not apply if the car is not for personal use or if the contractual obligation exceeds $25,000. Figure 7.3 contains a sample disclosure statement issued by the Federal Reserve Board. It requires the leasing company (the lessor) to disclose in writing specific information about a consumer lease before you (the lessee) sign the lease agreement.

The Closed-End Lease

The **closed-end lease** is also sometimes called the *net* or *walkaway* lease. You make fixed periodic payments based on your estimated usage. When your lease expires, you simply return the car and pay a surcharge for mileage in excess of your estimate. Unless you have seriously damaged the vehicle, given it more than normal wear, or driven it more miles than the lease permits, you are not responsible for the value of the vehicle at the end of the lease term. Because the lessor is taking the risk as to what the value of the car will be when you return it, your lease payments generally will be higher than they would be under an open-end lease.

Closed-end lease: Your costs are determined at the time you lease the car. Under most circumstances, you are not responsible for the value of the car at the end of the lease.

The Open-End Lease

The **open-end lease** also has fixed periodic payments; however, the total cost remains unknown until the end of the leasing period. This is because the periodic payments are based on the estimated resale value on the returned car, sometimes called the estimated *residual value*.

When you return the vehicle, the lessor will appraise it and compare the appraised value with the residual value stated in the lease. Under the Consumer Leasing Act, you have the right, at your expense, to obtain an independent appraisal by someone agreed to by both you and the lessor. If you get an independent appraisal, you and the lessor are bound by it.

If the appraised value of the car is the same as, or greater than, the residual value specified in the lease disclosure, you owe nothing. (Your contract will determine whether you get a refund for any excess value. You can ask the lessor to include the right to a refund in your contract.) Alternatively, if the appraisal indicates that the vehicle is worth less than the specified amount, you may have to pay all or a portion of the difference. This cost is often called an *end-of-lease payment*.

You may be able to bargain for lower periodic payments if you agree to have a higher residual value put on the vehicle. Of course, setting a higher residual value increases your risk of having to make a large payment at the end of the lease. To ensure that consumers will not unknowingly enter into agreements with exorbitant end-of-lease payments, the

Open-end lease: The total cost of the lease is unknown until the end of the lease, when the estimated resale value of the car is determined.

Consumer Leasing Act requires that under most circumstances the end-of-lease payment can be no more than three times the average monthly payment on the lease. However, higher payments can be collected if you agreed to pay a greater amount, there was unreasonable wear or excessive use, or the lessor wins a lawsuit seeking a higher amount.

Evaluating a Car Lease

Leases are difficult for even professionals to competitively evaluate. Therefore, it is no wonder that consumers with little training in finance can often find leases confusing. Of course, buyer confusion provides profit opportunities for unethical dealers. The best way to think about leasing is that you are taking out a loan, but instead of borrowing money, you are borrowing a car. You are paying for the use of the car in three ways. First, there are prepayments that are made at the time of the loan. Second, there are monthly installments and, third, there is a balloon payment, which is a much larger payment at the end of the loan. The balloon payment consists of the value of the returned car at the end of the leasing period or, if you buy the car, the purchase price at the end of the leasing period.

Unfortunately, federal statutes do not treat a lease like a loan. Accordingly, the lessor does not have to reveal an APR. In addition, the language in leases may be difficult to understand. The "Keys to Vehicle Leasing" contains a helpful glossary. Leases, however, may contain terms for which there are no standard definitions. The terms *lease rate* or *money factor* should not be confused with an interest rate. These are just proprietary numbers that the lessor uses to calculate your monthly payment.

The **gross capitalized cost** (Figure 7.4, entry 8) is the negotiated price for the car, including any other items you are going to finance over the term of the lease, such as taxes, fees, service contracts, insurance, and any prior credit or lease balance. Be sure to check the appropriate box to get an itemized listing of the specific components of gross capitalized cost. The **adjusted capitalized cost** is equal to the gross capitalized cost less any up-front payments included in **capitalized cost reduction** (entry 9). Capitalized cost reduction can consist of cash payments, a net trade-in balance, and rebates. In the current example, the capitalized cost reduction of $3,500 includes a $2,500 trade-in and a $1,000 cash payment. Notice that the amount due at delivery will exceed the capitalized cost reduction (entry 6b). It may include several other items, such as the initial monthly payment, title and registration fees, a security deposit, and insurance premiums.

A capitalized cost reduction is, in effect, an advance payment on the lease. It may or may not be required by the lessor. If you trade in your old car, the capitalized cost reduction may be set equal to the value of the trade. The more you pay down initially, the lower your periodic payments will be. However, if you make a high initial payment in order to reduce your periodic payments, you lose one important advantage of leasing—the lower initial cost.

The adjusted capitalized cost will be paid back over the life of the lease or at the end of the lease. At the end of the lease you give back the car and the lessor recaptures the residual value in the car. The **residual value** is equal to the car's initial market value less the depreciation in market value that occurs over the term of the lease. The depreciation and any other amortized amounts will be paid off uniformly over the term of the lease. In addition to these costs, you will have to pay for financing the carrying cost on the vehicle. This is similar to finance charges on a loan and is listed as a rent charge (entry 1D). However, you should not confuse the two. With a loan, you are building equity in a vehicle. With a lease, you own nothing at the end of the lease.

Be sure you understand how early termination (entry 14) and end-of-lease charges (15 and 17) will be determined. The Consumer Bankers Association reports that about 43 percent of auto leases are terminated early. In addition to simply desiring a new car,

TOPIC **LINKS**

Get a copy of "Keys to Vehicle Leasing" and review a sample disclosure statement.

Gross capitalized cost: The cost of the car and other items included in the leasing contract.

Adjusted capitalized cost: Gross capitalized cost less up-front payments.

Capitalized cost reduction: Up-front payments including cash, trade-in, and rebates.

Residual value: The car's market value at the termination of the lease.

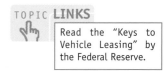

TOPIC **LINKS**

Read the "Keys to Vehicle Leasing" by the Federal Reserve.

Federal Consumer Leasing Act Disclosures

Date _00100100_

Lessor(s) _Dealer or Leasing Company_   Lessee(s) _J. Smith_   **①**

Amount Due at Lease Signing or Delivery (Itemized below)" **②** $ _4,241.94_	**Monthly Payments** Your first monthly payment of $ _256.94_ is due on _00100100_ , followed by _47_ payments of $ _256.94_ due on the _1st_ of each month. The total of your monthly payments is $ _12,333.12_ **③**	**Other Charges** (not part of your monthly payment) **④** Disposition fee (if you do not purchase the vehicle) $ _400.00_ _-0-_ Total $ _400.00_	**Total of Payments** (The amount you will have paid by the end of the lease) $ _16,368.12_ **⑤**

* Itemization of Amount Due at Lease Signing

Amount Due At Lease Signing:

Capitalized cost reduction	$ _3,500.00_
First monthly payment	_256.94_
Refundable security deposit	_350.00_
Title fees	_75.00_
Registration fees	_60.00_
_____	_-0-_
Total $	_4,241.94_ **6a**

⑥ How the Amount Due at Lease Signing will be paid:

Net trade-in allowance	$ _2,500.00_
Rebates and noncash credits	_-0-_
Amount to be paid in cash	_1,741.94_
Total $	_4,241.94_ **6b**

⑦ Your monthly payment is determined as shown below:

⑧ Gross capitalized cost. The agreed upon value of the vehicle ($ _21,500.00_) and any items you pay over the lease term (such as service contracts, insurance, and any outstanding prior loan or lease balance) .... $ _22,300.00_

If you want an itemization of this amount, please check this box. ☑

⑨ Capitalized cost reduction. The amount of any net trade-in allowance, rebate, noncash credit, or cash you pay that reduces the gross capitalized cost................................. − _3,500.00_

Adjusted capitalized cost. The amount used in calculating your base monthly payment............ = _18,800.00_

Residual value. The value of the vehicle at the end of the lease used in calculating your base monthly payment.............. − _12,350.00_

Depreciation and any amortized amounts. The amount charged for the vehicle's decline in value through normal use and for other items paid over the lease term .... = _6,450.00_

⑩ Rent charge. The amount charged in addition to the depreciation and any amortized amounts .... + _5,295.00_

Total of base monthly payments. The depreciation and any amortized amounts plus the rent charge........ = _11,745.00_

⑪ Lease payment. The number of months in your lease................. ÷ _48_

Base monthly payment .... = _244.69_

⑫ Monthly sales/use tax .... + _12.25_

+ _-0-_

⑬ Total monthly payment .... =$ _256.94_

---

⑭ Early Termination. You may have to pay a substantial charge if you end this lease early. <u>The charge may be up to several thousand dollars.</u> The actual charge will depend on when the lease is terminated. The earlier you end the lease, the greater this charge is likely to be.

⑮ Excessive Wear and Use. You may be charged for excessive wear based on our standards for normal use [and for mileage in excess **⑯** of _15,000_ miles per year at the rate of _.15_ per mile].

⑰ Purchase Option at End of Lease Term. [You have an option to purchase the vehicle at the end of the lease term for $ _12,350.00_ [and a purchase option fee of $ _150.00_ .

Other Important Terms. See your lease documents for additional information on early termination, purchase options and maintenance responsibilities, warranties, late and default charges, insurance, and any security interest, if applicable

Figure 7.4   *Federal Consumer Leasing Act Disclosures*   Source: Federal Reserve Board of Governors.

early termination can be triggered by theft or accident. Regardless of the reason for termination, you may be responsible for depreciation in the market value of the car and for additional special charges upon breaking the lease. Be sure you understand just how much you will owe if you decide to return the vehicle before the scheduled expiration of the lease. With an open-end lease it is important that you know how the residual value will be determined and whether it is a wholesale or resale price.

A Lease/Buy Comparison

Given this array of numbers, it is difficult to figure out just how much this lease is costing you. This would be a nice number to have, if you want to comparison shop leases or make a lease/buy comparison. Let us concentrate on the numbers listed on the disclosure statement and assume that other expenses such as maintenance and insurance would be similar under either decision. Figure 7.5 contains a worksheet for examining the lease/buy decision. Costs are separated into three distinct categories: initial expenses when the lease or purchase is initiated, continuing periodic monthly expenses during the lease or loan, and final expenses when the lease is terminated or the loan paid off.

The data from the disclosure statement have been used to complete the leasing side of this worksheet. On the buy side, it is assumed that an identical dealer package can be purchased for $22,300. Initial expenses on the purchase decision will consist of a $5,000 down payment ($2,500 trade-in and $2,500 cash) and other related sales expenses. Given the large down payment and the up-front sales tax, the initial expenses of buying will exceed that of leasing.

The buy decision assumes the purchaser can finance the remaining cost of the auto ($17,300) with a 48-month loan at an APR of 8.5 percent and monthly payments of $426.42. Accordingly, the payments on the loan will cost $169.48 ($426.42 − $256.94) more per month. It is obvious that the lease will entail significantly lower monthly expenses. This and the lower initial payment are what often make leasing an attractive alternative to buying for many consumers.

There are various ways that final expenses could have been handled. The worksheet analysis assumes that at the end of the lease the car is turned in resulting in a $400 disposition fee. For simplicity, it is assumed that the security deposit is returned and there are no other adjustments for excessive wear or residual value. At the end of the lease you own nothing. At the end of the loan you own the car. On the buy side it is assumed that the owner sells the car and nets the residual value ($12,350) less selling costs ($400).

If you total up all explicit, out-of-pocket expenses, it appears that the consumer saves $1,640 ($16,368 − $14,728) by buying rather than leasing. However, this does not take into account the time value of money. If you leased, you could have invested the savings on initial expenses ($1,968) over the 48-month period. At a 6 percent after-tax annual interest rate, this would have generated compound interest income of $532. Moreover, you could also have invested the monthly differential of 169 over 47 months, providing an additional $989 in interest income. This implicit interest income could either be subtracted from the leasing alternative as an implicit benefit of leasing or added to the cost of purchasing as an implicit cost of purchasing. In the worksheet it has been added to the cost of purchasing. In this example, buying is still the better alternative, but by a smaller amount.

Economists like to say there is no such thing as a free lunch. If you cannot afford to purchase a new car, you probably should not be leasing it. You are going to pay for the cost of using the car; it is just a matter of how. The real problem with leasing is that the lower up-front and periodic payments tempt us to drive a more expensive car. Over the long run we may end up spending a lot more on depreciation and finance charges than we would have if we had purchased a more reasonably priced car.

Figure 7.5

A Lease/Buy Comparison Worksheet

Leasing

Initial Expenses

Capitalized cost reduction	$3,500.00
First monthly payment	$256.94
Refundable security deposit	350.00
Title fees	75.00
Registration fees	60.00
Sales taxes	0.00
Total explicit initial cost	$4,241.94

Monthly Expenses

Base monthly payment	$244.69
Monthly sales/use tax	12.25
Total monthly payment	$256.94
Months	47
Total continuing explicit costs	$12,076.18

Final Expenses

Excessive mileage charge	$0.00
Excessive wear and tear	0.00
Adjustment for overestimated residual value	0.00
Security deposit	(350.00)
Disposition fee	400.00
Miscellaneous items	0.00
Total explicit final costs	$50.00

Total Explicit Expenses

Initial Expenses	$4,241.94
Monthly Expenses	12,076.18
Final Expenses	50.00
Total explicit costs	$16,368.12

Buying

Initial Expenses

Down payment and trade-in	5,000.00
Title fees	75.00
Registration fees	60.00
Sales tax	1,075.00
Total explicit initial costs	$6,210.00

Monthly Expenses

APR	8.5%
Initial amount financed	$17,300.00
Monthly loan payment	$426.42
Months	48
Total continuing explicit costs	$20,467.95

Final Expenses

Loan payoff	$0.00
Estimated residual value	(12,350.00)
Sales costs	$400.00
Total explicit final costs	($11,950.00)

Total Explicit Expenses

Initial Expenses	$6,210.00
Monthly Expenses	20,467.95
Final Expenses	(11,950.00)
Total explicit costs	$14,727.95

Implicit Cost of Purchasing

After-tax interest rate	6%	
Excess up-front cost of buying	$1,968.06	
Lost interest income		$532.34
Excess monthly payment	$169.48	
Lost interest income		988.66
Total lost interest income		$1,521.00
Total relevant cost of buying		$16,248.95
(Total explicit cost plus total lost interest income on purchase alternatives)		

TOPIC **LINKS**

Download this worksheet or use a lease/buy calculator.

Additional information on leasing can be found in a pamphlet published by the Federal Reserve Board entitled "Keys to Vehicle Leasing." Copies are available on the Internet. If you plan to lease, be sure to avoid high-pressure sales tactics. You need to carefully consider all of the costs outlined here and review your buying alternative. The Federal Reserve suggests that you follow a five-step process.

1. Don't directly enter into negotiations on a lease. First, identify the lowest price that the dealer will accept for the car. This will represent the capitalized cost.
2. After you have determined the best price you can get, then separately negotiate the value on any trade-in you may have. Given your anticipated down payment and trade-in, you can then estimate net capitalized cost.
3. Check all sources of financing to determine the best interest rate and your needed monthly payments under the purchase option.
4. Check out the resale value from industry publications.

5. Finally, enter into negotiations for the lease. You should now have all the information you need to use the lease/buy comparison worksheet and make an informed decision. Be wary of last-minute changes in the deal that don't leave you time to recheck your calculations. This is when consumers are most susceptible to high-pressure sales techniques that result in wasted dollars.

WHAT IF YOU BOUGHT A LEMON?

TOPIC **LINKS**

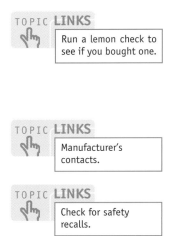

Run a lemon check to see if you bought one.

TOPIC **LINKS**

Manufacturer's contacts.

TOPIC **LINKS**

Check for safety recalls.

Your chance of purchasing a new car with serious problems is about one in 800. Your chance of purchasing a car with at least a few defects is apparently much higher. Most of the complaints in the first year should be covered by the new-car warranty. To ensure that they are corrected, you should be prepared to deal with new-car defects and know how to seek remedial action.

The suggested procedure is to discuss the problem with the dealer first, allowing the firm an adequate opportunity to repair the defect. If the dealer is unwilling to honor the warranty or is taking an unreasonable amount of time to correct the problem, contact the manufacturer. At the auto company, the person to contact first is often called the *zone representative* or the *area service manager*. If you still do not receive satisfaction, your next step is to contact the consumer representative at the company's headquarters. If neither the dealer nor the manufacturer responds to your request, you may consider going to small claims court, entering arbitration, or hiring an attorney.

Whichever alternative you choose, be prepared to supply adequate records on all your attempts at repair or replacement. Accordingly, be sure you receive a repair slip each time you return the car for service. The receipt should be legible and should contain an accurate statement of your complaint, the date of service, and the attempted repairs. If the dealer suggests you do not need a repair slip because the car is under warranty, insist on your right to receive one. Also retain copies of all relevant correspondence and a diary recording each related conversation, including the date, the name of the person with whom you discussed your problem, and a summary of what was said.

Secret Warranties

Secret warranty or policy adjustment: An understanding between manufacturers and retailers that certain defects will be repaired at no cost only when confronted with strong consumer complaints.

Warranties were examined previously in the section on the electronic market. Everything stated there holds true for automotive warranties as well. One additional item, however, commonly known as the **secret warranty,** seems to be unique to the automotive industry. It takes effect after the written warranty has expired. Under a secret warranty, the manufacturer repairs certain defects only when customers complain. Other, more docile, customers are not told about this policy and are unfairly charged for repairs.

The industry prefers the term **policy adjustment** or *after-warranty assistance* to *secret warranty.* Given the way the auto industry treats customers, it is a good idea to complain whenever you think your problem results from faulty workmanship or design. You should ask the zone representative whether policy adjustments have been made on similar problems and whether a policy adjustment would cover your current defect. The Center for Auto Safety collects information on policy adjustments. It may be able to supply you with information on how a manufacturer has previously dealt with similar defects.

TOPIC **LINKS**

Contact the Center for Auto Safety and review the NHTSA complaints database.

Alternative Dispute Resolution

If you have a problem with a new car and do not receive satisfaction from the dealer or the manufacturer's representative, or if you are dissatisfied with repairs made on a used car, your next step is to consider an alternative dispute resolution program. Ford and Chrysler have their own dispute resolution programs. Most of the auto manufacturers cooperate with the Better Business Bureau's (BBB) Autoline program (see Figure 7.6).

Most consumer protection agencies, such as the Better Business Bureau, will first attempt to resolve the disagreement through mediation. In mediation, an attempt is made to have the parties to the dispute reach their own agreement. If that doesn't work, arbitration may be entered into. **Arbitration** is a process for settling disputes in which an impartial third party listens to arguments made by both sides and suggests a remedy that may be binding or nonbinding. In consumer-related disputes, the Federal Trade Commission sets down rules to ensure that the arbitration procedure is, in fact, impartial. In the BBB Autoline program the arbitrator's decision is binding on the manufacturer but not on the consumer. If you accept the decision, you waive your right to sue the manufacturer in court.

Entering arbitration has two significant advantages over using the court system: The process is relatively speedy, and there is little or no cost to the individual. However, there are also some disadvantages. The arbitrators need not be lawyers or knowledgeable mechanics. Thus, they may not fully understand your problem or your rights as a consumer. Furthermore, they will not award punitive damages or compensatory damages related to such incidentals as lost wages or medical bills resulting from a defective car. Without your own lawyer, you may not know whether you would be entitled to such payments in the regular court system. In addition, by entering arbitration you may be accepting a potential decision that is legally binding. You should realize that your chances of coming out of arbitration with a better offer than that provided by the dealer or manufacturer's representative are only about 50–50.

Arbitration: A process for settling disputes in which an impartial third party mediates and suggests a binding or nonbinding remedy.

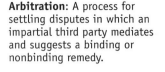

TOPIC **LINKS**

Arbitration programs.

Lemon Laws

Nearly all states have lemon laws to protect buyers of new cars. A few states even have lemon laws regulating the sale of used cars. In general, lemon laws declare that if a car dealer does not repair substantial defects covered by the new-car warranty within a reasonable period of time, the owner may be entitled to a comparable new car or a refund. A

TOPIC **LINKS**

Know your state's lemon laws.

BBB Autolite
See the Autoline Web site for a list of manufacturers that participate in the program.
www.bbb.org

Autocap (Automotive Consumer Action Program)
Administered through National Automotive Dealers Association, handles 15 makers of imports.
www.nada.org

Chrysler and Ford have their own boards for handling complaints:
Daimler Chrysler Motors Customer Relations
www.chrysler.com
Ford Dispute Settlement Board
www.ford.com

State-run arbitration boards
Many states have arbitration boards that help enforce the lemon laws. State-run boards exist in Connecticut, Florida, Hawaii, Maine, Massachusetts, New York, New Jersey, Texas, Vermont, Washington, and the District of Columbia. Contact your state consumer-protection office for information.

Figure 7.6

Arbitration Programs

reasonable time is usually defined as four trips to the repair shop for the same problem or a total of 30 days in the repair shop. If the manufacturer or dealer does not supply a new car, the customer may go to court after attempting to arbitrate the matter. If your state does not have a lemon law, you can still go to court to enforce performance of express and implied warranties under the Magnuson-Moss Warranty Act, discussed earlier in this chapter.

Key Terms

adjusted capitalized cost (p. 184)
arbitration (p. 189)
"as is" (p. 174)
base price (p. 177)
capitalized cost reduction (p. 184)
certificate of registration (p. 180)
certificate of title (p. 179)
closed-end lease (p. 183)
consumer durables (p. 171)
cost of operation (p. 181)
cost of ownership (p. 179)
credit life insurance (p. 178)

dealer sticker price (p. 177)
depreciation (p. 180)
express warranty (p. 175)
extended warranty (p. 175)
full warranty (p. 175)
gross capitalized cost (p. 184)
guarantee (p. 174)
implied warranty (p. 174)
invoice price (p. 177)
lemon protection (p. 175)
limited warranty (p. 175)
Magnuson-Moss Warranty Act of 1975 (p. 175)

Mail Order Merchandise Rule (p. 173)
marginal cost (p. 182)
Monroney sticker price (p. 176)
net replacement cost (p. 171)
open-end lease (p. 183)
policy adjustment (p. 188)
puffery (p. 175)
residual value (p. 184)
secret warranty (p. 188)
service contract (p. 175)
sunk cost (p. 182)
warranty (p. 174)

FOLLOW-UP ON THE Steele FAMILY

Reread the chapter-opening vignette.

1. When the Steeles decide to replace the family car, what factors should they consider when deciding whether to purchase a new or a used car?
2. Why are the monthly lease payments typically lower than the monthly loan payments on a comparable car? How would leasing affect the Steeles' financial plans?
3. What factors should the Steeles take into consideration when weighing the lease/buy decision?

Problems and Review Questions

1. What special characteristics and budgeting problems do consumer durables present?
2. How is net replacement cost defined?
3. How do you protect yourself against online fraud?
4. What is the Merchandise Mail Order Rule?
5. Why should you be cautious about entering into person-to-person auctions on the Internet?
6. What is the difference between an express and an implied warranty?
7. Does an item sold "as is" carry an implied warranty?
8. What requirements must a warranty satisfy before it can be labeled *full?* How do these differ for a limited warranty?

9. You purchase a stereo system from a local department store on the basis of the salesperson's assurance that this system is a "good buy." You later find out that it wasn't such a good buy. The same product is being sold elsewhere at a much lower price. Does the salesperson's statement constitute an express warranty? What action do you now take?

10. Suppose you purchase a CD player and later find that it does not play mp3 files. The sales clerk assured you it would. What can you do?

11. What is the single greatest cost associated with owning and operating a car? How do you distinguish an ownership cost from an operating cost?

12. What is the difference between a closed-end lease and an open-end lease?

13. What is a capitalized cost reduction? What role does it play in determining the adjusted capitalized cost?

14. You commute 20 miles each day in your own car, and the estimated operational cost per mile is 15 cents. If you used the mass-transit system, the same trip would cost you $2. Should you leave your car at home and ride the public transport?

15. Your new station wagon has 14,000 miles on the odometer. The new-car warranty expired at the 12,000-mile mark. Yesterday, while you were driving the car to school, the rear axle broke. The dealer tells you it will cost over $1,000 to have the problem fixed because the warranty has expired. What do you do?

16. Explain secret warranties and lemon protection.

Case 7.1
Ann Barnard Considers Alternative Holding Periods

Ann Barnard typically buys a new car and trades in the old one every four years. Because new cars are so expensive, she has recently been considering a change in her buying habits. She would like to know how much she might save in depreciation costs if instead she purchased a new car every five years.

Questions
1. Using a new-car price of $20,000 and assuming the market value will depreciate by 50 percent over the next four years, calculate the annual cost of depreciation given her present buying habits. Now calculate the annual cost of depreciation under the proposed change. Assume the market value will depreciate by 55 percent over the next five years. What is the annual cost savings? What is the cost savings over the five-year holding period?
2. What other factors should Ann Barnard consider before she changes her buying behavior?

Case 7.2
The Reeds Examine the Lease/Buy Decision

The Reeds are considering the purchase or lease of a $20,000 car. They have used the worksheet in Figure 7.4 to evaluate the relevant costs. They estimate that the initial expenses for leasing are $1,000 and the initial expenses for purchasing are $5,000. They could lease the car for 48 months for a total monthly expense of $200. If they purchase, they could obtain a 48-month loan at an 8 percent APR with monthly loan payments of $366.19. The final expense on the lease side of the ledger is zero. The returned security fee just offsets the disposition fee. If they sell the car, the net residual value after selling costs is $13,000. Over the next few years they expect to earn a 5 percent after-tax return on their investments.

1. Before considering the time value of money, is it better to lease or buy?
2. After considering the time value of money, is it better to lease or buy?

Exercises to Strengthen Your Use of the Internet

(Internet links for the following exercises can be found at **www.prenhall.com/winger.**)

Exercise 7.1 Which Is Better: A New or Used Auto?

Go to the "Which Is Better, New or Used Car?" calculator at the Yahoo Finance Center. This calculator lets you compare the annual cost of depreciation and finance costs on a new car versus those on an old car. Compare the average annual cost of a new car and a one-year-old car. You will no doubt be amazed at the cost difference. Be sure to go to the Average Cost Per Year ($) link. You will find a good explanation of the financial calculations and the time value of money. Don't overlook the other interesting calculators: auto loans versus home equity loans, rebate versus special dealer financing, and lease versus purchase.

Q. Using the same loan rate, what is the average cost per year on a $20,000 new car versus a three-year-old used car?

Exercise 7.2 How Much Is My Car Worth?

The Kelly Blue Book contains estimates on the market price of used cars. The Web site provides price estimates on both new and used cars. It contains price information on almost every make of car and every price option you can think of. Best of all, it is totally free.

Q. Select a make and model that hasn't changed much over the last five years, such as the Toyota Camry. Using today's pricing data from the Kelly Blue Book, estimate how a new car is likely to depreciate over the next five years. Assume you drive the car 20,000 miles a year and that you keep it in good condition.

Exercise 7.3 Find the Monthly Cost of an Auto Lease

The "Should I Lease or Purchase?" calculator at the Yahoo Finance Center lets you compare the monthly payments on a purchase versus a lease.

Q. For the car of your choice, what is the monthly lease payment on a 24-month lease versus the monthly loan payment on a 24-month loan?

Exercise 7.4 Check Out Vehicle Recalls

Autosite has an online database that helps you track down manufacturer's recalls on most cars. Especially when safety-related recalls are necessary, manufacturers will try to locate present owners and their vehicles. However, with a public that is always on the move, it is possible to lose track of owners of even recently purchased vehicles.

Q. Enter a make and model into the database. What are the outstanding recalls on this car? Are any of them safety related?

Exercise 7.5 Checking Out the BBB Autoline

The BBB Autoline Program helps manufacturers and consumers resolve disputes through mediation and arbitration. Check to see if your car or your family's car is covered by this program. At this site you can also electronically file a complaint against a manufacturer. You can review the complaint from under "How to Contact BBB Autoline."

Q. What kinds of disputes are handled by BBB Autoline?

Exercise 7.6 Does Your State Have a Lemon Law?

BBB Autoline provides information on state-specific lemon laws. You can find out whether your state has such a law. If it does, you can get information on how the law is applied and under what conditions you may be entitled to full reimbursement.

Q. Is there a lemon law in your state? If so, what's covered and how is it applied?

8

Housing

THE COST OF SHELTER

OBJECTIVES

1. To determine how much you can afford to spend on housing

2. To estimate whether it is financially more attractive to buy or to rent

3. To explain the real estate transaction from appraisal to closing

4. To understand the many kinds of home mortgages

5. To know how to handle a potential foreclosure

TOPIC **LINKS**

Follow the **Topic Links** in each chapter for your interactive Personal Finance exercise on the Web. Go to: **www.prenhall.com/winger**

Steele FAMILY

Arnold and Sharon are currently carrying a 15-year, fixed rate mortgage on their home. This loan resulted from a loan renegotiation several years ago when interest rates appeared low. However, since then rates have fallen even further. The monthly payments to service the current mortgage are around $1,525, which represents a serious strain on the Steeles' budget. The Steeles have scaled back some of their goals—a family trip to Hawaii, for example—in order to attain sufficient monthly savings for their other important goals. Arnold and Sharon wonder, though, if they should perhaps renegotiate again for another mortgage. They could obtain an adjustable rate mortgage with a 25-year term and a current contract rate of 7.5 percent. The loan would be for $154,000 and it would have current monthly payments of about $1,138.

A saving of almost $400 a month is not trivial and could go a long way toward the Hawaiian vacation or any other goal the Steeles might consider. Of course, there are several drawbacks. First, the Steeles would have closing costs of $1,171. They will add this amount to the existing mortgage balance of $152,829. This means they will have no additional cash outlay; still, it is a cost they must pay. Second, although 7.5 percent is a lower rate than the current rate on the mortgage, the rate is annually adjustable and could move up in the future.

Housing decisions, because they have a significant impact on the household budget, can often be difficult ones. This is especially so if you are a first-time buyer or seller. So much rides on the correct decision that it is important to thoroughly familiarize yourself with both the housing market and the home loan market.

Every period has its economic uncertainties. Each generation thinks that it is living in the most unsettling of all times. Unfortunately, clarity only accompanies historical hindsight. On the brink of an international crisis, a downturn in economic activity, and rising prices, the future does not appear clear. All of these factors have an impact on housing markets. In addition, housing markets will be affected by many other variables, such as regional migration, the age structure of the population, and consumer tastes. A home is probably the largest single investment you will make. With so much uncertainty and with so much at stake, it is essential that you investigate before you buy.

Housing Affordability Index: Published by the National Association of Realtors®, it is related directly to the ability of a median-income family to purchase a median-priced home.

The National Association of Realtors® publishes the **Housing Affordability Index** presented in Figure 8.1. When the median family income is enough to qualify for a conventional loan on an existing median-priced home, the index assumes a value of 100. When the index rises, more families find it easier to purchase and finance the typical home. For example, when the index rises to 110, those earning about 90 percent of the median family income will now qualify for a loan on a median-priced home.

The Housing Affordability Index (HAI) reached a low point at the beginning of the 1980s. Since then, the trend has been generally upward. Inflation has been brought under control, and interest rates have taken a significant drop. Figure 8.2 illustrates the fall in mortgage rates from double-digit levels in the late 1980s. The decline in interest rates combined with the slower rise in house prices has made housing significantly more affordable for the typical home buyer. The Housing Affordability Index is now at a high of about 140.

TOPIC **LINKS**

Find the latest data on the HAI.

While becoming more affordable, housing has also become less of the investment vehicle it once was. As Figure 8.3 indicates, the median sales price of existing housing after adjustment for the declining value of the dollar has only moderately increased over the last decade. A median-priced home is the one that separates the bottom 50 percent from the top 50 percent. The statistical median house is about the same age each year. The sales price of an actual home that ages from year to year would most likely have declined in inflation-adjusted dollars over this same period. Nationwide statistics, however, do not reveal the great variability in regional and local markets. Purchasing a home may still be a wise decision, but prospective home buyers should carefully examine the local market conditions. In today's market, consumers must fully weigh the benefits, costs, and risks of home ownership.

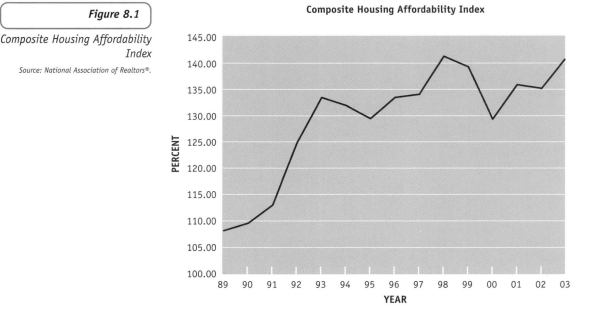

Figure 8.1

Composite Housing Affordability Index

Source: National Association of Realtors®.

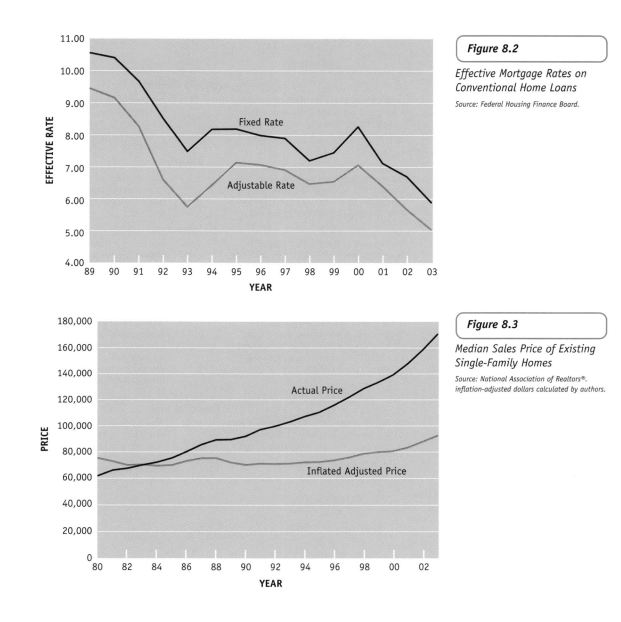

Figure 8.2

Effective Mortgage Rates on Conventional Home Loans

Source: Federal Housing Finance Board.

Figure 8.3

Median Sales Price of Existing Single-Family Homes

Source: National Association of Realtors®. inflation-adjusted dollars calculated by authors.

RENT OR BUY?

TOPIC **LINKS**

Check out the latest housing market conditions.

You have little choice in the matter: You need shelter. However, the ways in which you may satisfy that need are practically unlimited. Like most decisions, this one must take into account your preferred lifestyle and your financial constraints. You can decide on a rental that places minimal demands on your time or finances. You can purchase a single-family home, thus taking on all the responsibilities of maintenance and a home mortgage. Or you may prefer to purchase a condominium or a cooperative, with characteristics falling somewhere between those of a rental unit and those of a single-family home. Obviously, your choice will, and should, depend on what makes you feel most comfortable. All we can do is point out the various advantages and disadvantages concerning your choice of shelter.

Figure 8.4 outlines some of the lifestyle considerations surrounding the choice. The following discussion will be concerned with the financial considerations. We do not mean to

Figure 8.4

Rent Versus Buy: Personal Considerations

Renting	Buying
Lifestyle Choices	
Landlord may place restrictions on pets, guests, and children. There also may be restrictions on how you may redecorate your rental unit.	For condos and co-ops, similar restrictions may exist in the bylaws. The single-family home provides the most freedom in choice of lifestyle. You need only abide by city zoning ordinances.
Privacy	
You may be bothered by both other tenants and the landlord. The landlord will have rights to inspect the premises and to show the unit to prospective tenants.	You can have as much or as little privacy as you want, depending on the type of home ownership you choose.
Maintenance	
Maintenance costs will be included in your rental payments. With a responsible landlord, you will be free of maintenance concerns. With an irresponsible landlord, your only remedy may be to move.	You alone are responsible. You must budget for maintenance expenses and be prepared to do it yourself or hire a capable person.
Mobility	
At the end of the leasing period you simply pack up and leave. If you must move before the lease is up for renewal, you usually can negotiate a mutually agreeable termination.	Selling costs may be considerable, including sales commissions and fixing-up expenses. You are at the mercy of the marketplace. If home demand is down, you must either accept a lower price or incur carrying costs until the market improves.
Financial Risk	
The only risk you face is the possible loss of your personal property in the rental unit. This risk can be covered by renter's insurance.	Your home is also an investment. You can insure it against natural disasters and most other risks. However, you cannot insure against a forced sale at below market price resulting from the loss of your job.

imply that the financial decision is the most important one. The financial decision is an objective one that we can help you analyze. Your preferred living arrangement is a personal choice.

To find out whether you are a candidate for home ownership, you should first estimate how much you can afford. Given this information, you can then examine housing within your price range. Once you understand what the market has to offer, you can decide whether it is financially more advantageous to buy or to rent.

Determining What You Can Afford

The following formulas and related worksheets indicate the highest-priced home you can afford. They do not intend to suggest that you should borrow the maximum amount a bank will lend you. When buying a home, you are committing yourself to fixed future expenses and future maintenance. While shopping, be sure to get information on what current owners are paying for utilities and property taxes. You can then estimate the future expenses you will be locking in. Given these expenses, prepare a sample budget. You may find that, even though you can afford this home, you may not want to cut back on the other expenditures that enrich your lifestyle.

The general rule of thumb for determining how much you can afford either to rent or purchase is that you spend no more than 25 percent of your after-tax income on housing expenses. For buyers, this usually implies a home purchase price of about two and one-half times after-tax income. This is only a rule of thumb; the actual guidelines used by lending institutions can be a lot more complicated.

A worksheet incorporating the housing expense and repayment test set down by the Federal Home Loan Mortgage Corporation, an agency that purchases and resells home mortgages, is contained in Figure 8.5. You begin by entering your annual and monthly gross income on lines 1 and 2. This includes all before-tax income from normal and regular sources.

Next, multiply the housing expense-to-income ratio on line 3 by your monthly gross income on line 2, and enter the result on line 4. This indicates the total amount you may devote to housing expenses. A maximum housing expense-to-income ratio of 0.28 is used in the example.

The Federal Home Loan Mortgage Corporation (popularly called Freddie Mac) recommends that your monthly housing expenses not exceed 28 percent of gross monthly income, the amount you earn before taxes. Furthermore, it suggests that your total monthly debt payments, including housing expenses, not exceed 33 to 36 percent of your gross monthly income. Most lenders will attempt to abide by these ratios. However, you may find a few who are willing to surpass the recommended ratios if you have proven yourself creditworthy. FHA-insured mortgages, discussed later in this chapter, limit housing expenses and debt payments to, respectively, 29 percent and 41 percent of gross income. The existing debt ratios for homeowners (see Figure 8.6) are much lower than these limits.

Figure 8.5

How Much House Can You Afford?

1. Annual gross income	$75,600.00
2. Monthly gross income (divide line 1 by 12)	$6,300
Housing Expense Test	
3. Housing expense-to-income ratio	× 0.28
4. Allowable housing expenditure (multiply line 2 by line 3)	$1,764
5. Estimated nonmortgage housing payment	−340
6. Affordable monthly mortgage payment under housing expense test (subtract line 5 from line 4)	$1,424
Debt Repayment Test	
7. Debt repayment-to-income ratio	0.36
8. Allowable debt payment (multiply line 2 by line 7)	$2,268
9. Monthly installment debt and alimony	$474
10. Total nonmortgage expense and installment debt repayment (add line 5 and line 9)	$814
11. Affordable monthly mortgage payment under debt repayment test (subtract line 10 from line 8)	$1,454
Your Affordable Home Purchase	
12. Affordable monthly mortgage (lesser value of line 11 or line 6)	$1,424
13. Monthly payment per $1,000 mortgage (see Table 8.1)	$7.34
14. Your affordable mortgage (divide line 12 by line 13 and multiply by $1,000)	$194,068
15. Fractional amount borrowed	÷ 0.80
16. Your affordable home purchase (divide line 14 by line 15)	**$242,585**

TOPIC **LINKS**

Download worksheet or try online worksheet at Freddie Mac.

Household Debt Service Ratio
The household debt service ratio (DSR) is an estimate of the ratio of debt payments to disposable personal income. Debt payments consist of the estimated required payments on outstanding mortgage and consumer debt.

All Families	12.98%

Financial Obligations Ratio (FOR)
The financial obligations ratio (FOR) is a broader measure than the debt service ratio. The FOR includes automobile lease payments, rental payments on tenant-occupied property, homeowners' insurance, and property tax payments.

All Families	18.09%
Homeowners	15.54%
Homeowners–mortgage debt only	9.60%
Homeowners–consumer debt only	5.94%
Renters	31.10%

Line 5 includes all your nonmortgage housing expenses. These will consist of mortgage insurance premiums, property insurance, real estate taxes, and, when applicable, homeowner's association or condominium maintenance fees. Subtracting nonmortgage housing expenses (line 5) from line 4 indicates your affordable monthly mortgage payment under the housing expenses test (line 6).

The debt repayment test is used to ensure that other claims on your paycheck do not interfere with your ability to meet your mortgage payment. An allowable debt-to-income ratio of 0.36 is used in the example. If you plan to place 10 percent or less down on the purchase price, use the lower limit of 0.33. On line 9 include all installment debt with more than 10 payments remaining, in addition to any other regular claims on your income, such as alimony payments. Adding in nonmortgage expenses and subtracting the total from the allowable debt payment on line 8 provides your affordable monthly mortgage payment under the debt repayment test.

You must satisfy both the home expense and debt repayment test; therefore, your affordable monthly mortgage will be equal to the lower of the values on line 6 and line 11. The next step is to determine how much you can borrow, given your ability to cover the monthly mortgage payments on line 12. To estimate this, you first need to know the current initial interest rates on home mortgages. You will find that interest rates differ by lending institution, type of mortgage, and size of down payment. However, after a few calls to local financial institutions, you should have some idea what the going market rate is. You then can use this rate to find your monthly payment per $1,000 of mortgage loan in Table 8.1. Enter this value on line 13. In the example, it is assumed that the annual interest rate on an expected 30-year loan with a 20 percent down payment is 8 percent. This produces the monthly payment per $1,000 of $8.05 on line 13. Divide line 12 by line 13, and then multiply the result by $1,000 to obtain an estimate of your affordable mortgage on line 14.

The home purchase price will be equal to the amount borrowed plus the down payment. Given a 20 percent down payment, the mortgage will equal 80 percent of the selling price, and the affordable home purchase price on line 16 is $242,585.

Types of Housing

Since World War II, the U.S. Congress has pursued a policy of fostering home ownership through subsidies and tax breaks. That policy has largely succeeded. About two-thirds of housing units are now owner-occupied.

Table 8.1

Monthly Payment per $1,000 of
Mortgage Loan

Contract Interest Rate (%)	Duration of Loan (Years)					
	5	10	15	20	25	30
12	22.24	14.35	12.00	11.01	10.53	10.29
11½	21.99	14.06	11.68	10.66	10.16	9.90
11	21.74	13.78	11.37	10.32	9.80	9.52
10½	21.49	13.49	11.05	9.98	9.44	9.15
10	21.25	13.22	10.75	9.65	9.09	8.78
9½	21.00	12.94	10.44	9.32	8.74	8.41
9	20.76	12.67	10.14	9.00	8.39	8.05
8	20.28	12.13	9.56	8.36	7.72	7.34
7	19.80	11.61	8.99	7.75	7.07	6.65
6	19.33	11.10	8.44	7.16	6.44	6.00
5	18.87	10.61	7.91	6.60	5.85	5.37

TOPIC **LINKS**

Use an online monthly payment calculator.

Home ownership varies directly with age, income, and net worth. Between ages 25 and 34, 46 percent of households own the home they are living in. By age 55 to 64, ownership has risen to about 80 percent. Household income and net worth both increase with age, so housing becomes both more affordable and more tax advantageous, because of federal income tax deductions for mortgage interest and property taxes.

The typical household starts out in a rental unit. With an increase in income and the accumulation of the necessary down payment, families tend to purchase their first home when the head of the household is around age 30. And when they do purchase, the overwhelming choice is the traditional single-family home. Your household, however, need not be typical. Choose the types of housing and the type of occupancy that best fits your lifestyle and financial plan.

Apartment Housing

Although any style of living unit can be rented, it is usually the apartment we think of first. Large apartment complexes may offer attractive amenities such as swimming pools, tennis courts, and clubhouses. Outside of a cooperative or condo, such amenities would be difficult for the average homeowner to afford.

For mobile individuals demanding minimal responsibilities and an environment in which social relationships are nurtured, a large apartment complex may be desirable. This group seems to be the one to which new apartment construction is designed to appeal.

Condominium Housing

Condominium housing can offer the extras of apartment living along with the rewards of home ownership. Strictly defined, **condominium** does not refer to a particular type of housing. It stands for a unique type of ownership where part of the property is individually owned and part is owned in common with other members of the condominium complex. You own your living unit and have a shared interest in other areas of the condominium site, such as recreational and maintenance areas. This means you will be responsible not only for the financing and upkeep of your individual unit, but you will also be assessed charges for the financing and upkeep of the common areas. Before you purchase, you should fully understand what these charges are and how they will be determined in the future.

As an owner, you are a member of the condominium association and will be able to vote for directors in whom most of the governing powers will be vested. Condominiums are created by the laws of the state where they are located. The laws provide a legal framework for

Condominium: A form of ownership in which there is an individual ownership interest in the living unit but a shared ownership unit in the common areas.

the operations of the directors and for the conditions and restrictions imposed on a property. Although this framework will differ from state to state, in all states you have a right to receive copies of the basic documents in which the legal and economic rules of the condominium are set out.

Cooperative Housing

As in a condominium, several owners share an undivided interest in cooperative housing. However, a **cooperative** has a corporate form. Instead of purchasing the individual living unit, you purchase stock in the corporation and then lease the living unit from the corporation. The corporation owns the living units and carries the mortgage on them. Its expenses are covered by the rents set in the lease agreements. As a stockholder, you can vote for the board of directors. One major problem associated with cooperatives is that you must receive the consent of the board of directors before you can transfer your stock and lease.

Single-Family Housing

When you purchase a single-family home, you take on all the responsibilities of finance and maintenance that go with it. You are your own landlord and maintenance person and must budget your money and time accordingly. When something needs to be fixed, you must be ready to do it yourself or have the funds to hire someone else.

Multifamily Housing

If you are considering purchasing a multifamily dwelling, you are looking for an investment that also satisfies your own need for shelter. The financial considerations concerning investment in real estate are not covered in this text. A specialized course in real estate can provide you with the needed financial tools.

Mobile Homes

Over 90 percent of mobile homes are not very mobile. They travel only from the manufacturer to the dealer and finally to a housing site, where they usually remain permanently affixed. For this reason, the industry prefers the term *manufactured home*. Because the homes are constructed at the factory, the cost per square foot of living space is considerably less than for on-site construction.

The mobile home may be placed on a solitary plot or within a mobile home park. Parks often have common recreational areas and offer many of the conveniences of large apartment complexes. Typically, mobile home parks rent sites using long-term lease agreements. However, there are a few condominium mobile home developments where you purchase the site and then pay a monthly maintenance fee to cover the cost of the common areas.

Because the market price of mobile homes has typically depreciated with age, financing has been a problem. Mobile homes are usually financed with a 20 percent down payment, a personal property loan of 10 to 15 years duration, and an interest rate a few percentage points above that on conventional home mortgages. For those who qualify, federally insured mortgages for longer durations and with lower down payments are available through the Federal Housing Administration (FHA) and the Veterans Administration (VA).

A Cost Comparison

When you purchase a home, you are undertaking a sizable investment of your own money. The financial question is, would you be better off renting and investing your funds elsewhere? The answer will depend on expected future housing prices, the expected return on

Beware Predatory Lending

The growth in predatory lending has come to the attention of state and federal authorities over the last few years. Predatory lenders target the old and the poor. Through fraud and deception, predatory lenders entice homeowners into highly unfavorable second mortgages. This is often done in conjunction with the sale of home repairs that are either never or shoddily performed.

These predatory lenders deal in the market for "subprime" loans. These are high interest rate loans to low-income borrowers with poor credit histories and low credit scores. Predatory lenders hide from consumers the facts they need to make an informed decision. According to the Federal Trade Commission, predatory practices have included:

Loan flipping	A process in which the borrower's loans are repeatedly refinanced over a short period of time with no gain to the borrower.
Equity stripping	The loan is designed to fail because it is based on the equity in the property and not the borrower's ability to pay
Packing	Adding credit insurance or other "extras" to increase the lender's profit on a loan

Don't be pressured or harassed into taking out a home loan. If you feel that you or a relative has been a victim of any of these predatory lending practices, contact your state Attorney General's office or the Federal Trade Commission.

financial investments, the length of time you expect to stay in one location, and the expected tax advantage from home ownership.

The Tax Advantage

Several immediate and long-term tax advantages are associated with buying a home. If you itemize deductions—and you probably should if you have a home mortgage—both the state and local taxes you pay on the property and the interest you pay on the mortgage may be deductible from your adjusted gross income when you calculate your federal taxable income. This means that if you are in the 28 percent marginal tax bracket, each dollar you pay in property taxes and interest saves you 28 cents in federal income taxes. Naturally, the higher your marginal tax rate, the greater is the income tax advantage. As a renter, you may find these items included in the price of the rent, but you as a renter cannot take them as a deduction on your income tax return.

TOPIC **LINKS**

IRS on Home Mortgage Interest Deduction.

Mortgage interest is fully deductible only on first and second homes, if total home mortgages for couples filing a joint return do not exceed $1 million. Special tax treatment accorded capital gains provides an additional long-term tax advantage. You may exclude up to $250,000 ($500,000 if filing jointly) of the gain from your taxable income. This exclusion may be applied to each sale of a home so long as you owned the home for two years and used it as your main home for two of the last five years. The exclusion is proportionately reduced for shorter periods of ownership.

TOPIC **LINKS**

IRS rules on buying and selling your home.

Finally, there is a hidden tax advantage that is often overlooked. Suppose you could rent your present home for $500 a month; this is the market worth of the shelter that you are receiving. This value is part of the return from the investment in the home and may be thought of as an implicit rent paid to and received by yourself. However, payments to yourself are not considered income for tax purposes. Thus, the implicit rental income accompanying home ownership remains tax free.

Buying versus Renting

Figure 8.7 shows a worksheet for comparing the relative costs of buying and renting a home. The worksheet contains entries for a one-year comparison and a five-year comparison. Both periods are considered because it is most likely that the best choice depends on the length of time spent at one location. The sample data are based on a home that could be purchased for $110,000 or rented for $700 per month plus utilities. If purchased, it is assumed the buyer would place 20 percent down and borrow $88,000, to be paid back over 30 years at an annual percentage rate of 6 percent. It is also assumed that all prices, including the market price of the home, will rise at 3 percent a year.

To calculate the gross gain or loss from buying in Figure 8.7, we first estimate the appreciation in the value of the home over the holding period. Looking at the first-year

Figure 8.7

Buy Versus Rent: Cost Comparison

TOPIC **LINKS**

Download worksheet.

GIVENS:			
BUYING		**RENTING**	
Home purchase price:	$110,000	Rent:	$700 a month plus utilities
Mortgage:		Renters' insurance:	$50 a year
Principal:	$88,000		
Term:	30 years		
Interest rate:	6% APR		
Monthly payment:	$527.60		
Selling expense:	7% of selling price	**COMMON FACTORS**	$527.60
Closing costs after taxes:	$2,500	Annual fuel and utilities:	$2,400
Annual property taxes	$2,100	Marginal tax rate:	28%
Annual homeowners repair		Taxes on capital gain:	$0
and maintenance:	1,200	Before-tax return on investment:	6%
Annual homeowners' insurance:	$500	Inflation rate:	3%

ONE-YEAR COMPARISON		
	Buying	Renting
Gross gain or loss		
Buying		
Appreciation:	$ 3,300	
Selling expenses:	(7,931)	
Capital gain or loss:	($ 4,631)	
Taxes on capital gain:	0	
Initial closing costs after taxes:	(2,500)	
Renting		
Interest earned after taxes:		$ 1,058
	————	————
Total Gross Gain (1)	($ 7,131)	$ 1,058
Annual Expenses		
Buying		
Mortgage interest after taxes saved	($ 3,780)	
Property taxes after taxes saved	(1,512)	
Repair and maintenance	(1,000)	

Figure 8.7

(continued)

Renting		
Rent		($ 8,400)
Common expenses		
Fuel and utilities	(2,400)	(2,400)
Insurance	(500)	(50)
Total Annual Expenses (2)	($ 9,192)	($10,850)
Total Gain or Loss (Gross gain (1) + annual expenses (2))	($16,323)	($9,792)

You Save $6,531 by renting

FIVE-YEAR COMPARISON

	Buying	Renting
Gross gain or loss		
Buying		
Appreciation:	$17,520	
Selling expenses:	(8,926)	
Capital gain or loss:	$ 8,594	
Taxes on capital gain:	0	
Initial closing costs after taxes:	(2,500)	
Renting		
Interest earned after taxes:		$ 5,769
Total Gross Gain (1)	$ 6,094	$ 5,769
Annual Expenses		
Buying		
Mortgage interest after taxes saved	($18,392)	
Property taxes after taxes saved	(8,027)	
Repair and maintenance	(5,309)	
Renting		
Rent		($44,597)
Common Expenses		
Fuel and utilities	($12,742)	(12,742)
Insurance	(2,655)	(265)
Total Annual Expenses (2)	($47,125)	($57,604)
Total Gain or Loss (Gross gain (1) + annual expenses (2))	($41,031)	($51,835)

You save $10,804 by buying

comparison, the assumed appreciation rate of 3 percent is equal to $3,300. The capital gain or loss at the sale of the home is equal to the appreciation less selling expenses. These selling expenses include commissions, advertising fees, legal fees, and loan charges paid by the seller. The largest selling expense is likely to be the sales commission. In Figure 8.7, selling expenses are 7 percent of the selling price.

The gross gain or loss on the sale of the home will be equal to the capital gain or loss less capital gain taxes and the after-tax closing costs you incurred when you purchased the home. Losses on the sale of your home are not deductible and, as previously discussed, there is generally no tax on the appreciation. The exceptions include a gain on a home held less than two years and a gain exceeding the exemption. Therefore, it is likely that the capital gains tax is zero. The initial closing costs you incurred at the time of purchase will also reduce your realized gain. Some of these initial expenses, such as property taxes and mortgage points, may be tax deductible. Therefore, these expenses may be reduced for tax adjustments.

The gross gain from renting is based on the assumption that if you did not buy, the $22,000 down payment and the initial closing costs of $2,500 would remain in an investment fund paying an annual interest rate of 6 percent. This investment would provide interest income of $1,470 before taxes. However, with an assumed marginal tax rate of 28 percent, interest earned after taxes is $1,058 = ($1,470 × (1 − 0.28)).

The related expenses of home ownership and renting are listed next. Mortgage interest payments can be taken from an amortization schedule prepared by your lender or any of the many online calculators on the Internet. This schedule will specify your yearly repayments on the loan and your yearly interest payments (for an example, see Table 8.2). On the present loan, mortgage interest payments for the first year are $5,251. Assuming you itemize deductions, the actual interest expense after taxes is $3,780 = ($5,251 = (1 − 0.28)). A similar tax adjustment should be made for property taxes.

The five-year comparison employs the same basic assumptions as the one-year comparison. The annual mortgage rate is 6 percent, and all prices, including fuel, insurance, maintenance, taxes, and rent, are assumed to rise at a 3 percent annual rate.

Such analyses, including this example, commonly show that renting appears the better alternative over the short run, whereas ownership is cheaper over the long run. The high turnover cost of buying and selling a home makes renting the better short-term choice. On the other hand, inflation protection and tax advantages make buying the optimal long-term choice.

All other things remaining the same, the following changes will make owning a home more attractive:

- A reduction in mortgage interest rates
- An increase in the expected future price of housing
- An increase in your marginal tax rate
- An increase in rents
- A decrease in the rate of return on financial investments

THE REAL ESTATE TRANSACTION

A home is most likely the largest single purchase you will make. It is also the largest single asset you are likely to own. The equity in the family home accounts for a surprisingly large 44 percent of household net worth. Because it is so important and because few of us buy and sell homes often enough to become experts on the subject, you should seek the advice of experienced professionals. You may want to rely on an appraiser, a real estate agent, a home inspector, and an attorney.

The Appraisal

TOPIC LINKS
Review an appraisal form.

As a buyer or a seller, you need information on market price. Housing prices depend on many factors, the principal ones being size, construction, age, and location. The last factor

Table 8.2

Amortization Schedule for a
Fixed Rate Mortgage

Loan amount: $88,000
Annual contract rate: 6%
Term (years): 30
Monthly payment: $527.60

Year	Principal Repayment	Interest Payment	Ending Principal Outstanding
1	$1,081	$5,251	$86,919
2	$1,147	$5,184	$85,772
3	$1,218	$5,113	$84,554
4	$1,293	$5,038	$83,261
5	$1,373	$4,958	$81,888
6	$1,458	$4,874	$80,430
7	$1,548	$4,784	$78,883
8	$1,643	$4,688	$77,240
9	$1,744	$4,587	$75,495
10	$1,852	$4,479	$73,643
11	$1,966	$4,365	$71,677
12	$2,087	$4,244	$69,590
13	$2,216	$4,115	$67,374
14	$2,353	$3,978	$65,021
15	$2,498	$3,833	$62,523
16	$2,652	$3,679	$59,871
17	$2,816	$3,516	$57,055
18	$2,989	$3,342	$54,066
19	$3,174	$3,158	$50,893
20	$3,369	$2,962	$47,523
21	$3,577	$2,754	$43,946
22	$3,798	$2,533	$40,148
23	$4,032	$2,299	$36,116
24	$4,281	$2,051	$31,835
25	$4,545	$1,786	$27,291
26	$4,825	$1,506	$22,466
27	$5,123	$1,209	$17,343
28	$5,439	$893	$11,904
29	$5,774	$557	$6,130
30	$6,130	$201	($0)
Totals	$88,000	$101,938	

should not be underestimated. There may be a wide spread in the selling price of identical houses in two different locations. Remember, you are really buying more than a home. You are buying into a neighborhood, a score of community services, and a school system. Only someone very familiar with the local housing market may be able to appraise all these and other relevant factors.

Professional appraisers may be located in the Yellow Pages under *Real Estate Appraisers*. Mortgage lenders can also provide you with a list of competent appraisers. In all cases, ask for credentials and references. The appraiser should be state licensed or certified.

Mortgage lenders will conduct an appraisal, but you should not rely on this procedure to determine the market value of your potential home. The lender's interest and yours are not the same. The lender wants to determine if the value of the house exceeds the amount

TOPIC LINKS

Check out the Neighborhood Explorer™ for socioeconomic data on your neighborhood.

borrowed by some safety margin. An independent appraisal may be necessary, because, as a buyer or a seller, you need to know that you are paying or receiving the market value.

The Real Estate Agent

Unless you as a buyer have a special agreement with the real estate agent, the agent will be representing the seller. Many people fall into a comfortable relationship with the agent who is showing them homes and, in the course of casual conversation, reveal too much about what they are willing to pay. Because the agent's interest must be with the seller, this information may be later used to undermine the buyer's negotiating position.

TOPIC **LINKS**
National Association of Exclusive Buyer Agents

If you would like someone to represent your interest, you must enter into a contract with a buyer's agent. The National Association of Exclusive Buyer Agents is comprised of agents that work exclusively for the buyer. An exclusive buyer agent works for a firm that does not take listings or represent sellers. Nonexclusive agents may represent both buyers and sellers and may have conflicting interests. A buyer agent can help you select a home by providing information on relative home values and the local community. There is no set method for paying a buyer agent. Payment may be a flat fee, an hourly fee, or a percentage of the purchase price. Be sure you understand how the agent is to be compensated.

As a seller you can choose to use a real estate agent or not. Only about 15 percent of all house sales are made without an agent. However, with an agent's commission at about 6 to 7 percent of the sale price, selling the home yourself can appear to be an attractive alternative. To make the best decision, think in terms of earning the commission rather than saving it. You will have to take on the work of advertising and showing the home and dealing directly with potential buyers. This work can be both time consuming and, for some people, emotionally draining.

TOPIC **LINKS**
Check out sales on your street.

Be sure that the agent you choose to sell your home is a member of the Multiple Listing Service (MLS). This will provide information on your home to all other real estate agencies in your area who are also members of the MLS. Because of fee-splitting arrangements among MLS members, every agent has an interest in selling your home.

The Listing Agreement

TOPIC **LINKS**
View a sample listing agreement.

You will be asked to sign a **listing agreement.** This is a contract between you and the real estate agent. It provides the agent with authority to act as your salesperson in return for a commission on the sale of the home. Important items on the contract will consist of the listing price, the commission, a description of the property, any terms and conditions for sale, duration of the listing, and exclusivity of the listing. The last item will determine whether you have the right to retain other sales agents during the term of the listing agreement.

Listing agreement: A contract between the seller and the real estate agent providing the agent with authority to represent the seller in return for a commission on the sale.

Exclusive right to sell: Entitles the agent to a commission no matter who sells the property.

Exclusive agency agreement: The agent has an exclusive right to broker the property but may agree to share the commission with other agents. If you locate the buyer yourself, you don't pay a commission.

There are three basic types of listing arrangements: the exclusive right to sell, the exclusive agency, and the open agreement. The **exclusive right to sell** entitles the agent to a commission regardless of who sells the property. Under an **exclusive agency agreement,** the seller agrees to retain one agent, but the agent collects the commission only if it is sold with the help of the agent. If you locate a buyer, you don't pay a commission. In both of the foregoing agreements the agent can co-broker the property, offering to split the commission with any other agent who can help find a buyer. With an **open listing agreement** the agent receives a commission only if he or she discovers a buyer. If you or another agent sells the home, you don't owe a commission to the agent who listed your home.

Beware of clauses that automatically extend the listing period, prohibit recording (public notice) of the listing agreement, or contain a net listing agreement. Each of these can result in serious problems for the seller. Automatic extensions beyond the typical 90-day period reduce the agent's incentive to sell your home in a timely manner. Public notice may be required if the contract is misrepresented. A **net listing agreement** provides the seller with a predetermined net price from the sale of the property. The real estate agent receives the difference between the actual sale price and the net price promised the seller as commission.

Some real estate agencies will offer special inducements in an effort to get your home listing. These may turn out to be less valuable than first appearances would suggest. For example, some agencies will agree to buy your home if it cannot be sold by a specified time. Unfortunately, the price at which they are willing to purchase the home may be substantially below the price at which they are listing it. In addition, you may be still charged a commission, even though the home was purchased by the real estate agency at a low market price. Finally, the agreement may bind you to purchase a new home through this same agency, which will, of course, collect a commission on that transaction.

Open listing agreement: Any agent can broker your home. The commission goes to the agent who locates a buyer. If you sell your home, you don't pay a commission.

Net listing agreement: Provides the seller with a predetermined amount of money from the sale of the property.

The Home Inspection

Instead of depending on a warranty as insurance against defects, get information on potential problems before you purchase. A thorough inspection by a qualified housing inspector should uncover problem areas that would otherwise go unnoticed. A home inspection will cost about $400, but this will vary by the extent of the inspection. For this amount, you should receive a written report stating the condition of the home and its component systems.

The American Society of Home Inspectors (ASHI) trains and certifies qualified individuals. They may be found in the Yellow Pages under *Building Inspection Services, Inspection Bureaus, Engineers*, or *Real Estate Inspectors*. Be sure the inspector you hire has nothing to gain from your purchasing the home. The inspector should not, for example, run a remodeling firm or depend on a real estate agency for support. Ask for the names of previous customers and insist on being present during the home inspection. The person you hire should be able to answer all questions you may have during the inspection.

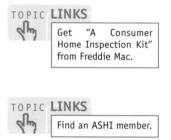

TOPIC **LINKS**

Get "A Consumer Home Inspection Kit" from Freddie Mac.

TOPIC **LINKS**

Find an ASHI member.

The Purchase Contract

Verbal offers to purchase real estate are not binding. The offer to purchase a home is made on a document entitled *Contract to Purchase, Purchase Agreement*, or *Deposit Receipt*. There is no standard contract. When both the buyer and the seller have agreed to all the conditions in the purchase contract, it becomes a binding agreement that creates rights and obligations for both parties. Consequently, request a blank copy before you sign and have an attorney review it. Most real estate transactions are closed, however, without the aid of an attorney. Unfortunately, too many people consult an attorney only when they want to get out of a disagreeable contract. Such remedial action can be very costly.

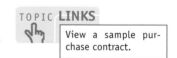

TOPIC **LINKS**

View a sample purchase contract.

Reviewing the Contract

You and your attorney should carefully examine the purchase contract to make sure it contains the following:

- The purchase price, the down payment, and the type of financing. Beware of an "escalator" clause that permits the builder to increase the price because of future cost increases.
- Anticipated closing costs and prepaid items and who will pay them.
- A description of the property and a list of all items being sold with the house. For new construction, plans and specifications should be included, and you should carefully review these with your architect and home inspector.

- A statement as to who is responsible for the property from the date of the contract to the date the property is conveyed to you.
- The amount of the deposit and the conditions under which the buyer or the seller might void the contract. For example, failure to buy or sell another house, inadequate financing, an unsatisfactory inspection report, or failure to obtain a marketable title may all be good reasons for voiding the purchase contract.
- A stated date after which the offer lapses if not accepted.

The process leading to the sale of a home begins when the buyer makes an offer to purchase, with a signed purchase contract and a commitment of earnest money. The seller may then accept the offer, reject the offer, or make a counteroffer by altering some or all of the terms on the purchase contract. Likewise, the buyer may then accept the counteroffer, reject it, or make another counteroffer. This process continues until the two sides either terminate negotiations or agree upon a sale.

Earnest money: Money deposited by the buyer, to be kept by the seller if the buyer does not abide by the terms of the offer to purchase. It demonstrates the buyer's good faith in the offer.

The buyer's deposit of **earnest money** demonstrates that the offer is made in good faith. If the offer to purchase is not accepted or lapses, the earnest money should be returned to the buyer. If the seller accepts the offer to purchase, a third party—either a broker, a title company, or an escrow agent—will hold the money in a trust account until the sale is closed or the contract is broken. Should the buyer fail to purchase the home as indicated in the contract, the seller can keep the earnest money. On the other hand, if the seller breaks the contract, the deposit is returned to the buyer. When the sale goes through, the deposit is applied to the buyer's down payment on the purchase.

The Title Search

Deed: A written instrument transferring title of real estate to the buyer.

Title search: An examination of public records in order to determine who may have enforceable claims on the property.

Marketable title: Legal evidence of a right to property that is free of claims from other parties.

The **deed** is a written document that transfers title, or ownership, to the buyer. However, the deed does not show who else might have rights to the property. In the **title search,** an attorney examines the public records to determine if others may have enforceable claims on the property. At the completion of the search, the attorney will render an opinion as to whether **marketable title** exists. A marketable title is free of all claims from other parties.

The mortgage lender will conduct a title search. However, the fact that you are granted a loan does not necessarily mean the title is free of all defects. A loan may still be granted if the lender feels assured that the full value of the loan can be repaid in spite of minor defects in the title. In addition, if the search is deficient, you may have no claim against the attorney. The attorney is financially responsible only to the client. If the lender ordered the search, the lender is the client and not you. For this reason you should have an independent examination.

Title insurance: Protects the insured against defective title.

The mortgage lender will require that you purchase **title insurance.** This insures the bank, not you, against a defective title. To protect your interest in the title, you can obtain owner's title insurance. You will save money by purchasing this coverage at the same time you buy the lender's policy. As with all insurance, coverage can vary. Read the insurance contract carefully to be sure it covers all defects in title, both in and out of the public record.

The Closing

Closing: The meeting at which the sale is finalized and the title is transferred.

Immediately before you are about to complete your home purchase, schedule a final walk-through to ensure that everything is as it should be. The meeting at which the purchase and the mortgage are finalized is called the **closing.** The seller receives payment. The buyer undertakes the mortgage and receives the deed. By mutual agreement between the buyer and the seller, actual possession of the property may take place at this time or at some later date. Whoever closes the sale is required to report the terms of the sale to the IRS in order

Government Charges

Prorated taxes
Recording fees
Transfer taxes

Lender Charges

Appraisals
Attorney fees (lender)
Credit report
Document preparation
Flood zone determination
Hazard (homeowner's) insurance
Inspections (lender)
Land survey
Mortgage insurance
Origination fees
Points
Prepaid interest
Title insurance (lender)
Title search

Other Sale-Related Charges

Attorney fee (buyer)
Inspections (buyer)
Real estate agent sales commission
Title insurance (buyer)

Figure 8.8

A Checklist of Potential Closing Costs

to ensure compliance with tax law. Costs due at this time are called **closing,** or **settlement, costs.** These typically add up to between 2 and 4 percent of the purchase price. A sample list of these costs is given in Figure 8.8.

Closing, or settlement, costs: Payments due at closing.

Government Charges

At the date of the closing, property-based taxes will be prorated to the buyer and seller over the current tax period. In addition, there may be various state and local charges on the transfer and the recording of the transfer. These charges are usually modest, but in some states these fees can run as high as 1 percent of the sale price.

TOPIC **LINKS**

View sample closing costs.

Lender's Charges

The buyer generally pays lender's charges. They include the lender's cost of processing the loan, plus related costs such as property appraisals and inspections. Title charges include the costs of title search, title insurance for the lender, and document preparation. A single premium paid at this time will keep the policy in force until the house is sold again.

The Real Estate Settlement Procedures Act requires that the lender give you a good faith estimate of your closing costs within three days of receiving your loan application. The origination fee to start processing your loan cannot be more than 1 percent of the mortgage amount. Other fees they may charge include appraisal fees, inspection fees, and attorney fees.

Points, also called discount points, may be included. Points are considered prepaid interest and are charged when the interest rate is below the yield required by lenders that buy mortgage securities. One discount point is equal to 1 percent of the amount borrowed. For example, on an $80,000 mortgage, 1½ discount points are equal to $1,200.

Points: Prepaid interest; one point is equal to 1 percent of the amount borrowed.

Contract rate: The interest rate applied to the unpaid balance on the home mortgage.

This has the effect of reducing the amount borrowed from $80,000 to $78,800. You still, however, owe the bank the unpaid balance of $80,000. Consequently, paying points raises the annual percentage rate (APR) on the loan above the **contract rate,** the rate applied to the unpaid balance for calculating your monthly mortgage payments. This difference arises because the APR calculates payments as a percentage of $78,800 (amount borrowed), whereas the contract rate calculates payments as a percentage of the amount owed ($80,000).

Mortgage		$80,000
Points (1 1/2)	(1.5%) × ($80,000) =	$1,200
Amount borrowed	($80,000 − $1,200) =	78,800
Contract rate		6.00%
Interest payment	($80,000 × 6.00%) =	$4,800
APR	($4,800/$78,800) × 100 =	6.09%

Lenders may offer mortgages with identical APRs but with different contract rates. The loan with the lower contract rate would have more points up front. Should you prefer one mortgage over the other? The answer may depend on how long you intend to hold the home. Points push the interest payments to the front of the mortgage. If you are planning to move in a few years, you may prefer to defer interest into the future when you no longer own the home.

If the loan is closed before the last day of the month, the lender will want the borrower to prepay the balance of that month's interest. The lender may also require the borrower to prepay mortgage and hazard insurance. On some loans, particularly those with low down payments, the lender requires the borrower to set up and periodically fund a reserve account for paying insurance and property taxes. This account, called an *escrow account*, ensures that these payments will be made on time.

Other Sale-Related Charges

These may include the cost of your attorney, title insurance coverage for the buyer, and any home inspections arranged by the buyer or seller. The seller typically pays the broker's commission on the sale of the home. It currently runs about 6 or 7 percent of the sales price, but the exact percentage is negotiable.

Warranties

Homes, like other goods, will be covered by unwritten implied warranties set down in state law. Written warranties may also accompany the sale. These fall into two categories; the first are builders' warranties on newly constructed homes, and the second are home buyers' warranties on the resale of existing homes. Neither of these warranties relieves you from the duty of conducting a full and adequate home inspection before you buy.

Builders' warranties are meant to assure the buyer that the new home is structurally sound. The buyer receives a 10-year warranty covering a list of defects that decrease in number as the home ages. During the first year almost all defects in workmanship and materials are covered. In the second year the list of guaranteed items is substantially shorter, and in the remaining eight years only major structural defects are covered.

There have been problems with builders' warranties. Consumer groups have been highly critical. They charge that policies have been issued on poorly built homes. Moreover, the claims process may be complicated and lengthy, often forcing the consumer to deal with the original builder who was responsible for the faulty construction.

The second type of warranty, the warranty on the resale of an existing home, is similar to an extended service contract. Rather than covering the structural integrity of the home, it insures the major home appliances included in the sale. Typically, it lasts for only six months to a year. This provides the buyer with some assurance that he or she will not have to incur the cost of a new furnace or water heater soon after purchasing the home. Be warned that most policies include high deductibles on service calls and may even exclude preexisting mechanical problems. There is no standard format for resale warranties; therefore, policy coverage may vary widely.

FINANCING THE PURCHASE

You can shop around for a home mortgage at a variety of financial institutions, including commercial banks, mutual savings banks, mortgage companies, and savings and loan associations. You can contact the lending institutions directly or you can employ a mortgage broker to shop for you. If you deal with a broker, the fee for the broker will likely be passed on to you as either a separate broker's fee at closing or in the form of a higher APR. Be sure to contact several lenders and mortgage brokers. A small reduction in the interest rate can result in significant savings. On a $100,000 30-year mortgage, a ½ percent reduction in the contract rate can reduce your future interest payments by more than $12,000.

Today's mortgage market is highly competitive. Lenders offer both fixed and adjustable rate loans and several ways in which each of these loans may be structured. Ask the loan officer to explain each of the loan options and discuss how each might fit your own financial situation. The decision is an important one. A typical mortgage will commit you to interest payments that, over the life of the loan, can equal as much as three times the original amount borrowed.

The larger your down payment, the lower the interest rate, and the longer the term of the loan, the smaller is the monthly mortgage payment. The typical home buyer makes a 20 percent down payment on a 30-year mortgage. However, with mortgage insurance you may obtain a home mortgage with as little as 5 percent down.

The annual percentage rate (APR), explained in Chapter 6 on consumer credit, is the most important disclosure. It takes into account the interest rate and other credit charges, such as mortgage insurance, points, and loan origination fees, into a uniform measure of cost. Unfortunately, the published APR on adjustable rate loans must be based upon the initial interest rate. Since the future interest rate on the loan may differ from the initial interest rate, the APR in the mortgage contract will not likely reflect the interest costs you will actually incur. Therefore, on adjustable rate loans, the lender is also required to describe the circumstances that will lead to rate changes and to give an example of the payment changes that can occur. For such loans, the circumstances under which rates may change are as important as the APR.

Realistically, it is impossible to present every repayment scenario for many adjustable rate loans. Loan officers will ordinarily try to be helpful, but time constraints may prohibit them from providing you with a complete examination of the proposed loan. Therefore, some previous knowledge of mortgage instruments may greatly aid you in the search for a home mortgage. The mortgage comparison checklist in Figure 8.9 should prove helpful when reviewing the characteristics of the available mortgages.

TOPIC **LINKS**

Obtain the latest rates on home mortgages.

TOPIC **LINKS**

Download a comprehensive checklist from the FED.

Fixed Rate Mortgages

As seen in Figure 8.10, most homes are financed with fixed rate mortgages. **Fixed rate mortgages** have an interest rate and monthly payments that remain constant over the life

Fixed rate mortgages: Home mortgages on which the interest rate and monthly payment remain constant over the life of the loan.

Figure 8.9

Mortgage Comparison Checklist

Lender
Loan type (fixed or adjustable)
Annual percentage rate
Duration (years)
Percentage down payment
Application fee
Points
Title insurance
Prepayment penalty
Other closing fees
Mortgage insurance
Initial interest rate
Initial monthly mortgage payment
Balloon payment

Additional Information on Adjustable Rate Loans
Interest adjustment index
Adjustment period
Periodic rate cap
Aggregate rate cap
Periodic payment cap
Negative amortization (Y/N)
Adjustable duration (Y/N)

Figure 8.10

Characteristics of Home Mortgages, 2001

Source: American Housing Survey National Tables, U.S. Census Bureau.

Type of Payment Plan	Percent of Total
Fixed rate and payment	90.99%
Adjusted rate mortgage	5.01%
Adjusted term mortgage	1.28%
Graduated payment mortgage	0.97%
Other and not reported	1.74%
Current Interest Rate	
Less that 6 percent	2.7%
6 to 7.9 percent	65.0%
8 to 9.9 percent	26.0%
10 to 11.9 percent	4.4%
12 and above	1.7%
Term of Primary Mortgage at Origination or Assumption	
12 years or less	6.63%
13 to 17 years	16.62%
18 to 22 years	5.81%
23 to 27 years	3.05%
28 to 32 years	63.55%
33 years or more	2.33%
Variable	2.01%

of the loan. For example, if you borrowed $88,000 at 6 percent for 30 years, you would have level monthly payments of $527.60 over the entire 30-year period. Part of each monthly payment will go to the repayment of **principal**—the amount owed—and part will go toward payment of interest on the principal.

With a fixed rate mortgage, you are protected against future increases in mortgage rates. Rising mortgage rates are likely to happen during periods of increasing inflation. However, less risk for you means more risk for the lender. Lenders offset this risk by charging a higher rate on fixed rate mortgages than the initial rate they charge on adjustable rate mortgages. Fortunately, a fixed rate mortgage does not necessarily lock you into a high rate when market rates are falling. On most fixed rate loans, you can pay off the remaining balance on the loan at anytime without penalty.

When you repay a loan by periodic payments, you are said to **amortize** your debt. Table 8.2 contains an amortization schedule for a fixed rate loan. During the first years of the loan, most of the mortgage payment will go toward paying interest on the principal. As the amount owed declines, a larger percentage of the mortgage payment will go toward paying off the principal. Near the end of the loan period, almost the entire mortgage payment will serve to reduce the outstanding principal.

Principal: The remaining balance on the amount borrowed.

Amortize: To satisfy an obligation by periodic payments of interest and principal.

Adjustable Rate Mortgages

The distinguishing feature of **adjustable rate loans** is that the interest rate on the loan is not fixed over the entire life of the loan. This feature is about the only common characteristic of adjustable rate loans; there are almost as many types of them as there are homes. To add to the confusion, they come under various names—such as variable and flexible rate loans.

Adjustable rate mortgages carry an initial interest rate below the rate offered on a standard fixed rate mortgage. The difference between the initial rate on fixed and variable

Adjustable rate loans: Home mortgages on which the interest rate is periodically adjusted over the term of the loan.

loans can vary widely as credit market conditions change. As Figure 8.2 indicates, the differential has fluctuated between ½ and 2 percentage points in recent years.

The Federal Trade Commission suggests you examine all of the following when shopping for an adjustable rate mortgage:

TOPIC **LINKS**

FTC Home Financing Primer

- The initial interest rate
- How often the rate may change
- How much the rate may change
- The initial monthly payments
- How often payments may change
- How much payments may change
- The mortgage term
- How often the term may change
- The index to which rate, payment, or term changes are tied
- The limits, if any, on negative amortization

Interest Rate Adjustment Period and the Adjustment Index

The interest rate on the remaining loan balance may be changed after a specified period. The period between one rate change and the next is known as the **interest rate adjustment period.** The majority of adjustable rate loans have an adjustment period of one year. The change in the rate is tied to the change in an **interest rate adjustment index** that tends to mirror the general movement in interest rates throughout the economy.

Interest rate adjustment period: The time between potential adjustments in the interest rate applied to the outstanding loan balance.

Interest rate adjustment index: The index to which changes in the mortgage interest rate are related.

Several different interest rate adjustment indexes are commonly included in mortgage contracts. You can check out the history and volatility of the most used indexes at HSH Associates (www.hsh.com). Financial analysts tend to favor the use of the National Average FHLB Mortgage Contract Rate as an interest rate index, because it seems to be less volatile than the other indexes.

To determine the contract interest rate on the outstanding mortgage balance, lenders add a few percentage points, called the **margin,** to the index rate.

TOPIC **LINKS**
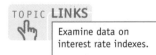
Examine data on interest rate indexes.

Index rate + margin = contract interest rate

Margin: The amount added to the index rate in order to calculate the interest rate on the mortgage contract.

For example, suppose an index rate such as the National Average FHLB Mortgage Contract Rate was 7.5 percent at the time of adjustment and the margin was 2 percentage points. The contract rate applied to the outstanding loan balance would be 9.5 percent. The margin may differ from one lender to the other, but it is usually constant over the life of the loan.

At periodic dates specified in the mortgage contract, the contract rate will be recalculated to reflect changes in the indexed rate. Using the current example, suppose the index rate fell from 7.5 percent to 7.25 percent at the next rate adjustment. With a 2 percent margin, the contract rate will decline from 9.5 percent to 9.25 percent. Lenders have been known to incorrectly determine the interest rate readjustment; therefore, you should locate information on the index and check the lender's calculation.

TOPIC **LINKS**

Get an ARM Check Kit from HSH Associates.

Teaser rate: An abnormally low initial interest rate meant to attract borrowers.

A few lenders offer **teaser rates,** which are a promotional gimmick. Over some initial period a reduced margin is used to calculate the adjustable rate. When this period ends, a higher margin is used to compute the rate over the remaining term of the loan. This produces an upward adjustment in the flexible rate independent of any change in the interest rate adjustment index.

Rate Cap

Some loans may have rate caps that limit the movement in your interest rate. These typically limit increases but may also limit decreases in the rate. A **periodic rate cap** limits changes during any one adjustment period. Suppose you had a 1½ percent periodic cap, and the underlying index rate rose by 2 percent. The adjustable rate applied to the outstanding loan balance would be limited to a 1½ percent increase during this adjustment period. However, the unused ½ percent may be applied during the next adjustment period.

An **aggregate rate cap** limits changes over the entire life of the loan. If you had a 5 percent aggregate cap on your mortgage rate, then no matter how high the financial index rose, a mortgage with an initial rate of 7 percent could never go above 12 percent. By federal law, all adjustable rate mortgages must have a lifetime ceiling on the contract rate. There is no federal limit on how high the cap may be, although most states do set limits.

Periodic rate cap: Limits the movement on changes in the interest rate during any one interest rate adjustment period.

Aggregate rate cap: Limits the total change in the interest rate over the entire term of the loan.

Payment Cap

A **payment cap** limits changes in your monthly loan payments. Under a payment cap, it is possible for the interest rate on your adjustable rate loan to increase while your monthly payments either remain unchanged or do not increase as much as required by the interest rate adjustment.

Don't assume you don't have to pay the higher interest. Suppose you take out a 30-year, $88,000 mortgage at an initial interest rate of 8 percent and an annual adjustment period. At the 6 percent rate your initial monthly payments are $527.60. If, at the end of the first year, the interest rate rises to 8 percent, the monthly payments would ordinarily increase to $645.71. However, if the yearly adjustment under the payment cap is less than $118.11 ($645.71 − $527.60), then the monthly payments will not increase to the level required to completely discharge the loan in the remaining 29 years. The difference between your monthly payment under the cap and the required payment may be made up in one of several ways. The term of the loan can be lengthened beyond the initial 30-year agreement. Alternatively, the term might remain unchanged, but the lending institution might require an additional lump-sum payment at the time the mortgage is to be paid up. Still another method is for future monthly payments to be increased. The lending institution should specify in the mortgage contract the method it plans to use.

In the current example, the amount outstanding on the mortgage at the end of the first year will be $86,919.35. At an annual percentage rate of 8 percent, interest payments alone amount to $579.46 per month. If the payment cap keeps the monthly payment from rising beyond $579.46, **negative amortization** will result. This term simply means that instead of your debt getting smaller over time, it will get larger. You will owe the lending institution more at the end of the year than you did at the beginning. Obviously, this situation can create problems for both you and the lending institution. For this reason, only a small percentage of mortgage contracts permit negative amortization. In all other cases, the payment cap cannot hold monthly payments to less than the interest owed on the outstanding loan balance.

Payment cap: Limits changes in the monthly mortgage payment.

Negative amortization: The resulting increase in the amount owed when the monthly payment is less than the interest due on the previous balance.

Convertible Features

Lenders have recently been promoting **convertible mortgages.** These are adjustable rate mortgages that can be converted into fixed rate mortgages during a specified time period, usually between the thirteenth and sixtieth months of the loan. The fixed rate will be determined by rules set down in the mortgage contract. If you elect to make the conversion, the lender will charge a fee that, most likely, will be equal to either a stated dollar amount or a percentage of the outstanding loan balance.

Convertible mortgage: An adjustable mortgage contract that permits the borrower to convert to a fixed rate contract at some point during the term of the loan.

The rate on the fixed rate loan may depend on the value of the interest adjustment index at the date of the conversion. If you believe that interest rates will decline, then a convertible mortgage would allow you to get the benefits of an adjustable rate loan today and the expected benefit of a lower rate on a fixed rate loan at a future date.

You should be careful not to place too much value on the conversion feature. Adjustable rate loans rarely carry penalties for paying off a loan before it is due. Therefore, even with an ordinary adjustable rate loan, you always have the choice of paying it off and refinancing with a fixed rate loan. If you refinance, however, you will be charged closing costs and points on the new loan. The real value of the conversion feature is, consequently, the difference between the conversion fee and traditional refinancing charges.

Specialized Mortgage Formats and Creative Financing

Most borrowers will end up with either a basic fixed rate or adjustable rate mortgage. During times of tight credit and high interest rates, however, both lenders and borrowers have demonstrated an increasing willingness to experiment with new financial instruments. Two of the less common formats that can be found in the market are graduated payment mortgages and shared appreciation mortgages.

Graduated payment mortgage (GPM): A mortgage with scheduled increases in monthly payments over the term of the loan.

On a **graduated payment mortgage (GPM),** monthly payments rise gradually (usually over 5 to 10 years) and then remain level for the remainder of the loan. The lower initial monthly payments allow individuals to borrow larger amounts than they ordinarily would. The government offers FHA insurance on GPMs to aid young low-income families who expect their income to rise in the future. Unfortunately, the low monthly payments in the early years can result in negative amortization. This can create a financial problem if you have to relocate in the first few years after your home purchase. In addition, a graduated payment mortgage will have a slightly higher interest rate than a comparable-level payment loan, generating greater interest payments over the life of the loan.

TOPIC LINKS
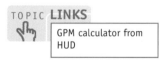
GPM calculator from HUD

Shared appreciation mortgage (SAM): In return for lower monthly payments the lender shares in the home's appreciated market value.

With a **shared appreciation mortgage (SAM),** you get a below-market contract rate on a loan that lets you qualify for a larger mortgage on a larger home than you would with a traditional mortgage. However, the bank becomes your partner on any future appreciation in the market value. Typically, the lender receives between 30 to 60 percent of the home's appreciation. If the home goes down in value, the bank gets none of the equity. Increases in the home's value due to significant improvements are not shared, nor are the selling costs incurred by the homeowner. If you have not sold the home by the end of the mortgage, you still have to come up with the money to pay for the lender's share in the home's appreciation.

Reading the Fine Print

In addition to understanding the economic characteristics of the loan, you must also understand the legal ramifications. This means reading the fine print and carefully examining each clause.

Acceleration clause: The loan repayment is accelerated if you miss a payment.

The **acceleration clause** will allow the lender to speed up the rate at which the loan comes due if you miss a payment. Be sure you understand how and when this clause becomes operative. Also be wary of an acceleration clause that then permits the lender to foreclose on the loan "without notice."

A **due-on-sale clause** requires immediate repayment of the loan when the property changes hands. Such clauses are common and have been enforced by the courts. If you do not have a due-on-sale clause, then you may have an **assumable mortgage.** This mortgage may be transferred to the buyer at the time of sale. However, a credit review of the buyer and a fee may be required by the lender. In a tight credit market, an assumable mortgage at a relatively low contract rate can attract buyers.

The prepayment clause indicates how early payment on the loan will be handled. The loan contract could impose a **prepayment penalty** if you repay the loan early for reasons other than the sale of the home. This clause is generally not permitted on adjustable rate loans.

On some loans, the lending institution adds to the monthly mortgage payment an amount to cover home insurance or property taxes. The lender accumulates these funds in what is called an **escrow account.** When the insurance or property taxes become due, the lender will pay these bills out of the funds in the escrow account. By doing so, the lender ensures that these obligations are being met.

An escrow account is required when the mortgage is insured by the Federal Housing Administration or the Veterans Administration or when the loan is for 90 percent or more of the value of the house. In all other situations, the need for an escrow account is negotiable between the borrower and lender.

If possible, you should avoid setting up an escrow account. In most places the lending institution will pay no interest on the funds held. In the 14 states where lenders are required by law to pay interest on escrow accounts, the rate paid is typically less than the rate on a passbook savings account. You can do better by holding these funds in your ordinary savings account and paying your taxes and insurance directly. If you have an escrow account, you should contact the lending institution to see if it can be closed.

Due-on-sale clause: The outstanding balance on the loan must be repaid when you sell the home.

Assumable mortgage: The buyer replaces the seller as the borrower on the existing mortgage contract.

Prepayment penalty: A penalty incurred by the borrower if the mortgage balance is prepaid for any reason other than the sale of the home.

Escrow account: An account held by the lender into which the borrower deposits funds in order to ensure that the homeowner's expenses will be paid.

Insured Mortgages

The term *conventional financing* is used for mortgages that are neither government insured nor guaranteed. Conventional mortgages may have **private mortgage insurance** on high-risk loans to protect the lender in the event you default on the loan. If you take out a conventional home mortgage with less than a 20 percent down payment, private mortgage insurance is a required addition to your monthly mortgage payment. The insurance protects the lender from losses resulting from a defaulting borrower. Thus, private market insurance enables lenders to extend loans to individuals who do not have the necessary funds for the typical down payment.

The cost of this protection is not cheap. The fee varies depending on the down payment and the size of the mortgage but typically ranges from $240 to $1,200 annually. Understandably, borrowers prefer to see these premiums end as soon as possible.

Typically, there is no need for private mortgage insurance when your equity in the home reaches 20 percent. However, many homeowners do not know that they may request cancellation of the insurance when home equity reaches this level. In addition, lenders have been slow to honor such requests.

Given the high cost of private mortgage insurance, you would be better off to avoid it. You might consider putting off a purchase until you have the 20 percent down payment or even consider a temporary personal loan at a higher interest rate in order to fund a 20 percent down payment.

Mortgage insurance may also be arranged through either the Federal Housing Administration (FHA) or the Veterans Administration (VA). These programs make nonconventional mortgages available to individuals who might otherwise be considered poor credit risks.

Private mortgage insurance: Protects the lender when borrowers default on the mortgage.

TOPIC **LINKS**

MICA Insurance Cancellation Kit

Federal Housing Administration (FHA)

FHA mortgages are not government loans. **FHA mortgage insurance** protects the lender against loss on the mortgage, thereby permitting the lender to offer more liberal credit terms to families who could not otherwise afford a home.

FHA mortgage insurance: Federally backed insurance protecting lenders against nonrepayment of mortgage.

TOPIC **LINKS**
Check current FHA insurance limits.

The FHA insures mortgages when both property and borrower meet certain standards. Information on current requirements can be found by contacting the FHA or lenders that provide FHA-insured loans. If you are eligible, you may borrow up to a government-set maximum with a relatively low down payment of no more than 5 percent of the purchase price.

Veterans Administration (VA)

TOPIC **LINKS**
Get the latest limits on VA loan guarantees.

All veterans and current members of the Armed Services are entitled to loan guarantees through the Veterans Administration. The stated purpose of the program is to help veterans finance the purchase of reasonably priced homes at favorable rates of interest. With a VA loan you do not need a down payment. The guarantee encourages lenders to make bigger loans with a smaller down payment than they otherwise could, because the government guarantees repayment of up to 50 percent of the loan and a legislatively set dollar maximum. However, the VA requires that borrowers have a debt repayment-to-income ratio of 41 percent or less.

Refinancing

If you took out a mortgage at a high interest rate, and rates have since come down, you should consider the possibility of refinancing the loan. Your first step is to contact your current lender concerning refinancing. If you have been a good customer, the lender may be willing to reduce some of the up-front closing costs associated with refinancing. Your up-front expenses will consist of a possible prepayment penalty on the old loan and points and origination costs on the new loan. Your future savings will consist of lower monthly mortgage payments. To determine whether you should refinance, you must estimate your payback period, that is, the length of time required for your future savings to cover your up-front expenses. With the average family moving once every seven years, you most likely should not refinance if the payback period is longer than seven years.

TOPIC **LINKS**
Download worksheet or try an online calculator.

Because loans may be written in so many ways, the proposed new loan is likely to differ by more than just the interest rate. You must also weigh these additional factors into your decision to refinance. For example, you may be considering giving up a high fixed rate mortgage for a currently low adjustable rate mortgage. This exchange may be profitable if rates stay low. Whether such an exchange is attractive to you depends on how much risk you are willing to accept.

TOPIC **LINKS**
Download a calculator for biweekly mortgages.

Figure 8.11 contains a worksheet for calculating the approximate payback period. To calculate your monthly savings at the lower interest rate, the new monthly payment should be based on the outstanding loan balance and the remaining term on the old loan. Given a refinancing cost of $1,987 and savings on monthly mortgage payments of $97.92, the reduction in mortgage payments would pay for the cost of refinancing in about 21 months. This is only an approximate payback period, because it does not consider the differential tax treatment for mortgage interest and closing costs or the different rates at which low- and high-interest mortgages pay back principal.

You should recognize that the tax treatment of points differs for refinancing. On the initial home mortgage, the IRS has decided you can deduct all points representing prepaid interest in the year the loan is taken out. For refinancing, however, the deduction must be spread out over the term of the mortgage. In the current example, you would have an annual itemized deduction of $39.35 = $787/20 years. Of course, if you sell the home

Figure 8.11

Refinancing: Calculating the Approximate Payback Period

Current Loan		
Amount borrowed	$ 88,000	
Outstanding balance	$ 78,698	
Original term (months)	360	
Remaining term (months)	240	
Annual contract rate	9.00%	
Present monthly payment		$708.07
New Loan		
Initial balance	$ 78,698	
Term (months)	240	
Annual contract rate	7.00%	
New monthly payment		610.15
Monthly savings		$ 97.92
Initial Cost of Refinancing		
Origination fee	$ 100.00	
Closing costs	1,100.00	
Points (1%)	786.98	
Total initial costs	$1,986.98	
Divided by monthly savings	÷ 97.92	
Approximate payback period (months)	20.29	

before the mortgage is paid off, any remaining nonitemized points may be deducted in the year of the sale.

What If You Can't Meet Your Mortgage Payments?

The unexpected can happen. You can lose your job, or your business can enter troubled times. Whenever the possibility exists that you may be unable to meet your future mortgage payments, your first step is to contact the lending institution. If you do not meet your scheduled payments, the lender probably has the right to demand immediate payment on the remaining loan balance. Failure to meet this demand may result in **foreclosure.** This legal process terminates your rights to the property and forces its sale. You receive any excess of the sale price over the amount needed to discharge the loan. Of course, because of the immediacy surrounding the sale, the price may be relatively low, leaving you with little or nothing in return. This process also involves costs and risks for the lending institution; therefore, you may both benefit by avoiding foreclosure. This is why you should contact the lending institution before you actually have to miss payments. It is possible that, through a renegotiation of the loan, the monthly payments can be reduced. This can be accomplished by stretching out the term of the loan, postponing repayment of principal, or even negative amortization.

Selling a home in a declining housing market can be a serious problem for borrowers with low down payments. The potential sales price may be less than the outstanding mortgage balance. In this case, the lender may be willing to enter into a *compromise* or *short sale*, in which the lender agrees to receive less than the full value of the mortgage. This permits the mortgager to sell the house for less than the original loan amount.

When your lending institution appears uncompromising, you may still be entitled to some special help if you have a federally insured FHA or VA loan. If a potential foreclosure seems likely, you should consult an attorney. Under the bankruptcy code you may be able to force the lending institution to accept a proposed repayment plan or at least delay the forced sale until you can sell the property at a favorable price.

Foreclosure: A legal process that terminates your rights to a mortgaged property and forces its sale.

Saving
money $

Biweekly Mortgages

Most mortgages require that you repay the loan in monthly installments. You may have the choice, however, of obtaining a biweekly mortgage, on which you make a repayment once every two weeks. If you decide on a biweekly mortgage, you will end up making 26 biweekly payments during the year. When the biweekly payment is set equal to one-half the monthly payment, the total annual value of the biweekly payments will equal 13 monthly payments instead of the traditional 12.

With the extra monthly payment you will reduce the term of the mortgage and eliminate a good chunk of your future interest payments. In the accompanying table, it can be seen that the higher the interest rate on the loan, the more interest you save and, therefore, the earlier you pay off the loan. On a 30-year, $100,000 mortgage with an annual contract rate of 7 percent, a biweekly loan with a periodic payment of one-half the monthly mortgage payment would pay off after about 24 years;

BOX 8.3

at a 9 percent rate it would pay off after only about 22 years. The corresponding interest savings range from $46,299 to $60,417. At first glance, a biweekly mortgage looks like an excellent idea.

Are these savings really a net benefit? Your interest expense is less because you are paying off the mortgage at a faster rate. By using these dollars to pay off your mortgage at an earlier date, you give up the option of either investing these funds elsewhere or using them to reduce higher-cost debt. The optimal strategy will depend on which alternative provides the greatest after-tax savings or return. You are only really better off by the difference between mortgage interest not paid and what these funds could have earned in an alternative investment. If your returns are higher elsewhere, the correct strategy is to extend your mortgage payments.

Surprisingly, you don't need a biweekly mortgage to pay off your loan balance at a faster rate. Most traditional mortgage contracts allow you to make partial prepayments of principal at your discretion, thus providing you with greater flexibility than a similar biweekly loan. You probably already have the choice of making or not making a thirteenth monthly payment.

Annual Contract Rate (%)	Monthly Payment*	Biweekly Payment	Total Number of Payments	Term of Biweekly Mortgage (years)	Total Interest on Monthly Mortgage	Total Interest on Biweekly Mortgage	Interest Saved?
9.00	$804.62	$402.31	569.83	21.92	$189,664	$129,247	$60,417
8.00	733.76	366.88	593.81	22.84	164,155	117,857	46,299
7.00	665.30	332.65	616.40	23.71	139,509	105,046	34,463

*Monthly payments on a 30-year $100,000 mortgage.

Key Terms

acceleration clause (p. 216)

adjustable rate loans (p. 213)

aggregate rate cap (p. 215)

amortize (p. 213)

assumable mortgage (p. 217)

closing (p. 208)

closing costs (p. 209)

condominium (p. 199)

contract rate (p. 210)

convertible mortgage (p. 215)

cooperative (p. 200)

deed (p. 208)

due-on-sale clause (p. 217)

earnest money (p. 208)

escrow account (p. 217)

exclusive agency agreement (p. 206)

exclusive right to sell (p. 206)

FHA mortgage insurance (p. 218)

fixed rate mortgages (p. 211)

foreclosure (p. 219)

graduated payment mortgage (GPM) (p. 216)

Housing Affordability Index (p. 194)

---

interest rate adjustment
index (p. 214)
interest rate adjustment
period (p. 214)
listing agreement (p. 206)
margin (p. 214)
marketable title (p. 208)
negative amortization
(p. 215)

net listing agreement
(p. 207)
open listing agreement
(p. 207)
payment cap (p. 215)
periodic rate cap (p. 215)
points (p. 209)
prepayment penalty
(p. 217)

principal (p. 213)
private mortgage
insurance (p. 217)
settlement costs (p. 209)
shared appreciation mort-
gage (SAM) (p. 216)
teaser rate (p. 214)
title insurance (p. 208)
title search (p. 208)

Reread the chapter-opening vignette.

**FOLLOW-UP
ON THE**

**Steele
FAMILY**

1. The Steeles are considering substituting a fixed rate loan for the adjustable rate loan they presently have. What factors should the Steeles consider before exchanging one type of loan for another?
2. The Steeles plan to use the reduced monthly interest payments to fund a savings plan. However, by exchanging a 15-year loan for a 30-year loan they will build up equity in their home at a slower rate. What factors should they consider before lengthening the term of their present loan?
3. Help the Steeles in their decision making by drawing up a list of the potential benefits and the potential costs of mortgage refinancing.

**Problems and
Review
Questions**

1. What is the relationship between market rates of interest and affordable housing?
2. If your income after taxes is $28,000 per year, and you expect to pay about $100 per month on utilities, about how much can you afford to spend on monthly rental payments?
3. Given an affordable monthly mortgage payment of $650, and a mortgage interest rate of 9 percent on a 30-year loan, what is the size of the affordable mortgage? Given this affordable mortgage, and a 10 percent down payment, what is the affordable purchase price?
4. How does a cooperative differ from a condominium?
5. Suppose you had $6,000 in mortgage interest payments during the year and you were in the 28 percent marginal tax bracket. What is the real cost of the mortgage interest payments after tax considerations? Suppose you had $6,000 in rental payments during the year and you were in the 33 percent marginal tax bracket. What is the real cost of the rental payments after tax considerations?
6. Suppose housing prices rise at a 5 percent annual rate over the next five years. If a house now costs $100,000, how much will it bring after five years and the payment of a 6 percent sales commission?
7. What are the tax advantages attached to home ownership, and under what conditions will long-term capital gains on the sale of a residence be tax free?
8. What occurs at *closing?* Give three items that would be included in closing costs.
9. A lender is offering an 11 percent fixed rate mortgage, requiring a down payment equal to 20 percent of the home's purchase price. The lender estimates that closing costs should be equal to $500 plus 4 points. How much will closing costs be on a $120,000 home?
10. What are the relative advantages of fixed and adjustable rate loans?
11. What are some important characteristics of adjustable rate loans that you should examine carefully?

12. An adjustable rate mortgage has a yearly interest rate adjustment cap of 1 percent. If the indexed rate moves up by 1½ percent in the first year, and ½ percent in the second year, how much can the interest rate on the remaining loan balance move up after the first year, and after the second year?

13. Suppose you expect your income to increase significantly over the next few years. You would like to purchase a home that more closely fits your future income status rather than your present circumstances, thereby avoiding relocation expenses in a few years. What types of mortgages might be of interest to you?

14. You are thinking of retiring in about 15 years. You would like to purchase a home now but would like to have it paid off before retirement. You plan to live on reduced income during retirement, so the tax deductions on mortgage interest would not be significant at that time. What types of mortgages might be of interest to you?

15. What does the term *conventional financing* mean? What government programs exist for nonconventional financing?

16. Whom does private mortgage insurance protect, and why is it sometimes required?

17. Name two government organizations that can help you obtain a home mortgage with a relatively small down payment.

18. Why does the lender obtain title insurance?

19. What is the distinguishing feature of a convertible home mortgage?

20. What is foreclosure, and how might you avoid an impending foreclosure?

Case 8.1
How Much House Can Kim and Dan Bergholt Afford?

Kim and Dan Bergholt are both government workers. They are considering purchasing a home in the Washington, D.C., area for about $280,000. They estimate monthly expenses for utilities at $220, maintenance at $100, property taxes at $380, and home insurance payments at $50. Their only debt consists of car loans requiring a monthly payment of $350.

Kim's gross income is $55,000 per year and Dan's is $38,000 per year. They have saved about $60,000 in a money market fund on which they earned $5,840 last year. They plan to use most of this for a 20 percent down payment and closing costs. A lender is offering 30-year variable rate loans with an initial interest rate of 8 percent given a 20 percent down payment and closing costs equal to $1,000 plus 3 points.

Before making a purchase offer and applying for this loan, they would like to have some idea whether they might qualify.

Questions
1. Estimate the affordable mortgage and the affordable purchase price for the Bergholts.
2. Suppose they do qualify; what other factors might they consider before purchasing and taking out a home mortgage?
3. What future changes might present problems for the Bergholts?

Case 8.2
Should the Bergholts Choose the Rental Option?

The real estate agent tells the Bergholts that if they don't care to purchase, they might consider renting. The rental option would cost $1,400 per month plus utilities estimated at $220 and renter's insurance of $25 per month.

The Bergholts believe that neither of them is likely to be transferred to another location within the next five years. After that, Dan perceives that he might move out of government service into the private sector. Assuming they remain in the same place for the next five years, the Bergholts would like to know if it is better to buy or rent the home. They expect that the price of housing and rents will rise at an annual rate of 3 percent over the next five years. They expect to earn an annual rate of 5 percent on the money market fund. All other prices, including utilities, maintenance, and taxes are expected to increase at a 3 percent annual rate. After federal, state, and local taxes, they get to keep only 55 percent of a marginal dollar of earnings.

Questions

1. Given the information in this and the previous case, estimate whether it is financially more attractive for the Bergholts to rent or to purchase the home over a five-year holding period. (Assuming the contract interest rate of 8 percent, monthly interest payments over the five-year period would total $87,574.)
2. Suppose it turns out that they have to relocate after one year. Which is the preferred alternative after one year? (Interest payments over the first year would equal $17,852.)

Exercises to Strengthen Your Use of the Internet
(Internet links for the following exercises can be found at **www.prenhall.com/winger**.)

Working Out on the Web

Exercise 8.1 How Much House Can You Afford?
The Finance Center has several calculators to help you with your housing decision. Two that fit nicely into the discussion in the text are the "What Home Can I Afford?" worksheet and the "Am I Better Off Renting?" worksheet. The mortgage worksheet gives you a range of possible outcomes based on how much you are willing to put down and your lender's attitude toward risk.

Q. Given the sample data, vary the interest rate from 6 percent to 9 percent. How does the affordable home price change as the interest rate changes?

Exercise 8.2 Rent or Buy?
Return to the Finance Center Web site and click on the worksheet, "Am I Better Off Renting?" The graph on the rent/buy worksheet is a real plus. With one glance you can observe the year in which the cost of renting begins to exceed the cost of buying. As we state in the text, buying is likely to be the preferred alternative the longer you plan to stay in one place. With this worksheet graph, you can easily determine the point of indifference between buying and renting.

Q. Use the sample data in the "Am I Better Off Renting?" worksheet but vary the appreciation rate on homes from 3 to 5 percent. Also vary the interest rate on the mortgage from 7 to 9 percent. How do these changes affect the decision to buy or rent? How many years would you have to live at the same location for you to be financially indifferent to buying versus selling?

Exercise 8.3 Evaluating the Neighborhood
The market value of a home depends on more than just the number of rooms. To a large extent, the price of a home depends on the community it is located in. Coldwell Banker has a nationwide chain of real estate firms. In addition to providing online listings of homes, it also provides summary data on neighborhoods to help you evaluate the community. You can access this information through its Neighborhood Explorer (TM).

More difficult to use, but with much more detailed data, is the TIGER Map Service or the FFIEC Census Report from the U.S. Census. Both sites permit you to obtain socioeconomic data by zip code. They are most helpful when comparing neighborhoods within a city. You can try them out by comparing your own neighborhood with some other well-known community.

Q. Using either of these online sites, compare the socioeconomic data on your own neighborhood with that from zip code 90210, the famous Beverly Hills community.

Exercise 8.4 Generate an Amortization Table

The mortgage calculator from Bloomberg.com generates an amortization table indicating the remaining balance on your loan after each mortgage payment. It also indicates how much you must increase your monthly payment for you to pay off the mortgage at an earlier date. A $100,000, 30-year mortgage at 7.5 percent APR would require monthly payments of $699.21.

Q. How much more would you have to pay per month if you wanted to repay your mortgage in 20 years? How much interest would you save by paying off the mortgage in 20 rather than 30 years? (Go to the full table.)

Exercise 8.5 Comparing Monthly Payments on Fixed and Adjustable Rate Loans

The Bank Rate Monitor publishes the national averages for 30-year fixed and one-year adjustable rate loans. Use these rates to calculate the monthly payment on a $100,000, 30-year mortgage with a mortgage calculator. Enter the average current contract rate on 30-year fixed rate mortgages and one-year adjustable rate mortgages.

Q. How would monthly payments on a $100,000 loan differ for fixed rate and adjustable rate mortgages given current market rates? If adjustable rates remained unchanged, how much would this save you in interest payments?

Exercise 8.6 Interest Savings on a Biweekly Mortgage

HSH Associates' Mortgage Calculator can also be used to calculate the payoff on a biweekly mortgage.

Q. Given the 30-year fixed rate mortgage you used in the previous exercise, how much sooner would you pay off this mortgage with biweekly payments? How much would you save in interest payments?

Exercise 8.7 Calculating a Rate Adjustment

HSH Associates provides ARM Check Kit for calculating the rate change on a variable rate mortgage. On the index histories page you can find recent information on the most popular ARM indexes.

Q. Which mortgage would have a lower contract rate: one using the weekly rate on the 10-year Treasury security with a two-point margin, or one using the national mortgage contract interest rate with a one-point margin? The answer is likely to vary with the most recent economic conditions.

Exercise 8.8 Comparing Future Payments Under Fixed Rate and Adjustable Rate Mortgages

This site from Belmont National Bank has several mortgage comparison calculators. The fixed rate versus adjustable rate calculators are great for comparing the worst-case outcome for an adjustable rate mortgage versus what would occur with a fixed rate mortgage. Assuming maximum upward adjustments each period, it indicates at what point the fixed rate mortgage becomes the optimal choice.

For example, the program indicates that given a 30-year fixed rate mortgage at 8.75 percent and a 30-year annually adjusted mortgage with an initial rate of 4.75 percent, an annual cap of 2 percent, and a lifetime cap of 6 percent, the fixed rate would be more cost-effective by the end of the seventh year. This assumes that the ARM increases by the maximum each year and that other costs (fees and points) are comparable.

Q. How would the break-even year change if the fixed rate mortgage had a 9.5 percent contract rate?

PART 4

Investing for the Future

GROWING YOUR FINANCIAL RESOURCES

Chapter 9
Financial Markets and Institutions: *Learning the Investment Environment*

Chapter 10
Investment Basics: *Understanding Risk and Return*

Chapter 11
Stocks and Bonds: *Your Most Common Investments*

Chapter 12
Mutual Funds and Other Pooling Arrangements: *Simplifying and (Maybe) Improving Your Investment Performance*

The next four chapters deal with investments. They explain different investment alternatives, discuss investment strategies, and describe important aspects of the investment process. Above all, they continuously alert you to the trade-off between the return you can expect from an investment and the degree of risk you must take to earn it. According to many financial advisers, failure to understand this trade-off is the single most important reason investors lose with their investments—and these losses are often catastrophic in relation to the investors' net worths. To succeed as an investor, you need an understanding of investment risk and realistic expectations of investment return.

Along with considering investment risk and return, you must also ask whether or not you should be investing in the first place. Of course, the answer depends on how broadly we define *investment*. If it includes assets held for liquidity or to accommodate your lifestyle, the answer is you should be investing immediately and constantly. On the other hand, if we follow a narrower definition and include only those assets we hold for the specific purpose of increasing our net worths, then investment should come *only after* we have provided for adequate liquidity and have enough insurance to protect us against unexpected losses.

A key to successful investing is to understand *why* you are investing. Is it to provide for retirement? Educate your children? Buy a new car three years in the future? Or are you simply looking for a way to lower your income taxes? Your answers to these questions help determine the type of investment vehicles you should choose. This notion of linking specific investments to specific savings goals was introduced in Chapter 2 in the discussion of planned savings. Throughout Part 4, we will continue to stress the importance of having clearly defined investment objectives.

9

Financial Markets and Institutions

LEARNING THE INVESTMENT ENVIRONMENT

OBJECTIVES

1. To identify the basic investment alternatives

2. To understand the nature of securities markets, distinguishing between organized exchanges and the over-the-counter market

3. To recognize important legislation that protects investors

4. To learn how to select a stockbroker and how to choose an investment account

5. To know how to take an investment position and how to place investment orders

6. To recognize and use various sources of investment information

Steele FAMILY

Arnold and Sharon Steele have become deeply concerned about their ability to accumulate sufficient funds for Nancy and John's education and for their eventual retirement. They realize that successful investing will play an important role in achieving their goals but, unfortunately, they do not have a strong background in investment fundamentals and techniques.

Presently, the Steeles' investment portfolio consists of 400 shares of InChemCo common stock, which Arnold has acquired through the company's stock-purchase incentive plan (InChemCo is Arnold's employer) and 200 shares of Fidelity Fund (a mutual fund). The Steeles had almost doubled their money in InChemCo and were up over 50 percent in Fidelity until the stock market dropped sharply in 2000. Their investments lost most of the previous gains and have shown little recovery since then. Although they still have some profit, the amount is quite small and is probably no more than the Steeles could have earned by putting their money in savings accounts. In fact, Arnold and Sharon are wondering if switching their funds into such accounts might be their best step.

Before making any move, though, the Steeles want to know much more about the investing process. Should they use a stockbroker? If so, what kind—full service or discount? How frequently should they trade? Should they trade on the Internet? Are stocks better investments than bonds? Is a mutual fund a better alternative than owning stocks or bonds directly? What type of mutual fund might best meet their investment objectives? The list of questions is extensive.

The Steeles are first-time investors, clearly amateurs in a game that is supposedly dominated by professionals. Perhaps you too are a first-time investor; if so, you might find the investment process bewildering and fearsome. Reading news items in the *Wall Street Journal* or watching *CNBC News* on cable convinces us that finance people speak a foreign language. Worse yet, there seems to be no logic in their stories. For example, a reporter announces, "The government's most recent employment figures hint strongly that a recession is coming." This must be bad news, right? Wrong. She then goes on, "Encouraged by the recent data, the stock and bond markets soared to new highs."

Fear not. The language isn't that hard to learn, and, believe it or not, there really is some sense in most investment news. This chapter will get you started by describing investment alternatives and by explaining important investment markets and institutions. Although you won't be an investment professional four chapters later, you certainly will know enough to make sound investment decisions.

GOALS AND INVESTMENT ALTERNATIVES

Our investment goals differ. If you are a young person starting a career, you may want to achieve a goal different from that of people preparing for retirement. You are concerned with building an estate; they are concerned with preserving what they have. You may be willing to sacrifice current income; they might depend on it to meet living expenses. Obviously, an investment that's good for you may be totally inappropriate for them. Before starting an investment program, define your goals as clearly as you can, then indicate specifically how an individual investment is related to those goals. Goal definition is made easier when you understand yourself better: that is, when you are aware of your investment needs. Then you can look at the basic investment alternatives.

What Are Your Needs?

Surprisingly, perhaps, earning a return on an investment is not the only need many people try to satisfy from investing. The pleasure associated with many investments derives from your using them (your home) or simply owning them (your antiques). Also, if you are looking for a dollar return, this goal has to be further defined to state whether you want more now or more later: that is, a current versus a future return. And people are quite different in their tax situations and attitudes toward risks.

Tangible and Intangible Investments

The first major classification of investments is based on whether an asset is tangible or intangible. Tangible assets, also called hard assets, are things you can (but don't necessarily) use or enjoy while owning them. Houses, antiques, gold coins or bullion, diamonds and other precious stones, land, and even certain automobiles are examples of **tangible investments.** Some people might object to referring to some of these as investments, since your main reason for buying them is not to earn a return, but that's not an important distinction. Anything that has the potential to increase in value over time is an investment, regardless of its other characteristics. If you can sleep on it, drive it, and enjoy looking at it, all the better. In fact, many Americans have found over the years that their most profitable investments were the tangible ones, particularly their homes. During the 1970s, you would have done much better owning the average home than the average common stock, but in the 1980s and 1990s, the situation was exactly the reverse. Another factor important to some people is the greater personal control they have with tangible investments. If you invest in an apartment complex, for example, you can decide what the rents will be or how much upkeep to provide. If you invest in an apartment complex indirectly, say, through a limited partnership or a corporation, someone else makes those decisions for you. If you like to control things, you have a mental disposition for tangible investments.

Tangible investments: Investments that can provide enjoyment in use as well as an investment return.

Intangible investments:
Financial assets that provide claims to tangible assets or the earnings they provide.

Intangible investments, also called financial or paper assets, are actually claims to tangible assets or the earnings those assets produce. For example, a share of common stock is a claim against the issuing corporation's assets and an entitlement to any dividend or other distributions the corporation might make.

Current Versus Future Return

Some investments offer a return the moment you invest in them—a savings account, for example. Others pay a return less frequently. Most bonds pay interest twice a year, and most stocks that pay dividends usually do so four times a year. Dividends, interest, or any other type of asset income you receive on a regular basis during a year is called a **current return.** Many people prefer owning investments that offer current return, since it supplements their other income. Retirees, for example, often depend on current investment income to meet living expenses.

Current return: Dividends, interest, or other types of asset income received on a regular basis.

Some investments, however, offer no current return whatsoever. Your only return comes about if you can sell the investment to someone else (or have it redeemed by the issuer) at a price greater than what you paid for it. Since this exchange takes place in the future, it is called a **future return** or simply a capital gain. The common stocks of many growth companies have never paid dividends and probably will not for some time in the future. Investors buying these stocks realize that their only return will be from price appreciation over time. These kinds of investments appeal to investors who do not want or need current return but instead are investing to achieve future goals. The Steeles fall into this category.

Future return: A return expected in the future resulting from the potential sale of an asset that has appreciated in value.

Some investments offer both current and future returns. For example, if you buy a share of IBM common stock for, say, $100, you will receive a yearly dividend of $0.72, giving you a 0.72 percent current return on your investment. Obviously, you would be looking for a better return than this in buying IBM, and you would hope to get it through price appreciation. Your target might be 14 percent a year. An investment's **total return** is the sum of its current and future returns, and, in the IBM example, this would be 14.72 percent. Before making an investment, then, you should decide what proportion of total return you want as current return and what proportion as future return.

Total return: Sum of current return and future return.

Your Income Tax Situation

Having read Chapter 4, you know the importance of income taxes in overall financial planning. As you move into higher tax brackets, you have a greater incentive to choose investments that avoid or defer taxes. For example, interest on municipal bonds is not subject to federal income tax, but interest on a U.S. Treasury bond is. Suppose for a $1,000 investment you could earn $60 a year in the municipal bond or $80 in the Treasury bond. Which do you prefer? With no taxes to consider, your answer should be out in an instant—the Treasury bond. But suppose you are in a 28 percent tax bracket; now your choice is less clear. The Treasury bond would yield $57.60 after taxes, but the municipal bond would yield $60, clearly making it a better pick.

Your Attitude Toward Risk

Your attitude toward risk will also shape your investment horizons. Some of us are by nature **risk averters.** We feel extremely uncomfortable in risky situations and prefer to avoid them or at least expect adequate compensation for undertaking them. Going back to the choice between the two bonds above, it could be that an investor in a 28 percent tax bracket would still prefer the Treasury bond to the municipal, not on the basis of after-tax return, but simply because it is a less risky investment. He reasons that an issuing municipality has a far greater chance of defaulting on its interest or redemption obligation than does the U.S. Treasury, and to him, the after-tax greater return is not worth the added risk.

Risk averters: Investors who prefer to avoid risk or at least expect adequate compensation for undertaking risky investments.

Finance News

Human Frailties: Why Smart People Make Dumb Investments

Is intelligence a guarantee of stock market success? Not hardly! Unfortunately, many investors' cranial capacities are often overshadowed by their emotions, perceptions, and downright bad habits. Following is a discussion of three serious character flaws that many of us share and that can have devastating effects on our portfolios.

We Never Learn

During the previous bull market all we heard was how things are different this time. Why? Because of the revolutionary changes forged by the Internet, fiber optics, and technology in general. Forget a company's earnings; if it's in technology, its stock price can go only one way—up. Gee, that's the same story (ex the Internet and fiber optics) we heard back in the early 1970s. The rage at that time was the "nifty fifty," 50 companies guaranteed to hit and stay in the stratosphere. For fun, take a look at where Xerox and Polaroid (two of the darlings) are today. For more recent humor, look at the price chart of almost any Internet or fiber-optic company. Lucent, for example, traded at $100 in late 1999 and at $0.90 by October of 2002.

We Have Unrealistic Perceptions

An absolutely amazing statistic is one found in a Consumer Federation of America/Primerica poll (October 1999) that many

BOX 9.1

respondents felt that winning a state lottery (40 percent) was a more probable way of accumulating $500,000 during their lifetimes than saving and investing (30 percent). How many of those respondents understood the true odds of winning a large lottery (10 million to 1)? Probably none, but even if they did it is unlikely that many would stop buying lottery tickets and start investing. The perception is that you can only get rich through some fortuitous event, such as winning the lottery. This same outlook extends to many investors, who hope to get rich by buying the next Microsoft at $2 a share and selling it (usually within a year) at $200.

We Binge on Excessive Optimism and Pessimism

The stock market is no place for emotional binges, yet that seems to be the order of the day on Wall Street. Few of us are immune from feeling good when the market is booming and becoming depressed when it tanks. However, how we feel should not affect how we invest, yet it often does. In recent years the cable news networks have provided additional drama for investors, who watch "breaking" news stories almost every hour. Unfortunately, too many investors then chase after certain securities that supposedly will thrive or perish by whatever events are reported in the stories.

What are investors to do then? Are we expected to act as machines when it comes to investing, removing all emotions from the process? The honest answer is "yes." Save emotions and feelings for your friends and family members where they are appreciated and do some good. When it comes to investing, be cold and calculating. In future years your friends and family members will be glad that you did.

Just as there are risk averters, there are also **risk seekers**—but these aren't foolish people. Risk seekers also expect additional return for undertaking risky investments, although they don't demand as much as risk averters. To them, a marginally better return of 1 percent might be enough to buy the municipal bond. Both risk-seeking and risk-averting approaches can be satisfied in investment markets. In fact, investor differences help make these markets function as smoothly as they do.

Risk seekers: Investors who will undertake risky investments for less compensation than that demanded by risk averters.

Basic Investment Alternatives

There are many different kinds of investments, and Table 9.1 summarizes their return and risk characteristics by five categories. The rankings assigned to each (A++ is the best and F− the worst) reflect your authors' opinions. Your instructor might have different rankings. Reaching a ranking everyone agrees with is impossible; for one thing, it depends on the period of time you use to measure risk or return, and for another, the techniques one uses

TOPIC **LINKS**

Broaden your understanding of the investment process.

Table 9.1

Investment Alternatives

Investment	Dividends, Interest, Rents (Current Return)	Potential Price Appreciation (Future Return)[a]	Rank[b] Total Return	Rank[b] Total Risk
I Investments held primarily for liquidity: savings accounts, money market deposit accounts and mutual funds, U.S. Series EE and HH bonds, and certificates of deposit	Yes	No	C	A+
II Securities with long or no maturity				
Bonds and notes:				
U.S. Treasury issues	Yes	No	C+	A
Municipal and state government issues	Yes	No	B−	A−
Corporate issues	Yes	No	B	A−
Preferred stock	Yes	No	B−	B+
Common stock	Some	Yes	A−	B−
III Pooling arrangements				
Mutual funds:				
Income funds	Yes	No	B	A
Growth funds	Some	Yes	A	C
Balanced funds	Yes	Yes	B+	B
Investment trusts	Yes	Yes	B+	B
Limited partnerships	Some	Yes	B	C−
IV Contractual claims				
Warrants and rights	No	Yes	A+	D
Put and call options	No	Yes	A+	D
Commodity and financial futures	No	Yes	A++	F−
V Tangible assets				
Real estate:				
Personal residence	No	Yes	A	A
Others	Usually	Yes	B+	D
Gold and other metals	No	Yes	B+	D
Jewelry and collectibles	No	Yes	A−	F

[a]This does not consider price appreciation that is embedded in the investment, such as that sold on a discount basis: e.g., U.S. Treasury bills, U.S. Series EE bonds, and zero coupon bonds. Nor does it include cyclical price variation arising from interest rate changes.

[b]Rank is based on a typical investment, but there are many variations within each class. Returns are ranked from low (C) to high (A), and risks are ranked in opposite order—low (A) to high (F).

to measure each can differ. Table 9.1 simply provides a rough idea of these two characteristics. Also, the ranking is for a typical investment within the class, but there are many variations within each class. For example, a typical common stock is riskier than a typical corporate bond, but not every common stock is riskier than every corporate bond. A share of IBM common stock might be far less risky than a bond issued by Fly-by-Night Airlines. A detailed discussion of each of these kinds of investments is presented in the next five chapters, but a brief overview of all is a helpful start.

Investments Held for Liquidity

Chapter 3 explained investments that satisfy your liquidity needs. Remember from that discussion that there are degrees of liquidity, ranging from checking and savings accounts that are almost perfectly liquid to certificates of deposit that have penalties for early withdrawal. Also, while we give these investments a return rank of only a C, bear in mind that they frequently have done far better than some of the other investments with higher ranks, particularly during high-inflation periods.

Securities with Long or No Maturities

By maturity, we mean the length of time you must wait before the issuer agrees to redeem the security. Corporate and government bonds, which represent creditorship claims—that is, the issuer borrows money from you and promises to repay it in the future—have maturities ranging from one to over 30 years. Common stock and most preferred stock, which represent ownership claims—that is, you are a part owner of the business—have no maturities. The issuing corporations never redeem them, and the only way you can recover your cost is by selling them to someone else. Of course, there is no guarantee you will sell at the same price you paid for them; you might get more, you might get less. When we say in Table 9.1 that there is no appreciation with bonds and preferred stock, we mean that such appreciation is not what investors *expect* from these securities *when they are issued*, since the interest or dividends they pay are fixed and cannot grow. However, their prices do fluctuate with respect to changes in interest rates overall. Therefore, it is possible to have capital gains—or capital losses—with them.

Because of price volatility, bonds, preferred stocks, and common stocks are all considered risky, but common stocks are the riskiest of the three, and all can be very risky during unsettled economic times. None of these are suitable investments if there is a possibility you may need to sell them to raise cash. They are more appropriate for long-term investment.

Pooling Arrangements

A pooling arrangement allows you to achieve greater diversification for your investment dollar than if you attempt to buy individual securities. For example, one share of a mutual fund gives an ownership interest in perhaps as many as 100 different common stocks. Pooling arrangements also provide professional investment management. Not only do you reduce risk through diversification, you might also improve your return.

Contractual Claims

A contractual claim gives you a legal right or obligation to buy or sell something at a given price within a given period of time. Warrants and rights are issued by corporations, and they usually entitle you to buy a certain number of shares of the issuing corporation's common stock. Put and call options are similar to warrants and rights except that they are issued (written) by individuals. A *call* entitles buyers to buy, and a *put* entitles them to sell, shares of a corporation's common stock. People who buy options pay a price for them, since they are actually privileges, not obligations. If you buy an option entitling you to buy, say, 100 shares of General Motors stock at $60 a share, you are not forced to make the purchase; and if GM's stock price fell below $60, you would choose not to. So the most you can lose is what you paid to buy the option.

Commodity and financial futures are like options, but they differ in one important aspect. Rather than being a privilege to buy or sell something, they are an obligation to do so. If you enter into a futures contract on, say, 5,000 bushels of corn at a price of $3.00 per bushel, you are obligated to comply with that agreement regardless of what happens to the price of corn. Even if it falls to $2.00 a bushel, you must buy it at $3.00; thus, your losses with futures contracts are not limited as they are with options. Your potential future return with options and futures is extremely high—but so are your losses, and that is why we rank them highest in risk.

Tangible Assets

Only a few of the many tangible assets are listed in Table 9.1. We have singled out the personal residence from other real estate because it has been such a good investment for so many people. Perhaps our risk assessment is too favorable, but in many cases the prices of homes have not been as volatile as prices of common stocks or even U.S. Treasury bonds. Other real estate, particularly raw land, is another story.

The demand for gold, other metals, and jewelry and collectibles is highly erratic over time. All these kinds of investments are exceptionally risky. With some, such as collectibles, you need specialized knowledge to compete in their markets.

SECURITIES MARKETS

On a normal day about a billion shares of stock are traded on the New York Stock Exchange. Assuming an average price of $40 a share means that about $40 billion worth of securities change hands on just this one exchange and just for common and preferred stocks and warrants. Add to this the combined total values of options, commodity futures, bonds, notes, and all short-term debt securities and you begin to see the magnitude of the securities industry.

Organized Exchanges

Organized exchange: A physical place where securities are traded.

Facilitating the exchange process is the **organized exchange,** which is usually understood as a physical place where buyers and sellers—or their representatives—face each other in making transactions. Each exchange has a floor that is arranged to trade specific securities at specific locations. Only members of an exchange are authorized to make trades, and only securities listed on the exchange are traded.

The New York Stock Exchange

New York Stock Exchange (NYSE): Largest organized exchange in the world.

The **New York Stock Exchange (NYSE)** is the largest organized exchange in the world. Most large U.S. corporations, as well as many large foreign companies, have their shares listed there. To be listed, a company must meet certain requirements and pay rather stiff annual fees, but many firms are willing to do so since listing is often regarded as a sign of financial strength and prestige. Over 3,000 firms are listed on the NYSE with an aggregate market value of around $10 trillion (as of mid-2004). Approximately 80 percent of the market value of all shares traded in the United States are traded on the NYSE; clearly, it earns its nickname—"the Big Board."

TOPIC **LINKS**

Visit the NYSE.

Order Execution on the NYSE

Organized exchanges are fascinating places to visit. What appears to be utter chaos is actually an efficient system for transferring billions of dollars' worth of securities each trading day. Figure 9.1 shows order execution on the NYSE and introduces its members who may be involved in the process. To be a member, you must buy or lease a "seat."

Commission Brokers Commission brokers are employed by stockbrokerage firms. Assuming you deal with Merrill Lynch and have placed a market order to buy 100 shares of Xerox, your representative will transmit the order to one of Merrill Lynch's commission brokers on the floor of the exchange. Suppose that, at the same time, someone else places an order to sell 100 shares of Xerox through her broker, Smith Barney. Both commission brokers would then go to the post where Xerox is traded. For an actively traded issue, such as Xerox, there will be a number of brokers and traders bidding to buy or sell shares. All of

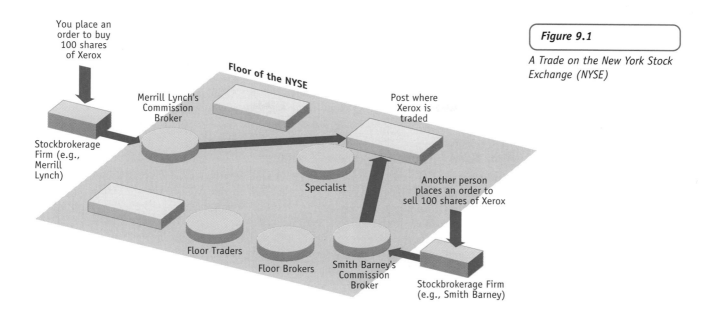

You place an order to buy 100 shares of Xerox

Floor of the NYSE

Merrill Lynch's Commission Broker

Post where Xerox is traded

Stockbrokerage Firm (e.g., Merrill Lynch)

Specialist

Another person places an order to sell 100 shares of Xerox

Floor Traders

Floor Brokers

Smith Barney's Commission Broker

Stockbrokerage Firm (e.g., Smith Barney)

Figure 9.1

A Trade on the New York Stock Exchange (NYSE)

them will try to get the best possible price, either for their customers or for themselves. In effect, shares are auctioned to the highest bidders. (The NYSE and similar markets are thus called *auction markets*.) Perhaps the Merrill Lynch and Smith Barney brokers settle a trade at $10 a share. The entire transaction may be completed in less than 10 seconds.

Specialists Specialists play a number of critical roles in the trading process. They are expected to maintain an orderly and continuous market in the six or seven stocks assigned to them. To keep wide swings in price from occurring, they must buy or sell for their own accounts. For example, assume that when your commission broker arrives at Xerox's trading post, no other broker or trader is there to trade Xerox. Then it is the specialist's responsibility to trade. Another responsibility for the specialist is to maintain the limit books, which contain all limit orders clients have placed with their brokers. (Limit orders will be explained shortly.) Because of the inside information specialists have, it is possible for them to profit handsomely at the expense of outside investors. The NYSE, however, insists that customers' interests come first and specialists' second. This rule is monitored constantly for compliance and enforced rigorously because the integrity of the specialist is critical to maintaining customer confidence in the system.

Specialists: Members of organized exchanges responsible for maintaining orderly and continous markets.

Floor Brokers and Floor Traders Floor brokers are not associated with any particular stockbrokerage firm but serve as independent operators. They assist commission brokers by executing orders on their behalf for a fee. They also serve stockbrokerage firms that do not own seats on the floor. Floor traders operate strictly for themselves, hoping their position on the floor will help them trade stocks profitably.

The American Stock Exchange

The **American Stock Exchange (Amex)** is very similar to the NYSE in terms of physical layout and trading details, but it has easier listing requirements. Often called the "junior board," the Amex is younger than the NYSE and has less prestige. A good number of its listed securities are from relatively unknown companies nationally, and a fairly large percentage are energy oriented. The Amex has had considerable success with the introduction of exchange traded funds (explained in Chapter 12). These have become very popular.

American Stock Exchange (Amex): Another (smaller) organized exchange in New York City.

TOPIC **LINKS**

Visit the Amex.

Regional Stock Exchanges

Along with the two major exchanges, there are regional stock exchanges, such as the Cincinnati Stock Exchange and the Pacific Coast Stock Exchange. Regional exchanges list securities of companies within their geographic areas, but very often these securities also are traded on the NYSE or Amex. In this respect they are duplicates, and it is hard to justify their existence. Together, all the regional exchanges account for a little less than 10 percent of all trading on organized exchanges.

Organized Options and Futures Exchanges

Options are also traded on organized exchanges, such as the Chicago Board Options Exchange, the American Option Exchange (part of the Amex), the Philadelphia Option Exchange, the Pacific Coast Exchange, and the New York Stock Exchange. Options are traded in a manner similar to stock trading.

There are over a dozen organized commodity exchanges in the United States and Canada, and others throughout the world. Trading on commodity exchanges differs somewhat from trading on stock exchanges. It takes place by public outcry and through a complicated series of hand signals. You might have seen pictures of commodity trading and wondered how anything is ever accomplished in what appears to be bedlam. If you have an opportunity to visit any organized exchange—but particularly the commodity exchanges—don't pass it up; although free, they are sufficiently entertaining to be worth an admission charge.

TOPIC **LINKS**

Read a few NASDAQ quotes.

Over-the-Counter Markets

Over-the-counter (OTC) market: Securities trading via electronic communications.

NASDAQ: Name of the electronic communications system used in the OTC market.

Trading over the counter sounds like an illegal activity—but it's not. In fact, in terms of the number of different stocks traded, it is the largest securities market, surpassing the NYSE and Amex combined. In contrast to an organized exchange, the **over-the-counter (OTC) market** consists of a network of securities dealers who trade securities through an extensive communication system called **NASDAQ** (National Association of Securities Dealers Automated Quotations System). In addition to common and preferred stocks and warrants, all government and many corporate bonds are traded in the OTC market. Any securities dealer can buy or sell through NASDAQ, and many stockbrokerage houses make their own portfolio rather than acting as an agent of a customer. Most OTC stocks are of relatively small and unknown companies; however, some giant firms such as Microsoft and Intel trade on the NASDAQ.

REGULATION OF THE SECURITIES INDUSTRY

The nature of the securities industry has offered disreputable people considerable opportunities to defraud investors. Since 1933, important laws have been passed to protect investors; in addition, the industry has initiated reform through self-policing efforts. You have much greater protection now than in the past, but it would be a mistake to think fraud no longer exists or to believe losses you might suffer are the fault of your broker. It is important to know your rights and your obligations before you invest.

Federal Legislation

Federal laws form the backbone of investor protection. The important federal acts are explained in the following sections.

The Securities Act of 1933

The Securities Act of 1933 calls for full disclosure of new securities to be traded in interstate commerce. Such securities must be registered with the Securities and Exchange Commission (SEC, an independent agency of the Federal government), which approves their sale. To receive approval, the applicant must provide the SEC with economic and financial data relevant to the firm and the new offering. It does so in the form of a **prospectus.** After the SEC has determined that the prospectus represents adequate disclosure of all material information affecting the company's value and after the SEC has approved the registration, the company must provide the prospectus to any potential investor. Misrepresentation or fraud in preparing the prospectus can be the basis for lawsuits by investors and the SEC against the issuing corporation, its directors, stockbrokers handling the issue, and even public accountants who assisted in its preparation.

Stiff penalties and possible jail sentences have done much to provide investors with reliable and relevant prospectuses. However, SEC approval in no way assures the issues will be successful. Many new firms have prepared impeccably clean prospectuses and then gone into bankruptcy. The message is clear if you are considering investing: Obtain a prospectus; read it thoroughly, particularly the section explaining risk factors; and believe what it says. Some investors seem to think a prospectus is a mere formality; it isn't. It is a helpful document and should be regarded as such.

Prospectus: Document describing a new security issue.

Review the SEC's Assistance and Complaints area.

The Securities Exchange Act of 1934

The Securities Exchange Act of 1934 extended regulation to securities that had already been issued. With this provision, it brought under government regulation almost all aspects of the security markets. It required all securities traded on organized exchanges and the exchanges themselves to be registered with the SEC (which it established). It outlawed fraud and misrepresentation by anyone engaged in the sale of securities, including stockbrokers and their representatives. It forbade price manipulation, and it required registered firms to file with the SEC both a detailed annual report (called a **10-K Report**) and quarterly financial statements. It stipulated that annual reports be provided to shareholders, and it also established guidelines for security trading by insiders, the intent being to prevent them from taking advantage of their privileged information.

10-K Report: Detailed financial report that must be filed with the Securities and Exchange Commission; also available to shareholders.

The Maloney Act of 1938

The Maloney Act of 1938 required trade associations in the securities industry to register with the SEC. Only one—the National Association of Securities Dealers (NASD)—has been formed and registered. The NASD is the self-regulating arm of the securities industry. It establishes and enforces a professional code of ethics and is responsible for testing and licensing dealers.

The Investment Company Act of 1940

The Investment Company Act of 1940 brought regulation to investment companies, which we more frequently call mutual funds. Such companies are required to register with the SEC and provide shareholders with adequate information about the company's activities. A subsequent amendment to the act forbade paying excessive fees to fund advisers.

The Investment Advisors Act of 1940

The Investment Advisors Act of 1940 requires anyone providing advice to investors (for a fee or other compensation) to register with the SEC and indicate his methods of investment analysis. As an investor, keep in mind that registration does not improve the quality of advice offered or in some other manner guarantee its usefulness. Some advisers advertise their registration, perhaps with the intent of impressing potential clients. Do not be impressed—virtually anyone with sufficient funds can pay the fee to register.

The Securities Investor Protection Act of 1970

The Securities Investor Protection Act protects investors from financial losses that might result from the failure of their broker. It created the Securities Investor Protection Corporation (SIPC), which insures an investor's account up to $500,000 for securities held and up to $100,000 in cash holdings. Most brokerage firms are members of the SIPC and contribute to its funding. It has been particularly helpful to discount brokerage firms in their efforts to overcome investor reluctance to deal with out-of-town brokers.

Some investors believe that the SIPC protection extends to any losses on securities they hold while a broker is in financial difficulty. This is not true. SIPC guarantees only that your securities eventually will be delivered to you or to another broker. Losses or gains during the time the failing firm's arrangements are being sorted out are the investor's. For example, SIPC only guarantees delivery of 100 shares of GM, if that is what you held with a failing broker; it does not guarantee a price for those shares. GM might have been worth $80 a share when your broker ceased to operate but be worth only $50 a share when you eventually have access to the shares.

The Sarbanes-Oxley Act of 2002

The Sarbanes-Oxley Act (SOA) is intended to curb a number of abuses that mushroomed during the boom of the late 1990s. The Act mandates a set of reforms to enhance corporate responsibility and financial disclosures, and to combat corporate and accounting fraud. It also created the Public Company Accounting Oversight Board, known as the PCAOB. The full impact of this legislation has yet to be determined, although early signs indicate it is significantly affecting the disclosure of information. On the negative side, some company owners complain that complying with the law is time consuming and potentially expensive, leading them to question the value of being a publicly traded company.

Among the provisions of SOA are those intended to make financial analysts more responsive to investors and less so to the companies that pay their salaries and bonuses, some of which often run into the millions of dollars. The Act requires brokerage firms and/or their analysts to disclose whether they own shares in the companies they are rating, or are involved (or expect to be involved) in investment banking of such companies. In short, if analysts stand to gain from favorable ratings, they must disclose the nature of their relationships. The securities industry has already paid over $1.4 billion to regulators to settle past grievances, and the penalties for future violations are expected to be steep.

State Law and Self-Regulation

State security laws actually predate federal law. Kansas passed the first "blue sky" law in 1911, and all states now have similar legislation. These laws attempt to keep investors from being defrauded by promoters selling securities worth no more than a piece of blue sky. State laws (patterned after the federal laws) apply to *intrastate* securities sales. Although federal laws apply to *interstate* sales, the SEC can be contacted for any expected fraudulent activity in securities trading.

In addition to federal and state regulation, the securities industry has its own internal regulatory process. Most of this is found in the National Association of Securities Dealers' Rules of Fair Practice, Code of Procedure, and Uniform Practice Code. These three documents cover a wide range of trading activities, specifying rules and appropriate conduct guidelines for NASD members.

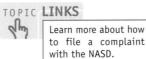

TOPIC **LINKS**

Learn more about how to file a complaint with the NASD.

An extremely important part of self-regulation is the process of **binding arbitration.** If you have a complaint against your broker for not handling a transaction properly, or for pressuring you to invest in securities totally inappropriate for your investment objectives, or for any suspected misconduct, you can appeal to any of the organized exchanges, the NASD, or the American Arbitration Association, for binding arbitration to resolve the problem.

Binding arbitration: A method of resolving disputes among stockbrokers and customers.

Claims less than $10,000 are usually resolved quickly by one arbitrator, but claims above the amount involve more complicated procedures. As its name implies, binding arbitration decisions are final. When considered against the only alternative for seeking a resolution—hiring your own attorney and filing a suit—binding arbitration makes a great deal of sense, since it is much cheaper and faster.

USING THE SERVICES OF A STOCKBROKER

Most financial investments are bought and sold with the assistance of a securities dealer, usually called a stockbroker, or broker for short. (A major exception are mutual fund shares, which are discussed in Chapter 12.) The first step is to select a broker and to choose either a cash or a margin account. Then you must know whether to take a long or a short position. Finally, you need to distinguish among various types of orders.

Selecting a Stockbroker

Finding a stockbroker is not difficult. The number of brokers available has grown considerably since the industry was deregulated in 1974. In recent years, even commercial banks and savings and loans have entered the stockbrokerage business, and the chances are good that some of these institutions, along with traditional stockbrokers, are located in your

Saving
money $

BOX 9.2

Who Is Your Best Protector Against Dishonest Brokers? You!

Humberto Cruz, who writes a very timely and useful syndicated column on personal finance, noted recently a statement made by Arthur Levitt, Chairman of the Securities and Exchange Commission: "No group of regulators can possibly protect investors against their own inability, against their own unwillingness to protect themselves." No truer words could have been spoken.

Certainly Mr. Levitt does not mean that you shouldn't use the courts or regulators to seek restitution if you think you have been injured by a dishonest or incompetent broker or financial adviser; rather, his warning seeks to alert you that, even with all these protections, you still can suffer substantial financial losses. If you lose $10,000 to an incompetent who

takes your money but winds up penniless, what consolation is it to you if he or she spends some time in jail but never repays your loss?

Mr. Cruz points out that if you are thinking of hiring an investment adviser, ask to see his or her Adviser Registration Form (ADV), both Parts I and II. Advisers must provide you with Part II, which shows the adviser's qualifications and experience, but Part I is equally important because it shows the adviser's history of disciplines, convictions, or no-contest pleadings over the past 10 years. Be skeptical of anyone with a shady Part I regardless of how wonderful their qualifications appear or how successful they tell you they have been at managing other people's money. It goes without saying that you should never use a person who is not registered or who is reluctant to provide Part I to you. Also, after you have selected an adviser be prepared to regularly monitor his or her performance. If you ignore performance reports or tell the adviser to "go ahead and do what you think is best," you are asking for trouble.

community. The major distinction between stockbrokers is whether they are considered a full-service or a limited-service (usually called a discount broker) firm.

Full-Service Stockbrokers

Full-service stockbroker: A stockbroker who provides a wide range of services, including research and advice, but generally charges high commissions.

As the name implies, a **full-service stockbroker** provides a wide range of investment products—usually any you can think of—along with recommendations from its research department on which securities to buy or sell. Full-service firms, such as Merrill Lynch or Smith Barney, are probably the ones you recognize. The greatest benefit a full-service broker can offer you is advice on selecting stocks and managing your portfolio. As we shall soon see, you pay for these services through substantially higher commissions. If you fail to use them, you are, in effect, wasting your money.

You should know that a broker's sales representative (the person you probably call your "broker") is a salesperson first and an investment adviser second. This person may call you frequently to inquire about your investment needs. Of course, frequent calls can lead to frequent buying and selling, which, in turn, reduces your investment profits or adds to your losses. A conscientious full-service broker will discourage frequent transactions (called "churning the account") and will, instead, become familiar with your investment objectives and help you arrange a portfolio to achieve them.

TOPIC **LINKS**

Visit two full-service brokerage houses.

Discount Brokers

Discount broker: A stockbroker who provides most services except research and advice and offers low commissions.

The advent of the **discount broker** after deregulation introduced important changes in the stockbrokerage business. The discounter emphasizes only one thing—low commissions. And, as Table 9.2 shows, these can be substantially below commissions charged by full-service brokers. As you can see, brokers' commissions vary widely, and you should ask for a commission schedule before opening an account. Also, many brokers will negotiate fees, depending on how often you trade and the dollar value of your account.

Internet Trading

TOPIC **LINKS**

Compare two firms specializing in Internet trading.

The very hottest trend in the stockbrokerage business is trading securities over the Internet. While the discount brokers have pioneered this revolution, full-service brokers also offer this service to meet the competition. There are several reasons why many investors desire Internet trading. The first and undoubtedly the most important is very low commissions: some brokers offer rates as low as $8 a trade, regardless of the stock's price or the number of shares traded (up to some very high limit, such as 5,000 shares). Another attractive feature is easy account access to place orders and to review your holdings and the status of orders you have placed. Also, most of the Internet firms have excellent Web sites, which provide market data and news along with stock research. If you think you can manage your own investment portfolio, you definitely should have an Internet broker.

Table 9.2

Illustrative Stockbrokerage Commissions: Common Stock Transactions

| Transaction | Value of the Transaction | Commissions: Cost and Percentage of Value | | | | | |
| | | Full-Service Broker | | Well-Known Discounter | | Internet Trades with a Smaller Discounter | |
		$	%	$	%	$	%
10 shares @ $35	$ 350	18	5.1	35	10.0	8	2.30
200 shares @ $25	5,000	130	2.6	89	1.8	8	0.16
500 shares @ $18	9,000	225	2.5	107	1.2	8	0.09

Source: Advertised rates and telephone inquiry.

Round Lots and Odd Lots

The basic trading unit when placing orders is 100 shares. Orders for 100 shares, or multiples of 100 shares (e.g., 300 shares) are called **round lots;** orders for a fraction of 100 shares are called **odd lots.** So an order for 250 shares involves one round lot of 200 shares and an odd lot of 50 shares. There is no specific disadvantage in dealing in odd lots, although you should realize that most stockbrokers have a minimum commission amount, regardless of order size. So a trade with a low dollar amount will lead to a high commission as a percentage of the trade amount.

Round lots: Orders for 100 shares or multiples of 100 shares.

Odd lots: Orders for fewer than 100 shares.

Kinds of Accounts

Having picked a stockbroker, you should next open an account. This doesn't take much time. If you are married, it's a good idea to open a joint account, with each spouse having authority to initiate orders. Your account can be either a cash account or a margin account.

TOPIC **LINKS**

See how you can open an account online.

Cash Account

A **cash account** is similar to a regular charge account used by many retailers, except you must pay for securities you purchase within three working days after the purchase is made. So, if you buy on Monday, you have three days to come up with the cash. The same time frame applies when you sell securities; that is, you must deliver shares sold within three working days. Some brokers will ask for an initial deposit before executing orders; others will not. If you wish, the broker can have your shares mailed to you, or you can choose to let the broker hold them. Holding your own shares prevents problems that might arise if the

Cash account: A stockbrokerage account similar to a regular charge account.

broker goes bankrupt or experiences other difficulties, but you must take steps to safeguard them, and a safe-deposit box is the only really safe place.

Actually, holding shares may not be possible in the future. Plans are currently in progress to do away with stock certificates, and your ownership interest would be shown only in so-called book-entry form.

Margin Account

Margin account: A stockbrokerage account that allows borrowing from a stockbroker using securities as collateral.

A **margin account** sounds mysterious to the uninformed. Actually, it is nothing more than a loan the broker makes to you using your securities as collateral to support the loan. Here's how it works.

Initial margin requirement: An amount that must be deposited when buying securities on margin; the current rate is 50 percent.

Say you open a margin account by depositing $3,000. (All brokers require a minimum deposit for a margin account, and the Board of Governors of the Federal Reserve System requires an **initial margin requirement** of 50 percent of the value of securities purchased.) Then you buy 100 shares of ABC stock at $50 a share. Thus, you bought $5,000 worth of stock, ignoring commissions, with a $3,000 deposit; obviously, the other $2,000 came from your broker. Now, what happens if the stock goes up or down in value? No problem, if it goes up. You can sell whenever you like and repay the $2,000 loan *plus interest* and pocket the difference. If it goes down, keep one simple fact in mind—the loss is all yours. You don't share it with the broker. So if ABC goes down to $30 a share and you then sell, the broker still gets $2,000 *plus interest* and you still pocket the difference—$1,000 in this case. You lose $2,000, which is $20 ($50 − $30) a share times the 100 shares.

Maintenance margin requirement: A minimum equity required in an account to continue using a broker's loan.

Perhaps the mystique surrounding margin trading is the possibility of getting a margin call (this means your broker calls and asks for more money) if the price of a security falls below a certain level, called the **maintenance margin requirement.** This requirement varies among firms but cannot be less than the minimum of 25 percent of the market value of your securities set by the Board of Governors of the Federal Reserve System. If a broker had, say, a 30 percent requirement, this means the security in our previous example could go no lower than $28.57 a share before you would get a margin call. The way you get the above number is as follows:

Step 1 Divide the broker's loan by 1.0 minus the maintenance margin requirement; that is $2,000.00 (1.0 − 0.3) = $2,000.00/0.7 = $2,857.14.

Step 2 Divide your answer by the number of shares held: $2,857.14/100 = $28.57.

Since you still owe the broker $2,000, your equity in the account is $857.14 ($2,857.14 − $2,000.00). As a check on your math, your equity should be 30 percent of the market value of your securities. In this example, 30 percent of $2,857.14 is $857.14, so our math is correct.

Leverage: Using borrowed funds, such as with a margin account, to buy securities.

Using a margin account magnifies your gains or losses, as would any loan you use to buy securities. In the previous example, if you had used your own funds, you could have purchased only 60 ($3,000/$50) rather than 100. Thus, if the price of the stock had gone up or down by $10, for example, your gain or loss would have been $600 rather than $1,000. A loan allows you to **leverage** your investment, which automatically increases the range of possible returns, which in turn is synonymous with more risk. Keep that in mind: Leverage always increases risk.

Kinds of Positions

Long position: A purchase of securities.

Short position: Sale of securities you don't own.

After you open an account with a broker, the next step is to begin trading. Brokers refer to this as opening a position, and there are two kinds you can take: a **long position,** meaning you buy securities, and a **short position,** meaning you sell securities (that you don't own).

A long position is what you typically associate with investing: You buy, and then own, securities. A long position can be viewed as buying now and selling later. In contrast, with a short position, you sell now and buy later. This seems confusing, and certainly more mysterious than a margin account. How can you possibly sell securities you don't own? The broker helps you accomplish this by lending the securities to you. Here's how it works.

Mechanics of a Short Position

Suppose you think KLM stock is overvalued at $40 a share and sure to go down in price over the next year. Your strategy is to sell 100 shares now at their high price and then buy them a year later after their price has fallen. You call the broker and tell him you wish to short-sell 100 shares of KLM. He will execute your order in exactly the same fashion as if you already owned the shares, and the buyer will receive 100 shares from your broker. Where did your broker get the shares? He probably borrowed them from other clients who own KLM shares and hold them in margin accounts. Is the broker adding risks to these clients by lending their shares? No, because the broker will insist that you deposit sufficient margin to cover potentially adverse price movements. In the above example, you would have to deposit at least 50 percent, or $2,000. You could deposit more if you wanted to, but it would be foolish to do so, since your deposit does not earn interest.

If you guessed correctly about KLM's price and it declines to $30 a share, you close out your short position by buying the stock and returning the borrowed shares to your broker. Your account was credited $4,000 when you sold them, and you need only $3,000 to buy them back. The $1,000 difference is your gain. If you deposited $2,000 to initiate the short sale, your account would now have $3,000 in it. If you guessed incorrectly about KLM and its price went up to $50 when you decided to close your position, you would lose $1,000 and your account would have only $1,000 left in it.

Short Position Risks

Is a short position any riskier than a long one? Probably so, because the long-run trend of stock prices has been upward, and you're betting against the trend with a short sale. Moreover, you lose all earnings potential on your margin deposit, and you also must pay any dividends declared on stocks sold short. If KLM declared a $1.00 per share dividend while you were short, you would have to pay $100. (You probably are wondering if this means that two dividends are paid on the same stock—one by you and one by KLM. Yes, because the person who loaned the shares expects to receive a dividend, as does the person who bought them from you.)

Kinds of Orders

You place an order when you wish to buy or sell securities. Your order will be executed either on the floor of an organized exchange, such as the New York Stock Exchange, or between brokers in the over-the-counter market. You can place three kinds of orders: a market order, a limit order, and a stop order.

Market Order

A **market order** instructs your broker to buy or sell securities at the best possible price. At the time you make a transaction, the broker will give you an up-to-the-minute price of a security. For example, you might call wishing to buy 100 shares of Alcoa. The broker will use his quotation terminal to find the last price paid for a share of Alcoa; assume it was $50. If you then instruct the broker to buy or sell Alcoa "at the market," you are placing a market order. Are you guaranteed a price of $50? No, even though your order may be executed in less than two minutes, Alcoa's price could change during that time.

Market order: An order to buy or sell securities at the market price prevailing when the order is executed.

Your Broker—Your Banker

Let's suppose a minor financial emergency arises and you need to raise cash rather quickly. Should you see your local banker? You might, but a quicker route might be to tap into a margin account you establish with a stockbrokerage firm.

Many people are hesitant to have a margin account, since such accounts are used typically by aggressive investors as a source of funds to buy more securities. Used in this fashion, a margin account clearly adds risk to a portfolio. However, there is nothing preventing you from having a margin account without borrowing. Used this way, you establish a reservoir of readily available credit.

Suppose you have securities worth $5,000 in the account and no broker's loan against them. With a phone call you could arrange to borrow up to $2,500 and have the money almost immediately. Furthermore, the interest charged by the broker is usually at the prime rate plus 1 or 2 percent. Compared with other sources of consumer credit, that can be a steal. At this writing, the broker's loan cost about 9.5 percent versus about 19 percent on a bank credit card.

There are two problems to consider. Since you never have to pay off the principal on a broker's loan (barring a margin call), theoretically you can finance forever whatever it is that prompted the loan. If this is an item that decreases in value and needs to be replaced periodically, obviously, not reducing the loan in proportion to the depreciation value will keep you from accumulating enough funds to finance an eventual replacement. And there is the problem or a margin call. If the value of your securities falls appreciably, the broker will require a deposit of additional funds. As a hedge here, you should consider borrowing less than maximum allowable—for example, never more than 30 percent of the total value ($1,500 in the foregoing example).

Limit Order

Limit order: An order to buy or sell securities at a specific price.

A **limit order** sets the price that you are willing to pay for a security. For example, if Alcoa's price is very volatile, you may fear that it could increase during the time it takes to execute a market order. If $50 a share is the top price you want to pay, you would use a limit order specifying that price. Limit orders remain in effect until they are either canceled or executed. Some investors do not want limit orders to remain "alive," so they place day orders, which are limit orders that are automatically canceled at the end of the day they are placed. Limit orders are not that important for actively traded issues such as Alcoa, since the large number of buyers and sellers usually keeps the stock's price from fluctuating widely within a short period of time. However, shares of less actively traded stocks are different. Perhaps as few as 200 or 300 shares trade each day, and substantial price changes are then possible. Limit orders are more appropriate here.

Stop Order

Stop order: An order that is triggered by the market price of a security; often used to stop losses.

A **stop order** (often called a stop-loss order) is a market order that is triggered by the market price of a security. It is used to protect profits or limit losses. Suppose you bought Alcoa at $50 and its price subsequently increased to $80. You would have a nice profit but might not wish to sell, because Alcoa's price could go still higher. You could then place a stop-loss order on Alcoa at a price of, say, $75. If its price continued to rise, the order would be meaningless; but if its price fell to $75 (the trigger), the stop-loss order would become a market order. Again, you would not be guaranteed a $75 price, but only the best price your broker could get, which might be higher or lower, as is the case with all market orders. Stop orders are used by investors who do not wish to watch their securities closely or make frequent selling or buying decisions. (Stop orders can also be used to buy securities.) Also, some investors use such orders because they feel they lack adequate discipline to make correct decisions during emotionally charged periods. As a security's price falls, you are often tempted not to sell because you convince yourself it's bound to increase again. Consequently, you sit and watch as the price falls—perhaps back to the original purchase price, eliminating your entire gain. With a stop order, you make the selling decision without the emotional atmosphere created by a falling price.

Do Things on Paper First

TOPIC **LINKS**

Set up a portfolio and track your favorite stocks.

Now that you have information about accounts, positions, and orders, should you begin investing immediately? We don't think so. It is often a good idea to have a trial period in which you make investments on paper. This is especially true if you plan to pick your own securities. This trial period, if you do it seriously, will familiarize you with the mechanics of investing and will give you firsthand experience with price volatility. Of course, you can always mimic a trial period by going back in time and selecting securities and then seeing how your selections would have fared, but this experience is often not the same as investing for future periods. In general, we have some background on the general market or specific securities, which is bound to influence our investment decisions. (Most of us like to cheat by picking known winners!)

Keep Honest Records

The whole experience will be useless if you fail to keep honest records. It's surprising how much we wish to avoid admitting—even to ourselves—the mistakes we make. If you pick a stock and its price goes down, then measure your loss as carefully as you might measure a price increase. If the stock or bond pays dividends or interest, note that, too, along with the date it's received. In this dry run you would buy all the risky securities you might want to buy later. Include options and futures contracts in your portfolio if you are thinking of buying them. It is better to understand their enormous risks now rather than later, when it can cost you dearly.

Evaluate Your Performance

After a time, say, three months, you should designate a cutoff date and measure your performance for the period. A form, such as the one illustrated in Figure 9.2, is helpful in doing this.

As you see, the investor (Cindy Lipton) narrowed her investment choices to five common stocks. Cindy assumed she had about $5,000 to invest and planned investing about $1,000 in each security. When the quarter ended, she was somewhat surprised with the results and very glad she started investing with a dry run. As you see, she lost $206.57 for the quarter, and this figure doesn't include commissions she would incur if she actually wanted to sell out on March 31. Cindy was woefully underdiversified. Even though she bought five securities, three are in the computer industry—Apple, Hewlett-Packard, and IBM.

Notice the relatively high total commissions in relation to the total amount invested: about 3.5 percent ($172/$4,983.75). This wouldn't be too bad if Cindy planned to hold the portfolio for some time, but it is very high if she plans to turn it over every quarter. If she did, the commissions alone would probably consume all her gains.

Cindy's quarterly rate of return of −4.2 percent indicates that if her performance remained the same, she would lose 16.8 percent (about 1/6) of her original investment in one year. Needless to say, this loss is considerable, and Cindy concluded that she needed more experience before investing on her own.

FINDING INVESTMENT INFORMATION

Most investment decisions require some research. Even if you decide to limit your investing to mutual funds or other pooling arrangements, you still must evaluate the alternative funds available. And if you make your own investment decisions, your research must be

NAME: _Cindy Lipton_

REPORTING PERIOD: _1/1/05 – 3/31/05 (13 weeks)_

Securities	(1) No. of Shares, Bonds, etc.	(2) Purchase Price per Unit	(3) Total (1) × (2)	(4) Commissions	(5) Total Invested (3) + (4)	(6) Closing Prices	(7) Total Closing Market Value (6) × (1)	(8) Gain or (Loss) (7) – (5)	(9) Dividends or Interest	(10) Total Gain or Loss (8) + (9)
1. Apple Computer	23 shares	$42.75	$ 983.25	$ 35.00	$1018.25	$49.00	$1127.00	$ 108.75		$ 108.75
2. Lucent	190 shares	5.25	997.50	35.00	1032.50	4.25	807.50	(225.00)		(225.00)
3. Hewlett-Packard	60 shares	16.50	990.00	35.00	1025.00	16.00	960.00	(65.00)		(65.00)
4. Exxon	22 shares	45.50	1001.00	36.00	1037.00	49.50	1078.00	41.00	11.00	52.00
5. IBM	8 shares	105.00	840.00	31.00	871.00	98.00	784.00	(87.00)	9.68	(77.32)
6.										
7.										
8.										
9.										
10. Money Market Fund										
			$ 4811.75	$ 172.00	$ 4983.75		$ 4756.50	(227.25)	$ 20.68	$ (206.57)

Supplementary Information:

A   Interest on margin balance = $_____ — _____ (amount borrowed × margin rate)

B   Dividends on stock sold short = $_____ — _____

Gain (Loss) This Period:

1   Dollar return = Column (10) − (A) − (B) = $_____ (206.57) _____

2   Rate of return = dollar return ÷ Column (5) = _−0.0415 (−4.2%)_

3   Rate of return annualized = rate of return for the period × 52/N (N = number of weeks held) = _____ −16.8% _____

Figure 9.2

A Portfolio Summary Sheet

ambitious. Information is the key to good research, and the sections to follow provide an overview of available sources.

Company Sources

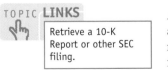

TOPIC LINKS

Retrieve a 10-K Report or other SEC filing.

As noted earlier, companies are required by the SEC to provide shareholders with annual and quarterly financial reports. Companies must also provide 10-K Reports if they are requested. A 10-K Report is a detailed compilation of a company's financial performance for the previous year. It presents the same data found in a company's annual financial report but may include other information not found there, such as asset depreciation methods or officer compensation levels.

Considerable information can be found in company reports. In addition to financial data, these documents contain discussions of past results and plans for the future. The corporate officers who provide these statements want to present their company in its most favorable light. Thus, caution is necessary.

Investment Advisory Services

There are thousands of individuals registered with the Securities and Exchange Commission (the SEC). These people have licenses to offer (for a fee, usually) investment advice. But don't assume that their government licenses guarantee good advice. Some is good, but much isn't; or at least, it's no better than what you can find free at the library.

Library Sources

Most libraries contain three excellent investment services: *Moody's, Standard & Poor's*, and *Value Line*. Of course, you can also subscribe to each and have it delivered to your home, but they are relatively expensive. Among other things, each offers a manual containing financial data for several thousand companies and a weekly newsletter that reports on economic trends and specific industries and companies. Each also recommends stocks to purchase or avoid. To become familiar with all their publications, you should visit your local or school library and ask the reference librarian to show them to you. Certainly, if you are doing any research on an individual company's securities or on an industry, include one of these publications.

Advisory Services You Pay For

There are many investment advisers who offer a weekly or monthly newsletter. Some also offer "hotline" connections that allow you to call for their up-to-the-minute advice, or they might call you if there is an important change in their opinions. You pay handsomely for these services, and the logical question is, Are they worth it? It is difficult to answer that question. To begin with, you have to evaluate them on a risk-adjusted basis. Many tout that they beat the market, but it isn't clear that they do so, after considering risk. They tend to do well in bull markets (an expression meaning rising prices), but not so well in bear (falling-price) markets. Finally, unless you have sufficient funds to offset their advisory fees—which can be as high as $500 a year—their cost is simply too high in relation to the amount you invest.

Newspapers and Magazines

Many investors find a considerable amount of information in newspapers and magazines. This information includes investment stories and articles that might stimulate your interest as well as financial data. Most of the newspapers and magazines mentioned below are available at libraries.

The Wall Street Journal

The *Wall Street Journal* is a newspaper published each work day. Many investors subscribe to the *Journal* or read it at their offices or libraries. It is not exclusively investment oriented but rather covers a wide range of business and economic topics. Practically every issue has at least one story of relevance to most investors along with extensive price and trading information on a wide range of securities. It would be fruitless to attempt to describe this publication in detail; you simply must read an issue to appreciate its comprehensive coverage of investments. An interesting part of the *Journal* is its daily report on various market indicators, such as the Dow Jones Industrial Average (DJIA). The DJIA is perhaps the most widely watched market index in the United States because of its historical significance. Because it covers only 30 individual stocks, it is not considered a comprehensive market index. The S&P 500 Stock Index also has wide appeal, and it is far more representative of the overall market and differs in its method of computation.

TOPIC **LINKS**

See the *Wall Street Journal's* Interactive Edition; also, see its Classroom Edition.

Barron's

Barron's, a sister newspaper to the *Journal*, is published weekly and is exclusively investment oriented. It has regular columns dealing with different aspects of investing and a market laboratory section in each issue. In addition, it features stories on different companies, reports interviews with security analysts and other investment advisers, and offers refresher articles on different aspects of investing.

Investor's Business Daily

Investor's Business Daily (IBD) is a daily newspaper devoted exclusively to investment news. It provides full coverage of trading activity of stocks, bonds, options, futures, and mutual funds. *IBD* is similar to Section C of the *Journal* except that its coverage, in some respects, is more thorough. For example, it provides graphic displays of 30 stocks of interest on the NYSE, Amex, and OTC market each day; in addition, it highlights one company for extensive analysis, both graphic and in terms of the company's underlying fundamentals. If you are interested exclusively in investment news, you might consider *IBD* as an alternative to the *Journal*.

Magazines

A number of good magazines provide investment information and ideas. *Forbes* is exclusively investment oriented. Its stories and regular features usually are realistic in outlook, often forewarning investors of potential problems with various investments. Its annual survey of mutual funds is well worth the price of that issue.

Financial World is similar to *Forbes* but less extensive and perhaps less conservative in outlook. Although not a get-rich-quick magazine, it takes a more positive view than does *Forbes*.

Fortune magazine usually features in-depth articles on different companies or industries. These articles provide excellent background material but are not geared directly toward investing. Nevertheless, the articles are timely, as are the regular monthly columns.

Money magazine covers a wide range of financial planning topics, including investing. Its investment articles often provide personal investment stories—almost always of success—that are interesting and thought-provoking. After reading *Money*, you get the impression that becoming wealthy through investing is a simple task, involving little risk. More articles on investment failures would help temper that impression.

Internet Data Sources

TOPIC **LINKS**

Visit Yahoo and FTcom.

There are so many excellent sources of investment information on the Internet that many investors use little else. We mentioned earlier that most brokerage houses offering Internet trading also offer market data and information on specific companies. But you don't need a brokerage account to access other really great sites. Yahoo Stock Quotes, for example, provides much more than stock quotes; it also offers market news, company financial data, access to 10-K and 10-Q reports, price charts, company profiles, analysts' earnings forecasts, and other information. Another excellent site is FT.com. It has even more detailed information than Yahoo with respect to international financial news.

If you have never used an Internet site to obtain financial information, visit one of the preceding sites and take time to click on and examine the various features. If you are "into" investing, you could spend the better part of a day reviewing the available data. In one sense, there is too much, which makes the following two chapters so very important—you must learn how to interpret and understand the mass of information now so readily available.

American Stock Exchange (Amex) (p. 233)	leverage (p. 240)	over-the-counter (OTC) market (p. 234)
binding arbitration (p. 237)	limit order (p. 242)	prospectus (p. 235)
cash account (p. 239)	long position (p. 240)	risk averters (p. 228)
current return (p. 228)	maintenance margin requirement (p. 240)	risk seekers (p. 229)
discount broker (p. 238)	margin account (p. 240)	round lots (p. 239)
full-service stockbroker (p. 238)	market order (p. 241)	short position (p. 240)
future return (p. 228)	NASDAQ (p. 234)	specialists (p. 233)
initial margin requirement (p. 240)	New York Stock Exchange (NYSE) (p. 232)	stop order (p. 242)
		tangible investments (p. 227)
intangible investments (p. 228)	odd lots (p. 239)	10-K Report (p. 235)
	organized exchange (p. 232)	total return (p. 228)

Key Terms

FOLLOW-UP ON THE Steele FAMILY

Reread the chapter-opening vignette. In common with thousands of beginning investors each year, the Steeles know virtually nothing about investing. Perhaps you are in a similar position, and perhaps after reading this chapter, your knowledge has expanded. Answer the following questions, playing the role of financial adviser to both the Steeles and yourself.

1. On a scale of 1 to 5 (5 representing the highest degree of risk aversion), where do you rank the Steeles? Where do you rank yourself?
2. The Steeles are contemplating opening a stockbrokerage account. Help them in the selection process. Is the type of broker you recommend for them the same as you would choose for yourself? Explain why or why not.
3. Should the Steeles open a cash account or a margin account? Explain and also discuss which type of account is the better choice for you.
4. Explain which of the three media choices—Internet, cable news (such as CNBC), or newspapers—is the best source of investment news for the Steeles. Assume they will devote no more than two hours a week to the task. Which source(s) do you like to use? How much time do you devote to the task? Is this amount too much or too little, in your view?

Problems and Review Questions

1. How do tangible and intangible investments differ, and what investor needs can be satisfied with tangible investments?
2. What is an investment's total return? What type of investors prefer a current return? Who might prefer a future return?
3. Compare an organized exchange with the over-the-counter market.
4. Distinguish among commission brokers, floor brokers, and floor traders. Explain a critical role played by specialists on the floor of an organized exchange.
5. What is NASDAQ?
6. Very briefly highlight the six federal laws (discussed in this chapter) regulating the securities industry.
7. Explain a prospectus and a 10-K Report.
8. What are the differences between a full-service broker and a discount broker? Identify a round lot and an odd lot.
9. How does a cash account differ from a margin account?
10. What is an initial margin requirement? If its value is 0.50, and if you have $10,000 to invest, you can buy securities with a total market value of $_____.

11. What is a maintenance margin requirement? Assume that you bought 100 shares of Acme, Inc., at $100 a share. If the maintenance margin requirement is 0.30, at what price would your broker give you a margin call? What does a margin call mean?

12. Allen Gold thought Exxon's common stock was far overpriced at $45 a share; therefore, he executed a short sale on 100 shares. How did his stockbroker assist in arranging this short sale, and how much profit (ignore commissions) will Al make (or lose) if: (*a*) Exxon goes down to $40 a share, or (*b*) it goes up to $50 a share? Does Al have to put up any money for this short sale? Would you recommend short selling as a routine practice over the long run? Explain.

13. Explain market, limit, and stop orders. In what situations would investors use stop orders? Explain.

14. Identify three investment advisory services usually available at most libraries.

15. Identify three financial newspapers and four financial magazines.

Case 9.1
Rose Geisler's Investment Plan

Rose Geisler, a college graduate in electrical engineering, has a good position with a major electronics firm. Her current annual salary is $65,000, and, since Rose is single with no financial obligations, she plans to invest all her savings (around $11,000) in common stocks. Rose has done some research on security selection, and she feels capable of picking her own stocks. At present, she likes the technology sector and also thinks companies in the auto industry will do well.

At the advice of her former personal finance instructor, Rose has decided to have a trial run before she actually invests. So she has selected three stocks—Intel, Microsoft, and GM—and has tracked their performances for six months. The results follow:

	Intel	Microsoft	GM
1. Purchase price per share	$60	$80	$40
2. Number of shares purchased	50	50	100
3. Commissions	$85	$85	$80
4. Closing prices	$50	$65	$50

Questions

1. Using a format similar to the one illustrated in this chapter, show the results of Rose's experiment.

2. Calculate the following: (*a*) the portfolio's dollar gain or loss, (*b*) the rate of return for the six-month period, (*c*) the annualized rate of return. Evaluate the portfolio's performance. Do you have any advice for Rose? Explain.

Case 9.2
Should the Delaneys Open a Margin Account?

Pat and Ed Delaney are a married couple with two children. Both have professional positions, and their joint income is over $70,000 a year. Their net worth is well over $100,000, and they have excellent liquidity with very little short-term debt.

The Delaneys want to start an investment program by investing in growth stocks. They believe their situation calls for the services of a full-service broker who will guide their selections. One of the brokers they interviewed urged them to open a margin account, since the amount they wanted to invest initially—$10,000—was not enough, in her opinion, to achieve adequate diversification. She put together a list of 10 stocks and urged the Delaneys to invest $2,000 in each one.

Questions

1. Assuming the Delaneys would pay 12 percent a year on the broker's loan associated with the margin account, determine their net annual return (expressed as a percentage of the amount they invest) if their stocks paid a current dividend of 5 percent and increased in market value by 20 percent. Make a similar calculation assuming a current dividend of 5 percent and a decrease in market value of 20 percent. (Ignore commissions in both your calculations.) What advice do you have for the Delaneys about leverage?

2. Suppose the broker has a maintenance margin requirement of 30 percent. Ignoring dividends and commissions, how low could the market value of the Delaneys' holdings go before they would get a margin call? For simplicity in calculations, assume they bought 2,000 shares of only one stock at $10 a share.

3. What other advantage(s) might the Delaneys have with a margin account? Given their particular situation, do you recommend one for them? Explain.

Exercises to Strengthen Your Use of the Internet

(Internet links for the following exercises can be found at **www.prenhall.com/winger**.)

> **Working Out on the Web**

Exercise 9.1 Investment Mistakes

Salomon Smith Barney has a site dedicated to providing investor information and education. At the home page click on "Services," and then "Investor Education," and then "Smith Barney University."

Q. Choose "10 Common Errors in Investing." What is the first error discussed in this section?

Exercise 9.2 What Is Your Risk Tolerance?

Merrill Lynch can help you with risk assessment, particularly in terms of understanding risk tolerance levels. At the home page, select "Individual Investor," then "Financial Education," and then "Risk Assessment."

Q. Read the tutorial on "Risk Tolerance" and then indicate the five risk categories specified. In which category do you think you belong?

Exercise 9.3 See Order Flow on the NYSE

The New York Stock Exchange has a useful site. Click on "NYSE Market Trac" and choose "Order Flow."

Q. How many trading posts are on the floor?

Exercise 9.4 What's Happening to NASDAQ?

NASDAQ maintains a lively market page that tracks trading activity during the day.

Q. Compare the NASDAQ Index to the DJIA. Are they moving in the same direction?

Exercise 9.5 Advice from the SEC

An important source of securities regulation is the Securities and Exchange Commission (SEC). Visit its site for considerable information, beginning with "Investor Information." Scroll down and click on "Complaint Center."

Q. How can you file a complaint with the SEC?

Exercise 9.6 Trading over the Internet

Some firms specialize in Internet trading. See what E-Trade offers. Click on "Account Services" and then "Open An Account" and choose "Power E*TRADE."

Q. What is the minimum investment amount needed to open a margin account?

10

Investment Basics:

UNDERSTANDING RISK AND RETURN

OBJECTIVES

1. To grasp the nature of risk and its sources and to relate risk to investment return

2. To see the importance of diversification and to understand how it reduces investment risk

3. To understand how to accomplish adequate diversification, both among asset groups and within an asset group

4. To grasp the concepts of required return and expected return and to see how they are used in security selection

5. To become familiar with important methods and issues involved in establishing a portfolio and making changes over time

TOPIC LINKS

Follow the **Topic Links** in each chapter for your interactive Personal Finance exercise on the Web. Go to: **www.prenhall.com/winger**

Beginning investors like the Steeles often find it difficult to select securities that are appropriate for them. Inexperience is partly to blame, but the core problem is an inability to recognize how much potential return a particular investment offers and the kind and degree of risk they must take to earn the return. You often hear people say, "Oh, I wouldn't put my money in common stocks—they're far too risky. I'll stick to conservative savings accounts." Keeping your money in a safe place might provide short-run security, but what do you give up in the long run? In 30 or 40 years, will these people accumulate a sufficient nest egg for retirement?

Investing is very serious business. It is not an activity that you should begin without preparation or with preconceived notions such as "stocks are too risky." Your goal is not to avoid risk altogether or to bet your life savings on one investment's performance; rather, you should attempt to create a portfolio of investments that connect suitably to all your investment goals and to your individual risk-tolerance level.

RISK AND RETURN

Our review of investment alternatives in Table 9.1 reveals that investments with higher returns also have higher risks. Economists tell us there is no such thing as a free lunch, and in the investments arena that is certainly true. This positive direct relationship between risk and return can be called the **iron law of risk and return**, and it serves as a good forewarning: If you are seeking high returns, be prepared to undertake high risks.

Iron law of risk and return: The strong positive correlation between higher investment return and greater risk.

What Is Risk?

You probably have an intuitive understanding of **risk** as the possibility of losing some or all of your investment. Games of chance are considered very risky because you can lose your entire bet. Most stocks and bonds are risky because their prices might decline after you buy them, and some may even go into bankruptcy, costing you practically your entire investment. This is the dismal side of risk, but there is also a bright side. You wouldn't invest in a risky venture unless you anticipated a high return. Therefore, an evaluation of risk must consider these high returns as well as losses, and it is actually better to view risk as a range of possible returns—positive and negative. The greater this range, the greater an investment's risk.

Risk: Often thought of as a possibility of loss; but a better definition is variability of return.

An Example of Return Variability

The concept of risk as return variability is illustrated in Figure 10.1, which shows three hypothetical $1,000 investments. Investment *A* is a deposit in a savings account promising to pay 10 percent interest for the upcoming year. Assuming the deposit is FDIC insured, you are virtually certain of getting back $1,100 at the end of the year and earning a return of $100. Investment *B* is a U.S. Treasury bond that pays interest of $120. If you bought the bond for $1,000 and sold it for the same amount a year later, you would get back $1,120. But this result is not assured. Suppose instead that the bond's price could go up or down by $50 during the year. In the first case, your total return would be $170 ($120 + $50); in the second it would be $70 ($120 − $50). Investment *C* is a speculative common stock that pays no dividends. Your only return is through price appreciation. If its price increased by 30 percent over the year, you would make $300 on your $1,000 investment. If the price decreased by 10 percent, you would lose $100.

A is a risk-free investment since it has no range; that is, it has only one outcome. *C* is the riskiest investment, since it has the widest range of possible returns ($400). *B* has some risk, since its range of returns is $100. Estimating the range of possible returns provides a good approximation of risk, and it is often used for that purpose.

Risk and Time

It is often felt that investment risk is influenced by the passage of time, and there are two perspectives on the issue. First, the greater the time before an investment's return is

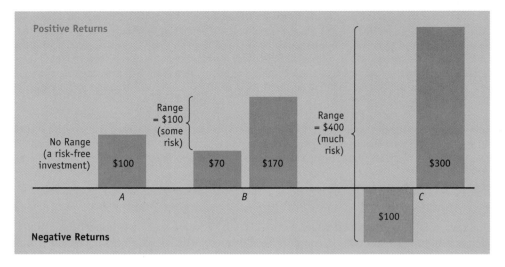

Positive Returns

No Range
(a risk-free
investment) $100

Range
= $100
(some
risk)

$70 $170

Range
= $400
(much
risk)

$300

A   B   C

$100

Negative Returns

expected, the riskier the investment—all things considered. The rationale is simple: We never know what the future holds, and the further we extend our projections, the more likely they are to be wrong. This principle implies greater variation in returns on long-term investments than on short-term ones.

The second perspective is somewhat different. Here, we ask the question, Are we more likely to achieve an investment goal by holding an asset for a shorter or a longer period of time? Of course, the answer depends very much on the type of asset held. Consider a risky one, such as common stocks. Suppose that common stocks have shown an average yearly return of about 12 percent over the past 70 years or so. We would like to invest in them and hope to earn the average yearly rate in the future. Are we most likely to achieve this goal by holding stocks for one week, one year, or 10 years? You probably guessed the last choice—and you are right. The longer the investment horizon, the greater the odds of earning the average rate. This is why we realize that holding stocks for short periods of time is risky. This message was driven home very forcefully by "Black Monday"—October 19, 1987—when the stock market fell about 23 percent. The prospect of losing 23 percent of your portfolio in *one* day is indeed evidence of considerable risk, which is why financial planners urge us to hold common stocks only if we have relatively long investment horizons.

Sources of Risk

What factors make an investment risky, that is, widen its range of possible returns? The various sources of risk can be placed into two groups: those associated with changing conditions of the overall economy and those related to changing conditions of the issuers of the securities.

Changing Economic Conditions

Inflation risk: The risk that an investment's return may fall short of the inflation rate.

Practically every investment's return is influenced by changes in economic conditions. First, many investments have **inflation risk,** which means that their returns may not keep pace with the rate of inflation. Any investment that pays a fixed number of dollars of return is subject to inflation risk because the purchasing power of your fixed return declines during inflation. Most government and corporate bonds fall in this group, explaining why investment advisers suggest not buying them if you expect inflation to increase.

Second, many investments are subject to **business cycle risk.** Economic growth seldom takes place in an even-keel manner. Usually, there is a period of rapid expansion followed by a period of recession. The profits of most businesses tend to follow these cycles, and so do the prices of their common stocks. The prices of real estate and other tangible assets also move in step with the economy, and their returns are similarly influenced by it.

Closely related to both inflation risk and business cycle risk is **interest rate risk.** This risk has to do with the relationship between the price of a fixed-return security that has already been issued and returns available on newly issued, similar securities. For example, suppose you bought a government bond for $1,000 that paid $100 a year in interest, a yield of 10 percent. What would happen, though, if a month later, because of tightened credit conditions, the government began issuing new bonds that yielded 12 percent? The bond you bought would still yield only 10 percent, but if you tried to sell it, nobody would be willing to give you $1,000 for it, since they could just as easily buy newly issued bonds paying $120 interest on $1,000. The buyer would expect the same percentage return on yours as he or she could get with any other bond of that type, so you would have to sell yours at a loss. At a price of $833, for example, your bond would also have a current yield of 12 percent, as calculated next:

$$0.12 = \frac{\$10}{\$83}$$

Thus, you would lose $167 ($1,000 − $833) by holding the bond during a period of rising interest rates. Interest rate risk has become increasingly important in recent years because interest rates have been so volatile.

Changing Conditions of the Issuer

Even in very good economic times, some firms go bankrupt; and in bad times, many do. You may buy the stock of a promising growth company anticipating a high return over time but then find that, because of poor management, the firm does not do well. In addition to this **management risk,** other sources of risk have to do with the issuer's condition. First, the company's line of business presents certain risks, usually called **business risk.** Making personal computers in the 1990s is inherently riskier than selling consumer perishables such as food. Another source of risk has to do with the way a company raises capital. Firms that borrow heavily are inherently riskier than those that issue mostly common stock. During periods of economic stress, the firm with a large amount of interest due its bondholders will be more vulnerable to bankruptcy than a firm without such payments. This risk is often called **financial risk,** and corporate financial managers attempt to minimize its impact, considering the firm's need for expansion capital.

How Much Return Do You Need?

Having looked at risk, let us turn our attention to return. Suppose you are willing to undertake risk. How much return should you realistically expect to receive for doing so? The answer to that question for a specific investment is called the investment's **required rate of return.**

But, if someone were to ask you what you think is a reasonable required return estimate for various financial assets, you might find it hard to answer. Should you earn 10 percent on common stocks, or 30 percent, or 5 percent, or what? While there is no completely satisfactory answer to the question, let's take a look at some relatively recent historical

Business cycle risk: Fluctuations in an investment's return resulting from fluctuations in the business cycle.

Interest rate risk: The risk that the price of a fixed-return asset will decline if interest rates rise.

Management risk: Poor earnings performance of a firm associated with poor management.

Business risk: Risk associated with a company's product or service lines.

Financial risk: Risk associated with the use of considerable debt in a company's financing arrangement.

Required rate of return: A realistic estimate of the minimum return an investment must offer to be attractive, given its degree of risk.

TOPIC **LINKS**
Visit the NAIC Internet site //www.better-investing.org.

returns on two kinds of assets: common stocks as represented by the S&P 500 stock index and 90-day U.S. Treasury bills. Treasury bills are a cashlike asset, mentioned in Chapter 5. Common stocks are covered in the next chapter. Table 10.1 shows returns over the period from January 1, 1970, through December 31, 2003 (34 years).

While an actual return in any future year may be very different from an historical average return, nevertheless, there is some evidence that the average annual return over many future years, say the next 31, will not be considerably different from the average of the past 34 years. However, there can be some difference. For example, as mentioned earlier, the arithmetic average return for common stocks over the past 75 years or so is around 12.0 percent. The average for the period covered in Table 10.1 is 11.30 percent, about 0.70 percent less.

The Returns

Even a cursory review of Table 10.1 shows why so many investors favor common stocks, particularly for long holding periods. Stocks earned 4.07 percent more than bills. Many people find it hard to evaluate percentage rates of return in comparing investments. A far more forceful presentation is to show the accumulation of wealth, given the investments' returns. Notice that $1,000 invested on 1/1/1970 would have grown in value to $38,078 for common stocks, and $10,739 for bills. We should note that for the accumulated amounts, calculations assume that any dividends and interest received on the investments were immediately reinvested when received. Clearly, common stocks dominate bills, almost to such a large extent that you wonder why investors ever invest in the latter. If you review other data in Table 10.1, you probably can make a guess.

	Stocks			Treasury Bills			Table 10.1
	Average Annual Return	Added Wealth	Total Wealth	Annual Return	Added Wealth	Average Total Wealth	
Initial Investment, 1/1/1970			$ 1,000			$ 1,000	
Five-year periods:							
1970–1974	−2.39%	$ −114	886	7.45%	$ 432	1,432	
1975–1979	14.83	883	1,769	9.64	837	2,269	
1980–1984	14.81	1,760	3,529	10.11	1,404	3,673	
1985–1989	20.36	5,385	8,914	7.90	1,699	5,372	
1990–1994	8.70	4,613	13,527	6.64	2,036	7,408	
1995–1999	28.56	33,978	47,505	5.24	2,156	9,564	
Four-year period, 2000–2003	−5.38	−9,427	38,078	2.92	1,175	10,739	
34-year average return	11.30%			7.23%			
Best year	37.40%			14.10%			
	(1995)			(1981)			
Worst year	−26.50%			1.00%			
	(1974)			(2003)			
Return range	63.90%			13.10%			

Returns and Wealth Accumulations from Stocks and Treasury Bills, 1970–2003

Source: Federal Reserve Bank of St. Louis (accumulation data available at the Fed's Web site, FRED® (http://www.stls.frb.org/fred/).

The Risks

Clearly, common stocks are the riskier investment, with a return range of 63.90 percent, compared to 11.30 percent with bills. Moreover, the single largest one-year loss (−26.50 percent) was with stocks; indeed, there was even a loss over a full five-year period (−2.39) from 1970 to 1975 and over the four-year period (−5.38) 2000 through 2003. Losses of such magnitude attract investors to bills and other debt securities. But unless you have a very low risk tolerance level, you should seriously consider a portfolio heavily weighted with stocks—the longer your investment horizon, the greater the weight.

Risk Premiums

The difference between an investment's return and the return on Treasury bills is called a **risk premium.** Common stocks' risk premium as measured by the 34-year averages is 4.07 percent (11.30 percent − 7.23 percent). This number is very low in comparison to the risk premium calculated over a much longer period of time, which is about 8.0 percent (12.0 percent stock return average minus 4.0 percent Treasury bill return average). There are ongoing heated debates among financial experts as to the proper risk premium value to use in stock analysis. Some feel that a premium of 3 to 5 percent is appropriate, while others favor the long-run average of 8.0 percent. We will not develop these arguments here; however, we will use the 8.0 percent number later in this chapter and also in the next chapter. Keep in mind that a lower value may change any conclusions that we reach about a stock as we will show.

Risk premium: The difference between an investment's required return and the return on U.S. Treasury bills.

THE REWARDS OF DIVERSIFICATION

The advice "Don't put all your eggs in one basket" is particularly applicable in the area of investments. By holding a **portfolio,** which is simply a group of assets held at the same time, certain risks can be avoided. In the short run, you might be lucky and do very well with one or two investments; but eventually luck reverses itself, and profits turn to losses.

Portfolio: A group of assets held at the same time.

Diversification: A portfolio attribute that can reduce investment risk.

Unquestionably, an important part of a sound investment program is adequate **diversification**. Next, we explain diversification and show how it applies to investing in common stocks.

Why Diversification Works

Diversification creates a synergistic quality in a portfolio in the sense that the portfolio's risk can be much less than the sum of the risks associated with all the securities it holds. In other words, you might hold two assets that by themselves are very risky but when held together create a very low-risk portfolio. The key to risk reduction is the correlation of returns between the two assets. We need an example.

An Example of Return Correlation

Figure 10.2 shows the returns from two hypothetical assets—A and B—over time. In each case, the return varies from 5 to 15 percent, and each asset has an average return of 10 percent. If you held either A or B, you would have a fairly risky asset since the range of returns (5 to 15 percent) is quite large. But look what would happen if, rather than investing all your money in one or the other, you allocated it evenly between the two.

You should see that whenever A's return is decreasing, B's return is increasing, and vice versa. Under the ideal arrangement assumed in our example, your return in the portfolio of A and B would always equal 10 percent. For example, when A's return is 15 percent, B's is 5 percent, and the average of the two is 10 percent. In effect, you have a no-risk asset—the portfolio—that provides as good a return as the average return over time from either A or B, individually. If you are a rational investor, you should prefer holding the portfolio as opposed to holding only one of the assets.

Returns from assets A and B are perfectly, negatively correlated; that is why you can eliminate risk by holding the two together. Perfect negative correlation seldom, if ever, exists in the real investment world; nevertheless, significant risk reduction is achievable even if asset returns are simply *poorly* correlated. There are many examples of poor correlation.

When Diversification Is Less Effective

You probably already grasp the situation when diversification may not work effectively—when asset returns are highly, positively correlated. Indeed, if returns are perfectly, positively correlated, they are clones of each other and there is nothing to be gained by holding both. For example, suppose that every time gold's price increases, silver's price increases

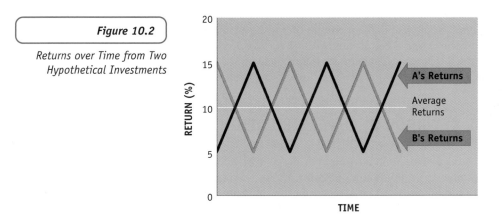

Figure 10.2

Returns over Time from Two Hypothetical Investments

by a proportionate equal amount; and, the same correlation holds for price decreases. (Silver and gold returns are highly positively correlated but not perfectly so.) In this situation, if your interest in the metals is strictly one of investing for price appreciation, then there is no benefit to investing in both. Select gold or silver and look for another commodity with returns that correlate poorly with theirs.

Return Correlations Among Key Financial Assets

Statistical correlation studies have measured the degree of return correlation among the key financial assets—stocks, bonds, and Treasury bills. Their findings indicate rather poor correlations among the major groups, particularly between stocks and Treasury bills. These findings lend support to the conventional recommendations of financial planners that you should diversify among stocks, bonds, and bills (or other highly liquid assets). Although, compared with an all-stocks portfolio, such diversification lowers your average return over time and reduces your wealth accumulation, it adds far greater return stability.

Diversification Guidelines

Diversification is so critical to successful investing that certain guidelines should be followed. The objective is to achieve a reasonable portfolio return while simultaneously reducing return variability as much as possible.

Diversify Among Intangibles and Tangibles

Not only should you diversify among the key financial assets, you should further diversify between financial and tangible assets, such as real estate or commodities. For example, during the inflationary 1970s, common stocks did very poorly while gold showed excellent returns. Its price appreciated from around $35 an ounce early in the decade to over $850 in 1980. Since the early 1980s, the situation has reversed: Stocks have boomed while gold has busted.

Diversify Globally

Recent investment studies clearly demonstrate the importance of investing on a global basis. Cross-country diversification reduces portfolio risk and frequently *increases* portfolio return. This is the best of both worlds. The explanation is that economies throughout the world do not expand and contract together. So there may be good times in the United States while Europe and Asia are lagging. This mix sets up the poor return correlations needed to reduce risk.

Moreover, certain parts of the world are growing much more rapidly than others: for example, South America and the Pacific Basin region compared with the United States. By investing in these parts of the world, you not only diversify but you also pick up the higher returns that typically accompany rapid growth.

Diversify Within Asset Groups

This is perhaps the most important rule. Some people take the view that you should "put all your eggs in one basket and watch the basket very closely," but for most of us that is a prescription for poverty. Few investors are so clever that they can identify the specific assets that will boom in the upcoming period. Indeed, the majority of professional money managers fail to do as well as an unmanaged stock index such as the S&P 500. An old market pro was once asked how much diversification an investor should have. His answer: Keep diversifying until you can sleep at night. Not bad advice, but we'll be more precise in the next section.

APPLYING A RISK-RETURN MODEL

Although it's interesting (and sometimes even fun) to study financial theory and investment returns, it's far more profitable to be able to apply what we learn. In this regard, theorists have developed certain techniques that many practitioners have used successfully. One approach is derived from the so-called capital asset pricing model (CAPM, for short). The CAPM can be applied to investing in any type of asset, but it has been used most extensively in common stock investment. Our discussion will be limited to that area.

Eliminating Random Risk

When you hold a limited number of stocks, you open yourself to all the risk factors discussed previously; that is, you are taking on risks associated with the overall economy as well as those associated with individual firms. A portfolio eliminates these latter risks. If you like the personal computer industry and put all your "apples" into Apple Computer, you rise or fall with this one stock. By putting half your money into Apple and the other half into, say, Dell you divide the risks associated with these two firms. If Apple fails in market acceptance, Dell might prosper. Of course, both might prosper or both might fail, but the probabilities are greater for one prospering or failing.

Studies have shown what happens to risk as you increase the number of stocks in a portfolio. A fairly typical outcome is shown in Figure 10.3. This is a hypothetical, randomly constructed portfolio with individual securities drawn by chance from the S&P 500 Stock Index. What do you find interesting in the figure?

First, notice the extent to which risk can be reduced by holding only a few stocks in a portfolio. With only five, you can cut your risk almost in half. After 20, you have virtually eliminated all the risk that can be eliminated, which is called **random risk.** Second, no matter how much you diversify, you cannot eliminate all risk (individual stock returns are poorly, but not negatively, correlated), and that which remains is called **market risk.** In other words, even if you owned all the stocks in the S&P 500, you still could expect considerable return variation over time, as we have discussed.

Random risk: Risk associated with any single asset; it can be reduced by holding the asset in a portfolio.

Market risk: Risk associated with unpredictable movements of the overall market; it cannot be reduced by a portfolio.

Managing Market Risk

Since you cannot eliminate market risk, the next best step is to manage it. By managing risk, we simply mean that you receive sufficient return over time to compensate you for

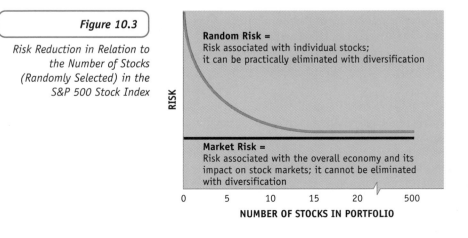

Figure 10.3

Risk Reduction in Relation to the Number of Stocks (Randomly Selected) in the S&P 500 Stock Index

Part 4   Investing for the Future

undertaking it. A general but very, very important first rule is: *If you invest in stocks as risky as the overall market, you should receive a risk premium equal to that of the overall market.* Recall our discussion earlier about risk premiums, and how the overall market has averaged about an 8.0 percent risk premium over a long period of time. Now we put that information to use. Suppose you are contemplating investing in the overall market (either by selecting 20 stocks randomly or by buying a mutual fund that approximates the market). What is your required return for one year? Step 1: Determine what the rate will be on risk-free, one-year U.S. Treasury bills. Step 2: Add the risk premium, and you have your answer. For example, if the U.S. Treasury bills rate is 5.0 percent, the required market return is 13.0 percent (5.0 + 8.0). Although simple, it is nevertheless a sound approach for estimating a required return. Assuming you invest, are you guaranteed the 13.0 percent return? Of course not. It could be much higher or much lower, as we saw in Table 10.1.

A second, and equally important, rule in investment risk management is: *If you invest in stocks more or less risky than the overall market, you should expect a risk premium greater or less than the overall market premium in direct proportion to the greater or lesser risk taken.* Common sense tells us we should receive a higher return if we take greater risks, but, unfortunately, it doesn't tell us *how much* higher. More sophisticated—but not difficult to understand—techniques are needed to answer that question.

Estimating a Stock's Risk

The first step now is to determine the risk of an individual stock in relation to the overall market. This is done with a statistical figure called **beta.** A stock's beta measures the

Beta: A statistic that measures the responsiveness of an asset's return in relation to changes in the overall market return.

Table 10.2

What Beta Values Mean

Range of Beta Values for a Stock	What It Means
Less than zero; that is, a negative beta	The stock's price moves in the opposite direction from the market; very few stocks have negative betas over extended periods of time.
Zero	The stock's return is independent of the market; this could be a risk-free U.S. Treasury security, where return is guaranteed regardless of the market's performance.
Zero to +1.0	The stock's price moves in the same direction as the market but not as much; stocks with betas less than 1.0 are considered conservative investments.
Equal to +1.0	The stock has the same risk as the market; if you bought all beta 1.0 stocks, your portfolio's return and risk would be the same as if you bought the overall market.
Greater than +1.0	The stock's price moves in the same direction as the market but by a greater percentage amount: buying these stocks increases your risk relative to the market.

responsiveness of its return over time to that of the overall market. For example, if Apple Computer's beta is +1.5, it means that if the stock market goes up 10 percent, Apple's common stock goes up 15 percent; if the market goes down 10 percent, Apple goes down 15 percent. A beta value indicates relative risk, with higher betas meaning greater risk. Table 10.2 summarizes ranges of beta values and their meanings, and Table 10.3 shows a wide array of betas of companies, some of which might be familiar to you.

Betas are not difficult to calculate, although the method involves a type of statistical analysis that may not be familiar to you. Fortunately, betas are available from a number of sources, such as the one used in the nearby Internet exercise.

TOPIC **LINKS**

Find Microsoft's beta.

Estimating a Stock's Required Return

After determining a stock's beta value, you can then estimate its required return. Considerable historical evidence shows that stock returns over time are related to their beta values;

Table 10.3

Estimated Beta Values for Various Companies

Company	Ticker Symbol	Major Business	Beta Value
Avon	AVP	Cosmetics	0.6
Barrick Gold	ABX	Gold mining	0.4
Citigroup	C	Global banking	1.4
DPL	DPL	Electric utility	0.5
Ebay	EBAY	Internet auction site	1.7
Exxon-Mobil	XOM	Oil refinery	0.4
Gillette	G	Razor blades	0.4
Intel	INTC	Computer memory chips	2.1
Kellog	K	Packaged foods	−0.1
Micron Technology	MU	Computer memory chips	2.4
Sirius	SIRI	Satellite radio	3.9
Southwest Airlines	LUV	Major airline	0.9

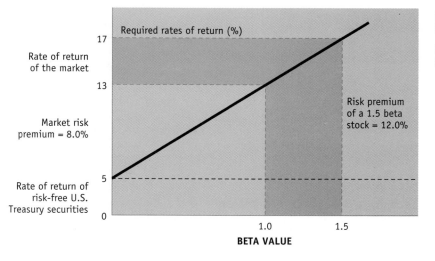

Figure 10.4

Required Rates of Return in Relation to Beta Values

specifically, risk premiums are shown to be directly proportional to beta values. The following equation expresses this relationship:

Stock risk premium (%) = stock's beta value × market risk premium (%)

If a stock has a beta of +1.5, its risk premium should be 12.0 percent:

12.0% = 1.5 × 8.0%

The total required return on a stock consists of the risk premium plus the expected return on risk-free Treasury securities. If this latter rate is 5.0 percent, the stock's total required return is 17.0 percent (5.0 + 12.0). The diagram in Figure 10.4, which incorporates the figures we have just used, is a convenient way to express and summarize the important relationship between required return and risk.

The Importance of the Risk-Free Rate of Return

You should understand the important role played by the rate of return on U.S. Treasury bills. All required rates of return depend on it, and if it changes, so will these rates. For example, if this rate went up to 10.0 percent, all other rates would similarly increase by 5 percent; the market return will now be 18.0 percent, and a 1.5 beta stock will be 22.0 percent.

Making Stock Selections

Finding a stock's required return does not answer the question of whether the stock should be bought or sold. To make these decisions we need a stock's **expected total return**. This is a return that investors believe they will actually earn with the stock in the upcoming investment period. We will discuss this return in detail in the next chapter; for now, let's work with it as a given.

    Consider three investments—A, B, and C—shown in Table 10.4. They differ substantially in risk, as measured by their beta values, and in expected returns. How would you rank them in terms of appeal? Would you take C because it offers the highest return? Some investors might, but it would be a mistake.

Expected total return: An actual return that investors expect to earn on a stock in an upcoming period.

	Stock	Beta Value	Required Rate of Return	Expected Rate of Return	Alpha Value	Decision
Table 10.4	A	0.35	7.8%	10.0	+2.2%	Definitely accept, expected rate well exceeds required rate
Selecting Stocks by Comparing Required Rates of Return with Expected Rates of Return	B	1.50	17.0%	14.0	−3.0%	Definitely reject, expected rate is far below required rate
	C	2.00	21.0%	21.0	0.0%	A borderline case, flip a coin to make your choice

Look for a Stock's Excess Return

Alpha: A measure of a stock's appeal, calculated by subtracting required return from expected return.

Actually, A is the best investment. Why? Because it offers the highest **alpha** value, which is the difference between expected return and required return; that is,

$$\text{Alpha} = \text{expected return} - \text{required return}$$

Alpha values can be positive, as they are with investments A and C, or negative, as with investment B. Any stock with a negative alpha value should not be bought, and you might consider selling if you already own it. Stocks with positive alpha values are buying opportunities, with greater alphas indicating greater investment appeal.

Stock A with its 2.2 percent alpha value seems a good investment. Stock C's situation is not overwhelming; as noted in the table, you might flip a coin to make a choice here.

TOPIC **LINKS**

See an application of the CAPM called the Dividend Discount Model.

Is Selecting Stocks This Easy?

The answer to this question is a resounding no. The CAPM technique is very simple, which makes it appealing; but there are several problems to consider. First, beta may not always measure a stock's risk appropriately, particularly when a company is undergoing dramatic changes in business or financial risk. A beta calculated from historical data may not reflect the riskiness of the new firm. Second, as we shall see in the next chapter, estimating a stock's expected total return is very difficult. Third, the 8 percent risk premium we are using places a heavy risk burden on stocks B and C. Suppose we used a lower rate of, say, 4 percent. Then B's required return is only 11.0 percent [5% + 1.5 (4%)] and C's is 13 percent [5% + 2.0 (4%)]. Now, each should be regarded as solid buys.

Despite all the criticisms, though, the technique is useful if it does nothing more than force us to consider both risk and return in the investment selection process. Equally important, it highlights the need to earn higher returns if you take greater risks. If you invest your money in roller-coaster (high beta) stocks, you should at least get the thrill of the ride (a high return).

BUILDING AND CHANGING A PORTFOLIO

Although the need to diversify in building a portfolio is important, there are other issues to also consider. First, assets selected must be suitable to meet the investor's objectives. You will understand this topic better after you have become more familiar with the wide variety of investments available; so our discussion of selecting assets is deferred to Chapter 12. But other issues can be addressed now. In the following sections, we discuss the topics of acquiring and selling securities over time.

Dogs of the Dow: Using a High-Yield Method to Select Stocks

Beating the market is not easy—just ask over half of all professional money managers who come up short each year. Surprisingly, one very simple method has a good track record and a rapidly growing number of converts. Even some mutual funds offer the method, if you prefer to avoid even the slight details of investing on your own.

What do you need to do? At the beginning of each year find the 10 (of 30) stocks in the Dow Jones Industrial Average (DJIA) with the highest dividend yield. You could use a copy of the *Wall Street Journal* or *Barron's* to find the 10 highest yielders, or make life easy and go to the "Dogs of the Dow" Web site (**www.dogsofthedow.com/**), which provides the names each day. It also provides performance results along with much other information. Actually, you can begin investing anytime; you don't have to wait until the beginning of a year.

Regardless of how you get the 10 stocks, invest an equal amount in each at the start of a year, then sit back and reap.

From 1972 through 1995, this method has scored an average annualized return of 17.7 percent versus only 11.9 percent for the overall DJIA. However, from 1999 through 2003, it underperformed the Index, 5.1% to 6.1%. Still, this is a fairly good performance. Why does it do so well?

High-yielding stocks often represent so-called turnaround situations. A company, such as Sears at one time, may fail to keep up with its competitors in terms of market share of production efficiencies. As a result the stock price plummets; but the company has ample cash and continues paying a decent dividend. So the dividend yield rises, and the company makes the top 10 list. Often these companies solve their problems—as Sears did—and their stock prices rebound sharply.

Would the high-yield method work in pinpointing other potential turnarounds? Sure, but be careful. Stocks in the DJIA are large blue chips that have the resources to make drastic operational changes. If you find a small company with a high yield, it may never turn around; instead, it may lower or cut its dividend altogether. Now, your high-yielder is a no-yielder, and its price might fall sharply. It is much simpler to limit your choices to the DJIA.

Acquiring Securities

As funds become available to acquire securities, how should we do it? Two methods are often advised by financial planners—dollar cost averaging and routine investment plans.

Dollar Cost Averaging

Dollar cost averaging (DCA) is a mechanical method of investing in securities. Table 10.5 shows how it works. As you see, the idea is quite simple. You establish an investment plan calling for equal dollar investments at regular intervals. By following the plan, you then buy securities at a wide range of prices, and, over time, you will have an

Dollar cost averaging (DCA): A method of investing that calls for a constant amount investment at regular time intervals.

(1) Date	(2) Shares Purchased	(3) Price per Share	(4) Total Shares Held	(5) Total Cost	(6) Average Cost (5)/(4)	(7) Cumulative Profit (Loss) [(3) × (4)] − (5)
1/1	100.00	$10	100.00	$1,000	$10.00	$ 0
2/1	83.33	12	183.33	2,000	10.91	200
3/1	125.00	8	308.33	3,000	9.73	(533)
4/1	100.00	10	408.33	4,000	9.80	83
5/1	166.67	6	575.00	5,000	8.70	(1,550)
6/1	100.00	10	675.00	6,000	8.89	750

Table 10.5

Illustration of DCA, Assuming $1,000 Invested Each Month

TOPIC **LINKS**

Review an example of dollar cost averaging.

average cost somewhere between the highs and the lows. In this example, the average cost after six months is $8.89 per share. The mechanical nature of the plan keeps investors from using their own judgment to determine buying points or from buying a given number of shares (rather than investing a given number of dollars) at regular intervals.

A supporter of this plan believes that investors' judgments usually are wrong, because they are guided by emotions or incorrect assessments of the market situation. In the enthusiasm of a bull market (rising prices), we tend to invest too heavily; in the gloom of a bear market (falling prices) we don't invest at all. Following this approach, the average cost of purchased shares is much higher than the average with DCA.

Routine Investment Plans

Dividend reinvestment plans (DRIPs): Plans offered by corporations that allow shareholders to reinvest cash dividends.

There are a number of ways to make investments on a regular basis. Many companies have **dividend reinvestment plans (DRIPs)** that enable investors to reinvest dividends they receive from a company's stock to buy more of the company's shares. Since dividends are paid at regular quarterly intervals, a DRIP accomplishes the same end as dollar cost averaging on a quarterly basis. A similar routine investment process arises if you own mutual fund shares and choose to reinvest dividends and capital distributions rather than receiving them in cash. Many mutual funds also encourage routine investing by offering plans that automatically transfer a certain amount of funds each week (or other period) from your checking account to the mutual fund.

All the preceding plans are effective primarily because they put savings and investment first, rather than last, in your budget. But they are not substitutes for sound investment selection in the first place. You don't want to dollar cost average with a poor stock or use the DRIP of a company with no future. The downside of regularity in investing is that we might not review our holdings as often as we should.

TOPIC **LINKS**

Find detailed information on dividend reinvestment plans.

Selling Securities

The decision to sell securities may be as difficult to make as the decision to buy them. There are a number of factors to consider. They are discussed next.

The Security Becomes Overvalued

Let's suppose that you bought stock A, which we discussed previously and showed to be a good value within the CAPM framework. Suppose that its price was $20 a share when you bought it, but it's now $50 a share. The CAPM might now indicate that it's overvalued and should be sold. Surely, one important reason to sell a security is if we believe that it is no longer attractive relative to other securities that could be purchased.

TOPIC **LINKS**

Learn more about MITTS and other similar securities by visiting the Amex Web site at **www.Amex. com.** Click on "Structured Products," then "Index Notes."

Selling for Tax Reasons

The tax law often encourages security sales. For example, suppose that you bought shares of GM stock, which subsequently declined in value. You now have a $3,000 loss. Should you sell? If you do, you establish a loss that can be used to offset other income on your tax return, saving you taxes. The amount depends on your marginal tax rate: At a 28 percent rate, you save $840 ($0.28 \times 3,000$).

Investment advisers say that you should not sell securities *simply* to save taxes; nevertheless, in certain situations it makes good sense. For example, you may think that Ford and Chrysler are just as attractive as General Motors; by selling the latter and buying one of the former, you will save enough in taxes to allow you to buy more shares. Changing investments for tax reasons is referred to as a **tax swap.** Swaps are very popular but more so with bonds than with stocks.

Tax swap: Selling a security to establish a tax loss and then reinvesting funds in a similar security.

Your Investment Objectives Change

Over time, it is likely that your investment objectives will change. You might want more current income as opposed to price appreciation, or you might want less portfolio risk. Clearly, changing objectives require the sale of certain securities and the purchase of others.

Economic Changes and the Portfolio

A frequently debated issue in portfolio management is whether your investment activities should ignore economic conditions or be managed in ways to exploit expected changes. The argument is referred to as buy-and-hold versus market timing.

Buy-and-Hold Strategies

As the name implies, a **buy-and-hold strategy** means you do not attempt to enhance your portfolio return by "trading with the investment cycle." People advocating the buy-and-hold approach argue that economic cycles cannot be forecasted. Since you can't forecast cycles, there is no way you can consistently benefit by trading in anticipation of them, and all you do is make your stockbroker wealthy by trying. Buy-and-hold advocates stress the importance of *carefully constructing* a well-diversified portfolio to begin with rather than continually *changing* one to improve performance.

The growing evidence that economic cycles cannot be forecasted certainly supports this view. Even the so-called experts have been consistently off their forecast targets, often

Buy-and-hold strategy:
A method of portfolio management that does not attempt to trade securities over economic status.

by so much that any random forecasting device forecasted as well. If you like the idea of simply building and then holding a portfolio, there is no reason to be defensive about its simplicity.

Market-Timing Strategies

Market timing: A method of portfolio management that changes a portfolio's composition in relation to expected market changes.

Market timing attempts to change a portfolio's composition in anticipation of expected changes in returns among different investments. Timing strategies range from the complex to some that are very simple. A simple one usually involves going back and forth between a common stock mutual fund and a money market fund. The simpler versions are growing in popularity, and certain advisers now specialize in offering timing advice or in managing portfolios based on their timing methods.

Since no evidence overwhelmingly supports even professional market timers, you should think twice before attempting your own timing techniques. If a formula appeals to you, our advice again is to try it on paper first and evaluate it critically. If it seems to work, then consider investing in a mutual fund family that allows you to switch among individual funds at little or no cost. (Fund switching is explained in Chapter 12.)

Key Terms

alpha (p. 262)
beta (p. 259)
business cycle risk (p. 253)
business risk (p. 253)
buy-and-hold strategy (p. 265)
diversification (p. 256)
dividend reinvestment plans (DRIPs) (p. 264)
dollar cost averaging (DCA) (p. 263)
expected total return (p. 261)
financial risk (p. 253)
inflation risk (p. 252)
interest rate risk (p. 253)
iron law of risk and return (p. 251)
management risk (p. 253)
market risk (p. 258)
market timing (p. 266)
portfolio (p. 255)
random risk (p. 258)
required rate of return (p. 253)
risk (p. 251)
risk premium (p. 255)
tax swap (p. 264)

FOLLOW-UP ON THE

Reread the chapter-opening vignette.

1. Do you agree with the financial consultant that the Steeles' portfolio is not adequately diversified? Explain your answer.
2. How likely is it for the Steeles to earn annual returns of 30 to 50 percent for the next *several* years? How likely are they to earn those returns *consistently* in the future? Discuss your answers.
3. Arnold and Sharon have been watching the financial news networks, such as CNBC. The commentators and guests generate a considerable amount of energy, which can be conducive to frequent trading. Explain if you feel the Steeles should be active traders, holding securities perhaps no longer than several months, or even several weeks.
4. Explain if you feel that dollar cost averaging and dividend reinvestment plans might be better alternatives to the frequent trading strategy discussed in question 3.

1. How would you define risk to someone who doesn't have a grasp of investment fundamentals? Do you think the best definition is "Risk is the chance of losing money"? Explain.
2. Explain two views that you might take relating risk to time. Which is the more appropriate if you are a long-term (over 10 years) investor?
3. Drew Dugan is considering investing in one of three securities listed in the following table. Drew isn't familiar with return or risk and would like you to explain the data. Also, he would like your opinion on which security to invest in; he generally considers himself a risk-seeking individual.

	Securities		
	A	B	C
Highest expected return	50%	15%	30%
Lowest expected return	−30%	10%	−20%
Most likely return	20%	12%	22%

4. What sources of risk are associated with the overall economy? What sources are associated with individual issuers of securities? Explain two perspectives of the relationship of risk to time.
5. From 1970 through 2003, which financial investments—stocks or Treasury bills—were the more and the less risky? Explain and provide evidence for your answer.
6. What investment implications can you derive from the information in Table 10.1? Express your answer from the perspectives of a young investor (mid-20s) and an older investor (mid-50s) nearing retirement.
7. Explain an investment's risk premium. Is there some "set" number to use in stock analysis? Explain.
8. People often understand through common sense that diversification reduces risk. But explain *why* diversification works and when it works most effectively. Also indicate when it may not be effective.
9. Briefly explain three diversification guidelines.
10. How many securities must you hold for adequate diversification? Does diversification eliminate all risk, or does some remain? Explain.
11. What is meant by managing risk, and how is the beta concept used in this effort?
12. Dan Stramm thinks if you invest in common stocks, you ought to get three times as much return as you would if you invest in Treasury bills. Do you agree with Dan? If not, explain how you would estimate a required return for common stocks.
13. How do you calculate a stock's alpha value? How do you use it to select stocks?
14. Explain dollar cost averaging and why it may be helpful for certain investors. What is a dividend reinvestment plan, and what advantage does it offer? Also briefly explain several other routine investment techniques.
15. Briefly explain three reasons for selling securities.
16. Explain a market-timing strategy, comparing it with a buy-and-hold strategy.

Case 10.1
Selecting Stocks for Bart Parks

Bart Parks is a bachelor, 33 years old, with a good income and a reasonable net worth. Bart has about $20,000 invested in individual common stocks, most of them recommended by his broker, Buzz Bushkin. He's done well with Bushkin over the years, and he is particularly pleased that Bushkin always gives him a list of several stocks to choose from, instead of just one. Bart has saved another $3,000 for the market and has asked Bushkin for a new list, which follows. Bushkin recommends Alpha Dynamics, but Bart is concerned with this selection because he has heard that Alpha's latest product—an automatic envelope opener—has not met huge market acceptance.

Bart has turned to you for help, and in response you have gathered the following data on expected returns and betas.

Security	Current Price	Expected Return	Beta
Bushkin's alternatives			
Alpha Dynamics	$ 10	25%	2.0
Beta Depressants	18	5%	0.3
Gamma Globulins	6	27%	3.1
U.S. Treasury bills	—	5%	0.0
A market index fund	16	13%	1.0

Bart doesn't consider himself either excessively risk averting or risk seeking, but he does expect a return commensurate with the degree of risk inherent in a security. Also, Bart's current holdings give him adequate diversification, so that need not concern him in selecting a stock now. Finally, Bart uses a market risk premium of 8 percent.

Questions
1. Calculating alpha values, explain if you agree or disagree with Bushkin's selection.
2. Should the information Bart has heard about Alpha's new product be a concern in his selection? Explain.
3. Assuming that Bart takes Bushkin's advice, calculate the commission he will pay and compare this with the commission he probably would pay to a discount broker.

Case 10.2
Arlene Elton Considers Dollar Cost Averaging

Arlene Elton has been investing in LKV Aeronautics common stock over the past six months. She bought 300 shares initially at $25 a share. A month later, after a nice move by LKV, she bought another 300 shares at $35 a share. LKV then went into a tailspin over the next three months, and at the end Arlene considered selling all her shares at $15 a share. She's glad she didn't, though, because the stock rebounded in the last month and is currently selling at $30 a share. Arlene has saved some more money and is now thinking of buying 200 more shares. Before buying them, she has decided to talk to a friend, Mark Hatfield, who also invests in stocks. Mark uses dollar cost averaging. He thinks Arlene should also consider this technique. Indeed, he is convinced that dollar cost averaging almost guarantees successful investment results over time.

Questions
1. Assuming that Arlene goes ahead with her plan to buy 200 more shares of LKV, she will have invested $24,000 to buy 800 shares. Suppose that instead she had invested $4,000 each month over the six months and purchased shares at the following prices: $25, $35,

$30, $20, $15, and $30. Set up a table that shows the number of shares purchased each month, the total value of her holdings, and her profit or loss after the purchase.

2. Compare Arlene's actual performance with the performance from dollar cost averaging. Calculate the average share cost each way, and use the values in your discussion.

3. Do you think Arlene is the type of person who should use dollar cost averaging? Explain.

4. Do you agree with Mark that dollar cost averaging guarantees good investment results? Explain.

Exercises to Strengthen Your Use of the Internet

Working Out on the Web

(Internet links for the following exercises can be found at **www. prenhall.com/winger**.)

Exercise 10.1 Learn More About Risk and Return

Go to AAII's home page and choose "Investment Basics" then choose "FAQs."

Q. Which type of investment has the greatest risk as measured by the standard deviation?

Exercise 10.2 What's the Market Doing?

Many excellent Internet sites provide information on individual securities and the markets over all. One of the best is **Ft. com**. At the home page review the performances of the popular indexes throughout the day. Then click on "Standard and Poors" to view the day's graphic of this index. Click on "Interactive Charting" to find performance graphics for other periods of time.

Q. What has been the highest value for the S&P 500 over the past five years?

Exercise 10.3 What's Intel Doing?

Go to Yahoo's Finance site and find out what Intel is doing by entering its symbol (INTC) in the block. Along with the most recent price, other information appears. Click on "Chart."

Q. What are Intel's earnings per share and P/E ratio?

Exercise 10.4 Does P&G Have a Dividend Reinvestment Program (DRIP)?

DRIPS are very popular. You can find a list of companies with dividend reinvestment programs at the Netstock Direct site. Enter P&G's symbol (PG).

Q. Does P&G (PG) have a DRIP? What is the minimum number of shares you need to participate in the DRIP program?

Exercise 10.5 How Does Dollar Cost Averaging (DCA) Work?

DCA is a popular investment strategy that avoids the perils of "playing the market."

Q. Review the DCA example provided by Sun At its home page, choose "Planning Tools." . In each example, calculate the total profit or loss over the six-month period with dollar cost averaging. Compare these amounts to profit or loss, assuming the full $3,000 was invested at the beginning of the period.

11

Stocks and Bonds

YOUR MOST COMMON INVESTMENTS

OBJECTIVES

1. To identify basic shareholder rights and the means by which corporations make distributions to shareholders

2. To recognize the investment opportunities in various types of stocks, such as growth stocks or income stocks

3. To understand how to determine the investment appeal of a stock using various valuation techniques and the price-to-earnings approach

4. To understand corporate bondholders' rights and the payment characteristics of corporate bonds

5. To identify different types and payment characteristics of U.S. Treasury securities, U.S. agency securities, and municipal bonds

6. To know how to calculate a bond's current yield, yield to maturity, and present value

7. To understand default risk and interest rate risk associated with bond investments

8. To become familiar with preferred stock, recognizing its characteristics and investment quality

TOPIC **LINKS**

Follow the **Topic Links** in each chapter for your interactive Personal Finance exercise on the Web. Go to: **www.prenhall.com/winger**

After considerable deliberation, the Steeles have decided to manage their own investment program. They intend to direct most of their savings into mutual funds, although they also plan to build their own portfolio of common stocks, most likely through dividend reinvestment plans. Regardless of the specific investment approach they use, Arnold and Sharon are fully aware that they must increase their knowledge of the two most popular investment vehicles—stocks and bonds. At the present they know very little about each.

The Steeles don't understand fully the differences between a stock and a bond. Bonds seem to offer much better cash returns, and Arnold and Sharon wonder if perhaps they might be better investments than stocks. Then there is preferred stock; what makes it "preferred?" They have a general idea that common stocks are considered the best vehicle for growth, but surely not all common stocks can be considered "growth" stocks.

Arnold and Sharon want to learn enough about investing to achieve a basic understanding of how to evaluate most stocks. They don't hope to become experts, but they do want to be able to understand a company's relative strengths and weaknesses. Additionally, they want to know how to evaluate particular types of bonds. For example, should they buy corporate bonds or Treasury bonds? They have heard that municipal bonds are great for certain investors. Would they be in this category? Finally, should they buy bonds with short or long maturities?

The Steeles have some work ahead of them. So do you, if you intend to be an active investor. The rewards, though, may be worth the effort. For one thing, you won't pay professional management fees and other expenses associated with a managed account, such as a mutual fund. And for another, you may show better investment returns. Often so-called "amateur" investors outperform the pros, not because they are smarter but because they bring simplicity to the process and tend to hold their investments for much longer periods of time. For example, many people still hold shares of Wal-Mart or Microsoft from the time these companies first went public. Some are now millionaires, thanks to these investments.

Of course, you can argue that these people were lucky—not informed investors. Sure, luck plays a role, just as it does in a poker game. But you wouldn't sit down at a poker table to test your luck unless you were very familiar with how to play the game. The same is true in investing, and this chapter will familiarize you with the most important "chips" in the investment game—stocks and bonds.

AN OVERVIEW OF COMMON STOCKS

Everybody likes to get in on the ground floor of an emerging growth company, such as Intel or Microsoft. To do this you must buy a company's **common stock.** Although it is riskier than bonds or preferred stock, it gives you a stake in the company's future—for better or worse. A $100 investment in Microsoft's shares in 1986 was worth about $29,000 in mid-1998! And it is safe to say that, with few exceptions, you should buy common stock only when you are willing to risk that its future price will exceed its current price; if you don't think that will happen, then you should invest in something else. Essentially, most common stocks are for the future, but in varying degrees; some are completely growth oriented, others are far less so. This chapter explains common stock investing. Perhaps it will help you find the Microsofts of the future; but even if it doesn't, it should make you a more informed investor.

Common stock: Shares that give you an ownership interest in a company.

Characteristics of Common Stock

Becoming an informed investor begins by learning common stock's basic characteristics. The important ones are explained in the following sections.

Shareholders' Rights

Suppose you were thinking of buying 100 shares of Meadwestvaco Corporation (a paper and forest products company with other diversified interests) at around $30 a share in mid-August 2004. Along with receiving a stock certificate evidencing your ownership, you would have an interest of 0.0000005 (100/201,200,000) in the company. Although your holding is a minuscule one, you are nevertheless an owner of Mead. And, although you have far less power than someone owning a million shares, you have identical privileges, which are explained below. (As this text was going to the printer, Mead sold a substantial amount of its assets and announced that it will change its name to NewPage Corp.)

The Right to Vote In most cases your voting right gives you one vote for each share of common stock you own, although some stock is classified as nonvoting. In contrast to voting in political elections, in a corporation you can assign your vote to someone else through a **proxy.** So if you can't make the annual stockholders' meeting where voting takes place, you can return it with your signature, either giving or not giving authority to vote your shares. It is hard to get excited over a voting right if you own 0.0000010 of a company. However, if you and several friends are contemplating going into business and forming a corporation to do so, then be very careful about who owns how many shares and how these shares might be voted in controversial decisions. Hardly anything is more powerless than a minority interest in a corporation, even if that minority is 49 percent. Make

Proxy: An assignment of your voting rights to someone else.

sure in these situations to have an attorney's advice before the corporation is formed and shares are distributed.

The Preemptive Right Your right to maintain a proportionate interest in a company is called the **preemptive right.** If Mead wanted to sell 20 million more shares of common stock to raise capital, you would have the right to buy 10 (0.0000005 × 20,000,000) more shares.

The Right to Share in Earnings or Asset Distributions Your obvious intent for investing in a company is to receive a return. With common stock you have the right to participate (in proportion to the number of shares you own) in any distribution of earnings or assets. This right is limited, however. For example, most states prohibit any distributions that would impair the firm's capital and subject its creditors (usually bondholders) to greater risk. In addition, if the corporation has any preferred stock outstanding, any current or past unpaid dividends must be paid on it before any distributions are made to common stockholders. This means that, as a common stockholder, you come last in line, behind bondholders and preferred stockholders. You are said to have a **residual claim;** that is, you get what is left. Although this sounds dismal, actually, getting what is left is why you buy common stock in the first place. Bondholders and preferred stockholders have prior claims, but the amounts they are entitled to are fixed each year; that is, regardless of how well (or poorly) the company does, the amount they get is the same. In contrast, the amounts available to common stockholders vary in direct proportion to the company's profits. Figure 11.1 illustrates this relationship.

The hypothetical company has bonds outstanding requiring $5,000,000 a year in interest and preferred stock requiring $3,000,000 a year in dividends. This represents $8,000,000 of fixed obligations that must be paid before any earnings are available to

Preemptive right: A right to maintain your proportionate interest in a company.

Residual claim: The claim against assets or earnings of common stockholders; the claim comes after the claims of bondholders and preferred stockholders.

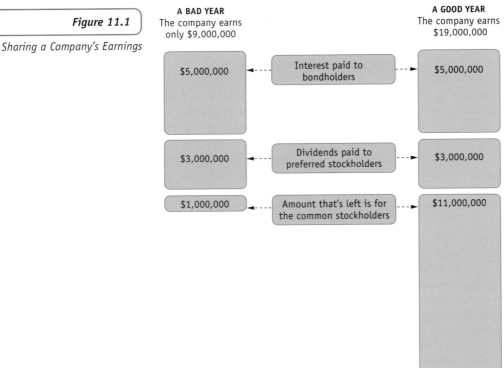

Figure 11.1

Sharing a Company's Earnings

common stockholders. If the corporation has a bad year and earnings are only $9,000,000, common stockholders' claims will be $1,000,000. If the corporation has a good year and earnings are $19,000,000, the bondholders' and preferred stockholders' distributions will still total $8,000,000, but common stockholders' claims will now be $11,000,000. It should be noted that the corporation might not pay out all the common stockholders' claims in dividends. In fact, most companies retain a portion of the earnings and reinvest them in the business. For example, in the good year just described, perhaps $5,000,000 would be paid in dividends and $6,000,000 retained. In the bad year, it is possible that no dividends would be paid. However, many companies continue paying common stock dividends, even in very poor years. Mead, for example, had earnings of $1.99 a share in 1999 and paid a dividend of $0.65 per share. Although its earnings fell to $1.58 per share in 2000, it actually increased the dividend to $0.68 a share.

Distributions to Shareholders

Although shareholders have a right to share earnings, this does not mean that the corporation pays its shareholders each year a cash amount equal to the annual earnings. Actually, there are various types of distributions corporations make, some in cash and some in shares of the company's stock.

Cash Distributions As the name implies, cash distributions are cash payments the corporation makes to its shareholders. By far the most common type of cash distribution is the **regular dividend.** Many corporations pay dividends on a regular basis. For example, Mead Corporation paid an annual dividend of $0.50 per share from 1991 through mid-1995, when it increased the amount to $0.56. Mead has increased the dividend steadily since then.

Regular dividend: Cash distribution made to shareholders on a regular basis, usually each quarter.

Although less popular, many companies have begun **periodic share repurchases** as a way of distributing cash to shareholders. These plans offer shareholders the right to sell shares back to the corporation at a set price, which is higher than the market price at the time the repurchase offer is made. In effect, regular repurchases offer the same cash advantage to shareholders as regular cash dividends as long as they don't mind reducing their holdings in the company. (You have the option of selling shares or not.) There can be tax advantages as well with share repurchase.

Periodic share repurchases: Corporate repurchase of shares having a similar effect as cash dividends.

Noncash Distributions In many cases, corporations' managements want to reward shareholders but cannot do so because the business does not have sufficient cash. Frequently, noncash distributions are made, which include stock dividends and stock splits. With a **stock dividend,** you don't receive cash; instead, you receive shares of the company's stock. For example, if you owned 100 shares of Mead and the company declared a 10 percent stock dividend, you would get an additional 10 shares. Are stock dividends attractive? Not really, because every stockholder gets a proportionate increase in shares. All you then have are more shares of stock but no more assets or greater earning potential for the company. As a result, the day a stock dividend is paid, the price of the stock goes down by the same percentage as the percentage increase in the number of shares. Instead of having 100 shares of Mead at, say, $30 a share, you would have 110 shares at $27.27 a share.

Stock dividend: A dividend paid by issuing additional shares of a company's stock.

Closely related to a stock dividend is a **stock split.** Here, a company simply gives you and all other stockholders more shares of stock. Two-for-one splits are the most common, which means the number of shares you own doubles. (Mead accomplished a two-for-one stock split in December 1997.) Are stock splits by themselves desirable? No, for the same reasons stock dividends aren't. Granted, many companies that have done well, such as Microsoft, sometimes split their shares to lower the stock's price and broaden its market appeal. But it's not the split that adds value, it is the underlying strength of the company.

Stock split: Giving additional shares of stock to current stockholders.

Opportunities in Common Stocks

Your opportunities to earn a return with common stocks are as varied as the many different kinds of corporations that issue them. You can buy very conservative stocks with low risk, or you can find those that are extremely risky. The total return you can expect over the long run should reflect your willingness to assume risk—the more you take, the higher your potential return. The following are the different kinds of stocks most investors buy.

Growth company: A company with expected earnings growth greater than the growth of the overall economy.

Growth Companies The earnings and dividend-paying potential of a **growth company** are expected to grow at a rate faster than the growth rate of the overall economy. The price of its common stock should also grow rapidly in the future. Of course, there are all sorts of growth companies. Microsoft is one, BEA Systems is another. Microsoft represents less risk than BEA Systems, because it has a good history of achieving growth, and its chances of continuing to do so in the future are very good. BEA Systems, on the other hand, is a relative newcomer to the computer software industry, but it may have the more rapid growth. If you are interested in buying growth stocks, get as many recommendations as you can from brokers or other advisers, and narrow down the field to 10 or 15 companies that appeal to you.

Income stocks: Stocks that pay high dividends in relation to their market prices.

Income Stocks As their name suggests, **income stocks** pay high dividends in relation to their market prices and offer good current rates of return. However, they vary considerably in risk, so be sure to review that characteristic before investing. Because of their capabilities for paying regular cash dividends, public utilities are often considered the best income stocks. In recent years, their dividend yields have been in excess of 7 percent, and some also offer reasonable growth prospects. They are not without risks, though, as investors learned with public utilities that have not been permitted to use nuclear reactors.

Blue chip: A low-risk stock that reliably provides investors with the expected dividend or growth.

Blue Chips The popular expression **blue chip** really doesn't tell you much about a stock. It usually refers to low-risk stocks—those you can count on to deliver the dividend or growth you expected when you bought them. It also usually refers to what are called *high-capitalization stocks*, which means the issuing corporations are very large companies with many millions of shares outstanding. Being a blue chip doesn't guarantee success, however. The New York Central Railroad was the bluest of the blue in the 1920s and bankrupt in the 1960s.

Cyclical stocks: Stocks that are highly responsive to changes in the business cycle.

Cyclical Stocks **Cyclical stocks** are more responsive to changes in the business cycle than are other stocks. Companies in the capital goods industries, such as the Mead Corporation, are good examples of cyclical stocks. Investors like to "play" cyclical stocks by buying them in recession periods and then selling out as the economy improves. Sounds easy, but it isn't, because it is almost impossible to know when the stock's price is at the bottom of its cycle.

Special situation: Any potentially profitable investment opportunity, but often referring to a possible takeover.

Special Situations Anything can be a **special situation,** but the most common is when one company is expected to take over another. Almost always these takeovers result in a substantially higher price for the stock of the company taken over. For example, Lotus Development's price was about $30 a share in 1995, when IBM announced it would offer $65 a share. If you can get in on a takeover shortly before the event takes place, the profit opportunity is enormous. Naturally, the trick is to know if and when a takeover will occur. If you don't have inside information, you must rely on opinions of so-called experts in identifying takeover situations. Very often these opinions are no better than random guesses. Other special situations could involve changes in key managers, favorable or unfavorable legal opinions, granting of a license or patent, a new and unexpected invention, and many others. All these events can change a company's financial outlook dramatically and its stock price accordingly.

Stock Quotations

Stock quotations are reported in major financial newspapers, such as the *Wall Street Journal*, and in many local newspapers. At a minimum, the quotes usually provide the stock's closing price (the price of the last trade of the day) and the number of shares traded (called "volume"). Additional information may include the highest and lowest prices of the day and of the previous 12 months, the change in price from today's closing price to the closing price on the previous trading day, the dividend yield, and the P/E ratio (explained shortly). Figure 11.2 illustrates a quote for Mead prior to its merger with Westvaco.

TOPIC **LINKS**

Find a stock's quotation.

While newspaper quotes are still useful, investors today clearly use the Internet much more often to obtain quotes and much additional information about a stock. Moreover, these quotes are available throughout the trading today. As an exercise, you should access the Yahoo! Web site. Click on "Finance" and then enter a stock symbol (say, MWV) in the "Quote" box. Then observe the rich amount of information available, both on the current page and on other options available from that page. If you are not sure of a stock's trading symbol, you can find it by clicking on "Symbol Lookup" at the Quote box.

You probably will not understand many of the notations. Some are explained later in this chapter, but you can also access a glossary that defines a large array of terms and expressions. On the Finance page, access "Glossary" at the Education heading under Investing. As in most activities, practice will improve your skills. So, as we suggested in Chapter 9, put together a simple portfolio and measure your success over some designated period of time. Actually, you can create a portfolio at the Yahoo! Finance that is automatically updated throughout the trading day. The site does all the work, but we see that as a disadvantage in your learning stage. After you gain expertise, delegate the work to the site.

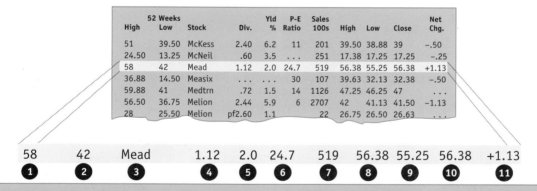

| 52 Weeks | | | | Yld | P-E | Sales | | | | Net |
High	Low	Stock	Div.	%	Ratio	100s	High	Low	Close	Chg.
51	39.50	McKess	2.40	6.2	11	201	39.50	38.88	39	−.50
24.50	13.25	McNeil	.60	3.5	. . .	251	17.38	17.25	17.25	−.25
58	42	Mead	1.12	2.0	24.7	519	56.38	55.25	56.38	+1.13
36.88	14.50	Measix	. . .	. . .	30	107	39.63	32.13	32.38	−.50
59.88	41	Medtrn	.72	1.5	14	1126	47.25	46.25	47	. . .
56.50	36.75	Melion	2.44	5.9	6	2707	42	41.13	41.50	−1.13
28	25.50	Melion	pf2.60	1.1		22	26.75	26.50	26.63	. . .

58	42	Mead	1.12	2.0	24.7	519	56.38	55.25	56.38	+1.13
1	2	3	4	5	6	7	8	9	10	11

1. The highest price per share paid in the past year, $58 for Mead.

2. The lowest price per share paid in the last year. Mead's lowest price was $42.

3. The company's name, which is usually abbreviated. For example, McKess is McKesson and Robbins, a pharmaceutical company.

4. The indicated regular dividend in the current year based on what the company has paid in the last quarter or six months. Some companies also pay extra dividends in good earnings years, but these are not shown. Mead's regular dividend was estimated at $1.12 a share.

5. The current yield, which is found by dividing the current year regular dividends by the closing price of the stock. Mead's current yield is 2.0 percent.

6. The price-earnings ratio, which is the company's earnings over its last fiscal year divided into the closing price of the stock. Mead's ratio is 24.7.

7. The number of shares sold on that day, in hundreds. For example, 519 means 51,900 shares of Mead stock.

8. The highest price paid for the stock that day. Mead's was $56.38.

9. The lowest price paid for the stock that day. Mead's was $55.25.

10. The last price paid that day. Mead's was $56.38.

11. The difference between the closing price that day and the closing price of the previous day. For example, Mead's closing price on the previous day was $1.13 lower than its closing price on the reported day.

Figure 11.2

How to Read Stock Quotations

FUNDAMENTAL ANALYSIS OF COMMON STOCKS

TOPIC **LINKS**

Access fundamental data.

What is a stock worth? In mid-August 2004, Mead was selling at around $30. Was it worth that much, or was it worth more, or less? These are very difficult questions to answer, but investors must at least try; otherwise, securities could sell at any set of prices. You may choose not to undertake value analysis on your own, but even if you rely on professional analysts' opinions, you should be familiar with their techniques. We will consider two basic approaches—application of the CAPM (introduced in the previous chapter) and a price-to-earnings analysis. The section concludes with a discussion of book value. Much of the discussion uses information provided in Table 11.1, which compares Mead with two other companies, Gillette and Intel. All of the data were readily available from the Yahoo! Finance Internet site.

Application of the CAPM

In the previous chapter we learned that a stock offers two pertinent returns: (1) a required return, which reflects its individual risk and a risk premium for the overall stock market, and (2) an expected return, which reflects what you as an investor believe the stock will offer in terms of a cash dividend or potential price appreciation. The required return concept was developed thoroughly in the previous chapter; now let's turn our attention to the expected return.

Recall from Chapter 10 that the expected total return, TR, is the sum of current return, CR, and future return, FR; that is,

$$TR = CR + FR$$

Current return (also called the "yield") can be expressed in ratio or percentage form. For example, if you expected to receive a $0.98 dividend on a share of Mead over the next

Company Ticker Symbol	Mead MWV	Gillette G	Intel INTC
1. Current (mid-2004) stock price	$30.00	$41.00	$22.00
2. Dividends per share (DPS):			
(a) paid over previous 12 months	$ 0.92	$ 0.65	$ 0.16
(b) estimated for next 12 months	$ 0.98	$ 0.74	$ 0.19
3. Earnings per share (EPS):			
(a) earned over previous 12 months	$ 0.61	$ 1.55	$ 1.10
(b) expected over the next 12 months	$ 0.68	$ 1.83	$ 1.37
4. Estimated five-year average annual EPS growth	7.0%	13.9%	15.5%
5. Price/Earnings (P/E) ratio:			
(a) based on previous 12-month EPS	49.2	26.5	20.0
(b) based on expected 12-month EPS	44.1	22.4	16.1
6. Book value per share	$23.06	$ 2.45	$ 6.02
7. Market to book ratio (line 1 divided by line 6)	1.30	16.73	3.66
8. P/E to growth (PEG) ratio (line 5b divided by line 4)	6.30	1.61	1.04
9. Beta value	1.06	0.36	2.12
10. Weighted average analysts' recommendations (1.0 = highest rank, 5.0 = worst rank)	2.60	2.50	2.10

Table 11.1

Selected Financial Data for Three Companies

12 months, and if you paid $30 a share, your expected current return would be 3.3 percent, calculated as follows:

$$CR\% = \frac{\$0.98}{\$30.00} = 0327 \text{ or } 3.3\%$$

Earnings as a Source of Dividends

All dividends must come eventually from earnings. If a corporation's dividends exceed the sum of its current earnings and earnings it has accumulated in the past, then it is actually liquidating itself. It is relatively easy for potential investors to estimate a current dividend, because it is also relatively easy to estimate both a company's current earnings and the proportion of those earnings it is likely to distribute. Moreover, many companies indicate what the current dividend will be. But it is not so easy to estimate future earnings and future dividends. How much Mead will earn per share in 2006 or 2008 is not an easily answered question. Nor is it easy to know the company's future policy with respect to dividend distributions. Mead might undergo a complete change in the nature of its business, and this change might demand more cash, forcing Mead to cut the proportion of its earnings it pays in dividends.

Expressing Future Return in the Total Return Equation

Bringing future return into the total return equation is done most easily by expressing it as a percentage return, and the most commonly used percentage is the company's expected *annual growth* in dividends (or earnings) in the future. So, if you thought Mead's dividends would grow at a 7.0 percent annual rate each year in the future, this is its future return percentage. Add this to the current return percentage to arrive at the total return percentage; that is,

$$TR\% = CR\% + FR\% = 3.3\% + 7.0\% = 10.3\%$$

It makes sense to include the dividend growth factor since a stock with a growing dividend should be worth more than one without growth. Moreover, the growth factor allows you to make return comparisons among different stocks with different current return characteristics. For example, Mead's $0.98 dividend will grow to $1.37 in five years at Mead's growth rate of 7.0 percent. But Gillette's $0.74 dividend will grow to $1.42 in five years. Of course, Gillette's advantage grows larger each year thereafter.

Was Mead Worth $30 a Share?

To answer this question, recall from the previous chapter the concept of alpha, which is calculated as follows:

Alpha = expected return − required return

Greater positive values of alpha signal greater investment appeal; conversely, negative alpha values indicate stocks that should not be bought and perhaps should be sold, if you already own them.

Figure 11.3 summarizes the evaluation of Mead. Short-term Treasury bills yielded about 1.5 percent when the analysis was undertaken. Notice in Table 11.1 that we use Mead's expected growth in earnings, because it generally is the best estimate of future dividend-paying capacity.

Figure 11.3

*Comparing Mead's Required
Rate of Return with Its
Expected Rate of Return,
Mid-August 2004*

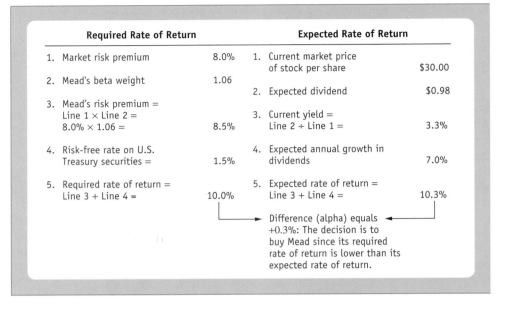

Required Rate of Return		Expected Rate of Return	
1. Market risk premium	8.0%	1. Current market price of stock per share	$30.00
2. Mead's beta weight	1.06	2. Expected dividend	$0.98
3. Mead's risk premium = Line 1 × Line 2 = 8.0% × 1.06 =	8.5%	3. Current yield = Line 2 ÷ Line 1 =	3.3%
4. Risk-free rate on U.S. Treasury securities =	1.5%	4. Expected annual growth in dividends	7.0%
5. Required rate of return = Line 3 + Line 4 =	10.0%	5. Expected rate of return = Line 3 + Line 4 =	10.3%

Difference (alpha) equals +0.3%: The decision is to buy Mead since its required rate of return is lower than its expected rate of return.

Figure 11.3 shows that Mead has a positive alpha value of 0.3 percent. Mead, then, represented a "buy" at the time of the analysis. However, the alpha value is not so large that we classify Mead as a "strong buy." Investment analysis is not rocket science, and it's quite possible that the estimate of Mead's 7.0 percent growth rate is too optimistic.

Financial Analysts' Opinions

Line 10 in Table 11.1 summarizes the opinions of financial analysts who follow the three stocks. These are trained professionals who use a variety of analytical techniques to determine the investment quality of a stock. While their opinions are certainly worth reviewing, you shouldn't buy a stock simply because it has a high rating since the stock may not fit your investment objectives. Moreover, analysts tend to be somewhat optimistic in their growth projections. Also, be careful of a recommendation if it is made by only one or two analysts. It is better to have a weighted average of, say, six or more analysts. The weighted average recommendations in Table 11.1 reflect more than a dozen analysts for each stock. As you see, Intel receives the highest recommendation of the three. While interpretations can differ, you might consider a 1.0 to 2.0 rating as a buy recommendation, a 2.0 to 3.0 rating as a hold (if you currently own the stock), and anything over 3.0 as a sell rating (if you own the stock).

Price-to-Earnings Analysis

Price-to-earnings analysis:
A method of valuing common stocks based on a company's expected future earnings.

Earnings per share (EPS):
A company's total earnings divided by the total number of shares of common stock outstanding.

Price-earnings (P/E) ratio:
The price of a company's stock divided by the company's earnings per share.

A **price-to-earnings analysis** is a somewhat simpler and more direct approach than the CAPM method. Basically, analysts who follow this approach feel that the price of a share of a company's stock depends entirely on the company's future **earnings per share (EPS).** EPS is simply the company's total earnings divided by the total number of shares of common stock outstanding.

Analysts also use a **price-earnings (P/E) ratio,** which reflects how much a stock is worth in relation to its EPS; that is,

$$P/E \text{ ratio} = \frac{\text{stock's price}}{\text{EPS}}$$

Financial Analysts: Do They Help or Hinder?

Financial analysts are professional people whose main function is to evaluate companies with respect to their financial strengths and weaknesses. The end product of their work is a research report that includes rating companies as to whether they are buys, holds (if you already own them), or sells. Some analysts are independent operators, but most are employed by large financial institutions, particularly large stockbrokerage firms. On balance, analysts do a good job and are an important component in the overall investment process. Certainly, their efforts make the process more efficient than it would be in their absence. However, in recent years problems have surfaced that should prompt investors to be cautious when following analysts' opinions.

Appearing before the House Financial Services Sub-committee, Chairperson of the SEC, Laura Ungar, testified that nearly 30 percent of analysts whom the SEC surveyed owned shares in companies they covered. On the face of it, this should not necessarily be cause for concern; indeed, you can make a case that "putting their money where their mouths are" makes analysts' opinions more credible. However, the SEC report also noted that some analysts made between $300,000 and $3.5 million trading *against* their own advice—selling their shares while telling us to buy. Surely, an ethical issue seems at play here.

Another study, involving four years of data, prepared by Investars.com (a subscription online investment service) showed that investors lost 53.34 percent by following the advice of analysts whose firms led or comanaged an IPO versus a loss of 4.24 percent by following nonaffiliated analysts. (IPO stands for initial public offering—the first time a company's shares are sold to the public.) Although the latter figure is hardly encouraging, the former is absolutely dreadful.

The securities industry has paid over $1.4 billion to settle claims arising from past abuses, and congress passed the Sarbanes-Oxley Act in 2002 in an attempt to curb abuses in the future. How has Sarbanes-Oxley worked so far? While a full evaluation will take time, we do know that the distribution of analyst ratings has changed dramatically. In early May 2004, about 9 percent of all ratings were "sell" or "under perform"; in 2000, not even 1 percent were in these categories. Some indication remains, though, that investment banking clients are viewed more favorably than nonclients. If you are considering investing in a particular company, you should review not only the overall ratings for the company but determine if your broker's rating is in step with most others, and if the firm has any financial connections with the recommended company. You are entitled to that information and should ask for it.

So if a stock earns $1.50 per share and if a P/E ratio of 12.0 seems appropriate for valuation purposes, rearranging the foregoing equation shows that the stock's price should be $18.00 a share:

$$\text{Stock's price} = \text{EPS} \times \text{P/E ratio}$$

$$\$18 = \$1.50 \times 12$$

A price-to-earnings analysis is only as good as the analyst's estimates of EPS and the P/E ratio. Further discussion of each is needed.

Use Future (Not Past) EPS Amounts

Past earnings, though interesting from a historical perspective or in helping to forecast future earnings, are not integral in the valuation process. In a sense, past earnings have already been distributed or used by the company. So their impact on the company's value has already been felt. But future earnings can influence this value by being greater or less than past earnings. To use a sports example: You wouldn't pay a top price for athletes who are in the twilight of their careers, no matter how great they may have been in their prime. This seems a bit harsh, but the investment world is brutal. The moment a stock fails to live up to investors' expectations, its price falls dramatically as they rush to "dump" the stock.

What Is an Appropriate P/E Value?

Determining a P/E ratio to apply to future EPS amounts is unquestionably the most troublesome task in using a price-to-earnings analysis. We must carefully distinguish between a *calculated* P/E ratio and an *appropriate* P/E ratio to use. For example, Mead's P/E ratio of 49.2 is based on past year's earnings (line 3a). Similarly, the P/E ratio of 44.1 reflects the expected next year EPS amount. Both are calculated ratios. Now, analysts may use these P/E ratios in a comparative way to determine if a company is over or undervalued. For example, other paper companies may show P/E ratios (based on next year's earnings) of, say, 25 or less. In this comparative sense, then, Mead's ratio is rather high.

Continuing the example, let us say that the other paper companies' P/E ratios have an average value of 25. If we think this average should apply to Mead, then we are using an appropriate ratio to value Mead, and we call the resulting number Mead's **fundamental value.** In the example, it is $17.00 To reinforce the concept:

> **Fundamental value:** A stock value based on the underlying strengths of a company.

$$\text{Fundamental value} = (\text{appropriate P/E ratio}) \times (\text{next year's EPS})$$
$$= 25 \times \$0.68$$
$$= \$17.00$$

Since Mead is selling at $30 a share, it is clearly overvalued and should be sold. Of course, you can question if using the average is a reasonable approach. To the extent that there might be considerable manufacturing, marketing, and financial differences among the firms, using an average accomplishes very little. Still, if not the average—then what?

The PEG Ratio

Some analysts think that a company's future growth rate (expressed as a number rather than as a percent) should serve as a reasonable estimate of an appropriate P/E ratio. Applying this logic to Mead leads to a very low value of $4.76 (7 × $0.68), since Mead's growth rate is only 7.0. In common with most price-to-earnings approaches, this one also fails to consider a stock's riskiness. Two companies with equal earnings and growing at the same rate may have very different market values if they differ in risk.

Despite its shortcomings, analysts often compare a company's P/E ratio to its growth rate. This comparison is called the **PEG ratio.** Mead's PEG ratio is calculated next:

> **PEG ratio:** The ratio of a stock's P/E ratio to the expected annual rate of growth of earnings per share (EPS).

$$\text{PEG ratio} = \text{P/E ratio} / \text{growth}$$
$$= 44.1 / 7.0 = 6.30$$

All other things held equal, the lower the number, the more attractive the stock. The basic idea is not to pay too much for growth. For example, Gillette's PEG ratio is 1.61 and Intel's is 1.04. Unfortunately, there is no simple answer to the question of what is "too much." While Intel's ratio is attractive, it also is the most risky of the three companies, as measured by beta.

Fundamental Value and Book Value

> **Book value:** A company's net worth divided by the number of common stock shares outstanding.

Investors often refer to a company's **book value,** which is determined by dividing a company's net worth by the number of shares of common stock outstanding. The net worth of a business is measured in the same way that someone's personal net worth is measured; that is, net worth equals total assets minus total liabilities. (Refer to Chapter 3 if you need to review the concept.) Table 11.1 shows Mead's book value in line 6. As you see, Mead had a book value of $23.06 at mid-August 2004.

How about $766 Million for a $100 Investment?

Sounds like a scam, until we provide some background. First, it would have taken 198 years to earn that return—1802 through 2000. And, if you held on through 2002, your wealth would have declined to $459 million. Oh well, easy come, easy go! Actually, you might be surprised at the rate of return over the 200-year period. Unless you have some experience with the time value of money, you are likely to guess a fairly high rate, say 20 percent. Actually, the rate is *only* 7.9 percent.

Robert D. Arnott provided this information in an article in the *Financial Analysts Journal* (March/April 2003). Mr. Arnott also puts forth an equally interesting insight on the return components: 5.0 percentage points (or 63.3 percent of the total return, 5.0/7.9) is attributable exclusively to dividend yield, while the balance (36.7 percent) arose from an inflation return, rising valuation levels, and the real growth in dividends. We can view the 5 percent dividend return in a way similar to how we view the yield on bonds; for example, a 5 percent coupon bond selling at par.

Mr. Arnott makes a strong case that the findings are somewhat at odds with the perspective we typically take on common stock investments. We tend to justify their rather low current dividend yields on the argument that dividend growth is far more important. However, that seems not to be the case. Mr. Arnott further points out that since 1965, the inflation-adjusted growth of earnings and dividends of stocks in the S&P 500 stock index has been exactly *zero*. (We should note, though, that simply matching the inflation rate since 1965 is no small accomplishment. Moreover, bond coupon payments never grow and bond returns are always eroded by inflation.)

Several lessons might be drawn from this analysis. Mr. Arnott shows concern with the overall stock market because the dividend yield on stocks (around 2 percent in mid-2004) is far below the historical average of 5 percent. So, it seems we are asking for considerably higher growth rates in the future than we have experienced in the past. At a micro level, the lesson for young adults might be to focus much of your attention when selecting stocks on their current dividend yields and capacity to sustain those yields in the future. Don't ignore earnings and dividend growth, but don't fixate on them either.

Book Value's Limitations

If Mead's book value is only $23.06, why should anyone pay $30? The answer is that book value often is a poor estimate of fundamental value. Book value reflects the historical costs of a company's assets, which may be poor indicators of the current or replacement costs of those assets. Moreover, what a company paid for an asset may have little connection to the asset's ability to generate future cash inflows to the company. Also, perhaps the most valuable of all assets—a company's goodwill—is not even shown on its balance sheet. What is the brand name Coca-Cola worth? If you guess "a lot," you are correct; it's probably worth far more than all of Coke's other assets combined. Yet it is not listed on Coke's balance sheet. These limitations make book value a poor estimate of fundamental value in most cases.

Market-to-Book Ratios

However, it would be a mistake to conclude that book value has no use whatsoever. If, over time, the price of a company's stock increases (or decreases) more rapidly than its book value increases (or decreases), we might want to know why. If there is no underlying explanation, then perhaps the stock is being overvalued (or undervalued) in the market. So analysts often examine a company's **market-to-book ratio,** which is simply market price divided by book value. Mead's ratio is 1.30 as shown in line 7 of Table 11.1.

Market-to-book ratio: The market price of a common stock divided by its book value.

Most stocks have market-to-book ratios greater than 1.0, and these values change considerably over time. For example, since 1960, the average ratio for the 500 stocks in the Standard & Poor 500 Stock Average (the S&P 500) has varied from 1.13 (1982) to 6.98 (2000).

All other things equal, analysts prefer low market-to-book values rather than high values. Indeed, some analysts feel that you will find more undervalued stocks if you limit your analyses to companies with low ratios. If you follow their advice you might be attracted to Mead, and you probably would ignore Gillette and Intel. Many other analysts argue that could be a big mistake. Their view is probably the correct one, since there is no reason to limit your perspective in searching for good investments. Try to apply the CAPM or price-to-earnings method to any company. Be careful, though, if a company seems terribly undervalued. Our introductory treatment of valuation cannot cover all possible problems. If you are going to make your own stock selections, you really should learn more about investments. Taking an investments course at a university would be very helpful.

CORPORATE-ISSUED BONDS

Corporations raise far more money selling bonds to investors than they do selling common stocks. Think of a bond as an IOU: that is, as a piece of paper proclaiming the fact that its issuer acknowledges owing you money and agreeing to repay your loan at some future date along with interest at periodic intervals. This idea seems simple enough, but there are numerous details that must be addressed, particularly with corporate bonds.

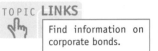

TOPIC **LINKS**

Find information on corporate bonds.

Your Rights as a Bondholder

Bond indenture: Document accompanying a bond issue—a contract between the issuer and bondholders.

Just as stockholders have certain rights, so do bondholders. Bondholders' rights are described clearly in a document that accompanies each bond issue—the **bond indenture.** The indenture is actually a contract between the issuing institution and the bondholders. In some respects it is similar to a loan agreement you sign when you borrow from a bank. Since it is impossible for the issuer to have an individual contract with each bondholder, the indenture acts as a comprehensive contract covering all bondholders. To see that the issuer lives up to its agreements in the indenture, a trustee (which is usually a large commercial bank) is appointed to represent bondholders.

Protective covenants: Restrictions placed on a bond issuer designed to strengthen the bondholders' position.

Mortgage bonds: Bonds secured by collateral.

Because of the risk of bankruptcy, many bond indentures contain **protective covenants** (restrictions) to strengthen the bondholders' position. Perhaps the best protection is provided by **mortgage bonds,** which are secured by collateral. In the event of bankruptcy, the bondholders' interest is protected by the pledged property, which does not have to be shared with other creditors or stockholders.

Debentures: Bonds not secured by collateral.

Bonds without supporting collateral are called **debentures,** and there are still other bonds that offer even less protection. These are called **subordinated debentures.** If you buy this kind of bond, your claim to assets in liquidation are subordinated to (meaning they come after) the claims of another issue.

Subordinated debentures: Bonds with claims given to other bond issues.

Payment Characteristics of Bonds

Fixed return: A return of a specific dollar amount each year, characteristic of bonds and preferred stock.

Regardless of who issues them, bonds have many similar characteristics. The most important of these is the **fixed return.** Let's look at the return components in greater detail.

Face Value

Face value: An amount for which a bond is redeemed at maturity.

The **face value** of a bond is the amount for which the issuer agrees to redeem the bond at its maturity. When a bond is issued, it has a set life; for example, a 25-year bond means the bond may not be redeemed by its issuer until 25 years after the date it is issued.

Practically all corporate bonds sold to the public have the same face value—$1,000—although some (mostly those issued by various governments) have higher face values. When a bond series is issued, the issuer attempts to adjust its interest rate so that it can be sold *at par*, which means it is sold at the face value. However, bonds issued in the past and currently traded on bond markets may have market prices completely different from their face values, because interest rates may have increased or decreased since their issuance.

Semiannual Interest Payments

Most bonds pay interest twice a year and are referred to as **coupon bonds.** The amount of interest you receive is stated on the bond and expressed as a percentage of par value. For example, a 12 percent bond pays $120 a year ($1,000 × 0.12) in interest, or $60 each six months. This rate is often called the **coupon rate.** This term is a carryover from the past, when most bonds were coupon bonds and you received interest by clipping coupons from the bond and presenting them to a bank for payment. Since all corporate bonds now are registered, rather than coupon bonds, the interest checks come directly to you, or to your broker if your certificates are held at a firm.

Coupon bonds: Bonds that pay periodic interest.

Coupon rate: Stated interest rate on a bond.

Zero Coupon Bonds

A **zero coupon bond** (zero, for short) is a bond that pays no semiannual interest; you earn interest by buying the bond at less than face value and receiving face value at redemption. For example, you buy a bond for $940 today and have it redeemed for $1,000 one year later. The interest earned is $60 in this case, and the percentage return (yield) is 6.383 percent ([$60/$940] × 100). Zero coupon bonds have increased considerably in popularity in recent years, primarily because investors like to hold them for retirement funds.

Zero coupon bond: A bond that pays no periodic interest; all interest is earned at the bond's redemption.

Zeros are issued in a wide array of maturities, some as long as 40 years. For any given yield, the longer a bond's maturity the bigger the difference between its price and its redemption value, called the *discount*. So, a two-year zero with a 6.38 percent yield would have a price of $883.60 and a discount of $116.40 ($1,000.00 − $883.60). We'll discuss valuation methods for both coupon bonds and zeros more fully later in this chapter.

Retirement Methods

Although many bond issues have long maturities, in reality most such bonds are retired (terminated) long before their maturity dates. There are three retirement methods: redemption at maturity or by a call from the issuer, through the operation of a sinking fund, or with a conversion of the bond into shares of the issuer's common stock.

Redemption at Maturity or Earlier

As mentioned earlier, the issuer agrees to redeem your bond at its maturity. However, many corporate bonds (and some government bonds) can be redeemed earlier at the discretion of the issuer. These **callable bonds** allow the issuer an earlier redemption, and such redemption usually takes place at a price above face value. For example, a bond may be callable at $1,100. Corporations attach calls to bonds to give them greater flexibility in future financing. However, the call feature may be a disadvantage to investors, who should review the call situation before buying a bond.

Callable bonds: Bonds that can be redeemed before their maturities.

Sinking Funds

Another retirement method involves the use of a **sinking fund,** which consists of reserving funds for the purpose of gradually retiring bonds before their maturity. Most sinking funds operate through a plan stipulating that a portion of the bonds in a bond issue be retired each year. This gradual retirement of an issue provides greater safety to bondholders as opposed to having all the bonds redeemable at one time.

Sinking fund: A system for gradual retirement of a bond issue.

The Convertible Feature

A particularly attractive bond to potential common stock investors is the convertible bond. A **convertible bond** may be redeemed, but it may also be converted into shares of the issuing corporation's common stock. For example, a bond may convert into 20 shares of the company's common stock. Convertible bonds are quite different from conventional bonds.

Convertible bond: Bond that can be converted into shares of the issuer's common stock.

They offer potentially higher returns by virtue of their conversion privilege, but they are also riskier.

Investing in Corporate Bonds

After you have a reasonable understanding of bond valuation techniques, you might decide to be a corporate bond investor. At this point, you must become familiar with the mechanics of making your investments.

Trading Costs

The cost to trade corporate bonds can be quite high. First, you typically buy bonds through a stockbrokerage firm and, of course, pay a commission. The amount varies from one firm to the next, but expect to pay a cost of $25 to $40 per bond if you buy one bond. The cost per bond goes down substantially if you increase the size of your order.

Most securities, including bonds, are traded in the market at bid and asked prices. A bid price is the highest price a buyer is willing to pay to buy a bond; the asked price is the lowest price a seller will take to sell it. The asked price is always higher than the bid price, and the difference is called the *spread*. So if you buy a bond, you will pay the asked price, but you receive only the bid price when you sell. The trouble with bonds is that the spread often is large, sometimes as much as $50 per bond. Obviously, the spread adds to your trading cost and certainly discourages frequent trading. As with common stocks, if you invest in bonds you should have a long investment horizon.

Pooling Arrangements May Be Best

Along with the potential for high trading costs, bond investors must constantly be on guard to determine if their bonds have been called. Failing to meet a call does not mean you lose the value of your bond, but it does mean that you lose any interest payments that were scheduled to be made after the call date.

All things considered, investing in bonds should perhaps be left to investment professionals. Not only can they operate with much smaller trading costs and follow individual bond issues more closely, but they also are able to diversify far more effectively. We are better off by simply investing in a mutual fund, or other pooling arrangement, that invests in bonds. We'll cover these investment vehicles in the next chapter.

GOVERNMENT-ISSUED BONDS

As noted earlier, corporations raise huge sums of money each year by selling bonds, but government units raise even more. You have heard of the national debt, which the government is trying to reduce. We discuss the variety of government-issued bonds in the following sections.

U.S. Treasury Securities

TOPIC **LINKS**

Find information on a Treasury Direct Account.

U.S. Treasury securities are the most popular investment vehicles in the world. They are owned by investors throughout all parts of the world and are actively traded 24 hours a day. Treasury securities are issued in three forms: Treasury bills, with maturities of one year or less; Treasury notes, with maturities from 2 to 10 years; and Treasury bonds, with maturities from 10 to 30 years. Treasury bills are held for liquidity purposes as discussed in Chapter 5, so we will focus on bonds and notes. Also, the term *Treasury bonds* (T-bonds, for short, or simply Treasuries) is often used to describe both notes and bonds, and we will

Type of Bond	2001	2004
Corporate bonds: best quality	6.93%	5.47%
medium quality	7.69	5.95
U.S. Treasury bonds	5.58	5.07
General obligation municipal bonds	5.26	4.51

make no distinction between the two in our discussion. With the exception of maturity, notes and bonds are identical.

T-Bond Payments

T-bonds are issued only in coupon form, and they pay semiannual interest. As with corporate bonds, par value is $1,000, and interest payments depend on the coupon rate. For example, an 8 percent bond pays $40 interest each six-month period. Since T-bonds have no default risk, their yields always are lower than all other comparable-maturity bonds. Table 11.2 shows a variety of bond yields in 2001 and 2000 and, as you see, Treasuries' yields are the lowest in each year with the exception of municipal bond yields. An income tax advantage explains this oddity, and we'll discuss it later.

Simplifying FINANCIAL Planning

BOX 11.3

Buy Treasuries Directly

Investors throughout the world consider U.S. Treasury–issued securities the bedrock of safety. Actually, from a safety perspective a Treasury security is the same as currency itself; the major difference is that one pays interest and the other does not. Despite the advantages, unfortunately, small investors seldom buy Treasuries, primarily because they are unaware of how easy it is.

That might change in the future, though, since buying Treasuries now can be done directly through the Treasury, eliminating the middleman and the usual buy/sell commissions. Over 1 million Americans are currently using the Treasury Direct program, and the number is growing rapidly.

It's simple to sign up: Get an application form from the nearest Federal Reserve Bank or one of its branches. Or download a copy from the Bureau of the Public Debt's Internet site **www.publicdebt.treas.gov**. Fill out the form, being careful to include your Social Security number and your bank's nine-digit "routing transit" number (call your bank if you aren't sure of the number).

Treasuries are sold at auctions, and you must be sure to submit the application before the auction day. Information about upcoming auctions will be available at the Federal Reserve Bank. Your application is referred to as a "noncompetitive tender," which means that you agree to accept the average yield that arises from competitive bidding at the auction.

After the purchase you now have a Treasury Direct account. Interest paid on the securities each six months will be forwarded to your bank, as will the redemption of the securities at their maturity. What could be easier? Finally, a brief summary of Treasury securities is shown next.

Security Name	Maturity	Minimum Investment	Interest Information
U.S. Treasury bills	Up to 1 year	$1,000 (cashier's check)	Interest is earned via a discount from $1,000
U.S. Treasury notes	2–10 years	$1,000–$5,000 (personal check)	Interest is paid semiannually
U.S. Treasury bonds	10–30 years	$1,000 (personal check)	Interest is paid semiannually

U.S. Treasury Strips

U.S. Treasury Strips: Zero coupon bonds derived from U.S. Treasury coupon bonds.

Although the Treasury does not issue zero coupon bonds, it provides a mechanism that allows large brokerage firms to create such bonds, and these are called **U.S. Treasury Strips** (STRIPS, for short). The creation process is somewhat involved and of little concern to investors; however, they are indeed concerned that STRIPS also be free of default risk. And they are. As with zero coupon corporate bonds, but to a much greater extent, Treasury Strips are an appealing vehicle for retirement investments.

U.S. Treasury Inflation-Indexed Bonds

Inflation-indexed Treasury bonds: Bonds issued by the U.S. Treasury with redemption values that are adjusted each year for inflation.

In 1996, the Treasury issued a new class of bonds, called **inflation-indexed Treasury bonds.** This new bond is unique in that its redemption value will be adjusted each year to keep pace with inflation. For example, assume that on January 2, 2006, you bought one of the new bonds at its face value of $1,000. Suppose, then, that inflation for 2006 is determined to be 3 percent; then the redemption value of the bond is adjusted upwards to $1,030. Such an adjustment would occur each year until the bond's maturity. So, if inflation was 10 percent in 2007, the bond's redemption value would be increased to $1,133 ($1.10 \times \$1,030$).

The assurance that your investment's value will not be ravaged by inflation is clearly an advantage over traditional bonds with fixed redemption amounts. But, of course, there is a catch: The inflation-indexed bonds offer lower coupon interest payments than conventional Treasuries. The extent of the difference varies over time and was around 2.0 percent at mid-August 2004 on the 30-year bond.

U.S. Agency Bonds

Agency bonds: Bonds issued by agencies of the federal government other than the Treasury.

Agencies of the federal government besides the Treasury also issue notes and bonds, which are referred to as **agency bonds.** There are two types of agency bonds—those that are virtually identical to Treasury bonds and those related to mortgage and other forms of lending. The former are referred to as conventional agency bonds, and the latter are called mortgage-backed bonds.

Conventional Agency Bonds

Conventional agency bonds have the same features as coupon Treasury bonds, and their prices are also reported in the financial pages. Although considered by most investors to be also free of default risk, these bonds usually offer a slightly higher yield. The difference is explained by poorer liquidity in the sense that there is less trading of agency bonds and greater bid-asked price spreads. Investors who do not trade bonds frequently perhaps can ignore this lack of liquidity and go for agencies' better yields.

Mortgage-Backed Bonds

Mortgage-backed bonds: Agency bonds that "pass through" interest and principal payments from a pool of mortgages.

Certain agencies of the federal government are involved in the credit industry. For example, you may buy a home and finance it with a mortgage loan from a local bank. Although you may never know it, the bank might sell the mortgage to the Government National Mortgage Association (GNMA), which buys many similar loans and holds them in what is called a "pool." GNMA then issues bonds to investors on the basis of the payments being collected in the pool. The cash collected by the pool is distributed (said to be "passed through") to the investors; in this fashion, the bonds are supported by the mortgages and so are called **mortgage-backed bonds.** Such bonds issued by the GNMA are called "Ginnie Maes." Although not a mortgage loan, your student loan has probably been sold by the lending bank to the Student Loan Marketing Association, which creates bonds (called "Sallie Maes") that are supported by pools of student loans. The complexities of mortgage-backed bonds offer a strong incentive to invest in them through a mutual fund rather than on your own.

Municipal Bonds

Municipal bonds (referred to as munis) are bonds issued by state and local governmental units to finance their capital spending programs. An average of about $200 billion of municipal bonds are issued each year, and they are very popular with investors in high tax brackets.

Types of Municipal Bonds

If a muni bond issue is supported by the full taxing authority of the issuing governmental unit, it is a **general obligation (GO) bond;** if it is supported only by the revenues that a particular capital project generates, it is a **revenue bond.** In general, GO bonds offer better protection than revenue bonds and, therefore, are safer investments. As you might guess, GO bond yields, such as those shown in Table 11.2, are a bit lower than revenue bonds.

Munis are issued in coupon and zero coupon form with face values usually $5,000. You should realize that munis can have default risk even though they are issued by a government. It is not uncommon for municipalities to default on their bond issues.

The Income Tax Advantage

Any interest received from a municipal bond is free of federal income tax. This is a major advantage for munis versus taxable bonds. The muni yields in Table 11.2 are the lowest of all shown. However, to put them on a comparable footing with the other bond yields, you need to adjust for the income tax differential. To do this, we calculate a muni's **pretax equivalent yield,** which is the yield a taxable bond must offer before taxes to have the same after-tax yield as the muni. The pretax equivalent yield (*PTEY*), considering a 28% investor's marginal tax rate (*MTR*), is calculated as follows:

$$PTEY = \frac{\text{muni yield}}{1.0 - MTR}$$

So the 5.26 percent muni yield in 2001 has the pretax equivalent yield of 7.31 percent (5.26%/[1.0 − 0.28] = 5.26%/0.72). A similar calculation for 2000 provides 6.26 percent (4.51%/0.72). When adjusted for taxes, the muni yields in Table 11.2 are among the highest each year.

RETURN AND RISK CHARACTERISTICS OF BONDS

Clearly, there are reasons why bond investment is so popular. Although young people tend to favor common stocks, seeking their long-term growth, other investors are drawn to the more certain cash payments bonds offer. But there is substantial risk in bond investing, and informed investors of all ages must understand its sources and how it operates. The following sections explain both return and risk characteristics of bonds.

Expected Return from Bonds

If you bought a bond at its face value when it was issued and eventually redeemed it at its face value, then your return would consist exclusively of the semiannual interest payments

Municipal bonds: Bonds issued by state and local governments.

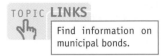
TOPIC **LINKS**
Find information on municipal bonds.

General obligation (GO) bond: A municipal bond supported by the full taxing authority of the issuing governmental unit.

Revenue bond: A municipal bond supported by the revenues of a particular project.

Pretax equivalent yield: A pre-tax yield a taxable bond must offer to have the same after-tax yield as a municipal bond.

you would receive each year. The preceding situation may not happen, however. You may buy the bond for more or less than its face value; doing that leads to a capital loss or gain if you hold it to maturity. Or you may sell the bond before maturity, and the price you receive will probably be different—perhaps quite different—from your purchase price. Therefore, just as with common stocks, a bond's return may consist of both a current return and a future return. Each must be considered in evaluating investment performance.

Current Return or Current Yield

Current yield: A bond's annual interest divided by its market price.

The current return with a bond comes from the semiannual interest payments. This is often expressed in percentage form and is called the **current yield.** To calculate the current yield, all you need to do is divide the annual interest by the current market price of the bond. Suppose you have a bond that pays $120 a year interest: If its current market price is $1,000, then its current yield is 12 percent ($120/$1,000). If its price is $900, its current yield will be 13.3 percent ($120/$900). The formula is

$$\text{Current yield} = \frac{\$I}{\$P}$$

where

I = annual interest

P = current market price

If you refer to the financial section of many newspapers, you will notice that current yields are reported for corporate bonds. Although that information is helpful, you usually want to know more about a bond's return than the current yield. You also want to determine its yield to maturity.

Yield to Maturity

Yield to maturity: A yield measurement that considers a bond's annual interest plus price appreciation or depreciation if the bond is held to maturity.

In addition to current yield, bond investors often are interested in a bond's **yield to maturity,** which may differ from current yield. A yield to maturity is the return you would earn by buying a bond today and holding it until it is redeemed by the issuer. A precise calculation of yield to maturity requires the use of a financial calculator, but a close approximation is possible using the following formula:

$$\text{Yield to maturity} = \frac{\$I + (\$1,000 - \$P)/N}{(\$P + \$1,000)/2}$$

where

I = annual interest

P = current market price

N = number of years remaining to maturity

It is assumed that the bond has a face value of $1,000. Let us return to the bond mentioned previously and assume that its market price is $900 and that it has five years to maturity. Its yield to maturity is 14.7 percent, as calculated next:

$$\frac{\$120 + (\$1,000 - \$900)/5}{(\$900 + \$1,000)/2} = \frac{\$140}{\$950} = 0.147, \text{ or } 14.7\%$$

Present Value of a Coupon Bond

Bond investors often determine a bond's present value. This task is performed quickly with a financial calculator, but it can also be accomplished with present value tables. Recall from Chapter 2 that a present value is simply a discounted future value. To review, if you expected to receive $1,000 one year from today, and if you felt you could earn 10 percent interest on your money, then the $1,000 has a present value of $909.10. You find this amount by multiplying the future value by the present-value-of-$1 factor from Table A.3 in the Appendix at the end of the text. Referring to that table, go to the 10 percent column and the period 1 row; you read 0.9091, and 0.9091 × $1,000 = $909.10.

Remember that discounting is simply the opposite of compounding. So if you invested $909.10 today to earn 10 percent for one year, your accumulation (compounded value) is $1,000 ($909.10 × 1.10 = $1,000).

Table 11.3 shows the present value calculation for the five-year coupon bond we are discussing, using a 15 percent interest rate. The bond has a present value of $899.46, which is approximately its price of $900. Notice that the bond provides two sources of cash inflow: (1) the annual interest of $120 for five years, and (2) the $1,000 redemption value at the end of the fifth year. For simplicity, we assume that the bond pays annual, rather than semiannual, interest. Also, interest is assumed to be paid at the end of each year.

A Quicker Method for Finding Present Value

Table 11.3 is used to illustrate the process of finding a coupon bond's present value. However, a quicker solution uses the present-value-of-$1-annuity table (Table A.4 in the Appendix at the end of the text). There are two operations. First, from Table A.4 find the present value of a $1 annuity for 15 percent and 5 years; it is 3.3522. Multiply this number by the annual interest to find the present value of the coupon interest cash inflows— $402.26 (3.3522 × $120). Second, find the present value of the future redemption value, which has already been done in Table 11.3. The value is $497.20. Add the two present values to arrive at the total present value of $899.46. This quicker method is very desirable if you are examining bonds with long maturities.

TOPIC LINKS

See an example of bond yields and prices.

Present Value of a Zero Coupon Bond

Finding the present value of a zero coupon bond is very simple since there are no coupon interest payments to consider. The only cash inflow to discount is the future redemption

Year	Cash Inflow to Investor		PV of $1 Factor ($i$ = 15%)*	Present Value of the Cash Inflow
1	Interest	$ 120	0.8696	$104.35
2	Interest	120	0.7561	90.73
3	Interest	120	0.6575	78.90
4	Interest	120	0.5718	68.62
5	Interest	120	0.4972	59.66
5	Redemption	1,000	0.4972	497.20
			Bond's present value = total =	$899.46

*PV of $1 factors are found in Table A. in the Appendix at the end of the text. Look in the 15 percent column.

Table 11.3

Finding the Present Value of a Bond

value of $1,000. For example, the present value of a five-year zero discounted at 15 percent is $497.20. Once again, you find this value in Table 11.3.

Present Value and Yield to Maturity

If the bond's cash inflows are discounted by the bond's yield to maturity, the present value is the same as the bond's price. Indeed, the yield to maturity should be viewed as the precise discount rate that equates a bond's price to the sum of its discounted future cash flows. For most practical purposes, 15 percent can be considered the true yield to maturity on the coupon bond since $899.46 is almost $900. Also, we can see that the 14.7 percent estimate using the approximation method is a fairly close estimate.

However, a bond's future cash inflows can be discounted using any rate that the investor feels is relevant. For example, suppose that you are convinced that interest rates will fall in the future and that very shortly our example coupon bond will have a yield to maturity of only 9 percent. What will be its new present value? To find the answer, simply consult Table A.3 in the Appendix at the end of the text and obtain PV of $1 factors from the 9 percent column. Substitute these values for those in Table 11.3 and calculate the new present value. Your answer should be $1,116.65. So, if you are right in your assessment of future interest rates, this bond's price will increase by $216.75 ($1,116.75 − $900.00). But if you are wrong, its price will fall. This potential price volatility is unquestionably a serious risk element that deserves more attention.

Risks of Bond Investment

If you buy a bond, you face two major sources of risk. First, unless you are investing in Treasury or agency bonds, the bond's issuer may default on paying interest or redeeming the bond at maturity. Second, all bond prices, regardless of issuer, are sensitive to changes in the overall level of interest rates.

Default Risk

Default risk: Probability of receiving bond interest and redemption payments.

Default risk has to do with the probability of actually receiving the promised interest and redeeming the bond at face value. If the probabilities of both of these happening are high, the bond is considered low risk; if the probabilities are low, the bond is risky. As we saw earlier in the chapter, default risk depends in large measure on the protections provided in the indenture. All things considered, a subordinated debenture is much riskier than a mortgage bond. But default risk also depends on the financial strength of the issuer. You probably would be safer with a Sears or Du Pont subordinated debenture than a mortgage bond issued by Fly-by-Night Airlines using a dilapidated hangar or vintage airplane as collateral.

Very frankly, very few investors are sufficiently skilled to do their own bond safety analysis; it is far better to rely on professional rating services. The major sources are Standard & Poor's and Moody's and their manuals can be found in most public libraries.

TOPIC **LINKS**

Visit a ratings service company.

Interest Rate Risk

Interest rate risk: Price volatility of a bond in relation to changes in market rates of interest.

After you purchase a bond, your investment will be subject to **interest rate risk.** This risk results from the fact that if credit conditions tighten or loosen after your purchase, interest rates in general will go up or go down. Along with these changes, the market price for your bond will also change, as we have already demonstrated. The primary factor determining how risky a bond is in relation to interest rate changes is its maturity; the longer the maturity, the greater the price volatility and risk. This is seen best through the use of an example.

Table 11.4

Changes in Market Prices of
Three Bonds in Response to
Changes in Interest Rates

	Market Prices		
Yield to Maturity	**1-Year Bond**	**5-Year Bond**	**20-Year Bond**
9%	$1,028	$1,117	$1,274
12%	1,000	1,000	1,000
15%	974	900	812

Change in Yield to Maturity	Change in Market Prices		
Down by 3%	$ +28	$+117	$+274
Up by 3%	−26	−100	−188

Let us assume that you are considering three different bonds each with a 12 percent coupon rate: One matures in one year, another in five years (our previous example bond), and the third in 20 years. Assume further that each is currently selling for $1,000, meaning each has a yield to maturity of 12 percent. Now assume that after you purchase each one, yields to maturity on identical new bonds (1) increase to 15 percent or (2) decrease to 9 percent. Let us see what would happen to the market prices of the three bonds. The new market prices can be calculated using the discounting techniques for finding present values that we just explained. Table 11.4 shows the results. As you see, if yields to maturity rise to 15 percent, your loss is greatest with the 20-year bond and least with the one-year bond; but if interest rates fall, you enjoy the biggest gain with the 20-year bond and, again, the least with the one-year bond. It should be clear that your greatest exposure to risk is with long-maturity bonds.

PREFERRED STOCK

Preferred stock represents another type of fixed-income investment. It is often called a hybrid security because it has characteristics of both common stock and bonds. It is unfortunate the word *preferred* is used to describe this type of security, for it suggests that in some way it must be superior to common stock. Although preferred stock is certainly different from common stock, it isn't necessarily preferable.

Preferred stock: A hybrid security with characteristics of both common stock and bonds.

Characteristics of Preferred Stock

Most of preferred stock's characteristics make it similar to bonds, except one: By law it is considered a form of equity ownership. Therefore, preferred stockholders rank behind bondholders in terms of asset distributions in the event of liquidation. If a corporation files bankruptcy, all its creditors' claims must be settled before any payments can be made to preferred stockholders.

Dividend Features
Like common stock, preferred stock is paid a dividend, not interest. However, the dividend is usually a fixed amount, and it is often expressed as a percentage of par value (which is usually $100), similar to how interest is paid on bonds. For example, an 8 percent preferred stock would mean that an $8-a-year dividend is paid on each share of stock. Even though a preferred stock has a par (or face) value of $100, its price in the marketplace could be quite

BOX 11.4

No Reason to Settle for 90 Percent

If you are holding SERIES EE (savings) bonds as a long-term investment, you probably should consider other Treasury bonds. To begin with, the return on five-year Treasuries is likely to average 1 to 2 percent less than the return on 20- or 30-year Treasuries; then, you receive only 90 percent of that return. So the return that you finally receive is about the equivalent, on average, of what you might earn in very short-term Treasury bills. We shouldn't complain about receiving the Treasury bill yield if we are holding savings bonds for liquidity purposes, but this yield is not adequate for long-term bond investment.

Unfortunately, many families *do* hold savings bonds for long periods of time. For example, parents and relatives like to give them as gifts to small children with the usual warm feeling that the bonds can help much later in the recipients' lives. Then, too, the convenience of buying savings bonds leads many

people to buy them for their retirement. Sadly, these long-term holdings will not produce the accumulations that other bonds could.

True, savings bonds have other appealing features, such as federal income tax avoidance if they are used for certain educational purposes and if the owners meet certain conditions. But these other features do not apply to many investors, so they are worth nothing. If you want to hold Treasury bonds as a long-term investment, and if there are no unique advantages applicable in your case, then go after all the yield—not just 90 percent.

It's relatively easy to buy bonds directly from the Treasury without a commission, and your broker can buy them for you in a flash. The broker's commission will be insignificant in the long run when it's compared with savings bonds' smaller yields. Also, there are a number of very good mutual funds specializing in Treasury bonds. Tell Grandma and Grandpa and aunts and uncles that opening a custodial mutual fund account for the kids (a five-minute task) will be as warmly appreciated as savings bonds.

Cumulative, noncumulative: Feature of preferred stock indicating if nondeclared dividends will (cumulative) or will not (noncumulative) carry forward to future years.

different, depending again upon the overall level of interest rates. Some preferred stocks do not have par values; they simply state the dollar amount of dividend.

Preferred dividends can be **cumulative** or **noncumulative.** Cumulative means that if a dividend is not declared in one year, it accumulates and must be paid in a future year before any dividend can be paid on the common stock. With noncumulative stock, a missed dividend is lost forever. It is important to know that a corporation is not required legally to pay preferred dividends. In contrast to bond interest, which becomes a legal liability of a corporation the moment it is due, preferred dividends are not liabilities until they are declared.

Preferred Stockholders' Rights

As mentioned previously, preferred stockholders do not enjoy the same legal protections as bondholders do. However, there are similarities. For example, preferred stock is issued under an offering agreement, and many protective covenants are written into it. Some agreements go so far as to give voting rights to preferred stockholders (which they almost never have) if the common stockholders fail to live up to the terms of the agreement or are unable to manage the business profitably. However, these restrictions are rare. You are better advised to think of preferred stock as a considerably weaker instrument than a bond with respect to your protections in bankruptcy.

The Convertible Feature

Convertible preferred stock: Preferred stock that converts into shares of the issuer's common stock.

A growing number of new preferred stocks are convertible. Just as in the case of convertible bonds, **convertible preferred stock** converts into a given number of shares of the company's common stock. In recent years, the convertible feature has replaced the participating feature as a "sweetener" to help sell the preferred.

Expected Return from Preferred Stock

The expected return from nonconvertible preferred stock is calculated in the same way as the expected return on bonds. You receive a fixed annual dividend (usually paid quarterly), which is the current return, and you may have a future capital gain or loss if you sell the preferred for a price more or less than your purchase price. It must be noted, though, that most preferred stock does not have a maturity date when the corporation must redeem it. It is said to be issued in perpetuity. Therefore, you cannot calculate a yield to maturity, but you can calculate a current yield in the following way:

$$\text{Current yield} = \frac{\$D}{\$P}$$

where

D = annual dividend

P = market price of the preferred stock

A preferred stock paying $2 a year in dividends and having a market price of $18 would have a current yield of 11.11 percent ($2/$18). This is the same calculation we made to find a bond's current yield. Although the preferred stock may not have a redemption date, it may have a call option attached, allowing a corporation the right to call the shares if it wishes to. Finally, preferred stock has the same degree of price risk as bonds, given similar maturities.

Key Terms

agency bonds (p. 286)
blue chip (p. 274)
bond indenture (p. 282)
book value (p. 280)
callable bonds (p. 283)
common stock (p. 271)
convertible bond (p. 283)
convertible preferred stock (p. 292)
coupon bonds (p. 283)
coupon rate (p. 283)
cumulative (p. 292)
current yield (p. 288)
cyclical stocks (p. 274)
debentures (p. 282)
default risk (p. 290)
earnings per share (EPS) (p. 278)
face value (p. 282)
fixed return (p. 282)
fundamental value (p. 280)

general obligation (GO) bond (p. 287)
growth company (p. 274)
income stocks (p. 274)
inflation-indexed Treasury bonds (p. 286)
interest rate risk (p. 290)
market-to-book ratio (p. 281)
mortgage-backed bonds (p. 286)
mortgage bonds (p. 282)
municipal bonds (p. 287)
noncumulative (p. 292)
PEG ratio (p. 280)
periodic share repurchases (p. 273)
preemptive right (p. 272)
preferred stock (p. 291)
pretax equivalent yield (p. 287)
price-earnings (P/E) ratio (p. 278)

price-to-earnings analysis (p. 278)
protective covenants (p. 282)
proxy (p. 271)
regular dividend (p. 273)
residual claim (p. 272)
revenue bond (p. 287)
sinking fund (p. 283)
special situation (p. 274)
stock dividend (p. 273)
stock split (p. 273)
subordinated debentures (p. 282)
U.S. Treasury Strips (p. 286)
yield to maturity (p. 288)
zero coupon bond (p. 283)

Reread the chapter-opening vignette.

1. Knowing the Steeles' financial background, particularly their financial goals, do you feel that most of their money should be invested in stocks or bonds? Discuss.
2. Suppose your preceding answer is "stocks." Indicate what types of stocks are most appropriate for the Steeles. For example, is Mead a better choice than Intel or Gillette? Discuss. (You might want to dig a bit more deeply into these three companies. From the Internet, find a price chart that goes back as far as 1998. How have the prices of these stocks done since then?)
3. Suppose your preceding answer is "bonds." Indicate what types of bonds are most appropriate for the Steeles. Recommend specific bonds, such as "a corporate bond with a 20-year maturity" or "a Treasury STRIP with a 10-year maturity." Explain your choice(s).
4. Assume the Steeles have done their research and subsequently invest in several companies. What financial information should they use to monitor their results? You can limit your answer to Internet sources. Indeed, you need go no further than financial data available through Yahoo!'s Finance URL listings.

Problems and Review Questions

1. Explain your rights and return potential as a common stockholder, bondholder, or preferred stockholder. Discuss whether one of these is better than the other two.
2. Suppose you and two friends are considering forming a corporation to produce and market computer software programs that each partner has written. Explain whether you think you should be concerned about voting rights and the preemptive right, assuming each shareholder receives 1,000 shares.
3. Magna Corporation has the following securities outstanding: 1,000,000 shares of common stock, 200,000 shares of $2.50 (annual dividend) preferred stock, and $10,000,000 of 15 percent bonds. Calculate earnings per share available to common stockholders if Magna earns:
   (a) $5,000,000
   (b) $2,200,000
   (c) $1,000,000
4. Compare a regular cash dividend with a periodic share repurchase. Which has greater appeal to you? Explain.
5. Explain a stock dividend and further explain if you would prefer it to a cash dividend. What are stock splits, and how desirable are they?
6. Bartholomew Industries' common stock indicates a dividend of $2 a share next year, and its dividend has been growing at an annual rate of 15 percent. If its stock has a current market price of $40 a share, calculate your total expected return on the stock.
7. Bartholomew Industries' (see Question 6) common stock has an estimated beta of 2.2. Assuming you could earn 9 percent on U.S. Treasury securities and the market risk premium is 8 percent, should you buy the stock? Explain, using your answer from Question 6 here.
8. Tartan Corporation has the following 10-year data:

Number of common shares outstanding	1,000,000
Average annual earnings	$2,635,000
Average market price of the common stock	$20/share

(a) Securities analysts think Tartan will earn $5 million next year and have 1,200,000 common shares outstanding. What price do you expect for its common stock next year? Begin your answer by calculating a P/E ratio.

(b) Calculate the market-to-book ratio using your answer to part (a) and assuming a book value of $10 a share.

(c) If the price of Tartan's stock is currently $30 a share, explain if you think it's a good buy.

9. Explain the following stock quotation.

| 52 weeks | | | | | | | | | |
High	Low	Stock	Div	Yld.	P/E	High	Low	Close	Net Chg.
17.75	7.13	AAR	.44	3.1	18	14.13	14	14.13	0.13

10. Is a bond a loan? If it is, who is the borrower and who are the lenders?

11. What is a corporate bond indenture? Differentiate among a mortgage bond, a debenture, and a subordinated debenture.

12. Using a bond's face value and coupon rate, explain how the amount of semiannual interest is determined.

13. Indicate three ways that a bond may be retired.

14. Explain a convertible bond. Would you be inclined to buy such a bond if it were issued by a growth company? Discuss.

15. Why do U.S. Treasury bonds have the lowest yields of all bonds?

16. What is a U.S. Treasury Strip?

17. Calculate the yield to maturity for the following bonds (each has a par value and redemption value of $1,000):

(a) 8 percent coupon rate, 10-year maturity, $1,200 price

(b) 12 percent coupon rate, 20-year maturity, $800 price

18. Using appropriate tables found in the Appendix at the end of the text, determine the present value of the following bonds (each has a redemption value of $1,000):

Bond	Annual Coupon Interest	Maturity (Years)	Yield to Maturity
A	$120	10	8%
B	60	20	8
C	zero	20	10

19. Suppose the yields to maturity for bonds A and B increase to 10 percent. Calculate the new present value of each, and, comparing it with your answer to Question 18, discuss which bond has the greater interest rate risk.

20. What is meant by default risk, and how do investors usually determine how much a bond might have?

21. The following five bonds all have the same maturity and coupon rate. Also shown are five yields. Match the yield to the bond.
    (a) Municipal   10%
    (b) Treasury   8%
    (c) Corporate, best quality   9%
    (d) Corporate, medium quality   7%

22. What feature of a municipal bond is particularly appealing? Suppose you have a marginal tax rate of 28 percent, and a municipal bond offers a yield of 5 percent. Would you prefer this bond to a similar quality corporate bond with a yield of 6.5 percent? Show why or why not.

23. What is a cumulative preferred stock?

24. If a preferred stock (issued in perpetuity) has a price of $20 a share and pays an annual dividend of $1.50 a share, what is its current yield? Can you calculate its yield to maturity? Explain. Could you experience a capital gain or loss with this stock? Explain.

Case 11.1
Ed Driessen's Stock Pick

Ed Driessen is in a management trainee program at Leyton and Leyton Company, a manufacturer of business forms and accounting systems. During his first month on the job (January 2006), Ed was assigned to the sales department to become familiar with its operations. In reviewing customer accounts, Ed happened to notice a substantial increase in orders from Antogen, Inc., a hospital supplies company with diverse interests in that area. Since most of these orders were for invoices, purchase orders, and other forms related to sales, Ed reasoned that Antogen might be on the verge of increasing its sales and profits rapidly. If this were to happen, its common stock might be a very good buy.

Before buying, however, Ed thought it would be a good idea to research the stock at the local library. One day during his lunch hour, he stopped there and gathered some data and made a photocopy of Antogen's price chart. (The data and the chart are shown here.) Ed isn't quite sure how to use all this information, but a friend of his indicated that it shows fairly good performance and that Ed's investment should work out well for him. Ed is ready to buy the stock but would first like your opinion. He is single and has good insurance coverage, and his position with Leyton and Leyton seems very secure and promising for the future.

Questions
1. Assume that at the time Ed asks your advice, the rate of return on U.S. Treasury bills is 5 percent and that a market risk premium of 8 percent seems appropriate. Using the 1996–2005 dividend growth rate, do you think Ed should buy the stock? Explain your answer. Suppose you use the dividend growth rate indicated for 2006 and 2007 instead of the 1996–2005 rate; what is your answer then? Which rate do you feel is the more appropriate? Explain.
2. Rather than using a dividend approach, suppose you prefer to judge a stock's value by using a price-to-earnings analysis. Based on the available data, does this approach indicate the stock is a good buy? Explain your answer.
3. Does the stock's price chart help you in making a decision? Explain.

4. What do you think of Ed's hunch? Do you feel he has information that might not be available to investors in general? Does the information given suggest that other investors are not aware of Antogen's prospects for growth? Explain.

5. All things considered, do you think Ed should buy the stock? Defend your answer. (Assume that Ed already has adequate diversification.)

Data for Antogen, Inc.

Current market price per share: $50

Earnings per share (EPS):
  Average annual growth
  1996–2005: 10%
    2005 actual $3.60
    2006 estimated $4.30
    2007 estimated $5.20

Dividends per share:
  Average annual growth
  1996–2005: 10%
    2005 actual $1.00
    2006 estimated $1.20
    2007 estimated $1.44

Average price/earnings (P/E) ratio:
  1996–2005   10
  2005   12
Current beta estimate: 1.5

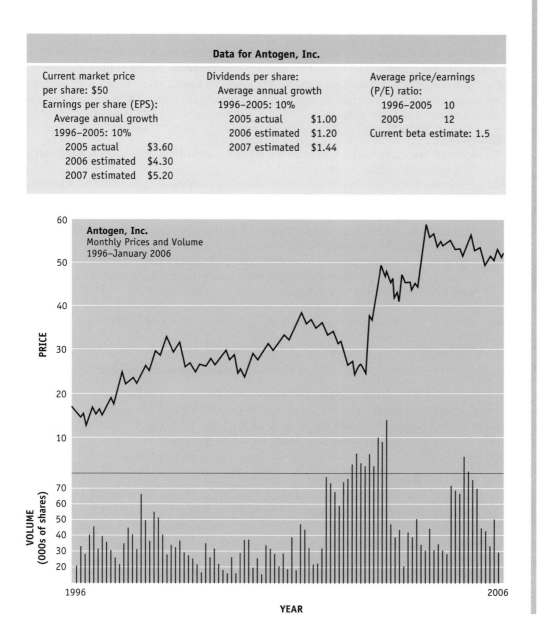

Antogen, Inc.
Monthly Prices and Volume
1996–January 2006

PRICE

VOLUME (000s of shares)

YEAR

Case 11.2
Brendan Hoyt Speculates About Bonds

Brendan Hoyt has been fortunate to accumulate about $50,000 of savings, currently held in a money market fund. Brendan is single and has a good position that pays over $80,000 a year. He has no serious financial obligations. He is reluctant to speculate in the stock market because he has a poor background in security analysis, but he believes he can forecast future interest rates with moderate success.

Brendan is convinced that interest rates will fall two percentage points very shortly. His friend, Tina Tobe, has told Brendan that if he really can forecast interest rates, he should speculate in the bond market. He can limit his bond selections to Treasuries, so he doesn't have to worry about possible defaults. Tina says that he should buy Treasury Strips with a 20-year maturity and a yield to maturity of 10 percent. Brendan likes the idea but fails to see why STRIPS are Tina's choice. He thinks he should select bonds with the highest yields to maturity, and right now those are 10-year bonds with a 14 percent coupon rate (coupon interest of $140 annually) and with a yield to maturity of 12 percent.

Questions
1. Brendan needs your help. Calculate the present value of the zero coupon bond and of the 14 percent coupon bond.
2. Assuming a $50,000 investment, how many of each bond type could he buy if he invested the entire amount in one or the other?
3. Assume that Brendan forecasts correctly and that each bond's yield to maturity declines by two percentage points. Determine the new present value for each bond and then further determine which bond provides the greatest profit opportunity.
4. Assume that Brendan guesses incorrectly and each bond's yield to maturity increases by two percentage points. Again, determine new present values and indicate which bond suffers the largest loss. What advice can you offer Brendan?

Working Out on the Web

Exercises to Strengthen Your Use of the Internet
(Links for the following exercises can be found at **www.prenhall.com/winger**.)

Exercise 11.1 How Are the Dogs of the Dow Doing?
Many investors rely on a company's dividend yield as a guide for selecting companies. Read about a popular approach called Dogs of the Dow. Click on "Performance" to compare the approach to the overall Dow Jones Industrial Average.
Q. For the current year, are the Dogs of the Dow beating the overall market?

Exercise 11.2 How Is Mead Doing?
A number of excellent sites provide both quotes and company data. Perhaps the best is Yahoo! Finance. Enter Mead's symbol, MWV, in the request block and receive the price quote. Click on "Company News" to see if any news items occurred recently. Choose "Charts" to get a great price chart. Choose "Research" to find recommendations on securities analysts.
Q. What is Mead's average recommendation? Compare it to the industry mean.

Exercise 11.3 Help for the Bond Investor
You can find information about all kinds of bonds—corporates, Treasuries, and municipals—with Bonds On Line, available at Yahoo! Finance (choose "Bonds" then Screener"). Find the answer to the following question, choosing "Corporates."

Q. Suppose you want a bond with a maturity between 10 and 20 years and a coupon rate of 5 to 8 percent. Enter these data. What list of corporate bonds does the search suggest?

Exercise 11.4 How Can I Buy Treasuries Without Paying a Broker's Commission?

The Federal Reserve Bank of New York provides information on buying Treasury bonds. At the home page, click on "Treasury Direct" for information and forms.

Q. What two ways are available to acquire securities forms?

Exercise 11.5 What Are My Savings Bonds Worth Right Now?

Stay at the foregoing Federal Reserve site, go back to the home page, and click on "Savings Bonds." Now click on "Redemption Calculator" and find the series that you own.

Q. Use the Redemption Calculator. What is the redemption value for a savings bond from issue date January 1998 to issue date Jan 2002? Choose $25 face value ($12.50 investment).

12

Mutual Funds and Other Pooling Arrangements

SIMPLIFYING AND (MAYBE) IMPROVING YOUR INVESTMENT PERFORMANCE

OBJECTIVES

1. To understand why pooling arrangements are important alternatives to direct investment

2. To identify the important characteristics of open-end and closed-end mutual funds

3. To be able to evaluate a mutual fund within a risk and return framework

4. To recognize the characteristics of unit investment trusts and real estate investment trusts and how each differs from mutual funds

5. To understand the basic framework of limited partnerships and why they appeal only to a limited number of investors

6. To learn the basics of portfolio construction and maintenance and appreciate why mutual funds simplify the process

TOPIC **LINKS**

Follow the **Topic Links** in each chapter for your interactive Personal Finance exercise on the Web. Go to: **www.prenhall.com/winger**

Steele FAMILY

The Steeles invested in the Fidelity Fund several years ago, primarily on the recommendation of a friend. They were surprised and delighted at the ease of opening and maintaining their account. They chose to reinvest dividends and other cash distributions from the fund, and by so doing they have accumulated 200 shares of the fund, worth about $6,800. They like Fidelity's services and quarterly reports, but the fund's performance since their initial investment has been modest and, after doing some basic research, they now are unsure if they have invested in the right fund for their investment objectives.

Arnold and Sharon thought that mutual fund investing would be rather simple, but it hasn't turned out that way. They are amazed at the large number of funds available, even within narrow categories, such as *growth* funds. Moreover, many funds tout the superiority of past performances, making it difficult to separate the real winners from the losers. Also, the Steeles have learned that some funds' shares trade in the financial markets just as individual stocks do. Maybe these funds are better alternatives to the conventional ones, such as the Fidelity Fund. Finally, they noticed there are wide differences among funds in terms of commissions to buy or sell them, operating costs incurred in managing the funds, and the frequency of trading undertaken by fund managers. Perhaps some or all of these factors are important in selecting a fund.

In future years, the Steeles envision investing most of their available savings in mutual funds, primarily to ensure adequate diversification. Given the eventual size of this investment, they realize the importance of gaining knowledge to become sophisticated fund investors.

In common with the Steeles, many investors become overwhelmed in mutual fund investing. Also, like the Steeles, many find themselves in potentially inappropriate funds for their investment objectives. Some people harbor an illusion that mutual funds have little investment risk. Ignoring diversification advantages, mutual funds are as equally risky as the underlying securities in which the funds invest. When technology stocks tanked in the recent bear market, many technology funds showed similar losses. Although it may be virtually impossible to lose all your money in a good fund, it's not impossible to lose a great deal. Knowing more about mutual funds should help you make better decisions when investing in them.

The important characteristics of mutual funds and other pooling arrangements are explained in this chapter. Actually, the term *mutual fund*, or simply *fund*, is often used in a generic sense to describe any pooling arrangement. There are legal distinctions among the different arrangements, but our focus is on their investment differences.

MUTUAL FUNDS

A **mutual fund** is an investment company that invests its funds in securities issued by other entities, such as corporations or governmental units. When you buy shares of a mutual fund, you are buying a proportionate interest in the fund's securities. As a simple example, if a fund owns 100 shares each of IBM, Exxon Mobil, and General Motors and if you own 10 percent of the fund's outstanding shares, then you effectively own 10 shares in each of those corporations. The value of a mutual fund share—called its **net asset value (NAV)**—depends on the values of its underlying securities; in the preceding example, those are IBM, Exxon Mobil, and General Motors. Suppose that, on a particular day, the following market values existed; then NAV is calculated as follows, assuming the fund has no liabilities:

Mutual fund: An investment company that invests in securities issued by corporations or governmental units.

Net asset value (NAV): The net value of one mutual fund share determined by the net market value of the shares the fund owns.

(1) IBM—$120/share × 100 shares	=	$12,000
(2) Exxon Mobil—$80/share × 100 shares	=	8,000
(3) GM—$70/share × 100 shares	=	7,000
(4) Value of the fund's portfolio	=	$27,000
(5) Number of shares outstanding in the fund	=	1,000
(6) Net asset value (NAV) per share = (4) divided by (5)	=	$ 27

Owning 10 percent of the shares outstanding means you own 100 shares and the value of your investment is $2,700 ($27 × 100). Surely, the first bit of information you want when considering a mutual fund's shares is its NAV per share.

Characteristics of Mutual Funds

To many investors, the single biggest advantage of a mutual fund—after diversification—is its professional management. As discussed in Chapter 11, determining which securities to buy and deciding when to buy and sell them are very difficult decisions—and time consuming if you take them seriously. By investing in a mutual fund, you transfer these problems to someone else, who may have better training to handle them. Mutual funds charge for these services, but the charges are quite minimal and usually worth it. Before looking more closely at mutual fund selection, you should first understand some characteristics of mutual funds.

Load Versus No-Load Funds

A **load fund** is one that charges commissions on the shares you buy; a **no-load fund** does not charge commissions. In a load fund, the price you pay for a share is called the offer

Load fund: A mutual fund that charges commissions on share purchases.

No-load fund: A mutual fund with no purchase commissions.

price, and it is higher than NAV, the difference being commission. In a no-load fund the price you pay is NAV. (We should point out that mutual funds typically have some liabilities outstanding at any point, and these are deducted from the funds' assets to arrive at *net* assets; however, these liabilities are inconsequential in comparison with assets.) Mutual funds' NAVs are reported in most newspapers, as indicated in Figure 12.1. Most listings do not indicate if the fund has a load or is a no-load. You must find this information elsewhere, such as through a fund's Web site.

Obviously, with commissions, you should be concerned with whether load funds outperform no-loads. On balance they do not. There have been spectacular performers on each side—but there also have been dreadful losers, and most studies show their average performances to be about the same, on a risk-adjusted basis. So why buy a load fund? There is no compelling reason to do so, unless you receive other advantages, such as investment advice. If you invest regularly, saving commissions gives you that much more money invested, and over the long run these extra amounts will produce a substantial addition to the value of your holdings.

In addition to the commission, or front-end load, some funds also have a redemption charge, or rear-end load. The Emerging Markets Fund, for example, illustrated in Figure 12.1 has a 1.5 percent redemption charge. The increasing popularity of funds, coupled with their apparent success, prompted many funds to begin front- and rear-end loads. Also, redemption charges tend to discourage frequent trading in and out of the fund.

Open-End Versus Closed-End Funds

An **open-end fund** issues shares at their NAV to anyone caring to buy them and, equally important, is also willing to redeem shares at their NAV. For example, if you held shares in any of Fidelity's funds, you could have sold them back to the funds at any time. You

TOPIC LINKS

Visit Fidelity's and Vanguard's Web sites.

Open-end fund: A fund that issues or redeems shares at their NAVs.

Figure 12.1

Typical Listing of Mutual Funds

A fund family—you have the advantage of free switching within this family.

r means a redemption fee is charged.

Within this grouping, Fidelity offered 76 different funds; it offered about 175 funds in total.

	NAV	NAV Chg.
Fidelity Invest:		
A Mgr	16.21	−.02
Balanc	15.46	−.05
BluCh	45.36	−0.30
Canad r	19.74	+.06
CapAp	21.97	−.17
Cplnc r	7.37	+.02
CngS	387.50	−1.02
Contra	43.77	−.20
CnvSc	20.47	−.10
DisEq r	22.93	−.10
Em Mkt r	7.56	−.04
Eq Inc	52.16	−.22
EQll	22.83	−.07
Europ r	25.27	−.14
Exch	245.51	−1.04
Fidel	30.37	−.14
Trend	51.73	−.32
USBl	10.74	−.01
Utility	15.29	−.10
Value	52.46	+.07
Wrldw	14.96	−.10

generally buy or sell shares directly from or to the fund, rather than through a stockbroker. Of approximately 8,000 total mutual funds in existence, about 6,800 are open-end funds, and their greater popularity is due in part to the assurance investors have in always being able to sell their shares at NAV. They are also widely advertised, and the load funds are promoted by sales representatives.

A **closed-end fund** is different in a number of respects. First, it has a relatively fixed number of shares outstanding. Second, you buy these shares as you would buy shares of any other corporation; that is, its shares are traded on organized exchanges or in the over-the-counter market. Third, because the fund neither buys nor sells shares to the public, you must buy or sell them from or to another party, which further means you are not guaranteed their NAV as either a seller or a buyer. Finally, these funds are seldom promoted, so chances are good you won't know much about them unless you do research on your own. However, quite a few closed-end funds are available with a variety of investment objectives, and Figure 12.2 shows just a few.

Discounts on Closed-End Funds Enhance Their Appeal

A major point of interest about closed-end funds is the size of premium or discount, which is the difference between their market prices and their NAVs. As you see in Figure 12.2, some of the funds were selling at premiums while others were selling at discounts. More often than not, these funds sell at discounts, which enhances their investment appeal. For example, suppose you can buy Adams Express at an 8 percent discount. To keep things simple, suppose Adams Express held securities that offered a 10 percent current return. If you invested $100 in these securities directly, you would get $10 in dividends or interest. But you need to invest only $92 in Adams Express to get a $10 return. Rather than a 10 percent rate of return, your rate is 10.87 percent ($10/$92). This is a sizable increase in return for no increase in intrinsic risk. You should realize, though, that the size of the discount varies over time, and it could increase after you invest. This means the market price of your shares declines relative to NAV, and if you then sell, you do so at a loss, or at a relatively smaller gain than would have been the case had the discount remained the same.

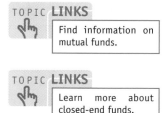
	N.A. Value	Stock Price	% Diff.
Bond Funds			
Cigma Invmt Sec	18.60	16.95	−8.9
Fortis Securities	7.94	7.95	+0.1
Hatteras Income	14.87	14.00	−5.9
Montgomery St	19.39	19.08	−1.6
Diversified Common Stock Funds			
Adams Express	19.29	17.33	−10.2
Gabelli Equity	9.91	11.08	+11.8
Source Capital	55.19	61.20	+10.9
Tri-Continental	24.19	21.40	−11.5
Specialized Equity and Convertible Funds			
Bancroft Conv.	21.72	21.19	−2.4
Engex, Inc.	13.36	14.01	+4.9
Germany Fund	9.10	8.30	−8.8
Korea Fund	12.87	10.32	−19.8
Taiwan Fund	11.33	10.41	−8.1

Negative difference means the shares sell at a discount; positive difference means they sell at a premium.

Conservative growth and income funds.

Many closed-end funds invest in foreign securities.

Figure 12.2

Typical Partial Listing of Closed-End Funds

Want to Invest in a Mutual Fund? Just Do It!

The most popular investment vehicle over the past 10 years must be the mutual fund. From $135 billion invested in 1981, there was over $8.0 trillion invested in 2004. This is remarkable. Equally remarkable, though, is the number of people who feel that mutual funds are good investments but, for one reason or another, do not invest in them or who do so only through a broker. Why?

In a recent survey, some respondents indicated that they didn't know where to look to find a fund. Others didn't think the "hassle" of investing in a fund on their own was worth it, so they let their brokers find one for them. Many felt nervous about venturing into an unknown situation and, therefore, left their money in bank savings accounts.

What these people need desperately is more confidence in themselves and a "power of positive thinking" attitude. In short: just do it, and here are four simple steps to get started.

1. Two large fund families are Fidelity (800-544-8888) and Vanguard (800-662-7447). Each has an excellent Web site. Use either to get started; when you become more knowledgeable, you might use the many other fund families that are available. If you want to start with a very small investment, use 20th Century Ultra (800-345-2021), which has no minimum investment requirement.
2. Call and ask for information on any three or four of their most popular funds (either no-load or loads less than 5 percent) that match your investment goal. Review them as well as you can and pick one. The application takes about three minutes to complete.
3. Regardless of how much money you have to invest, make a small initial commitment. The idea is simply to get in the game, not to find the ideal fund right at the start.
4. Invest regularly, which you can do in two ways. First, check the automatic reinvestment boxes on the application form, both for dividend and capital gain distributions. Second, arrange to have an amount automatically deducted from your checking or savings account and invested in the fund each month. Most fund families provide this service.

Prospectus: A document describing a fund in considerable detail.

Shareholder report: A statement showing how a fund has performed in the past and the securities it currently owns.

International fund, global fund: A fund that invests in foreign securities.

Sector fund: A fund that invests in only one industry.

Maximum capital appreciation fund: A fund that uses a variety of strategies in an effort to earn high returns.

Index fund: A fund that attempts to match the return on a market index.

Money market fund: A fund that invests in money market instruments issued in large denominations.

The Fund's Objectives

It is obviously important to select a fund that is attempting to achieve the same investment goal you are. If you call or write a fund, you will be sent a **prospectus** and a **shareholder report.** The prospectus describes the fund in detail, and the shareholder report indicates how the fund has performed in the past and the securities it currently holds. Risks associated with investing in the fund are also discussed, and they should be read as thoroughly as material describing the fund's objective and its past performance.

Figure 12.3 indicates the more common fund objectives. As you see, there are a number from which to choose. While growth, income, and balanced funds are the most popular, many investors use the other funds also. **International funds** and **global funds** allow you to invest in foreign countries, where returns have often been higher than in the United States. **Sector funds** make it possible to invest in one industry if you think that industry will do better than the overall economy. **Maximum capital appreciation funds** use a number of investment strategies in an effort to earn high returns. For example, some look for companies that might be acquired (at high prices) through takeovers. Some invest in distressed companies (even bankrupts) that are expected to recover.

A particularly interesting fund is an **index fund.** It invests in securities that constitute a market index, such as the S&P 500 Stock Index. Its sole objective is to earn the return the index earns. Beginning investors often feel they can do better than a simple index, which has no investment strategy or approach. In actuality, however, many investment professionals do not perform as well as an index. Studies indicate, for example, that fully two-thirds of equity mutual funds underperform the S&P 500 on a risk-adjusted basis.

A particularly popular fund is the **money market fund.** There are several reasons for this popularity. For one thing, these funds are known as dollar funds, which means you always buy or sell shares at $1.00 each. Actually, the fund is a form of checking account,

Figure 12.3

Types of Mutual Funds

Type of Fund	Objective	Primary Investment Securities
Growth	Price appreciation over time	Common stocks
Income	High current return	Bonds, preferred stocks
Balanced	Moderate growth plus moderate current return	Bonds, preferred and common stocks
Money market	High liquidity plus higher current return than bank savings accounts	Money market securities
Maximum capital appreciation	Exploit opportunities to earn high returns	Varies, depending on strategy
Sector	Invest in one industry	Common stocks
International	Earn returns in countries outside the U.S.	Common stocks
Global	Earn returns in both the U.S. and foreign countries	Common stocks
Index	Earn returns equal to a market index, such as the S&P 500	Common stocks or bonds; depends on the index

allowing you to write checks against your balance in the account. You earn interest daily and can withdraw all funds credited to your account at any time. Withdrawals can be made by telephone or wire but are more frequently made by checks. The usual minimum withdrawal is $500, but some accounts allow checks for any amount. The big appeal is the earnings on the account. In contrast to some checking accounts that pay no or low interest, these funds usually offer rates that are about the same as those earned on liquid money market instruments.

Important Mutual Fund Services

Along with a professionally managed and well-diversified portfolio, mutual funds offer other appealing features. Some of the more important services are described below.

Reinvestment Plans

A **reinvestment plan** allows you to automatically reinvest the fund's dividends and capital gain distributions into additional shares of the fund. You choose the amount you wish to reinvest: It can be all or only a fraction of the total distributed. Many investors like to receive dividends in cash but prefer having capital gain distributions reinvested. When you fill out an application to buy shares, you indicate how you wish to handle reinvestment.

Reinvestment plan: An option a fund investor can choose to have cash distributions used to acquire more fund shares.

Transactions by Telephone or over the Internet

Once you have completed an application, you can buy or sell shares by calling a toll-free telephone number or by accessing your account over the Internet. You can also arrange to have funds wired to your bank, which eliminates delays with checks in transit. If you sell shares and have the funds wired, they can be in your interest-earning bank account the next day.

Fund Switching

Fund switching: An option allowing fund investors to switch among funds within a fund family.

Fund switching allows you to withdraw money from one fund to reinvest in another, so long as the two funds are members of the same family (Fidelity, for example). If the fund is a no-load, this feature is particularly attractive for investors trying market-timing techniques. In general, switches up to a certain number can be made without charges; however, you will pay commissions on a load fund. Be sure to determine your fund's policy before you begin making switches.

Adaptability to IRAs

Most mutual funds make attractive IRAs (the IRA is discussed in Chapters 4 and 16). This is so because of the wide range of investment objectives available and their relatively low administrative costs, which usually are less than $20 a year (some funds offer them free). To open an IRA, all you need to do is indicate your intent to the fund, and you will be sent a simple document for your signature. This document, along with the completed application form to the fund, automatically makes your investment an IRA.

Selecting a Mutual Fund

Once you have defined clearly your investment objective, you will find many funds available for your choice. Picking one or two is a difficult task. You can get started by looking at a fund's historical performance and comparing it with its risk. Use a beta value (if one is available) in this effort. Other steps to take include reviewing the fund's current holdings, comparing its expenses in relation to its earnings or to the market value of its securities, and seeing how often it buys and sells securities (called the fund's portfolio turnover).

Evaluate Performance

A fund must indicate its past performance in its financial reports to shareholders. Figure 12.4 shows data for Fidelity Fund, a very large, open-end growth and income fund that is part of the Fidelity family. This report is typical of reports all mutual funds provide investors, although Fidelity's report is particularly useful in that it discusses how to evaluate performance.

Average Annual Total Return (AATR) The average annual total return (AATR) is a difficult calculation and cannot be solved accurately without time-value-of-money techniques. Fortunately, fund reports provide the values. Fidelity's 10.62 percent average annual total return for 10 years is the rate you would have earned by investing $10,000 ten years ago and having that grow to $27,380 by August 31, 2004. This is a good return and, as you see, it was a bit less than the return on the S&P 500 index.

Growth of a $10,000 Investment and Cumulative Total Return Figure 12.4 shows that $10,000 invested in the Fidelity Fund on September 1, 1995, would have grown to $27,380 over the 10-year period ending August 31, 2004. Most funds provide this information, sometimes in graphic form and year by year. Fidelity shows such a graph along with the numeric data. Some funds also provide the so-called cumulative total return percentage. Fidelity did in previous annual reports but apparently has stopped doing so. Actually, this return percentage is easily calculated if we know beginning and ending values for an investment: simply divide the ending value by the beginning value and subtract the number 1.0, then multiply by 100 percent. Fidelity's cumulative total return is 173.8 percent ($27,380/$10,000 = 2.738; 2.738 − 1.0 = 1.738; 1.738 × 100% = 173.8 percent).

Figure 12.4

Fact Sheet for the Fidelity Fund

I. Performance and Risk	Fidelity Fund	S&P 500 Index	Lipper Growth and Income Funds Average
A. Annual Returns (as of 12/31/03)			
1 Year	27.26%	28.69%	27.61%
5 Years	– 0.58	– 0.57	– 1.47
10 Years	10.62	11.07	9.65
B. Growth of $10,000 (9/1/95-8/31/04)	$27,380	not provided	not provided
C. Beta Statistic (as of 8/31/04)	0.94	1.00	not applicable

II. Ratings	Morningstar	Lipper
1 Year	3 Stars (5 is Best)*	722 out of 1240 Similar Funds
5 Years	3 Stars	549 out of 799 Similar Funds
10 Years	3 Stars	101 out of 281 Similar Funds

* Overall rating based on 3-, 5-, and 10-year performances

III. Top 10 Holdings (26.1% of Aggregate Value)
- Microsoft
- General Electric
- Pfizer
- Citigroup
- American International Group
- Exxon Mobile
- Gillette Company
- 3M Company
- American Express
- Tyco

IV. Other Data (Year Ended 6/30)	2004	2003	2002
Expense ratio	0.59%	0.61%	0.53 %
Portfolio turnover rate	53.0%	32.0%	155.0%

Adapted from: Fidelity Investments (Fidelity.com): choose investment products, then mutual funds, then Fidelity funds, then Fidelity Fund (symbol FFIDX). Annual returns are found in the Prospectus.

The Reinvestment Assumption A key input in determining both the average annual total return and the cumulative total return is the assumption of immediate reinvestment of fund distributions. To illustrate the situation, let's look at the example for a hypothetical fund shown in Table 12.1. Although funds actually make quarterly distributions, we will assume that all distributions were made at midyear and then reinvested at the average NAV for the year. We also assume that one share was owned at the beginning of each year.

Table 12.1

Calculating a Fund's Average Annual Return

	Year 1	Year 2
(1) NAV, beginning of year	$15.42	$17.93
(2) NAV, end of year	$17.93	$16.30
(3) Average NAV = [(1) + (2)]/2	$16.68	$17.12
(4) Distributions during the year	$ 1.85	$ 0.74
(5) Shares acquired during the year = (4)/(3)	0.111	0.043
(6) Shares owned at year end	1.111	1.043
(7) Value of shares owned at year end = (2) × (6)	$19.92	$17.00
(8) Change in value during the year = (7) − (1)	$ 4.50	−$ 0.93
(9) Average annual total return = (8)/(1)	+29.2%	−5.2%

The cumulative total return can also be determined from the foregoing data. You had 1.043 shares of the fund at the end of year 2 for each share that you owned at the beginning of that year. Since you actually owned 1.111 shares at the year's beginning, you would have owned 1.158773 (1.043 × 1.111) shares at year-end. And the total value of those shares is $19.70 (1.158773 × $17.00). Your initial investment at the beginning of year 1 was $15.42, so your gain is $4.28 ($19.70 − $15.42). The cumulative total return over the two-year period is 27.76 percent ([$4.28/$15.42] × 100).

The year-to-year changes in returns shown in Table 12.1 reveal the riskiness of investing in the fund; clearly, going from a +29.2 percent return to a −5.2 percent return suggests quite a bit of risk. Risk is often incorporated into an analysis by determining a fund's beta value and using it to adjust the average annual total return ($AATR$), as shown in the following examples.

Risk-Adjusted Return Professionals who evaluate mutual fund performance often make comparisons among funds using the risk-adjusted rate of return ($RAROR$). One very simple way to calculate this follows:

$$RAROR = \frac{AATR}{\text{fund's beta weight}} - \text{S\&P 500 return}$$

From Figure 12.4 we see that Fidelity Fund's beta was at 0.94, which means it was somewhat less risky than the overall market. Using Fidelity Fund's 10-year $AATR$ and the S&P 500 10-year $AATR$, we have

$$\text{Fidelity's } RAROR = \frac{10.62}{0.94} - 11.07 = 11.30 - 11.07 = +0.23\%$$

The +0.23 percent indicates the amount the Fidelity Fund overperformed the S&P 500. A positive number indicates a good performance; and the larger the positive number, the better the performance. Of course, a negative number indicates poor performance. We conclude, then, that Fidelity Fund's performance was slightly ahead that of the S&P 500 index.

Review the Fund's Current Portfolio

At this point, you should look at each fund's current holdings. If you invest in a number of different funds, you should be concerned with the specific companies in which the funds invest. This will help you determine the extent to which you are diversified. At an extreme, imagine that all your funds are invested in the same companies. In that case it would make no sense to own all the funds since one fund would be sufficient. Furthermore, you probably would have much less diversification than you think you have. Reviewing the fund's portfolio will help you evaluate your degree of diversification. As Figure 12.4 shows, the Fidelity Fund held 10 investments that totaled 26.1 percent of the fund's aggregate value; altogether, the fund held 126 different companies. On balance, the fund seems reasonably diversified; but you should be cautious to invest in a similar fund if its top 10 holdings were approximately the same as the Fidelity Fund's.

Examine Expenses and Portfolio Turnover

Managing a mutual fund involves certain administrative expenses. The greater these expenses, the fewer resources the fund has to invest or make shareholder distributions. These expenses are usually related to the size of the portfolio and the frequency of security purchases and sales. This frequency is measured by a turnover percentage. (For example, if a fund replaced 10 percent of its holdings with new holdings, its turnover would be 10 percent.) Figure 12.4

shows Fidelity's data for three years: 2002, 2003, and 2004. It is important, by the way, to express expenses as percentages of average net assets because funds are quite different in size, and a large fund naturally has higher expenses than a small one. The ratio of expenses to average net assets for most equity funds is around 1.0 percent. Fidelity's ratios are well below that figure, indicating that management controls expenses rather well.

Review a Fund's Ratings

Two excellent ratings services evaluate fund performance—Morningstar and Lipper Analytical Services. Each has a Web site that you can review if you would like more information on how their ratings are derived. How they report ratings is simple in both cases. Morningstar assigns a number of stars with five indicating the best performance. Lipper shows the rank of the fund in relation to all others in its peer group. Figure 12.2 shows that Fidelity is a three-star performer according to Morningstar. Its Lipper rank varies depending upon the time period over which returns are measured. Fidelity's 10-year ranking is fairly good, but its 5- and 1-year rankings are less impressive. Actually, these ratings somewhat confirm the conclusion we reached using the RAROR—that the Fidelity Fund performs about as well as the overall market.

Ratings are very helpful and you are well advised to use them before investing. However, you should not place excess emphasis on ratings based on short time periods. Many funds pursue investment strategies that produce high returns in certain economic environments, but very poor returns in other situations. If you chase after funds always showing the highest ratings, you might be investing at the end of the boom cycle. Naturally, you then are stuck with poor returns that often follow the good ones. Many financial planners favor long-run evaluations—3-year periods and longer.

Select Mutual Funds

You can get help in selecting mutual funds from a number of sources, including financial advisory services that charge fees. More readily available sources, though, include *The Wall Street Journal, Barron's, Money, Business Week*, and *Forbes. Money* has a "Fund Watch" column appearing in each monthly issue. In addition, it ranks a large number twice a year, reporting each fund's 1-, 5-, and 10-year performance along with a risk rating. It also gives each fund's address and phone number, making it easy for you to get information. Also, there are a number of Internet sites that provide fund data, including risk factors and performance results. Yahoo! provides a complete review of a fund's performance, comparing it to performances of other funds with similar investment objectives.

TOPIC **LINKS**

See a review of the Fidelity Fund.

OTHER POOLING ARRANGEMENTS

Although mutual funds are clearly the dominant pooling arrangement, other forms have arisen to meet special considerations. We review four relatively popular arrangements: unit investment trusts, real estate investment trusts, limited partnerships, and investment clubs.

Unit Investment Trusts (UITs)

A **unit investment trust (UIT)** is similar in some respects to an open-end mutual fund, but there are important differences. As Figure 12.5 shows, a UIT is formed when an originator, a large financial firm (such as John Nuveen and Company) creates a portfolio of assets and then sells trust units to individual investors. In most cases you can sell your units back to the trust at their NAVs, which may be quite different—higher or lower—from their original cost to you. Basically, this is how an open-end mutual fund works. The big difference is that the original portfolio of securities remains intact until they are redeemed or the trust

Unit investment trust (UIT): A pooling arrangement similar to an open-end fund; however, the investment portfolio is relatively fixed (unmanaged) over the fund's life.

Figure 12.5

Formation of a Municipal Bond Unit Investment Trust

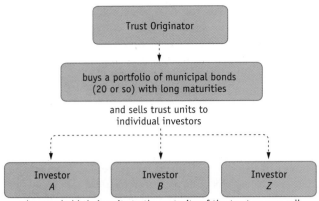

Trust Originator

buys a portfolio of municipal bonds (20 or so) with long maturities

and sells trust units to individual investors

Investor A Investor B Investor Z

who may hold their units to the maturity of the trust or may sell back to the originator—but at current market value, not at original price paid.

Saving money $

BOX 12.2

Focus on Loads and Annual Expenses

You have $1,000 to invest and are considering mutual funds. Two have come to your attention. Fund A has an 8.5 percent load and typically incurs operating expenses at 2 percent of net assets; Fund B is a no-load fund with an expense ratio of 0.25 percent. If each fund manager earns, say, 12 percent each year before expenses, how much better off are you with Fund B? Answers are in the table that follows.

B's advantage is anything but trivial, but you probably think this example is stretched to make a point. It is somewhat, but not completely. There are funds with loads as high as 8.5 percent, and you certainly can find two funds with that much difference in expense ratios.

Saving money, then, is simple: First, ignore all load funds; second, select only those no-load funds with low operating expense ratios. But, as with all simple plans, there are a few

hitches. First, by eliminating all load funds you cut out a few super performers, such as Fidelity's Magellan Fund—one of the best performers of all funds over the past 15 years. By relaxing the rule to exclude only high-load funds (loads over 5 percent), you keep most of the better performers, including Magellan.

Second, many load funds are sold by stockbrokers who also provide investment and portfolio management advice. Notice in the table that the load has far less importance with long holding periods. Paying $820 over 20 years may not be an excessive amount if the broker provides useful advice.

The table clearly shows that operating costs are the real villain in the long run. Indeed, some studies have shown that selecting funds with low cost ratios is the most consistent method of selecting funds that are likely to perform well in the future. One mutual fund family, Vanguard, emphasizes low costs, and its funds typically have the lowest ratios in the industry. Not surprisingly, its funds—particularly its index funds—are consistently among the better performers.

| Years After Investment | Accumulation: | | B's Advantage | Advantage Due to: | |
	Fund A	Fund B		No Load	Low Costs
1	$1,007	$1,120	$ 113	$ 95	$ 18
10	2,373	3,106	733	265	468
20	6,156	9,646	3,490	820	2,670

is dissolved. The trust is, thus, an unmanaged fund, reducing administrative expenses considerably, but you do pay a commission (usually 4 percent) to the trust originators.

Exchange-Traded Funds

Exchange-traded funds (ETFs) are a variation of the UIT model. The major difference is that trust units (more popularly referred to as shares) trade in the securities markets. In this respect they are similar to closed-end funds. However, in common with UITs and in contrast to closed-end funds, the portfolio of assets held by ETFs remains fixed. ETFs have grown rapidly in popularity for a variety of reasons:

1. Since they are market traded, investors can enter and exit positions very rapidly, intraday if they so desire. In contrast, most mutual funds settle only at the day's closing net asset value.
2. Investors can use margin to acquire the shares. This may not be possible with mutual funds.
3. They have very low expense ratios, often under 0.3 percent with some as low as 0.18 percent.
4. They are more tax efficient. Mutual funds pass their capital gains to investors each year, adding to investors' tax liabilities. With ETFs, investors can choose to hold their positions, thereby not incurring taxable gains. Over a long period of time, this deferral of taxes can significantly increase wealth.
5. Of course, investors incur brokerage commissions in trading ETFs. However, these commissions could be far less than a front- and/or back-end load on a mutual fund. Clearly, frequent trading usually diminishes wealth no matter what security is traded.

Most ETFs are designed either to track a broad market index or a market segment.

Exchange-traded funds: Fixed portfolios of securities that trade in the securities markets.

TOPIC **LINKS**

Learn more about ETFs.

Broad Market ETFs

Broad market ETFs are by far the most popular. The first offered was one that tracked the S&P 500 stock index. Its trading symbol on the American Stock Exchange is SPY and it is referred to as a "spider" (acronym for Standard and Poor's Depository Receipt). Shortly after Spiders, an ETF tracking the Dow Jones Industrial Average—called a "diamond" (symbol, DIA)—was introduced. Although actively traded, diamonds have been far less popular than spiders. However, each has been eclipsed completely with the introduction of the ETF that tracked the 100 largest stocks traded through NASDAQ. Called the "Qs" (after their trading symbol, QQQQ), trading in these shares often averages over 80,000,000 shares a day, making it perhaps the most popular stock traded.

In addition to the S&P 500 spider, the Amex trades other ETFs that track almost every major market index, such as those representing small and intermediate-sized companies. ETFs have been created also to track stock indexes in other countries, making global diversification possible for individual investors. Actually, with ETFs investors can create virtually any type of highly diversified stock portfolio they desire. Of course, the diversification exists only as to having an adequate number of individual stocks; for example, the 100 different companies in the Qs provide excellent company diversification. However, you still have an investment that is not broadly diversified among many different kinds of stocks. The 100 companies are largely technology oriented. Any decline in that market segment will mean similar declines in the Qs, as their owners well know from the previous market downturn.

Market Segment ETFs

Market segment ETFs are designed to track the performances of specific market sectors. For example, the S&P 500 index is broken down into nine sectors—consumer staples, consumer cyclicals, consumer services, basic industries, financials, utilities, energy, industrials, and technology—and an SPDR fund has been created for each one. In addition, Barclays Global Investors has created similar ETFs—called iShares—on over 20 different sectors, including real estate, health care, and chemicals.

Merrill Lynch has created a somewhat different type of ETF, called "holders." The difference arises in that a trust unit can be converted at the holder's option into a fixed number of shares of the companies included in the holder. The trust unit actually consists of 100 shares of the holder, and trades cannot be for less than 100 shares. The first fund consisted of 16 Internet companies, including Yahoo!, AOL, Amazon, eBay, and 12 others. Initiated at the peak of the Internet frenzy, this ETF (symbol, HHH) quickly became a very popular way to diversify among leading Internet companies that were trading at extremely high prices. At its peak, the share price of HHH was about $175. A year or so later it traded at $27.91. Nevertheless, holders have achieved some degree of popularity, and Merrill Lynch has now introduced 17 others, each tracking a different market segment. The biotechnology and semiconductor holders have become very popular.

Real Estate Investment Trusts (REITs)

TOPIC **LINKS**

Review different types of holders.

Real estate investment trust (REIT): A pooling arrangement (similar to a closed-end mutual fund) that invests in real estate and real estate mortgages.

A **real estate investment trust (REIT)** is a type of closed-end investment company similar to closed-end mutual funds explained earlier. To be considered an investment company for tax purposes, the REIT must derive 70 percent of its income from real estate and distribute no less than 90 percent of its income as cash dividends. Many REITs are publicly held, which means that their shares are traded on organized exchanges or in the over-the-counter market. In effect, you buy or sell their shares as you would the shares of any other public corporation. This feature makes REIT shares very marketable but not necessarily liquid, since their prices are often as volatile as those of other stocks.

Differences Among REITs

Equity trusts: REITs specializing in investing in real estate.

Mortgage trusts: REITs specializing in mortgage lending.

REITs differ in a number of respects. First, some invest in buildings, shopping centers, warehouses, and many other kinds of properties. These are called **equity trusts,** and they earn income from renting space to tenants. Other REITs do not invest in properties but instead invest by lending funds to others; that is, they make loans (usually mortgage loans) to builders and developers. These are called **mortgage trusts.** A second difference has to do with the manner in which a REIT finances itself. Some are financed entirely with owners' equity, having no long-term debt whatsoever. Others make extensive use of borrowed funds, which increases their leverage.

Since REITs differ so much in both the kinds of investments they make and how they are financed, they also differ considerably in their expected return and risk characteristics. Some are extremely safe, while others are very risky. Before investing, you should research their underlying fundamentals, by either doing the work yourself or asking your broker for a research report and an opinion on which ones seem appropriate for your investment objectives.

The Return from a REIT

As noted earlier, 90 percent of a REIT's earnings must be distributed as dividends. The current return on many REITs is, therefore, fairly high but also volatile, a factor you should not overlook if a stable return is important to you. Similar to the NAV of a mutual fund, the equity per share (*EqPS*) of a REIT can be determined by dividing assets minus liabilities by the number of shares outstanding; that is,

$$EqPS = \frac{(\text{REIT assets} - \text{liabilities})}{\text{REIT shares outstanding}}$$

EqPS is an important figure to investors who want to know if the market price of a REIT share is selling at a discount or premium to it. You should understand, however, that assets are measured at their book—rather than appraised—values. If a REIT acquired properties some years ago, there is a good possibility that book value will be substantially below appraised value. So it is important not to attach excessive importance to the *EqPS* figure.

Investment Appeal of REITs

Many financial planners feel that a portion of your portfolio should be invested in certain types of assets to hedge against inflation. Real estate has been particularly effective in this capacity, and people who buy homes not only achieve living space but also add an important asset to their portfolios.

Unfortunately, not all investors are homeowners. REITs (of the equity trust variety) should be even more appealing to them. If you are a renter, consider seriously a REIT investment. A good place to begin your search for information is the National Association of REITs, 1129 20th Street NW, Suite 705, Washington, D.C. 20036 (telephone 1–800–3NAREIT).

TOPIC **LINKS**

Learn more about REITs.

Limited Partnerships

A **limited partnership** is a legal arrangement that combines features of a corporation and a general partnership. The formation of a limited partnership is illustrated in Figure 12.6; as you see, limited partnerships engage in a wide variety of business activities. However, owning and managing real estate is the most important.

A limited partnership is similar to a corporation in that most investors (called *limited partners*) are inactive in management of the business, preferring instead to turn over these responsibilities to a person called the *general partner*. It resembles a partnership in that profits or losses from the business are passed directly to the partners rather than being profits or losses of the business itself.

Limited partnership: A pooling arrangement that combines features of a corporation and a general partnership.

Liquidity with Limited Partnerships

While some limited partnerships issue shares (such as the Boston Celtics basketball team) that trade in the securities markets, most limited partnership interests cannot be sold in any readily available markets. If partnership interests are held by the public and if the promoter is a large stockbrokerage firm, they might be able to find a buyer, but there is no guarantee.

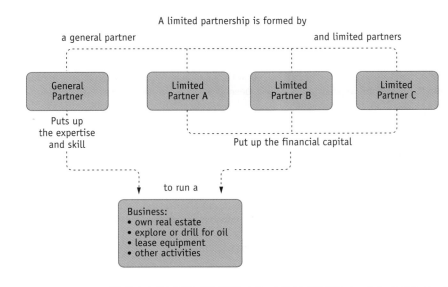

Figure 12.6

Formation of a Limited Partnership

If the partnership is privately held, selling your interest may be extremely difficult. You might wait until the partnership is dissolved to recover your original investment plus any capital appreciation. Obviously, if liquidity is an important concern, then a limited partnership interest is not a suitable investment.

The Tax Situation with Limited Partnerships

The 1986 Tax Reform Act eliminated many of the tax advantages previously associated with limited partnerships. The act's loss limitation rules stipulate that any loss from a limited partnership can be used to offset gains from other limited partnerships, but any combined net loss cannot be used to offset other forms of income, such as earned income or portfolio income. (See Chapter 4 for a review of the loss limitation rules.)

Investment Potential

The income tax situation seriously limits the investment quality of many real estate limited partnerships. Without any particular tax advantages to consider, you should evaluate this investment no differently than you would all other passive investments, such as stocks or bonds. However, evaluation might be more difficult since cash flows from the business, including its eventual liquidation, are difficult to estimate. In today's environment it is probably good advice to avoid all limited partnerships unless you are skilled at interpreting the materials they provide.

Finance News

BOX 12.3

What's a Hedge Fund?

Average investors seldom hear about hedge funds. They wonder, then: "Are these the really good funds—the ones my broker reserves for his or her wealthy clients?" Well, hedge funds certainly are for the wealthy since investors must have a net worth of $1.0 million, or $200,000 to invest. You might think this excludes you from the hedge fund industry. It might directly, but not necessarily indirectly, since hedge funds are rapidly gaining popularity among institutional investors. So, your retirement fund, or even your university, might have some of its money in such a fund. Estimates at mid-2004 put the amount invested in hedge funds at $650 to $800 billion.

Hedge funds are very different from other types of funds. First, they are usually structured as limited partnerships. Another difference is that fund managers usually receive compensation in the form of a profit share (often 20 percent), which is typical of most limited partnerships. Also, the rules for withdrawing cash from the partnership are more rigid than with mutual funds.

The term "hedge" suggests the funds pursue investment strategies designed to lower periodic investment risk, and many do just that. After the market crash in 2000, this feature began to appeal to investors. However, some funds do not hedge; rather, they seek profits in certain market segments, such as fluctuating exchange rates. This single theme can make them very risky. Consider the case of Long Term Capital Management, a so-called leveraged fund. At one point it had $4 billion in assets and almost as much in borrowed money. Its managers, often called financial geniuses, thought they could predict future interest rates. The geniuses were wrong and resulting losses led to a $3.6 billion bail out by the Federal Reserve. This debacle, along with other abuses, has moved the SEC to propose strict new guidelines for the hedge fund industry, which has been virtually unregulated since its beginning in 1949.

As with the mutual fund industry, some hedge fund returns have been excellent while others have been dismal. The weekly financial newspaper Barron's, reports regularly on fund performances should you be inclined to research them. Actually, you shouldn't feel too badly about being excluded from the market. If the fund does indeed hedge against risk, it probably will do so by forgoing potential return. As a young adult investor who, ideally, is investing for the long term, you should not seek a lower-return investment simply because it lowers periodic risk. Now, when you are ready to retire, you can weigh risk more heavily into the return–risk equation. By that time, you might also have the financial resources to meet the stringent financial requirements for entry.

You can, of course, rely on a financial adviser, but be careful if that person receives a commission from the partnership in which you invest. At the very least, have the adviser explain (in writing) the return and risks you can expect and why the partnership is suitable for your investment objectives. Investment scams frequently take on the appearance of legitimate business activities, many cloaked in the mystique of the limited partnership. Put simply, you can't be too cautious. All things considered, small investors are well advised to simply avoid limited partnerships altogether.

Investment Clubs

For many people, an **investment club** is the ideal way to achieve diversification: It gives them an opportunity for fun and fellowship, along with a possibility of profit. Most investment clubs invest in common stocks, although you can find a range of investment objectives. Some of the clubs have excellent performance records, and their members take a most serious attitude toward finding good investments.

You invest in a club by paying monthly dues, usually in the $25 range, which are then used to buy securities selected by the membership. Most clubs reinvest dividends and capital gains. Securities are often recommended for purchase by members given the task of researching a specific company or industry, and this is perhaps the most enjoyable part of being a member. You can expect divergent opinions and robust discussion in any club in which members take their investments seriously.

Investment club: A pooling arrangement characterized usually by a small number of members, monthly meetings and dues, and regular investment (and social) activities.

TOPIC **LINKS**

Find information on investment clubs.

CONSTRUCTING AND MAINTAINING YOUR PERSONAL PORTFOLIO

Now that we have examined the two most popular direct investments—stocks and bonds—and the popular pooling arrangements, it is time to put it all together by considering your personal portfolio. Investors share many common characteristics, but in a sense each investor is unique in terms of his or her risk attitude and financial goals. A portfolio suitable for you may be totally inappropriate for your parents.

Portfolio Construction

A portfolio should begin with a plan that considers your risk-tolerance level and your investment objectives. Then, specific investments are selected and combined to achieve the objectives within the risk tolerance specified. An important reason why many investors have so little success is that they do not specify concrete investment objectives. General goals, such as "making a lot of money," are too ambiguous to be of much help. We all want to make money—but over what period of time and subject to what degree of risk?

Figure 12.7 illustrates the portfolio construction process for three different types of investors. (Of course, other types are possible.) It is assumed that each investor owns a home and has adequate liquid assets and insurance. If any of these conditions are not met, then a different asset portfolio would be recommended. For example, if a home was not owned, then it would be desirable to allocate 30 to 40 percent to real estate (or some other form of investment with inflation-hedging capacity), possibly REITs, and cut back proportionately in the other asset categories.

Aggressive Investors

As an aggressive investor, you are likely to have a high risk-tolerance level and generally prefer future return to current return. We assume in this example that you have no specific

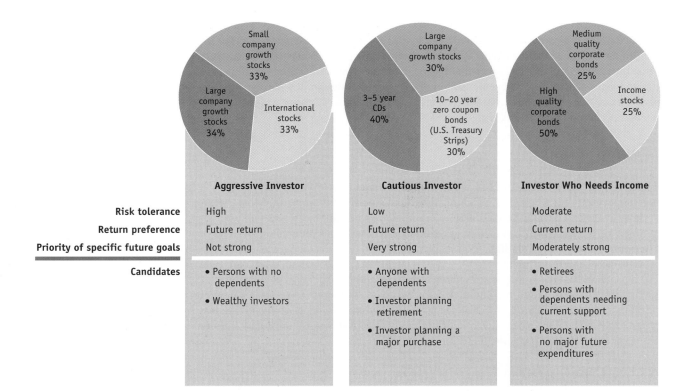

	Aggressive Investor	**Cautious Investor**	**Investor Who Needs Income**
Risk tolerance	High	Low	Moderate
Return preference	Future return	Future return	Current return
Priority of specific future goals	Not strong	Very strong	Moderately strong
Candidates	• Persons with no dependents • Wealthy investors	• Anyone with dependents • Investor planning retirement • Investor planning a major purchase	• Retirees • Persons with dependents needing current support • Persons with no major future expenditures

Figure 12.7

Portfolios are designed to meet specific investment objectives. These differ, depending on circumstances and the investor's risk tolerance. Three cases are shown. The asset weights in each portfolio should be considered as broad approximations, since more exact amounts would require detailed information about specific investors. Also, it is assumed that the investor owns a home, has sufficient funds to meet liquidity needs, and has adequate life insurance.

future goals with high priorities; although that assumption could be relaxed with respect to a retirement goal. As you see, the recommended asset mix is one-third each for large company growth stocks, small company growth stocks, and international stocks. Many excellent mutual funds offer these kinds of stocks, and you should diversify by owning two or three funds in each category. It is very important to make sure of the fund's investment objective. For example, the Fidelity Fund we have been reviewing would not be a good choice even though it has a good performance history. It is a growth *and income* fund, not simply a growth fund.

Although the recommended mix of assets will provide some degree of diversification, particularly with the international stocks, your portfolio still will have a high degree of market value volatility. However, if you hold the portfolio for a reasonably long period of time (say, 10 years or longer), you should show a good accumulation of value.

Cautious Investors

A cautious investor generally has a low risk-tolerance level but, more important, also attaches a high priority to accumulating sufficient sums of money to achieve certain future goals. If you are planning for a major expenditure in five years, or retirement in 10 years, and you want to be sure that sufficient funds are available to meet that target, then your portfolio must be constructed accordingly.

In our example, 70 percent of your funds are invested in assets with predetermined accumulation amounts—bank-issued certificates of deposit (CDs) and U.S. Treasury Strips. (Of course, the maturities of these investments would match the horizon dates of your goals, which may not be the same as those in the example.) You could use mutual funds to acquire the Treasury Strips, or you could purchase them directly through a broker.

Even though you have a strong priority for achieving future goals, it often makes sense to put some of your funds into a growing asset, such as large company growth stocks, since you do not need current return. Clearly, this move adds an element of risk to your future accumulation amount, and you should not make it if your future plans are in a sense "set in stone." But such rigidity is not common with many investment goals. You might plan $10,000 for a nice vacation in four years, although any amount between $8,000 and $12,000 will do; adding a growth asset gives you a good shot at the higher amount but also brings a possibility for the smaller one.

Investors Who Need Income

If you need income from your investments, you must select vehicles that provide high current returns. Our example assumes that you have a moderate risk-tolerance level. So you could place half your funds in high-quality corporate bonds and divide the other half

Saving
money $

BOX 12.4

Can You Profit from Market Overreactions?

Before answering this question, let's review a good example of overreaction. Until April 2004 the commercial real estate sector of the stock market was enjoying a decent up-trend over the past 12 months, as shown by the following graph. (The Vanguard REIT index is a mutual fund that invests in a wide range of real estate investment trusts, known as REITs. A REIT, in turn, is a type of investment that invests directly in income-producing properties.) Then, as you can see, the bottom fell out.

In general, commercial real estate is a fairly stable industry that does not experience wide swings in revenues or costs. In short, it has fairly stable and predictable cash flows because of the nature of its business, which involves long-term lease arrangements. Why, then, did investors all of a sudden decide in early May that the industry was worth almost 20 percent less than it was in early April? What could have changed so much in one

month? The answer: a monthly government economic report that investors felt foreshadowed increases in future interest rates, and interest expense is a major item in real estate finances.

As it turned out, the fear of rising rates was largely overblown and, as the graph shows, the industry eventually rebounded to the early April level. Even if higher rates did emerge, their impact on the real estate industry should not have led to a 20 percent decline in profitability. Many observers see this as a clear example of overreaction.

True, but many are viewing it with the benefit of hindsight, not foresight. When everyone else is selling, it takes courage to go the other way. Still, overreactions offer good entry points if you are looking for certain market sectors in which to invest. It is probably sound advice to limit your search to broad market sectors rather than individual stocks, since often some stocks fall sharply for very good reasons such as a bad earnings report or a government probe. The prices of many of these stocks never rebound—indeed, they often go much lower—and the overreaction was justified.

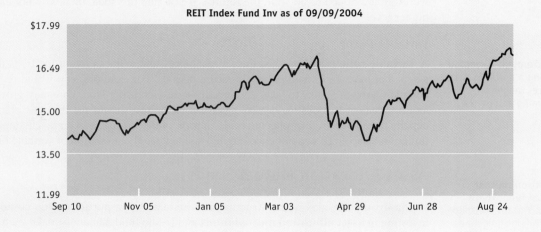

REIT Index Fund Inv as of 09/09/2004

between two moderately riskier investments—medium-quality corporate bonds and income stocks. This mix should provide a return of one to two percentage points more than if you invested in very safe bonds, such as U.S. Treasuries. Of course, if you have a very low risk-tolerance level, then the Treasuries would be more appropriate.

Mutual funds are definitely the best route for the recommended investments here. As we noted in Chapter 11, bond investment is somewhat complex and can be expensive for small amounts invested. You will have no trouble finding very good bond funds. Those offered by the Vanguard Group are particularly appealing because Vanguard features low operating costs and no front-end loads. Several studies have shown that performance differences among fixed-income funds are explained mostly by variations in fund expenses. So find funds with low expenses and you are likely also to find funds with good performance potential.

Maintaining Your Portfolio

Over time, the values of assets in your portfolio are likely to change; some assets will increase in value while others decline, or increase less rapidly. Of the three investor types discussed above, fluctuations would be most likely for the aggressive investor. As the investment values change, the portfolio weights will also change. For example, the aggressive investor's small company growth stocks might show substantial increases over several years and become, say, 50 percent of the portfolio's total value. Clearly, it may be necessary to rebalance the portfolio. Several rebalancing approaches are used—a constant ratio plan and a variable ratio plan.

Constant Ratio Plan

Constant ratio plan: A method of rebalancing a portfolio that restores each component to a preset percentage.

As the name implies, a **constant ratio plan** adjusts the portfolio back to its target weights—a third in each asset category for the aggressive investor example. So you would sell some of the small company growth stocks and reinvest in the large company growth stocks and the international stocks, assuming that each was under 33 percent. To avoid excessive trading, you might do rebalancing only once a year or when one asset exceeds a predetermined limit, say 40 percent. Rebalancing might be done more often with mutual funds if switches among funds are free.

Some investment advisers feel that rebalancing your portfolio not only keeps the portfolio in line with your investment goals but also has the advantage of selling some assets that have appreciated (perhaps excessively) in value and buying those that have not fared well (but are hoped to do so in the future). If you like this idea, then why not carry it to a higher level?

Variable Ratio Plan

Variable ratio plan: A method of rebalancing a portfolio that places greater weight on underperforming assets in a restoration.

A **variable ratio plan** does just that; it rebalances, but it stacks the proportions in favor of assets that have performed poorly in recent periods. For example, you would reduce small company growth stocks to, say, 25 percent while increasing large company growth stocks and international stocks to, say, 37.5 percent each. You should see that this plan not only departs from your original plan but is also a form of market timing. Our discussion of market timing in Chapter 10 was not encouraging, and neither is our opinion of variable ratio plans.

Asset Allocation Mutual Funds

Asset allocation mutual funds: Mutual funds that operate with certain portfolio component weight guidelines.

If you dislike the idea of constructing and maintaining a portfolio, you could consider investing in **asset allocation mutual funds** and let the fund managers make such decisions for you. These funds operate within certain guidelines as to component weights of their portfolios. For instance, Fidelity has a number of such funds, each having a different objective. Its Asset Manager fund, for example, seeks high total return with relatively low risk. Its target asset weights are 40 percent common stocks, 40 percent bonds, and 20 percent short-term securities, and it adjusts its portfolio to fluctuate around those weights. Although we don't know its actual strategy, it is likely to be a version of a constant or variable ratio plan.

TOPIC **LINKS**

Review Fidelity's Asset Allocation funds.

Asset allocation funds are appropriate for investors with broadly defined investment objectives, such as our above aggressive investor. Unfortunately, there is some evidence suggesting that their returns are not very good, when measured in a risk-return setting. Much of their poor performance arises from poor market-timing results, the very area in which they supposedly are better than the average small investor.

Mutual Funds Management in the 401(k) Retirement Plan

A typical 401(k) plan offered by many employers allows employees to invest in a wide array of mutual funds. While legal and operational details of such plans are discussed in Chapter 16, it is helpful to discuss here the topic of managing mutual funds you might own in a plan. The topic is important because there is growing evidence that many employees are not managing their investments wisely. Some critical problems are addressed next.

Rejecting Participation in the Plan

Many employees choose not to participate in 401(k) plans, even when employers agree to match, partially or wholly, their contributions. If you turn down such an offer from an employer who wholly matches your contributions, in effect, you give up the opportunity to double your money immediately. No one can match that performance investing outside a plan. True, you can eliminate the 401(k) management problem by simply not participating, but it could be the worst retirement and investment decision you make.

Holding a Single Fund

Too many employees choose only one fund in which to invest. Often they select the fund based on its previous year's performance. Each of these actions can be a mistake. First, it is difficult for one fund to accomplish a variety of objectives. For example, even an index fund of, say, the S&P 500 stocks does not provide adequate significant international exposure or any exposure to small- and medium-sized businesses. So, even if you desire a 100 percent stake in common stocks, you should choose perhaps three or four different equity funds to gain broader diversification. Second, when you choose a fund, you should review a number of factors as we have explained in this chapter and not simply focus on what the fund did last year. Very often, last year's hot fund is this year's dud, particularly if the fund follows a narrow theme, such as investing in Internet stocks.

No Coordination Between In-Plan and Out-of-Plan Investments

Remember that your 401(k) investments are a part of your overall portfolio. Often it is helpful to coordinate the two areas and not treat each as a separate investing activity. For example, outside the plan you might have money invested in savings accounts, CDs, and other relatively safe vehicles, while you invest totally in growth stocks within the plan. It could be better from an income tax point of view to reverse the process. Since you defer taxes with in-plan investments, you can choose a good bond fund with a high current return; meanwhile, outside the plan you can buy growth stocks on your own or invest in growth funds that try to minimize taxes. In a sense, a good growth stock such as Microsoft has a built-in tax deferral since it pays no dividends, and you can avoid a capital gains tax by simply not selling. Putting Microsoft in your 401(k) accomplishes nothing by way of tax deferral.

An important operational rule is that you should choose retirement-directed investments based upon diversification considerations, your tolerance for risk, and your proximity to a retirement date. After you have constructed such a plan, then consider income tax or other implications of how the investments should be held.

Trying to Time the Markets

401(k) plans have created a whole new class of market players—individuals who think they can time the market. So, they rush to sell when the market sinks and then scramble to get back in when it rises. Regrettably, the ease of switching investments in a plan (often, you can do it over the Internet) without any income tax effects is conducive to a trading habit. But the evidence on how well traders perform these timing decisions indicates more failure than success. Market timing's primary risk to the young investor is that it too often puts you out of the market, usually at critical times when prices advance sharply.

Excessive Conservatism

Several studies of 401(k) investors have been revealing. Along with poor diversification, many investors choose ultraconservative investments such as fixed-income annuities. These are not older investors nearing retirement; rather, they are young investors with very long investment horizons. Moreover, these investors are not choosing annuities for tax reasons, as discussed above, since practically all of their investments are in the 401(k) plan.

Being too conservative can be the most tragic mistake you make in investing. If you have forgotten the power of compounding over long periods of time, you need to review the section covering the topic in Chapter 2. And, if you ask people who have invested properly in a 401(k) plan for the past 20 years, they will tell you that compounding is not just a textbook lesson. Indeed, they already may have joined the ranks of 401(k) millionaires.

Key Terms

asset allocation mutual funds (p. 318)
closed-end fund (p. 303)
constant ratio plan (p. 318)
equity trusts (p. 312)
exchange-traded funds (ETFs) (p. 311)
fund switching (p. 306)
global fund (p. 304)
index fund (p. 304)
international fund (p. 304)

investment club (p. 315)
limited partnership (p. 313)
load fund (p. 301)
maximum capital appreciation fund (p. 304)
money market fund (p. 304)
mortgage trusts (p. 312)
mutual fund (p. 301)
net asset value (NAV) (p. 301)

no-load fund (p. 301)
open-end fund (p. 302)
prospectus (p. 304)
real estate investment trust (REIT) (p. 312)
reinvestment plan (p. 305)
sector fund (p. 304)
shareholder report (p. 304)
unit investment trust (UIT) (p. 309)
variable ratio plan (p. 318)

FOLLOW-UP ON THE Steele FAMILY

Reread the chapter-opening vignette.

1. What type of fund (as to fund objective—such as growth, income, index) do you feel is appropriate for the Steeles, given their investment goals? Explain your answer.
2. What type of fund (as to fund structure—such as open-end, closed-end, exchange-traded) do you feel is appropriate for the Steeles, given their backgrounds and willingness to manage their investments?
3. The stockbroker with whom the Steeles have had discussions is encouraging them to invest in several balanced funds sponsored by her firm. Each has a 4.5 percent front-end

load and operating costs of 1.2 percent annually. Would you advise the Steeles to follow her suggestion? Explain and indicate any additional information you would like to have about the funds.

4. Refer to Figure 12.7. Of the three types of investors shown there, which is the most fitting for the Steeles? Explain. Also, if you feel that none of the three is appropriate in the Steeles' case, design a portfolio that you think is better.

1. What is a mutual fund? Define NAV, and explain how it is calculated.
2. What is the difference between a load and a no-load fund? Is one a better performer than the other?
3. What is the difference between an open-end and a closed-end fund? Which type might show a discount? Is a discount an advantage or disadvantage? Explain.
4. Kim Karnes is thinking of buying the three mutual funds that follow:

	NAV	Offer Price	Closing Price on NYSE
Alpha	10.50	N.L.	—
Beta	21.00	22.90	—
Gamma	30.75	—	$26.25

But Kim doesn't know what any of the preceding figures mean. Help Kim by explaining the difference in the three funds.

5. Identify nine different fund objectives. Explain which appeals most to you.
6. Briefly explain four important services provided by mutual funds.
7. Distinguish between a fund's cumulative total return and its average annual total return over a given time period, say five years.
8. Metro Fund had a cumulative total return of 150 percent over the past four years. If you invested $1,000 in the fund four years ago, how much is your investment worth today?
9. What roles do a fund's operating costs and portfolio turnover rate play in terms of fund evaluation? Explain.
10. You bought 100 shares of an open-end mutual fund one year ago at $10 a share. You received a $0.50 per share distribution six months ago when the fund's NAV was $12.50 a share. If the fund's NAV at the end of the year was $12 a share, calculate your rate of return on the fund for the year.
11. Provide a brief explanation of the following, indicating their advantages and disadvantages:
    (a) a unit investment trust
    (b) an exchange-traded fund
    (c) a real estate investment trust
    (d) a limited partnership
    (e) an investment club
12. Explain how your risk-tolerance level and investment objectives influence the construction of your personal portfolio.
13. Indicate the type of securities or mutual funds that you believe are suitable for an aggressive investor whose primary investment goal is capital accumulation over the long term. Contrast your advice in that case to the advice you would give a person with a low risk-tolerance level who seeks current income.
14. Explain constant and variable ratio plans. Which is actually a form of market timing? Explain.
15. Describe an asset allocation fund. What type of investor might be interested in such funds?

16. Maria Gomez has recently been hired by a major corporation with a 401(k) plan. She thinks she will not participate, though, because she believes she can earn better returns investing on her own. What insight can you offer Maria?

17. Is holding a single fund in a 401(k) plan a good strategy, particularly if that fund was a super performer last year?

18. Explain a situation highlighting the importance of coordinating investments within and out of your 401(k) retirement plan.

19. Helmut Bosh, a 22-year-old recent college graduate, has a low risk tolerance. He has signed up with his employer's 401(k) plan but has chosen to put all his money in a annuity guaranteeing a 5 percent annual return. Evaluate Helmut's strategy.

Case 12.1
The Byron's Search for a Mutual Fund

Lorrie and Dave Byron are saving for their children's education. They estimate they will need about $10,000 a year for a six-year period beginning nine years from now. The Byrons have sufficient liquidity and will not need these investment funds until then. They have decided that mutual funds represent the best investment vehicle for them, and they are currently trying to select one for their first investment of $3,000.

Lorrie is impressed with the Sun Income Fund, which invests mainly in fixed-income securities. Lorrie notes that it has a good history of making distributions and that its rate of return last year (2005) was 17.0 percent. Dave disagrees with Lorrie's selection; instead, he favors the Ambrux Capital Appreciation Fund. It invests heavily in the common stock of growth companies, and it distributes very little each year, preferring rather to reinvest capital gains. He argues that since they will not need distributions, it doesn't make sense to invest in a fund that features them. He also notes that Ambrux's rate of return last year was 33.4 percent, a much better performance than Sun's.

Lorrie agrees that growth might be a better investment goal than high current income, but she thinks it doesn't matter how much a fund distributes, since they will elect to have all distributions reinvested in the fund anyway. Her preference for the Sun Fund rests mostly with her feeling that it is less risky—and she thinks the beta values for each support this view.

Questions
1. Using the data below, calculate the rates of return for each fund for 2004 and 2005. Your figures for 2005 should agree with the values given in the case. Calculate the average rate of return for the two-year period for each fund.

2. Show how much their $3,000 investment would be worth as of December 31, 2005, assuming it was invested in one or the other fund. Assume that distributions during the year were used to acquire additional shares at the average NAV for the year.

3. Assuming that each fund is no-load and that the two funds are similar in other important respects, which do you recommend for the Byrons? Explain the reason(s) for your choice. Be sure to comment on the issue of distributions from the funds.

4. Explain whether you think it might be a good idea for the Byrons to divide their investments between the two funds.

	Sun Income Fund	Ambrux Capital Appreciation Fund
NAV:		
December 31, 2003	$16.50	$12.50
December 31, 2004	15.00	11.00
December 31, 2005	16.00	14.00
Distributions per share:		
2004	$ 3.00	$ 0.50
2005	1.50	0.60
Current beta value	0.60	1.20

Cliff Swatner is single, 33 years old, and owns a condominium in New York City worth $250,000. Cliff is an attorney and doing well financially. His income last year exceeded $90,000, and he has sufficient liquid assets to supplement his condominium and other tangible assets. Several years ago, Cliff began investing in stocks and bonds. He made his selections on the basis of articles he read describing good investment opportunities. Some have worked well for Cliff, but others have not. Cliff has never taken the time to evaluate his portfolio performance, but he feels it isn't very good. Cliff currently has about $90,000 invested. He has been dating a woman lately and hopes to marry her in three years, at which time he will need $20,000 for marriage expenses and a honeymoon. Cliff's only other objective is to accumulate funds for retirement, but he does not have a specific dollar target for this goal. Cliff feels that he has a moderate risk-tolerance level.

Questions
1. Explain some disadvantages of Cliff's current investment approach.
2. Construct a portfolio for Cliff, limiting your selections to mutual funds (assume that he sells his current stock and bond holdings). Make sure your plan indicates specific dollar amounts for each portfolio component.
3. Explain how Cliff should rebalance his portfolio periodically, indicating how frequently rebalancing should be done.

Exercises to Strengthen Your Use of the Internet
(Internet links for the following exercises can be found at **www.prenhall.com/winger**.)

Exercise 12.1 Does Fidelity Have a Growth Fund?
Many mutual fund families, such as Vanguard's, have Web sites. For another great site, visit the Fidelity Investment Center. Click on "Mutual Funds" and then click on "Fidelity Funds" for comprehensive information, including performance measurements, on any Fidelity fund. Funds are grouped by objective, and you must choose a fund through this criterion. For example, choosing "growth," you get a list of the specific funds that are growth oriented. Click on the fund that interests you.
Q. How many growth funds does Fidelity offer?

Exercise 12.2 What Are Closed-End Funds?
Closed-end funds offer certain advantages and disadvantages in relation to open-end funds. Go to "Statistics and Research" and choose "Closed-End Funds."
Q. How many closed-end funds are there? Are bond funds more numerous than stock (equity) funds? (Click on "Portfolio Composition.")

Exercise 12.3 How Many Stars Does the Berger Select Fund Have?
A premier mutual fund evaluation service is Morningstar, which also provides a Web site Morningstar Fund Reports. You can browse the alphabetical index at no charge and find the Morningstar rating for many funds.
Q. What's the rating for the Berger Select Fund? Click on "B" and keep scrolling until you find the fund.

Exercise 12.4 How Are the Qs Doing?
Exchange-traded funds have become very popular. Visit the Amex Market Site and click on "Exchange Traded Funds," and then on "Broad Based Indexes."
Q. Scroll down to Nasdaq-100 Index Tracking Stock.^{SM} What was the performance of QQQQ in 2003? Also, what is the most popular stock in the index?

Exercise 12.5 Where Can You Find a High-Performing REIT?

The National Association of Real Estate Investment Trusts can help answer this question and also provide much more information about REITs. On the home page, click on "Data Library," then "Performance Data," then "Performance by Company."

Q. What is the total return for the most current year for industrial/office properties?

Exercise 12.6 Want to Join an Investment Club?

If your answer is yes, or if you simply want to learn more about investment clubs, or if you want to find some sound ideas on investing in general, visit the National Association of Investment Clubs site.

Q. How can you find an investment club to join?

Protecting Your Wealth

INSURANCE AND RETIREMENT PLANNING

Chapter 13
Property and Liability Insurance: *Protecting Your Lifestyle Assets*

Chapter 14
Health Care and Disability Insurance: *Protecting Your Earning Capacity*

Chapter 15
Life Insurance and Estate Planning: *Protecting Your Dependents*

Chapter 16
Retirement Planning: *Protecting Your Leisure Years*

Financial security is the major theme in this section. You want to be secure from uncertain financial losses, and you want to ensure that you are comfortable in your later years. To accomplish these goals you have to adopt a strategy that both preserves your current assets and plans their future growth.

This section begins with a brief review of insurance basics in Chapter 13. Property and liability insurance protects what you have today. Property loss coverage protects you from financial loss as a result of either nature's perils or human negligence. Health and disability insurance, examined in Chapter 14, protects you and your family from the disastrous financial consequences that accompany a major illness or injury. Life insurance provides support for dependents at the death of a household provider. In Chapter 15 you will estimate your life insurance needs. Life insurance can also serve as a vehicle for accumulating retirement savings and a means for the orderly transfer of a death estate. You will estimate your retirement needs and structure a plan for satisfying those needs in Chapter 16.

Insurance is one area in which a wrong purchase is very easy to make. The objectives are complicated, the terminology is confusing, and the sales agent may not be working in your best interest. Moreover, if you buy without adequate forethought, your mistake will become apparent only after it is too late. What good does it do to realize you purchased the wrong kind or amount of insurance after the auto accident, after the home fire, or after the disabling illness? Insurance is purchased for many reasons. However, the basic and most important purpose of insurance is to protect you against financial catastrophe.

13

Property and Liability Insurance

PROTECTING YOUR LIFESTYLE ASSETS

OBJECTIVES

1. To review the foundations of insurance coverage

2. To understand the primary components of the homeowners' and auto insurance packages

3. To list and explain the standard formats for homeowners' insurance policies

4. To learn how to evaluate your auto and home insurance needs

5. To be able to find and fill any gaps in your homeowners' and auto coverage

TOPIC **LINKS**

Follow the **Topic Links** in each chapter for your interactive Personal Finance exercise on the Web. Go to: **www.prenhall.com/winger**

It is unfortunate that many people wait until after an accident or catastrophe to closely read the provisions in their property and casualty insurance coverage. Some will find that their homeowners' or auto policy covers more than they expected. Others may feel cheated, having less coverage than they thought or receiving less reimbursement than they expected. With a little forethought and financial planning, you can protect yourself from financial harm due to either the negligence of others or the vagaries of nature.

In this chapter we will examine both homeowners' and auto insurance. Each is a package of component policies covering disasters at home or on the road. Both can provide nonoverlapping protection against property loss and personal liability. **Property loss insurance** reimburses you for damage to your property due to accidental or natural circumstances or due to the negligence of others or yourself. By negligence we mean the failure to exercise the care expected of a prudent person. **Personal liability insurance** provides protection from claims against you resulting from the financial harm your negligence may cause others.

Property loss insurance: Reimburses you for damage to your property due to accidental or natural circumstances or due to the negligence of others or yourself.

Personal liability insurance: Protects you against claims from the financial harm your negligence causes others.

FUNDAMENTAL INSURANCE CONCEPTS

Property insurance is only part of a bag of tools you can use to manage financial risk. To understand how this tool and others, such as health, disability, and life insurance, can best be applied, you should first review a few basic concepts in insurance and risk management. Given this foundation in the principles of insurance, the information provided in this and subsequent chapters should help you avoid many of the major financial catastrophes that can occur.

Risk

It is impossible, and probably not even desirable, to eliminate all risk from your life. Every day brings you unexpected pleasures and unforeseen disappointments. Without them, life would be bland and unexciting. That new job can be rewarding or frustrating. The new car can provide hours of enjoyment or hours in the shop. Everything you do involves some risk.

You willingly undertake certain risks because they provide the possibility of financial gain. In the stock and bond markets you accept **speculative risks** in the hope that you will receive a compensating return on your investments. Speculative risk exists when both gain and loss are possible.

Speculative risk: Exists when there is the opportunity for both gain and loss.

There are some risks, however, that you certainly could do without. These risks provide only the opportunity for loss, with no possibility of gain. Examples include the risk that your home might burn to the ground or that your car might go off the road. Each represents a potential financial drain on your resources and is said to contain pure risk. **Pure risk** exists when only loss is possible and the loss is the result of accidental circumstances. You may undertake certain precautions to reduce these risks, such as keeping a fire extinguisher in your home and driving only in good weather. However, individual action may not be enough to significantly reduce pure risk. In some circumstances, group action in the marketplace may be necessary. It is pure risk we seek to protect against when we purchase insurance.

Pure risk: Exists when only loss is possible and the loss is the result of accidental circumstances.

Pooling of Risk

All market insurance involves a pooling of risk. For each of us individually, the future is highly uncertain. However, when we combine many individuals, functioning under similar circumstances, future events affecting the group as a whole become highly predictable. It is difficult to forecast with any certainty whether you will have an auto accident on a given weekend. However, it is not too difficult to predict how many accidents will take place nationally on that weekend. This ability to forecast with great certainty the likelihood of events for large numbers of individuals allows us to join together and pool our risks.

If we can estimate total losses suffered by a given group of individuals, then we know the necessary amount of financial reserves that will reimburse these same individuals for their expected losses. When group members share the cost of this reserve by each paying what is termed a *premium*, they share the group's losses. Each member is committed to paying a certain premium but is also freed from the possibility of a larger financial loss. The premium represents the cost of the risk transfer.

The premium should be based on the average loss experience for the group as a whole. When using past loss experience to project future losses, insurance companies must be wary of adverse selection. **Adverse selection** is the tendency for those with higher than average risk to desire insurance coverage. If, over time, those at high risk either purchase insurance or continue coverage to a greater extent than those at low risk, then average losses must rise. The insurance company will then find that the premiums it has collected do not adequately cover the losses it had insured. If the insurance company is unable to meet its obligations, it is insolvent. This may result in widespread financial loss and great hardship for many policyholders who had paid premiums for nonexisting protection. It is hard to think of a greater tragedy than to have suffered a loss, only to find that the insurance protection you were depending on is not there.

Underwriting is the process of selecting and classifying risk exposure. The person who does this is called an *underwriter*. It is the underwriter's responsibility to guard against adverse selection by denying coverage to those who are at greater risk than that of the insured group. This can lead to negative publicity for the insurers, who are often accused of being heartless because they deny coverage to those who most need it. In doing this, however, the underwriter is protecting not only the interest of the insurance company, but the underwriter is also guaranteeing the continued protection of the many policyholders who are relying on this company to be there in time of need.

Obviously, if everyone in the group suffered a loss at the same time, the reserves could not cover all the losses. Consequently, we cannot successfully insure ourselves against risks that affect the group as a whole; we can only insure against risks that are personal in nature. For this reason, private market insurance does not cover losses resulting from wars, nuclear accidents, or floods. Where such insurance does exist, it is viable only when backed by a government with the power to levy taxes and print money.

In the marketplace, the insurance company manages the reserve pool of funds. In doing so, it incurs some transaction costs and some financial risks. The company must receive adequate compensation for processing and policing the many claims and for assuming the risk that the pooled reserves may not be adequate to meet all of the claims. Consequently, insurance companies will receive more in premiums than they pay out in claims. This doesn't mean that insurance is a bad deal. It does mean there is an expected cost attached to using the marketplace. Therefore, you should decide whether the transfer of risk is worth the additional cost before purchasing insurance.

Insurable Interest

In order to have an **insurable interest,** you must be related to the insured event in such a way that if the event occurs, you will incur a financial loss. Without this requirement, you would be **gambling,** not purchasing insurance. For example, I cannot purchase insurance against loss of the space shuttle. I have no financial interest in the enterprise. If it were lost, I would not suffer any financial harm. An agreement whereby I would receive payment if the shuttle were unsuccessful would be a gamble rather than an insurance contract. However, companies having payloads aboard the shuttle can and do enter into insurance contracts dependent on the shuttle's success. The financial loss these companies would suffer if the shuttle mission were unsuccessful represents an insurable interest.

Adverse selection: The tendency for those with higher than average risk to seek or continue insurance coverage.

Underwriting: The process of selecting and classifying risk exposure so that an insurance company may decide which applications for insurance it will accept.

Insurable interest: An interest in which you may experience financial loss and an interest for which you can purchase insurance protection.

Gambling: Wagering on a risky event in which you have no insurable interest.

Indemnification

Another way in which insurance differs from gambling is that payment under an insurance contract should not exceed the value of the loss. At most, insurance is meant to provide **indemnification;** that is, a return to your financial status before the loss. You should not receive a net financial gain when an insurance policy pays off. For this reason, you should not insure an article for more than it is worth. Overinsurance is a waste of money, because an insurance company will not pay out more than the market worth of the loss.

Indemnification: The restoration of the financial state that existed before you incurred a loss.

Of course, no fair market value can be placed on a human life. Consequently, the amount of life insurance we can take out on ourselves and our relatives is practically unlimited. The concept of indemnification, however, is important when we take out life insurance on our business associates. In business relationships, the amount of life insurance must be limited by the amount of financial harm.

Risk Management

Risk management consists of identifying, evaluating, and determining how to handle your risks. Your health, property, and ability to generate income are constantly at risk from numerous sources. You need to enumerate these risks and then determine how threatening each is to you and to your family's financial survival. You must then choose the best method or combination of methods for dealing with each of your risk exposures. There are four basic techniques for managing risk: risk reduction, risk avoidance, risk transfer, and risk retention.

Risk management: The process of identifying, evaluating, and deciding how to deal with risk.

Risk Reduction

You engage in **risk reduction** when you lower the probability of a loss by taking preventive action. Examples of personal risk reduction include the use of car bumpers, football helmets, seat belts, and smoke and burglar alarms. Each reduces the probability of major property damage, the probability of loss of life, or both.

Risk reduction: Reducing the probability of loss through preventive action.

Risk Avoidance

Risk avoidance involves reducing or eliminating the probability of a loss by avoiding the cause of the loss. If you avoid smoking and the heavy use of alcohol, you avoid severe risks to your health.

Risk avoidance: Reducing or eliminating risk through behavior modification.

Risk avoidance is termed a conservative strategy because it calls for a change in our behavior. Sometimes, the cost of changing our behavior is just too high for us to accept. You could avoid the risk of flying by not flying, but this would limit both your business career and your vacation alternatives. Furthermore, you must be careful that the avoidance of one risk does not increase another. By not flying, you may be accepting greater risks by driving.

Risk Retention

When the cost of eliminating the risk far exceeds the benefits of eliminating the risk, your best decision may be **risk retention.** This can be true for both major losses and minor losses. For example, it would be prohibitively expensive—if not impossible—to insure your property against loss to war or insurrection. Consequently, you must assume the risk.

Risk retention: Accepting risk as the least costly, best course of action.

You can insure against the cost of appliance repairs with a service contract. The expected cost of repairs, however, is typically much less than the cost of the service contract. In addition, when the appliance does need repairs, it is usually a minor inconvenience rather than a major financial catastrophe. Your optimal strategy is to retain small risks but transfer the large ones.

Risk Transfer

By purchasing an insurance contract, you engage in **risk transfer.** With life, health, auto, and homeowners' insurance the associated risks of major financial loss are transferred from you and your family to the insurer. Transferring risk is an important tool for eliminating major risks that cannot be feasibly disposed of through risk reduction or avoidance. No matter how moderate and healthful your lifestyle may be, there is still the possibility of a disabling sickness or premature death. The resulting expense and loss of income could lead to drastic changes for both you and your family. For protection against risks such as this, transferring risk through insurance is the best risk management strategy.

HOMEOWNERS' INSURANCE

The homeowners' insurance package usually provides better protection, at a lower cost, than the sum of its parts. Over the years, homeowners' policies have evolved into a few standard formats that seem to serve adequately the needs of the typical homeowner or renter. In order to fully understand the differences among homeowners' policies, you first must know some standard insurance terminology and the basic elements of a homeowners' policy.

The Terminology of Homeowners' Policies

You will find that most homeowners' policies are written in a clear and straightforward style. In fact, if you can't understand your policy and your insurance agent can't provide an adequate explanation of your coverage, you may have sufficient reason for finding another insurer. However, even the best-written policies contain some points that require an explanation to help you fully realize what you have purchased and how you are protected.

All Risks Versus Named Perils Insurance

The policy should indicate whether you have **all risks coverage** or **named perils coverage.** The type of coverage need not remain the same throughout the policy. You may find that some items come under all risks insurance and others come under named perils insurance. All risks protection doesn't necessarily cover you against all risks. It does protect you against all risks that are not specifically excluded in the policy. Named perils insurance is just what the term implies: It covers only risks that are specifically stated in the policy. Therefore, with all risks protection you should see a list of circumstances not covered, whereas under named perils you should see a list of circumstances that will be covered.

The difference is important, because each places special obligations on the insurer and the insured. Under all risks coverage, the insurance company is responsible for showing that your loss was not due to one of the specific exemptions stated in the policy. Alternatively, under named perils coverage, it is your responsibility to demonstrate that your loss was due to one of the named perils.

Replacement Cost Versus Actual Cash Value

The policy should indicate whether you will be reimbursed for losses at replacement cost or actual cash value. When the insurance company agrees to pay **replacement cost** on damaged goods, you receive the amount needed to replace new for old, with no deduction for depreciation. Depreciation is equal to the decline in market value, the difference between the purchase price of a good and its current market value. For example, if the roof on your home is destroyed, replacement cost coverage will pay for the construction of a new roof, regardless of the age of the old one.

Actual cash value is equal to replacement cost minus depreciation. If the typical roof lasts 20 years and yours is destroyed in the tenth year, under actual cash value reimbursement you would receive only 50 percent of the funds needed to replace the roof. This could place you in a very unfortunate position if you did not have the additional funds needed to repair the structural damage to the home. Without a roof over your head, you would need to rent some place to live. In addition, you would still be responsible for the mortgage payments on the home. Failure to pay could wipe out a good portion of your remaining equity in the home. For this reason, most homeowners' policies provide for reimbursement at replacement cost for structural damage and reimbursement at actual cash value for the contents. Moreover, additional living expenses while the structure is being repaired may be partially or totally reimbursed.

> **Actual cash value:** Market value, which is equal to replacement cost minus depreciation.

Replacement Cost Provision

Homeowners' policies contain a provision that requires the homeowner to provide **coinsurance** when the dwelling unit is insured for less than 80 percent of replacement value. Replacement value is the cost of rebuilding the home from the foundation up. It should be approximately equal to the price of a similar new home minus the cost of the lot and foundation.

The following example shows how a coinsurance clause works. Suppose the replacement value of your home is $100,000. If your insurance coverage on the dwelling is at least $80,000, the insurer will pay the full cost of repairing covered damages to the dwelling, up to the face amount of the policy. However, if your protection is for less than $80,000, you

> **Coinsurance:** Requires the homeowner to become a coinsurer when the home is insured for less than 80 percent of its replacement value.

will receive less than full replacement cost. You would, in effect, become a coinsurer by having to pay the difference when repairing the structure.

Let's look at a specific example. Suppose a fire in the kitchen causes structural damage that would cost you $10,000 to repair. If you carry $50,000 of insurance on a home with $100,000 replacement value, you fall below the 80 percent requirement. In this situation the amount you would receive from the insurance company would be calculated under the following formula:

$$\frac{\text{Amount of dwelling protection}}{80\% \times \text{replacement cost of dwelling}} \times \frac{\text{cost of damage at}}{\text{replacement cost}} = \text{insurance payout}$$

$$\frac{\$50,000}{80\% \times \$100.000} \times \$10,000 \qquad = \$6,250$$

The payout is reduced by the ratio of your actual protection to the 80 percent requirement. Thus, you would receive only $6,250, less the deductible on the policy.

There is one important exception to the preceding analysis. If the actual cash value of the loss were greater than the $6,250 calculated under the coinsurance formula, then the insurer would reimburse at actual cash value up to the policy limits. For example, if the actual cash value of structural damage to the kitchen, equal to replacement cost minus depreciation, is estimated at $8,000, you will receive $8,000 rather than $6,250. Notice that this reimbursement is still less than $10,000 replacement cost, the amount received by a comparable fully insured homeowner.

Coinsurance may seem like a scheme designed to cheat homeowners, but it actually serves a useful purpose. Most losses are for much less than the replacement value of the home. Without the coinsurance clause, some homeowners might be tempted to reduce insurance costs by carrying less than full coverage on the home, leaving them with inadequate coverage in the case of total destruction.

Inflation Guard Endorsement

With rises in the general price level, the cost of replacing your home should also increase. This means that unless you periodically increase the face amount of dwelling protection, your coverage will eventually fall below 80 percent of the replacement cost of the home. To protect against this deficit, you can include an **inflation guard endorsement** that periodically increases the face amount of dwelling protection. The increase may either be set at an agreed-upon percentage or tied to an index of construction costs.

Be careful, because the inflation guard endorsement does not necessarily mean that you have the right amount of coverage. Even with the endorsement, it is still your responsibility to make sure that there is neither too much nor too little dwelling protection.

Inflation guard endorsement: Periodically increases the face amount of dwelling protection to reflect market prices.

Deductible Clause

A **deductible clause** limits payments to damages that exceed a given dollar loss. For example, a $100 deductible means that payments will be made only for damages exceeding $100, and then the amount of the payout will be reduced by $100. Under a $100 deductible, you would receive $400 back on a $500 loss. By including a deductible, the insurer eliminates the cost of handling many small claims. This saving can be passed on to the homeowner through lower insurance rates. Including deductibles in your policy is an excellent way of holding down your insurance costs.

Deductible clause: Limits reimbursement to damages in excess of deductible.

Some policies contain a *disappearing deductible*. For example, the insurer might agree to pay 111 percent of the excess of any loss over $50, up to losses of $500. If you suffer a loss of $150, the insurer will pay you 111 percent of $100, or $111. If your loss is $500 or more, you will receive complete reimbursement.

Mortgage Clause

You will discover in the **mortgage clause** that payments for damages to the dwelling and surrounding structures are made to the mortgagee if the mortgagee is named in the policy. The mortgagee is the lender, not you. The lender may hold the money to pay for repairs or to pay off the loan if the house is not rebuilt.

Mortgage clause: Insurance payments for structural damage are made to the mortgage holder.

Other Insurance and the Apportionment Clause

If you have more than one insurance policy, each will pay only for damages up to their proportionate share of coverage. The **apportionment clause** makes it impossible for you to collect more than 100 percent of your losses by having multiple policies.

Because of the significant cost advantage of having all your homeowners' protection under one policy, you are not likely to want dual coverage. This clause is important, however, when you have additional coverage on a business conducted in the home. In this situation it may be unclear whether a particular loss is to be covered under your homeowners' insurance or your business insurance. Whoever pays, the apportionment clause makes sure you will not collect more than 100 percent of the value of the loss.

Apportionment clause: Apportions financial responsibility among multiple insurers so that the insured cannot collect more than 100 percent of the loss.

Subrogation Clause

Most insurance policies, both homeowners' and auto, contain a **subrogation clause** that places your right to sue for recovery after the insurer's. If the insurer pays you for a loss, it can then seek to recover its payments from the party who caused the harm. You are entitled to sue for and collect only amounts that exceed those you have received from the insurer. Likewise, the insurer cannot sue for or collect more than you were paid under the insurance coverage.

Subrogation clause: Places your right to sue after the insurer's.

Property Coverage

Homeowners' policies contain two sections: Section I on property coverage and Section II on liability protection. The first section includes a discussion of your coverage for losses to the dwelling unit and your personal belongings. It states the method for determining reimbursement and the types of losses covered. Subsections A, B, C, and D in Section I are organized by type of property loss and typically begin with a discussion of coverage on the dwelling.

Coverage A—Dwelling Protection

Dwelling protection generally protects you against damage to the structure resulting from fire, lightning, civil commotion, smoke, hail, vehicle damage, aircraft damage, riot, and explosion. Unless the dwelling has been unoccupied for the previous 30 days, you may also be covered for damage resulting from vandalism and malicious mischief. Loss from earthquake, flood, nuclear accident, and war will be specifically excluded.

The face amount of your dwelling protection is the most important number in the homeowners' policy. As stated previously, to avoid coinsurance payments, you should set the face amount at or above 80 percent of the cost of rebuilding. The amount of dwelling protection is also important because most of your other property loss limits will be stated as a percentage of the amount of insurance carried on the dwelling.

Dwelling protection: Protects against structural damage to the home.

Coverage B—Appurtenant Structures

Appurtenant structures: Structures other than the dwelling unit.

Structures other than the dwelling unit are called **appurtenant structures.** They include the garage, the storage shed, and even the mailbox. These will usually be covered for losses up to 10 percent of the amount on the dwelling unit.

Coverage C—Contents

Unscheduled personal property: Items not specifically listed as insured on the policy.

The loss of **unscheduled personal property**—items that are not specifically listed in the policy—from theft or damage at the home will generally be covered for about 50 percent of the dwelling coverage. This coverage is not as generous as it sounds. First, reimbursement is usually set at actual cash value, and second, there are much lower limits on specific valuables. If your valuables exceed these limits, you can take out additional insurance coverage by attaching a personal property floater to your homeowners' policy.

Many policies cover computer equipment for up to $5,000 damage, regardless of whether it is used for business. Some companies, however, may refuse to pay for damage to business-related property such as computers, fax machines, and printers unless they are covered by an optional rider insuring a home business. In addition, coverage limits on portable computers away from home may be much less.

One aspect of a homeowners' policy that most people overlook is the protection it provides away from home. If you read this subsection, you will likely find that your personal property away from home is covered for at least 10 percent of the value of the personal property on the premises.

Coverage D—Loss of Use

This often-unnoticed subsection on additional living expenses can prove extremely helpful in the event of serious loss. If a covered loss leaves your home uninhabitable, it will pay for the additional expenses necessary to retain your normal living standards. The limit on this might be expressed as 10 to 20 percent of dwelling protection prorated for the amount of time spent out of the house, or the limit might be stated as a period of time over which additional expenses will be paid.

Totaling Up the Coverage

It is unlikely that a single catastrophe would permit you to collect up to each of the previously stated limits. However, if such a disaster did occur, the total reimbursement could be considerably greater than the face amount of the homeowners' policy. On a policy with a face amount of $100,000 in dwelling protection, the maximum payout is as follows:

Dwelling	$100,000
Appurtenant structures (10%)	10,000
Unscheduled property on premises (50%)	50,000
Unscheduled property off premises (5%)	5,000
Additional living expenses (20%)	20,000
Total coverage	$185,000

In addition, you might also receive payment for the following incidentals:

- Theft of items from cars
- Credit card and check forgery
- Debris removal

- Emergency removal
- Fire department charges
- Necessary repairs after loss
- Damaged trees, shrubs, plants, and lawns

Exclusions on Property Loss Coverage

In most policies, the following classes of property are specifically excluded from contents coverage, either because they are nonpersonal in character or because they are more appropriately covered by other types of policies:

- Articles described separately in a personal articles floater or insured elsewhere
- Animals, birds, or fish
- Motorized land vehicles and electronic communication and sound devices attached to them
- Aircraft and parts
- Property of roomers, boarders, and tenants
- Property in an apartment regularly rented to others
- Property rented or held for rental to others
- Business records

Liability Coverage

Liability coverage, explained in Section II of the homeowners' policy, protects you and your family from the financial harm your **negligence** causes others. When you take the proper precautions against harming others, you are exhibiting *due care*. Due care is the type of behavior that is expected of a reasonable person. Due care standards are defined by court decisions and legislative statutes. If you violate those standards, you become liable for any harm you may cause.

Usually people become liable because either they do not understand what is expected of them or they have a temporary lapse in judgment. For example, you might not realize that you have a responsibility to protect neighborhood children from attractive hazards on your property, like a swimming pool. On the other hand, you may realize you have a responsibility, but you forget to lock the gate to the pool when you leave home. In either case, you are liable for the potential harm. The three components of liability protection in your homeowners' policy consist of personal liability insurance, medical payments insurance, and insurance against physical damage to the property of others.

Liability coverage: Protects you and your family from the financial harm your negligence causes others.

Negligence: The failure to exercise due care, the care expected of a prudent person.

Coverage E—Personal Liability

The insurer will pay, up to the limits of protection, all legally obligated expenses for bodily injury or property damage, assuming you did not intentionally inflict them. In addition, the insurer will also pay defense and settlement costs if it decides to fight the payment in court. However, once the insurance company has paid up to the policy limits, it is no longer legally responsible for further damage payments or for the legal defense.

The generally recommended minimum is $300,000, but the standard limit under this section is $100,000. This is not much protection when your actions result in serious physical harm. For example, if you are sued for $150,000 and your liability coverage is for $100,000, the insurer might decide to pay $100,000 to the injured party, leaving you with the cost of defending against a potential $50,000 award.

Coverage F—Medical Payments Coverage

Minor injuries that occur on your property are covered by medical payments insurance, regardless of who is at fault. Off your premises, it pays for minor injuries that are caused by you. It doesn't pay the medical bills for you or your family, only the medical bills of others.

Most policies limit payments to a relatively small amount, $500 to $1,000 per person. While this is not major dollar protection, it nevertheless serves a useful purpose by providing the means and incentive for timely medical treatment. This protects both you and the insurer. Immediate inspection and documentation of the injury may prevent the filing of larger claims resulting from exaggeration or delayed medical action.

Damage to the Property of Others

Similar to medical payments coverage, property liability insurance pays for minor property damage, regardless of who is at fault. The limits are typically $250 to $500 per occurrence.

Exclusions on Liability Coverage

The homeowners' policy doesn't cover slander or libel, nor does it protect you against business-related liabilities. Professional practices need special malpractice insurance, and this need is generally recognized. Where problems occur, they usually have to do with defining a business. For example, if you take on an occasional babysitting job, you may or may not be covered under your homeowners' policy. However, if you regularly take in the neighbor's children for a fee, you probably will not be covered. If there is any question that your activities might constitute a business, check with your insurance agent.

If your child works part time delivering papers or mowing lawns, be sure your policy covers those activities. Most homeowners' policies will state that the business exclusion does not apply to occasional and part-time business activities of an insured person who is under 21 years of age.

In general, your liability coverage will not extend to accidents in your automobile or aircraft. It will cover boating accidents on boats having less than a stated horsepower and less than a given length. For these exclusions you will need specialized insurance.

Policy Format

The present homeowners' policy achieved its standard form in the 1950s. Today there are established formats into which almost all policies can be categorized. The coverage under each is outlined in Figure 13.1.

Basic Format (HO-1) provides the least coverage, insuring against the 11 most common perils on a named peril basis. Only a few of these policies are sold, because most homeowners correctly demand more adequate protection.

Broad Form (HO-2) also provides named perils coverage for both dwelling and personal property. However, it is broader than HO-1, including seven additional named perils. It is the second most popular homeowners' insurance package.

Special Form (HO-3) is now the most widely purchased form and is highly recommended for most homeowners. It provides all risks coverage on the dwelling and named perils coverage on the personal property. The typical excepted perils on all the risks coverage are flood, earthquake, war, and nuclear accident.

Contents Broad Form (HO-4) is for renters. The dwelling is not covered because it is the landlord's responsibility. Coverage on personal property is for the same named perils as under HO-2. There is also additional living expense coverage equal to 20 percent of the limit on personal property and protection on tenant improvements to the property equal to 10 percent of the personal property coverage.

Figure 13.1

Peril	Basic Format (HO-1)	Broad Form (HO-2)	Special Form (HO-3)	Contents Broad Form (HO-4)	Comprehensive Form (HO-5)	Condominium Form (HO-6)	Older Home Form (HO-8)
1. Fire or lightning							
2. Loss of property removed from premises endangered by fire or other perils							
3. Windstorm or hail							
4. Explosion							
5. Riot or civil commotion							
6. Aircraft							
7. Vehicles							
8. Smoke							
9. Vandalism and malicious mischief							
10. Theft							
11. Breakage of glass constituting a part of the building							
12. Falling objects							
13. Weight of ice, snow, sleet							
14. Collapse of building(s) or any part thereof							
15. Sudden and accidental tearing asunder, cracking, burning, or bulging of a steam or hot water heating system or of appliances for heating water							
16. Accidental discharge, leaking, or overflow of water or steam from within a plumbing, heating, or air-conditioning system or domestic appliance							
17. Freezing of plumbing, heating, and air-conditioning systems and domestic appliances							
18. Sudden and accidental injury from artificially generated currents to electrical appliances, devices, fixtures, and wiring (TV and radio tubes not included)			Dwelling Only				
All perils except flood, earthquake, war, nuclear accident, and others specified in your policy. Check your policy for a complete listing of perils excluded.							

Figure 13.1

Insured Perils Under Homeowners' Policies

BOX 13.2

Financial
PLANNING
for Young Adults

A Property Insurance Protection Checklist for College Students

When you headed off to school did you check to see if you had everything you needed? It's likely that you overlooked an important item: your property insurance protection. You can remedy that oversight by answering a few simple questions.

✓1. Is your personal property protected under your parents' homeowners' policy?

Most homeowners' policies cover the property of students away at college, but the coverage may not extend to off-campus housing. The easiest way to find out whether you are adequately covered is to discuss the matter with your family's insurance agent. If you are not covered under your parents' homeowners' policy, consider purchasing renters' insurance.

✓2. Do you have adequate overall property protection?

Personal property coverage is typically 50 percent of dwelling coverage. However, the limit on property away from home may only be 10 percent of personal property coverage. On a home insured for $200,000, personal property coverage would be $100,000, and coverage of property away from home would be $10,000. In most cases, this should be adequate. However, if more protection is needed an endorsement could be added to your family's homeowners' policy.

✓3. Have you taken a personal inventory?

A descriptive list of the important items in your apartment, along with approximate values, should be compiled. Keep the list somewhere other than at school; typically, the family home is the best place. If the apartment is broken into while you are not at school, you will be able to supply the authorities with an accurate list of property that may be missing.

✓4. Do you exceed the limits on specific classes of property?

Valuable property is more likely to be lost or stolen when it is away from home than when it is at home. Coverage for computers and related equipment is probably limited to $5,000. Jewelry typically has a lower limit of $1,000. Property that exceeds policy limits can be insured with a personal articles floater.

Comprehensive Form (HO-5) provides all risks coverage on both the dwelling and personal property. It differs from HO-3 in that HO-3 includes only named perils coverage for personal property. The Comprehensive Form has the most protection and is the most expensive of all policies. In place of HO-5, some insurance companies provide HO-3 with Comprehensive Endorsement HO-15.

Condominium Form (HO-6) is similar to renters' form HO-4. Like the landlord, the condominium association usually provides insurance for the building and other structures. This may not cover, however, the condominium owners' additions and improvements to the dwelling unit. Therefore, the Condominium Form covers the owners' interest in additions to the dwelling unit at replacement cost up to a set limit. Furthermore, additional living expenses are paid for up to 40 percent of the coverage on personal property, instead of 20 percent. The policy also provides for endorsements in the event the owner is assessed for property or liability losses not covered under the association's insurance.

Older Home Form (HO-8) is for homes with actual cash value substantially below their replacement cost. This form provides coverage at actual cash value rather than replacement cost. Coverage at replacement cost on older homes would provide an incentive for arson, and carry exorbitant premiums.

Comprehensive Endorsement Form (HO-15) extends the coverage offered under HO-3 by providing all risks coverage on contents. In combination with HO-3, it provides the same coverage as HO-5.

Specialized Insurance

To close a gap in protection from either a standard exclusion or an insurance liability limit, you might consider some of the following additions to your homeowners' policy.

Endorsement

An **endorsement** is a paragraph that amends the original policy. It is added to make the standard policy more closely fit your individual needs. Endorsements may also be used to change the kind of coverage. Most policies agree to pay actual cash value on personal property damage. With an endorsement for "replacement cost coverage," you could change that. The perils insured against may also be changed with an endorsement. As previously mentioned, the standard policy excludes damage resulting from earthquakes. At additional cost, an endorsement can provide financial protection from this calamity.

Coverage that exceeds standard policy limits on personal property may be included in an endorsement. In addition, a business pursuits endorsement could cover a small business in your home. Of interest to most homeowners is an "inflation guard" endorsement. As housing values rise, this endorsement automatically increases your coverage. It is a worthwhile addition, ensuring that you will not get caught short under the coinsurance clause.

Endorsement: An amendment to the basic policy extending or changing the type of insurance coverage.

Floaters

The term **floater** is left over from the industry's early days, when it specialized in marine insurance. Like the cargo on a ship, your valuables can be insured with a *personal articles floater*. This can take the form of a separate policy or an endorsement to the original policy. Under the unscheduled property coverage, fairly low limits are set on payments for damaged or stolen valuables. If you need coverage beyond these limits, you can acquire it with a floater.

In a floater, the property is *scheduled*. This means it is described in terms of type and quality, and its value is supported by a report from a professional appraiser or bill of sale. Personal articles floaters usually cover all risks with no deductible.

Floater: Schedules property for specific coverage.

An Umbrella Policy

Umbrella coverage is written over an underlying homeowners' policy and a family auto policy. It takes over when the liability limits on these policies are reached. For example, if your homeowners' policy covers liability losses up to $100,000, an umbrella policy can protect you from losses in excess of $100,000, up to $1 million or more.

An umbrella policy is often written on a "following form" basis, meaning it will follow the form of the underlying coverage on which it was written. Consequently, you will be insured for the same perils as in the underlying policy.

Umbrella coverage: Provides catastrophic protection that begins where basic coverage ends.

Earthquake Insurance

Earthquake insurance may be purchased as an endorsement to the homeowners' policy. In earthquake-prone areas such as California, this insurance carries a high premium and a high deductible. Because of the high premiums and attempts by insurers to cut back their exposure in this market, fewer homes than you might expect carry earthquake protection. At most, only about one in four California homes is covered.

In California, where insurers have been reluctant to sell earthquake insurance, the legislature passed a law requiring insurers to offer earthquake insurance along with normal homeowners' policies. In response, some insurers withdrew from the homeowners' insurance market. To remedy this situation the state legislature created the California Earthquake Authority (CEA) to provide catastrophic earthquake coverage. By law it is required to sell policies to all customers of insurers within the state. Rates on CEA coverage can be obtained online.

TOPIC **LINKS**
Check out your earthquake hazard.

TOPIC **LINKS**
Check out rates on CEA coverage

Flood Insurance

Because flood damage is an excluded peril under homeowners' policies, you will have to rely on the federal government's National Flood Insurance Program. Your community must participate in this program before individual homeowners are able to purchase government flood insurance. The federally guaranteed insurance is sold by participating private insurance companies. You can locate an insurer through your agent or by contacting the FEMA (Federal Emergency Management Agency).

When you apply for a home mortgage, a second mortgage, or a home equity loan, it is likely that your lender will require certification as to whether your home is in a Special Flood Hazard Area. If it is, you must acquire flood insurance before the loan can be closed. To ensure that your policy does not lapse from nonpayment, your lender can require that you deposit flood insurance premiums in an escrow account.

If your home is in an area no longer rated as a flood hazard region, then you can drop your flood insurance. But you might want to think twice about doing so; one-third of flood claims come from outside special flood-designated areas. Do not plan on obtaining flood insurance when you see the hurricane on the horizon. Unless the insurance is purchased when the property is acquired, there is a 30-day waiting period for coverage.

TOPIC **LINKS**

Locate a National Flood Insurance provider in your state.

Renters' Insurance

A survey by the Insurance Agents and Brokers of America (IIABA) found that 64 percent of respondents living in rental properties did not have property insurance. The most common reason was that they believed they were covered by their landlord's insurance. However, under most circumstances the landlord is not responsible for your property losses. If you add up the cost of your belongings, you might discover that an apartment fire or a burglary can leave you with significant uncovered property losses. In addition, if a visitor trips on your carpet and breaks a leg, you could be responsible for medical bills. The IIABA reports that the average cost of a policy is $12 per month for about $30,000 of property coverage and $100,000 of liability coverage. Some insurers let roommates hold down total cost by sharing policy coverage.

Home Office

With the advent of Internet access and mobile communications, more people than ever are spending at least part of their workday in a home office. Many more take homework from the office. Over one-third of the adult population engages in some work at home. Unfortunately, homeowners' policies do not protect you from business-related liabilities. In addition, business property coverage typically is limited to $2,500. Moreover, there are policy limits on computers and electronic equipment. If you use that laptop away from home, the limit may be as low as $250.

A small business in your home might be covered by a business pursuits endorsement added to your current homeowners' policy. However, for anything substantial you will need a separate business insurance policy to cover all business-related losses. Professional liability insurance, also called errors and omissions insurance, provides coverage for malpractice in the provision of services.

Selecting Homeowners' Insurance

Now that you understand the basics of homeowners' coverage, you should be able to compare policies and insurers. The following points should aid you in your selection.

- Shop for coverage. Market studies have found a wide range in prices for similar policies. It is worthwhile talking to several insurers before you select an insurer and the type of coverage that is right for you. Check the Web site for your state's department of insurance. Several states now compare prices on insurance products and publish the results on the Internet.

- Buy your homeowners' and auto insurance from the same insurer. Insurers often offer discounts for combined coverage.
- Select a high deductible. A high deductible can result in significant cost savings on premiums. You can self-insure the small risks.
- Periodically revise your coverage for increases in building costs. If you insure for significantly less than current replacement cost, you may be penalized under the coinsurance clause.
- Check out discounts. You may be able to lower your premiums by improving your home security and making your home more disaster resistant.
- Maintain a good credit record. A low credit score can result in higher premiums. It indicates to the insurer that you are not a responsible person.
- Review your limits on personal property. If the value of your personal property exceeds the limits on your policy, you might want to extend coverage with an endorsement.
- Insure for special circumstances. If you conduct part of your business at home, don't assume your business is covered by your homeowners' policy. Discuss your special circumstances with your agent.
- Check out the financial stability of the insurer. You want to feel secure that the insurer will be there when you need help.

TOPIC **LINKS**

Get a quote.

Making Sure You Collect on a Loss

Having adequate insurance coverage is not enough to ensure that you will receive appropriate compensation in the event of property loss. Policyholders with identical losses and identical coverage may receive different levels of reimbursement simply because they approach the claim process differently. Making good on a claim requires documentation, notification, and evaluation.

TOPIC **LINKS**

Compare California homeowners' premiums.

Documentation

The first step in filing a claim should be taken before the loss occurs. The loss must be documented. Of course, doing so is a lot easier while you still have your property in good condition.

When you apply for scheduled property coverage with a floater, you will be required to document the property's actual cash value. Be sure to update the appraisals whenever market prices change, including both upward and downward movements.

On unscheduled property coverage, evidence of worth need be supplied only after the loss. You are entirely responsible for documenting and describing your loss to the insurance company. Keep an inventory of your belongings, including a description of each item that indicates all identifying marks, the original purchase price, and the date of purchase. For the more expensive items you should include a copy of the bill of sale in your records. While taking inventory, check for items that might exceed the recovery limits on your homeowners' policy. Consider scheduling these goods with a floater. Take photos of every room in your house, or better yet, make a videotape tour of your home. Now take all of this documentation and store it in a safe place away from the home. If your house burns down, you don't want this destroyed with it.

TOPIC **LINKS**

Check ratings for financial stability.

Notification

When a property loss occurs, you should first contact the relevant civil authority, then take whatever steps are needed to protect your property from further damage. Your failure to notify the police or a credit card company in the event of theft may invalidate your coverage. Next, contact your insurer. Your agent should be able to inform you immediately whether you are covered, in addition to supplying information on what you should do next. Insurance agents are used to dealing with tragedies. At a time like this, the support they can provide in seeking alternative shelter or assistance with repairs and debris removal can be invaluable.

Before anything is repaired or removed, be sure you have fully documented the loss. Take photos of the damage. If you followed the previous advice, you will now have a set of before and after snapshots. Also, request copies of any police or fire reports on the damage, and get the names and addresses of any witnesses to the mishap.

Evaluation

If the insurer feels your claim may be covered, an adjuster will be sent to verify the claim and determine the amount of loss. You should supply the adjuster with copies of all the evidence of loss you have collected. Under most circumstances, a settlement offer will be made promptly. Don't be too hasty to accept. Take the time to review your inventory of damaged items and to search out the replacement cost on these goods.

Let the adjuster make the first settlement offer, and request an explanation of how the amount was determined. If you feel the offer is too low or you are denied payment on what you believe is a covered loss, you may state your case to the adjuster and ask that the settlement offer be reconsidered. If you still can't agree, you can demand that the settlement be submitted to arbitration. You and the insurer will be required to split the cost of the arbitrators' fees.

One less costly but potentially less effective action is to write your state's insurance commission. They are not likely to take action on an individual complaint. But if yours is one of many, the state commission may decide to look into the problem.

You may be able to deduct any unreimbursed casualty losses on your personal income tax return. Only sizable losses, however, are likely to lead to any significant tax savings. The rules for reducing your taxable income by the amount of the loss are quite strict. (See IRS Publication 547, "Casualties, Disasters and Thefts.")

Frequency of Claims

The Insurance Information Institute reports that homeowners file on average one claim every 11.2 years for average damages per claim of $3,752. Your claim will be included in the Comprehensive Loss Underwriting Exchange (CLUE). This is a shared industry-wide database that tracks claims. Filing a number of small claims can result in your insurer dropping your coverage or increasing your premiums. This is because it will affect your insurance risk score, which insurers used to assess your risk classification (see Box 13.2). This is another good reason for having a large deductible on your insurance policy. By avoiding a number of small claims you will hold down your risk score and your premiums.

AUTOMOBILE INSURANCE

Automobile insurance is meant to protect you against three risks: (1) bodily harm and property damage to others from negligent operation of the vehicle; (2) personal injury to you, your family, and guests riding in your car; and (3) damage or loss of your car due to fire, theft, or collision. Of the three, the first has the potential for the greatest financial loss.

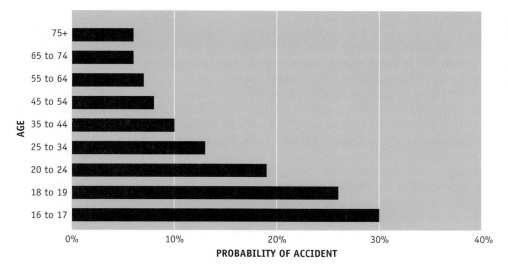

Figure 13.2

Probability of Licensed Driver Involved in an Auto Accident

Source: *U.S. Statistical Abstract, 2003.*

Who Needs Auto Insurance Coverage?

The simple answer is that if you drive a car, you do. There is a substantial chance of being in some kind of car accident over the next five years, and if you are an unmarried male driver under age 25, the odds are even higher (see Figure 13.2). In all states, liability insurance is mandatory. However, regardless of state requirements, it is just downright foolish to take a car on the road without adequate coverage. One accident can result in hundreds of thousands of dollars in claims against you and your estate.

Coverage Under Your Auto Policy

The standard policy covers you and other family members living with you. It also protects others when driving one of your covered cars and you and your family when driving someone else's auto.

The **personal auto policy** follows a standard format used by most insurers. Policy comparisons are fairly easy, because coverage is usually divided into identical parts listed in the same order. However, auto policies tend to be written in stilted language and are difficult to read. If your policy contains the terms *first party, second party*, and *third party*, just remember that the first party is you and the second party is the insurer. If you collide with another car, the driver of that car becomes the third party. Claims by you or your passengers are first-party claims. Those by the driver or passengers in the other vehicle are third-party claims.

Part A—Liability

The most important component of your auto insurance is liability coverage. It operates much the same as liability coverage under the homeowners' policy, except that it applies only to damages resulting from an auto accident. It pays for bodily injury and property damage you cause to third parties.

On a policy with a **split liability limit,** you will see the liability limits presented in the following format: 100/300/10. The first number indicates the maximum amount the insurer will pay for bodily injury to a single person. The second number is the maximum amount

TOPIC LINKS

Find the mandated minimum liability in your state.

Personal auto policy: Auto policy providing standardized coverage for families and individuals.

Split liability limit: Provides specific limits on liability coverage for a single individual, a single accident, and property damage.

TOPIC **LINKS**

Try an auto coverage analyzer.

Single liability limit: Provides a single limit that covers all bodily and property losses incurred in a single accident.

the insurer will pay for all injuries sustained in a single accident, and the last is the insurer's liability limit for property damage in a given accident. For example, suppose there were two riders in the other car. One sustained $210,000 in bodily injury and the other $80,000 in bodily injury. The insurer would reimburse the first rider for $100,000 and the second rider for the full $80,000 sought, since total payments are under the $300,000 limit for a single accident. In addition, the insurer would pay for damage to the other vehicle up to $10,000. You would be responsible for the excess liability, which would include $110,000 to the first rider and any property damage exceeding $10,000.

Some policies have a **single liability limit.** This means the insurer will pay up to this limit for each accident, regardless of how this amount may be divided among the injured and for property damage. When the single liability limit on one policy is the same as the limit per accident on a split liability policy, the single liability limit provides the better coverage. In the previous example, a single liability limit of $300,000 would have left you with little or no excess liability.

In addition to damages up to your policy limits, the insurer will also cover the cost of defending you in a lawsuit. This coverage will include such supplementary costs as legal and defense fees, premiums on appeal bonds, and limited reimbursement for bail bonds and lost earnings. However, once the company has reached your liability limits, perhaps through an out-of-court settlement with the injured party, then further legal costs are all yours.

A liability limit of $300,000 may sound like a lot of protection. It actually isn't. The damages suffered by a severely injured person who is unable to work can easily exceed this figure. You might suggest you don't need this much insurance because you don't have $300,000 in assets to protect. But the higher your protection, the less likely it is that you will have any excess liability above your insurance coverage.

Part B—Medical Payments

Medical payments coverage: Covers minor medical expenses for those riding in your car during an accident.

Injuries to you, your family, and guests riding in your car are insured under **medical payments coverage,** regardless of who is at fault. The coverage also applies when you or your family are riding in other vehicles or when one of your family members is hit by a car while walking. The typical limits on payments are low, between $500 to $5,000 per person. It is not meant to take the place of a good health insurance plan. In fact, if you have good health insurance, you should consider holding limits in this part to a minimum.

Some companies will include death and disability insurance under the medical payments section. A special life insurance or disability policy would take care of these contingencies with broader coverage than would a policy that covers only auto accidents.

Part C—Uninsured Motorists

Uninsured motorists coverage: Covers bodily injury to you or your family members from either an uninsured driver or a hit-and-run driver.

Uninsured motorists coverage is worthwhile low-cost protection, about $11 per year for a policy with 25/50/10 limits. In most states, damage to your auto is not covered under uninsured motorists. It primarily covers bodily injury to you or your family members from either an uninsured driver or a hit-and-run driver. The coverage also applies when riding in other cars or walking. For the policy to pay off, the other driver must be at fault.

You may want to carry this protection even when your state requires auto liability insurance, since there is no way the state can ensure that every driver is financially responsible. The need for this coverage is apparent when you consider that about 14 percent of drivers do not carry auto insurance according to the Insurance Research Council. Some financial planners advise clients do without uninsured motorist coverage if they have adequate health and disability insurance.

Underinsured motorists coverage: Protects you when the at-fault motorist is insured for less than the damages incurred.

In many areas you may purchase supplementary **underinsured motorists coverage.** This operates in the same manner as uninsured motorists, except that when the other motorist is insured for less than the damages, your policy pays for the difference up to specified limits.

Part D—Damage to Your Auto

Part D consists of two separate components, collision and other than collision. **Collision coverage** pays for damage to your car in a collision, regardless of who is at fault. If the other driver is responsible for damages, your insurer will seek reimbursement and refund the deductible if it is successful. **Other than collision coverage,** also called comprehensive auto coverage, provides all risks coverage on your car. Specifically included are such perils as fire, theft, falling objects, windstorm, flood, earthquake, and collision with an animal. Both coverages carry deductibles, and under either, the insurer has the option of paying for repairs or paying you for the actual cash value of a similar auto.

Because the actual cash value on older cars is small, it is generally recommended that you not purchase property damage insurance on cars five years or older or when your car is worth less than ten times the annual premium on collision and comprehensive coverage. The premiums do not justify the minimal benefits in case of loss. With newer cars, you can hold down your premiums by including higher deductibles. Again, the optimal strategy is to take on the small risks yourself and use the savings to transfer the big risks.

Collision coverage: Pays for damage to your car in a collision, regardless of who is at fault.

Other than collision coverage: All risks coverage on your car.

Exclusions

Most policies will exclude noninstalled sound and CB equipment from theft coverage. The chances of such accessories being stolen are just too high. You might consider covering these with a floater on your homeowners' policy.

A few other common exceptions are important to your personal liability coverage. Some are clear-cut, and others are not so obvious. If you think you might be subject to any of the following exclusions, you should discuss the matter with your insurance agent.

- Use of someone else's car without permission
- Use of a nonlisted car you own, except for a grace period during a trade-in
- Carrying passengers for a fee
- Driving a motorcycle
- Use of a company car
- Driving a noninsured car of a live-in relative
- Driving a rental car unless the policy states otherwise

No-Fault Insurance

No-fault insurance: Allows policyholders to recover financial losses from their own insurer regardless of who is at fault.

Several states have attempted to hold down the cost of insurance by introducing no-fault plans. A **no-fault insurance** plan is one that allows policyholders to recover financial losses from their own insurer, regardless of who is at fault. In return for receiving reimbursement from your own insurer, there may be restrictions placed upon your right to sue. You retain the right to sue only when your physical injuries are severe according to a **verbal threshold** or your medical expenses exceed a **monetary threshold.** In addition, your right to sue for nonmonetary losses such as pain and suffering may also be restricted. By eliminating the determination of fault and reducing the types of damages that may be litigated, no-fault insurance is meant to hold down insurance premiums.

Verbal threshold: Injured individuals may sue for reimbursement for physical injuries that satisfy this definition.

Monetary threshold: Injured individuals may sue for medical expenses that exceed this amount.

No-fault insurance has not always worked as intended. States with no-fault insurance tend to have higher auto premiums. Nonexisting or low thresholds have resulted in widespread first-party payments for small claims without curtailing costly legal suits. Insurance company representatives, however, continue to believe that no-fault insurance can be a success if properly written. They are now lobbying for a federal law that would impose a standardized no-fault insurance on all states.

Personal injury protection (PIP): Mandatory coverage in no-fault states that allows you to collect expenses for personal injury from your own insurer, regardless of fault.

Although the required minimum amount of coverage varies, in all no-fault states you are required to carry **personal injury protection (PIP).** This permits you to recover medical and hospital expenses, lost wages, and other injury-related expenses up to your policy limits from your own insurer, regardless of fault. However, because lawsuits are still possible, in most of these same states you also must carry personal liability protection.

Rental Coverage

Collision damage waiver (CDW): A waiver of the rental firm's right to charge you for damage to the rental.

Your personal auto policy may extend liability coverage to rental cars. It may even cover damage to a rental car. Your credit card may provide similar auto damage coverage. It is important to check before you rent. With this coverage you can avoid purchasing a **collision damage waiver (CDW)** when you rent a car. CDW looks like insurance, but it isn't. It is actually a waiver of the rental firm's right to charge you for damage to the rental. The cost of this limited protection can be very high, from $10 to $20 a day, which totals from $3,650 to $7,300 over a 365-day year.

Other Coverage

There are several supplemental coverages that some insurance companies make available. These are generally considered high-cost add-ons, and most consumer groups advise against their purchase. The most common is *rental reimbursement,* which covers a rental vehicle if your car is damaged or stolen. Insurance for *towing and labor* charges for road repairs can also be added. And if you really love your car, there is *auto replacement coverage* that insures that your car will be either repaired or replaced.

The Cost of Auto Insurance

The average cost of full auto coverage in 2001 was $718 per car, but the actual cost varied greatly across the nation. The average auto premium was higher in densely populated states such as New Jersey ($1,027) and lower in sparsely populated states such as Iowa ($513).

The cost of auto insurance can also vary widely from one company to another. As with homeowners' policies, most auto companies sell a standardized policy, making it easy to compare features and price. Moreover, it may be wise to shop for both homeowners' and auto insurance at the same time, since some companies provide a multiple-policy discount when both are purchased. Be sure to request the potental discounts listed in Table 13.1. To help with your shopping, use a checklist like that in Figure 13.3, listing the kind, amount, and cost of each coverage.

Check with your state's Department of Insurance. Several states provide buyers' guides and rate reporting services on the Internet. They should also be able to provide some background information on insurers in your state. Moreover, before you buy, be sure to review the financial stability of the insurer with one of the rating services such as Best's or Standard & Poor's.

The Rate Base

The cost of your insurance policy will depend on your risk class. It is based on factors over which you have some control, such as your driving record and your zip code, and others over which you have no control, such as your age and gender. If other drivers in your age group are accident prone, you are going to be charged more for insurance, independently of how good or bad a driver you happen to be. This may sound discriminatory, and in a sense it is. However, an efficient system of insurance requires the assignment of probabilities to groups of events. The insurance company must be able to discriminate, on the basis of experience, between apparent high-risk groups and low-risk groups. Otherwise, those in the low-risk group would subsidize the premiums for poor drivers.

Individual auto insurance premiums are determined in a two-stage process. First, each state is divided into territories, and each territory is assigned a base rate dependent on risk factors and costs within that region. Next, the base rate is multiplied by a value that is determined by the risks associated with the personal characteristics of the insured. Your risk classification will take into account each of the following factors: your age, sex, marital status, educational level, driving record, credit record, and even the kind of car you drive.

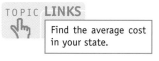

TOPIC **LINKS**

Find the average cost in your state.

TOPIC **LINKS**

See if there is a shopper's guide to auto and home insurance in your state.

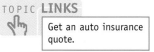

TOPIC **LINKS**

Get an auto insurance quote.

Discounts Offered for Cars with the Following Features	Discounts Offered for Insureds with the Following Characteristics
Antilocking brake system Antitheft devices Automatic seat belts or air bags High-level brake light	Away-at-school driver Carpool driver Driver training Good driving record Good student record Mature driver Multicar household Multipolicy household Nonsmoking driver Retired driver

Table 13.1

Typical Discounts Offered by Auto Insurers

Figure 13.3

Auto Insurance Comparison Checklist

	Limits	Deductible	Annual Rate
Company _____			
Liability	_____		_____
Medical payments	_____		_____
Personal injury protection (no-fault states)	_____		_____
Uninsured motorists	_____		_____
Underinsured motorists	_____		_____
Collision		_____	_____
Other than collision		_____	_____
Total Cost			_____

Discounts (see Table 13.1)

Type	Percentage Discount	Dollar Discount
1. _____	_____	_____
2. _____	_____	_____
3. _____	_____	_____
etc. _____	_____	_____
Total Dollar Discount		(_____)
Total Cost after Discount		_____

When discounts are offered (see Table 13.1), they are figured from the base rate, not from the individual auto insurance premium. A young male driver, for example, might receive a 10 percent discount for having taken driver education. If his base rate is $200 and his annual premium is $760, his discount will be $20, not $76.

Driving Record

One factor over which you definitely do have some control is your driving record. A chargeable accident (one that is your fault) or a serious driving violation will increase your premiums by 40 percent or more. A history of such behavior can cause your rates to double and may result in cancellation of your policy. You will then have to purchase very expensive insurance from a company specializing in high-risk drivers or from the *shared* market in your state. In this market, which is also called the *assigned risk* market, your policy is placed in a pool with those of other high-risk drivers. The insurance companies agree to jointly share the cost and risk of providing for the insurance needs of these drivers. In about half the states, these are known as FAIR (Fair Access to Insurance Requirements) plans.

Car Make and Model

It is obvious that a car requiring more expensive repairs will carry higher rates for property damage coverage than other vehicles. (See Figure 13.4 for the relative cost of property damage on selected autos.) What is not so obvious is that certain cars will carry higher rates for liability coverage and collision because the chances of you, your passengers, and others being seriously injured in this particular car are greater.

The relative mix of age groups driving a particular car should affect that car's risk exposure. However, even after we consider that factor, some cars are just more accident prone than others. The insurance companies have responded by providing discounts for cars in low-risk groups and surcharges for cars in high-risk groups. The next time you think about buying a car, it is probably wise to check with your insurance agent to find out how your planned purchase ranks. The insurance saving on an alternative purchase might more than outweigh any saving on purchase price.

TOPIC **LINKS**

Locate loss data on your car.

MAKE	MODEL	RELATIVE LOSS PAYMENT
Acura	RSX	213
Toyota	Celica	182
Toyota	MR2 Spyder conv.	142
Hyundai	Accent–4dr	123
Saturn	ION	91
Chrysler	PT Cruiser 4dr	73
Toyota	Camry–4dr	83
Saturn	LS	69

Figure 13.4

Auto Accident Checklist

Source: Highway Data Loss Institute, 2004.

Before, At, and After the Accident

The odds are overwhelming that you will be involved in at least one auto accident. Accordingly, having the correct coverage and understanding what you should and should not do can prove extremely rewarding.

Before the Accident

Adequate liability protection is a must. You should periodically review your policy to make sure that your family has the right kind and amount of coverage. Auto insurance information, including your policy number, agent, and telephone number, should be kept in the glove compartment. Any preprinted insurance forms allowing you to report the particulars of any accident, including a sketch of the scene should also be placed there.

At the Accident

If you are driving a car involved in a collision, you must stop the vehicle immediately. Do not, however, leave it in a position that creates a traffic hazard and causes another accident. Give your name and address, insurance information, and the registration number of the vehicle involved, to the other driver, any injured persons, and the arriving police officer. Obtain similar information of all persons involved in the accident and witnesses to the accident. Furthermore, get the name of the arriving police officer, and request a copy of the officer's accident report (see Figure 13.5).

Auto Accident Checklist

1. Stop the vehicle immediately and remain at the scene until a police officer arrives.
2. Give your name and address, those of the vehicle's owner, and the registration number of the vehicle to:
   (a) Any injured person.
   (b) The owner, operator, or attendant of any damaged vehicle.
   (c) Any police officer at the scene of the accident.
3. Obtain the name and address of the driver of the other vehicle, all passengers, and witnesses.
4. Obtain license numbers of all drivers involved.
5. Make notes of all significant circumstances surrounding the accident.
6. If there are serious injuries, make the injured person comfortable and phone for medical aid immediately. Under no circumstances should you move the injured person.
7. If you or any passenger in your car is injured, consult with your doctor immediately and encourage others to do so.
8. Obtain copy of the police officer's accident report.
9. File all accident report forms required by the state or local government.
10. Report the accident to your insurance company as soon as possible.

Figure 13.5

Auto Accident Checklist

Make notes of the circumstances concerning the accident, including the position of the cars before and after the accident, traffic signs, road and weather conditions, and road obstacles. Step off the skid points to measure them, and locate the point of collision. If you have a camera with you, photograph the damage and the accident scene.

Assist the investigating officer by providing all factual information when requested. Do not offer any opinion on the cause of the accident or admit any guilt or blame. If others are injured, your first reaction may be to feel responsible. On calmer reflection, you might realize the fault was not yours. If you are arrested, ask to meet with your attorney before offering any explanation.

Do not make any payments or accept any payments at the scene of the accident. A settlement offer should be considered only after you have discussed the matter with your agent and, possibly, an attorney.

If there are serious injuries, your first obligation is to seek medical aid. You may make the injured person more comfortable, but do not move the injured in any way that might aggravate a serious injury. Even if the accident was not your fault, if your actions contribute to the other person's injuries, you may be liable. If you think that you or anyone in your car might be injured, be sure to seek treatment immediately. You will be reimbursed under your medical payments coverage.

After the Accident

Report the accident to your insurance agent as soon as possible and file any written reports required under your state's motor vehicle statutes. Most policies require that you notify the company within one day of the accident. If you fail to satisfy this requirement, the insurer can later refuse to honor any claim resulting from the accident.

Keep track of all your accident-related expenses, including medical payments, lost wages, and additional traveling costs. These are all collectible damages when the other driver is at fault. If you think these losses may be sizable, seek the advice of an attorney. You may find that, in addition to the economic damages, you may also be able to collect for pain and suffering.

In a suit for damages, the plaintiff's attorney usually recovers a contingency fee. A few lawyers may be willing to work on an hourly basis, however. The contingency fee is normally 30 percent of the awarded damages, but the exact percentage is negotiable. This pays only for the lawyer. Whether you use an hourly basis or a contingency fee, there will be added expenses for such things as expert witnesses. These additional expenses must be paid whether you win or lose the case. Be sure to request that the lawyer first seek your approval before incurring any of these extra costs.

If the accident was your fault and it appears the damages awarded may exceed the liability limits on your policy, the insurer should inform you of this likelihood. You must then independently hire an attorney to take over when the insurer's participation ends and to make sure the insurance company has operated in your best interests.

Key Terms

actual cash value (p. 331)	coinsurance (p. 331)	floater (p. 339)
adverse selection (p. 328)	collision coverage (p. 345)	gambling (p. 328)
all risks coverage (p. 330)	collision damage waiver	indemnification (p. 329)
apportionment clause (p. 333)	(CDW) (p. 346)	inflation guard endorsement (p. 332)
appurtenant structures (p. 334)	deductible clause (p. 332)	insurable interest (p. 328)
	dwelling protection (p. 333)	liability coverage (p. 335)
	endorsement (p. 339)	

medical payments coverage (p. 344)
monetary threshold (p. 346)
mortgage clause (p. 333)
named perils coverage (p. 330)
negligence (p. 335)
no-fault insurance (p. 346)
other than collision coverage (p. 345)
personal auto policy (p. 343)
personal injury protection (PIP) (p. 346)

personal liability insurance (p. 327)
property loss insurance (p. 327)
pure risk (p. 327)
replacement cost (p. 330)
risk avoidance (p. 329)
risk management (p. 329)
risk reduction (p. 329)
risk retention (p. 329)
risk transfer (p. 330)
single liability limit (p. 344)

speculative risk (p. 327)
split liability limit (p. 343)
subrogation clause (p. 333)
umbrella coverage (p. 339)
underinsured motorists coverage (p. 344)
underwriting (p. 328)
uninsured motorists coverage (p. 344)
unscheduled personal property (p. 334)
verbal threshold (p. 346)

FOLLOW-UP ON THE Steele FAMILY

Reread the chapter-opening vignette.

1. Given the Steeles' assets (outlined in previous chapters), what types of property insurance should they have?
2. The Steeles are interested in holding down their property insurance costs. What strategies might satisfy this objective?
3. Given the Steeles' financial position (discussed in previous chapters), how much auto liability insurance should they carry?

Problems and Review Questions

1. How does gambling differ from purchasing insurance?
2. Explain the difference between all risks insurance and named perils insurance. List three perils not ordinarily covered under the basic homeowners' policy.
3. Which cost is greater: replacement cost or actual cash value? Why?
4. What items are typically insured for replacement cost?
5. What is the difference between unscheduled property and scheduled property? How is scheduled property insured?
6. Where would a homeowner obtain flood insurance?
7. How does a homeowner obtain earthquake coverage? Assess the pros and cons of obtaining earthquake insurance.
8. Larry recently started operating a mail-order business in the basement of his home. Unfortunately, a fire put an end to his dreams of success by destroying about $10,000 worth of goods that had been temporarily stored in his basement. Will his homeowners' policy cover the loss? Why or why not?
9. While on her newspaper route, Jane's daughter tosses a paper through a subscriber's front window, causing $300 in damages. Might Jane be covered by her homeowners' insurance?
10. Why is it important to insure your dwelling for at least 80 percent of its replacement cost? How does the coinsurance clause operate?
11. What is the most important component of your auto insurance coverage? Why?

12. Ruth had stopped for breakfast during a long morning drive to the ski slopes. While she was inside eating, someone broke into her car and made off with over $500 in ski equipment. What should she do? Under what policy might she be covered?

13. Last week Fred traded in his old junker for a new sports car. Not used to the fast response of a sports car, he accidentally drove it off a country road into a field, killing a cow. The car suffered extensive damage, and the farmer is demanding compensation for the dead cow. Fred had insurance on his old car. But he hadn't yet gotten around to informing his insurer of the trade-in. Will his old policy still cover him?

14. While riding to school on her bicycle, Ruth was run off the road by a hit-and-run driver. Except for a broken arm that is healing nicely, she was unhurt. Under which insurance policy and under what section of that insurance policy might her parents apply for reimbursement of medical expenses?

15. An engine fire destroys your car. Which coverage would reimburse you for the damage? What is the maximum amount you could collect under your auto policy?

16. While stopped for a red light on Main Street, Ralph's car was hit from behind by a negligent driver. Because he was in a state with no-fault insurance and since nobody was injured, he didn't think it was necessary to get the other driver's name and license number. Under what section of his auto policy is he covered?

17. Name several factors insurers consider when setting auto insurance rates. How might you hold down your auto insurance costs?

18. Peter is away at college and drives the family car only when he comes home on special occasions. How might Peter's family hold down the cost of their auto insurance?

19. Why is it wise to review your auto policy before you rent a car?

20. Why is uninsured motorists coverage sold in states that have laws requiring compulsory auto insurance?

Case 13.1
A Fire at the Pages'

It was around midnight when the smoke alarm woke Peter and Barbara Page. The fire had started in the attached garage and was already flaming when the fire department arrived. By the time it was out, the Pages' home had sustained damages that would take $20,000 to repair. In addition, their Honda, with a market price of $8,000, was totally destroyed.

When the Pages purchased their home, they took out a homeowners' policy with $60,000 worth of dwelling protection. Since then they have received several letters from the insurance company suggesting they increase the dwelling coverage. For one reason or another they just never got around to responding. Now the insurer tells them that because their coverage was for less than 80 percent of the home's replacement value, as determined by the replacement cost provision, the insurance company probably will not pay the full cost of repairs. To avoid coinsurance payments, they should have been carrying at least $90,000 in dwelling protection.

Questions
1. Given the position of the insurance company, what is the smallest reimbursement the Pages can expect?
2. Is there any chance they can collect for the destroyed auto? How much and from whom?
3. Suppose the Pages disagree with the insurer's cost estimates. What course of action should they follow?

Bob Brown was recently involved in a minor auto accident. His car was hit from behind, and he, in turn, slammed into the car in front of him. He would like someone to explain his coverage and show him where in his auto policy each of his losses might be covered. Help him out by doing that for each of the following items:

1. The cost of a medical checkup for his passenger, Ruth
2. The front and rear damage to his car
3. The damage to the car in front of him
4. The damage to the car behind him
5. The total amount of liability protection for bodily harm and property damage

Case 13.2

After the Accident

Exercises to Strengthen Your Use of the Internet

(Internet links for the following exercises can be found at **www.prenhall.com/winger**.)

Working Out on the Web

Exercise 13.1 Check the Financial Stability of Property Casualty Insurers

In the event of a major catastrophe, such as hurricane Hugo, property casualty insurers must have adequate reserves to cover the liabilities. The Insurance News Network provides Standard & Poor's ratings of property and casualty insurers and life and health insurers.

Q. Choose a company with a triple A rating and one that has a triple B rating. Determine why these companies are rated differently.

Exercise 13.2 Does Your State Publish a Rate Comparison Survey?

The National Association of Insurance Commissioners provides links to state insurance regulators. Go to the department of insurance for your state and review the helpful material at this site.

Q. Does your state provide a rate comparison survey of homeowners' insurance or auto insurance? What other useful information is available at this site?

Exercise 13.3 What Are the Minimum Liability Limits in Your State?

Each state requires car owners to purchase a minimum amount of auto liability coverage. This minimum amount is probably less than you should have. However, this may be what the other driver on the road has. Consequently, you should be aware of your state's minimum. This information can be found at the Insurance News Network on a page entitled "Minimum levels of required auto liability insurance." The minimums are listed in terms of split liability coverage. The information can also be found at Autopedia.

Q. What is the minimum split liability coverage in your state? Explain how the split liability limit is applied to bodily injury and property damage.

Exercise 13.4 What Is the Cost of Auto Insurance and How Much Coverage Do You Need?

This map from Insure.com provides the average cost of auto insurance in your state. The Coverage Analyzer at SmartMoney.com calculates how much coverage it thinks you need.

Q. What is the average cost of auto insurance in your state, and how much coverage do you really need?

Exercise 13.5 Will Your Car Be Stolen?

If thieves like your car, you will probably have to pay a high premium for coverage against theft. The Highway Loss Data Institute collects data on this and other factors that affect auto insurance premiums. Review "Injury, Collision and Theft Losses."

Q. How does the loss rating for your or your family's auto compare to that of the average auto? If your model year is not listed, use the closest model and year.

Exercise 13.6 Driver Death Rates

The Highway Loss Data Institute publishes driver death rates by make and model of car, which take into account the crash worthiness of the vehicle and the characteristics of individuals who drive a certain type of vehicle. Vehicles with higher death rates are likely to have higher insurance premiums.

Q. Check out the "Death Rates by Make and Model" *for the car you own or usually ride in. How does this car compare with the average vehicle in its class?*

14

Health Care and Disability Insurance

PROTECTING YOUR EARNING CAPACITY

OBJECTIVES

1. To describe the separate components of basic health care coverage

2. To discuss the need for major medical insurance

3. To list the important providers and insurers of health care

4. To compare and evaluate health care insurance plans

5. To list sources of disability income

6. To estimate your disability insurance needs

TOPIC **LINKS**

Follow the **Topic Links** in each chapter for your interactive Personal Finance exercise on the Web. Go to: **www.prenhall.com/winger**

Steele FAMILY

Like most families, the Steeles have been concerned about the rising cost of health care. They recognize the importance of having health insurance to protect against major medical emergencies. The Steeles obtain their health insurance coverage through Arnold's employer. He has a choice of joining either a traditional fee-for-service plan or a health maintenance organization. The employer covers the full cost of Arnold's individual coverage and for an extra $150 a month he receives family coverage. Over the past few years, the additional contribution for family coverage has risen significantly. Their hope is that when Sharon returns to full-time employment, she may be able to obtain less costly family coverage.

The Steeles are members of the HMO (health maintenance organization) but they do not have a flexible spending account. The Steeles have been generally satisfied with the HMO. However, copayments for doctors' visits and drug prescriptions will increase significantly. Moreover, dental visits and eyeglasses are not covered. Combined expenditures for copayments and noncovered health expenditures are expected to be above $1,500 next year.

Arnold's employer does not provide long-term disability income protection. Were Arnold to become ill, his short-term disability benefits would end after six months. Arnold and Sharon have discussed this possibility. They feel that if Arnold were permanently disabled, Sharon could return to full-time employment. Over all, the Steeles believe that they are prepared for any future medical emergency.

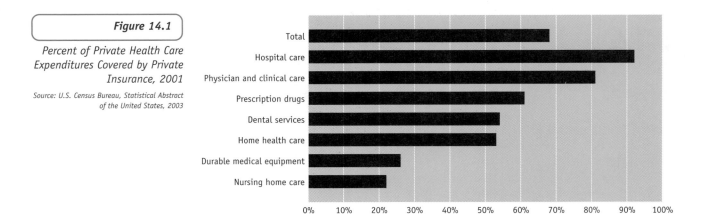

In terms of financial burdens, nothing is more devastating than a catastrophic illness. Serious illness or injury is difficult enough to deal with, even without the stress that medical bills and lost income can create. Having quality health and disability coverage can at least lessen the increasing financial hardship that accompanies injury and illness.

Over the past two decades, the price of medical care has risen at almost twice the rate of increase in all other prices. An increasing share of this rising burden has been covered by third-party payments through private insurance and government programs. Private health insurance now covers about 68 percent of all private consumer expenditures on health care. As indicated in Figure 14.1, this can range from a high of 92 percent for hospital care to a low of 22 percent for nursing home care.

The Bureau of the Census reports that about 85 percent of all Americans have some type of private or public health insurance coverage. Most of the private coverage is group coverage related to the past or current employment of a family member. Because health insurance coverage is primarily work related, young adults aged 18 to 24, who are more likely than other age groups to be unemployed, are also more likely to be without health insurance protection.

Many people with insurance are inadequately covered because they have the wrong kind or amount of protection. Adequate protection includes reimbursement for major medical expenses through health care insurance and compensation for lost income through disability income insurance. Protection against loss of income due to illness or injury is even less adequate than health care coverage. Apparently, most people feel either that the chances of becoming disabled are too small to require protection or that government programs will prove sufficient. As we will see, both assumptions are incorrect.

HEALTH CARE INSURANCE

Employment-related health insurance is often a very attractive deal. First, because of lower administrative costs and because of lower health risks than exist for the population as a whole, insurance companies will on average charge lower premiums for employer-sponsored health insurance. Second, more than half of the premiums are typically paid for by the employer. Finally, you and your family are probably eligible regardless of your physical condition.

You might think that most of us have little need to consider health insurance. You simply accept what the employer is offering. This assumption is incorrect. Today, many companies will offer their employees a choice among two or more health care plans with differing employee premiums and differing schedules of benefits. And, in families where both spouses are employed outside the home, these choices are greatly compounded. Not only must they compare the plans offered by their individual employers, they must also consider whether it is better for them to join their respective group plans separately or to participate in only one, listing the other as a dependent. No doubt the company personnel officer will help you compare and contrast the available options, but the final decision on what is best for you and your family must be yours. You alone can determine the adequacy of your group coverage and select a supplemental individual or family nongroup policy if you find a serious gap in your health care protection.

Types of Coverage

Unlike auto and homeowners' policies examined previously, there are no standard formats for most health care policies. This means that most plans will not provide an explanation of coverage that is broken down into the discrete components discussed later. However, after you read the policies closely and discuss them with insurers' representatives, you should be able to reorganize the benefits provided into a more comparable format. Most policies include **comprehensive health insurance** coverage providing both basic health care benefits and major medical protection.

Comprehensive health insurance: Provides both basic health care benefits and major medical protection.

Basic Health Care Coverage

Three components—hospital insurance, surgical insurance, and medical insurance—make up **basic health care insurance.** Each can be purchased separately, but they are usually combined and sold as a basic health care package.

Hospital insurance will help pay for room and board and other medical expenses while in the hospital. It can take the form of indemnity coverage, expense coverage, or service benefit coverage. *Indemnity insurance* provides for specific dollar payments made directly to you for each day you are in the hospital, regardless of your actual expenses. *Expense insurance* provides for cash reimbursement either to you or to the provider of health care, based on expenses actually incurred.

Hospital **indemnity insurance** typically ranks as least preferable. This is the type of hospital insurance most often sold on television and in newspapers. Although receiving $100 to $150 a day for each day you are in the hospital may sound attractive, it is not likely to cover even your room and board. In addition, many of these policies do not begin payments until you have been in the hospital a set number of days. With the average hospital stay a little over six days at an average charge of over $6,000, don't plan on collecting much from an indemnity policy that commences payments after the fifth day. Furthermore, your likelihood of being admitted to a hospital has steadily declined over the last decade as more surgeries are performed on an outpatient basis.

More adequate benefits are generally provided by **hospital expense insurance,** which pays for room and board up to a set daily maximum. In addition, hospital expense insurance should pay for other hospital-related expenses, such as laboratory procedures, surgical materials, and X-rays, typically stating payments for these items as a percentage of the maximum payment for room and board. This is not a trivial supplemental benefit. On average, such items can double the cost of a hospital stay.

Surgical expense insurance should cover the fees of the operating surgeon and the anesthesiologist. An expense-type policy might provide a list of covered operations along with the maximum amount to be paid for each. A preferred policy agrees to pay all surgical costs as long as these are **usual, customary, and reasonable (UCR)** for your geographic area. If you have a policy with this provision, be sure to find out whether your physician will accept this amount as payment in full. If the doctor will not, find out how much extra he or she is planning to charge you.

Basic health care insurance: Consists of hospital, surgical, and medical coverage.

Hospital insurance: Provides coverage for room and board and other medical expenses while in the hospital.

TOPIC **LINKS**

Check online data for most hospitals.

Indemnity insurance: Provides a specified dollar benefit regardless of actual cost.

Hospital expense insurance: Pays actual cost up to a daily maximum.

Surgical expense insurance: Covers the fees charged by the operating surgeon and anesthesiologist.

Usual, customary, and reasonable (UCR): The typical fee charged in your region for a specific good or service. Insurers will generally not provide reimbursement for expenses in excess of this amount.

Service benefit coverage:
Provides full reimbursement for covered services as long as costs are usual, customary, and reasonable.

Physicians' expense Insurance:
Insurance coverage for general nonsurgical physician care at the office or hospital.

Copayment: A payment by the insured covering less than the full cost of the service; the remainder is paid by the insurer.

TOPIC **LINKS**

Review a physician's credentials.

Major medical insurance:
Provides protection after limits on basic health care coverage have been exceeded.

Coinsurance: A requirement that the insured pay a certain percentage of the medical expenses incurred.

Service benefit coverage is the preferred approach to reimbursement for both hospital and surgical expenses. This type is provided by Blue Cross and many HMOs. For qualified and participating hospitals, full reimbursement for covered services is made directly to the health care provider. With service benefit insurance you don't have to constantly keep track of hospital costs in order to ensure adequate coverage. The one drawback is that you may have to stay in a qualifying hospital to receive 100 percent reimbursement.

Physicians' expense insurance, also termed *regular medical insurance*, provides payments for general nonsurgical physician care at the office or in the hospital. Traditional insurance has used an indemnity approach, paying you so much for each visit. Because you are likely to visit a doctor's office several times during the year, such insurance is relatively expensive. It has proved efficient, however, as one component of a comprehensive health care plan offered by a health maintenance organization (HMO). Under an HMO, office visits may be fully covered, or you may be required to make a small copayment. A **copayment** is a dollar fee covering less than the full cost of the service. Its purpose is to limit unnecessary use.

Prescription drug coverage has become an increasingly important part of health insurance. Average household expenditures on prescription drugs were $497 in 2001. As seen in Figure 14.1, private insurance has covered only about 61 percent of these expenditures. This percentage can vary significantly among households, with the elderly paying much more. For this reason the government has recently created a drug prescription program for the elderly. It is discussed in the Medicare section of this chapter.

Major Medical Coverage

The one component of health care insurance you should not do without is **major medical insurance,** because it eliminates the greatest risk to your financial health. Basic health care coverage may not pay all of your health care expenses, either because particular services are not covered or because you have exceeded the limits on coverage. Major medical is the backup you need when catastrophic illness strikes. If, after reimbursement under basic health care insurance, your health care expenses exceed a stated deductible, major medical will pick up part of the overage. Most policies have a **coinsurance** clause under which the insurer pays 80 percent of the overage and you pay the other 20 percent. The better policies put a dollar limit, perhaps $2,000, on your out-of-pocket expenses. Your payments after 20 percent coinsurance and a $2,000 limit are illustrated in Figure 14.2 In

---

Figure 14.2

Sample Illustration of Major Medical Coverage

	Cost	Basic Health Payment	Overage
Hospital bill	$5,200	$3,000	$2,200
Physician services (office visits)	840	—	840
Surgical services	2,400	1,900	500
Prescription drugs	760	—	760
Total	$9,200	$4,900	$4,300
		Minus individual deductible	−100
			$4,200
			× .20
		Coinsurance	$ 840

You pay the lesser of the deductible ($100) plus the coinsurance ($840) or $2,000.

---

this example, health care costs total $9,200, of which basic health coverage pays $4,900, leaving a total overage of $4,300. After a deductible of $100 and a coinsurance payment of $840, your total out-of-pocket expenses would be $940. According to the terms of this policy, the amount you pay normally cannot exceed $2,000 per year.

Long-Term Care Coverage

With recent attempts by government, hospitals, and insurers to reduce the average hospital stay, nursing or rehabilitative care at home or in a skilled nursing facility is becoming increasingly important. Where traditional coverage for such services does exist, it applies only to services absolutely required by the illness or injury. Insurers will not typically pay for care that is primarily personal or custodial. Medicare and most traditional health care insurance limit nursing care to a fixed number of days in a skilled care facility. As seen in Figure 14.3, almost half of nursing home care is paid for out of pocket.

This lack of coverage can leave families with annual nursing home bills of from $30,000 to $60,000. An extended stay can easily deplete an estate and force you to rely on the health care provider of last resort—Medicaid. The insurance industry has responded by offering specialized long-term care policies. In addition, the government has provided tax preferences for long-term care premiums and policy payouts.

Long-term care policies sold by commercial insurers are typically indemnity policies that pay up to a set daily limit for nursing home expenses and home health care. To qualify for custodial care under these policies you must demonstrate that you can no longer care for yourself. This is usually defined in terms of "activities of daily living," or ADLs. This includes bathing, continence, dressing, eating, toileting, and mobility. Although policies differ, you may qualify for benefits if you cannot do at least two or three of these tasks.

Long-term care policies: Provides payments for long-term custodial care.

Long-term care policies are expensive, especially for the aged. The older you are when you first purchase long-term care coverage, the more the policy costs. This is because your chances of needing benefits are greater as you age. Moreover, even high premiums are no guarantee that you will get the anticipated benefits. Some insureds have mistakenly thought their policies covered custodial care, whereas the contracts covered only the more restrictive skilled or intermediate care.

Dental Insurance

Dental insurance is a nice fringe benefit if it is included in your group plan and paid by your employer. One of the fastest-growing forms of insurance, dental insurance is similar to other

Dental insurance: Primarily covers the cost of preventive care, with coinsurance on nonroutine dental work.

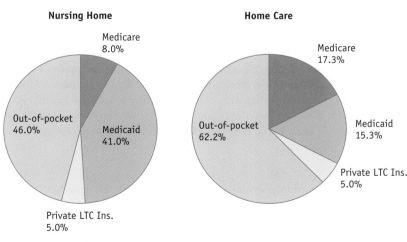

Total Long-Term Care Spending in 2000 is $100 Billion

Figure 14.3

Sources of Payment for Long Term Care, 2000

Source: Office of the Actuary, National Health Statistics Group

kinds of health insurance. Many plans require a deductible, have maximum reimbursement limits, or have copayments. One major difference is that dental insurance covers the cost of preventive care, usually paying all of the fees for routine checkups and cleanings, but only partial payment for corrective care.

If your dental insurance is not part of your overall health insurance plan, it may not be cost-effective to buy the insurance on your own. You should be able to plan for these expenses in your yearly budget. Moreover, expensive dental surgery to correct birth deformities or injuries is in most cases already covered under the surgical expense component of the basic health care package.

Specific Disease and Accident Insurance

Widely sold through the media, specific disease insurance is one policy you should definitely not purchase. Not only is it likely to be a poor bargain, it also makes no financial sense. Why would you want a policy that covers you if you have cancer but pays nothing if you have a heart attack? You need broader coverage that pays out no matter what the cause of illness. Companies offering such policies are playing on our fears of a dreaded disease.

Although accident insurance is often sold by reputable major insurers, the reasons against purchasing it are much the same as those for not purchasing specific disease insurance. The purpose of health care insurance is to reduce your financial risks. Gambling on the cause of future illnesses and injuries does not serve that purpose.

Important Provisions

No matter what type of health care coverage you may have, certain provisions will indicate the quality of your insurance coverage. In general, those with shorter waiting periods, fewer exclusions, and higher policy limits offer better protection.

Waiting Period Under Preexisting Conditions Clause

Preexisting conditions clause: Excludes from coverage certain medical conditions that existed before the policy was initiated.

All individual policies and some group policies will contain a **preexisting conditions clause,** which excludes from coverage certain types of injuries and illnesses that began before the policy was issued. These conditions may later be covered after a specified **waiting period.**

Waiting period (health care): Preexisting conditions may be covered after this period of time.

This clause is a common means of denying payment. You may be better off keeping a less-than-satisfactory policy rather than waiting the necessary time before you are fully covered under a new policy. Also, beware of policies that do not waive the preexisting conditions clause after a given period of time.

Guaranteed Renewability

Guaranteed renewability: Guarantees coverage up to a specified age upon payment of premiums, although future premiums may increase.

Unless you are purchasing temporary coverage to bridge a gap between group insurance policies, you should consider purchasing insurance that is guaranteed renewable until age 65. **Guaranteed renewability** means that no matter what your health, your coverage will continue so long as you pay the premiums. The company can increase rates for a given class of insureds, but cannot increase your individual premium for any reason.

Policy Limits

The maximum amount the insurance company will pay out is particularly important on the major medical portion of your coverage. The limit may hold for each benefit period, usually a calendar year, over a lifetime, or for each illness or accident. Never purchase a policy with a limit of less than $250,000 on hospitalization payments for a given illness or accident per benefit period or less than a lifetime maximum of $500,000. The likelihood of huge medical expenses, although small, does exist.

Waiver of Premium

This clause waives your premium payment should you be unable to work because of illness or injury. If your health insurance policy does not contain this provision, you must plan for these payments under your disability income protection.

Exclusions

Some injuries and illnesses will not be covered even when there is no medical history of them. For example, intentionally self-inflicted injuries, injuries covered by workers' compensation, mental illness, or injuries resulting from war or military service are typically excluded. Such elective procedures as cosmetic surgery and dental treatment may be covered only if the condition being treated results from birth defects or accidental injuries.

Some policies will cover maternity expenses, and others will exclude them. Although a maternity plan may be helpful if you are planning an addition to your family, it is not necessary financial protection. After all, you should be able to budget adequately for these expenses over at least a nine-month period. Of much greater importance is how your policy handles the costs of childbirth complications and the costs of treating birth defects.

For most types of policies the Newborns' and Mothers' Health Protection Act of 1996 (NMHPA) prohibits health insurers from restricting your hospital stay for childbirth to less than 48 hours after a vaginal birth and 96 hours after a caesarian birth. You can be forced to leave earlier if the attending provider permits it. The act, however, does not require that your insurer offer maternity coverage. It only ensures that you have a prescribed time for recuperation when it is covered by your policy.

Finance News

Health Savings Accounts

A Health Savings Account (HSA) can cut your medial bills. Contributions by you are tax deductible whether or not you itemize and contributions by your employer are excluded from your gross income. The savings earn tax-free interest and remain in your account until you use them. Moreover, the account remains with you when you change employers. HSAs are new; therefore, only a few employers provide them. Most accounts are being set up by the self-employed or those without employer-provided health insurance.

Funds in the account may be used to pay for qualified medical expenses (see IRS Publication 502, "Medical and

BOX 14.1

Dental Expenses") that are not covered by your health insurance policy. To qualify for an HSA you must have a high deductible health policy (HDHP) and you must not be covered by other significant health insurance or Medicare. Eligibility requirements and contribution limits can be found at **www.irs.gov** and **www. eHealthInsurance.com**. Basically, you cannot have a comprehensive health insurance policy that covers minor expenses. Self-insuring minor expenses with your savings account and covering larger expenses with major medical are excellent ways of managing your health care costs.

Funds can be withdrawn from the account for nonmedical reasons. Like an IRA, withdrawals for nonqualified expenses are taxed as income and are subject to a 10 percent penalty before age 65. After age 65, an HSA could also be used as a source of retirement funds.

Insurance Providers

Twenty years ago fee-for-service plans covered almost the entire market. Emerging home maintenance organizations were providing coverage for a small market segment, and preferred provider organizations and point-of-service plans were largely unheard of. In an attempt to hold down the rising cost of medical care, alternative strategies for health care reimbursement have been implemented.

Managed care is the current term applied to a health insurance plan that puts together a coherent network of providers. Your primary-care physician usually serves as the gatekeeper to this network. It is the gatekeeper's job to guide you through the network so as to ensure that you receive appropriate medical care in the most efficient and inexpensive way.

Many companies have introduced the managed care concept to hold down the heavy cost of medical care and the rising level of health insurance premiums. The three basic cost-containment features employed by managed care plans are preadmission certification for hospital stays, utilization review for the appropriateness of care, and second opinions for non-emergency surgical procedures. Each of these features limits you or your doctor's choice of medical care. The hope is that eliminating unnecessary or excessively costly choices will provide you with better health care for each dollar spent.

Managed care: A health program that manages the services you receive in an attempt to provide adequate care while containing costs.

Fee-for-Service (FFS)

Fee-for-service health insurance providers offer the greatest choice of health care services. They are also the most expensive, costing about $2,000 more than alternative managed care type plans. You choose your doctor and the hospital. The insurer reimburses service providers at your community's UCR (usual, customary, and reasonable) rates. The UCR is based on fees charged in your local area and is typically set at a level that would provide complete reimbursement for bills submitted by most physicians. Your physician may require a supplemental fee arrangement under which you will pay any excess charges not paid by your insurer.

Fee-for-service health insurance: The insured selects a provider of medical care and is then reimbursed for covered medical expenses.

Fee-for-service providers typically require deductibles and coinsurance payments. However, total out-of-pocket expenses may be limited under the major medical provisions.

HMOs

A **health maintenance organization (HMO)** differs from the other insurers because it is not only the provider of insurance but also the provider of the health care. The HMO premium represents a prepayment for future medical services, which are then provided as needed at little or no out-of-pocket cost.

There are two basic types of HMOs: the group-staff arrangement and the individual practice arrangement. The **group-staff HMO** provides services at one or more locations with salaried physicians. The **individual practice arrangement (IPA) HMO** contracts with private physicians who maintain their own offices and then pays them on a fee-for-service schedule. Individuals then choose from among the participating physicians for their needed medical services. IPAs generally offer a greater choice of physicians and more conveniently located medical services. They are slightly more costly than group-staff HMOs.

An HMO is likely to cover more basic health care benefits than a fee-for-service plan. Some advocates of HMOs have suggested that they are better than traditional insurers because they concentrate on preventive rather than curative medicine. Because the physician has a financial interest in seeing you remain healthy, you supposedly receive better preventive care and, therefore, remain healthier. Critics argue that the physician also has a financial incentive to hold back medical care. There is evidence that hospital stays are shorter for patients of HMOs, but the reasons are unclear. As of now, it is not possible to

Health maintenance organization (HMO): Provides comprehensive health care services on a prepaid basis. It is both an insurer and a provider of health care.

Group-staff HMO: Delivers health services at one or more facilities through groups of physicians working on a salaried or contractual basis.

Individual practice arrangement (IPA) HMO: Physicians maintain their own offices and then are reimbursed by the HMO for services performed.

make any generalizations about the quality of care provided by any particular category of health care plans.

Point of Service (POS)

Recently, some HMOs have begun to offer a **POS (point-of-service) plan.** Under an open-ended plan, you may select non-HMO providers if you are willing to incur additional costs in the form of higher deductibles and coinsurances. This provides a health care alternative for those who find that they are dissatisfied with the HMO's choice of providers.

PPOs

Virtually nonexistent in the mid-1980s, **preferred provider organizations (PPOs)** currently enroll about 40 percent of the participants in employer-sponsored plans. A PPO is only a provider, not an insurer. It works either directly with an employer or through the employer's insurer to provide medical services at less than customary rates to the company's employees. Those who choose a PPO option may still be able to utilize non-PPO services at increased cost. This is not true for persons who belong to an *EPO (exclusive provider organization)*. They must receive care from an affiliated provider or pay the entire cost themselves.

Point-of-service plan (POS): An HMO plan in which members may use providers outside the HMO but incur additional cost in the form of a deductible or coinsurance payment.

Preferred provider organizations (PPOs): Selectively offered health care services providing care to insureds at a lower out-of-pocket cost.

EMPLOYMENT-RELATED HEALTH CARE INSURANCE

About 88 percent of private insurance is employment related. In most cases the employer subsidizes the cost. Access is generally limited to employees who pay part of the monthly premium. The U.S. Bureau of Labor Statistics found that in 2003 the average monthly contribution was $60 for single coverage and $229 for family coverage. It covered 18 percent of the cost for single coverage and 30 percent of the cost of family coverage. This represented a significant annual after-tax fringe benefit; the cost of the average plan ranged from $4,000 for single coverage to $9,160 for family coverage.

Figure 14.4 lists the percent of workers who have access to various types of employer-sponsored health care plans. For many people, health insurance selection is tied to employment selection. As a result, a few individuals in ill health may be deterred from looking for a job. They fear that employers, concerned about rising medical costs, may be reluctant to hire them. The Americans with Disabilities Act of 1990 provides some help to these prospective workers by setting down hiring restrictions on businesses. Basically, an

	MEDICAL CARE	DENTAL CARE	VISION CARE	DISABILITY BENEFITS	
				Short-term Disability	Long-term Disability
Worker Characteristics					
All	60	40	25	39	30
White-collar occupations	65	47	28	41	42
Blue-collar occupations	64	40	25	45	21
Service occupations	38	22	15	21	11
Full-time	73	49	30	46	38
Part-time	17	9	7	11	5
Union	57	43	24	69	28
Nonunion	38	23	9	36	30

Figure 14.4

Percent of Workers with Access to Health Care and Disability Plans in Private Industry, 2003

Source: National Compensation Survey, U.S. Bureau of Labor Statistics

employer cannot deny a person a job because of potential insurance claims or higher insurance premiums. Preexisting conditions, however, can be excluded from coverage as long as these same exclusions are applied to all other workers.

Even a uniformly applied preexisting condition clause can deter workers from changing jobs. In response to that concern, the Health Insurance Portability and Accountability Act (HIPAA) limits the period that insurers could deny or limit coverage because of a preexisting condition to 12 months. Moreover, employees who have not experienced a significant lapse in coverage cannot be forced to wait through more than one 12-month period during their entire work life.

Interim Coverage

Previously, workers who lost their jobs were also likely to lose their health insurance protection. To remedy this doubly disastrous situation, Congress now requires employers with 20 or more workers to provide terminating employees with continued health care coverage under a law called COBRA. This must be made available to those ex-workers who cannot obtain either alternative group insurance or Medicare coverage. The employer may charge you for the insurance, but in most instances the cost to you cannot be more than 102 percent of group insurance rates.

Mandated continuation periods are listed in Figure 14.5. When the continuation period ends, the group coverage must be convertible to an individual policy. Although the individual policy can have a higher price and provide fewer benefits, it still may be wise for you to exercise your conversion rights. An entirely new policy would exclude preexisting conditions and require a waiting period before full coverage began. The continuation and conversion of previous health insurance coverage can be used to eliminate any gaps in coverage due to a change in employment or marital status.

Family members also have a right to request a continuation of benefits for three years with the right of conversion thereafter. The circumstances under which benefits would be continued include death of the covered worker, separation or divorce from the covered spouse, or loss of dependent status by a child of an insured parent.

Specialized Health Care Accounts

New government regulations on tax-advantaged employee benefits have allowed employers to experiment with new types of plans that might save costs.

A few employers now offer **defined-contribution health plans.** These plans can vary widely. Generally, the employer provides a voucher or set amount of money for you to purchase

TOPIC **LINKS**

Review quotes on health insurance policies.

Defined-contribution health plans: Employer provides a fixed amount of dollars for the employee to individually purchase health insurance.

Figure 14.5

Continuation Period for Group Health Insurance

Qualifying Events	Beneficiary	Term of Coverage
Termination	Employee	18 months
Reduced hours	Spouse	(For individuals who qualify for
	Dependent child	Social Security disability benefits, special rules extend coverage an additional 11 months)
Employee entitled to Medicare	Spouse	36 months
Divorce or legal separation	Dependent child	
Death of covered employee		
Loss of "dependent child" status	Dependent child	36 months

individual insurance in the marketplace. If your employer's contribution is less than the cost of the policy, you are responsible for the rest. This is favorable for young individuals in good health. However, older workers are likely to be charged more, and those with chronic illnesses may find it impossible to obtain health insurance.

Many employers now offer employees the option of setting up **flexible spending health care accounts,** also called *cafeteria plans*. These are meant to complement an existing health insurance plan. An IRS-approved account permits employees to voluntarily contribute pretax dollars to the account. The monies may be used to purchase various types of disability and health insurance. They may also be used to pay for deductibles and co-insurance expenses not covered by your health insurance plan. Exactly how the funds may be spent will depend on the particular plan and IRS restrictions. On the negative side, any funds not distributed for qualified expenses by the end of the year are forfeited. You must use it or lose it (see Box 14.3).

"Health savings accounts" are different from flexible spending accounts. You can only combine a health savings account with high deductible health insurance. The main advantage over flexible spending accounts is that the funds carry over from year to year and from employer to employer. (See Box 14.1 for more on health savings accounts.)

Flexible spending health care accounts: Employee funded accounts for paying health care expenditures with pretax dollars.

Workers' Compensation

All states have **workers' compensation** programs that help pay for medical expenses and lost income resulting from work-related illnesses or injuries. However, not all workers are covered nor is coverage required in all states. You should ask your employer whether you

Workers' compensation: State programs providing health and disability income coverage for work-related illnesses and injuries.

Financial PLANNING for Young Adults

BOX 14.2

Insurance Options for Young Adults

Young adults between ages 18 to 24 are more likely to be without health insurance than any other group. Luckily, they are less likely to need medical care than their elders. However, they are more likely to find themselves with catastrophic injuries that can leave them with a lifetime of medical bills and any illness that requires a hospital stay can result in thousands of dollars in bills. The lack of insurance among young adults is the direct result of their labor market experience. They have a higher unemployment rate and job turnover rate than the rest of the labor force.

As long as you remain a student and below a certain age (generally age 25) you are likely to be covered under your parent's health insurance. This coverage lapses when you are no longer a full-time student. Young adults who are in the workforce, therefore, are likely to find themselves without coverage during periods of unemployment and job search.

This gap in coverage could be filled by either extending previous employment-related coverage or by purchasing an interim health insurance policy. As discussed in this chapter, workers

have a right to retain their health coverage for some time after they leave employment. This right also extends to dependents who were covered under their parent's policy, but are no longer eligible because they are no longer in school. If you are a young worker who is unemployed or without coverage in your new job, continuing coverage under your parent's plan is a good idea. To extend this coverage, you must pay the full cost to the employer plus a 2 percent administrative fee. Unfortunately, a comprehensive health care plan could be too costly for someone who is unemployed.

University health plans that cover about one-quarter of college students typically end a few months after graduation. However, some schools allow students to extend coverage for an additional limited period.

Another option is to purchase interim coverage for only major medical. This does not cover preexisting conditions and should only be used for limited periods of job search and unemployment. eHealthInsurance found that the average monthly cost for single major medical coverage was $125 in 2004. But if all you need is temporary coverage, you can purchase a nonrenewable short-term policy for as little as $50 a month.

---

are covered. If you are, the type and amount of benefits you may receive are set down in state laws. Your personnel office or the state compensation office can provide you with a schedule of potential benefits.

Workers' compensation provides no-fault insurance for workplace injuries. You are covered regardless of fault. In return for the no-fault coverage, the employer's liability is limited by a prescribed schedule of benefits. Employees, however, are not restricted from filing lawsuits against third parties, such as a product manufacturer, that may have contributed to the injury or in special situations from suing an employer that was grossly or intentionally negligent.

Publicty Health Services

Medicare and Medicaid are federal programs designed to improve the health of the indigent and the elderly.

Medicaid is neither an insurer nor a provider of health care. It is a joint federal–state effort to cover the medical expenses of the indigent. Unless you find yourself in this group, you will not have contact with Medicaid services. The coverage and quality of the services offered differ from state to state. Information can be obtained at your state's welfare office.

In one way or another, **Medicare** concerns us all. We either have a relative who is affected by the program, or we will eventually consider enrolling ourselves. A federal health insurance program for those 65 or older or those with chronic kidney failure or certain other disabilities, it consists of two parts: Part A is hospital insurance and Part B is medical insurance. Current coverage limits can be found at the Medicare Web site. The hospital insurance is financed through the Social Security taxes you pay while you work. The medical insurance is voluntary and is partly paid by premiums from those who choose to participate. These programs are administered through the Social Security Administration. You should contact a local office for information and applications.

Both Medicare hospital and medical insurance are a good buy at the time you become eligible. Medicare will, however, leave some serious gaps in your health care coverage. You can consider closing them with a private supplemental health insurance policy. Medicare includes substantial deductibles and coinsurance payments. In the event of catastrophic illness, these payments could deplete the investment portfolio generating your retirement income.

Medigap Insurance

Medigap insurance is designed to fill the gap between expenses that are covered by Medicare and those that are not. It is sold by private insurers. A medigap policy that places a realistic limit on deductibles and coinsurance payments is an excellent choice. Furthermore, if you purchase a medigap policy within six months of turning age 65 and enrolling in Medicare Part B, federal law now states that you cannot be turned down or charged extra because of your health status or medical condition. And once you have coverage, a medigap policy may not be canceled or a renewal refused because of your ill health.

Under directions from the U.S. Congress, the National Association of Insurance Commissioners (NIAC) has developed 10 standardized policies. Medigap insurers can promote only those policies as supplemental Medicare insurance; all must sell at least a basic policy that addresses the major gaps in Medicare benefits.

Medicaid: A joint federal-state-sponsored program covering medical expenses for the indigent.

Medicare: A federal health insurance program for those age 65 or older, or those with certain sicknesses or disabilities.

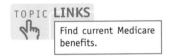

TOPIC **LINKS**

Find current Medicare benefits.

Medigap insurance: Private insurance meant to partially or totally cover those health care expenses that are not reimbursed by Medicare.

Medicare + Choice

If you wish, you can receive your Medicare benefits from a private insurer by obtaining a policy through the Choice Program. These policies also close many of the gaps in Medicare coverage. In fact, it is illegal for an insurer to sell you medigap coverage if you are insured through the Choice Program. Choice plans can take various forms. They include both managed care plans and traditional fee-for-service plans. At the Medicare Help Plan Compare site, you can review and compare the costs and coverage of plans in your area.

TOPIC **LINKS**

Compare medigap policies.

Medicare Prescription Drug Card

Medicare recently introduced a drug discount program. This is not pharmaceutical insurance. Medicare contracts with private insurers to provide an approved discount card. For low-income consumers the card provides limited credit for drug expenditures. For all cardholders it provides discounts that are expected to trim drug prices by 10 to 15 percent. The card can cost up to $30 annually and discounts and available pharmacies can differ by card issuer. Therefore, it is important to check out the discounts at the Medicare Web site before you buy. Be aware that companies can change their discounts at anytime.

Individually Selected Health Care Insurance

Group coverage is generally less expensive than individual insurance. If you are one of the few who cannot take part in a group plan at work, look into group policies offered through fraternal and professional organizations. But be careful. Some insurers advertise their policies as part of a group plan but provide none of the expected cost savings. When the identifiable group is not likely to be in any better health than the population as a whole, there is little reason to believe the policy is a good buy.

Cost of Coverage

Most group insurance plans offer expensive comprehensive health coverage that includes basic health and major medical benefits. Individual policies cost 30 to 40 percent more, with a comprehensive family policy costing over $5,000 a year. You can hold down this expense by purchasing only major medical coverage with large deductibles and making out-of-pocket payments for your basic health needs. Increasing the deductible from $100 to $1,000 can cut your premiums by 40 to 50 percent. If you set aside an emergency fund, you can use those resources to self-insure against unexpected basic health costs. Meanwhile, the major medical insurance provides you with the backup protection you need in case of catastrophic illness or injury. Review the checklist in Figure 14.6 before shopping for private health insurance.

TOPIC **LINKS**

Check accreditation status of health care organizations.

Even healthy persons may find it difficult to purchase comprehensive individual coverage including maternity and mental health benefits. If you have a specific health problem, you will encounter additional difficulties. You are likely to be denied coverage, charged an additional risk premium, or offered a policy that specifically excludes coverage for your preexisting condition. Different insurers apply differing restrictions on coverage for those in less than perfect health; therefore, it pays to shop around. Remember, purchasing health insurance after your illness or accident is like trying to purchase fire insurance after the fire.

Figure 14.6

Checklist: Shopping for Private Health Insurance

✓ **Comparison Shop**
Coverage and costs differ widely.

✓ **Check for Preexisting Condition Exclusions and Beware of Giving Up an Existing Policy**
Statements such as "no medical examination required" do not relieve you of a preexisting condition clause.

✓ **Be Aware of Maximum Benefits and Major Medical Coverage**
You need insurance to avoid major financial losses.

✓ **Check Your Right to Renew**
Avoid policies that permit the company to cancel policies on an individual basis.

✓ **Know with Whom You Are Dealing**
Check out both the agent and the company.

✓ **Don't Put Up with High-Pressure Sales Tactics**
High-pressure sales tactics typically indicate high commissions, high cost, and low quality.

The Insurance Company

Be sure to investigate the financial soundness of the medical insurer. A bankrupt insurer could leave you financially ruined. In many states commercial insurers are covered by a state guarantee fund that protects policyholders if an insurer gets into financial trouble. Technically, however, Blue Cross/Blue Shield companies are not viewed as insurance companies and, thus, are not covered by the guarantee funds in most states.

In the event they become insolvent, HMOs that are federally qualified by the Health Care Financing Administration must carry insurance to cover the unpaid bills of patients. They are also required to include clauses in all contracts with doctors and patients prohibiting the providers of medical services from collecting directly from patients.

TOPIC **LINKS**
Check the financial condition of an insurance company.

TOPIC **LINKS**
Shop online for health insurance.

Saving
money $

BOX 14.3

A Flexible Spending Account for Medical Expenditures

Employer-provided flexible spending accounts generally permit you to allocate a portion of your salary for this purpose. Sometimes employers match employee contributions or contribute a fixed amount. If tax-qualified, the salary dollars paid into this account are tax exempt. These dollars may then be used to pay for expenses that would be deductible from personal income taxes under IRS guidelines.

One popular use of flexible spending accounts is to pay for the deductibles and coinsurance on health insurance plans. The money placed in the flexible spending account can be used to pay the difference between the employee's medical expenses and the amount paid for by the company's health plan. Normally, you would have to earn $138.89 in taxable income to

pay for a $100 deductible if you were in the 28 percent marginal tax bracket and your total medical expenses for the year did not exceed 7.5 percent of your family's gross income. Using tax-exempt dollars through a flexible spending account would result in savings of $38.89, regardless of your proportional medical expenses.

As employers increase deductibles and coinsurance payments in order to hold down the increasing cost of medical insurance, the tax savings provided by flexible spending accounts become greater. There is, however, one significant drawback. At the end of the year, any unused funds you have allocated to this account are forfeited. You either use it or lose it.

For persons engaging in personal financial planning, this should not be a serious problem. If you review previous budgets and your upcoming medical needs in the pro forma budget, you should be in a good position to estimate your flexible account needs conservatively and obtain the maximum tax advantage.

DISABILITY INCOME PROTECTION

Only those workers with dependents need life insurance, but every worker needs disability income protection. Young workers often purchase life insurance while ignoring the much greater risk of disability. This is especially unfortunate because your chances of suffering a serious disability are surprisingly high. The Social Security Administration estimates that a 20-year-old has over a 20 percent probability of experiencing an insured disability before reaching age 65 (see Figure 14.7). Since the requirements for an insured disability are rather strict, it is likely that many more individuals will experience a significant earnings loss at some point in their work life. In fact, over one-fifth of 55- to 64-year-olds state that they have a work disability that limits the kind or amount of work they do.

Long-term disability insurance that bridges at least part of the gap between when short-term benefits end and retirement begins is provided to approximately 30 percent of the workforce. In smaller establishments only about one-fifth of employees are similarly covered. Those without long-term disability protection must rely entirely on Social Security benefits or a declining bank account. Furthermore, few will be able to collect the Social Security benefits they may be depending on. The rules are quite strict. You must be able to prove that the disability is total and will last for at least one year or terminate in death. Nothing is paid out for partial disability unless it is preceded by a period of total disability. And if you do qualify, benefit checks do not begin until at least six months after you become disabled.

Sources of Disability Income

If you become disabled, you will probably have to rely on a variety of sources for support. The following are some common means of support used by the disabled during periods of reduced market income.

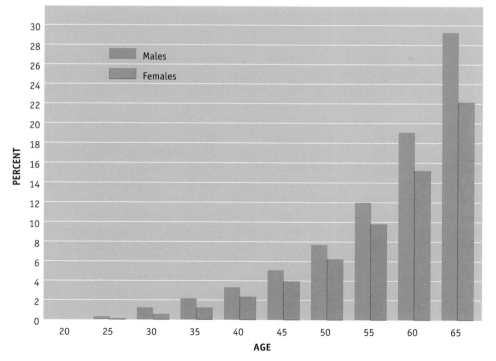

Figure 14.7

Probability of Social Security Insured Disability from Age 20 to Given Age

Source: U.S. Department of Health and Human Services, A Death and Disability Life Table for the 1966 Birth Cohort.

Disability Income Insurance

Disability income insurance:
Partially replaces lost income during a period of defined disability.

TOPIC **LINKS**

Locate providers of disability income insurance.

As with health care insurance, the cheapest **disability income insurance** is obtained through group coverage sponsored by employers. Group benefits are typically integrated with Social Security payments and workers' compensation to provide a level of benefits dependent upon current wages. This usually does not exceed 60 percent of salary.

Individual disability income policies generally provide a set dollar amount of coverage. Premiums may be stated in terms of each $100 of monthly disability benefits purchased. Various endorsements and riders are available to tailor the policy to individual needs. For example, the amount of benefits may be dependent upon whether you qualify for Social Security disability benefits.

Both short-term and long-term disability income plans are available. *Short-term coverage* usually begins immediately after an accident but has a short waiting period for disabilities resulting from sickness. Benefit payments may then continue for six months, or at most, two years. *Long-term disability* income insurance has a longer waiting period, but benefits will continue for either a stated number of years or until age 65.

The conditions for receiving disability payments are generally more stringent under long-term disability insurance and may even change with the duration of the disability. For example, you may be considered disabled over the first two to five years if you cannot perform the duties of your current occupation. Payments after this period, however, may continue only if you are unable to engage in any occupation for which you are reasonably fitted by education, training, or experience.

Private disability benefits may or may not be taxable. Specifically excluded are payouts related to military service and terrorist attack. Also, if you pay for premiums on an individual policy with after-tax dollars, the benefits are not taxable. Alternatively, payouts from group employment policies funded with pretax dollars are taxable. Payments received from private sources, including both company plans or individually purchased disability insurance, do not reduce your Social Security disability benefits. However, public benefits from programs such as workers' compensation may lower your Social Security benefits. These are reduced if the combined payments from all public programs exceed 80 percent of your average current earnings.

Social Security

TOPIC **LINKS**

Social Security Disability Planner

To be considered disabled under the Social Security law, you must have a physical condition that prevents you from doing any substantial gainful work and that is expected to last 12 months or result in death. In 2004, if you could earn over $810 a month in gross wages (higher if blind) after deductions for medical services and equipment required because of your impairment, you were considered capable of substantial gainful employment. The disability must be expected to last at least one year or result in death. You may not receive benefits for a partial disability or short-term disability. Moreover, benefits do not begin until six months after the onset of the disability.

Obviously, these requirements rule out Social Security payments for all but the severely and, apparently, permanently disabled. Because you and your family could suffer a severe reduction in income and still be ineligible for disability income from Social Security, you will likely have a need for private disability income insurance. Plans that integrate private benefits and Social Security benefits provide additional income security by increasing the monthly payout if you do not qualify for governmental benefits.

To be eligible for Social Security disability benefits, you must have accumulated 20 quarters of coverage within the last 10 years. However, younger workers can be eligible with fewer credits. You earn a quarter of coverage for each $900 (in 2004) of wages you receive, with a four-quarter maximum for one calendar year. You are also automatically enrolled in Medicare, the government's health insurance program, after two years of disability benefits.

The Disability Planner at the government's Social Security Web site should help you determine potential government-funded disability benefits. You, your dependent children, and a caretaking spouse may all be eligible for benefits. The basic disability benefit is received by the disabled worker. Mothers caring for dependent children under age 16 and earning no more than an annually determined maximum would additionally receive 50 percent of the basic monthly disability benefit. Children under 18 years of age would also get 50 percent of the basic benefit. However, there is a cap on the total benefits a household can receive. Sample benefits are listed in Table 14.1.

When you decide to try reentering the workforce, your Social Security benefits need not end immediately. You may be eligible for a certain trial period in which you will continue to receive unreduced disability benefits. The cost of rehabilitation and the fear of losing Medicare coverage have deterred some beneficiaries from rejoining the workforce. Under a new Ticket to Work Program, workers receive a Ticket that may be used to obtain vocational rehabilitation, job training, and other support services. They also retain their Medicare coverage for a substantial time period after they return to work.

Workers' Compensation

If the disabling injury or illness is work related, you may also be entitled to disability benefits under your state's workers' compensation statutes. These laws hold employers strictly liable for injuries in the workplace. This means that the employer is responsible, regardless of who is at fault. In return for assuming strict liability, compensation paid by employers is limited to mandated amounts. The benefits vary from state to state and are generally set equal to a given percentage of the average weekly wage within the state.

Specific types of injuries, such as loss of an arm, may come under the state's definition of permanent partial disabilities. For such injuries, the worker may receive a lump-sum payment or weekly payments for a limited time.

Many states also provide maintenance and benefits for workers undergoing rehabilitation. Workers' compensation or related programs may handle this coverage. Again, specifics can be provided at your state's workers' compensation office.

Pension Plans

Instead of purchasing separate group disability insurance, some employers will incorporate a disability option into the existing pension plan. If you are disabled before normal retirement age, you may be able to receive an immediate pension under a disability clause in the pension plan. The method for calculating monthly benefits may or may not differ from that used for normal retirement. However, even at reduced benefit levels, this alternative may be desirable.

	Current Annual Earnings			
	$20,000	**$40,000**	**$80,000**	**$160,000**
	Monthly Disability Benefit			
Worker alone	805	1,256	1,827	2,009
Family maximum	1,274	2,324	3,243	3,537
	Percent of Income Replaced by SSA Benefit			
Worker alone	48%	38%	27%	15%
Family maximum	76%	70%	49%	27%

Table 14.1

Estimates of Monthly Disability Benefits from the SSA Quick Benefits Planner

Source: SSA Quick Planner, based on 35-year-old worker qualifying for disability benefits

Also look for a waiver of contributions clause. Under this option the employer will continue to contribute to your pension plan for as long as you are disabled. Thus, at normal retirement age you could collect the full retirement pension even though you had not worked up until normal retirement age.

Accident Insurance

Accident insurance: Pays a set dollar amount in the event of physical dismemberment.

Also called *dismemberment insurance*, **accident insurance** pays the insured a set dollar amount for the loss of life, limb, or sight. It pays nothing when the physical loss is caused by an illness rather than an accident. Furthermore, the amount paid is unrelated to your actual income loss. Its major selling point is its low price. One company charges $2 a month for $150,000 of accident life, with smaller payments for dismemberment. The price is low because your chances of collecting are small.

Waiver of Premium or Payment Clauses

Life and health insurance policies should be examined for clauses that waive future premium payments in the event of disability. If you have mortgage life insurance on your home or credit life insurance on a car loan, be sure also to examine these for a disability clause.

Savings

If you have not adequately planned for your disability income needs, you may have no choice but to rely on accumulated savings. An emergency fund may provide support in the short run. Over an extended period, you may have to consider disposing of assets that were held for long-term purposes. You may be able to borrow against the cash value on a life insurance policy. For those who are severely disabled or terminally ill, some life policies provide an early payout while you are still alive. Retirement accounts are another potential source of support in times of extreme need. Normally, early withdrawals from tax-advantaged accounts before age 59½ trigger tax penalties. However, the penalties may be waived if you are disabled or if the withdrawals were made to satisfy qualifying medical expenses.

Insurance Clauses Affecting Disability Benefits

The quality of your disability insurance protection will depend on more than just the promised monthly benefits. It will be determined largely by the duration and conditions under which the benefits will be paid.

Definition of Disability

How disabled must you be before you can collect benefits? The answer depends on the exact wording in the insurance contract. A policy that considers you disabled if you cannot perform the main duties of your regular occupation is better than one that considers you disabled if you are unable to engage in any occupation for which you are reasonably suited by education and experience. For example, a surgeon suffering the loss of a hand would be considered disabled under the first definition, but not necessarily under the second, if he or she could practice some other medical specialty. Obviously, both of these are better than a policy that considers you disabled only when you cannot engage in any type of paid work. The definition of disability may depend on the duration of your condition, requiring a strict interpretation over longer periods.

Most policies provide for some compensation in case of partial disability. Some definitions of partial disability are related to income loss, while others are defined in terms of the physical handicap. In many policies, however, you must experience a period of total disability before you collect partial benefits. The level of partial benefits may be equal to a set percentage of total disability benefits or geared to the income loss created by the partial disability. For example, if you earned $2,000 a month before the disability and now earn $500 a month, you have suffered a 75 percent reduction in income. If the maximum monthly benefit under the insurance policy is $1,000, you will receive a partial benefit equal to 75 percent of the $1,000 maximum monthly benefit. In this situation, partial disability benefits are $750 per month.

Elimination or Waiting Period

The time between the onset of the disability and the beginning of disability payments is the **disability elimination or (or waiting) period.** The longer the elimination period, the less likely you are to collect and, therefore, the lower your premium.

A good method of holding down your insurance costs is to opt for the longest elimination period you feel comfortable with. An emergency fund of highly liquid assets would permit you to continue to meet your financial obligations during this time. This is a highly rewarding strategy. Increasing the waiting period from 7 days to 60 days can reduce premiums by more than 50 percent; from 7 days to a year reduces them by more than 65 percent.

Be sure you understand how the policy handles intermittent disabilities. If you are disabled and then return to work after recuperating, must you again go through a waiting period if you have a relapse? Most policies don't require another elimination period if you are disabled by the same cause within six months after returning to work.

Disability elimination (or waiting) period: The time between the onset of the disability and the beginning of disability benefits.

Benefit Period

Depending on the policy, benefit payments may last one, five, ten years, or until age 65. Your greatest financial risk is a lifetime disability. The best risk-reduction strategy is to opt for the policy with the longer **benefit period** and to hold down your premiums by choosing a longer elimination period. If this strategy proves too expensive, policies with shorter benefit periods may be used to protect income during a readjustment period or during the financially demanding childrearing years.

Benefit period: The duration of disability benefits.

Coordination of Benefits Clause

Many policies use a **coordination of benefits clause** to state the maximum disability income you may receive from all insurance sources, both public and private. The maximum is usually stated as a percentage of your current income. This is to ensure you do not earn more by owning multiple policies and not working.

Coordination of benefits clause: Ensures that disability benefits received from all sources are not greater than either some defined amount or a maximum percentage of previous earnings.

Social Insurance Substitute

The **social insurance substitute** may be included as a rider or as part of the basic policy. In the event you are disabled but still do not satisfy the strict requirements for Social Security benefits or are not covered by workers' compensation, this provision will replace those benefits with private insurance payments. This is a highly desirable provision because it eliminates an important source of uncertainty regarding your total disability payments, thus permitting you to estimate more accurately potential disability income.

Social insurance substitute: Provision of private disability income benefits in the event that social insurance benefits are not forthcoming.

Provision for Rehabilitation

Some policies explicitly provide for the continuation of benefits while you are in a rehabilitation program. This provision ensures that your benefits will not be terminated if you enter a work-related program. Some policies even state that tuition and equipment expenses for such programs will be covered. If you are disabled, and your policy does not contain this provision, you should check with the insurance company anyway. They may be more than willing to cover these expenses. After all, they have an incentive in seeing you return to gainful employment.

Renewability

The disability policy should be renewable without evidence of insurability; however, renewability provisions do vary.

The most unfavorable provision is found in policies that are **class cancelable.** This means the insurance company has the right to cancel an entire class of policies. For example, it can cancel all policies written before a specific date or within a specific state. If you are in poor health, this action can leave you in the position of finding expensive alternative coverage.

Next best are policies that are guaranteed renewable. These cannot be canceled as long as you pay your premiums; however, the premiums can increase. Better yet are policies that are *guaranteed renewable and noncancelable*. Such a provision gives you the right to renew your policy at the same premium.

Inflation Protection

A policy written to cover a certain percentage of your salary will provide some inflation protection. That is, as your salary increases, your insurance protection will increase correspondingly. If you are instead purchasing insurance that provides fixed-dollar payments, an *option to purchase* rider should be considered. It permits you to purchase additional protection in the future without evidence of insurability.

Ensuring that you have the appropriate level of protection at the beginning of the disability provides only partial protection against inflation. If your dollar benefits are unchanged during the period of disability, then inflation will erode the real worth of these payments. Social Security benefit payments are adjusted for increases in the cost of living, so that at least a portion of your disability payments will receive inflation protection. However, some disability policies provide for a dollar-for-dollar reduction in benefits to offset increases in Social Security payments, thus leaving your total compensation from Social Security and private disability insurance unchanged. A policy that establishes the company's dollar payments at the beginning of the disability and that does not permit future reductions in these payments is preferred. Better yet is one with a cost-of-living rider that automatically adjusts dollar payments during the disability period for inflation.

Determining Disability Income Insurance Requirements

Your disability income requirements will depend on the duration and severity of the disability. For disabilities lasting six months or less, you may have to rely on sick leave, short-term group disability benefits provided by an employer, or workers' compensation if the disability is work related. Lacking those, an emergency fund equal to six months' wages can provide the needed support through this interim period. For disabilities lasting longer than six months, you will have to consider your income needs until, typically, age 65, when retirement benefits begin. A good rule of thumb is that you should plan to replace about 60 to 70 percent of your lost gross income. This figure is based on the

Figure 14.8

Estimating Your Monthly Disability Insurance Needs

1. Income replacement requirements
   (60%–70% of gross income lost) _____
2. Spouse's income _____
3. Employer-provided disability benefits _____
4. Individually funded benefits _____
5. Social Security benefits _____
6. Total integrated benefits (_____)
7. Additional disability insurance needed _____

assumptions that some of your disability benefits will be nontaxable and that you will no longer incur work-related expenses. (Employer-provided benefits will be largely taxed, but privately purchased disability benefits will be tax free.) In any case, you may find it difficult to replace a larger percentage of your income through private insurance, since most insurers do not want to provide an incentive for not working.

Starting with your monthly income replacement requirements on line 1 of Figure 14.8, you can then reduce this amount by potential sources of disability income. If you are married, you might include spousal support. The personnel office at your place of work should provide you with an estimate of employer-provided benefits. Individually funded benefits would include investment income and benefits from individually purchased disability income protection.

The Social Security Administration will provide you with a "Personal Earnings and Benefit Statement" that lists potential disability benefits. You can also use the Benefits Planners at its Web site for an estimate of your disability benefits on line 5. Sample results for the Benefits Planner are listed in Table 14.1. You should notice that benefits replace a smaller percentage of lost income as market earnings increase.

Your total integrated benefits are listed on line 6. This is not necessarily equal to the sum of lines 2 to 5. You must examine each of your policies for coordination of benefits clauses and social insurance substitute riders. Participation limits set down in these sections of the disability policies may limit your total integrated benefits to less than the summed total of lines 2 to 5.

If you subtract your total integrated benefits from your total income replacement requirements on line 1, you will have determined your need for additional income insurance protection on line 7. You may be able to satisfy this need through additional individual or group insurance. If you do purchase additional insurance, make sure its benefits will not be offset by a reduction in prospective payments under your present policies.

Be sure to periodically review your disability income needs and your health care plan. You should also review your plans at all of life's major changes. A marriage, the birth of a child, or a divorce may require different strategies. You may not be able to avoid the pain and suffering accompanying an accident or ill health, but with proper planning you should be able to reduce the accompanying financial risks.

TOPIC **LINKS**
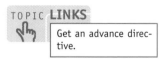
Use the Benefits Planner.

TOPIC **LINKS**
Get an advance directive.

Having a Living Will

Breakthroughs in medical science now make it possible to extend life far beyond what we had thought likely only a few decades ago. But advances in the extension of life do not always go hand in hand with improvements in the quality of life. For those who worry about being kept alive in a vegetative state with little or no chance of recovery, the "living will" can be the answer.

A living will is really not a will at all. It is a medical directive indicating the type of life support you are willing or unwilling to receive in the event you are unconscious or in a coma and unable to speak for yourself. In most states it is a legal document and, therefore, the state you live in may specify the precise form it must take. In order for a living will to be effective, it must state your wishes precisely, so that your intent is clear.

The Patient Self-Determination Act of 1991 requires that all institutions receiving Medicare or Medicaid funds inform patients upon admission of their right to sign an "advance directive." This includes a living will in which you have the right to refuse life-sustaining treatment and a health care power of attorney in which you appoint someone to make health care decisions for you if you are unable to. You don't have to sign an advance directive, but if you do, a record of it should be kept in your medical file.

The time to make these decisions, however, is not upon entry into a health care facility. By that point you may be incapacitated and your family may be in crisis. It is better to plan for such emergencies well in advance, when both your health care and financial concerns can be combined into a fully integrated plan. In addition to a living will and a health care power of attorney, this plan should include a last will and testament and a durable power of attorney. Similar to the health care power of attorney, the durable power of attorney enables a designated guardian to manage your financial and legal matters if you are unable to.

Review these documents periodically to ensure that they still conform with your wishes. As you get older or your family situation changes, the kind of medical care you desire may also change.

Key Terms

accident insurance (p. 372)

basic health care insurance (p. 357)

benefit period (p. 373)

class cancelable (p. 374)

coinsurance (p. 358)

comprehensive health insurance (p. 357)

coordination of benefits clause (p. 373)

copayment (p. 358)

defined-contribution health plan (p. 364)

dental insurance (p. 359)

disability elimination period (p. 373)

disability income insurance (p. 370)

fee-for-service health insurance (p. 362)

flexible spending health care accounts (p. 365)

group-staff HMO (p. 362)

guaranteed renewability (p. 360)

health maintenance organization (HMO) (p. 362)

hospital expense insurance (p. 357)

hospital insurance (p. 357)

indemnity insurance (p. 357)

individual practice arrangement (IPA) HMO (p. 362)

long-term care policies (p. 359)

major medical insurance (p. 358)

managed care (p. 362)

Medicaid (p. 366)

Medicare (p. 366)

medigap insurance (p. 366)

physicians' expense insurance (p. 358)

point-of-service plan (POS) (p. 363)

preexisting conditions clause (p. 360)

preferred provider organizations (PPOs) (p. 363)

service benefit coverage (p. 358)

social insurance substitute (p. 373)

surgical expense insurance (p. 357)

usual, customary, and reasonable (UCR) (p. 357)

waiting period (disability) (p. 373)

waiting period (health care) (p. 360)

workers' compensation (p. 365)

Reread the chapter-opening vignette.

FOLLOW-UP
ON THE

Steele
FAMILY

1. How might the Steeles hold down their out-of-pocket health care expenses?
2. Should the Steeles consider supplementing their employer coverage with privately purchased health or disability insurance? Why or why not?
3. Suppose Arnold lost his job. What options would the Steeles have for continuing or replacing their present coverage?

Problems and Review Questions

1. What kinds of insurance provide protection against the financial consequences of illness and injury?
2. What is the difference between hospital indemnity insurance and hospital expense insurance? Which is the preferred coverage? Explain why.
3. What is the difference between medical insurance and major medical insurance? Which is more important? Why?
4. Suppose you have $5,000 of health care expenses that are not covered by your basic health insurance. You have a major medical policy with $500 deductible and 20 percent coinsurance. What are your out-of-pocket expenses?
5. For certain procedures, a fee-for-service plan agrees to pay the physician a UCR fee. What does UCR stand for and how is this fee determined?
6. How does an HMO differ from traditional fee-for-service insurance? How would you go about comparing the relative benefits of fee-for-service insurance and an HMO?
7. How does an HMO differ from a PPO?
8. Which health insurance plans allow you to choose your primary care physician?
9. Name the two government programs that provide health care benefits. Which one is run entirely by the federal government?
10. Where do most individuals obtain group insurance coverage?
11. Which age group is most likely to be without health insurance?
12. How does Social Security define "substantial gainful employment"? Explain how definitions of disability contained in private insurance policies can determine the quality of the insurance protection.
13. It is impossible to purchase disability insurance covering 100 percent of lost income. Why?
14. What part does the elimination period play when planning for adequate disability income protection?
15. Discuss some disability income protection strategies that can help you cope with the erosion of benefits due to inflation.
16. What type of nursing home care is traditionally not reimbursed under health insurance plans?
17. What is the purpose of a living will?
18. What should comprehensive health insurance cover?
19. How can an employer-sponsored flexible spending plan help save you tax dollars? How can you lose dollars with a flexible spending plan?
20. What is meant by managed care?

The Hurleys have narrowed their choice of disability insurance for Mr. Hurley down to two policies. They cost the same and are identical except for those differences outlined in the following table. They are guaranteed renewable and have an elimination period of 15 days.

	Policy 1	Policy 2
Monthly benefit	$500	$300
Benefit period	10 years	To age 65
Maximum replacement from all sources	Lesser of $2,000 a month, or 60% of income	60% of income

Mr. Hurley is currently 35 years of age with two children. Over the next 10 years his child-rearing responsibilities should end. His current job pays $30,000 a year and is covered by Social Security. He calculates potential family disability benefits from Social Security at about $900 a month while the children are still at home. He is currently in line for an upper-level management position. Should he get it, his salary will increase substantially.

Questions
1. From the Hurleys' point of view, discuss the relative merits of each policy. Which would you recommend?
2. Which policy provides the better inflation protection? Why?
3. Do these policies provide adequate income replacement for the Hurleys?
4. Suppose the Hurleys must limit the amount spent on disability insurance to the cost of these policies. Are there any changes in coverage that might lower their risk without increasing their premiums? Explain.

As long as Walter Simon was a full-time student he was covered under his parents' health insurance policy. He recently dropped out of school, which effectively eliminated him from his parents' plan. Since then he has worked in a number of temporary jobs, none of which included employer-provided health care coverage. However, he is covered by workers' compensation when on the job. He recently enrolled in a hospital expense insurance plan that will pay him $100 a day for each day he remains in the hospital after an initial three-day stay. For a minimal fee he has also purchased accident insurance that pays him set dollar amounts for a long list of possible injuries.

Walter is pretty pleased with himself. By buying low-cost insurance policies he believes he has been able to obtain comprehensive health care coverage at minimal cost.

Questions
1. Does Walter have good reasons to be pleased with his current health care coverage?
2. What health insurance alternatives should Walter consider?

Exercises to Strengthen Your Use of the Internet

(Internet links for the following exercises can be found at **www.prenhall.com/winger**.)

Exercise 14.1 Comparison Shopping for Health Care Plans

Test your ability to evaluate health insurance policies at the Health Care Shopper. Here you will find a list of HMOs, PPOs, and POSs in your area. Full plan descriptions are provided along with monthly fees.

Q. Select an HMO and a PPO, and determine which one provides the better basic health care coverage and which one provides the preferred major medical coverage. Which is the better plan for you? Why?

Exercise 14.2 Obtaining Comparative Data on Hospitals

QuadroMed Corporation has created the American Hospital Directory. It is a database of information on hospitals. The raw data were collected by the government. QuadroMed created a convenient online database for accessing this information. It provides a free service and a subscription service for using this database. The free service provides only summary data. However, this is probably sufficient information for most consumers. You can also search a database at the Joint Commission on Accreditation of Healthcare Organizations to review your hospital's accreditation status.

Q. Check on a hospital in your area. What is the average length of stay in this hospital? Is it accredited by some reviewing agency?

Exercise 14.3 Review a Living Will

Rio Grande Free-Net serves up a Healthcare Guide to medical care resources on the Web. If you dig down through the menus, you will find a page on "Advanced Directives." Consider whether this document reflects your own wishes. Other links to forms can be found at the U.S. Living Will Registry.

Q. What would you put in an advanced directive that reflects your own wishes?

Exercise 14.4 Get a Report Card on Your Local Managed Care Plans

The National Committee on Quality Assurance has derived a system called HEDIS for rating managed care providers. It accredits those health care plans that meet its standards. Find out about the accreditation standards and determine whether the managed care plans in your area are accredited at this Web site. You can search the database or download the entire list of accredited plans.

Q. Select a managed care plan in your area. Is this an accredited plan?

Exercise 14.5 Obtaining an Estimate of Social Security Disability Benefits

If you didn't obtain a copy of your Social Security benefits in the previous chapter, you can do it now to determine your disability benefits. You can now obtain an estimate of your Personal Earnings and Benefit Estimate Statement from Social Security Online. You will receive a reply to your electronic request by snail mail.

Q. What are your estimated monthly disability benefits? If you don't have your own statement, you can review the sample statement at Social Security Online.

15

Life Insurance and Estate Planning

PROTECTING YOUR DEPENDENTS

OBJECTIVES

1. To calculate your life insurance protection needs

2. To understand the important provisions in a life insurance policy

3. To describe the major kinds of life insurance

4. To be able to choose the type and amount of protection that is best for you

5. To understand the purpose of a will and what happens if you die without a will

6. To be able to plan for the orderly transition of a death estate

TOPIC **LINKS**

Follow the **Topic Links** in each chapter for your interactive Personal Finance exercise on the Web. Go to: **www.prenhall.com/winger**

Steele FAMILY

Each year Arnold receives a personal benefits statement from his employer that lists the dollar value of all his fringe benefits. These consist of legally required benefits, such as Social Security and unemployment insurance, and elective employer-paid benefits, such as pension plan, medical insurance, and group term life insurance. Arnold is always amazed to find that these benefits represent a significant portion of his total compensation.

One of the benefits that currently concerns the Steeles is the employer-provided term life insurance of $90,100. Arnold's employer provides employees with term insurance protection equal to one and a half times their annual salary. The only other life insurance the Steeles have is a $50,000 cash value policy on Arnold that he purchased from a fellow classmate shortly after graduation. The policy's cash value is $4,000 against which he has taken a low-interest $2,000 loan. Lately, he has been wondering whether he has sufficient death protection. He tried out a number of life insurance calculators while surfing the Internet. They all seem to indicate that he needs more protection than he has. He is not sure he should trust these calculations. After all, most of these Web sites have a financial interest in selling him additional protection.

Arnold and Sharon have not totally ignored their own mortality. Before the children were born, they had separate wills drawn up naming each other as primary beneficiary. If something happened to either one of them, the entire estate will go to the surviving spouse. Given that they are both professionals, they have not given life insurance much thought. If need be, they expect that either Arnold or Sharon could generate enough income to support the children.

Life insurance is a topic that most people would rather not discuss. Anything that questions our own mortality is almost always distasteful. In addition, we confront a special language we don't understand and costs that are difficult to compare. Moreover, we are sometimes subjected to high-pressure sales tactics from aggressive life insurance agents. It would be very nice if the whole problem of life insurance would just go away. Unfortunately, avoidance is often not the best policy.

A more positive attitude can produce substantial rewards. Life insurance is an integral part of a well-thought-out financial plan. It can provide your dependents with security against possible financial hardship resulting from your premature death. Without life insurance, these contingencies must be covered by your present savings. If you first had to accumulate substantial savings before providing this security, you might be overly cautious in your career decisions and your financial investments.

The life insurance decision requires a considerable amount of effort. You must first examine the reasons why you need life insurance. If you feel you need additional insurance, you must then decide on the appropriate kind and amount of insurance protection. This means gathering information on the life insurance market. Life insurance policies differ widely in both cost and coverage, and you can easily misunderstand what is offered you. Finally, you must be able to compare costs to satisfy your insurance needs at the lowest possible cost. Most people do not devote this much effort to the life insurance decision. This is the reason for the industry adage, "Life insurance is sold, not bought."

Similar attitudes affect estate planning. In addition, there is the erroneous belief that only the rich have to worry about estate planning. Tax exemptions are generous on death transfers. But estate planning is more than just limiting tax liability. Its main purpose is the orderly transition of your assets. Without specific instructions, heirs can find themselves in legal entanglements that waste needed resources.

ESTIMATING YOUR LIFE INSURANCE NEEDS

The two most important reasons for buying life insurance are that it can serve as a convenient means of saving and it can provide financial security for dependents. You must judge its performance as a form of savings against all alternative methods. However, there is no substitute for the death protection it provides. You may *want* to use life insurance as a savings vehicle, but you need it for the insurance protection.

Young adults are often sold life insurance when they graduate from college. Many times, these policies are purchased from other recently hired and inexperienced alumni. The insured later tend not to review the adequacy of their coverage. The paradoxical result is that those who don't need protection have too much, and those who really need the protection have too little. To avoid this situation, sit down and calculate your life insurance needs at least once every three years. Also, recalculate whenever your family undergoes a significant change, such as the birth of a child or the purchase of a home.

Be sure to estimate the insurance needs for each adult in the family unit. In most families both spouses are in the job market. Consequently, the absence of either parent can mean a significant decline in family income. Even when the absent spouse is a full-time homemaker, the financial consequences should be considered. Replacing the services of a homemaker can be expensive.

The needs of survivors may be many and varied. All estimates of need, however, must focus on three basic considerations: a transition fund, a maintenance fund, and specialized needs funds. The dollars to cover all of these expenses must come either from the liquidation of your family's present net assets or from your life insurance proceeds. After you decide what assets might be used to support your survivors, any needs in excess of this amount must either remain unsatisfied or be covered by life insurance. The accompanying worksheets and text will help you judge your life insurance protection needs and the adequacy of your present coverage.

TOPIC **LINKS**

For a quick estimate, use an online life insurance calculator.

The Transition Fund

Transition fund: Funding or expenses that will be incurred at the time of death.

Expenses that are related directly to the death and that must be paid for at the time of death may be budgeted for in the **transition fund.** This fund should also include any liabilities that would be convenient or preferable to liquidate at this time. The typical items included in a transition fund are listed on the sample worksheet in Figure 15.1.

Funeral and Burial Costs

The price of a funeral and burial can vary widely, depending on your style of departure. A standard funeral and burial cost between $4,000 and $7,000. However, you can hold this expense down to about $1,000 if you decide on an inexpensive cremation.

TOPIC **LINKS**
See "Funerals: A Consumer Guide."

Estate Taxes

Both the state and the federal government may collect taxes on the death estate. These are discussed in Chapter 4 on taxes.

Under federal estate tax laws, an unlimited amount may be transferred to your spouse tax free. If you have a substantial estate and a nonspousal estate transfer, you will have to estimate your tax liability at this point. This is particularly important if you own a business. Covering the tax liabilities will allow your beneficiaries to avoid a forced sale in a possibly depressed market.

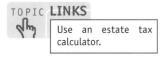

TOPIC **LINKS**
Use an estate tax calculator.

Probate Costs

The lawyer who wrote your will can probably estimate the probate costs associated with the validation of your will and the distribution of your estate. As a second-best estimate, you may calculate probate costs at 4 percent of the value of the assets distributed through the probate process. For example, you would incur about $6,000 on an estate with $150,000 in assets. These assets should not include life insurance proceeds, since life insurance payouts to beneficiaries other than the estate avoid probate.

Uninsured Medical Costs

Your estimate of uninsured medical costs will depend on the quality of your health insurance coverage (see Chapter 14). You can generally count on the cost of your medical care at death exceeding deductibles on your medical insurance policy. Therefore, enter any deductibles as an uninsured medical cost. In addition, you might enter another $500 to $1,000 for expenses that are medically related but not covered by medical insurance. Consequently, if you had a $300 deductible on your medical insurance, you might conservatively enter $1,300 for uninsured medical costs.

Figure 15.1

Transition Fund Worksheet

	Sample Entries
1. Funeral and burial costs	$6,000
2. Estate taxes	-0-
3. Probate costs	6,000
4. Uninsured medical costs	1,300
5. Outstanding loans due	16,000
Total transition fund	$29,300

Outstanding Loans Due

The amount you enter under *outstanding loans due* will be equal to the value of the loans you would like to see paid off at the time of your death. Generally, it is a good idea to include any consumer-type loans you may have. These are probably at high rates of interest and will represent an unnecessary burden on your dependents. If you had $1,000 payable on your charge cards and a $15,000 auto loan, you might enter $16,000 for outstanding loans due.

The outstanding balance on a home mortgage may or may not be included in the transition fund. The payments on any loan that is not included in the transition fund must be covered under the family maintenance fund.

The Family Maintenance Fund

The most important of your insurance protection needs is the **family maintenance fund.** It will insure the viability of the dependent family unit. The size of the fund will reflect the level of living you would like to see maintained. You want to budget an amount at least large enough to eliminate the need for major financial adjustments. On the other hand, you don't want to budget an amount that makes you worth more to your family dead than alive.

Using a computer spreadsheet, you should be able to arrive at a good estimate of the needed support for survivors. The following steps and the worksheet in Figure 15.2 will lead you through the computations.

Step 1: Calculate the monthly expenses for the dependent family unit. If you keep a family budget, you can estimate the monthly living expenses for the surviving family members on the basis of these data. Be sure to include all items that are jointly consumed and exclude only those items that are independently consumed by the insured. For example, the home must still be heated and maintained, but the family may no longer need that second car.

If you have not kept track of your monthly expenses, or you find it difficult to identify marginal expenses for the insured, use data based on average family budgets. Various studies tend to support the percentage of income consumed by the head of household presented in Figure 15.3. To estimate the amount spent for the exclusive support of the insured, multiply total family take-home pay by the appropriate percentage. If you subtract the resulting amount from the family's take-home pay, you are left with the approximate expenditures necessary to provide for the continued support of the surviving members in a typical household.

The entries in Figure 15.2 assume combined take-home pay of $5,000 per month and a family with three dependent children. Consumption by one of the adult family members in

Family maintenance fund:
Funding for the ongoing support of dependent family members.

TOPIC **LINKS**

Download life insurance planning worksheets.

		Sample Entries
Step 1. Monthly survivors' expenses		$ 4,000
Step 2. Monthly survivors' take-home pay	$ 670	
Step 3. Monthly survivors' benefits	1,980	
Total contribution by survivors		− 2,650
Step 4. Monthly maintenance requirement		$ 1,350
Step 5. Calculate size of maintenance fund		× 12
(a) Annual requirement		$ 16,200
(b) Multiply by annuity factor		× 9.1622
Family maintenance fund		$148,428

Figure 15.2

Family Maintenance Fund: Needs Approach

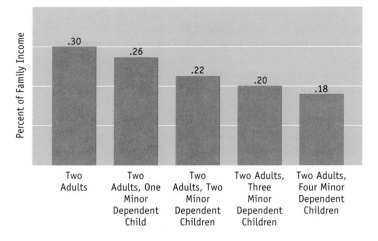

Figure 15.3

Family Head's Consumption Expenditure as Percentage of Family Income

a three-child family would be equal to 0.20 × $5,000, or $1,000 per month. Therefore, the dependent family would require $4,000 per month in maintenance expenditure.

You may want to add in any additional expenditures the family might incur with the death of the insured. This may include additional homemaking expenses and lost fringe benefits. For example, many workers receive family medical insurance as a fringe benefit, but this coverage may lapse at their death. In this situation, the monthly cost of medical insurance should be added to living expenses in order to assure the family's continued protection.

Step 2: Calculate total monthly survivors' take-home pay. You will have to estimate the amount the surviving family members can contribute to their own support. After the death of the insured, survivors may find new sources of income. On the other hand, the additional homemaking responsibilities placed on the surviving spouse may reduce that person's ability to participate in the labor market. The example in Figure 15.2 assumes that the surviving spouse will bring home part-time earnings of $670 per month. This represents expected earnings after taxes and other payroll deductions.

Step 3: Calculate total monthly survivors' benefits. It is likely that your survivors may be eligible for monthly Social Security death benefits. To be eligible, you must either have recent employment or a history of past employment. Given a fully insured status, a wide range of close relatives might qualify for benefits. These may include:

- A widow, widower, or divorced spouse at normal retirement age or reduced benefits as early as age 60. A disabled widow, widower, or divorced spouse can get benefits at ages 50 to 60.
- A widow, widower, or divorced spouse at any age if she or he takes care of your child who is under age 16 or disabled.
- An unmarried child under 18 (or up to age 19 if he or she is attending elementary or secondary school full time). Your child can get benefits at any age if he or she was disabled before 22 and remains disabled. Under certain circumstances, benefits can also be paid to your stepchildren or grandchildren.
- A dependent parent age 62 or older.

The Social Security Administration (SSA) mails out annually a "Personal Earnings and Benefit Estimate Statement" to most workers age 25 and older. This statement lists potential benefits available for survivors. If you do not have a statement, you can request one online or you can use the online calculator for a quick estimate. Some sample

	Current Annual Earnings			
	$20,000	**$40,000**	**$80,000**	**$160,000**
Monthly Benefit				
Child	614	962	1,389	1,524
Spouse caring for child	614	962	1,389	1,524
Spouse at full retirement age	819	1,283	1,852	2,032
Family maximum	1,274	2,324	3,242	3,558
Percent of Income Replaced by SSA Benefit				
Child	37%	29%	21%	11%
Spouse caring for child	37%	29%	21%	11%
Spouse at full retirement age	49%	38%	28%	15%
Family maximum	76%	70%	49%	27%

Source: SSA Quick Calculator, based on 35-year-old worker qualifying for disability benefits.

Table 15.1

Estimates of Monthly Death Benefits from SSA Quick Calculator

estimates from the quick calculator are listed in Table 15.1. Each child should receive the indicated benefit so long as total family payments are less than the indicated maximum. In that case, benefits are proportionately reduced to each survivor so that total benefits do not exceed this limit.

TOPIC **LINKS**

Use the SSA death benefits calculator.

Benefits paid to a surviving spouse with children are significantly reduced if he or she has significant market earnings ($11,640 before age 65 and $31,080 thereafter in 2004). In addition, benefits paid to a dependent child end at age 18 and benefits paid to the caretaking spouse end when the child reaches age 16. The surviving parent then enters a "blackout" period during which benefits are discontinued. Later, when he or she reaches age 60, benefits may again be paid under a widow(er)'s pension.

If you have a private insurance plan that provides monthly survivors' benefits, you will want to add this to any Social Security benefits to arrive at total survivors' benefits. For example, if Social Security provides $1,880 per month and a private pension plan provides $100 per month, then total monthly benefits will be $1,980.

Employer-sponsored retirement plans will often provide some type of benefit for the surviving spouse. In fact, when retirement annuities are offered employees, both preretirement and postretirement spousal survivorship benefits are in most instances required under the Retirement Equity Act of 1984. These benefits are mandatory and can be withdrawn only with the consent of the nonemployee spouse.

Step 4: Calculate the monthly maintenance requirement. The monthly maintenance requirement is equal to the difference between the expenditure needs of the dependent family unit and the support provided by potential income and benefits. To calculate this amount, add survivors' take-home pay in step 2 and survivors' total benefits in step 3, and subtract the sum from total monthly expenses in step 1. For the sample data, the monthly maintenance requirement is $1,350.

The requirement may change over time. However, some of the changes may offset each other; for example, Social Security benefits are reduced as children become self-supporting. Thus, your estimate of a monthly maintenance requirement for the present age structure of your family may hold up reasonably well until the youngest child reaches age 16. If the surviving spouse does not expect to become self-supporting after the youngest child reaches age 16, you may want to calculate a separate monthly maintenance requirement for the surviving spouse over the years that Social Security benefits are blacked out or include early retirement benefits in a specialized fund.

Do Children and Young Adults Need Life Insurance?

The quick answer is a definite no for children and a maybe for young adults. Life insurance can replace lost market earnings and provide financial security for survivors. The death of a child is a tremendous emotional loss, but it is typically not a financial loss. The government estimates that it costs the typical household more than $130,000 to raise a child to age 18. This doesn't include lost market earnings or the cost of a college education.

Life insurance agents often target young adults who have just graduated from college. This is the time to start building for the future and life insurance is presented as an important part of the needed foundation. Do you really need the death protection at this point in your life? A single individual with no family or parents to support may receive sufficient protection through employer-provided group term insurance. After all, the only real cost to your survivors would be funeral and burial expenses.

If you don't need the death protection, what about buying cash value insurance as an investment? To answer this question, you must compare it with other investments. In particular, you should compare it with other tax-advantaged investments such as tax-qualified retirement accounts. It may seem strange to start thinking about retirement when you have just entered the workforce. However, the dollars you put aside today are going to buy a lot more retirement benefits than those you purchase tomorrow.

Young adults with families or parental obligations will need life insurance. Moreover, they probably need a lot more than they might realize. The death of either spouse in a young family with children is a huge financial loss. The affordable answer for most young families is low-cost term protection on both spouses.

The deciding factor on the right strategy is the financial need of your survivors. If you are single without financial obligations, think about retirement planning first. If you have family obligations, be sure you have an adequate amount of life insurance.

TOPIC **LINKS**

Use an online annuity calculator.

Step 5: Calculate the size of the maintenance fund. The monthly maintenance requirements must be paid out of the maintenance fund. In estimating the appropriate size of the maintenance fund, you should consider two important facts: one, with inflation, monthly expenses will rise over time; and two, the maintenance fund will be invested and will earn an interest return. You have to estimate a real rate of return. The real return on your funds is equal to the market rate of interest less the rate of inflation. For example, if these funds can be invested at an annual rate of 5 percent and the rate of inflation is 3 percent, then the real return on your assets is about 2 percent $(5 - 3)$. The larger the expected real return on the maintenance fund, the smaller is the amount of needed funding. To find the size of the needed maintenance fund you can use a financial calculator, our online worksheet, or the annuity tables at the end of the text.

For the current example, assume that the real return on the fund will be 2 percent and the fund will need to last 10 years, when the youngest child reaches the age of majority. In Table A.4 the present value of a $1 annuity that earns 2 percent a year and pays out for 10 years is $8.9826. This is the present value of an inflation adjusted $1 annuity that will pay out at the end of each of the next 10 years.

Unfortunately, this is not quite what you need. You really need a payout at time of death and then a payout at the beginning of each of the subsequent nine years. An *annuity due* is an annuity that pays out at the beginning of each year. To find the value of a 10-year annuity due of $1, you find the value for a nine-year annuity of $1 and then add one for the immediate payment. In the current example, a nine-year annuity of $1 that earns a 2 percent real return has a present value of $8.1622. Therefore, the present value of this $1 annuity due would be $9.1622 ($1 + $8.1622). This is the annuity factor you enter in Figure 15.2.

$$9\text{-year annuity of }\$1\text{ at }2\% \ = \ \$8.1622$$

$$\text{Payment at beginning of first year} \ = \ \underline{1.0000}$$

$$10\text{-year annuity due of }\$1\text{ at }2\% \ = \ \$9.1622$$

Try not to be too optimistic when assuming an after-tax return on your death estate. Although you may be an experienced investor, it is your survivors who will be making the investment decisions. Furthermore, you should not employ an interest assumption that requires speculative investments. Your life insurance objective is to reduce risk, not to increase it.

Specialized Funds

You might consider setting up various specialized funds to meet temporary needs that are not covered by the maintenance fund. Special funds for emergencies, education, and retirement are definitely worth thinking about and are listed on the specialized fund worksheet in Figure 15.4.

An Emergency Fund

You may want to be fairly generous in estimating the size of your emergency fund, since emergencies might be more difficult to handle in a single-parent household. A good rule of thumb is three to six months of the survivors' expenses included in Figure 15.4. If most of these expenses are guaranteed by survivors' benefits, a multiple of 3 might be sufficient.

An Educational Fund

College students over 18 years of age are no longer entitled to survivors' benefits under Social Security. Therefore, if you plan to provide a college education for your children, you should consider the need for an educational fund. Tuition and fees, room and board, books and supplies, transportation, and personal expenses for a resident student are now about $11,000 per year at public institutions. Thus, a four-year college education can cost about $44,000.

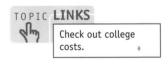

TOPIC **LINKS**

Check out college costs.

Figure 15.4

Specialized Fund Worksheet

		Sample Entries
Emergency fund		$ 12,000
Educational fund		
Cost per child	$44,000	
Number of children	× 3	
		$132,000
Retirement fund		
Annual requirement	$ 5,000	
Multiply by 20 years	× 20	
		$ 100,000
Other funds		-0-
Total specialized fund		$244,000

A Retirement Fund

If you think that pension benefits from private plans and Social Security might not provide enough support for the surviving spouse, you might want to set an additional amount aside in a retirement fund to eliminate this deficiency. If you multiply the annual deficiency in support times 20 years, you will have a decent estimate of the amount needed in the retirement fund, assuming retirement at age 65. If you want payments to begin during the "blackout" period on Social Security benefits, you will need a larger multiple. More accurate techniques for estimating a retirement fund are contained in Chapter 16 on retirement and pension planning.

The Insurance Protection Gap

Once you have estimated the total needs of the dependent family—consisting of the transition fund, the maintenance fund, and specialized funds—the next task is to determine how these needs will be met. Figure 15.5 contains a worksheet for calculating the insurance protection gap.

Funding sources will consist of:

1. *Financial investments.* These should be counted at present market value after taxes. Include your personal portfolio, plus any lump-sum distributions from retirement plans that pay out upon death.
2. *Tangible goods.* You may have some items the family will no longer require. These should be valued at their market price after taxes and selling costs. Do not include lifestyle assets that will be utilized by the survivors.
3. *Life insurance.* The face amount of your present policies, minus outstanding loans on those policies, is available for future support. Include any group coverage you have at work, plus the $255 death benefit under Social Security.

Funding needs less funding sources represents your survivors' unfunded needs. You obviously will have to provide sufficient insurance protection for your survivors' unfunded needs. However, covering only unfunded needs may not protect your survivors adequately from immediate financial hardship. Your survivors may be hard-pressed to convert the funding sources into cash in order to meet immediate death-related expenses such as estate

---

Figure 15.5

Worksheet: The Life Insurance Gap

	Sample Entries	
Funding Needs		
1. Transition fund	$ 29,300	
2. Family maintenance fund	148,428	
3. Specialized fund	244,000	
Total funding needs		$421,728
Less Funding Sources		
1. Financial investments	$ 56,000	
2. Tangible goods	10,000	
3. Life insurance		
(a) Group insurance	$ 50,000	
(b) Individual insurance	-0-	
(c) Social Security	255	
Total sources		($116,255)
Unfunded Needs		$305,473
Unfunded Estate Liquidity		0
Life Insurance Protection Gap		$305,473

---

taxes. For this reason, you should check your funding needs and sources in Figure 15.5 to ensure that your liquid resources—those readily convertible into cash—are sufficient to cover the transition fund, which should include all immediate death-related expenses. The deficiency in liquid resources must be entered under unfunded estate liquidity.

Your survivors' unfunded needs plus their unfunded estate liquidity equals your **life insurance protection gap.** If a gap exists on your worksheet, it is time to consider additional life insurance coverage.

Life insurance protection gap: Unfunded needs plus unfunded estate liquidity.

THE SPECIAL LANGUAGE OF LIFE INSURANCE POLICIES

A life insurance policy is a contract between you and the insurance company. As with all contracts, you should read it carefully and understand it fully before you sign. This may require some tenacity on your part, since many companies provide sample policies only with great reluctance. Furthermore, to understand the agreement you must first master the special language of the life insurance industry. However, the efforts are worth the trouble. Purchasing the wrong kind of insurance or the wrong type of policy can prove costly.

The Basic Policy

In return for amounts paid to the insurance company while you are living, the life insurance agreement obligates the company to pay out a stated amount at the time of your death. Although policies differ widely in language and coverage, the basic agreement should contain some common terminology.

Face Amount

The dollar amount stated on the face of the policy is the **face amount.** In the absence of special provisions or additions, the face amount minus any outstanding loans on the policy is the amount paid out at death. Special provisions, such as an accidental death clause, which increases the payout when death is due to accidental circumstances, may affect the actual payout at death.

Face amount: The dollar amount of life insurance protection stated on the face of the policy.

Face Amount of Policy + Accidental Death Benefit − Outstanding Loans = Death Benefit

Cash Value − Outstanding Loans − Surrender Charges = Surrender Value

Cash and Surrender Value

The **cash value** of a life insurance policy is equal to the savings accumulated during the existence of the policy contract. Not all insurance policies have a cash value; only those that allocate a part of each year's premium to savings do. In many insurance policies, the insured may borrow against the policy's cash value at an interest rate either specified in the policy or set periodically by the insurance company. Closely related to the policy's cash value is its **surrender value.** This is the amount returned to the policyholder when coverage is terminated. Typically, the surrender value of the policy is equal to the cash value plus surrender dividends, minus outstanding loans and surrender charges.

Cash value: An amount equal to the savings accumulated during the existence of the policy contract.

Surrender value: The amount returned to the policyholder when coverage is terminated.

Lives Covered

Most policies are taken out on the life of one person and are called **single life policies.** There are, however, policies with more complicated coverage. A **joint life policy** covers more than one person. With this policy coverage, the face amount is paid out at the first death. This may be important to a family that desires to replace the income lost at the death of either spouse. In this case, a $100,000 joint life policy can be considerably less expensive

Single life policy: Covers a single life and is payable at the end of that life.

Joint life policy: Covers more than one life but pays out at the death of the first.

than a single life policy of $100,000 on the husband and a single life policy of $100,000 on the wife.

A **survivorship joint life** policy operates in the reverse manner. It pays out on the death of the last individual in the group. This policy is particularly useful in estate planning, when taxes must be paid at the death of the surviving spouse.

Many insurance companies issue what is commonly called a **family policy** or family rider. It provides coverage for several family members in one policy. The coverage provided generally consists of whole life insurance on the primary breadwinner and small amounts of term protection on the children, including those born after the policy is issued. Coverage on the children is usually convertible into whole life insurance when the term protection ends at some stated age.

Premium

The periodic payment made to the insurance company is called the **premium.** Depending on the particular policy, this payment may be made on an annual, semiannual, monthly, or even weekly basis. A service charge is usually added for premiums that are paid other than annually.

Dividend

Insurance may be purchased from either mutual insurance companies or stock insurance companies. Typically, the mutual insurance companies issue participating policies, and the stock insurance companies issue **nonparticipating insurance.** A few stock companies do write policies with limited participation, however.

Participating insurance gets its name from the fact that policyholders participate in the earnings and mortality experience of the insurer. If the mutual insurance company pays out less in claims than it expected, the policyholders participate in this good fortune by receiving back the surplus funds in the form of what is called a **dividend.** This dividend is considered a partial return of your initial premium and is therefore nontaxable.

If the company had only unexpected gains, participating insurance would be a great buy. However, policyholders may participate in both unexpected gains and losses. Mutual insurance companies tend to charge higher premiums than stock insurance companies in order to create a fund to cover any unexpected costs. Should these costs occur, dividends need not be paid out. A dividend payment is not guaranteed, and payments will fluctuate with the earnings experience of the mutual insurance company.

Beneficiary

The person or instrument (e.g., a trust fund) that receives the proceeds of the policy when you die is the **beneficiary.** If two or more individuals are to share the proceeds, then they are known as *cobeneficiaries.* You may also specify a primary beneficiary and a contingent beneficiary. The **contingent beneficiary,** also termed the *secondary beneficiary,* receives the proceeds if the primary beneficiary dies before you do. You may name more than one person as either a primary or a contingent beneficiary. For example, suppose Arnold Steele takes out a policy naming his wife, Sharon, as primary beneficiary and their two children, Nancy and John, as contingent beneficiaries. If Sharon dies before Arnold, the children, or more likely a trust fund for the children, will receive the insurance proceeds.

Special Provisions

The worth of a life insurance policy will depend on more than just the policy's face amount or cash value. It will also be influenced by the various specialized provisions contained in

---

Survivorship joint life: Covers more than one life and pays out on the death of the last.

Family policy: Covers several family members in one contract.

Premium: The periodic payment made to the insurance company.

Nonparticipating insurance: Future net premiums are not dependent upon the earnings and mortality experience of the insurer.

Participating insurance: Policyholders participate in the earnings and mortality experience of the insurer through dividend adjustments.

Dividend: A partial return of premium dependent upon the earnings of the insurer.

Beneficiary: The individual who receives the proceeds from the life insurance policy.

Contingent beneficiary: The one who receives the proceeds if the primary beneficiary dies first.

Living Benefits Insurance and Life Settlements

The availability of living benefits provisions, also called accelerated death benefits, has expanded rapidly over the last few years. More than 18 million Americans now have these provisions in their policies. Playing on the fear of the high cost of long-term health care, living benefits insurance is meant to allay that concern by either providing for your survivors in case of sudden death or providing for you in case of a protracted illness.

In most cases the payment of living benefits reduces potential death benefits, but not necessarily on a dollar-for-dollar basis. A partial prepayment of benefits while living may entail the elimination of potentially larger future death benefits. On one such policy, patients given 18 to 24 months to live can get from 50 to 75 percent of the policy's face value. However, acceptance of this partial sum wipes out all death benefits, in effect placing a very high opportunity cost on the prepayment of death benefits.

There are also viatical companies that purchase the insurance policies directly from the policyholders. (The word *viatical* comes from the Latin word *viaticum*, meaning provisions for a journey.) They typically pay the dying only about 50 to 80 cents on the dollar. Such high discounts on future payments might be avoided by arranging private loans from relatives in return for naming them as beneficiaries on the policy.

You don't have to be terminally ill to sell your insurance policy. The industry is increasingly engaging in what are termed "life settlements." You sell your policy to an investor who pays the premiums on the policy and collects the payout. This can be an ideal solution for those who no longer need the insurance protection or who do not want to continue paying premiums. For older insured, the market value of the life settlement can exceed the surrender value on the policy. Even term policies that have no cash value may be of interest to an investor in life settlements. Consequently, it may be a preferred alternative to either surrendering the policy or letting your coverage lapse.

---

the policy and the addition of any options, also called **riders,** to the insurance contract. The features you are most likely to encounter are described in Figure 15.6. Some of these provisions are determined by state law, and others can be added by the insured.

Rider: A specialized provision meant to modify or extend coverage in an insurance contract.

KINDS OF INSURANCE PROTECTION

Life insurance can be grouped into two basic categories: term and cash value. Most policies can be easily classified under one of these headings. A few, however, such as universal life, discussed later in this chapter, have the characteristics of both term insurance and cash value insurance.

Term Insurance

Term insurance provides only death protection. A term policy does not build up a cash value. If the insured discontinues premium payments, the coverage simply lapses after a specified grace period. Life insurance agents sometimes attempt to discourage people from purchasing term insurance by suggesting that if they survive the period of coverage, they have, in effect, paid for nothing, since the policy has no residual value. This is not true. They have paid for and received a reduction in the financial risks associated with the possibility of dying. Such risk reduction is not costless, nor is it valueless.

As we will see, there are many kinds of term insurance. Some are sold under the name *term insurance* and others are not. In addition, some policies that are sold under the *term*

Term insurance: Has no cash value buildup; provides only death protection.

TOPIC **LINKS**

Get term insurance quotes.

Figure 15.6

Checklist: Special Provisions of Life Insurance Policies

Provision	Description
Accelerated death benefits	Also known as living benefits. Predeath benefits that may be triggered by catastrophic illness or terminal illness.
Accidental death benefit	This option provides that, if the death of the insured is accidental, the death benefit will be some multiple of the face amount of the policy. If it doubles the face amount, it is sometimes known as a *double indemnity* provision.
Convertibility	You can exchange one kind of insurance for another without a medical examination. For example, your term insurance policy might be convertible to a specified amount of whole life at each age.
Cost-of-living adjustment	Automatically increases both the face amount of the policy and the premium. You have the right to reject this inflation-adjusted coverage, but if you do so, you may forfeit your right to all future cost-of-living adjustments in the face value of the policy.
Disability waiver of premium	If you become disabled, this rider requires the insurance company to take over premium payments on the policy. It usually takes effect six months after the beginning of the disability period.
Grace period	If you stop making payments and the cash value of your policy is depleted, coverage must cease but not until the specified grace period ends. This period is usually 31 days.
Guaranteed insurability	Allows you to increase the face amount of the policy by stated amounts and at specified dates without a medical examination. A worthwhile option for those who expect a future increase in insurance protection needs.
Incontestability	Prohibits the insurance company, after some period of time, from challenging your unintentional mistakes and omissions on the insurance application.
Nonforfeiture clause	This clause ensures that you will not lose the cash value of your policy if you cease making payments. The cash value may be disposed of in one of three ways: You may receive it in cash; you may use it to extend premium payments of the life insurance coverage; or you may use it to purchase a reduced amount of paid-up life insurance.
Renewability	Allows you to renew your coverage without a medical examination. However, your premiums for subsequent periods may be higher.
Settlement option	This provision determines how the face amount of the policy will be paid out. The choice of settlement option can also be left to the beneficiary.

label are not true term policies. The distinguishing feature of a term policy is that it does not have a savings component. Under a true term policy, the entire premium pays for death protection. Therefore, term provides the greatest amount of death protection for each premium dollar.

Because of tax advantages extended to employer-provided term life insurance, this is the type of group life insurance that is typically provided to nearly all workers in medium and large firms. The face amount of the employer-supplied insurance is on average equal to about one-and-a-half times the employee's annual salary. This coverage is particularly attractive to older workers. Current law prohibits employers from providing such workers with less insurance protection than younger workers, even though the cost of a given face amount of term protection may be much greater for this group.

Level Benefit and Increasing Premium or Renewable Level Premium

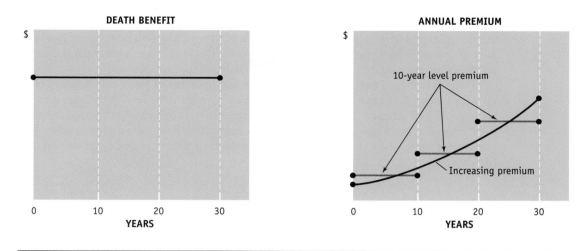

Decreasing Benefit and Constant Premium

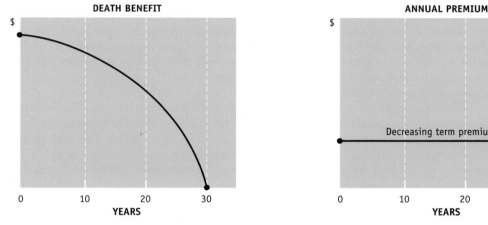

Figure 15.7

Structure of Term Policy Coverage and Premiums

Increasing-Premium Term

Each year as you age, you experience a greater risk of mortality. Therefore, a pure term policy that provides a level death benefit must have increasing premiums in order to offset age-related risks. Yearly **renewable term** is the most common type of increasing-premium term. Figure 15.7 illustrates the premium structure for a representative policy. Renewability indicates that a policy may be extended without proof of insurability such as a medical exam. The renewability provision may last for some specified number of years or until you reach some specified age, typically age 65. Since the premium covers only death protection, it is lowest in the early years. Consequently, it is ideal for families with young children who need large amounts of insurance protection at minimal cost. After age 65, term protection may be nonexistent or prohibitively expensive.

Renewable term: Term insurance that may be periodically renewed over some defined term without a medical examination.

Level-Premium Term

There are also *level-premium term* policies for 5-, 10-, and 15-year periods that may be renewable for subsequent periods. The level-term policies hold the premium constant over the specified period by requiring a higher premium than yearly term in the early years and a lower premium than yearly term in the later years. The lower premiums at the end of the policy's term are paid for by the overcharges in the earlier years.

Policies that hold the premium level over a large number of years may actually build up a cash value in the early years. *Life-expectancy term* provides level premiums over the insured's life expectancy. The leveling of the premium over this extended period creates a cash value that increases and then declines to zero at the termination of the policy. The same holds for *term-to-age-65* (or 70), which provides a shorter period of protection than life-expectancy term.

Decreasing Term

Decreasing term: A term policy with level premiums but decreasing death protection.

Decreasing term is usually packaged as a one-year renewable policy. Its premium remains constant over time. The increased risk of mortality is reflected in a declining amount of death protection, so your insurance coverage automatically decreases as you age. It is useful for those who can anticipate a declining need for insurance protection.

Group Mortgage Life and Credit Life

Group mortgage life: A policy designed to pay off the remaining balance on the mortgage at death.

A form of decreasing term insurance, **group mortgage life** is designed to pay off the remaining balance on a mortgage. The death benefit declines as the remaining balance on the mortgage falls. As with traditional decreasing term insurance, the premium remains level over the term of the mortgage. The face amount at any time may not exactly equal the remaining balance, so, if you die, the beneficiary will receive an amount only approximately equal to the remaining balance.

Group mortgage life is sold through the bank that holds your mortgage. The bank collects a commission from the insurance company for functioning as a sales agent. The bank also benefits in another way: It is the beneficiary on the insurance policy. This arrangement ensures that the mortgage is paid off at your death. Your family will have no say in how the proceeds are spent. If you have a low-interest mortgage, paying it off may not be the wisest use of insurance proceeds.

Credit life insurance: Prepays a remaining loan balance at death.

Group mortgage life is only one form of **credit life insurance** that pays off your loan balance at death. Too many consumers purchase credit life because they wrongly believe that it is a required condition for a loan. You have probably received numerous solicitations for credit life protection on auto loans, credit card balances, and personal loans. Consumer organizations suggest you just say no to all of these offers. They generally believe that these are bad deals, with consumers only receiving 42 cents in benefits on each dollar spent. The typical term life policy should provide a much better payback.

Deposit Term

Deposit term insurance: Returns a lump-sum amount at the end of the term of protection; not true term insurance.

What has been advertised as **deposit term insurance** is not true term insurance, because it has a savings component. With a typical deposit term policy, you are supposedly purchasing something similar to 10- or 15-year renewable term. Each year you pay a term premium on the policy. However, during the first year of coverage you pay an extra premium, which is the deposit. At the end of the coverage period you may get back an amount equal to double the extra premium paid during the first year. This represents the saving component. In reality, the deposit you made in the first year may be going to pay the sales commission received by the agent. The insurance company is able to pay you back a lump-sum amount after 10 years because over the 10 years you have paid a higher-than-standard premium on the term protection. When these excessive premiums are taken into account, the rate of return on the first year's deposit is much less than it at first appears. Also, if you terminate the policy before a specified number of years, you may lose the deposit. Most insurance analysts have been highly critical of deposit term and suggest you avoid purchasing this type of policy.

Cash Value Insurance

Cash value insurance functions both as death protection and as a savings vehicle. There are many reasons why people purchase cash value insurance: The periodic premium payments provide a convenient method for accumulating savings; the cash value may be a comparatively attractive investment; and, for most insurance products, the cash buildup is relatively safe. In some states the cash values and death benefits may even be protected from creditors.

Cash value insurance: Insurance that provides both death protection and cash value buildup.

If a cash value policy is terminated, you receive the cash value buildup less any surrender charges and outstanding loans. Such payouts may trigger tax liabilities; however, these may be conveniently handled by transferring the funds into retirement annuities. Also significant for your later years is the fact that cash value insurance can continue to provide death protection after term insurance has expired. Consequently, cash value insurance is an important tool in estate planning, supplying needed funds to pay estate taxes and an efficient method for transferring wealth to your heirs. Furthermore, under recently introduced policy options, some insureds may receive benefits before death in order to offset the unexpected cost of catastrophic illness.

One characteristic that often attracts people to cash value policies is that the insured may borrow from the insurance company an amount equal to the cash value at an attractive rate of interest. If the insured should die while owing money on the policy, the amount paid to beneficiaries will be reduced by the amount of the loan.

Figure 15.8 illustrates the death benefit and the death protection for a hypothetical cash value life policy with a face amount of $100,000. It is assumed that there are no special provisions, such as an accidental death benefit, that provide for an additional payout under special circumstances. The death benefit is equal to the face amount less any outstanding policy loans at the time of death. The actual death protection, the insurance component, is equal to the face amount less the policy's cash value. It is also equal to the death benefit less the net cash value (cash value less outstanding policy loans). An increase in the policy's cash value reduces the risk to the insurance company.

	Death Benefit*	Death Protection	Cash Surrender Value
Face amount	$100,000	$100,000	
Cash value		–30,000	$30,000
Outstanding loans	–10,000		–10,000
Surrender charges			–500
	$90,000	$70,000	$19,500

Figure 15.8

Death Benefit and Death Protection for a Hypothetical Policy

*Does not include additional amounts that may be paid out under an accidental death provision.

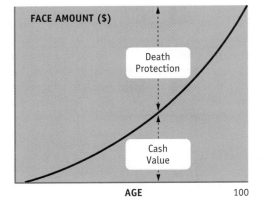

Figure 15.9

FACE AMOUNT ($)

Death
Protection

Cash
Value

AGE   100

Level-Premium Whole Life

Whole life or straight or ordinary life: Cash value insurance with level lifetime payments.

Whole Life

With **whole life,** also called **straight** or **ordinary life,** premium payments are level over the lifetime of the insured. On a cash value policy the amount of death protection is equal to the difference between the policy's face value and its cash value. Figure 15.9 indicates how the cash value and the death protection vary over the term of the policy. In the early years, much of the premium must go toward purchasing the death protection component. As the cash value builds up, and the required death protection declines, more of the premium can be added to the cash value. Thus, the buildup in cash value will be more rapid in the later years. At age 100 the cash value of the policy equals the face amount, and the insured receives the face amount if he or she is still living. The rise in the cash value is predetermined, and the insured is often presented with a schedule indicating what the cash value of the policy will be at each year of age.

TOPIC **LINKS**

Comparison shop for whole life insurance.

Limited payment life: Cash value insurance with level premiums over a limited number of years that provides insurance protection over an entire lifetime.

Limited Payment Life

Under a **limited payment life** policy, premium payments remain level up to a certain age, usually 65, and then cease. However, the insurance protection remains effective over the entire life span. This protection is accomplished by charging higher premiums than on a comparable straight life policy over fewer payment years in order to provide a more rapid buildup in cash value. The insurance company then uses part of the interest earned on the cash value to provide continued protection after premium payments terminate. The allocation of death protection and cash value is illustrated in Figure 15.10.

Endowment life: Rapid buildup of cash value, with payoff of face value after a set number of years.

Endowment Life

An **endowment life** policy pays off its face value after a set number of years, thus providing rapid cash value buildup with death protection. With past changes in the tax law, the cash value buildup on most traditional endowment policies no longer qualifies for tax deferral. Consequently, such policies are rarely sold anymore.

Modified whole life: Level premiums with varying death protection tied to life-cycle needs.

Modified Whole Life

Most families require less insurance protection in later years. **Modified whole life** attempts to fit the needs of the family throughout the life cycle by automatically reducing the death benefit as the insured ages. As in a whole life policy, the premium payments remain level for life. However, premium payments on a modified life plan will be lower than those on a whole life policy providing identical protection in the early years.

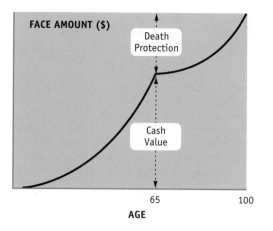

FACE AMOUNT ($)

Death
Protection

Cash
Value

65   100

AGE

Figure 15.10

Limited Payment Life

Adjustable Life

Under an **adjustable life** plan, both the premium payments and the face amount of the policy are adjustable. You are allowed to change coverage as need varies and to change premium payments as income varies. The basic idea seems to be a good one, but this plan has some characteristics you should be wary of.

The face amount of the policy may be increased only by specified amounts at specified time intervals. Unless the policy contains a guaranteed insurability rider, you may have to take another medical exam when you desire to increase the face amount. In addition, a sales charge may be built in to pay the insurance agent a second commission when you increase the insurance coverage. With the added sales charge and the medical exam, increasing the face amount of an adjustable life policy may cost about as much as taking out a new whole life policy.

The premiums are adjusted by allowing the insured to move between term protection and cash value protection. When the insured's income increases, higher premiums can be paid in order to build up cash value. During periods of financial distress, premiums can be cut by opting for lower-cost term protection. The implicit assumption is that when you can afford it, you purchase the more expensive cash value insurance.

Adjustable life: The face amount of this policy may be adjusted by specified amounts at defined time intervals.

Universal Life

Unlike traditional whole life, **universal life** permits flexible premium payments, affecting the size of the cash buildup. The premium payment on universal life is often called a *contribution* and, within certain limits, is voluntary. Out of this contribution the insurance company deducts a charge for term insurance protection and the cost of management. The remainder is deposited in an interest-bearing account. The interest earned either is determined periodically by the insurance company or is tied to an agreed-upon index.

You receive periodic reports on a universal life policy indicating the cost of the term protection, the management expenses, and the earned return on cash value. This provides a significant advantage over traditional whole life, where you may have no idea how much you are really paying for death protection or how much you are really earning on the policy's cash value. Given the more detailed information on a universal life policy, you are in a better position to judge the relative merits of purchasing term insurance separately and investing the difference.

Those who have compared universal life with traditional whole life have concluded that universal life does generally provide a better return on the invested cash value. Indeed, the primary reason for consumer interest in universal life has been the high advertised rate on the investment account. However, there are additional attractions. Within limits set by

Universal life: Permits flexible premium payments, affecting the size of the cash buildup.

Borrowing Your Cash Value

The cash value on your life insurance can represent a convenient source of liquidity. In most cases, you can promptly tap the cash value with a policy loan. Since the loan is 100 percent collateralized by the policy's cash value, there is no need for a credit check or other financial inquiries that can delay a typical bank loan.

To your advantage, policy loans need never be repaid, and policy loan rates are often substantially below those on other consumer financing. On the negative side, loans will reduce the death benefits, which is probably the primary reason you purchased life insurance in the first place.

When deciding on a policy loan, you should be sure to look at the true opportunity cost of borrowing, which may exceed the policy loan rate. The cash value on your life insurance will earn interest and grow over time. However, if you borrow against the policy, the cash value is used as collateral for the loan. Because the loan may be made at an interest rate that is below what the insurance company can earn on its invested assets, this may reduce the rate earned on the policy's cash value. This practice is called "direct recognition."

For example, suppose you have a universal life policy currently earning 8 percent on cash value, on which you may obtain a policy loan for 5 percent. If you decide to borrow against the policy, the insurance company may reduce the rate earned on the collateralized portion of the cash value to only 3 percent, thus forcing you to give up an additional 5 percent return on the cash value. The true opportunity cost of borrowing is, therefore, equal to 10 percent, the policy loan rate of 5 percent plus the reduced interest rate on the cash value of 5 percent.

When deciding whether to borrow in order to invest your funds elsewhere, the true opportunity cost and not the policy loan rate, is the starting point for comparison purposes. Tax considerations, of course, can make comparative valuations much more complicated. Interest earned on the cash value is tax deferred until the policy is surrendered. If the policy is never surrendered, income taxes need never be paid on the death benefits.

---

the company and the government, the insured may borrow against the accumulated cash value. Furthermore, most universal life policies allow the insured to increase the death protection, although another medical examination may be required.

On all policies that have an interest-sensitive cash buildup, you should critically evaluate seller illustrations of future benefits. These may be based on assumed rates of return that never materialize. Through the 1980s and into the 1990s, interest rates have generally been on the decline. In retrospect, illustrations using historically high rates have been incorrect.

Variable Life

Variable life: Permits selective investment of cash in a market portfolio that determines the cash value in the policy.

In many ways, **variable life** is similar to universal life. Like universal life, it has a term insurance component and an investment component. A minimum death benefit is guaranteed by the term insurance, while the cash value buildup and additional death benefit protection depend on the performance of selected market portfolios of stocks, bonds, or money market funds. You may be permitted to decide how the cash value will be allocated among the available portfolios and when funds should be switched between portfolios.

If your market portfolio does poorly, the cash value buildup will be less than with either whole or universal life. The speculative risk associated with variable life reduces its ability to secure the financial future of your survivors. Variable life should be compared with other tax-advantageous investments and only secondarily looked upon as death benefit protection. The government recognizes its speculative characteristics by requiring that only registered security dealers be permitted to sell this policy. As on universal life policies, management fees and early withdrawal penalties should be examined closely.

Variable life provides less flexibility than universal life. Annual premiums are fixed by the insurer. Regardless of how the market may look, you must contribute to at least one of the policy's portfolios to keep the policy in force. In contrast, universal life permits you to vary the amount you contribute each year and even to skip payments when there is sufficient cash value to cover the cost of insurance protection.

Variable-Universal Life

Variable-universal life is also sold under various other names, such as universal life II. It combines the flexible premiums permitted under universal life with the investment selection permitted by variable life. Depending on your outlook, you can say it blends the best or the worst of each. By allowing both contributions and investments to vary, it becomes a more flexible speculative investment. However, like a traditional variable life policy, if your cash value falls far enough, you may be required to contribute additional funds or lose your family's insurance protection. Furthermore, a forced payout of cash value will require the immediate payment of all deferred tax. This may present a severe hardship for those who have borrowed against the policy's cash value. After repaying those loans, they may have nothing left with which to pay the tax bill.

Variable-universal life:
Combines the flexible premiums of universal life with the investment selection of variable life.

SELECTING THE RIGHT POLICY

Policy selection may be looked upon as a three-step process.

1. Determine your life insurance needs.
2. Select the type of policy that best fits those needs.
3. Comparison shop specific policies and companies.

By now you should have an understanding as to how much insurance you need and information on the various types of policies that may satisfy your needs. You should be in a good position to select the appropriate insurance vehicle and comparison shop the best price.

Selecting the Type of Policy

Once you have determined your death protection needs, it may be easy to decide on the type of insurance protection you need. Young families with small children are going to need large amounts of death protection. Unfortunately, it is these same families who are on tight budgets and can ill afford to pay high premiums for life insurance. They need to get the greatest amount of insurance protection per dollar spent, and that means purchasing term insurance. It is a mistake to settle for less than needed protection today, in the expectation of some investment return in the future.

Cash value insurance should be looked upon as an alternative to term insurance for those who can comfortably afford it. If you can, then you may want to consider purchasing cash value insurance as a supplement to your investment portfolio or as part of your estate plan. As part of your investment portfolio, it should be evaluated like any other investment.

Term or Cash Value Insurance?

Commissions are significantly higher on cash value insurance than on term insurance. Consequently, insurance agents have stronger incentives for selling cash value insurance. This may lead them to exaggerate the benefits of cash value policies and understate the benefits of term insurance. The unique benefit of cash value insurance is the savings feature. It is often promoted as a method of forced savings for retirement and as a can't-lose proposition. If you die, you have the insurance protection; if you live, you have the savings. Unfortunately, the savings have often accumulated at unattractive rates of interest.

Term Plus a Saving Plan

For many years Consumers Union has suggested that individuals would be better off purchasing lower-cost term and investing the difference. One such plan is illustrated in Table 15.2. You would have $25,000 worth of death protection if the face amount of the term policy plus the amount in the savings account averaged $25,000 over each year. This is the way payments are allocated in Table 15.2. Assuming the side savings fund earned a 5 percent annual return after taxes, the amount in the side savings fund would equal $5,677.44 after 10 years.

If the amount in the side savings fund after the specified time period is greater than the after-tax surrender value on the cash value policy, then purchasing term and investing the difference should be the preferred option.

Unbundled Whole Life

Consumers have been increasingly purchasing term rather than cash value insurance. The industry has responded by introducing universal life, variable life, and, finally, variable-universal life. These insurance policies presently control about one-fifth of the market.

As previously discussed, each of these products unbundles the insurance premium into a payment for death protection and a contribution to savings; thus, they do exactly what the critics of whole life have suggested. They combine term and a side savings account into one convenient package. The important benefit is that you know how much you are paying for term protection and how much of a return you are earning on your investment. This is a significant benefit over traditional whole life, where it may be difficult to understand what you are paying for and what you are getting in return.

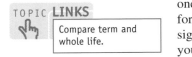

TOPIC **LINKS**

Compare term and whole life.

On all policies, such as universal, variable, and variable-universal, that have an interest-sensitive cash buildup, it is important to examine the historical returns of the companies' market portfolios. These returns should be compared with returns on other investments, such as mutual funds, that have similar levels of risk. But remember, past returns are no guarantee of similar future returns. Illustrations of future premiums and cash buildup based upon historically high returns may be overly optimistic.

The quality of the coverage will depend upon both the cost of the underlying term insurance and the return on the cash value. If you are paying for expensive term coverage, a high return on the cash value may be no bargain. The insurance company will subtract

---

Table 15.2

Buying Term and Investing the Difference at 5% After Taxes

Year	Term Rate per $1,000	Term Expenditures	Annual Deposit	Term Protection[*]	End-of-Year Side Savings
1	$2.57	$63.12	$482.38	$24,517.62	$ 506.50
2	2.75	65.93	479.57	24,013.93	1,035.37
3	3.00	70.62	439.63	23,525.00	1,548.75
4	3.15	72.60	432.40	23,018.85	2,080.21
5	3.31	74.37	425.38	22,494.41	2,630.87
6	3.51	77.16	417.34	21,951.79	3,200.62
7	3.79	81.08	408.17	21,391.22	3,789.22
8	4.05	84.22	399.78	20,811.00	4,398.45
9	4.35	88.13	390.62	20,210.93	5,028.53
10	4.75	92.69	378.56	19,592.92	5,677.44

[*]The term protection plus the amount in the side savings fund will equal about $25,000 each year.

Part 5 Protecting Your Wealth

from each premium the cost of insurance protection and a sales commission; what is left goes to build cash value. If you consider the sales commission on the savings component, your actual return may be much less than the advertised rates. Commissions on universal life policies vary from 5 percent to 90 percent of the first year's premium. Moreover, there may be significant charges if you surrender your policy in the early years.

Weighing the Tax Advantage of Cash Value Insurance

A major selling point for cash value insurance has been the tax advantage for individuals in high tax brackets. The interest earned on the policy's cash value avoids taxes at the time it is credited to the savings component. A 9 percent tax-sheltered yield on the cash value is equivalent to a 12.5 percent taxable yield for someone in the 28 percent marginal tax bracket. However, if you decide to surrender the policy, you will have to pay tax on the interest earnings at that time. One alternative is to borrow against the cash value instead of surrendering the policy. But, again, you may run into problems. Both the company and the government can limit the amount you may be permitted to borrow.

The basic tax rule is that if you surrender a policy, you must pay taxes on the difference between the value of savings and the cost of the policy. The cost of the policy is equal to the sum of premiums paid less the sum of dividends received. However, the immediate tax impact may be avoided if you engage in an IRC Section 1035 exchange. To qualify for a nontaxable exchange, you must roll over the cash value into another life insurance policy or an annuity contract. The exchange of life insurance for a retirement annuity can provide supplementary income if you no longer need insurance protection in your later years.

TOPIC **LINKS**

Download IRS forms and publications.

All life insurance, whether it be whole life or term, provides certain tax benefits at death. Beneficiaries can receive a tax-free payout. In addition, if the insurance contract is properly structured so that the insured gives up all rights of ownership, the proceeds can avoid estate taxes.

Comparison Shopping

Traditional whole life policies have been particularly difficult to compare, because insurance companies have not supplied information on the rate of return for the savings component. Also, life insurance agents have been known to misrepresent the actual cost of the policy. The agent would add up the premiums paid over the 20-year period and subtract from this amount the dividends received and the cash value at the end of the 20 years. The result would often be negative, erroneously indicating to the buyer that the insurance did not "cost" anything. Of course, this calculation ignores the time value of money. Had the consumer been depositing the net premiums into an account paying a competitive market rate of interest over the same period, the total amount in the account at the end of 20 years would have been much greater than the cash value of the policy at that time. The difference between the value in this imaginary account and the cash value of the policy at the end of the 20-year period represents the real cost of the life insurance policy.

Comparison Indexes

From the previous discussion, it should be apparent that when policies differ in premiums, cash buildup, and expected dividends, comparing their relative value is no easy task. Comparison indexes provide you with a single statistic for ranking the worth of different insurance illustrations. The National Association of Insurance Commissioners (NAIC) has promoted the use of the 10-year and 20-year **interest-adjusted net cost index,** sometimes called the **surrender cost index**. About three-quarters of the states now require that the insurance company provide you this information. The index takes into account annual premiums, annual dividends, and the cash accumulation at the end of a 10- and a 20-year

Interest-adjusted net cost index or **surrender cost index**: A useful industry-provided index for comparing the relative costs of similar life insurance policies.

TOPIC **LINKS**

Obtain a list of state insurance departments from the NAIC.

period. Assuming you can earn a 5 percent return on alternative investments, the index calculates the annual cost for a given dollar amount of insurance protection. The formula for the index is quite complex. However, all you really need to know is that the higher the index, the greater the cost of the insurance protection.

You must be careful not to use the index for comparing the relative cost of dissimilar policies. Most important, don't use the index to compare the cost of term insurance with the cost of cash value insurance. The cash value insurance will always appear cheaper if you do. The reason for this is simple. The interest-adjusted net cost index measures the cost of a given face amount of life insurance and not a given amount of death protection. If you purchase a term policy with a $10,000 face amount, you are receiving a full $10,000 of death protection over the period of coverage. On the other hand, when you purchase a $10,000 cash value policy, the amount of death protection is equal to the face amount of the policy less the policy's cash value.

The interest-adjusted net cost index also has another shortcoming. It is based on an assumed rate of return on savings of 5 percent. When market rates are above this amount, the net cost index will not perfectly reflect the relative value of two dissimilar policies. It will tend to understate the relative cost of policies that have higher current premiums but lower future premiums and higher future dividends.

Net payment cost index and yield comparison index (YCI): Indexes for ranking life insurance policies in terms of cost effectiveness.

In California, the Department of Insurance has replaced the interest-adjusted net cost index with the **net payment cost index** and the **yield comparison index (YCI).** These indexes take into account the interest credited, the estimated value of the death protection, and the expenses charged. The net payment cost index allows the consumer to rank policies in terms of cost per $1,000 of coverage. It assumes that you continue to pay premiums and do not withdraw the cash value. The YCI, which is a measure of cash value growth over the index period, is expressed as a percentage. A higher YCI indicates a better buy; however, it should not be confused with the rate of return on cash value.

The problem with all of these indexes is that they are dependent on policy illustrations. In most cases, illustrations are based on assumptions about interest rates, mortality rates, and policy lapses that are not guaranteed. Therefore, even though one policy might have a better index value than another, it may actually turn out to be more costly. Even with a comparison index, you must still examine the underlying assumptions.

The Insurance Company

Over the past decade the insured public has been as much concerned over the health of their insurance company as they have been with their own. The bankruptcies of a few large and several small insurers have stimulated these concerns. Although most people who were insured by those companies will eventually get most of their funds back, in the interim they will not be able to get at their assets or receive the high returns they had anticipated.

TOPIC **LINKS**

Review ratings of insurance companies.

Check the financial rating of the insurance company before you buy a policy. If you have cash value insurance, you should continue to monitor the financial health of the company for as long as you hold the policy. Providing the consumer with help on this matter are firms that rate the financial soundness of an insurance company. The five major rating services are A.M. Best Company, Fitch Ratings, Moody's Investors Service, Standard & Poor's Insurance Rating Services, and the Weiss Group. Publications issued by some of these services can be found at most university and public libraries. The top solvency rating given by each of these firms is shown in Figure 15.11. There has been much bickering among company representatives as to which firm does the best job of rating the insurance companies. Because ratings often differ by rating agency, it is a good idea to monitor several services.

Provision	Highest Rating	Criteria
A.M. Best Company www.ambest.com	A++	Superior ability to meet policyholder and other contractual obligations.
Fitch Ratings www.fitchrating.com	AAA	Strong capacity to meet contract obligations and commitments to policyholders.
Moody's Investors Service www.moodys.com	Aaa	Best quality and smallest degree of credit risk. The financial strength of these companies is likely to change, but changes are unlikely to impair their fundamentally strong position.
Standard & Poor's Insurance Rating Services www.standardpoors.com	AAA	Superior financial security on both an absolute and relative basis; they possess the highest safety and have an overwhelming capacity to meet policyholder obligations.
Weiss Group www.weissratings.com	A+	Excellent financial security; strong ability to deal with economic adversity.

Figure 15.11

Top Insurance Industry Ratings

Switching Policies

The general feeling among industry analysts is that the industry is basically sound, and that policyholders should be wary of insurance agents who exaggerate the difficulties faced by some insurers. This may be merely an unjustified attempt at "churning," replacing an existing policy with a new one simply to generate commissions. However, if your insurance company is down-rated, consider the associated benefits and costs of changing insurers. This is not an easy decision. If you surrender your policy, you may incur substantial surrender penalties and tax liabilities. The tax liabilities can be eliminated or deferred if you decide to switch your investment earnings into another policy and fill out a "1035 exchange form" with the new company. But there may be no way of avoiding additional high first-year commissions and another medical exam to prove insurability on a new policy. One intermediate step between doing nothing and switching insurers is to take out a policy loan. By borrowing against the policy instead of surrendering it, you at least enhance your own liquidity while avoiding surrender charges and protecting death benefits. If the company fails, you have a portion of your money; and if it recovers, you can always repay the loan.

TOPIC **LINKS**

Fill out a replacement questionnaire.

Participating Versus Nonparticipating Insurance

Historically, policyholders with participating insurance have done better than those with nonparticipating insurance. The major reason was the unexpectedly high interest rates during the late 1970s and early 1980s. Those with participating insurance received some of the benefits of the higher interest rates because mutual insurance companies passed on part of the higher return on their investment portfolios as dividends to policyholders. On the other hand, those with nonparticipating insurance often had cash values accumulating at a historically low rate set at the time coverage was initiated. In an effort to compete, stock insurance companies have been offering policies with a type of participation. Universal life and variable life are two such policies, because the policyholder participates in current market returns.

Some policy illustrations for participating life policies show *vanishing premiums* at a point in the future. The premium vanishes when the interest or dividend earnings become large enough to cover the premium. If dividends fall below those anticipated in the illustration, then the premium may not vanish. This fact was learned the hard way by many policyholders who purchased insurance in the 1980s when interest rates were higher. For a significant number, their expectations of vanishing premiums did not materialize, and some whose premiums had vanished found them reinstated as interest rates dropped.

Other Factors

You should recognize that life insurance will differ in cost because of policy riders. The riders attached to a contract play an important role in determining the worth of the policy to you and should be weighed carefully when making comparisons. The first step is to make sure you are not comparing apples and oranges. The second step is to take a close look at the apples. The same company may sell a high-commission and low-commission version of the same policy with identical riders. At times, unethical insurance agents have pointed to an independent survey indicating that their company's product was rated favorably, while forgetting to tell the prospective buyer that the rated policy was different from the higher-cost policy being offered.

If you deal through an independent life insurance agent, choose one who is a Chartered Life Underwriter. It will indicate that this individual has a minimum of three years' experience, has met basic educational requirements, and agrees to abide by a code of ethics. Ask the agent how much of each year's premium goes toward commissions. You may then inquire as to whether you might receive part of that commission as a rebate. This is a hot issue in the industry. Some insurance agents feel that commission rebates are unethical or illegal; others believe that rebates simply signal a competitive market.

Make sure you understand all of the assumptions that the company's illustration is based upon. The agent should explain how sensitive the illustration is to the underlying assumptions. In particular, you should request alternative illustrations of future dividends, premiums, and cash value based on guaranteed rates of return.

Ask for a specimen policy before you buy. When you receive the actual policy, read it carefully and be sure you understand every term. Also, find out the legally required cooling-off period during which you may change your mind and have your premiums returned without penalty. Finally, after you have decided to keep the policy, make copies for your beneficiaries. It is important that they understand the benefits they are entitled to and how the proceeds will be paid. Most policies offer settlement options consisting of either a lump-sum payment at death or an annuity for survivors. You may choose the settlement option or leave the choice to your beneficiaries.

ESTATE PLANNING

Death estate: Property and wealth transferred at death.

Upon death, the property you leave is termed your **death estate.** It should be large enough to provide for the care and support of the surviving spouse and children. However, all your planning and all your saving may accomplish little if your estate is squandered on legal costs or is transferred to the wrong individual. To make sure this does not happen, you will need some expert advice. Estate planning is not a do-it-yourself project. For small estates the help of an attorney may prove sufficient, but for large estates, especially those over $1 million, the aid of either an accountant or a financial planner specializing in estate transfer should also be enlisted.

The transfer of death estates can trigger tax consequences as discussed in Chapter 4 on taxes. These tax liabilities are scheduled to change erratically over the next few years, challenging the best of financial plans. In this section, we will limit the discussion to the methods of transfer and refer you to Chapter 4 for a discussion of potential tax liabilities.

Estate planning has two basic objectives: one, to transfer your assets at death in a manner consistent with your wishes, and two, to transfer those assets as intact as possible. The

Survivors	Division of Property
Spouse and one child	Spouse and child each receive one-half
Spouse and two or more children	Spouse receives one-third. The other two-thirds is divided equally among the children
Spouse and parents surviving, no children	Spouse receives 50–75% of estate, surviving parents receive the rest
Spouse surviving, no children, and parents deceased	Spouse receives 50–100% of estate, surviving brothers and sisters receive remaining balance
Parents surviving, no spouse or children	Parents receive all
Brother(s) and/or sister(s) surviving, no spouse or children, parents deceased	Brother(s) and/or sisters(s) receive equal shares

Figure 15.12

Possible Division of Estate Under Typical Intestate Provisions

first objective can be achieved through a well-thought-out will. Depending on the amount and nature of your wealth, the second objective can be either very simple or very difficult.

An overwhelming number of Americans die each year without a valid will. In these situations the deceased is said to have died **intestate.** When this occurs, the state supplies a ready-made will dividing the estate according to that state's laws of intestacy. The division is uniquely determined by each state, but the laws generally follow the format outlined in Figure 15.12.

Intestate: To die without a valid will.

The chance is very small that the state-mandated distribution of your assets will reflect your own desires. In fact, for many families with minor children, the distribution directed by the state is likely to run counter to the best interest of the family. Typically, under the laws of intestacy a surviving spouse with children receives only one-half to one-third of the estate. The rest is distributed to the children of the deceased. For those who have not yet reached the age of majority, court-appointed trustees will have to manage these funds in the children's interest. The surviving spouse may then be required to gain the agreement of the trustees on how and when these funds may be spent. For most families, this arrangement is undesirable and inconvenient. In addition, the associated administrative and legal costs may use up resources needed to support the surviving spouse and children.

The Last Will and Testament

A **will** is a legal declaration of how you wish your property to be disposed of at your death. It should be drawn up only with the supervision of an attorney knowledgeable in estate planning. The presence of an attorney is essential because there are myriad reasons for declaring a will invalid and contesting the distribution of the estate. For example, unless the will is properly witnessed, according to state-mandated guidelines, you may not have a valid will. Should the will be declared invalid for any reason, the estate will be distributed under the laws of intestacy. Furthermore, an improperly written will that does not foreclose future court proceedings may be more costly to your intended beneficiaries than dying with no will at all.

Will: A legal declaration of how you wish your property to be disposed of at your death.

TOPIC **LINKS**

View the wills of famous people and a sample will.

Your estate planning objectives will not be achieved if you simply write a will and then forget it. Review the document periodically to ensure that it reflects your current familial status and needs. Be sure to review your will whenever you change your state of residency or your family structure. Don't assume that just because you previously wrote a will with

Testate: To die with a valid will.

Testator: The male author of a valid will.

Testatrix: The female author of a valid will.

the help of a knowledgeable attorney that it is necessarily still valid. The laws differ among states, and a valid will in one state may be invalid in another.

A person who leaves a valid will is said to die **testate** and is referred to as either the **testator** or the **testatrix.** The correct suffix depends on whether the person is a male, requiring a *tor* ending, or a female, requiring a *trix* ending. You as the testator or testatrix can accomplish several objectives through the use of a will. You can name the executor for your estate. You can choose the guardian for your children. You can specify how your estate should be divided among beneficiaries. And finally, you can create investment trusts to provide for the future support and welfare of the beneficiaries.

Naming an Executor

Executor or executrix: The person who manages the distribution of the death estate according to the wishes expressed in the will.

Administrator or administratrix: The court-appointed manager of the death estate and will.

The person named in the will who manages your estate from the time of death until all the assets are distributed is called the **executor** or **executrix.** Because he or she is given extensive powers to handle your affairs and distribute your property according to your wishes, pick someone who is exceedingly trustworthy. Furthermore, discuss your choice with your potential executor, explaining what is required and who might provide additional information on the handling of your estate. This information should also be contained in the "letter of last instructions" discussed later. If you die without a will, or the named executor refuses to serve, the court chooses someone termed the **administrator** or **administratrix** to handle your estate. This choice may not coincide with your own desires.

An executor will normally be paid a fee for services performed, but the person you select may agree to serve free. More important, unless the will specifically states otherwise, the executor will be required to post a bond to cover any potential mismanagement of the estate. This is expensive and will eventually be charged to the estate. Assuming you have picked a trustworthy individual, you may waive the need for posting bond in the will.

Specifying Guardianship

For those who have children, the will is used to name a guardian in the event both parents die before the children reach the age of majority. As in the case of executor, make sure the proposed guardian will accept the assigned role. If you leave surviving children without a named guardian, or the named guardian refuses to serve, the court chooses one. In some cases this assignment provides the incentive for a lengthy and emotional custody battle among relatives. A potentially undesirable outcome is that guardianship of the children may be split. Consequently, brothers and sisters may grow up emotionally and physically separated from each other.

Dividing the Estate

In the will, you also indicate how your property should be disposed of. You may divide your estate up into percentage shares or provide for absolute dollar payments for each beneficiary. You may also make a specific **bequest,** also termed a **legacy,** leaving a specific item of property to a particular individual.

Most property is distributed under either a *per capita* or a *per stirpes* division. Suppose Arnold and Sharon Steele have two grandchildren by their son, John, as illustrated in Figure 15.13. Furthermore, assume John dies before his parents. At Arnold's and Sharon's subsequent death, how will their property be divided among the grandchildren and the surviving daughter, Nancy? The answer will depend on whether the Steeles specified a per capita or a per stirpes distribution in their will. In a **per capita division,** all of the survivors would share equally. One-third would go to Nancy, and one-third would go to each of the grandchildren. In a **per stirpes division,** each *branch* of the family would share equally. Nancy would receive one-half of the property, and each of John's children would receive one-quarter.

Bequest or legacy: Property given by a wish expressed in a will.

Per capita division: One in which the inheritance is divided equally among surviving family members.

Per stirpes division: One in which the inheritance is divided equally among branches of the family.

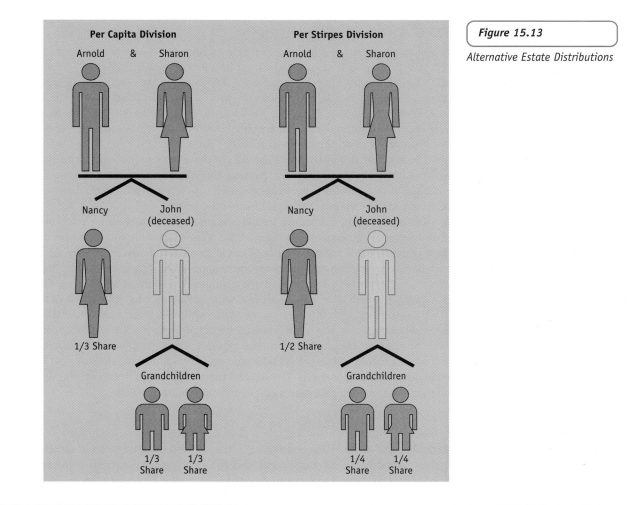

Figure 15.13

Alternative Estate Distributions

The way in which the estate is divided may affect estate taxes, inheritance taxes, and the income taxes of beneficiaries. In addition, there are some potential legal problems that should be considered. First, property cannot be left directly to minor children. If you have minor children, you will have to provide for their continued support through some kind of trust arrangement. An attorney can help you formulate one that reflects your intentions. Second, who is included and who is not included in your will may determine its validity. Under state law you may have no choice but to leave part of your estate to your spouse. Your failure to do so in your will may later provide the basis for contesting the will's validity.

Changing or Revoking the Will

Codicil: An amendment to an existing will, modifying or explaining specific items.

If you wish to change only a few specific items in the will, you can do so through a **codicil,** which is usually a one-page document indicating the desired changes in the existing will. Like the initial will, the codicil should also be drawn up and witnessed in a manner satisfying state law. Thus, an attorney should also be used when amending an existing will with a codicil.

For matters that require more than a few simple changes, the old will should be revoked and a new will written. The old will can be revoked by expressly stating so in the new will. What most people do not realize is that a previously valid will may be automatically revoked by a change in family status. Marriage, divorce, or the birth of a child can all automatically revoke an existing will. The exact result of this change will, again, depend on state law. Naturally, you should consult an attorney whenever family arrangements change.

The Letter of Last Instructions

Letter of last instructions: A document providing advice on the management of your death estate and the distribution of your assets.

If you desire, you can leave your relatives with a few well-chosen words, but not in the will. Everything in it is subject to legal interpretation and challenge. Therefore, to minimize the possibility of misinterpretation and conflict, do not include unnecessary statements. Your last words of wisdom or insult should be contained in the **letter of last instructions.** In it you might explain why you structured your bequests as you did, what you hoped to accomplish in the specified distribution of your assets, and what you hope your beneficiaries might accomplish in the future.

The letter of last instructions should also have a more practical objective. It can serve as a road map for your survivors, pointing the way to information on your estate. Since a road map is most useful at the beginning of a trip, inform your beneficiaries where it might be found and keep copies at several locations.

The letter of last instructions should contain an inventory of your assets and the location of important documents, beginning with the location of your will. You may want to keep a copy of the will along with the letter of last instructions. However, the original will should be kept on file at the attorney's office or, where applicable, at the county office with the register of wills and not in your safe-deposit box or home. It may take a while before the safe-deposit box may be opened after your death, and wills left at home have been known to disappear.

Be sure to provide information on life insurance policies, death and survivor benefits under pension plans, and your financial holdings. Such readily available information can save the executor considerable time and expense when taking inventory of your estate. Also provide the names of individuals who are familiar with the operation of your estate, such as your stockbroker, accountant, lawyer, and financial planner. The executor may have to rely on their help in the management and distribution of your assets.

Probate

Probate: A court process in which assets are transferred according to a will or the laws of intestacy.

Probate is the name for the court process in which assets are transferred subject to the will or the laws of intestacy. A special court, known as the probate court, exists to handle the transferal of death estates. The proceedings in this court may be divided into seven major steps.

1. Validation of will and appointment of executor or administrator
2. Informing heirs and claimants of death
3. Inventory and valuation of property and debts
4. Payments of claims against the estate
5. Determination and payment of taxes due
6. Determination of how the estate is to be divided and who are the legal heirs
7. Division and distribution of estate to heirs

In the first step the court determines whether a valid will exists. If there is one, the named executor oversees the rest of the process. In the absence of a valid will, the court will appoint an administrator to help manage the probate process.

Not all property is distributed through the will and the probate process. Property may be passed outside of the will. Since probate costs are usually equal to a percentage of the assets transferred, even a partial transfer of assets outside the will can result in cost savings. However, this need not result in any tax savings. Estate taxes are based on the value of the gross estate, which will include property transferred both within and outside of the will.

Transferring Your Estate Outside the Will

One way of transferring property and avoiding probate is to give your assets away while you are still living. Most of us would like to retain control over our property in case of future need, however, so this method isn't always desirable. There are ways in which property may transfer at death, thus leaving us with control while living and yet still avoiding probate. Joint tenancy, trusts, and contracts are the three most important ways in which this is accomplished. Each has advantages and drawbacks, and none should be entered into just to avoid probate. The indiscriminate use of these estate planning instruments could result in increased tax liabilities, increased estate management costs, and an undesirable distribution of your estate. Accordingly, each should be used with care and forethought, and never as a substitute for a will. Rather, they should be looked upon as individual instruments in your estate planning tool kit.

Joint Tenancy with Right of Survivorship

When property is held under the form of ownership called *joint tenancy with right of survivorship*, it automatically passes at death to the surviving co-owner. It is not distributed through the will and, therefore, avoids probate. In a **joint tenancy,** each owner has an undivided interest in the property, meaning that each has an equal right to make use of and enjoy the entire property.

Most estate planners tend to look upon joint tenancy unfavorably, because too many people use it as a substitute for a will. It is not. Even when most of your assets are held in joint tenancy, you still need a will to specify how the property is to be distributed at the death of the surviving owner. Joint tenants who are husband and wife might die simultaneously in an accident; only a will can specify how the jointly held property would then be disposed of.

Joint tenancy should not be confused with other forms of multiple ownership such as *tenancy in common* or *community property*. **Tenancy in common** is similar to joint tenancy in that each owner shares an undivided interest, even when each owns an unequal share. However, an important difference for estate planning is that the property does not necessarily pass to the co-owner(s) at death. Each owner can transfer his or her share in the tenancy in common as desired in both life and death. Thus, ownership will pass through the will the same as individually owned property.

Some states employ the concept of **community property.** This is property acquired during the marriage from the joint efforts of husband and wife. Each is assumed to share

Joint tenancy: A form of ownership in which each co-owner has an undivided interest in the property and the property passes to the co-owner at death.

Tenancy in common: A form of ownership in which each co-owner has an undivided interest in the property, but the property can be individually transferred.

Community property: Recognized in some states, it is property acquired during the marriage by the joint efforts of husband and wife.

equally in the ownership of such assets. Upon the death of either spouse, community property is treated much the same as in tenancy in common. The surviving spouse receives one-half of the property. The other half is disposed of through the will of the deceased spouse or through the laws of intestacy.

Trusts

Trust: A legal arrangement in which property is held by one party for the benefit of another.

A **trust** is an arrangement whereby the right to property is held by one party, the **trustee,** for the benefit of another, the **beneficiary.** The trustee is said to have a **fiduciary responsibility** to the beneficiary. This means that the trustee has a legal obligation to manage the trust in the best interests of the beneficiary. If the trustee does not honor this obligation, he or she may be held liable for any damages suffered by the beneficiary.

Trustee: The one who controls the property in a trust.

Beneficiary: The one who is to benefit from the trust.

The person who establishes and funds the trust is known as the **grantor.** The grantor may arrange for the trust to become operational either at his or her death or while the grantor is still alive. Each arrangement can play an important role in estate planning.

Fiduciary responsibility: A legal responsibility to manage the trust in the best interests of the beneficiary.

Testamentary and living trusts. A trust specified in the will and taking effect at death is called a **testamentary trust.** The most common reason for including a testamentary trust in a will is to provide for the support and care of dependent children. A minor cannot receive the proceeds from an estate directly. When property is left to a minor and the funds are not placed in a testamentary trust, the court will create a trust fund to manage the bequest in the minor's interest. By preempting the court, you can specify who will manage the fund, for what purpose the funds may be used, and when the funds may be paid out.

Grantor: The one who establishes and funds the trust.

Testamentary trust: A trust that takes effect at death.

Inter vivos or living trust: A trust that takes effect during the grantor's lifetime.

Since funding for a testamentary trust must be specified in the will, the trust funds are generally liable for both probate costs and estate taxes. An **inter vivos trust** is one established during the grantor's lifetime and is also termed a **living trust.** Funds in a living trust pass outside the will and the probate process, saving probate costs. This occurs because probate includes only those items held in the name of the deceased. The property in a living trust is held in the name of the trust.

Revocable and irrevocable trusts. Although funds in a living trust escape probate, they still may be taxable as part of the decedent's estate. The deciding factor for estate tax liability is whether the trust fund is *revocable* or *irrevocable.* A **revocable trust** can be changed or revoked by the grantor at any time. In reality the property still remains under the control of the person who established the trust and is, therefore, part of the deceased's taxable estate. The same is not true for an **irrevocable trust.** The terms of an irrevocable trust cannot be changed after it is established. Thus, the grantor loses all effective future control of the property placed in the trust, which eliminates future estate tax liabilities but creates immediate gift tax liabilities. Naturally, irrevocable trusts should be set up only after considerable forethought.

Revocable trust: A trust that can be changed or revoked by the grantor.

Irrevocable trust: A trust that cannot be changed by the grantor once it is established.

In a living trust, the grantor, the trustee, and the beneficiary may all be the same person. Setting up a revocable living trust can provide for your own welfare while you are still alive and then for the welfare of your survivors after your death. If you are considering setting up a revocable living trust, you would probably be better off if you first discussed the matter with an attorney specializing in estate planning. You will learn that this arrangement has both advantages and disadvantages. Property placed in the trust is not so easily exchanged as property outside the trust. Moreover, you may still need a will. Such things as naming a guardian for your children can be accomplished only through a will.

Contractual Transfers

Life insurance proceeds are directly assigned to beneficiaries in the life insurance contract, thus passing outside the will and probate. This represents a contractual transfer. Other investments such as retirement accounts and bank accounts may also be directly transferred to beneficiaries at death.

In states that have adopted the Uniform Probate Code, a bank account with the designation "Arnold Steele, payable on death to Sharon Steele," would pass directly to Sharon at Arnold's death. In other states the same type of transfer may be accomplished through a **trustee bank account,** also called a savings account trust or Totten trust. The designation for this type of account would be "Arnold Steele, as trustee for Sharon Steele."

Trustee bank account: An account that provides for contractual transfer at death.

Because no trust is actually created, the terminology used in setting up a trustee bank account is confusing. In the present example, Arnold would not owe Sharon any fiduciary responsibility. Moreover, Sharon would have absolutely no right to the bank account while Arnold is alive. However, at his death, the funds in the account would pass directly to Sharon, thus circumventing probate.

Life insurance and estate planning are to a large extent selfless acts. The time and effort you devote to proper planning show how much you appreciate those who have supported you. Be sure to revisit both of these topics every few years or when you experience a significant change. This will ensure the financial well-being of those who depend on your care and support.

Key Terms

adjustable life (p. 397)
administrator(trix) (p. 406)
beneficiary (p. 390, 410)
bequest (p. 407)
cash value (p. 389)
cash value insurance (p. 395)
codicil (p. 408)
community property (p. 409)
contingent beneficiary (p. 390)
credit life insurance (p. 394)
death estate (p. 404)
decreasing term (p. 394)
deposit term insurance (p. 394)
dividend (p. 390)
endowment life (p. 396)
executor(trix) (p. 406)
face amount (p. 389)
family maintenance fund (p. 383)
family policy (p. 390)
fiduciary responsibility (p. 410)
grantor (p. 410)
group mortgage life (p. 394)

irrevocable trust (p. 410)
interest-adjusted net cost index (p. 401)
inter vivos trust (p. 410)
intestate (p. 405)
joint life policy (p. 389)
joint tenancy (p. 409)
legacy (p. 407)
letter of last instructions (p. 408)
life insurance protection gap (p. 389)
limited payment life (p. 396)
living trust (p. 410)
modified whole life (p. 396)
net payment cost index (p. 402)
nonparticipating insurance (p. 390)
ordinary life (p. 396)
participating insurance (p. 390)
per capita division of property (p. 407)
per stirpes division of property (p. 407)
premium (p. 390)
probate (p. 408)
renewable term (p. 393)

revocable trust (p. 410)
rider (p. 391)
single life policy (p. 389)
straight life (p. 396)
surrender cost index (p. 401)
surrender value (p. 389)
survivorship joint life (p. 390)
tenancy in common (p. 409)
term insurance (p. 391)
testamentary trust (p. 410)
testate (p. 406)
testator(trix) (p. 406)
transition fund (p. 382)
trust (p. 410)
trustee (p. 410)
trustee bank account (p. 411)
universal life (p. 397)
variable life (p. 398)
variable-universal life (p. 399)
will (p. 405)
whole life (p. 396)
yield comparison index (p. 402)

Reread the chapter-opening vignette.

1. Are the Steeles likely to have too much or too little life insurance? About how much life insurance protection should a family like the Steeles have?
2. Should the Steeles consider purchasing life insurance on other family members besides Arnold? If so, who else in the family might need insurance protection?
3. If the Steeles were to purchase additional life insurance, what types of policies would best fit their current and future needs?
4. Arnold and Sharon both have wills. Given the relatively small size of their estate, is it necessary for them to engage in estate planning?

Problems and Review Questions

1. Explain the primary reason for having life insurance. For what other reasons might people hold life insurance?
2. What three funding categories are used to estimate life insurance needs? Explain the purpose of each.
3. Why might a family consider life insurance coverage for both spouses?
4. What types of family assets might be used to satisfy death protection funding requirements?
5. What is the difference between joint life and survivorship joint life?
6. One life insurance expert suggests that people should never buy participating life insurance, because the purpose of life insurance is to reduce risk, not to increase it. Discuss.
7. Renewability and guaranteed insurability are not the same. Explain the difference.
8. If a young family expects that its life insurance needs will increase in the near future, what policy options might they find desirable?
9. What is the distinguishing characteristic of term insurance? Why isn't deposit term true term insurance?
10. What kinds of insurance might offer the best protection against unexpected inflation? Explain why.
11. Suppose you wanted to leave your dependents with enough funds to pay off the home mortgage. Under what conditions would you prefer decreasing term insurance over group mortgage life, and vice versa?
12. If you perceive a need for insurance protection in your retirement years, might you prefer whole life over term life today? Why? Can you think of situations in which you might need insurance protection in your later years?
13. Suppose you took out a universal life insurance policy that charges a 20 percent sales commission on each dollar paid into the policy and pays a 10 percent annual return on the policy's cash value. What is the actual percentage return at the end of one year on each premium dollar placed in the savings component?
14. How does universal life differ from variable life? Which one entails greater risk?
15. What are the pros and cons of life insurance comparison indexes?
16. What are the basic objectives of estate planning?
17. What does it mean to die intestate? How might your estate be divided if you died intestate?
18. What can be accomplished only with a will? How would these matters be handled in the absence of a will? When certain changes occur, it is important that you review your will. What are these changes, and why is it important to review your will when they occur?
19. For estate planning purposes, what is the difference between *joint tenancy* and *tenancy in common?*
20. What is a trust? What obligation does the trustee have?

Sue and Tom Wright are both assistant professors at the local university. They each take home about $40,000 per year after taxes. Sue is 37 years of age, and Tom is 35. Their two children, Mike and Karen, are 13 and 11.

Were either one to die, they estimate that the remaining family members would need about 75 percent of the present combined take-home pay to retain their current standard of living while the children are still dependent. This does not include an extra $50 per month in child-care expenses that would be required in a single-parent household. They estimate that survivors' benefits would total about $1,000 per month in child support.

Both Tom and Sue are knowledgeable investors. In the past, average after-tax returns on their investment portfolio have exceeded the rate of inflation by about 3 percent.

Questions
1. Were Sue Wright to die today, how much would the Wrights need in the family maintenance fund? Explain the reasons behind your calculations.
2. Suppose the Wrights found that both Tom and Sue had a life insurance protection gap of $50,000. How might they go about searching for protection to close that gap?

David Lombard is considering the purchase of a $10,000 face amount, nonparticipating, whole life policy. The life insurance agent tells David that the $10,000 insurance protection really won't cost him anything. The annual premiums on the policy are $500, and at the end of 10 years the surrender value after taxes will be $5,000. Therefore, David can get back all of his premium payments at the end of the 10 years.

David decides to make some calculations on his own. He figures that if he deposited $500 annually in a savings account that had a 5 percent annual return after taxes, he would have $6,603.39 after 10 years. He wonders if the insurance policy is really the great deal the agent says it is.

Questions
1. How much is the death protection provided by the whole life policy really costing David?
2. How might David figure out whether term protection would be cheaper?
3. What other factors might David take into consideration when deciding between term and whole life?

Exercises to Strengthen Your Use of the Internet
(Internet links for the following exercises can be found at **www.prenhall.com/winger**.)

Exercise 15.1 Calculating Your Financial Worth to Your Dependents
The Life and Health Insurance Foundation for Education provides several different calculators for estimating insurance needs. The calculator for Human Life Value Analysis calculates the amount needed in the family maintenance fund to replace the support you will provide your family. The present value of the investment fund is based on an assumed interest rate, inflation rate, and tax rate.

Enter the following information: Assume a young married couple with a child and choose what you feel are appropriate values for the inputs.
Q. Given these assumptions, what is the net present value of the lost support from the death of either spouse?

Exercise 15.2 Calculating Your Insurance Needs

The Life and Health Insurance Foundation for Education also provides an Insurance Needs Calculator. You begin by entering the cash needs at death, the mortgage payoff, and anticipated college funding. To this amount it adds the present value of maintenance for the surviving spouse less current investments and existing life insurance.

Enter the amounts you think are appropriate for a married couple with two children and a 30-year-old head of household.

Q. If this family does not have any life insurance, what is the life insurance protection gap?

Exercise 15.3 Get a Quick Estimate of Future Social Security Benefits

Want to know how much your survivors will receive in Social Security benefits? Review your Personal Earnings and Benefit Estimate Statement. If you do not have one, you can order a copy at Social Security Online. You can obtain an instantaneous estimate by using its Quick Calculator.

Q. Assume a worker age 30 with a child. At the death of the worker, how much would the child receive in monthly payments?

Exercise 15.4 What Is Your Probability of Survival?

Life tables, like those included in the Social Security Statistical Tables published by the Social Security Administration, can provide estimates on your probability of survival. For a given age group they predict how many individuals are likely to survive to subsequent ages.

Q. Look at the life table. For an individual of your age and gender, what is your probability of survival over the next year? What is your probability of survival over the next 10 years? Hint: Given 100,000 males born alive, if 97,578 are alive at age 25 and 96,025 are alive at age 35, then the probability of surviving from age 25 to age 35 is .984 = (96,025 / 97,578).

Exercise 15.5 Playing the Longevity Game

How long can you expect to live? Northwestern Mutual Life's online life expectancy calculator factors in genetic and lifestyle characteristics to estimate your life expectancy. The probabilities of survival are based on data gathered by private life insurance companies and public agencies. Remember, you are calculating an average. This means that half the population with similar characteristics is expected to exceed this life expectancy and half is not.

Q. Enter you own characteristics. What is your life expectancy? Change one of the lifestyle characteristics you have control over. How does this change your life expectancy?

Exercise 15.6 Pricing Term Insurance

Numerous sites on the Web will provide a price quote on term insurance. Most, however, require that you be willing to provide the insurance company with some personal information. Price a $100,000 five-year term policy for yourself at age 25 and at age 45.

Q. How does your annual premium at age 45 differ from that at age 25?

Exercise 15.7 Checking the Ratings on Insurance Companies

Insure.com provides financial ratings on an extensive list of life and health insurance companies. The ratings are determined by both Standard & Poor's and Duff & Phelps Credit Rating.

Q. Choose one of the major insurers and see how the ratings from the two services compare. Do they both come to the same conclusion on claims-paying ability?

16

Retirement Planning

PLANNING FOR YOUR LONG-TERM NEEDS

OBJECTIVES

1. To evaluate the features of a company pension plan

2. To analyze alternative company retirement plans

3. To list individual tax-deferred methods of saving

4. To estimate your retirement needs

5. To learn how to establish a personal saving plan for retirement

TOPIC **LINKS**

Follow the **Topic Links** in each chapter for your interactive Personal Finance exercise on the Web. Go to: **www.prenhall.com/winger**

Steele
FAMILY

Arnold's parents visited over the holidays. They spent a few days with the Steeles before continuing on to Florida for their traditional winter vacation. Both Arnold and Sharon were impressed with how well Arnold's parents seemed to have planned their retirement. They have enough saved so that they can afford to take several trips each year. Arnold's parents spend a couple of weeks in a southern resort in the winter and take an extended camping trip out West in the summer.

Sharon's parents are self-sufficient, but they do not seem to have the funds to enjoy many extras. It has been a long time since they have seen the grandchildren. They do not travel much and rarely go out for entertainment. Her mom told Sharon that she enjoys staying home and really does not care to visit what she calls tourist traps. Sharon wonders if this is just a convenient excuse. The real reason may be that her mom and dad have to watch their pennies a lot more closely than Arnold's parents do.

Arnold and Sharon have discussed how they would like to remain active like Arnold's parents have. They know they need to start planning now if this is to become a reality. The only investments that have been specifically tagged for retirement are those in Arnold's defined-contribution plan at his place of work. The contributions are invested in a choice of bond funds and stock funds. Arnold has allocated 100 percent of his previous contributions to a government bond fund. On his last annual statement, the total value of this fund was only $21,000. However, he hopes to increase his contributions in the future. His maximum annual contribution to the plan fund is 10 percent. The employer matches the first 5 percent on a dollar-for-dollar basis. Over the past few years, he has contributed just enough (about $3,000) to receive the employer's matching contribution.

Sharon does not receive any employer-provided retirement benefits from her part-time employment. However, she expects to qualify for employer-provided retirement benefits when she returns to work full-time. As of now, the Steeles have put off planning for retirement until the future appears a little more certain.

Most financial planners will advise you to begin planning for retirement as soon as you enter the workforce. If you put off retirement planning until your forties and fifties, altering projected retirement benefits during your remaining working years will be much more difficult. In addition, you will have missed most of the tax advantages that come from funding tax-deferred retirement plans.

You probably realize this is good advice, but if you are in your early twenties and retirement is far off, you may find it very difficult to follow. Unless you have a crystal ball, forecasting more than a few years ahead is usually fruitless. Changes in tax rates, interest rates, inflation rates, and Social Security benefits may all upset well-made retirement plans. For this reason, a retirement plan should not be viewed as something set in concrete. It should change as circumstances change. And remember: the sooner you get started, the easier it will be to accommodate that plan to your changing financial environment.

Retirement planning should consider the family's needs and resources over the financial life cycle. Figure 16.1 illustrates a typical family's earnings and expenditures with respect to the age of the primary market worker. During the worker's twenties, thirties, and forties, both income and expenditures will likely increase. Savings accumulated during these early years will have more time to grow and accumulate tax-deferred returns until they are needed in retirement. Unfortunately, this is also the time when families like the Steeles experience the significant financial demands of childrearing, culminating with the high cost of a college education. In the worker's fifties, most of the children will have left the household, and savings will dramatically rise as expenditures drop. Saving will be easier at this time, but the money set aside will have fewer years in which to accumulate returns.

Earnings for the average market worker begin to decline in his or her early sixties as work time decreases and leisure time increases. Many individuals who retire from a full-time position find alternative employment as part-time workers. Self-employed individuals may experience no clear division between preretirement and postretirement years as they reduce their market efforts. Financially, retirement may be said to occur when expenses begin to exceed earnings. Retirement years are ones of dissaving, when the wealth accumulated over the preretirement years is slowly depleted. This dissaving is illustrated by the change in age-related net worth (assets − liabilities) of households in Figure 16.2.The standard of living in retirement will depend largely on the family's accumulated savings and, therefore, on plans begun and actions taken many years before.

Figure 16.1

A Typical Family's Earnings and Expenditures Over the Family Life Cycle

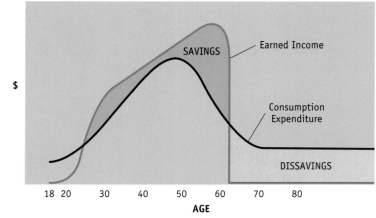

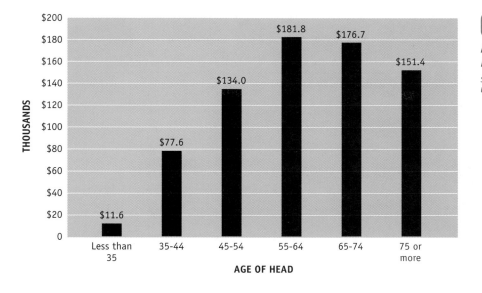

Figure 16.2

Median Net Worth by Age of Head of Household

Source: Survey of Consumer Finances: 2003 Update, Federal Reserve Board.

When and how much to save are personal decisions. There is not one "right" retirement plan for everyone. In saving for retirement, you are trading off present consumption for future consumption. How much you plan to save will depend on how much weight you place on each of these needs. Your retirement plan may be to consume everything today and leave nothing for tomorrow. As long as you realize that this decision means you will someday have to survive on minimal benefits provided under an uncertain system of Social Security, we have no quarrel with your choice.

In this chapter, we will first examine the traditional ways of saving for retirement. Once you understand how you can save, we address the question of how much you need to save to achieve your goals.

SAVING AND INVESTING FOR RETIREMENT

Is saving for retirement different from other types of saving? Like most questions in personal finance, this one can be answered with both a yes and a no. It is different because in many cases the government permits it to be treated differently. Qualified retirement savings receive special tax treatment. In most instances the tax isn't forgiven; it's just deferred until the funds are needed in your later years.

Retirement saving is also different because the funding need is not immediate. This means the savings can be channeled into less liquid investments that possibly penalize short-term withdrawals but pay a high return on long-term holdings.

Other than these two characteristics, saving and investing for retirement are the same as for any other purpose. Accordingly, investments for retirement should satisfy all of the guidelines for investments discussed in previous chapters. Most important, there should be a proper diversification of holdings, and the acceptable risk-return trade-off should depend on the size of your nest egg. Only after you have provided for a needed safety margin in your later years should you consider speculative deals with potentially more rewarding and more damaging outcomes.

TOPIC **LINKS**

Determine your risk profile.

Company Pension Plans

Company-sponsored retirement plans have become an increasingly important source of income for retired workers. Recent estimates by the Bureau of Labor Statistics reveal that 67 percent of all full-time employees have access to a retirement plan (see Figure 16.3).

Figure 16.3

Percent of Workers in Private Industry with Access to Pension Plans and Participating in Pension Plans, 2003

(Percentage participating in shaded row)
Source: National Compensation Survey, Bureau of Labor Statistics.

	All Plans	Defined benefit	Defined contribution
Worker Characteristics			
All	57	20	51
	49	20	40
White-collar occupations	67	23	62
	59	22	51
Blue-collar occupations	59	24	49
	50	24	38
Service occupations	28	8	23
	21	7	16
Full-time	67	24	60
	58	24	48
Part-time	24	8	21
	18	8	14
Union	86	74	45
	83	72	39
Nonunion	54	15	51
	45	15	40

Employee Retirement Income Security Act (ERISA): Federal act regulating funding and coverage guidelines for tax-qualified, employer-sponsored pension plans.

Qualified retirement plan: One that satisfies conditions set down in ERISA and therefore qualifies for special tax advantages.

TOPIC **LINKS**

Check out benefit guarantees at the PBGC.

TOPIC **LINKS**

Read "What You Should Know About Your Pension Rights."

The passage of the **Employee Retirement Income Security Act (ERISA)** in 1974 eliminated much of the uncertainty surrounding the payment of company benefits. ERISA sets down certain standards for funding of company-sponsored retirement plans, including guidelines for employee coverage and contributions. When a plan meets all of the government-mandated requirements, it becomes a **qualified retirement plan.** This means that taxes are deferred on employer contributions to the retirement fund and on interest earned by the retirement fund. Taxes do not become due until the benefits of the retirement fund are received by the employee.

A pension is nothing more than a promissory note. If you have a pension, what you have is a promise that you will receive certain payments at retirement. Before the passage of ERISA it was not uncommon to hear of workers nearing retirement losing all of the promised pension benefits they had been depending on. Some firms purposely terminated workers right before retirement so that they would not have to pay pension benefits. Other, better-intentioned firms found they simply could not afford to pay the promised benefits.

ERISA requires that all qualified pension plans be adequately funded. It established the Pension Benefit Guaranty Corporation (PBGC) to insure promised benefits against unexpected loss. However, an employee may still end his or her career without a pension. Furthermore, ERISA does not set standards for minimum benefits. At retirement you may find that your benefits are not as generous as you thought. For these reasons, and because the pension plan is often a valuable component of the salary package, it deserves close examination.

A careful study of the plan documents listed in Figure 16.4 will provide essential information on the operation of your pension plan. If you have trouble reading these documents, the personnel officer or plan administrator may explain the contents. Be sure you know the answers to the checklist questions in Figure 16.5.

The Advantage of Tax Deferral

Because qualified plans offer significant tax advantages, almost all company plans satisfy the ERISA requirements. To understand the advantages of tax deferral, look at the

Qualified Plan Documents

Participants in qualified plans are entitled to receive certain documents providing important information on the operation of the plan and their particular interest in the plan. In most cases, these documents will be routinely made available. If they are not, you should demand copies of the following:

Summary Plan Description This general overview of how the retirement plan operates should be written in a clear and understandable form. It contains essential information on the structure of the plan, explaining how benefits are calculated, when they may be received, and most important, how you might lose them.

Summary Annual Report It provides updated information on the plan and its financial status. If the pension fund depends upon an underlying portfolio of investments, it should indicate how well those investments performed over the previous year.

Personal Benefits Statement This may be included within the Summary Annual Report. It will indicate the total amount of your pension benefits that are currently accrued and vested. Each participant is entitled to receive an updated statement once a year. If you have not received one in the last 12 months the plan administrator (listed in the Summary Plan Description) must provide it within 30 days upon written request.

Statement of Deferred Vested Benefits for Terminating Employees If you leave your current employer, and you have a vested right to benefits, you should receive a statement describing those rights and benefits. Copies of this statement are kept on file by the Secretary of Health and Human Resources. If you lose your copy, or for some reason the firm will not provide you one, a duplicate is obtainable through the Social Security Administration upon written request.

example in Table 16.1. The comparison is based on an assumed flat tax rate of 28 percent. In Case One, the monies placed into the fund and the interest on the fund are taxed; in Case Two the tax is applied when the fund matures at the end of the 20-year period. In the first example, $2,000 in compensation is set aside each year for investment, but only $1,440 can be invested after taxes. Given an assumed pretax interest rate of 10 percent, the effective after-tax interest rate is reduced to 7.2 percent. After 20 years, this non-tax-deferred investment fund will accumulate to $64,683.27.

In Case Two, the full $2,000 of compensation can be invested at a pretax interest rate of 10 percent. Taxes on both the contribution and the investment returns are postponed until the funds are withdrawn. When the fund matures at the end of 20 years, taxes become due. This is the tax advantage provided by a typical tax-deferred company-sponsored retirement account or individual retirement account (IRA). Applying the same 28 percent

Checklist of Questions for Your Pension Plan Review

✓ What type of pension plan do I have (defined benefit or defined contribution)?

✓ Is it a qualified retirement plan covered by ERISA and insured by the PBGC?

✓ In order to participate, must I contribute to the pension plan? If so, how much?

✓ Can I make voluntary contributions to my employer's pension plan? What are the tax consequences of these contributions?

✓ Are my benefits fully vested? If not, how long must I remain employed before they are?

✓ How many years of credited service have I accumulated? How many hours do I have to work to earn a year of credited service?

✓ How is a break in service defined? What happens to my benefits if I have a break in service?

✓ What are my likely benefits at normal retirement age? How much would I receive at normal retirement age if I terminated employment today?

✓ How are my benefits at normal retirement age calculated? What is the benefit formula?

✓ Is there an early retirement age? If so, how are my benefits reduced for early retirement?

✓ If I become disabled before retirement, may I receive disability benefits through the pension plan?

✓ If I die, will my spouse or dependents receive any payout from my pension plan?

✓ What are the payout options at retirement? Can I receive a lump-sum distribution at termination or retirement?

✓ At retirement will I receive a single life annuity or a joint life annuity? If I am to receive a joint life annuity, how will benefits be reduced at the first death?

Table 16.1

The Power of Tax Deferral Under
a Flat 28% Tax Rate

TOPIC **LINKS**

Download worksheet
or use an IRA calcu-
lator.

Case One: No Deferral of Taxes

Year	Contribution after Taxes	Interest Income after Taxes (after-tax rate 7.2%)	Ending Balance
1	$1,440	$ 103.68	$ 1,543.68
2	1,440	214.82	3,198.50
3	1,440	333.97	4,972.48
•	•	•	•
•	•	•	•
•	•	•	•
18	1,440	$ 3,593.48	53,502.97
19	1,440	3,955.89	58,898.87
20	1,440	4,344.40	64,683.27
		Taxes due at maturity	(-0-)
		Ending year's balance after taxes	$ 64,683.27

Case Two: Deferral of Taxes (deductible IRA)

Year	Tax-Deferred Contribution	Tax-Deferred Interest Income (tax-deferred rate 10%)	Ending Balance
1	$2,000	$ 200.00	$ 2,200.00
2	2,000	420.00	4,620.00
3	2,000	662.00	7,282.00
•	•	•	•
•	•	•	•
•	•	•	•
18	2,000	9,119.83	100,318.00
19	2,000	10,231.80	112,550.00
20	2,000	11,455.00	126,005.00
		Taxes due at maturity	(−35,281.40)
		Ending year's balance after taxes	$ 90,723.60

Case Three: Tax-free Returns (Roth IRA)

Year	Contribution after Taxes	Interest Income (tax-free rate 10%)	Ending Balance
1	$1,440	$ 144.00	$ 1,584.00
2	1,440	302.40	3,326.40
3	1,440	476.64	5,243.04
•	•	•	•
•	•	•	•
•	•	•	•
18	1,440	6,566.28	72,229.09
19	1,440	7,366.91	81,036.00
20	1,440	8,247.60	90,723.60
		Taxes due at maturity	(-0-)
		Ending year's balance after taxes	$ 90,723.60

tax rate to the distributions, we find that you are still over $26,000 ahead on the tax-deferred investment. This is the power of tax deferral.

Case Three illustrates how funds would accumulate in a retirement plan with nondeductible contributions and nontaxable withdrawals. This is how taxes would accrue on a Roth

IRA. Contributions to the fund must be made out of after-tax income. However, returns on the fund and withdrawals from the fund are tax free. In this example, the available funds at the end of 20 years are the same as in Case Two. This is because we are assuming that the marginal tax rate remains the same over the entire 20-year period. Consequently, taking taxes out of the initial contribution provides exactly the same result as taking taxes out of the final distribution.

If your real income declines after retirement, then the marginal tax rate will likely be lower when the funds are finally withdrawn. This would increase the return in Case Two relative to Case Three. On the other hand, for the lucky few that might find themselves in a higher marginal tax bracket after retirement, Case Three would be the preferred choice. It is clear, however, that tax-advantaged funds are always preferred to no tax advantage as in Case One.

Defined-Benefit and Defined-Contribution Plans

All pension plans can be classified as defined-benefit plans, defined-contribution plans, or some combination of the two. As seen in Figure 16.3, most union workers have access to defined contribution plans, whereas white-collar workers are largely offered defined benefit plans. With the decline in union membership over the last few decades, a much larger share of the workforce has increasingly relied on defined contribution plans to fund their retirement years.

A **defined-benefit plan** specifies the monthly benefit you will receive when you reach retirement age. Each year the employer contributes to a retirement fund an amount necessary to pay for those promised future benefits. The present contribution is actuarially determined; that is, it is based on assumed investment returns and probabilities of survival. Defined-benefit plans are insured by a government agency, the Pension Benefit Guaranty Corporation (PBGC). Up to a given monthly limit, the PBGC insures the future payout of defined benefits. The PBGC does not insure benefits in defined-contribution plans.

Under a **defined-contribution plan** you are not guaranteed a specific benefit at retirement. Instead, your benefits will depend on the investment performance of the retirement fund. Employer contributions go into a separate retirement account for each worker, where they accumulate until retirement. The current value of this account should be indicated on the personal benefits statement (see Figure 16.3).

In most defined-contribution plans, the funds accumulated in the retirement account may be converted at retirement to an annuity that generates lifetime income. The cost of the annuity and the income generated by the annuity will depend on financial factors at the retirement date. Sometimes personal benefits statements for defined-contribution plans will contain an example of the monthly benefits that might be purchased with your retirement account. This example is only an illustration and should not be mistaken for a guaranteed monthly benefit.

Defined-benefit and defined-contribution plans have offsetting advantages and disadvantages as illustrated in Figure 16.6. With a defined-benefit plan, you know how much you will receive, but you don't know how much those dollars will be worth. Inflation can severely erode the purchasing power of benefits that currently appear quite respectable. With a defined-contribution plan, you know how much your retirement fund is currently worth, but you don't know how many dollars you will have at retirement. Remember, this will depend on future contributions and yet-to-be-determined investment returns.

Both defined-benefit and defined-contribution plans can be integrated with the Social Security system. When they are, your company's benefits and contributions may be less than expected. Defined-benefit plans can be written so that benefit payments from the plan are reduced as Social Security benefits increase. Defined-contribution plans sometimes include part of the Social Security tax in calculating the company's contribution.

Defined-benefit plan: A pension plan that specifies the monthly benefit you will receive at retirement age.

Defined-contribution plan: A pension plan that defines the current pension plan contribution. Future retirement benefits are dependent upon the underlying investments in the retirement fund.

Figure 16.6

Pension Unknowns

ACCUMULATION PHASE	GROWTH PHASE	DISBURSEMENT PHASE
Defined benefit plans		
How much is the employer contributing today?	When will the benefits vest? Will the pension fund be there when I retire?	How much will those defined dollar benefits be worth in the future?
Defined contribution plans		
How much do I need to contribute today?	When will the benefits vest? Will my funds earn an adequate return?	How many dollars will I have in the future?

Contributions

A few plans require mandatory contributions from employees who wish to participate in the company retirement plan. Those who elect not to participate should find out under what conditions, if any, they may later join. Most do not require employee contributions. However, many defined-contribution plans permit the employee to make a tax-advantaged voluntary contribution into a 401(k) account, discussed later.

Vesting

Accrued benefit: Pension benefits that have been accumulated because of previous credited service.

Vested benefits: Pension benefits that you are entitled to receive regardless of future employment.

When you participate in a pension plan, you accrue pension benefits. The **accrued benefit** is the benefit that a pension plan participant has accumulated to a particular point in time. Some or all of your accrued benefits may be lost if you leave your present employer. Your rights to your currently promised benefits will depend on whether they are *vested*. **Vested benefits** are not forfeitable for any reason other than death. You may be fired, or you may quit, but in either case you still retain the right to receive all vested retirement benefits.

All qualified pension plans must satisfy the vesting schedules in Figure 16.7. ERISA requires that all employee contributions to a retirement plan must immediately vest. However, there may be a specified waiting period before employer contributions are partially or fully vested. Employer contributions are subject to either cliff vesting or graded

Figure 16.7

Minimum Vesting Schedules

	Employer Contributions		Employee Contributions
	Nonmatching	Matching	100% Immediate Vesting
Cliff Vesting	Full vesting after 5 years of service, with no vesting before then	Full vesting after 4 years of service, with no vesting before then	
Graded Vesting			
20% vested after	3 years	2 years	
40% vested after	4 years	3 years	
60% vested after	5 years	4 years	
80% vested after	6 years	5 years	
100% vested after	7 years	6 years	

vesting. Under either schedule, minimum vesting is one year earlier if the employer has a policy of matching employee contributions. Many employers allow benefits to vest at a faster pace than is legally required.

Credited Service

For several reasons, you may have fewer years of credited service than calendar years of employment. Under all plans, you are credited with a year of service only if you have worked a sufficient number of hours within a 12-month period. The required number of hours, typically 1,000, can be found in the Summary Plan Description.

In the Summary Plan Description you will also find a definition for a break in service. Plans generally require that you work at least 500 hours per 12-month period to avoid a break in service. A break in service may delay the vesting of benefits and cause a forfeiture of nonvested benefits. Under federal law, qualified retirement plans cannot terminate nonvested benefits unless the break in service is greater than five years. Furthermore, firms cannot interrupt vesting for maternity or paternity leaves of one year or less.

Retirement Age

Most plans specify age 65 as **normal retirement age.** At this age, you are eligible to receive the full pension benefits. Many plans also specify an **early retirement age** at which you can retire with reduced benefits. A common requirement for early retirement benefits is the attainment of age 55 and the completion of 10 years of service. The reduction in benefits will depend upon the time interval between the early retirement age and the normal retirement age. You may be given a schedule of reduced payments or a formula for calculating the reduction factor.

For almost all occupations, the law forbids an employer from requiring you to retire at any age. If the normal retirement age is 65, you have a right to postpone receiving benefits until age 70. Furthermore, the company must provide you with additional retirement benefits for years of service beyond normal retirement age.

Normal retirement age: The age at which you are entitled to full retirement benefits.

Early retirement age: The earliest age at which you can retire with reduced benefits.

Calculation of Benefits

If you have a defined-contribution plan, the calculation of benefits at retirement age is simple. The value in the account determines either a lump-sum payout or the value of the retirement annuity. The funds available at retirement will depend on annual contributions to the account and investment returns on the account. Your employer may provide several investment funds into which your annual contribution may be deposited. These may range from short-term bond funds to high-growth equity funds. A benefit formula, typically expressed as a percentage of your salary, will determine how much is contributed by your employer each year. Most plans permit employees to make voluntary tax-advantaged contributions to the plan. In addition, a majority of employers match employee contributions with additional employer contributions.

With a defined-benefit plan, you must apply a specific formula contained in the plan documents to calculate your monthly benefits at retirement. Most defined-benefit plans compute benefits using a flat benefit, a unit benefit, or a cash balance formula. With a **flat benefit formula,** monthly benefits are equal to either a specific percentage of compensation or a specific dollar payment. Most plans use a **unit benefit formula,** where length of service is entered directly into the calculation of benefits. For example, the formula might state that your monthly normal retirement benefit will be $20 times your years of service. Alternatively, it might employ a percentage formula, such as 2 percent of salary times your years of service.

Flat benefit formula: Pension benefits are equal to a specified percentage of compensation or a specific dollar benefit.

Unit benefit formula: Pension benefits depend directly upon units of credited service.

Regardless of whether the flat or unit method is employed, you will receive better inflation protection when benefits are stated not in specific dollars but rather as a percentage of your salary. This is so because your salary at retirement should reflect the higher cost of living at that time. Percentage formulas use either the career average approach or the final average approach. With the *career average approach*, percentage benefits are based on your average compensation over all years of service. It is more common for plans to use the *final average approach*. This bases benefits on a percentage of your average compensation over the last three or five years. Since the final average approach responds more rapidly to an inflationary rise in wages, it is usually preferred.

Cash balance plan: A pension plan with defined cash value benefits.

Lately, many employers have adopted a specific form of a defined-benefit plan called a **cash balance plan** that looks like a defined-contribution plan (see Box 16.1). The cash balance plan defines promised benefits in terms of an account balance for each employee. Each year the account is credited by a dollar amount that depends on years of service and an interest rate that is either fixed or linked to some interest rate index. The market returns on the plan's underlying investments do not affect the stated accumulations of the employee, since a defined-benefit plan must have a promised benefit. When the employee retires, the account balance is converted into an annuity, or if the company plan permits, it is received in a lump-sum payment. Cash balance plans often permit employees who leave employment before retirement to receive the lump-sum value of the account balance.

There has been some dissatisfaction among older workers in companies that have converted an existing traditional defined-benefit plan to a cash balance plan. Traditional defined-benefit plans that base benefits on years of service, tend to favor older employees. When a company switches from a traditional defined-benefit plan to a cash balance plan, employees who expected to accumulate significant benefits at the end of their career may see that prospect eroded. In some firms, employees have sued employers for reducing what they perceived as promised benefits. To reduce dissatisfaction among experienced workers, some employers have permitted older employees the choice of accumulating future retirement benefits under the previous defined-benefit plan or the new cash balance plan.

Medical Benefits

You do not qualify for enrollment in the Medicare program until you are age 65. If you presently have health insurance through your employer and you plan to retire before age 65, be sure you have adequate alternative coverage between when you retire and when you and your spouse turn 65. The Kaiser Family Foundation reports that about 60 percent of retirees age 55 – 64 receive some assistance from their previous employer in obtaining and paying for health insurance.

Regardless of whether your employer subsidizes medical benefits for retired workers, you still may have the right to continued coverage under a group health plan sponsored by an employer with 20 or more workers. Your rights are set down in the Consolidated Omnibus Reconciliation Act of 1985 (COBRA). For 60 days after retiring, you may elect to continue group health coverage. If you make this election, you can extend the group health coverage for another 18 months, after which the group policy may be converted to an individual policy. The employer does not have to pay for your insurance after you leave employment. However, by continuing coverage under the employer-sponsored plan, you avoid having to satisfy preexisting conditions clauses that might exclude benefit payments under a new insurance plan.

When you do turn age 65, you most likely will qualify for enrollment in the Medicare program. Moreover, for six months after you turn 65, you cannot be denied private "medi-gap" insurance because of any preexisting illness. See Chapter 14 for details on both of these programs.

Finance News

BOX 16.1

Employers Expand the Number of Cash Balance Plans

Over the last decade, employers have been steadily replacing traditional defined-benefit plans with cash balance plans. A plan conversion can have a dramatic impact on benefits for older workers. In general, a defined-benefit plan credits a worker with future benefits for each year of service. Suppose a younger worker and an older worker are both promised additional monthly benefits at retirement based on their previous year of service. Assume this entitles each to an additional $10 a month in pension benefits beginning at age 65. Since the older worker is closer to retirement, that $10 a month annuity is a lot more attractive to the older worker than it is to the younger worker. It is also more costly for the employer. The present value of a $10 annuity that begins payouts 10 years from today is a lot more expensive than the present value of a $10 annuity that begins payments 30 years from now. Actuarially, traditional defined-benefit plans tend to be backloaded, with most of the benefits earned in the last years before retirement.

Many workers in traditional defined-benefit plans probably never realize that the value of the benefits each has earned over the previous year are significantly different. With a cash balance plan, the present value of the benefit is obvious. The worker's "hypothetical" account is credited with the present value of a future benefit. In addition, if the plan provides a cash-out option upon termination, the employee has a good dollar estimate of the lump-sum payment. This is especially beneficial for mobile younger workers who are changing jobs.

So, why do so many workers complain when an employer converts a traditional defined-benefit plan to a cash balance plan? The problem is that the conversion is usually accompanied by a change in the distribution of future benefit accumulations. If the new plan promises identical cash additions to both the younger and older workers' "hypothetical" accounts, this likely represents a reduction in benefits for the older worker.

In response to these plan conversions, workers have sued employers, arguing that the company breached a promise of future pension accruals. Typically, however, the law only protects previously earned benefits; it does not require the employer to provide future benefits. A few companies have responded by canceling a planned conversion; some have provided larger cash balance credits for older workers; and others have allowed older workers to choose between remaining in the old plan or going with the new cash balance plan. This is a difficult decision; however, your likelihood of making the right decision is better when you understand how the time value of money affects your pension benefits.

An example of how hypothetical traditional defined benefit and cash balance pension plans build value over an employee's career

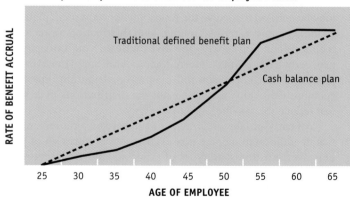

Disability Benefits

Most company retirement plans also include some type of disability income protection. Contributions by the company to the retirement plan may continue during periods of disability. In other situations, the plan may begin paying out monthly benefits at the onset of the disability, regardless of the employee's age. Furthermore, the monthly benefits may be computed under a more generous disability benefit formula. A review of the sections in Chapter 14 on disability insurance will help you determine the quality of this coverage.

Survivors' Benefits

Joint and last survivor annuity: Periodic benefits continue as long as you or your spouse is alive.

ERISA requires that if you die before your retirement benefits begin, the vested portion of your benefits must be used to provide death benefits for your spouse. It also mandates that married workers automatically be provided a **joint and last survivor annuity** at retirement, unless both spouses elect otherwise. This means that payments will continue as long as either you or your spouse is still alive, although the amount may be reduced after the first death. Federal law requires that monthly payments from the survivor's annuity be more than 50 percent, but less than 100 percent, of the amount paid when both the spouse and the participant were alive. The law also specifies that the benefits cannot be reduced if the surviving spouse remarries. The alternative is a **single life annuity,** for which all payments cease at the pensioner's death. The value of the single life annuity and the joint and last survivor annuity must be actuarially equivalent. That means that the total expected payouts under the two annuity options should be the same. Accordingly, since the potential benefit period under a single life annuity is less than a joint and last survivor annuity, the single life option will provide larger monthly benefits.

Single life annuity: All periodic payments cease at the death of the annuitant.

The choice is a difficult one. Do you select larger monthly payments over your life or lower monthly payments over both your life and your spouse's? Given life expectancies and interest returns, the two annuities are worth the same. Accordingly, if both you and your spouse need the cash flow generated by the joint and survivor annuity and you are both in average health, don't gamble on the single life annuity. You may do better under the single life annuity, but the odds are just as good that you will do worse, in which case the surviving spouse may suffer financial hardships.

Distributions

TOPIC **LINKS**

See IRS Pub. 575 "Pension and Annuity Income."

Distributions from a retirement account may occur for reasons other than just retirement. If you die, become disabled, leave your current employment, or suffer financial hardship, you may be entitled to receive the funds in your retirement plan. The distribution may consist of a single payment, termed a lump-sum distribution, or an annuity, a series of periodic payments. When you receive the distributions, you must pay ordinary income taxes on the proceeds from all tax-deferred accumulations. However, the tax consequences may be postponed further if you roll over the distribution into another tax-deferred retirement account. Generally, spreading out the distributions over your and your spouse's lifetime can reduce the tax due.

An early or late withdrawal of funds from a retirement account may trigger tax penalties in addition to income taxes. There is a uniform set of penalties on early and late withdrawals from almost all types of group and individual retirement accounts, including those discussed later in this chapter. An early withdrawal is defined as any withdrawal before age $59\frac{1}{2}$. With a few exceptions, such as death, disability, excessive medical expenses, or a lifetime annuity, a 10 percent tax penalty is levied on all early withdrawals.

The penalty on late withdrawals is much worse. Payouts from retirement funds must begin by April 1 of the next calendar year after you reach $70\frac{1}{2}$. In addition, these payouts must be large enough to distribute the fund over your own or your spouse's life expectancy. If you fail to meet the minimum required distribution, there is an onerous 50 percent tax penalty on the difference between the actual distribution and the minimum required distribution.

Other Company Retirement Plans

TOPIC **LINKS**

Contribution limits on retirement plans.

Companies may offer savings vehicles that differ from the pension format discussed above in one of two ways: One, they may not provide the same type of scheduled contributions or benefits expected of a long-term pension plan; or, two, they may be used to save for needs other than retirement. Such plans are often offered as a supplement to, rather than an alternative to, a typical pension plan. By not tying the employer or the employee into a scheduled set of contributions, they allow each to supplement the basic benefits afforded by the pension plan whenever possible.

ERISA specifies limits on the total amount contributed to company-sponsored retirement plans by both the employer and employee. The guidelines, recently expanded under the Tax Relief Act of 2001, are complicated but generous. Most middle-income taxpayers are not likely to be affected. Moreover, workers age 50 and older may be able to contribute more than the normal limits under what have been termed *catch-up* provisions.

401(k), 403(b) and 457 Plans

The name for each account is derived from the applicable section of the Internal Revenue Code. These plans are provided by private, (401(k)) nonprofit (403(b)), and public institutions (457), respectively. Under each of these plans, you may defer a portion of your compensation for retirement through a salary reduction agreement. Although you may currently owe Social Security taxes on the earnings, federal income taxes are deferred until you receive the money. Beginning in 2006, you may elect to have all or part of your contribution to these plans taxed like a Roth IRA. Under this option, the contributions would be out of after-tax income. However, all distributions from the account would be tax free.

Usually the employer provides a choice of investment vehicles into which the funds may be placed while earning tax-deferred returns. Furthermore, many employers offer matching contributions. These contributions, plus the current reduction in income taxes, typically make salary-reduction plans an excellent long-term investment.

Profit-Sharing Plans

A **profit-sharing plan** is a type of defined-contribution plan whereby the employer makes contributions into an individual employee's account according to a predetermined formula. Qualified profit-sharing plans must satisfy many of the same rules governing qualified pension plans. Unlike a pension plan, however, the employee may not have to wait until retirement to receive distributions. The plan can be set to pay out after a fixed number of years. One disadvantage for planning purposes is that the firm must contribute only when it earns a profit.

Profit-sharing plan: A defined-contribution plan in which contributions are contingent upon the profitability of the firm.

Employee Stock Ownership Plans (ESOPs)

An **employee stock ownership plan (ESOP)** can function in many different ways, but most operate like profit-sharing plans. The difference is that contributions are invested primarily in the employer's stock, and contributions are not necessarily dependent on profits. In addition, all distributions must be made in the form of stock.

An employee stock ownership program is an inappropriate instrument for retirement savings. Because most of the funds are concentrated in the stock of one company, it does not provide any safety through diversification. The value of the fund is likely to swing widely as the company's fortunes change. You could lose both your job and your savings at the same time. Fortunately, federal regulations allow certain employees nearing retirement to place part of their ESOP account in diversified investments.

Employee stock ownership plan (ESOP): A savings plan that provides employees benefits in the form of company stock.

Simplified Employee Pension Plans (SEPs)

Simplified employee pension plan (SEP): An employer-sponsored retirement plan utilizing individual retirement accounts.

A **simplified employee pension plan (SEP)** has advantages for both the employer and employee. For the employer, the paperwork and administrative costs are much less than under a qualified pension plan. For the employee, all amounts deposited in the SEP are immediately vested. As an alternative to a qualified pension plan, the SEP plan permits the employer to set up a tax-deferred individual retirement account for each employee.

Savings Incentive Match Plans for Employees (SIMPLE)

The SIMPLE may be set up as part of a 401(k) plan or as an IRA. This is a new tax-advantaged retirement plan for small employers. This allows employees to enter into a written agreement with their employer to defer some of their current income into a tax-advantaged retirement account. Over specified limits, the employer must also make matching contributions into this account.

Individual Retirement Plans

If you do not have a company retirement plan or you would like to supplement a company plan through additional private savings, the benefits of tax deferral can also be achieved through non-corporate-sponsored investments. The rules governing early and late withdrawals from individual retirement plans are generally the same as for company-sponsored plans. Distributions before age 59½ incur a 10 percent penalty tax. However, there are significant exceptions for withdrawals satisfying criteria related to hardship, medical expenses, disability, and death. Insufficient withdrawals after age 70½ suffer a 50 percent tax penalty.

Individual Retirement Accounts (IRAs)

Individual retirement account (IRA): An individual retirement account that qualifies for special tax treatment under IRS regulations.

The **individual retirement account (IRA)** is a trust or custodial account approved by the Internal Revenue Service. In a trust or custodial relationship, the funds are temporarily held by someone other than the investor. However, you as the investor may still retain control

---

Saving money $

BOX 16.2

Consolidating Pension Accounts through Rollovers

If you opened several IRAs over the last several years, or you have pension accounts from previous employers, you probably have trouble keeping track of your retirement savings. Many small accounts can also be costly, since each is likely to charge a management fee. By consolidating these accounts, you can simplify your bookkeeping and achieve economies of scale in your investments.

On tax-deferred retirement accounts, taxes become due when the funds are withdrawn. Taxes, however, can be deferred further if the funds are redeposited in another tax-deferred retirement account within 60 days. This tax-free transfer of assets from one retirement plan to another is termed a *rollover*. In order to ensure that you don't violate the 60-day limit, it is best to arrange a direct transfer from one account to another, so that you never have receipt of the funds.

A rollover is also useful for deferring taxes on a lump-sum distribution from a qualified retirement plan. A distribution of previously nontaxable contributions to retirement savings might occur upon termination of employment. In most cases, this can have severe tax consequences. If your age is less than 59½ years, you will have to pay both ordinary income taxes and a 10 percent penalty on funds you withdraw. Using a tax-free rollover, however, you can avoid the penalty by postponing receipt until after age 59½ and allow your savings to continue earning tax-deferred income.

If you decide to take the distribution and not roll it over, there are still some ways to hold your taxes down. Under certain circumstances, the 10 percent penalty might be avoided. These include disability, receipt of an annuity, exorbitant medical expenses, and payment under a divorce or separation agreement.

---

over how the funds are managed. The IRS approval indicates that the form of the IRA satisfies the requirements for special tax treatment. It does not suggest anything about the merits of investing in this particular account. Poorly managed IRAs can offer low returns and high risks while still maintaining IRS approval of their tax status.

For the majority of Americans, an IRA is probably the most convenient, and most tax advantageous, means to save individually for retirement. Taxes on income earned by funds in a traditional account are deferred until the earnings are withdrawn. For many workers the annual contributions are either partially or fully deductible against current income. This effectively defers taxes on the contribution until it is withdrawn from the account in later years.

For certain special circumstances an IRA may also be a convenient means of saving for shorter-term goals. As stated previously, there are several exceptions to the early withdrawal penalty. Three notable items are exceptions for qualified higher education expenses, excessive medical expenditures, and first-time home buyers. Withdrawals for these purposes have been discussed in previous chapters.

TOPIC LINKS

See IRS Pub. 590 "Individual Retirement Arrangements."

Eligibility

Every individual receiving earned income, or alimony, can contribute to an IRA. You may even open an IRA for a spouse with no earned income. Under the Tax Relief Act of 2001, the limits on the tax-deductible contributions are set to increase over the next few years according to the following schedule.

Year	IRA Contribution Limit
2005–2007	$4,000
2008 and after[a]	$5,000

[a]Indexed for inflation after 2008.

Under a catch-up provision, those age 50 and older are able to contribute additional amounts above the standard limits. Through 2005, they may contribute an additional $500. This limit will increase to $1,000 in 2006 and thereafter.

The Tax Relief Act of 2001 provides a tax credit for contributions to individual retirement accounts for low-income households. The following credits may also be applied to 401(k) plans and other types of employer-sponsored pension plans. The maximum eligible contribution is $2,000. Unfortunately, you cannot receive the tax credit if you are a full-time student or you are listed as a dependent on someone else's tax return. However, those just entering the job market are likely to qualify. This provides an incentive for early retirement planning by young workers.

Adjusted Gross Income		
Joint Filers	Singles	Credit Rate
$0–$30,000	$0–$15,000	50%
$30,000–$32,500	$15,000–$16,250	20%
$32,500–$50,000	$16,250–$25,000	10%
Over $50,000	Over $25,000	0%

Part or all of the IRA may be taken as an adjustment to gross income on your individual tax return. The full amount is deductible for those who are not covered by a retirement plan at work. For those who are, the size of the deduction will depend on adjusted gross income before the IRA deduction. The income ranges over which tax-deductible contributions are phased out are as follows.

Taxable Years Beginning In:	Phase-Out Range	
	Single Returns	Joint Returns
2005	50,000–60,000	70,000–80,000
2006	50,000–60,000	75,000–85,000
2007 and thereafter	50,000–60,000	80,000–100,000

Taxes on deductible IRA contributions are delayed, not forgiven. When contributions are withdrawn, taxes will become due on the portion of the withdrawal resulting from previously untaxed contributions and investment earnings. A deductible IRA contribution can be an excellent tax-advantageous investment for young adults with moderate incomes. They are able to capture both the immediate benefit of the tax reduction and the long-term benefit of tax deferral over the many years until retirement. As was demonstrated in Table 16.1, the benefits of tax deferral can be substantial.

Investments. You cannot invest your IRA funds in life insurance or in collectibles other than gold or silver U.S. coins. Nor can you borrow from the account, use it as collateral for a loan, or engage in investments that put you at risk for more than the value of the IRA. Other than these few rules, how you invest your IRA is a matter of considerable choice. You can place it in CDs, annuities, mutual funds, or real estate, or you can open a self-directed IRA through a brokerage house and organize your own portfolio of stocks and bonds.

The IRA is only one component of your investment portfolio. Where you should invest your IRA will depend on the risk-return trade-off that is acceptable to you and the diversity and risk in your non-IRA investments. In general, however, you probably want to consider investments that generate high ordinary income as candidates for inclusion in an IRA. Taxes are deferred on both deductible contributions and investment returns. It makes no sense to use the IRA for investments that generate uncertain tax-postponed capital gains, since taxes are already deferred.

Roth IRA

With a Roth IRA, contributions are not tax deductible. However, the returns on the account and qualified distributions from the account are tax free. Typically, a qualified distribution is any withdrawal from the account after it has existed for five years and you have attained age 59½.

Contribution limits are the same as for a traditional IRA, although these limits must be reduced by any amounts you have contributed to a traditional IRA. There is also a phase-out on allowable contributions for high-income individuals. However, the phase-out is much more generous than for tax-deductible contributions to a traditional IRA. For individuals with incomes in 2004 between $95,000 and $110,000 ($150,000 to $160,000 for married couples filing jointly) the allowable contribution is proportionately phased out.

For individuals who do not qualify for a tax-deductible contribution to a traditional IRA, the Roth IRA is a good alternative. In fact, for individuals who expect to be in a higher marginal tax bracket in their retirement years, a Roth IRA will provide greater benefits than a traditional tax-deductible IRA. The preferred retirement account will depend on the marginal tax rate during the accumulation phase and the marginal tax rate during the withdrawal phase. Assuming the same stream of contributions as in Table 16.1, the relative

Figure 16.8

The Relative Advantage of Traditional Tax-Deductible IRA*

Tax Rate in Payout Period	Tax Rate Accumulation Period			
	10%	15%	25%	35%
10%	0	$ 6,300	$ 18,901	$ 31,501
15%	$ (6,300)	0	$ 12,600	$ 25,201
25%	$ (18,901)	$ (12,600)	0	$ 12,600
35%	$ (31,501)	$ (25,201)	$ (12,600)	0

*Assuming an annual $2,000 contribution for 20 years and a lump-sum distribution in the twentieth year. The contribution to the Roth IRA is out of after-tax funds.

tax advantage of a traditional tax-deductible IRA to the Roth alternative for differing marginal tax rates is indicated in Figure 16.8. As also shown in Table 16.1, both accounts produce identical returns when the marginal tax rate remains unchanged. A Roth IRA may be an excellent choice for young part-time workers who owe minimal taxes.

Keogh (HR-10) Plans

If you derive any of your earnings from self-employment, you can set up a **Keogh (HR-10) plan.** Suppose you work by day for a corporation with a qualified corporate pension plan, but by night you run your own business. Part of the earned income from your self-employment may be tax-sheltered for retirement in a Keogh, even though you are already participating in the corporate retirement plan as an employee. Moreover, the limits on contributions to a Keogh are more generous than those governing IRAs.

Keogh (HR-10) plan: A tax-deferred pension account for self-employed individuals.

Retirement Annuities

In the early years of the family life cycle, when you have many responsibilities, it is important that you provide an estate for the protection of your survivors. In the later years, when you have fewer family responsibilities, it is more important to protect yourself against the possibility that your estate may run out before your death. Annuities can provide such assurance. These are often purchased as part of a tax-advantaged individual retirement plan.

TOPIC **LINKS**

See IRS Pub. 560 "Retirement Plans for the Self-Employed."

Annuity contracts sold by life insurance companies are a convenient means of saving for retirement and of providing security in retirement. Coinciding with these two objectives, annuities have two distinct periods: the accumulation period and the liquidation period.

Annuity contract: A contract that provides for some form of periodic payment.

During the **accumulation period** the principal builds through investments and returns on investments, while benefits are deferred. The annuity contract may allow the buyer to make a single investment (a single premium annuity) or a series of investments during the accumulation period.

Accumulation period: The term over which the principal in the contract is building.

You can purchase either fixed or variable annuities. The distinction has to do with the preservation of principal during the accumulation period. The value of a **fixed annuity** can only increase, whereas the value of a variable annuity can move both up and down. Typically, the interest rate on fixed annuities is guaranteed for a short period of time, such as a year. After this initial period, the interest rate can be changed at the discretion of the insurance company, so long as it doesn't fall below some guaranteed minimal interest rate, such as 3 percent.

Fixed annuity: An annuity in which the principal is guaranteed.

Variable annuity: The value of the annuity is dependent upon the market performance of a specified investment fund.

The principal in a **variable annuity** is invested in a portfolio of securities. Therefore, the value of a variable annuity will increase or decrease with the changing value of the underlying securities. The future worth of the annuity will depend on the portfolio's financial performance. If it does poorly, you could lose some or all of your principal.

Equity-indexed annuities are a hybrid product. The return on the cash value is linked to some market index, such as the Standard & Poor's 500 Index. You are guaranteed repayment of principal and a moderate annual return. In return for the reduced risk, you must share an increase in the equity with the insurance company. The policy may also place a cap on the maximum annual appreciation in your fund.

Liquidation period: The term over which the annuity pays out periodic benefits.

Annuity starting date: The date when the annuity begins periodic payments.

When the accumulation period ends, you can typically receive the accumulated cash value in a lump-sum payment or in the form of an annuity. In the **liquidation period** the owner receives the annuity benefit in monthly or annual installments. When you elect the type of payments to be received, you are said to annuitize the contract. The **annuity starting date** is the point in time when the liquidation period begins.

Immediate annuity: Payments begin one period from the current date.

Deferred annuity: Payments are deferred until some later time period.

An **immediate annuity** begins payments one period from the date it is purchased. How much income an annuity might purchase is indicated in Figure 16.9. Annuities that defer benefits until some later period are called **deferred annuities.** During the accumulation period, when benefits are deferred, taxes on the investment buildup of principal are also postponed. This makes deferred annuities a tax-advantageous savings vehicle. As with other retirement accounts, income taxes become due when the tax-deferred accumulations are withdrawn. Likewise, there is a 10 percent tax penalty on early distributions before age $59\frac{1}{2}$. The early withdrawal penalty does not apply in cases of death or disability or when payments are received as an annuity over the life of the annuitant or his or her spouse.

In addition to the penalties levied by the government on early withdrawal, the insurance company may impose a surrender charge in the early years. Some policies contain a

---

Figure 16.9

How Much Will $100,000 Buy?

Suppose you purchase a single life annuity with a single payment of $100,000. The monthly payments begin immediately and end at your death. How much would you receive each month? The answers below indicate that the older you are and the higher the rate of interest, the better your monthly benefits will be.

	Males		
		Starting Age	
Interest Rate	60	65	70
9%	$929	$1,026	$1,165
8%	866	964	1,103
7%	803	902	1,041
6%	741	840	979

	Females		
		Starting Age	
Interest Rate	60	65	70
9%	$847	$910	$1,005
8%	783	847	943
7%	719	784	882
6%	656	723	821

NOTE: Calculations are based on the 1983 Group Annuity Mortality Table published by the Society of Actuaries.

---

bailout provision that permits you to surrender the policy without charges if the rate paid on the annuity falls below some initially guaranteed rate. Together, tax penalties and surrender charges restrict the use of annuities to long-term savings objectives, such as retirement. Retirement annuities receive the same tax treatment as nondeductible IRA contributions, but there is no limit on the amount you may invest. Taxes on investment earnings are deferred until they are withdrawn during the liquidation period.

There are many ways you may collect the proceeds from the annuity. You can elect to receive a single life or a joint and last survivor annuity, already discussed in the section on survivors' benefits in qualified retirement plans. Under these options you are assured of receiving benefits no matter how long you (single life annuity) or you and your spouse (joint and last survivor annuity) may live.

Of course, if benefits are based entirely on survival, the possibility of an early death means you, the annuitant, may never receive the cost of the annuity in expected benefits. For this reason, many annuitants desire a *refund feature*. This guarantees that payments will continue until they have at least refunded the cost of the annuity. Should you die during the guaranteed period, payments would continue to your named beneficiary for the remainder of the guaranteed refund period.

The period of guaranteed payments need not coincide with the refund period. Annuities can be written to guarantee any number of payments. Of course, the longer the guarantee period, the smaller will be the annuity payment. A single life annuity with all payments ceasing at death will provide the greatest periodic benefit per dollar of cost.

Purchasing an annuity with guaranteed payments does not guarantee that the life insurance company selling the annuity will be around to make those payments. Given the recent volatility in financial markets and the long-term nature of the relationship, it is essential that you check out the financial stability of the company issuing the policy in *Best's Insurance Reports*.

Home Ownership

For many people, home ownership is an integral part of their retirement plan. They look forward to having the mortgage paid off and seeing an end to the monthly mortgage payments. Thus, equity in a home, equal to market value less the mortgage balance, represents an important source of savings for the elderly. The home ownership rate among those in the early retirement ages of 55 to 64 is close to 80 percent.

Obviously, owning a home is considered by many an important means of saving for retirement. Interest payments on the mortgage are tax deductible, and in most situations there is no tax on the capital gain. Consequently, home ownership can be an important source of savings for the future. There are, however, some potential disadvantages you should be aware of. Markets may rise and fall, and in efficient financial markets the past may be an inaccurate guide to the future. The housing market did very well in the 1970s as the baby-boom generation entered the age of home ownership. What might happen in the twenty-first century, when these same individuals retire and sell large homes that are no longer needed, is highly uncertain. In this potential market, those who rely on the equity in a home for financial support in retirement may be very disappointed.

The main point is that you should always attempt to reduce your risks through diversification. Don't rely on home ownership, or any other single investment, as the only source of retirement income. As one component in a comprehensive and diversified savings plan, it is likely to be a sound tax-advantageous investment.

Reverse Mortgages

Having a good chunk of your retirement savings locked up in your home can also be a problem if you need those savings for maintenance expenditures. A reverse mortgage could let you have your savings and your home at the same time. With a **reverse mortgage,** also called

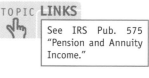

See IRS Pub. 575 "Pension and Annuity Income."

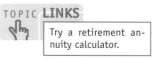

Try a retirement annuity calculator.

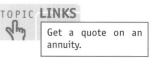

Get a quote on an annuity.

Check ratings for insurance companies.

See how much you can get from a reverse mortgage.

Reverse mortgage: Allows retirees to remain in their home while accessing the home equity for supplemental income.

an *equity conversion* loan, the equity in your home serves as collateral for the loan. What makes this loan unique is that repayment of principal and interest is deferred until the house is sold, regardless of when that may be. The loan may provide a line of credit, a lump-sum payment, or, as is the most common option, monthly disbursements. The monthly payout may extend over a fixed number of years or for as long as you remain in the home.

When the home is sold, the lender is repaid debt plus interest. Your obligation to the lender is limited by the value of the home at the time it is sold. The Federal Housing Administration (FHA) insures reverse mortgages up to specified limits, thus guaranteeing lenders that the equity would be sufficient to cover the amount owed at sale. The FHA also protects you by ensuring that your loan payments will continue if the lender defaults.

ESTABLISHING A PERSONAL RETIREMENT PLAN

We have already examined the various forms your retirement savings might take, but we have not yet answered the question of how much to save. The easy response is that you should save enough to meet your goals. All planning involves a statement of goals and a method for achieving those goals. In retirement planning the goal is a specific standard of living in your later years. Your standard is a personal decision.

Your present income, your ability and willingness to save, and your expected Social Security benefits will affect your goals. You might begin by setting a goal and then calculating how much you would have to save to achieve it. If the required savings appear out of line with your present abilities, then revise the goal and repeat your calculations. You should eventually arrive at a goal and a level of current savings that balance your immediate and future needs.

Financial planners often state that retirement planning should be thought of as a three-legged stool, with Social Security, company pensions, and private savings providing each of the essential supporting legs. The relative size of each leg is illustrated in Figure 16.10. As expected, the relative importance of Social Security benefits declines as retirement income increases. Those retirees with the highest income generate a larger portion of their support from private pensions and personal savings.

Social Security Benefits

You should have a Social Security card with your current name. If you change your name because of marriage or divorce, notify the Social Security Office and order a new card

Figure 16.10

Persons Age 65 or Older: Shares of Aggregate Income for the Lowest and Highest Income Quintiles, by Source, 2001

Source: Income of the Aged Chartbook, 2001,
Social Security Administration
www.ssa.gov/policy/docs/chartbooks/
income_aged/2001/

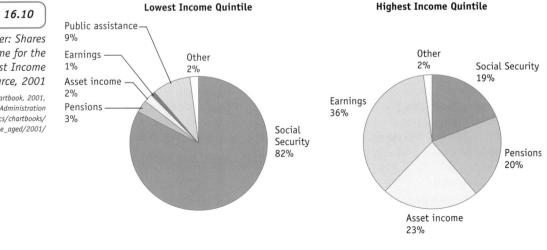

Lowest Income Quintile

Public assistance 9%
Earnings 1%
Asset income 2%
Pensions 3%
Other 2%
Social Security 82%

Highest Income Quintile

Other 2%
Social Security 19%
Earnings 36%
Pensions 20%
Asset income 23%

(Form SS-5). Your employer reports your earnings using the name you supply. For the Social Security Administration to correctly track your earnings, it is important that they have them listed under the correct name and Social Security number.

A record of your historic earnings will be contained in your personal Social Security Statement. These are automatically mailed to all persons age 25 and over who are not currently receiving benefits. If you have not received one, you can request a copy at the Social Security Administration Web site or by contacting the office nearest you. Review your record of historical earnings that are listed on this statement. It is estimated that one person in 13 has not had covered earnings credited correctly. This is unfortunate because future benefits depend on historic earnings.

The Social Security taxes you pay each year do not go into an investment fund where they accumulate for your retirement years. The Social Security tax is simply a transfer tax. It transfers income from working Americans to those receiving Social Security benefits. Congress is currently discussing options that would allow you to invest part of your Social Security contribution in an individual retirement account.

Because there is no investment fund, and because the government retains the power to tax, the system technically cannot go bankrupt. However, the average age of the population is expected to increase into the twenty-first century. There are currently 5 working persons for each elderly person; by the year 2030 there will be only 2.5 working persons for each elderly person. As this trend continues, the government will confront a difficult choice. It must either increase taxes on the working population or reduce benefits. In anticipation of future problems, some changes are already set to go into effect.

TOPIC LINKS

Visit Social Security Online

Retirement Age

For many years, the normal retirement age for full Social Security benefits has been age 65. You will probably have to wait a little longer. As indicated in Table 16.2, beginning in 2003, normal retirement age increases in installments until it reaches age 67 in 2027.

Additional incentives for delayed retirement should also hold down the cost of benefits. For each year you delay receiving benefits beyond age 65 up to age 71, benefits are increased. For those born after 1942, the yearly increase for delayed retirement is 8 percent.

There are no plans to change the early retirement age of 62. However, benefits at early retirement will eventually fall from 80 to 70 percent of monthly benefits at normal retirement age.

Retirement Benefits

To qualify for Social Security retirement benefits you must be "fully insured" at retirement. This requires 40 quarters of covered earnings (10 years). A quarter of earnings is defined as a minimum dollar amount, $900 in 2004, that is adjusted upward each year to reflect rising national wages. If you qualify for retirement benefits, other members of your family may also be entitled to monthly benefits. These may include

- your spouse age 62 or older
- your spouse under age 62, if she or he is taking care of your child who is under age 16 or disabled
- your former spouse age 62 or older and children up to age 18
- children ages 18 and 19, if they are full-time students through grade 12
- children over age 18, if they are disabled

Two-earner couples can each qualify separately for a pension, or one may qualify as a dependent on the other's earning record. A dependent spouse at normal retirement age will receive benefits equal to 50 percent of the benefits received by the retired wage earner. Whether you should qualify on your own record or your spouse's will depend on who generates more in retirement benefits.

Table 16.2		Retirement Age (Years/Months)		Age 62 Benefits as Percent of Basic Monthly Benefit*	
Year of Birth		Worker/ Spouse	Widow(er)	Worker	Spouse
1937 (same as prior law)		65/0	65/0	80.0	37.5
1938		65/2	65/0	79.2	37.1
1939		65/4	65/0	78.3	36.7
1940		65/6	65/2	77.5	36.2
1941		65/8	65/4	76.7	35.8
1942		65/10	65/6	75.8	35.4
1943		66/0	65/8	75.0	35.0
1944		66/0	65/10	75.0	35.0
1945–1954		66/0	66/0	75.0	35.0
1955		66/2	66/0	74.2	34.6
1956		66/4	66/0	73.3	34.2
1957		66/6	66/2	72.5	33.8
1958		66/8	66/4	71.7	33.3
1959		66/10	66/6	70.8	32.9
1960		67/0	66/8	70.0	32.5
1961		67/0	66/10	70.0	32.5
1962 and after		67/0	67/0	70.0	32.5

Normal Retirement Age and Age 62 Benefits

*Reduced retirement benefits will continue to be available to workers (and spouses) beginning at age 62 but at a greater reduction. For workers and spouses, the prior-law reduction factors ($^5/_9$ths of 1 percent per month for workers and $^{25}/_{36}$ths of 1 percent per month for spouses) are retained for the first 36 months of benefits before age 65 and a new factor ($^5/_{12}$ths of 1 percent) is applied for each additional month. For older survivors reduced benefits continued to be available at age 60 with the monthly reduction adjusted for each age cohort so as to maintain a 28.5 percent reduction at age 60—the same maximum reduction as occurred under prior law.

Source: *Social Security Bulletin*, July 1993, p. 30.

In a complicated manner, Social Security benefits are based on the amount you paid into the system and your age at retirement. Your estimate of future benefits in today's dollars will be contained in the personal benefits statement prepared by the Social Security Administration (SSA). You can use the online Social Security Quick Calculator to get a rough idea of your future benefits in today's dollars. A few sample estimates from the Quick Calculator are listed in Table 16.3. Benefits do not increase proportionately with covered earnings. Social Security benefits replace a declining percentage of market earnings as income increases.

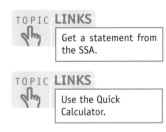

TOPIC **LINKS**
Get a statement from the SSA.

TOPIC **LINKS**
Use the Quick Calculator.

Table 16.3		Current Earnings			
		$20,000	**$40,000**	**$80,000**	**$160,000**
			Monthly Benefit		
Retirement age					
62 in 2004		$546	$821	$1,265	$1,422
		33%	25%	19%	11%
65 and 4 months in 2008		$747	$1,140	$1,178	$1,928
		45%	34%	26%	14%
70 in 2012		$1,019	$1,572	$2,326	$2,596
		61%	47%	35%	19%

Sample Estimates of Monthly Social Security Benefits, percent of income replaced on shaded line

Benefits in 2004 dollars of purchasing power as determined by SSA Quick Calculator for an individual who is age 62 in 2004.
Source: SSA Quick Calculator, http://www.ssa.gov/OACT/quickcalc/

Retirement Test

Before 2001, if you were under age 70 and earned too much income, you could see your Social Security benefits reduced. The retirement test no longer applies to individuals who have reached normal retirement age. When you reach normal retirement age, you can now earn wage income without fear of losing any of your benefits.

The retirement test, however, still holds for those who receive early retirement benefits. It deters individuals with earned income from applying for early benefits. In 2004, benefits were reduced by $1 for every $2 you earn above $11,640. The earned income limits are increased each year for changes in the average national wage.

Taxation of Social Security Benefits

Income from other sources will affect your Social Security Tax. Up to 85 percent of your Social Security benefits may be included in taxable income. The calculations for determining the taxable portion are complicated. A simplified rule is that if the total of nonbenefit income plus one-half of Social Security benefits exceeds $25,000 to $34,000 for single individuals and $32,000 to $44,000 for married couples, then 50 to 85 percent of the earnings could be taxed.

Cost-of-Living Adjustments

One particularly attractive characteristic of Social Security retirement pensions is that they are periodically increased to offset the rise in the price level. Most private pensions provide for fixed dollar benefits during retirement. Over time these constant dollar benefits will purchase fewer goods and services. Having Social Security as part of your retirement income ensures you will receive at least partial inflation protection.

Divorced and Surviving Spouse Benefits

Dependent spouses can receive 100 percent of the deceased spouse's benefits. If the dependent spouse was previously receiving spousal benefits at 50 percent of the basic monthly benefit, then total household income will decline by one-third after the death of the partner. Be sure to budget for these contingencies in your retirement plan.

Remarried spouses may qualify for widow's benefits, but they cannot receive both spousal benefits and widow's benefits. Divorced spouses may also qualify for benefits based on the ex-spouse's work record. They may even receive benefits before the ex-spouse applies for benefits and after the ex-spouse is deceased.

When Should You Begin Benefits?

Your need for financial support may determine when you begin your benefits. However, for many this will be a difficult financial decision. By delaying your retirement, you increase your monthly benefits but reduce the number of years that you receive benefits. The Quick Calculator at **www.ssa.gov** can be used to estimate when you break even by delaying retirement and thus increasing your monthly benefit. For example, if you retire at normal retirement age instead of early retirement age, you are likely to more than recover the benefits you lost in the early years with larger monthly benefits if you live beyond age 76. If you delay retirement between normal retirement age and age 70, you come out ahead if you live beyond age 82.

The optimal decision, however, will depend on more than just your survival probabilities. As discussed previously, early retirement benefits are reduced by the retirement test. Moreover, alternative income may increase the marginal tax rate on Social Security benefits at any age. Therefore, your earning capacity and the timing of alternative income streams will also influence your decision on when you should begin receiving your Social Security monthly benefit.

Estimating and Saving for Your Retirement Needs

You need to target your retirement needs and then estimate the annual savings necessary to meet that target. Each year, as new information becomes available, it can be incorporated into your retirement planning, and a new savings requirement can be calculated. Although the target may move each year, if you take the indicated steps you should arrive at your retirement goals. The calculations in this section use the financial tools discussed in Chapter 2.

Future Income Needs

Younger workers with many years until retirement cannot be certain about economic conditions between now and retirement. They can easily be sidetracked by dwelling on uncertainties. It is far better to gloss over them with simplifying assumptions, while building in a safety margin to cover potential misfortunes.

Figure 16.11 contains a worksheet that may be used for retirement planning by either a single individual or a household with a single market worker. In households where both spouses have separate retirement plans, and they expect to retire at different ages or dates, separate worksheets may be prepared by each market worker. In the current example we are assuming a married couple dependent upon the wages of a single market worker. The market worker plans to retire at age 67, at which time the spouse will be age 65.

Begin your analysis by entering your current salary on line 1. On line 2, estimate the percentage of that salary you would have to replace to retain an adequate standard of living during your retirement years. This figure should be based on the assumption that you will not have any work-related expenses or dependent children to support. The historic

TOPIC **LINKS**

Download worksheet or try an online site.

Financial
P L A N N I N G
for Young Adults

BOX 16.3

Participate in Your Company's Pension Plan

Young workers often make a serious financial mistake by not participating in their company's pension plan. An employer-sponsored defined-contribution plan may require a voluntary contribution before any matching contributions contributed by the employer are deposited in the account. This is often a good deal for at least two reasons. First, the funds you deposit reduce your taxable income today and generate tax-free compounding. Taxes are delayed until the funds are withdrawn. Second, if the employer matches your contributions, you receive a significant return on your initial investment. On a dollar-for-dollar match, you generate an instantaneous return of 100 percent on your investment. You can't find an investment better than that.

If you leave your current employment, any contributions you made are vested. At this time you can most likely receive these funds in a lump-sum distribution at any age. An early distribution before age $59\frac{1}{2}$ can trigger income taxes and a 10 percent tax penalty. However, even after the 10 percent penalty you may come out ahead if you received a dollar-for-dollar match on your previous contributions. Of course, that assumes the employer's contributions have vested. Check your vesting schedule. Especially with cliff vesting, it may be worth delaying your search for a new job.

You may also have penalty-free access to these funds at any age if you use them for a qualified purpose such as a down payment on a home or a medical emergency. A discussion of these exemptions can be found in IRS Publication 575, "Pension and Annuity Income."

Figure 16.11

Retirement Planning Worksheet

	Sample Data
1. Current salary	$ 60,000
2. Percentage of current salary you plan to replace	× 0.60
3. Retirement income target	$ 36,000
4. Minus vested defined benefits	(0)
5. Minus Social Security benefits	($ 17,503)
6. Required supplemental income from investment fund	$ 18,497
7. Income adjustment	
Number of periods until retirement:	30
Inflation rate:	3%
Future value of $1 (see Appendix Table A.1)	× 2.4273
Future value of supplemental annual income	$ 44,897
8. Required funding at retirement	
Number of periods of retirement income:	24
Net discount rate: (after-tax interest rate minus the inflation rate)	4%
Present value at retirement of a $1 inflation adjusted annuity due (see Appendix Table A.4)	× 15.8568
Lump sum needed at retirement to provide annual supplemental income	$ 711,926
9. Future value of current resources	
Years to retirement:	30
After-tax return on investments:	7%
Present retirement resources	$50,000
Future value of $1	× 7.6123
Future value of current resources	380,613
10. Additional savings needed at retirement	$ 331,313
Future value of $1 annuity to retirement (see Appendix Table A.2)	÷ 94.4608
11. Current level annual savings needed to achieve target	$ 3,507

rule of thumb is that you will need about 60 percent of your final salary to retain your current living standard during retirement. If you are planning on your home being fully paid for by then, this percentage may be reduced accordingly. Alternatively, if you intend to pursue an active lifestyle, as many retirees do today, you may want to input a higher replacement ratio of about 80 percent.

The retirement income target on line 3 will have to be covered by pension benefits or investment accumulations. To estimate the needed investment fund, first subtract annual pension benefits. Line 4 contains defined-benefit payments from corporate pension plans or independently purchased annuities. Enter only benefits that are vested and accrued—that is, future benefits you would receive at the expected retirement date were you to terminate employment and further contributions today. These should be estimated in terms of today's dollars. The purchasing power of future dollar benefits may be significantly eroded by future inflation.

Enter an estimate of your Social Security benefits on line 5. The Social Security Administration will provide an estimate of these benefits at normal retirement age and any other retirement age for which you may be planning. The estimates are in today's dollars, unadjusted for future inflation. Consequently, they may be entered directly into Figure 16.11 on line 5. If you do not have a personalized estimate prepared by the Social Security Administration, you can use the Quick Calculator at its Web site.

After subtracting annual payments under government and nongovernment pension programs, you have the annual income you must generate from investments in defined-contribution plans and individual investment accounts. This is in today's dollars. To find your income needs in future dollars, future rates of inflation must be taken into account. (Present value and future value computations can be complicated. In order that you might understand the methodology, we will calculate these values using the tables in the Appendix at the end of the text and the tools presented in Chapter 2. If you prefer an easier approach, the online worksheet will automatically enter the needed values.)

Appendix Table A.1 provides the future value of $1 compounded over various periods at several different rates of growth. If there are 30 years to retirement and you assume a 3 percent annual rate of inflation, what costs $1.00 today will cost $2.4273 at 30 years from now. When you multiply 2.4273 (the future value of $1) by $18,497 on line 6, you will find that you will actually need a supplemental dollar income of $44,897 in the year you retire.

Your Retirement Years

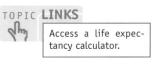
TOPIC **LINKS**

Access a life expec-
tancy calculator.

You must next estimate your retirement years. Table 16.4 contains unisex single and joint life expectancies published by the IRS. The single life expectancy represents the number of years an individual is expected to survive. Of course, 50 percent will live fewer years, and 50 percent will live more years. The joint life expectancy is based on two lives; the expected number of years until both are deceased is the joint life expectancy. Given a married couple age 67 and age 65 at retirement, their joint life expectancy at that date is 24.2 years, which is rounded off to 24 years. If you want to build in a safety margin, you can add a few years to your life expectancy.

Required Funding at Retirement

Appendix Table A.4 provides the present value of a $1 annuity payable over various periods. If you multiply the present value of a $1 annuity payable over your retirement years by $44,897, you can find how much you would need to fund this annuity at retirement. Of course, if you want your standard of living to remain constant, what you really desire is an annuity that begins at $44,897 and then is adjusted upward each year for any increase in the cost of living. The present value of an inflation-adjusted annuity can be found by using a net discount rate, which is approximately equal to the rate of inflation minus the rate of interest. For example, if you assume an after-tax return on your investments of 7 percent and a rate of inflation of 3 percent, then the net discount rate is 4 percent.

According to Appendix Table A.4, the present value of a $1 annuity payable for 24 years at a net discount rate of 4 percent is $15.2470. However, this is the present value of an annuity that pays out at the end of each year. What you really need in this example is a payment at the beginning of the year in which you retire, and then 23 future

Single Life Annuity
Life Expectancy
(Earnings Multiple)

Age	50	51	52	53	54	55	56	57	58	59	60	61	62	63	64	65	66	67	68	69	70
	33.1	32.2	31.3	30.4	29.5	28.6	27.7	26.8	25.9	25.0	24.2	23.3	22.5	21.6	20.8	20.0	19.2	18.4	17.6	16.8	16.0

Joint Life Annuity
Joint Life Expectancy
(Earnings Multiple)

Age	50	51	52	53	54	55	56	57	58	59	60	61	62	63	64	65	66	67	68	69	70
50	39.2	38.7	38.3	37.9	37.5	37.1	36.8	36.4	36.1	35.9	35.6	35.4	35.1	34.9	34.8	34.6	34.4	34.3	34.2	34.1	34.0
51		38.2	37.8	37.3	36.9	36.5	36.1	35.8	35.5	35.2	34.9	34.6	34.4	34.2	34.0	33.8	33.6	33.5	33.4	33.2	33.1
52			37.3	36.8	36.4	35.9	35.6	35.2	34.8	34.5	34.2	33.9	33.7	33.5	33.2	33.0	32.9	32.7	32.5	32.4	32.3
53				36.3	35.8	35.4	35.0	34.6	34.2	33.9	33.6	33.3	33.0	32.7	32.5	32.3	32.1	31.9	31.8	31.6	31.5
54					35.3	34.9	34.4	34.0	33.6	33.3	32.9	32.6	32.3	32.0	31.8	31.6	31.4	31.2	31.0	30.8	30.7
55						34.4	33.9	33.5	33.1	32.7	32.3	32.0	31.7	31.4	31.1	30.9	30.6	30.4	30.2	30.1	29.9
56							33.4	33.0	32.5	32.1	31.7	31.4	31.0	30.7	30.4	30.2	29.9	29.7	29.5	29.3	29.1
57								32.5	32.0	31.6	31.2	30.8	30.4	30.1	29.8	29.5	29.2	29.0	28.8	28.6	28.4
58									31.5	31.1	30.6	30.2	29.9	29.5	29.2	28.9	28.6	28.3	28.1	27.8	27.6
59										30.6	30.1	29.7	29.3	28.9	28.6	28.2	27.9	27.6	27.4	27.1	26.9
60											29.7	29.2	28.8	28.4	28.0	27.6	27.3	27.0	26.7	26.5	26.2
61												28.7	28.3	27.8	27.4	27.1	26.7	26.4	26.1	25.8	25.6
62													27.8	27.3	26.9	26.5	26.1	25.8	25.5	25.2	24.9
63														26.9	26.4	26.0	25.6	25.2	24.9	24.6	24.3
64															25.9	25.5	25.1	24.7	24.3	24.0	23.7
65																25.0	24.6	24.2	23.8	23.4	23.1
66																	24.1	23.7	23.3	22.9	22.5
67																		23.2	22.8	22.4	22.0
68																			22.3	21.9	21.5
69																				21.5	21.1
70																					20.6

Source: Internal Revenue Service, Publication 939, Unisex Tables V and VI, January 2003.

Table 16.4

Single and Joint Life Expectancies in Years

payments, each at the beginning of a subsequent year. An annuity that pays out at the beginning of each period is termed an *annuity due*. The present value of an *n*-period $1 annuity due can be found by taking the present value of an (*n* − 1)-period $1 annuity and adding 1 to it. Accordingly, the present value of a 24-period annuity due at a net discount rate of 4 percent is $15.8568. This is equal to $14.8568 (the present value of a 23-period annuity discounted at 4 percent) plus $1. Multiplying the present value of a $1 annuity due by the required supplemental income indicates that the lump sum needed at retirement is $711,926.

Future Value of Current Resources

Retirement needs may be funded by both previously accumulated resources and future savings. Current resources may consist of savings in defined-contribution plans and personal retirement accounts. Those resources you have already accumulated will continue to earn investment income until they are needed. If you assume that the annual after-tax return on your current resources is 7 percent, then Appendix Table A.1 indicates that $1 of present funding will grow to $7.6123 in 30 years. Therefore, the future value of present resources at retirement will be $380,613 ($50,000 × 7.6123). Thus, the additional savings needed at retirement will be equal to the difference between future needs and the future value of present resources, or $331,313 ($711,926 − 380,613).

Annual Retirement Savings

The future value of a $1 annuity is given in Appendix Table A.2. This indicates how much you would have in an investment fund after the given number of years if you deposited $1 in the account each year and the amount deposited earned interest at the indicated rate. For example, the future value of a $1 annual payment made over each of the next 30 years, where these payments earn an annual after-tax return of 7 percent, is $94.4608. Dividing $331,313 (the additional savings needed at retirement) by 94.4608, you will find that equal annual contributions of $3,507 will cover the shortfall in future funding needs. Unfortunately, equal annual contributions do not take into consideration the declining value of the dollar. Consequently, a $3,507 payment in the early years will be more burdensome than the same dollar payment in the later years when your earnings are likely to be greater because of productivity increases and inflation.

Suppose instead of level annual contributions, you wanted to assume increasing annual contributions. Your initial contribution could be less than $3,507, if you were to contribute a larger amount in the later years. Given a planned increase in your annual contributions, the online worksheet for Figure 16.9 will calculate a stream of increasing funding that will allow you to meet your savings target. For example, if you planned to increase your annual contribution by 3 percent each year, your initial contribution would begin at $2,389. After 30 years, the annual contribution would have risen to $5,629 and you would have created an identical fund of $331,313. Assuming a 3 percent rate of inflation, the real dollar value of your $5,629 contribution in the thirtieth year would be the same as your initial contribution of $2,389.

You may use either graduated contributions or level contributions to attain your retirement goals. The most important choice you can make is to plan and to plan early. Change some of the assumptions in the worksheet and notice how dramatically savings requirements can change. We tend to think that the market conditions that exist today will inevitably hold into the future. A brief review of historic market conditions should convince you that market returns and rate of inflation could change unexpectedly and dramatically. Periodic updates will ensure that you hit your targeted goals. The closer you get to retirement, the harder it is to overcome poor planning in your early years. Be sure to review your goals and savings each year to guarantee that you are on the right path.

accrued benefit (p. 422)

accumulation period (p. 431)

annuity contract (p. 431)

annuity starting date (p. 432)

cash balance plan (p. 424)

deferred annuity (p. 432)

defined-benefit plan (p. 421)

defined-contribution plan (p. 421)

early retirement age (p. 423)

Employee Retirement Income Security Act (ERISA) (p. 418)

employee stock ownership plan (ESOP) (p. 427)

fixed annuity (p. 431)

flat benefit formula (p. 423)

immediate annuity (p. 432)

individual retirement account (IRA) (p. 428)

joint and last survivor annuity (p. 426)

Keogh (HR-10) plan (p. 431)

liquidation period (p. 432)

normal retirement age (p. 423)

profit-sharing plan (p. 427)

qualified retirement plan (p. 418)

reverse mortgage (p. 433)

simplified employee pension plan (SEP) (p. 428)

single life annuity (p. 426)

unit benefit formula (p. 423)

variable annuity (p. 432)

vested benefits (p. 422)

Key Terms

Reread the chapter-opening vignette.

FOLLOW-UP ON THE

Steele FAMILY

1. Arnold has allocated all of his contributions in his retirement plan to a government bond fund. Is this choice consistent with long-term retirement planning?
2. The Steeles would like to plan for early retirement when Arnold reaches age 60 in 23 years. About how much would they have to save each year in order to afford a comfortable retirement?
3. Suppose the Steeles delayed retirement until Arnold is age 67 when he qualifies for Social Security benefits. How would this affect their savings decision?
4. If the Steeles decided to increase saving for retirement, what tax-advantaged investments might they consider?

Problems and Review Questions

1. "Retirement planning should be put off until you can accurately assess your latter-day needs." Do you agree or disagree with this statement? Explain.
2. What does the term *qualified* indicate when describing a pension plan? Why is it important that a pension plan be qualified?
3. What is the difference between a defined-benefit plan and a defined-contribution plan? What are the advantages and disadvantages of each?
4. Why is it important that benefits be vested?
5. How does cliff vesting differ from graded vesting?
6. Up to what age must the company provide you with additions to your retirement benefits? You cannot be forced into retirement before what age?
7. Which approach for calculating defined benefits responds more rapidly to the effects of inflation: the career average approach or the final average approach? Why?
8. How does a pension plan differ from a profit-sharing plan?
9. Which tax-deferred retirement plans could a self-employed individual take advantage of?
10. How do fixed annuities differ from variable annuities?
11. Why is it unwise to place the majority of your retirement savings into your home?
12. What is normal retirement age for Social Security benefits? How is this expected to change?
13. How are Social Security benefits reduced for part-time employment?
14. Are Social Security benefits tax free? Explain.
15. Why might you prefer a Roth IRA to a traditional IRA?

16. You want to change the mutual fund you have your IRA invested in. How might you change funds without triggering a tax on your withdrawal?
17. When might deferral of taxes on a retirement account be an unwise choice?
18. How does health care planning before age 65 differ from health care planning after age 65?
19. Does the nonemployee spouse have any rights to a pension plan participant's defined benefits?
20. Why do the ages 59½ and 70½ have special significance for qualified retirement plans?

Case 16.1
Steve Deutsch Plans for Retirement

Steve Deutsch's company pension and his expected Social Security benefits are his only sources of retirement income. He would like to retire in 10 years at age 62, but he is worried that these programs will not provide enough in early retirement benefits for him to live in his normal style. He figures he would need to generate an additional income of $10,000 from a supplemental investment fund for him to live comfortably in early retirement. He expects that the after-tax returns on his investments will average 9 percent, and future inflation will average 5 percent.

Questions
1. What is the target amount he would need in this investment fund?
2. What is his current savings target, given the target investment fund?
3. Where might Steve consider placing these additional funds for retirement?

Case 16.2
Janet Myrnic Considers Changing Jobs

Janet Myrnic has been offered an executive position at a competing firm. The salary is substantially above what her present employer is paying. Therefore, it is very likely she will accept the offer.

However, before leaving her old job, she would like to review her participation in that company's pension plan and understand her rights. She has participated in the company's defined-contribution plan for the last five years, during which the employer matched each dollar she contributed to the retirement fund. Combined contributions currently total $11,320.

Questions
1. Under graded vesting, what percentage of these benefits must be vested?
2. Suppose the entire amount in Janet's retirement account were fully vested; how much is she definitely entitled to receive in a lump-sum payment at termination of employment?
3. Assuming she leaves some funds in the retirement plan, what document should she receive at termination?
4. What are her investment options if she decides to receive a lump-sum payment?

Working Out on the Web

Exercises to Strengthen Your Use of the Internet
(Internet links for the following exercises can be found at **www.prenhall.com/winger**.)

Exercise 16.1 The Cost of Waiting
CNN Money has a calculator that demonstrates the power of tax deferral. Enter your monthly savings and your tax bracket, and it calculates how much more you would save at retirement by putting your funds in a tax-deferred account.

Q. Suppose you set aside $100 a month. How much will you have accumulated by retirement at age 65? Now suppose you delay the beginning of this savings plan for five years. How much less will you save by age 65 retirement?

Exercise 16.2 Roth IRA or Traditional IRA?

The Roth IRA Calculator from Moneychimp lets you compare accumulations and after-tax disbursements from a Roth IRA and a traditional IRA. Depending on your current income and relative marginal tax bracket in your retirement years, one of these IRAs may provide a more favorable outcome. Datachimp explains why different Roth calculators on the Web provide different accumulations.

Q. By assuming different marginal tax rates in the contribution and retirement years, provide an example in which the Roth IRA is the preferred investment vehicle. Now repeat your analysis and provide an example in which the traditional IRA is the preferred investment vehicle.

Exercise 16.3 How Long Do You Need to Plan For?

Insure.com provides life expectancy data. Look up your life expectancy for your current age. Choose a retirement age and find the life expectancy for that retirement age.

Q. Can you explain why your current life expectancy differs from your life expectancy at retirement?

Exercise 16.4 Selecting a Portfolio of Retirement Investments

How much you plan to save for retirement will depend on many factors. You have to consider your short-term needs, your present assets, and your attitude toward risk. The investor risk profiler from International Association of Registered Financial Consultants may give you some idea about which investments are right for you.

Q. How and why does the investment portfolio for the risk taker differ from the investment portfolio for the risk-adverse individual?

Exercise 16.5 How Much Do You Need to Save for Retirement?

Fidelity Investments has one of the best retirement planning calculators on the World Wide Web. It allows you to control almost every variable that will affect how much you need to save today to satisfy tomorrow's retirement needs. It does all of the difficult calculations for you. You input expected inflation and earnings, but it automatically calculates annual inflation-adjusted requirements. If you can't link up with Fidelity, try the Vanguard Investments Retirement Calculator.

Enter values that reflect either your current economic status or what your economic status will be when you begin full-time employment. Be sure to note the assumptions you enter into the calculator. Estimate how much you would have to save each year in order to fund what you consider a comfortable retirement.

Q. Change the retirement age from 65 to 55. How much more do you have to save each year to fund a comfortable early retirement?

Exercise 16.6 How Much Income Will $100,000 Buy?

ImmediateAnnuities.com lets you estimate the present cost of a future retirement annuity. The cost will depend on many factors. The major ones will be your present age and future retirement age, interest returns on the annuity accumulation, and the method of payout.

Q. Enter your gender and present age into the calculator. Find the cost of an immediate single life annuity that would pay out $1000 a month. Now find the cost of the same annuity at age 65.

Appendix

TIME-VALUE-OF-MONEY CONCEPTS

In Chapter 1 you were introduced to the basic concepts regarding the time value of money. This appendix provides greater detail about these concepts, and it also includes present value and future value of $1 tables.

FUTURE VALUE OF A SINGLE PAYMENT

Finding the future value, *FV*, of a sum of money invested today answers the question: "How much will my money grow if I invest it today and leave it in the investment for a specified number of time periods, assuming it earns a specified rate of return each period?" For example, $100 invested for three years and earning 10 percent each year grows to $133.10 as shown next.

$$FV \text{ end of year } 1 = \$100 + 0.10(\$100) = \$110.00$$

$$FV \text{ end of year } 2 = \$110 + 0.10(\$110) = \$121.00$$

$$FV \text{ end of year } 3 = \$121 + 0.10(\$121) = \$133.10$$

The year-by-year solution is long and unnecessary, because there are two much quicker solutions. If you have a calculator, simply use the *FV* of a single payment formula, which is

$$FV = PV(1.0 + i)^n \tag{A1}$$

where

FV = the future value

PV = the present value (the amount invested today)

i = the interest rate per period

n = the number of periods the PV is invested

In the preceding example, we have

$$FV = \$100(1.0 + 0.10)^3 = \$100(1.10)^3 = \$100(1.331) = \$133.10$$

The other approach for finding an *FV* is to refer to a future value (also called compound value) table. These are widely available, and they show the future value of $1 for various investment periods and rates. Table A.1 illustrates a future value table, and if you go down the left-hand column to period 3 (indicating three holding periods) and across to

Table A.1

Future Value (FV) of $1 at the End of n Periods: FV 5 (1.0 1 i)$^n

Number of Periods	1%	2%	3%	4%	5%	6%	7%	8%	9%	10%	12%	14%	15%	16%	18%	20%	24%	28%	32%	36%
1	1.0100	1.0200	1.0300	1.0400	1.0500	1.0600	1.0700	1.0800	1.0900	1.1000	1.1200	1.1400	1.1500	1.1600	1.1800	1.2000	1.2400	1.2800	1.3200	1.3600
2	1.0201	1.0404	1.0609	1.0816	1.1025	1.1236	1.1449	1.1664	1.1881	1.2100	1.2544	1.2996	1.3225	1.3456	1.3924	1.4400	1.5376	1.6384	1.7424	1.8496
3	1.0303	1.0612	1.0927	1.1249	1.1576	1.1910	1.2250	1.2597	1.2950	1.3310	1.4049	1.4815	1.5209	1.5609	1.6430	1.7280	1.9066	2.0972	2.3000	2.5155
4	1.0406	1.0824	1.1255	1.1699	1.2155	1.2625	1.3108	1.3605	1.4116	1.4641	1.5735	1.6890	1.7490	1.8106	1.9388	2.0736	2.3642	2.6844	3.0360	3.4210
5	1.0510	1.1041	1.1593	1.2167	1.2763	1.3382	1.4026	1.4693	1.5386	1.6105	1.7623	1.9254	2.0114	2.1003	2.2878	2.4883	2.9316	3.4360	4.0075	4.6526
6	1.0615	1.1262	1.1941	1.2653	1.3401	1.4185	1.5007	1.5869	1.6771	1.7716	1.9738	2.1950	2.3131	2.4364	2.6996	2.9860	3.6352	4.3980	5.2899	6.3275
7	1.0721	1.1487	1.2299	1.3159	1.4071	1.5036	1.6058	1.7138	1.8280	1.9487	2.2107	2.5023	2.6600	2.8262	3.1855	3.5832	4.5077	5.6295	6.9826	8.6054
8	1.0829	1.1717	1.2668	1.3686	1.4775	1.5938	1.7182	1.8509	1.9926	2.1436	2.4760	2.8526	3.0590	3.2784	3.7589	4.2998	5.5895	7.2058	9.2170	11.703
9	1.0937	1.1951	1.3048	1.4233	1.5513	1.6895	1.8385	1.9990	2.1719	2.3579	2.7731	3.2519	3.5179	3.8030	4.4355	5.1598	6.9310	9.2234	12.166	15.916
10	1.1046	1.2190	1.3439	1.4802	1.6289	1.7908	1.9672	2.1589	2.3674	2.5937	3.1058	3.7072	4.0456	4.4114	5.2338	6.1917	8.5944	11.805	16.059	21.646
11	1.1157	1.2434	1.3842	1.5395	1.7103	1.8983	2.1049	2.3316	2.5804	2.8531	3.4785	4.2262	4.6524	5.1173	6.1759	7.4301	10.657	15.111	21.198	29.439
12	1.1268	1.2682	1.4258	1.6010	1.7959	2.0122	2.2522	2.5182	2.8127	3.1384	3.8960	4.8179	5.3502	5.9360	7.2876	8.9161	13.214	19.342	27.982	40.037
13	1.1381	1.2936	1.4685	1.6651	1.8856	2.1329	2.4098	2.7196	3.0658	3.4523	4.3635	5.4924	6.1528	6.8858	8.5994	10.699	16.386	24.758	36.937	54.451
14	1.1495	1.3195	1.5126	1.7317	1.9799	2.2609	2.5785	2.9372	3.3417	3.7975	4.8871	6.2613	7.0757	7.9875	10.147	12.839	20.319	31.691	48.756	74.053
15	1.1610	1.3459	1.5580	1.8009	2.0789	2.3966	2.7590	3.1722	3.6425	4.1772	5.4736	7.1379	8.1371	9.2655	11.973	15.407	25.195	40.564	64.358	100.71
16	1.1726	1.3728	1.6047	1.8730	2.1829	2.5404	2.9522	3.4259	3.9703	4.5950	6.1304	8.1372	9.3576	10.748	14.129	18.488	31.242	51.923	84.953	136.96
17	1.1843	1.4002	1.6528	1.9479	2.2920	2.6928	3.1588	3.7000	4.3276	5.0545	6.8660	9.2765	10.761	12.467	16.672	22.186	38.740	66.461	112.13	186.27
18	1.1961	1.4282	1.7024	2.0258	2.4066	2.8543	3.3799	3.9960	4.7171	5.5599	7.6900	10.575	12.375	14.462	19.673	26.623	48.038	85.070	148.02	253.33
19	1.2081	1.4568	1.7535	2.1068	2.5270	3.0256	3.6165	4.3157	5.1417	6.1159	8.6128	12.055	14.231	16.776	23.214	31.948	59.567	108.89	195.39	344.53
20	1.2202	1.4859	1.8061	2.1911	2.6533	3.2071	3.8697	4.6610	5.6044	6.7275	9.6463	13.743	16.366	19.460	27.393	38.337	73.864	139.37	257.91	468.57
21	1.2324	1.5157	1.8603	2.2788	2.7860	3.3996	4.1406	5.0338	6.1088	7.4002	10.803	15.667	18.821	22.574	32.323	46.005	91.591	178.40	340.44	637.26
22	1.2447	1.5460	1.9161	2.3699	2.9253	3.6035	4.4304	5.4365	6.6586	8.1403	12.100	17.861	21.644	26.186	38.142	55.206	113.57	228.35	449.39	866.67
23	1.2572	1.5769	1.9736	2.4647	3.0715	3.8197	4.7405	5.8715	7.2579	8.9543	13.552	20.361	24.891	30.376	45.007	66.247	140.83	292.30	593.19	1178.6
24	1.2697	1.6084	2.0328	2.5633	3.2251	4.0489	5.0724	6.3412	7.9111	9.8497	15.178	23.212	28.625	35.236	53.108	79.496	174.63	374.14	783.02	1602.9
25	1.2824	1.6406	2.0938	2.6658	3.3864	4.2919	5.4274	6.8485	8.6231	10.834	17.000	26.461	32.918	40.874	62.668	95.396	216.54	478.90	1033.5	2180.0
26	1.2953	1.6734	2.1566	2.7725	3.5557	4.5494	5.8074	7.3964	9.3992	11.918	19.040	30.166	37.856	47.414	73.948	114.47	268.51	612.99	1364.3	2964.9
27	1.3082	1.7069	2.2213	2.8834	3.7335	4.8223	6.2139	7.9881	10.245	13.110	21.324	34.389	43.535	55.000	87.259	137.37	332.95	784.63	1800.9	4032.2
28	1.3213	1.7410	2.2879	2.9987	3.9201	5.1117	6.6488	8.6271	11.167	14.421	23.883	39.204	50.065	63.800	102.96	164.84	412.86	1004.3	2377.2	5483.8
29	1.3345	1.7758	2.3566	3.1187	4.1161	5.4184	7.1143	9.3173	12.172	15.863	26.749	44.693	57.575	74.008	121.50	197.81	511.95	1285.5	3137.9	7458.0
30	1.3478	1.8114	2.4273	3.2434	4.3219	5.7435	7.6123	10.062	13.267	17.449	29.959	50.950	66.211	85.849	143.37	237.37	634.81	1645.5	4142.0	10143.
40	1.4889	2.2080	3.2620	4.8010	7.0400	10.285	14.974	21.724	31.409	45.259	93.050	188.88	267.86	378.72	750.32	1469.7	5455.9	19426.	66520.	*
50	1.6446	2.6916	4.3839	7.1067	11.467	18.420	29.457	46.901	74.357	117.39	289.00	700.23	1083.6	1670.7	3927.3	9100.4	46890.	*	*	*
60	1.8167	3.2810	5.8916	10.519	18.679	32.987	57.946	101.25	176.03	304.48	897.59	2595.9	4383.9	7370.1	20555.	56347.	*	*	*	*

Note: n = number of periods; i = interest rate per period.

the 10 percent column, you find the number 1.3310. (Of course, this is the same number we have already calculated.) Since this shows the future value of $1, the final step is to multiply the *FV* of $1 by the amount of dollars invested, as we have already done.

FUTURE VALUE OF A STREAM OF EQUAL PAYMENTS (AN ANNUITY)

Very often an investment program calls for an equal amount invested each period. For example, suppose your budget allows a $100 investment each year. You are curious about how much you will accumulate at the end of three years, assuming you begin making payments at the end of each of the next three years. This total future value is calculated as follows:

FV of the payment made at the end of year $1 = \$100(1.10)^2 = \$100(1.21) = \$121.00$

FV of the payment made at the end of year $2 = \$100(1.10)^1 = \$100(1.10) = \$110.00$

FV of the payment made at the end of year $3 = $ $\underline{\$100.00}$

Total future value $= \underline{\underline{\$331.00}}$

Just as in the case of the *FV* of a single payment, you can use a formula to find the future value of a stream of equal investments—that is, of an annuity. It is

$$FV = \frac{[(1.0 + i)^n - 1.0] \times A}{i} \qquad (A2)$$

where, *FV*, *i*, and *n* have the same meaning as before, and $A = $ the amount of the annuity. Substituting the preceding values, we have

$$FV = \frac{[(1.0 + 0.10)^3 - 1.0] \times 100}{0.10} = \frac{[(1.10)^3 - 1.0] \times 100}{0.10}$$

$$= \frac{(1.331 - 1.0) \times 100}{0.10} = \frac{0.331 \times 100}{0.10} = \frac{33.10}{0.10} = \$331.10$$

There are also future value of an annuity tables that can be consulted for a quick answer. Table A.2 on page 449 is an example of such a table. To find the answer to the preceding example, again simply go down to period 3 and across to the 10 percent column to find the answer for the future value of a $1 annuity invested for three periods at a rate of 10 percent each period. It is 3.31. Multiply the amount of the annuity, $100, by this number to arrive at the correct answer: $331.00.

The preceding example assumes that the annuity payments begin at the end of the first period. However, you might encounter situations where the payments begin immediately. Let's assume that to be the case using the preceding example again. This change offers no particular problem: Simply assume four holding periods instead of three and then subtract 1.0 from the *FV* coefficient. In Table A.2 the coefficient for four periods at 10 percent is 4.641. Subtracting 1.0 from this gives 3.641, which is the future value of $1 invested for three periods with payments beginning immediately. So $100 invested in this fashion would grow to $364.10, a somewhat larger amount than in the previous illustration. Of course, this answer makes sense because your money is invested one year longer.

Table A.2

Future Value of $1 Annuity: $FV = £\dfrac{(1.0 + i)^n - 1.0}{i}$

Number of Periods	1%	2%	3%	4%	5%	6%	7%	8%	9%	10%	12%	14%	15%	16%	18%	20%	24%	28%	32%	36%
1	1.0000	1.0000	1.0000	1.0000	1.0000	1.0000	1.0000	1.0000	1.0000	1.0000	1.0000	1.0000	1.0000	1.0000	1.0000	1.0000	1.0000	1.0000	1.0000	1.0000
2	2.0100	2.0200	2.0300	2.0400	2.0500	2.0600	2.0700	2.0800	2.0900	2.1000	2.1200	2.1400	2.1500	2.1600	2.1800	2.2000	2.2400	2.2800	2.3200	2.3600
3	3.0301	3.0604	3.0909	3.1216	3.1525	3.1836	3.2149	3.2464	3.2781	3.3100	3.3744	3.4396	3.4725	3.5056	3.5724	3.6400	3.7776	3.9184	4.0624	4.2096
4	4.0604	4.1216	4.1836	4.2465	4.3101	4.3746	4.4399	4.5061	4.5731	4.6410	4.7793	4.9211	4.9934	5.0665	5.2154	5.3680	5.6842	6.0156	6.3624	6.7251
5	5.1010	5.2040	5.3091	5.4163	5.5256	5.6371	5.7507	5.8666	5.9847	6.1051	6.3528	6.6101	6.7424	6.8771	7.1542	7.4416	8.0484	8.6999	9.3983	10.146
6	6.1520	6.3081	6.4684	6.6330	6.8019	6.9753	7.1533	7.3359	7.5233	7.7156	8.1152	8.5355	8.7537	8.9775	9.4420	9.9299	10.980	12.135	13.405	14.798
7	7.2135	7.4343	7.6625	7.8983	8.1420	8.3938	8.6540	8.9228	9.2004	9.4872	10.089	10.730	11.066	11.413	12.141	12.915	14.615	16.533	18.695	21.126
8	8.2857	8.5830	8.8923	9.2142	9.5491	9.8975	10.259	10.636	11.028	11.435	12.299	13.232	13.726	14.240	15.327	16.499	19.122	22.163	25.678	29.731
9	9.3685	9.7546	10.159	10.582	11.026	11.491	11.978	12.487	13.021	13.579	14.775	16.085	16.785	17.518	19.085	20.798	24.712	29.369	34.895	41.435
10	10.462	10.949	11.463	12.006	12.577	13.180	13.816	14.486	15.192	15.937	17.548	19.337	20.303	21.321	23.521	25.958	31.643	38.592	47.061	57.351
11	11.566	12.168	12.807	13.486	14.206	14.971	15.783	16.645	17.560	18.531	20.654	23.044	24.349	25.732	28.755	32.150	40.237	50.398	63.121	78.998
12	12.682	13.412	14.192	15.025	15.917	16.869	17.888	18.977	20.140	21.384	24.133	27.270	29.001	30.850	34.931	39.580	50.894	65.510	84.320	108.43
13	13.809	14.680	15.617	16.626	17.713	18.882	20.140	21.495	22.953	24.522	28.029	32.088	34.351	36.786	42.218	48.496	64.109	84.852	112.30	148.47
14	14.947	15.973	17.086	18.291	19.598	21.015	22.550	24.214	26.019	27.975	32.392	37.581	40.504	43.672	50.818	59.195	80.496	109.61	149.23	202.92
15	16.096	17.293	18.598	20.023	21.578	23.276	25.129	27.152	29.360	31.772	37.279	43.842	47.580	51.659	60.965	72.035	100.81	141.30	197.99	276.97
16	17.257	18.639	20.156	21.824	23.657	25.672	27.888	30.324	33.003	35.949	42.753	50.980	55.717	60.925	72.939	87.442	126.01	181.86	262.35	377.69
17	18.430	20.012	21.761	23.697	25.840	28.212	30.840	33.750	36.973	40.544	48.883	59.117	65.075	71.673	87.068	105.93	157.25	233.79	347.30	514.66
18	19.614	21.412	23.414	25.645	28.132	30.905	33.999	37.450	41.301	45.599	55.749	68.394	75.836	84.140	103.74	128.11	195.99	300.25	459.44	700.93
19	20.810	22.840	25.116	27.671	30.539	33.760	37.379	41.446	46.018	51.159	63.439	78.969	88.211	98.603	123.41	154.74	244.03	385.32	607.47	954.27
20	22.019	24.297	26.870	29.778	33.066	36.785	40.995	45.762	51.160	57.275	72.052	91.024	102.44	115.37	146.62	186.68	303.60	494.21	802.86	1298.8
21	23.239	25.783	28.676	31.969	35.719	39.992	44.865	50.422	56.764	64.002	81.698	104.76	118.81	134.84	174.02	225.02	377.46	633.59	1060.7	1767.3
22	24.471	27.299	30.536	34.248	38.505	43.392	49.005	55.456	62.873	71.402	92.502	120.43	137.63	157.41	206.34	271.03	469.05	811.99	1401.2	2404.6
23	25.716	28.845	32.452	36.617	41.430	46.995	53.436	60.893	69.531	79.543	104.60	138.29	159.27	183.60	244.48	326.23	582.62	1040.3	1850.6	3271.3
24	26.973	30.421	34.426	39.082	44.502	50.815	58.176	66.764	76.789	88.497	118.15	158.65	184.16	213.97	289.49	392.48	723.46	1332.6	2443.8	4449.9
25	28.243	32.030	36.459	41.645	47.727	54.864	63.249	73.105	84.700	98.347	133.33	181.87	212.79	249.21	342.60	471.98	898.09	1706.8	3226.8	6052.9
26	29.525	33.670	38.553	44.311	51.113	59.156	68.676	79.954	93.323	109.18	150.33	208.33	245.71	290.08	405.27	567.37	1114.6	2185.7	4260.4	8233.0
27	30.820	35.344	40.709	47.084	54.669	63.705	74.483	87.350	102.72	121.09	169.37	238.49	283.56	337.50	479.22	681.85	1383.1	2798.7	5624.7	11197.9
28	32.129	37.051	42.930	49.967	58.402	68.528	80.697	95.338	112.96	134.20	190.69	272.88	327.10	392.50	566.48	819.22	1716.0	3583.3	7425.6	15230.2
29	33.450	38.792	45.218	52.966	62.322	73.639	87.346	103.96	124.13	148.63	214.58	312.09	377.16	456.30	669.44	984.06	2128.9	4587.6	9802.9	20714.1
30	34.784	40.568	47.575	56.084	66.438	79.058	94.460	113.28	136.30	164.49	241.33	356.78	434.74	530.31	790.94	1181.8	2640.9	5873.2	12940.	28172.2
40	48.886	60.402	75.401	95.025	120.79	154.76	199.63	259.05	337.88	442.59	767.09	1342.0	1779.0	2360.7	4163.2	7343.8	22728.	69377.	*	*
50	64.463	84.579	112.79	152.66	209.34	290.33	406.52	573.76	815.08	1163.9	2400.0	4994.5	7217.7	10435.	21813.	45497.	*	*	*	*
60	81.669	114.05	163.05	237.99	353.58	533.12	813.52	1253.2	1944.7	3034.8	7471.6	18535.	29219.	46057.	*	*	*	*	*	*

Note: n = number of periods; i = interest rate per period.

PRESENT VALUE OF A SINGLE PAYMENT

To find the present value, *PV*, of a single payment, you just reverse the process of finding a future value. Referring to Equation (A1), you simply rearrange terms to get

$$PV = \frac{FV}{(1.0 + i)^n} \text{ or } PV = FV \times \frac{1.0}{(1.0 + i)^n} \tag{A3}$$

Thus, the present value of 133.10 received three years from today is $100.

$$PV = \frac{\$133.10}{(1.0 + 0.10)} = \frac{\$133.10}{(1.10)} = \frac{\$133.10}{1.331} = \$100$$

Table A.3 on the following page shows a present value of $1 table. It is used in exactly the same manner as a future value table. The number in the period 3 row and 10 percent column is 0.7513, which is 1 divided by $(1.10)^3$. Multiplying 0.7513 by $133.10 gives $100.

PRESENT VALUE OF A STREAM OF EQUAL PAYMENTS (AN ANNUITY)

The following formula can be used to calculate the present value of a stream of equal payments to be received beginning at the end of the first period and assuming that each payment is discounted at the discount rate applicable each period.

$$PV = \frac{[1.0 - 1.0/(1.0 + i)^n] \times A}{i} \tag{A4}$$

If you receive $100 at the end of each of the next three periods, the present value of this stream is

$$PV = \frac{[1.0 - 1.0/(1.0 + 0.10)^3] \times \$100}{0.10} = \frac{[1.0 - 1.0/(1.10)^3] \times \$100}{0.10}$$

$$= \frac{[1.0 - (1.0/(1.331)] \times \$100}{0.10}$$

$$= \frac{(1.0 - 0.7513) \times \$100}{0.10} = \frac{0.24869 \times \$100}{0.10} = \frac{\$24.869}{0.10}$$

$$= \$2488.69$$

The same answer can be found by referring to a present value of an annuity table, such as the one in Table A.4 on page 452, and finding the value for $n = 3$ and $i = 10$ percent. This is 2.4869, and multiplying it by the $100 annuity gives $248.69. Figure A.1 on page 453 shows some applications of *FV* and *PV* techniques; exercises to test your understanding of the material follow.

Table A.3

Present Value of $1: PV = $\dfrac{1.0}{(1.0 + i)^n}$

Number of Periods	1%	2%	3%	4%	5%	6%	7%	8%	9%	10%	12%	14%	15%	16%	18%	20%	24%	28%	32%	36%
1	.9901	.9804	.9709	.9615	.9524	.9434	.9346	.9259	.9174	.9091	.8929	.8772	.8696	.8621	.8475	.8333	.8065	.7813	.7576	.7353
2	.9803	.9612	.9426	.9246	.9070	.8900	.8734	.8573	.8417	.8264	.7972	.7695	.7561	.7432	.7182	.6944	.6504	.6104	.5739	.5407
3	.9706	.9423	.9151	.8890	.8638	.8396	.8163	.7938	.7722	.7513	.7118	.6750	.6575	.6407	.6086	.5787	.5245	.4768	.4348	.3975
4	.9610	.9238	.8885	.8548	.8227	.7921	.7629	.7350	.7084	.6830	.6355	.5921	.5718	.5523	.5158	.4823	.4230	.3725	.3294	.2923
5	.9515	.9057	.8626	.8219	.7835	.7473	.7130	.6806	.6499	.6209	.5674	.5194	.4972	.4761	.4371	.4019	.3411	.2910	.2495	.2149
6	.9420	.8880	.8375	.7903	.7462	.7050	.6663	.6302	.5963	.5645	.5066	.4556	.4323	.4104	.3704	.3349	.2751	.2274	.1890	.1580
7	.9327	.8706	.8131	.7599	.7107	.6651	.6227	.5835	.5470	.5132	.4523	.3996	.3759	.3538	.3139	.2791	.2218	.1776	.1432	.1162
8	.9235	.8535	.7894	.7307	.6768	.6274	.5820	.5403	.5019	.4665	.4039	.3506	.3269	.3050	.2660	.2326	.1789	.1388	.1085	.0854
9	.9143	.8368	.7664	.7026	.6446	.5919	.5439	.5002	.4604	.4241	.3606	.3075	.2843	.2630	.2255	.1938	.1443	.1084	.0822	.0628
10	.9053	.8203	.7441	.6756	.6139	.5584	.5083	.4632	.4224	.3855	.3220	.2697	.2472	.2267	.1911	.1615	.1164	.0847	.0623	.0462
11	.8963	.8043	.7224	.6496	.5847	.5268	.4751	.4289	.3875	.3505	.2875	.2366	.2149	.1954	.1619	.1346	.0938	.0662	.0472	.0340
12	.8874	.7885	.7014	.6246	.5568	.4970	.4440	.3971	.3555	.3186	.2567	.2076	.1869	.1685	.1372	.1122	.0757	.0517	.0357	.0250
13	.8787	.7730	.6810	.6006	.5303	.4688	.4150	.3677	.3262	.2897	.2292	.1821	.1625	.1452	.1163	.0935	.0610	.0404	.0271	.0184
14	.8700	.7579	.6611	.5775	.5051	.4423	.3878	.3405	.2992	.2633	.2046	.1597	.1413	.1252	.0985	.0779	.0492	.0316	.0205	.0135
15	.8613	.7430	.6419	.5553	.4810	.4173	.3624	.3152	.2745	.2394	.1827	.1401	.1229	.1079	.0835	.0649	.0397	.0247	.0155	.0099
16	.8528	.7284	.6232	.5339	.4581	.3936	.3387	.2919	.2519	.2176	.1631	.1229	.1069	.0930	.0708	.0541	.0320	.0193	.0118	.0073
17	.8444	.7142	.6050	.5134	.4363	.3714	.3166	.2703	.2311	.1978	.1456	.1078	.0929	.0802	.0600	.0451	.0258	.0150	.0089	.0054
18	.8360	.7002	.5874	.4936	.4155	.3503	.2959	.2502	.2120	.1799	.1300	.0946	.0808	.0691	.0508	.0376	.0208	.0118	.0068	.0039
19	.8277	.6864	.5703	.4746	.3957	.3305	.2765	.2317	.1945	.1635	.1161	.0829	.0703	.0596	.0431	.0313	.0168	.0092	.0051	.0029
20	.8195	.6730	.5537	.4564	.3769	.3118	.2584	.2145	.1784	.1486	.1037	.0728	.0611	.0514	.0365	.0261	.0135	.0072	.0039	.0021
21	.8114	.6598	.5375	.4388	.3589	.2942	.2415	.1987	.1637	.1351	.0926	.0638	.0531	.0443	.0309	.0217	.0109	.0056	.0029	.0016
22	.8034	.6468	.5219	.4220	.3418	.2775	.2257	.1839	.1502	.1228	.0826	.0560	.0462	.0382	.0262	.0181	.0088	.0044	.0022	.0012
23	.7954	.6342	.5067	.4057	.3256	.2618	.2109	.1703	.1378	.1117	.0738	.0491	.0402	.0329	.0222	.0151	.0071	.0034	.0017	.0008
24	.7876	.6217	.4919	.3901	.3101	.2470	.1971	.1577	.1264	.1015	.0659	.0431	.0349	.0284	.0188	.0126	.0057	.0027	.0013	.0006
25	.7798	.6095	.4776	.3751	.2953	.2330	.1842	.1460	.1160	.0923	.0588	.0378	.0304	.0245	.0160	.0105	.0046	.0021	.0010	.0005
26	.7720	.5976	.4637	.3607	.2812	.2198	.1722	.1352	.1064	.0839	.0525	.0331	.0264	.0211	.0135	.0087	.0037	.0016	.0007	.0003
27	.7644	.5859	.4502	.3468	.2678	.2074	.1609	.1252	.0976	.0763	.0469	.0291	.0230	.0182	.0115	.0073	.0030	.0013	.0006	.0002
28	.7568	.5744	.4371	.3335	.2551	.1956	.1504	.1159	.0895	.0693	.0419	.0255	.0200	.0157	.0097	.0061	.0024	.0010	.0004	.0002
29	.7493	.5631	.4243	.3207	.2429	.1846	.1406	.1073	.0822	.0630	.0374	.0224	.0174	.0135	.0082	.0051	.0020	.0008	.0003	.0001
30	.7419	.5521	.4120	.3083	.2314	.1741	.1314	.0994	.0754	.0573	.0334	.0196	.0151	.0116	.0070	.0042	.0016	.0006	.0002	.0001
40	.6717	.4529	.3066	.2083	.1420	.0972	.0668	.0460	.0318	.0221	.0107	.0053	.0037	.0026	.0013	.0007	.0002	.0001	*	*
50	.6080	.3715	.2281	.1407	.0872	.0543	.0339	.0213	.0134	.0085	.0035	.0014	.0009	.0006	.0003	.0001	*	*	*	*
60	.5504	.3048	.1697	.0951	.0535	.0303	.0173	.0099	.0057	.0033	.0011	.0004	.0002	.0001	*	*	*	*	*	*

Note: n = number of periods; i = interest rate per period.

Table A.4

Present Value of an Annuity of $1 per Period for n Periods; $PV = \dfrac{1.0 - \dfrac{1.0}{(1.0+i)^n}}{i}$

Number of Periods	1%	2%	3%	4%	5%	6%	7%	8%	9%	10%	12%	14%	15%	16%	18%	20%	24%	28%	32%
1	0.9901	0.9804	0.9709	0.9615	0.9524	0.9434	0.9346	0.9259	0.9174	0.9091	0.8929	0.8772	0.8696	0.8621	0.8475	0.8333	0.8065	0.7813	0.7576
2	1.9704	1.9416	1.9135	1.8861	1.8594	1.8334	1.8080	1.7833	1.7591	1.7355	1.6901	1.6467	1.6257	1.6052	1.5656	1.5278	1.4568	1.3916	1.3315
3	2.9410	2.8839	2.8286	2.7751	2.7232	2.6730	2.6243	2.5771	2.5313	2.4869	2.4018	2.3216	2.2832	2.2459	2.1743	2.1065	1.9813	1.8684	1.7663
4	3.9020	3.8077	3.7171	3.6299	3.5460	3.4651	3.3872	3.3121	3.2397	3.1699	3.0373	2.9137	2.8550	2.7982	2.6901	2.5887	2.4043	2.2410	2.0957
5	4.8534	4.7135	4.5797	4.4518	4.3295	4.2124	4.1002	3.9927	3.8897	3.7908	3.6048	3.4331	3.3522	3.2743	3.1272	2.9906	2.7454	2.5320	2.3452
6	5.7955	5.6014	5.4172	5.2421	5.0757	4.9173	4.7665	4.6229	4.4859	4.3553	4.1114	3.8887	3.7845	3.6847	3.4976	3.3255	3.0205	2.7594	2.5342
7	6.7282	6.4720	6.2303	6.0021	5.7864	5.5824	5.3893	5.2064	5.0330	4.8684	4.5638	4.2883	4.1604	4.0386	3.8115	3.6046	3.2423	2.9370	2.6775
8	7.6517	7.3255	7.0179	6.7327	6.4632	6.2098	5.9713	5.7466	5.5348	5.3349	4.9676	4.6389	4.4873	4.3436	4.0776	3.8372	3.4212	3.0758	2.7860
9	8.5660	8.1622	7.7861	7.4353	7.1078	6.8017	6.5152	6.2469	5.9952	5.7590	5.3282	4.9464	4.7716	4.6065	4.3030	4.0310	3.5655	3.1842	2.8681
10	9.4713	8.9826	8.5302	8.1109	7.7217	7.3601	7.0236	6.7101	6.4177	6.1446	5.6502	5.2161	5.0188	4.8332	4.4941	4.1925	3.6819	3.2689	2.9304
11	10.3676	9.7868	9.2526	8.7605	8.3064	7.8869	7.4987	7.1390	6.8052	6.4951	5.9377	5.4527	5.2337	5.0286	4.6560	4.3271	3.7757	3.3351	2.9776
12	11.2551	10.5753	9.9540	9.3851	8.8633	8.3838	7.9427	7.5361	7.1607	6.8137	6.1944	5.6603	5.4206	5.1971	4.7932	4.4392	3.8514	3.3868	3.0133
13	12.1337	11.3484	10.6350	9.9856	9.3936	8.8527	8.3577	7.9038	7.4869	7.1034	6.4235	5.8424	5.5831	5.3423	4.9095	4.5327	3.9124	3.4272	3.0404
14	13.0037	12.1062	11.2961	10.5631	9.8986	9.2950	8.7455	8.2442	7.7862	7.3667	6.6282	6.0021	5.7245	5.4675	5.0081	4.6106	3.9616	3.4587	3.0609
15	13.8651	12.8493	11.9379	11.1184	10.3797	9.7122	9.1079	8.5595	8.0607	7.6061	6.8109	6.1422	5.8474	5.5755	5.0916	4.6755	4.0013	3.4834	3.0764
16	14.7179	13.5777	12.5611	11.6523	10.8378	10.1059	9.4466	8.8514	8.3126	7.8237	6.9740	6.2651	5.9542	5.6685	5.1624	4.7296	4.0333	3.5026	3.0882
17	15.5623	14.2919	13.1661	12.1657	11.2741	10.4773	9.7632	9.1216	8.5436	8.0216	7.1196	6.3729	6.0472	5.7487	5.2223	4.7746	4.0591	3.5177	3.0971
18	16.3983	14.9920	13.7535	12.6593	11.6896	10.8276	10.0591	9.3719	8.7556	8.2014	7.2497	6.4674	6.1280	5.8178	5.2732	4.8122	4.0799	3.5294	3.1039
19	17.2260	15.6785	14.3238	13.1339	12.0853	11.1581	10.3356	9.6036	8.9501	8.3649	7.3658	6.5504	6.1982	5.8775	5.3162	4.8435	4.0967	3.5386	3.1090
20	18.0456	16.3514	14.8775	13.5903	12.4622	11.4699	10.5940	9.8181	9.1285	8.5136	7.4694	6.6231	6.2593	5.9288	5.3527	4.8696	4.1103	3.5458	3.1129
21	18.8570	17.0112	15.4150	14.0292	12.8212	11.7641	10.8355	10.0168	9.2922	8.6487	7.5620	6.6870	6.3125	5.9731	5.3837	4.8913	4.1212	3.5514	3.1158
22	19.6604	17.6580	15.9369	14.4511	13.1630	12.0416	11.0612	10.2007	9.4424	8.7715	7.6446	6.7429	6.3587	6.0113	5.4099	4.9094	4.1300	3.5558	3.1180
23	20.4558	18.2922	16.4436	14.8568	13.4886	12.3034	11.2722	10.3711	9.5802	8.8832	7.7184	6.7921	6.3988	6.0442	5.4321	4.9245	4.1371	3.5592	3.1197
24	21.2434	18.9139	16.9355	15.2470	13.7986	12.5504	11.4693	10.5288	9.7066	8.9847	7.7843	6.8351	6.4338	6.0726	5.4509	4.9371	4.1428	3.5619	3.1210
25	22.0232	19.5235	17.4131	15.6221	14.0939	12.7834	11.6536	10.6748	9.8226	9.0770	7.8431	6.8729	6.4641	6.0971	5.4669	4.9476	4.1474	3.5640	3.1220
26	22.7952	20.1210	17.8768	15.9828	14.3752	13.0032	11.8258	10.8100	9.9290	9.1609	7.8957	6.9061	6.4906	6.1182	5.4804	4.9563	4.1511	3.5656	3.1227
27	23.5596	20.7069	18.3270	16.3296	14.6430	13.2105	11.9867	10.9352	10.0266	9.2372	7.9426	6.9352	6.5135	6.1364	5.4919	4.9636	4.1542	3.5669	3.1233
28	24.3164	21.2813	18.7641	16.6631	14.8981	13.4062	12.1371	11.0511	10.1161	9.3066	7.9844	6.9607	6.5335	6.1520	5.5016	4.9697	4.1566	3.5679	3.1237
29	25.0658	21.8444	19.1885	16.9837	15.1411	13.5907	12.2777	11.1584	10.1983	9.3696	8.0218	6.9830	6.5509	6.1656	5.5098	4.9747	4.1585	3.5687	3.1240
30	25.8077	22.3965	19.6004	17.2920	15.3725	13.7648	12.4090	11.2578	10.2737	9.4268	8.0552	7.0027	6.5660	6.1772	5.5168	4.9789	4.1601	3.5693	3.1242
40	32.8347	27.3555	23.1148	19.7928	17.1591	15.0463	13.3317	11.9246	10.7574	9.7791	8.2438	7.1050	6.6418	6.2335	5.5482	4.9966	4.1659	3.5712	3.1250
50	39.1961	31.4236	25.7298	21.4822	18.2559	15.7619	13.8007	12.2335	10.9617	9.9148	8.3045	7.1327	6.6605	6.2463	5.5541	4.9995	4.1666	3.5714	3.1250
60	44.9550	34.7609	27.6756	22.6235	18.9293	16.1614	14.0392	12.3766	11.0480	9.9672	8.3240	7.1401	6.6651	6.2492	5.5553	4.9999	4.1667	3.5714	3.1250

Note n = number of periods; i = interest rate per period.

Problem	Solution
1. Alicia invests $350 today and expects to earn 20% on the investment each year for the next 20 years. How much will she have?	Find the future value, *FV*, of $1 for 20% and 20 years; 38.337. Multiply 38.337 times $350 to get the answer; it is $13,417.95.
2. Manuel's uncle plans to give him a graduation present of $500 at graduation or $700 three years later if Manuel agrees to complete a graduate program. Considering the value of the gift only and assuming Manuel could invest at 8% in each of the three years, which is the better alternative?	You can use either future or present value of $1 tables. Using the former, find the *FV* for 8% and three years; it is 1.2597. The future value of $500 is $629.85 ($500 × 1.2597). Since this is less than $700, Manuel is better off waiting three years for his uncle's gift. If you use the present value of $1, you find the present value coefficient for 8% and three years; it is 0.7938. You then find the present value, *PV*, of $700, which is $555.66 (0.7938 × $700). Since the present value is greater than the immediate $500, Manuel should accept the future $700.
3. Gunther's stockbroker is trying to convince Gunther to purchase a security that will be worth $10,000 in 30 years. The cost of the security today is $1,500. Gunther isn't sure whether this is a good or bad investment but believes he could make a better decision if he knew the approximate rate of return on the investment. What is it?	You can find a rate of return by dividing the future value of an investment by its cost to arrive at a future value of $1 coefficient. Relate this coefficient then to the number of periods and the approximate value of *i*. You have a coefficient of 6.667 ($10,000/$1,500). Since the number of periods is 30, go across the 30 row until you come as close as possible to 6.667. As you see, the number corresponds to an *i* value of 6%, which is 5.7435. Since 6.667 is somewhat larger than 5.7435, you conclude the rate of return is greater than 6% but far less than 8% (in which case the coefficient would be 10.0620). As a rough approximation, you conclude it is about 6.5%. (You could use more accurate interpolation techniques, but such accuracy is not necessary in many cases. Moreover, for greater accuracy you should use expanded tables or an appropriate calculating device.)

Figure A.1

Some Applications of FV and PV Techniques

Exercises

1. You receive $500 in graduation presents and plan to invest it for your retirement in 40 years. Assuming you can earn 8 percent interest each year, how much will you have at retirement? (Answer: $10,862.) How much will you have if you could earn 12 percent each year? (Answer: $46,526.)

2. Suppose you cannot make an immediate investment for retirement but can afford $100 each year for the next 30 years, with the first payment starting in one year. Assuming a 14 percent investment rate each year, how much will you accumulate at the end of 30 years? (Answer: $35,678.) Suppose your target was to accumulate $50,000; how much must you invest each year? (Answer: $140.14.) Suppose your target was $50,000, but you had only 20 years and could earn only 10 percent each year. What would be your yearly contribution? (Answer: $872.98.)

3. You are thinking of buying a zero coupon bond. It matures in 10 years for $1,000, pays no yearly interest, and currently costs $200. You look at other similar bonds and see that they are yielding 16 percent. Since you feel the zero coupon bond should also yield 16 percent, the most you are willing to pay for it is _____. (Answer: $226.70.) Should you or should you not buy the bond? (Answer: Should.) Suppose you bought the bond and interest rates fell immediately afterward, such that your bond yielded only 10 percent based on its current market price. How much would its current market price be? (Answer: $385.50.)

4. You are thinking of buying an annuity to provide future income to your spouse in the event of your death. The insurance company selling the annuity offers two alternatives: The first calls for an immediate payment of $10,000, and the other requires annual payments of $1,500 for the next 10 years with payments beginning in one year. You are pretty sure you can invest your money at 6 percent interest each year for the next 10 years. If this is true, which alternative should you prefer? (Answer: The first, since the present value of the second is $11,040, which is greater than $10,000.) Suppose you could earn 10 percent; now which would be better? (Answer: The second; its present value is $9,217.)

Index

A

AARP, *see* American Association of Retired Persons
AATR, *see* Average annual total return
Acceleration clause, 156
Accident insurance, 372
Accrued benefit, 422
Actual cash value, 331
Additional dealer markup (ADM), 177
Adjustable life insurance, 397
Adjustable rate loans, 213
Adjustable rate mortgages, 213
Adjusted capitalized cost, 184
Adjusted gross income, 81
ADM, *see* Additional dealer markup
Adverse selection, 328
Affinity card, 146
Agency bonds, 286
Aggregate rate cap, 215
Alimony payments, 83, 84
Alpha value, 262
Alternative minimum tax (AMT), 93
Amateur investors, 271
American Association of Retired Persons (AARP), 18
American Society of Home Inspectors (ASHI), 207
American Stock Exchange (Amex), 233
Americans with Disabilities Act of 1990, 363
Amex, *see* American Stock Exchange
Amortization, 213
    debt, 213
    mortgages, 213
    negative, 215

AMT, *see* Alternative minimum tax
Annual percentage rate (APR), 143, 154, 156, 210, 211
Annuity(ies), 22
    approximation methods with, 29
    due, 25
    future value of, 25
    ordinary, 25
    present value of, 28
    tax-deferred, 101
Apartment housing, 199
APR, *see* Annual percentage rate
Arbitration, 189
ASHI, *see* American Society of Home Inspectors
"As is" sales, 174
Asset(s), 47
    allocation mutual funds, 318
    capital, 93
    investment, 49
    lifestyle, 49
    liquid, 48, 57
    management of current, 111
    paper, 228
Assumable mortgage, 217
ATM, *see* Automated teller machine
Automated teller machine (ATM), 113, 126, 152
Automobile
    cost of operation, 181
    cost of ownership, 179–81
    lemon laws, 189–90
    mass transit alternative, 182
    total cost of ownership and operation, 181–82
    warranties, 188

Automobile insurance, 342
    accident, 349–50
    collision coverage, 345
    collision damage waiver, 346
    cost of, 347–48
    coverage under policy, 343–46
    medical payments coverage, 344
    monetary threshold, 346
    need for, 343
    other than collision coverage, 345
    personal auto policy, 343
    personal injury protection, 346
    single liability limit, 344
    split liability limit, 343
    underinsured motorists coverage, 344
    uninsured motorists coverage, 344
    verbal threshold, 346
Automobile leasing, 182
    closed-end lease, 183
    lease/buy comparison, 186–88
    lease evaluation, 184–86
    open-end lease, 183–84
Automobile selection
    pricing information, 176–77
    rebates, 177–78
Average annual total return (AATR), 306
Average tax rate, 89

B

Balance sheet
    assets, 48–49
    liabilities, 29–50
    net worth, 50–52
    personal, 47
Balloon payment, 157
Bank
    credit cards, 146
    definition of, 117
    reconciliation, 122
Bankruptcy, 163, 164
Barron's, 246, 263, 309
Base price, 177
Basic health care insurance, 357
Beta value, 259
Binding arbitration, 237
Black Monday, 252
Blank endorsement, 120
Blue chip stocks, 274
Bond(s)
    agency, 286
    callable, 283

case study, 298
    convertible, 283
    coupon, 283, 289
    current yield, 288
    expected return from, 287
    face value, 282
    fixed return, 282
    general obligation, 287
    indenture, 282
    inflation-indexed Treasury, 286
    mortgage, 282, 286
    municipal, 99, 287
    return and risk characteristics of bonds, 287–91
    revenue, 287
    T-, 285
    U.S. Series EE, 52, 99, 102, 116
    U.S. Series HH, 117
    yield to maturity, 288
    zero coupon, 283
Bonds, corporate-issued, 282
    investing in, 284
    payment characteristics, 282–83
    retirement methods, 283–84
    rights as bondholder, 282
Bonds, government-issued, 284
    municipal bonds, 287
    U.S. agency bonds, 286–87
    U.S. Treasury securities, 284–86
Book value, 280
Bounced check, 122
Budgets, financial statements and, 46–78
    achieving goals through budgeting, 60–70
    balance sheet, 47–52
    budget, 60
    budget goals, 61
    budget worksheet, 62
    case study, 73, 74
    evaluating past financial performance, 53–60
    income statement, 52–53
Business cycle risk, 253
Business risk, 253
Business Week, 309
Buy-and-hold strategy, 265

C

Cafeteria plans, 365
Callable bonds, 283
Capital asset pricing model (CAPM), 258, 264, 276

Capital assets, 93
Capital gain, 92
Capitalized cost reduction, 184
Capital losses, 92, 100
CAPM, *see* Capital asset pricing model
Career planning, 9
Cash account, 239
Cash credit, 153
    contract, 153
    interest charges, 154–57
Cashier's check, 125
Cash management
    case study, 132, 133
    how account earns interest, 127–28
    meeting cash needs, 113–17
    strategy, 113, 128–30
    use of checking account, 117–26
Cash value insurance, 395
CD, *see* Certificate of deposit
CDW, *see* Collision damage waiver
Certificate of deposit (CD), 116, 316
Certificate of registration, 180
Certificate of title, 179
Certified check, 125
Charge account, regular, 143
Chargeback, 151
Charitable contribution, 85
Check
    bounced, 122
    cashier's, 125
    certified, 125
    stubs, 123
    traveler's, 125
    writing, 121
Checking account, 113
    procedures, 118
    right of survivorship, 119
    tenants in common, 119
Closed-end account, 143
Closed-end fund, 303
Closed-end lease, 183
Closing costs, 209
Coinsurance, 331, 358
Collision coverage, 345
Collision damage waiver (CDW), 346
Common stock(s), 271
    blue chip, 274
    CAPM, 276–78
    case study, 296–97
    cyclical stocks, 274

    distributions to shareholders, 73
    fundamental value and book value, 280–82
    growth company, 274
    income stocks, 274
    opportunities, 274
    PEG ratio, 280
    preemptive right, 272
    price-to-earnings analysis, 278–80
    proxy, 271
    quotations, 275
    residual claim, 272
    shareholders' rights, 271–73
    special situation, 274
    stock split, 273
Community property, 409
Compounding, 22
Compound interest, 22
Comprehensive health insurance, 357
Condominium, 199
Constant ratio plan, 318
Consumer durables, 170–92
    automobile selection, 176–82
    case study, 191
    leasing, 182–88
    lemon protection, 188–90
    major household purchases and electronic market,
        171–76
Consumer finance companies, 159
Consumer Reports, 171, 177
Consumption
    current, 4, 5
    future, 4, 5
    planning, 8
Continuous compounding, 128
Contract rate, 210
Convertible bond, 283
Convertible mortgages, 215
Convertible preferred stock, 292
Cooperative housing, 200
Copayment, 358
Cost(s)
    adjusted capitalized, 184
    auto insurance, 347
    closing, 209
    gross capitalized, 184
    marginal, 182
    net replacement, 171
    opportunity, 11
    probate, 382
    replacement, 330

Costs, *(contd.)*
    sunk, 53, 182
    usual, customary, and reasonable, 357
Cost of operation, 181
Cost of ownership, 179
Coupon bonds, 283, 289
Coupon rate, 283
Credit
    blocking, 152
    cash, 153
    counseling, 163
    history, 140
    life insurance, 178, 394
    sales, 141
    service, 136
    sources of, 157
    three C's, 138
    worthiness, 142
Credit account
    individual, 140
    joint, 140
Credit card(s), 146
    fraud, 149
    mistakes, 150
    secured, 141
    selection, 147
Credit management, short-term, 135–68
    arranging and using credit, 136–41
    case study, 166–67
    cash credit, 153–57
    obtaining credit and resolving credit problems,
        157–64
    sales credit, 141–53
Cumulative dividends, 292
Cumulative variance, 69
Current consumption, 4, 5
Current liability, 49
Current return, 228
Current yield, 288
Custodial account, 100
Cyclical stocks, 274

D

DCA, *see* Dollar cost averaging
Dealer sticker price, 177
Death estate, 404
Death taxes, 105
Debentures, 282

Debentures, subordinated, 282
Debit card, 152
Debt
    amortization, 213
    obligations, 49
    planning, 8
    problems, resolving, 162
    ratio, 58
    service coverage ratio, 60
Deductions
    itemized, 85
    standard, 84
Deed, definition of, 208
Default risk, 290
Defined-contribution health plans, 364
Dental insurance, 359
Dependency exemptions, 84
Deposit term insurance, 394
Depreciation, 27, 180
Disability elimination period, 373
Disability income insurance, 370
    benefit period, 373
    case study, 378
    class cancelable, 374
    clauses affecting benefits, 372–74
    coordination of benefits clause, 373
    requirements, 374–75
    social insurance substitute, 373
    sources, 369–72
    waiting period, 373
Discount broker, 238
Discounting, 26
    approximation methods with annuities, 29–30
    future and present values, 28–29
    present value of annuity, 28
    present value of single payment, 26–28
Dismemberment insurance, 372
Dissavings, 51
Diversification, 255–56
    guidelines, 257
    success of, 256–57
Dividend(s)
    cumulative, 292
    earnings as source of, 277
    noncumulative, 292
    regular, 273
    stock, 273
Dividend reinvestment plans (DRIPs), 264
DJIA, *see* Dow Jones Industrial Average
Dollar cost averaging (DCA), 263

Dow Jones Industrial Average (DJIA), 245, 263
DRIPs, *see* Dividend reinvestment plans
Due care, 335
Dwelling protection, 333

E

Earned Income Tax Credit (EITC), 88
Earnest money, 208
Earnings per share (EPS), 278
Earthquake insurance, 339
ECOA, *see* Equal Credit Opportunity Act
Economic trends
    continued instability in financial markets, 6–7
    continuing inflation, 5–6
    high and selectively rewarding tax system, 7
    persistent business cycles, 6
Educational fund, 387
EFTs, *see* Exchange-traded funds
EFTS, *see* Electronic funds transfer systems
EITC, *see* Earned Income Tax Credit
Electronic funds transfer systems (EFTS), 126
Electronic Fund Transfers Act, 152
Emergency fund, 387
Emergency reserves, 113–14
Employee Retirement Income Security Act (ERISA),
        418, 426
Employee stock ownership plan (ESOP), 427
Endorsement, 339
Endowment life insurance, 396
EPO, *see* Exclusive provider organization
EPS, *see* Earnings per share
Equal Credit Opportunity Act (ECOA), 138
Equity conversion loan, 434
Equity trusts, 312
ERISA, *see* Employee Retirement Income Security Act
Escrow account, 217
ESOP, *see* Employee stock ownership plan
Estate planning, 9, 404–11
    administrator/administratrix, 406
    bequest, 407
    case study, 413
    codicil, 408
    community property, 409
    death estate, 404
    executor/executrix, 405
    intestate, 405
    joint tenancy, 409
    last will and testament, 405–9

    legacy, 407
    letter of last instructions, 408
    per capita division of property, 407
    per stirpes division of property, 407
    probate, 408
    tenancy in common, 409
    testate, 405
    testator/testatrix, 405
    transferring estate outside will, 409–11
    will, 405
Estate taxes, 382
ETFs, *see* Exchange-traded funds
Exchange-traded funds (ETFs), 311–12
    broad market, 311
    market segment, 311–12
Exclusive agency agreement, 206
Exclusive provider organization (EPO), 363
Exclusive right to sell, 206
Expected total return, 259
Expenses, 52
    flexible, 53
    inflexible, 53
Expense variance, 69
Express warranty, 175
Extended warranty, 175

F

Fair Credit Reporting Act, 141
Fair Debt Collection Practices Act, 164
Family maintenance fund, 383
FDIC, *see* Federal Deposit Insurance Corporation
Federal Deposit Insurance Corporation (FDIC), 115
Federal Emergency Management Agency (FEMA), 340
Federal estate tax, 104
Federal gift tax, 104, 105
Federal Home Loan Mortgage Corporation
        (Freddie Mac), 197
Federal Housing Administration (FHA), 200, 217, 434
Federal income tax
    adjusted gross income, 84
    adjustments to income, 81–84
    alternative minimum tax, 93
    amount refunded or owed, 88
    capital gains and losses, 92–93
    determination of, 88–92
    getting outside help, 96–97
    gross income items, 80–81
    Internal Revenue Service, 94

Federal income tax, *(contd.)*
  students, 97–99
  taxable income, 84–85
  tax credits, 88
  tax liability before tax credits, 86–88
  taxpayer assistance, 94–96
Fee-for-service (FFS) health insurance, 362
FEMA, *see* Federal Emergency Management Agency
FFS health insurance, *see* Fee-for-service health
    insurance
FHA, *see* Federal Housing Administration
FHA mortgage insurance, 218
FICA taxes, 103
Financial independence, 5
Financial markets and institutions, 226–49
  case study, 248–49
  finding investment information, 243–46
  goals and investment alternatives, 227–32
  regulation of securities industry, 234–37
  securities markets, 232–34
  stockbroker services, 237–43
Financial planner, 13
Financial planning, 2–20
  achieving financial goals through planning, 7–11
  building block approach to, 13
  building blocks of success, 12–13
  career planning, 9–10
  case study, 15–16
  consumption and savings planning, 8
  debt planning, 8
  estate planning, 9
  income tax planning, 9
  insurance planning, 9
  investment planning, 9
  making financial decisions, 11–12
  reason for studying personal finance, 3–7
  retirement planning, 9
Financial ratios, 53
Financial resources
  growth of, 225
  organizing and managing of, 1
Financial risk, 253
Financial statements and budgets, 46–78
  achieving goals through budgeting, 60–70
  balance sheet, 47–52
  case study, 73, 74
  evaluating past financial performance, 53–60
  income statement, 52–53
Financial success, 3
Financial World, 246

Fitness of purpose, 174
Fixed rate mortgages, 210–11
Flexible expenses, 53
Flexible spending health care accounts, 365
Floater, 339
Flood insurance, 339
Forbes, 246, 309
Foreclosure, 219
Fortune, 246
401(k) retirement plan, 101, 319–20
Freddie Mac, *see* Federal Home Loan Mortgage
    Corporation
Full employment act for accountants, 7
Full-service stockbroker, 238
Full warranty, 175
Fundamental value, 280
Fund switching, 306
Future consumption, 4, 5
Future return, 228
Future value, 22
Future-value-of-$1 table, 24

G

Gambling, 328
GDP, *see* Gross domestic product
General obligation (GO) bond, 287
Global funds, 304
Global income, 80
GNMA, *see* Government National Mortgage Association
Goal setting, in financial planning, 61
GO bond, *see* General obligation bond
Government National Mortgage Association (GNMA),
    286
GPM, *see* Graduated payment mortgage
Grace period, 145
Graduated payment mortgage (GPM), 216
Gross capitalized cost, 184
Gross domestic product (GDP), 6
Gross income items, 80
Group-staff HMO, 362
Growth company, 274
Guarantee, 174

H

Health care accounts, flexible spending, 365
Health insurance, 356–68, 378
  basic, 357

case study, 378
comprehensive, 357
copayment, 358
employment-related, 363–68
fee-for-service, 362
guaranteed renewability, 360
important provisions, 360–61
individually selected, 367–68
point-of-service plan, 363
preexisting conditions clause, 360
providers, 362–63
service benefit coverage, 358
types of coverage, 357–60
waiting period, 360
Health Insurance Portability and Accountability Act
    (HIPAA), 364
Health maintenance organization (HMO), 358, 362
group-staff, 362
individual practice arrangement, 362
Health plans, defined-contribution, 364
Health savings accounts, 365
High-capitalization stocks, 274
HIPAA, *see* Health Insurance Portability
    and Accountability Act
HMO, *see* Health maintenance organization
Home equity loan, 158
Home office insurance, 340
Homeowners' insurance, 330
actual cash value, 331
all risks coverage, 330
apportionment clause, 333
appurtenant structures, 334
case study, 352
co-insurance, 331
collection on loss, 341–42
deductible clause, 332
disappearing deductible, 333
inflation guard endorsement, 332
liability coverage, 335–36
mortgage clause, 333
named perils coverage, 330
policy format, 336–37
property coverage, 333–35
replacement cost, 330
selection, 340–41
specialized insurance, 337–40
subrogation clause, 333
terminology, 330–33
umbrella coverage, 339
unscheduled personal property, 334

Hospital insurance, 357
Housing, 193–224
case study, 222–23
real estate transaction, 204–11
renting vs. buying, 195–204
Housing, financing, 211–20
adjustable rate mortgages, 213–16
fine print, 216–17
fixed rate mortgages, 211–13
insured mortgages, 217–18
refinancing, 218–20
specialized mortgage formats, 216
Housing, types of, 198
apartment, 199
condominium, 199–200
cooperative, 200
mobile homes, 200
multifamily, 200
single-family, 200
Housing Affordability Index, 194

I

Implied warranty, 174
Income, 52
global, 80
gross, 80, 81
nominal, 55
real, 55
stocks, 274
taxable, 84
variance, 69
Income statement, 52
contribution to savings, 53
expenses, 52–53
income, 52
Income tax, 104
planning, 9
return, 90–91
Indemnification, 329
Indemnity insurance, 357
Index fund, 304
Individual credit account, 140
Individual practice arrangement (IPA) HMO, 362
Individual retirement account (IRA), 83, 98, 101, 419, 429
Inflation, 5
compounding process, 32
guard endorsement, 332
hedge, 137

Inflation, *(contd.)*
   -indexed Treasury bonds, 286
   rates, 6, 54
   risk, 252
Inflexible expenses, 53
Inheritance tax, 105
Initial margin requirement, 240
Insurable interest, 328
Insurance
   accident, 372
   automobile, 342–50
   cash value, 395
   credit life, 178
   dental, 359
   disability income, 369–75, 378
   earthquake, 339
   flood, 339
   health care, 356–68
   home office, 340
   homeowner's, 330–42
   hospital, 357
   indemnity, 357
   life, 381–404
   major medical, 358
   Medigap, 366
   mortgage, 217, 218
   personal liability, 327
   physicians' expense, 358
   planning, 9
   property and liability, 326–54
   property loss, 327
   renters', 340
   risk, 327–29
   risk management, 329–30
   surgical expense, 357
   term, 391
   title, 208
Intangible investments, 228
Interest
   -adjusted net cost index, 401–2
   calculation of, 127
   compound, 22
   simple, 22
   student loan, 98
   teaser rate, 214
Interest charges
   acceleration clause, 156
   add-on clause, 156
   add-on method, 155
   annual percentage rate, 156

   discount method, 155
   simple interest method, 154
Interest rate(s)
   adjusted balance method, 144
   adjustment index, 214
   adjustment period, 214
   average daily balance method, 144
   previous balance method, 144
   risk, 253, 290
   two-cycle average daily balance method, 146
   volatility, 130
Internal Revenue Service (IRS), 80, 92, 94
International funds, 304
Internet
   budget information, 78
   cash management information, 134
   consumer durables information, 192
   credit management, information, 167
   financial markets and institutions, 249
   financial planning information, 18
   frauds, 172
   health care and disability insurance information, 379
   housing information, 223
   investment information, 269
   mutual funds, 323
   property and liability insurance information, 353
   retirement planning information, 444–45
   stocks and bonds, 298
   stock trading, 238
   tax information, 109
   time value calculations, 44
   time-value-of-money calculations on, 24
Internet Fraud Watch, 173
Inter vivos trust, 410
Investment(s)
   assets, 49
   clubs, 315
   current return, 228
   future return, 228
   intangible, 228
   leveraging of, 240
   most common, 270
   planning, 9
   tangible, 227
   total return, 228
Investment Advisors Act of 1940, 235
Investment basics, 250–69
   building and changing portfolio, 262–65
   case study, 268
   diversification, 255–57

risk and return, 251–55
risk-return model, 258–62
Investment Company Act of 1940, 235
Investment information, 243
    company sources, 244
    Internet data sources, 246
    investment advisory services, 245
    newspapers and magazines, 245–46
Investor's Business Daily (IBD), 246
Invoice price, 177
IPA HMO, *see* Individual practice arrangement HMO
IRA, *see* Individual retirement account
Iron law of risk and return, 251
Irrevocable trust, 410
IRS, *see* Internal Revenue Service
Itemized deductions, 85

J

Joint credit account, 140
Joint tenancy, 409

K

Kelley Blue Book Used Car Guide, 177
Keogh (HR-10) plan, 83, 101, 431

L

Lease
    closed-end, 183
    open-end, 183
    rate, 184
Lemon protection, 175, 188
Lender harassment, protection from, 164
Leverage, 240
Liability(ies), 47
    coverage, 335
    current, 49
    insurance, *see* Property and liability insurance
    management, 111, 169
    noncurrent, 49
Liability limit
    single, 344
    split, 343
Life-cycle planning, 7, 8
Life insurance
    adjustable life, 397
    beneficiary, 390

case study, 413
cash value, 389
categories, 391–99
contingent beneficiary, 390
dividend, 390
endowment life, 396
face amount, 389
family policy, 390
joint life policy, 389
language, 389–91
limited payment life, 396
modified whole life, 396
needs, 381–89, 413
nonparticipating insurance, 390
ordinary, 395
participating insurance, 390
policy selection, 399–404
premium, 390
protection gap, 388, 389
riders, 391
single life policies, 389
straight life, 395
surrender value, 389
survivorship joint life, 390
universal life, 397
vanishing premiums, 403
variable life, 398
variable-universal, 399
whole life, 395
Lifestyle assets, 49
Limited partnerships, 313–15
    investment potential, 314–15
    liquidity with, 313–14
    tax situation, 314
Limited warranty, 175
Limit order, 242
Liquid asset, 48
Liquid assets to take-home pay ratio, 57
Liquidity
    investments held for, 230
    management, 111
    ratio, 58
Listing agreement, 206
Living trust, 410
Load fund, 301
Loan(s)
    adjustable rate, 213
    home equity, 158
    refund anticipation, 95
    student, 98, 159

Local taxes, 103
Long position, 240
Long-term care policies, 359
Long-term disability income insurance, 370
Long-term financing, 169

M

Magnuson-Moss Warranty Act of 1975, 175, 190
Mail Order Merchandise Rule, 173
Maintenance margin requirement, 240
Major medical insurance, 358
Maloney Act of 1938, 235
Managed care, 362
Management risk, 253
Margin, 214
Margin account, 240
Marginal analysis, 11
Marginal cost, 182
Marginal tax rate, 89
Marketable title, 208
Market order, 241
Market risk, 258
Market timing, 265
Market-to-book ratio, 281
Master budget worksheet, 62
Maximum capital appreciation funds, 304
Medicaid, 366
Medicare, 366
Medigap insurance, 366
Merchantability, 174
MLS, *see* Multiple Listing Service
MMDAs, *see* Money market deposit accounts
Mobile homes, 200
Modified whole life insurance, 396
Money, 246, 309
Money, time value of, 21–45
    case study, 39–40
    compounding, 22–26
    discounting, 26–30
    goal planning, 31–36
Money factor, 184
Money market deposit accounts (MMDAs), 116
Money market fund, 116, 304
Monroney sticker price, 176
Monthly income and expense plan, 62, 66
Moody's, 245
Mortgage(s)
    acceleration clause, 216
    adjustable rate, 213
    amortization, 213
    assumable, 217
    -backed bonds, 286
    bonds, 282
    conventional financing, 217
    convertible, 215
    due-on-sale clause, 217
    escrow account, 217
    fixed rate, 210–11
    foreclosure, 219
    graduated payment, 216
    insurance, FHA, 218
    prepayment penalty, 217
    principal, 213
    rate caps, 215
    refinancing, 218
    reversed, 433–34
    shared appreciation, 216
    trusts, 312
Multifamily housing, 200
Multiple Listing Service (MLS), 206
Municipal bonds, 99, 287
Mutual fund(s), 301
    asset allocation, 318–19
    case study, 322
    characteristics of, 301–5
    closed-end fund, 303
    401(k) retirement plan, 319–20
    fund switching, 306
    global funds, 304
    important services, 305–6
    index fund, 304
    international funds, 304
    load fund, 301
    maximum capital appreciation funds, 304
    money market fund, 304
    no-load fund, 301
    open-end fund, 302
    prospectus, 304
    ratings, 309
    sector funds 304
    selection, 306–9
    shareholder report, 304

N

NASD, *see* National Association of Securities Dealers
NASDAQ, *see* National Association of Securities Dealers Automated Quotations System
National Association of Securities Dealers (NASD), 235, 236

National Association of Securities Dealers Automated Quotations System (NASDAQ), 234
National Automobile Dealers Association Official Used Car Guide, 177
National Credit Union Administration (NCUA), 115
NAV, *see* Net asset value
NCUA, *see* National Credit Union Administration
Negative amortization, 215
Negligence, 335
Negotiated order of withdrawal (NOW) account, 115
Net asset value (NAV), 301, 302
Net lease, 183
Net listing agreement, 206–07
Net payment cost index, 402
Net replacement cost, 171
Net worth, 47, 50
New York Stock Exchange (NYSE), 232, 233, 241
No-fault insurance, 346
No-load fund, 301
Nominal income, 55
Noncumulative dividends, 292
Noncurrent liabilities, 49
Nontaxable exclusions, 80
NOW account, *see* Negotiated order of withdrawal account
NYSE, *see* New York Stock Exchange

O

Occupational Outlook Handbook, 19
Odd lots, 239
Online auctions, 173
Open-end account, 143
Open-end fund, 302
Open-end lease, 183
Open listing agreement, 206, 207
Opportunity costs, 11
Ordinary annuity, 25
Ordinary life insurance, 395
Organized exchange, 232
OTC market, *see* Over-the-counter market
Overdraft, 122
Overdraft protection credit line, 158
Over-the-counter (OTC) market, 234

P

Paper assets, 228
Partnership, limited, 313

Passbook rate, 116
Payment cap, 215
PCOAB, *see* Public Company Accounting Oversight Board
PEG ratio, 280
Pension plans, 371
    accrued benefit, 422
    annuity contracts, 431
    cash balance plan, 424
    defined-benefit plan, 421
    defined-contribution plan, 421
    early retirement age, 423
    employee stock ownership plan, 427
    ERISA and, 418, 426
    fixed annuity, 431
    flat benefit formula, 424
    individual retirement account, 429
    joint and last survivor annuity, 426
    normal retirement age, 423
    profit-sharing plan, 427
    simplified employee pension plan, 428
    single life annuity, 426
    unit benefit formula, 424
    vested benefit, 422
P/E ratio, *see* Price-earnings ratio
Periodic rate cap, 215
Periodic share repurchases, 273
Personal auto policy, 343
Personal balance sheet, 47
Personal exemptions, 84
Personal injury protection (PIP), 346
Personal liability insurance, 327
Physicians' expense insurance, 358
PIP, *see* Personal injury protection
Plastic money, 146
Pocket money, 113
Point-of-service (POS) plan, 363
Policy adjustment, 188
Portfolio, 255
    case study, 323
    construction, 315–18
    maintenance, 318
POS plan, *see* Point-of-service plan
PPOs, *see* Preferred provided organizations
Preemptive right, 272
Preferred provided organizations (PPOs), 363
Preferred stock, 291
    characteristics of, 291–92
    expected return, 293
Pretax equivalent yield, 287

Price-earnings (P/E) ratio, 278, 280
Price-to-earnings analysis, 278
Principal, 213
Principle of diminishing marginal satisfaction, 5
Private mortgage insurance, 217
Probate, 382, 408
Profit-sharing plan, 427
Promissory note, 153
Property and liability insurance, 326–54
    automobile insurance, 342–50
    case study, 352–53
    homeowners' insurance, 330–42
    insurance concepts, 327–30
Property loss insurance, 327
Property taxes, 104
Prospectus, 235, 304
Protective covenants, 282
Proxy, 271
Public Company Accounting Oversight Board
        (PCOAB), 236
Puffery, 175
Pure risk, 327

R

Random risk, 258
Real estate
    closing, 208
    listing agreements, 206
    loan officers, 211
    points, 209
Real estate investment trusts (REITs), 312–13
    differences, 312
    investment appeal, 313
    return, 312–13
Real income, 55
Rebates, 177
Refund anticipation loan, 95
Regular charge account, 143
Regular dividend, 273
Reinvestment plan, 305
REITs, see Real estate investment trusts
Renters' insurance, 340
Replacement cost, 330
Required rate of return, 253
Residual claim, 272
Residual value, 184
Restrictive endorsement, 120
Retail installment contract, 153

Retirement
    age, 423
    fund, 388
    methods, 283
Retirement annuities
    accumulation period, 431
    annuity contracts, 431
    annuity starting date, 432
    deferred annuities, 432
    fixed annuity, 431
    immediate annuity, 432
    liquidation period, 432
    variable annuity, 432
Retirement plan
    company-sponsored, 417
    qualified, 418
Retirement planning, 9, 325, 415–45
    case study, 444
    establishing personal retirement plan, 434–42
    saving and investing for retirement, 417–34
Revenue bond, 287
Reverse mortgages, 433–34
Revocable trust, 410
Revolving credit account, 143
Risk(s), 251
    averters, 228
    avoidance, 329
    business, 253
    business cycle, 253
    default, 290
    financial, 253
    inflation, 252
    interest rate, 253, 290
    management, 253, 329
    market, 258
    premium, 255
    pure, 327
    random, 258
    reduction, 329
    retention, 329
    seekers, 229
    speculative, 327
    transfer, 330
Risk-return model, 258
    market risk, 258–61
    random risk, 258
    stock selections, 261–62
Roth IRA, 430
Round lots, 239

Rule of 72, 24
Rule of 78, 156

S

SAIF, *see* Savings Association Insurance Fraud
Sales credit, 141
    accounts, 143–46
    correct credit card mistakes, 150–52
    credit cards, 146–49
    debit cards, 152–53
    protection against credit card fraud, 149–50
Sales taxes, 104
SAM, *see* Shared appreciation mortgage
Sarbanes–Oxley Act (SOA), 236, 279
Savings, 5
    account, 115
    planning, 8
    positive contribution to, 51
Savings Association Insurance Fraud (SAIF), 115, 214
SEC, *see* Securities and Exchange Commission
Secondary beneficiary, 390
Secret warranty, 188
Sector funds 304
Secured credit card, 141
Securities Act of 1933, 235
Securities Exchange Act of 1934, 235
Securities and Exchange Commission (SEC), 235
Securities industry, regulation of
    federal legislation, 234–36
    state law and self-regulation, 236–37
Securities Investor Protection Act of 1970, 236
Securities Investor Protection Corporation (SIPC), 236
Securities markets
    organized exchanges, 232–34
    over-the-counter markets, 234
    specialists, 233
Securities sales
    interstate, 236
    intrastate, 236
Security agreement, 153
SEP, *see* Simplified employee pension plan
Service contract, 175
Service credit, 136
Settlement costs, 209
Shared appreciation mortgage (SAM), 216
Shareholder report, 304
Short position, 240
Short-term disability income insurance, 370

Simple interest, 22
Simplified employee pension plan (SEP), 428
Single-family housing, 200
Single liability limit, 344
Sinking fund, 283
SIPC, *see* Securities Investor Protection Corporation
SOA, *see* Sarbanes–Oxley Act
Social insurance substitute, 373
Social Security Administration (SSA), 384
Social Security taxes, 102
Special endorsement, 120
Speculative risks, 327
Split liability limit, 343
SSA, *see* Social Security Administration
Standard deduction, 84
Standard & Poor's, 245
State taxes, 103
Statute of limitations, 95
Stock(s), *see also* Common stock
    alpha value, 262
    beta value, 259
    blue chip, 274
    convertible preferred, 292
    cyclical, 274
    dividend, 273
    expected total return, 259
    high-capitalization, 274
    income, 274
    preferred, 291
    split, 273
Stockbrokerage firms
    accounts, 239–40
    discount, 238
    full-service, 238
    Internet trading, 238
    orders, 241–43
    positions, 240–41
    stockbroker selection, 237–39
Stop order, 242
Stop-payment order, 122
Straight bankruptcies, 164
Straight life insurance, 395
STRIPS, *see* U.S. Treasury Strips
Student(s)
    grants, 97
    loans, 98, 159
    tax credits, 98
    tuition and fees deduction, 98
    tuition programs, 98

Subordinated debentures, 282
Sunk cost, 53, 182
Surgical expense insurance, 357
Surrender cost index, 401–2

T

Tangible investments, 227
Tax(es), 79–109
    alternative minimum, 93
    case study, 108
    credit, 86, 88, 98
    death and transfer taxes, 104–6
    -deferred annuity, 101
    estate, 382
    federal estate, 104
    federal gift, 104, 105
    federal income tax, 80–99
    FICA, 103
    income, 104
    inheritance, 105
    local, 103
    planning to reduce income taxes, 99–102
    property, 104
    publications, 97
    rate, 87, 89
    refund, 89
    return, automatic extension, 94
    sales, 104
    service companies, 96
    Social Security taxes, 102–3
    state and local taxes, 103–4
    swap, 265
Taxable income, 84
T-bonds, 285
Teaser rate, 214
T&E cards, see Travel and entertainment cards
Tenants in common, 119, 409
10-K report, 235
Term insurance, 391
    credit life insurance, 394
    decreasing term, 394
    deposit term insurance, 394
    group mortgage life, 394
    renewable term, 393
Testamentary trust, 410

TILA, see Truth in Lending Act
Time value of money, 21–45, 446–53
    case study, 39–40
    compounding, 22–26
    discounting, 26–30
    future value of stream of equal payments, 448
    goal planning, 31–36
    interpolation techniques, 44–45
    present value of single payment, 450
    present value of stream of equal payments, 450
Title insurance, 208
Title search, 208
Total return, 228
Transition fund, 382
Travel and entertainment (T&E) cards, 146
Traveler's check, 125
Truncation, 124
Trust(s), 100
    beneficiary, 410
    equity, 312
    fiduciary responsibility, 410
    grantor, 410
    inter vivos, 410
    irrevocable, 410
    living, 410
    mortgage, 312
    real estate investment, 312
    revocable, 410
    testamentary, 410
    trustee, 410, 411
Truth in Lending Act (TILA), 138, 153
Tuition programs, 98

U

UCR costs, see Usual, customary, and reasonable costs
UIT, see Unit investment trust
Umbrella coverage, homeowners' insurance, 339
Underinsured motorists coverage, 344
Underwriting, 328
Uninsured motorists coverage, 344
Unit investment trust (UIT), 309
Universal life insurance, 397
Unsecured personal credit line, 158
U.S. Series EE bonds, 52, 99, 102, 116
U.S. Series HH bonds, 117

U.S. Treasury securities, 284
U.S. Treasury Strips (STRIPS), 286, 316
Usual, customary, and reasonable (UCR) costs, 357, 362

V

VA, *see* Veterans Administration
Value Line, 245
Variable life insurance, 398
Variable ratio plan, 318
Variable-universal life insurance, 399
Variance, 69
    cumulative 69
    expense, 69
    income, 69
Vested benefits, 422
Veterans Administration (VA), 200,
      217, 218

W

Wage earner plan, 164
Walkaway lease, 183
Wall Street Journal, 227, 245, 263, 309

Warranty, 174
    express, 175
    extended, 175
    full, 175
    implied, 174
    limited, 175
    secret, 188
W-2 form, 88
W-4 form, 88
Whole life insurance, 395
Will, 405
Workers' compensation, 365, 371

Y

YCI, *see* Yield comparison index
Yield comparison index (YCI), 402
Yield to maturity, 288
Your Income Tax (Lasser), 97

Z

Zero coupon bond, 283